The Complete Hardcore Punk Zine '79-'83

TOUCH AND GO

The Complete Hardcore Punk Zine '79–'83

TESCO VEE & DAVE STIMSON

Edited by Steve Miller

Bazillion Points

TOUCH AND GO
The Complete Hardcore Punk Zine '79—'83
Copyright (c) 2010 Bob Vermeulen & Dave Stimson
All rights reserved.

http://www.touchandgobook.com

Written by Tesco Vee & Dave Stimson
Executive editor: Steve Miller
Book design by Tom Deja
Cover by Bazillion Points

First published in 2010 by

BAZILLION POINTS BOOKS
61 Greenpoint Ave. #108
Brooklyn, NY 11222
USA
www.bazillionpoints.com

ISBN 978-0-9796163-8-9

Printed in China

TABLE OF CONTENTS

ESSAYS

"POISON PEN IN HAND AND PASSION IN OUR BRITCHES"

TESCO VEE

Oh the indelible mark the illustrious fanzine (root word: **fan**) hath left on cultural movements/ musical happenstances o'er the last six decades. The unofficial and unprofessional aspect of the homemade zine genre is what drew Masters Dave Stimson and Bob Vermeulen into the enterprise known as Touch and Go magazine three decades ago. Crafting a fanzine was certainly nothing new, but in mid-Michigan we were breaking ground, breaking wind, and generally feeling our way thru the process, with nothing to guide us but disdain for what was and a need for the new, whether "the new" meant **Black Flag, the Feelies, the Specials** ,or **Throbbing Gristle.**

The late '70s were musically heady times, a tumult of trends, a maelstrom of styles, talent, hype, fluff, and downright dreck. Doing T & G gave us a feeling of being musically svelte and relatively in the know compared to our fellow mitten-dwelling pongos. Dave's early targets included the stodgy Lansing rock station WILS, a local music reviewer named David Winkelstern (whom he more than once verbally reduced to smoking ash), hippies that seemed to grow from trees, and so many more defenseless invertebrates. All felt the double-barreled wrath of "The

Iceman," as he would later be known. I was the occasionally vitriolic, most times affable grade-school teacher, heavily armed with a penchant for the spoken word, a lust for vinyl, and a need to channel both pursuits into something tangible. It was this street-level pomposity, spirit of arrogance—a holier-than-thou hubris—and the awareness of being at the vanguard of some sort of musical revolution that would make T & G what it was: a bombastic, puerile, sophomoric, occasionally literary, resplendent publication spawned from the bent of two high-school chums who shared a boundless passion for the music.

My first foray into zinedom was the 999 Times (included in this book). Rudimentary but heartfelt, as you can see...okay, it sucked sloth cock! But ya gotta start somewhere, and somewhere was my fetid bedroom in my parents' house. Nick Cash and crew from 999 were far and away my fave of the UK corporate signings, and their live sets still rank high on my pantheon of stellar stageside experiences. I met and interviewed them over chow and became a fan for life. Christ, they played at Dooley's, a college frat bar in my benign home base of East Lansing, Michigan! That alone affords them entrance into the hallowed halls of cool.

I can't recall the exact moment that DS and I decided to do a zine, so don't ask. He had been the star running back in high school, me the long-haired band nerd/parking-lot burnout. But some years later we hooked up at a Coldcock show at Bookies in Detroit and decided it was time someone got off their literary keisters and started jotting down all of these punk/indie goin's-on. That someone, as we quickly figured out, was us. I already grasped that a serious musical shift was upon us when I happened into a newsstand and saw **the Bromley Contingent** in that now-famous scrum pile photo with **Rotten, Idol, Sioux,** and the rest. It wasn't long thereafter that I happened upon a little box of import 45s at a local record shop. At $3 a pop, I started my pile of ear candy. I musta bought half the box: Lurkers, Johnny Moped, Chelsea, Gen X, you name it; I could finally get a listen to all those mythical bands I had by then read so much about.

In search of our own Pet Sounds as well as potential fodder for the zine, we traveled back to **Bookies** (in the dead of winter in DS's unheated VW!), **Nunzio's, Menjo's, the Rainbow Ranch, Club DooBee, Bunches, Hobies;** anywhere in Michigan that was dumb enough to put on a punk show. We saw tons of bands both imported and domestic—**Stranglers, 999, Ramones, X, Subhumans, the Misfits** (many times), **Johnny Thunders, Gang of 4, the Fix, the Cramps, Negative Approach, Revillos, Necros, Minor Threat, Bad Brains, Effigies, DOA, Dickies, Black Flag**—holy crap, all these bands came to our little Midwestern pocket, and goddamn it, someone hadda document these proceedings!!

So with poison pen in hand and passion in our britches, we started layin' it all down on parchment. We sold our prog rock collections at a record store called **Flat, Black & Circular** (can I have my **Guru Guru** LPs back?) and traveled far and wide to unearth obscurities to review in our newfound platform. That groovy little ragazine kept us busy off and on for four years, and we took great pride in finding records nobody else would ever find and saying they ruled even if they sometimes didn't! Stores like **Schoolkids'** and **Wazoo** in Ann Arbor, **Dearborn Music** in Detroit, **Wax Trax** in Chicago—to which we would dutifully travel 220 miles monthly—fed our insatiable appetite for new and undocumented wax.

Call us **Kickboy Face, Chris D.,** or **Lester Bangs** wannabes. Call us literary hacks or punk rock protagonists as well. What we attempted to do was chronicle, lambaste, pass judgment on, extol virtue upon, and generally spin the whole musical movement on its head, and see what flew out. Looking back on the chronology of our sometimes stellar, oft times passable, and occasionally downright dung-filled 'n' tuneless aural taste buds, some question marks hover, exclamation marks burst, and our pride swells, hisses, and pops as we look back at what we called good/bad. The early issues are a testament to the fact that though only a $9,600-a-year schoolteacher in a small farm town, I dropped a princely sum to have **Melody Maker, Sounds,** and **NME** delivered weekly to my door, which still left me a full seven days behind the curve as far as the UK's flavor of the week, but still light-years ahead of my stateside brethren. Indeed, the heavy English tilt of the early issues would soon give way to the rumblings and grumblings of the burgeoning US hardcore scene.

And rightfully so.

First-wave NY bands that swelled the Sire roster left me cold for the most part. Oh, you had some exceptions with **Richard Hell, the Ramones,** and all, but it was mags like **Search and Destroy** and the Left Coast bands that more suitably tapped into the suburban angst thang and resonated musically with yours truly. **Dangerhouse, SST,** and **What?** were the labels that seemed to have their finger on the pulse beat of punk bombast, dropping gem after gem, and we thought it would never end: **the Weirdos, Dils, Controllers, Skulls, Deadbeats, Avengers, Middle Class, Negative Trend**—now that was fuckin' punk rock!

But **Slash** magazine was really what inspired DS and me to turn into gonzo guerilla scribes, banging out our diatribes on IBM Selectrics into the wee morning hours, ashtrays piled high with Lucky Strike heaters in our respective hovels. DS and I met to sit around and read each other's pages, laugh, slap ourselves on the backs, and read some more. Tumblers of cold gin later, it was time to pull the trigger and pronounce it an issue (that's right, it was all done separately, his stuff and mine, and we would meld 'em together just before publication). I'd sneak into the school where I taught and print these bad boys up on the school Xerox machine. My biggest fear was leaving one of these scurrilous, scandalous pages on the glass before leaving. I musta lifted that lid 15 times! Maybe one was stuck to the top, or fell in a crack. Thinking of the school secretary coming in on Monday morning and finding the Farrah page with cum gushing from her ears scared the living poop outta me!

The plaudits trickled in. Getting a postcard from Kickboy Face was too fuckin' cool and it read, "Thanks for Issue 1- Keep up the good work." It still hangs on my wall... Now that cat could form a sentence. It wasn't long before I realized that making fun of folk, even on the puny press run scale we operated on, left our suitably humiliated subjects ready to kill, and I deemed it necessary to change monikers. So after seeing a pic of Throbbing Gristle standing in front of a Tesco store in England I had my new handle and I was really ready to rumble.

Dropping $2 in the mail and actually getting **Black Flag's "Nervous Breakdown"** or **Fear's "I Love Livin' in the City"** in the mail a couple weeks later were moments of magic that are still etched in our craniums. Receiving the new Minutemen 7" with a note from D. Boon, or the infamous smashed **Teen Idles** with a note from Ian (and yes, we did tape it back together and still ascertained that it ruled), getting **GG Allin's** first horrible album and a personal hate note... Kiddies nowadays just don't realize the lengths that were necessary—the research involved, the gas and time and money, the exploration of dollar boxes in dusty back rooms—that would eventually culminate in the edification and illumination and inspiration that were busting out musically on a global basis, all running like a coveted undercurrent of cool, to be unearthed only by those inquisitive and hungry enough to see it for what it was: something that was rich and wondrous and can never exist again.

Eventually we started to do two-color offset covers courtesy of DS's classes at the local community college, where he printed the first **Necros** and **Fix** sleeves as well. The first issues were in laughably small runs of 100 copies, and eventually we started

making 200 of each and then 1,000 at the end. But we still managed to get 'em in the hands of anyone who might feed our habit: indie labels, record stores, other zines, and a fan or two hip or lucky enough to snag a copy.

If you wanted to get free zines in the mail, well then you needed your own zine; it was pretty simple. And eventually if you wanted to get free platters in the mail, you hadda put out yer own platters, and Touch and Go Records was born. You mostly know the story there—it became a label that defined the indie strain, one more element of the magazine's legacy. I forged some lifelong friendships out of all this, people I never would have met had I not beat the jungle drums of change, rattled some musical cages, and thrown away thousands of dollars pumping out this little rag.

There were some bumps along the way. The FBI found my ass when **Shane Williams**, aka **"The R&R Bankrobber,"** who was one of our contributors and a denizen of correctional institutions, was released and took up his old lifestyle. Those goddamn Fed gumshoes went door-to-door in my quiet little neighborhood with a picture of Shane holding a pound of muggles, telling those neighbors he was a friend of mine, and oh boy that went over like a fart in church with my neighbors. I knew it was time to get the hell out, and getting laid off from the teaching profession provided some added incentive, so me and Gerta loaded up the truck and moved from Michigan to the District—you know, DC—where with the help of Ian MacKaye I landed a job at a record store and kept the mag going solo for the last five issues.

The Internet in all its immediacy will see to it that neither an idea, nor a fanzine, will ever be allowed to percolate, fungate, and grow to fruition in this modern age. The Web will see to it that said idea is co-opted, bastardized, and rendered passé within 24 hours. I know this all reeks of an old buzzard ranting about the good old days of independent music, and for that you must forgive me. No, PISS OFF! If I could only make you feel the way it all made us feel as we watched it unfurl, listened to it, wrote about it, and chronicled it all in our little fanzine, (root word: **fan**), **Touch and Go.**

Footnote: The nature of shotgun journalism with a punk rock taint is that many images, photos, artworks were begged, borrowed, and stolen, cuz hell, who would ever see this besides a few slum-dwelling hipsters and miscreants?! Okay, so now it's a book and all ye of litigious persuasion please put your lawyers away if we nicked yer handiwork...or forgot to credit you...or turned your masterpiece into a shameless splash of con artistry for our own purpose. Those who we know about and can credit here for their fine contributions are as follows: Pushead for numerous contributions, John Crawford, Joel McCreery, Glen E. Friedman for his photos, Edward Colver, freie Peterson, Jim Saah, Marc Barie, Dave Stimson, Gerta Vee, and all of the many contributors who sent us stuff, records, etc. Thank you all.

Special thanks to Steve Miller and Christian Fuller, who, like Winston Churchill, never, never, never gave up until we sold this puppy; Ian at Bazillion Points; Tom Deja; Tim Gurchinoff, who took the original pages and with the help of Photoshop Pro, Lucky Strike nonfilters, Johnny Walker Black and, countless hours proved the old adage "You can't polish a turd...but you can paint it!" Thanks to Dave Stimson, Byron Coley, Henry Rollins, Ian MacKaye, Peter Davis, Steve Miller, Keith Morris, John Brannon, Corey Rusk, Joel McCreery, and Henry Owings for their recollections.

Tesco Vee

Please do not respond to any addresses listed herein except for the one below:

Tesco Vee
Box 26112
Lansing, MI 48909
www.tescovee.com

"YOU CAN IMAGINE HOW HANDICAPPED WE WERE"

And for me, that was the single biggest eye-opener in my catechism to the school of punk rock. **Kickboy** and **Chris D.**, along with a host of other writers, opened up a whole new world of music to me. The descriptions of the Masque and the shows that took place there made you burn with envy. This was Lansing we're talking about, not LA, and we didn't have anything close to a scene like that. Whoa, whoa, hang on there minute, Dave, there was no scene...nothing, zilch, nada... we had bupkis, is what we had. So you read the record reviews, and I'm not speaking out of turn here, the most important section in the magazine, it's not even close. Fortunately for us, **Flat, Black & Circular**, our local record emporium in East Lansing, carried a lot of the 45s reviewed in **Slash**. And if somebody pitched a tent over a particular record, you went out straightaway and bought the thing, and damn, if it wasn't the best thing you'd ever heard in your life! My early punk collection was built on those reviews.

In Michigan, Detroit and Ann Arbor were the only places that had anything going on. Remember driving down to some dorm on the University of Michigan campus and seeing

Destroy All Monsters for the first time. **Ramrods** also played, remember liking them a lot, but never saw any records. Started making trips to Bookies to see groups like **the Sillies, Cinecyde, the Pigs, the Boners, Nikki Corvette,** and others I've long since forgotten. It was around this time that the first issue of **White Noise** hit the newsstands. Modeled after **Slash,** it covered the local Detroit scene. A bit more form over substance, but hell, finally something a little closer to home.

Now Lansing was a hopeless backwater compared to Detroit, and Detroit was no New York or LA, so you can imagine how handicapped we were. Lansing's scene had an incredibly humble beginning; if you blinked, you missed it. We were instead feasting on descriptions of LA and the shows that took place there... Damn, where to start? Bob and I certainly weren't thinking about our legacy at the time, not by a long shot. No, we were simply living in the moment; that's what you do when you're young and think you know it all. And if you didn't agree with us, watch out, buddy boy, cuz you got ripped a new one in this little piece-of-shit rag. Now, and I can't stress this enough, T & G never would have happened if we (the Vee man and me) didn't have that shared, near-maniacal passion for the exact same music, and I mean the exact same music. Oh, and a taste for the perverse didn't hurt. Call it divine intervention or whatever, but our paths were meant to cross at precisely the same moment in the fall of '79, but hey, that's how destiny works, right?

Now we got there by different routes. Bob gave you his; mine probably started while I was finishing up a rather lackluster career at U of M in Ann Arbor during the spring of '77. I was absolutely clueless about any new musical revolution taking place, I'm buying jazz cutouts at Aura Sound in Ann Arbor, and I think I'm real smooth; what a dork. Anyway, a housemate says he'd

seen a flyer about some band playing up at the Roadhouse in a town north of A2 called Whitmore Lake. Never heard of the band, but what the hell, it was something to do. Well, the place was dead, maybe 20 people, if that, and the band turned out to be Sonic's Rendezvous Band. Didn't know it then, but that was the dawning of a new day, yes siree bob.

Upon graduation I moved back in with my folks outside of Lansing, but there was something in the air. **Flat, Black & Circular** had just opened, a pretty standard used-record store, but they carried 45s. Not the oldies shit your parents danced to, but by bands you never heard of, on labels like **Bomp** and **Dangerhouse.** And more importantly, they sold Slash, the magazine that we have both unabashedly gushed about here as being one of the motivating factors of our own little zine. On top of that demented and informed input, on Sunday nights in that fall of '77, at a pizza place way out on Waverly Road in the boondocks of Lansing, a cover band was rockin' these many bands that we were reading of in Slash. Yeah, you heard right, a cover band, and they called themselves **Toolbox.** I know it sounds ridiculous now, but anybody who was out there during that six- to eight-week stretch that autumn knows what I'm talking about. Toolbox was an education, and there's something to be said for seeing it live. **Ramones, Sex Pistols, Jonathan Richman**—hell, they even gave "Marquee Moon" a shot, just once, if memory serves.

As 1977 rolled into 1978 and nothing really took root, it seemed that Lansing would forever remain a stale and stodgy hard rock kind of town, so I packed my bags and moved out to New Jersey, to a job as a drug counselor that I would come to loathe, but I had a lot of free time on my hands. Obviously I was still reading Slash and buying lots of records. **Cheap Thrills** in New Brunswick, where I lived over Greasy

Tony's, and the countless shops of New York City made that easy, but the curious thing is that while I lived 30 minutes away, I never ventured into NYC to see shows. Don't know why really, but instead, I started hanging out at a tiny record store called the Music Scene in a mall in the Lehigh Valley at the intersection of Pennsylvania and Jersey. Huh? Yeah, I know, doesn't make any sense. It was there that I made a lasting friendship with a guy who worked there, Scott Steinberg.

In Scott, I had found a comrade in arms. It was all about the music, and we could shoot the shit for hours, and I do mean hours. This was also where I got my first taste of writing, if you want to call it that. He had a punk tip sheet called Indescribably Import that evolved into the Valley's first fanzine, Invasion. It gave me the opportunity to spew invectives, and I was more than happy to oblige. And we had plenty to write about. The 4th St. Saloon in Bethlehem held shows constantly during the spring and summer of '79. 999, Penetration, the Misfits, the Victims, the Mumps, and the UK Subs all played there. Pretty cool for a place that held maybe a hundred people. You want to have a scene to write about, ya gotta have a place where bands can play, and the 4th St. came up big every time. In retrospect, it was the golden age of punk rock in the Valley. I don't think the parallels between the 4th St. and our own Club DooBee outside Lansing are lost on anybody.

Which brings us back to that fateful meeting with the guy known to some as Tesco, to me as Bob. I had finally been shown the door where I worked in Jersey, and once again moved back to Michigan and in with my folks. I wouldn't say it was humiliating, but it was pretty damn close. All right, Dave, what the fuck are you gonna do now? Time for a career change. So I took some photography classes at our local community college, not knowing at the time that they would play a huge part in the magazine.

Now Bob doesn't recall the time we first met, but I do. It was actually twofold. I'm driving down Grand River, the main drag in East Lansing, and spot this tall dude walking down the sidewalk. Hey! Isn't that Bob from high school? Now remember, me and Bob ain't friends. Never were. We may have graduated the same year, but I don't think we said two words to each other the whole time, 'cept maybe, "Yo, douche, you're standing in front of my locker," answered with, "Oh pardon me... dick." Anyway, what caught my eye was what he carrying in his hand: the Weirdos' Who, What, When Where, Why LP. Well, well, well, we share the same taste in music. I only saw him though, that day, carryin' the goods. Our actual meeting took place shortly after at a former East Lansing disco dance joint called Rainbow Ranch, which was givin' over a night a week to the new wavers to have shows, play records, or whatever. I went down there to a show one night by myself. Bob was there with some friends. I sidled over. He was making some cutting remark about the bass player, a new addition to one of the bands on the bill, who was wearing platform shoes, silk bell-bottoms, and a puffy shirt. The kid was ripe for ridicule.

Bob and I got to talking and seemed to hit it off almost instantly. An invitation to spin some sides at his apartment in Williamston—shit, I lived in the 'burbs, but he lived in the country—followed. I don't remember much from that first visit, but Bob's drink of choice was Bombay Sapphire straight up—why I recall that and not much else is beyond me. I brought over a small stack of singles, you know, brand-new cutting-edge stuff to prove that I was a player. For the life of me, the only one that sticks in my mind is the Offs' "Johnny Too Bad." The idea of doing a fanzine was born in that apartment, maybe not that first night, but soon afterward. I'd like to take credit for suggesting the idea first, but after 30 years I don't really remember, and to be honest, who the fuck cares anyway?

Now you're holding the sum total of what we did during those brief two years we did this thing together. Some of the writing hasn't aged particularly well (I'm referring to my contributions only), but 20/20 hindsight will do that to ya. Enjoyed doing the covers; at least they don't come back to bite you in the ass. Made a lot friends along the way, most notably the members of **the Fix** and **Necros** (remember the Xanadu co-op show, guys?). Dick and Dave at FBC, George at Schoolkids' in Ann Arbor, Ian and Jeff at Dischord, and many, many more. However, I look back with a certain sense of melancholy. The passion I felt then, the excitement about nearly everything we did with the fanzine, simply isn't there anymore. I'm not suggesting that I have any regrets—far from it—but the passion of youth gets worn down with age: Touch and Go could only have been pulled off by a couple of guys in their twenties.

Let me take a moment to thank Steve Miller and Christian Fuller for getting this project off the ground and sticking with it...my parents, Roger and Mary Louise without whom yada, yada, yada...my brothers, Jim and Rog...Jerry Forrest at LCC...and finally Scott and Bob, for helping ignite that passion, for which I will be eternally grateful.

Dave Stimson (DS)
Arlington, VA
January 2010

"IN ITS UGLINESS, IT WAS THE PERFECT VEHICLE"

In its ugliness, it was the perfect vehicle to announce what was wrong with the tepid music that was heralded as good by such once-esteemed publications like Rolling Stone.

And in its parallel beauty, Touch and Go magazine, with its mimeograph aesthetic and its reliance on the profane, the obscene, and the unheard, was truly what it took for the times.

It was a fanzine, sure, but it was tinged with hate, a sure allure to us kids who were quickly getting acquainted with the emerging sounds from all geographic points circa 1979. Possession of a critical ear was as important as being a fan. And these two shit detectors/ scribes were as smart as any.

I picked up my first T & G at the local record emporium, Flat, Black & Circular, in the benign college village of East Lansing, MI. It was fall moving to winter 1979, and I was always scouring for something new imported by Jem, maybe a Damned single, perhaps a Dickies EP.

And there it was, issue #2 with Penelope Houston of the Avengers on the cover. It was jammed with cool crap; a fellow named DS seemed to possess the acerbic wit and the other, more literal one named Tesco was a bit more up-front but just as savage.

Soon I would have a little music combo of my own called the Fix that would allow me to meet these keyboard-crazed characters. DS was a thick-necked, broad-faced guy who appeared to always be studying on something. He was a star running back in high school, and his sturdy frame was still in gridiron shape. I guessed right away that he was one of those guys who was better off getting his aggression out in words. Anything else would really hurt someone. And no one was ever going to take him up on being struck down by his magazine grilling.

Tesco was thin and tall, and seeing him at a show was like seeing a tall bird lurching over everyone else. He always had the best view, in so many ways.

Together, their acid disdain for the crap and their love for the real deal drove us to distraction. The cool tunes they pimped pointed to punk progress. Every issue was jammed with cartoons, snide comments, bellicose rants, and one-liners that would be plastered, bannered, and tucked into the pages.

There has never been another publication to come close to what Touch and Go magazine did. The fact that it also launched the most prolific indy label in history is another part of its legacy. But the literary value of these here pages trumps even that. The world is a better place, our ears better served, because of those two guys from nowhere, Tesco and DS, who just did what they wanted and didn't worry what anyone else thought.

Steve Miller

MINOR THREAT REDUX

Ian: I can tell you how I first came across Touch and Go cuz I've never forgotten it: There was this store in Arlington called the Virginia Record and Tape Exchange run by a guy named Bill Asp. It was kind of a punky new wave shop and he had a pretty weird selection of fanzines, and being here in Washington we were so hungry for what was going on elsewhere in the country, and we were clued into the Dangerhouse and LA punk stuff. The Teen Idles had gone to California, so we had seen the Circle Jerks, Dead Kennedys, and Flipper, Vox Pop and the Mentors. One of the fanzines he has was Touch and Go, and on the cover was Penelope Houston, the Avengers

IAN MACKAYE

cover, and I remember thinking, "Whoa! Who the fuck knows who the Avengers are outside out of DC and West Coast?"

I couldn't believe it. I was so blown away. So we bought it and we were reading it and we thought, "This a really, really cool fanzine." So when we put the Teen Idles single out—which would have been December of 1980—we made a list of who to send it to. We sent it to Flipside and the Maximum Rocknroll radio show, Boston Rock and New York Rocker and some other ones like Mouth of the Rat. There weren't really zines in Washington at that time, so we mailed one of them to you, and we really didn't take into account what's involved with mailing something and just put it in a regular envelope or something. And then we get this letter back like, "Hey we got this record and

it was shattered but we taped it together, and what we can hear, because the needle jumps all over the fuckin' place, sounds cool!" And also I think you guys dug the cover.

TV: Oh ya.

Ian: We really worked hard on our covers and we were so happy that it connected with somebody outside of our world. It was really one of the first times that anyone outside of Washington really paid us any mind. The fact that T & G took an interest in us really blew us away, and I don't remember who called who first, but at some point we got on the phone. Did I talk to you before Corey or Barry of the Necros?

TV: I wanna think so, cuz it was about the time the Necros 7" came out.

Ian: Then you guys came down and I remember it very well, it was July of '81. You guys all pulled up on Beecher St. where we (brothers Alec and Ian) were still living at home, and I remember being so blown away by you guys and so happy to meet you, and there was that show at 9:30 with Youth Brigade/CJs/Minor Threat.

TV: Where you blew out your pipes during sound check.

Ian: You were there for that?

TV: Oh ya, we were there cuz I skipped the last day of school to be there. So with DS and me posturing as sort of know-it-alls in the mag, do you remember thinking, "These guys sound like real dicks?"

Ian: At first I thought these guys were like... and having met you I know it's true, you guys were punchy, with attitude and irreverents and you know your music well and have your opinions... but I also think there was a theme running thru the magazine that was juvenile and offensive in the same vein as Creem, Bomp, or Punk, where it's written in a childish fashion, but sets itself aside from the disgusting super-serious industry magazines who acted like they knew every damn thing about music... It was almost like a secret code... I mean we got it... and as irreverent as T & G was, I never thought it was a mean zine. The only time I thought it really got into the real mean stuff was the whole Maximum Rocknroll/Baboon Dooley (John Crawford). I tried to stay the fuck outta all that cuz it was pointless.

TV: Ya, I kinda let Crawford do his own thing and didn't even read 'em after awhile and just stuck 'em in. Which is funny cuz (Maximum Rocknroll honcho) Tim Yohannan and I got on great... He liked me and I think he was a closet Meatmen fan.

Ian: Suddenly there was this smear campaign against Tim. He called me up at some point and said, "What the fuck man you gotta step in and defend me!" and I don't wanna get mixed up in this. I thought the best thing to do was just walk away from all that. Not sure why John got such a bone up his ass about MRR. When you think that at the time there were 250 million people in this country and maybe 500–1,000 were even active hardcore punk people and were even aware of this stuff and not that many zine people and something like that feud just took on a life of its own... Now this shit gets played out on the Internet all the time.

TV: And then there was the TSOL fake feud! (The Meatmen song "TSOL Are Sissies" was just a joke, folks.)

Ian: Ya, that started as some incredible comic in T & G that showed these thugs with baseball bats and the caption was "DC Skins waiting for TSOL to arrive." (lots of laughter, fond recall, old timer-chuckles here) We thought it was funny cuz we're just a bunch of kids! Well, those guys got to

Washington and I walked downstairs at the 9:30. John Stabb, who sang for Government Issue, was a HUGE TSOL fan, especially the later, stuff when Jack was doing the clown stuff and Code Blue stuff. So he was saying TSOL was the greatest band, and we were saying, "We're gonna kick their ass," just to fuck with John. I didn't even know those guys. So I go downstairs and the minute I walk in I'm like, "Uh-oh"...and I wasn't counting on A) John was down there saying I was gonna kick their ass and B) that they would have seen the Touch and Go comic! Have you ever met TSOL?!

TV: Nope.

Ian: Yer a big guy, right? They are BIG, bigger than you. Very scary. So I walk in there and I'm 5'9", not a big guy, and these guys fuckin' stood me up so hard. They were like, "Come on, motherfucker! Come on, you gonna beat our asses?" and I'm like, "Whoa hold on," and I remember having to talk my way out of getting my face crunched by them!

TV: It's all my fault! I'm sorry, man!

Ian: Hey, it was funny...power of the pen. We were just fuckin' around! Then later we did a tour where we played in Lansing, and then we went out west where we played with the Dead Kennedys, Zero Boys, and MDC at this place called the Barn, and I came backstage and Ron and Mike from TSOL had Brian (Baker) up against the wall saying, "Minor Threat is gonna kick our ass, huh?!" TSOL would hear all this stuff while they were on tour, then we'd see them and straighten everything out...then they'd get back in the van and start hearing it all over again

(Discussion ensues about letter writing to zines and the blogs of today.)

Ian: Well, the people writing to zines weren't always erudite, but it did take some initiative to write a letter, stamp and mail it.

TV: Like sending $2 to Fear for their first single. I'm surprised Lee didn't just toss it and buy some beer. Sending money like that was a big leap of faith... but even punk rockers have principles... I don't remember ever getting ripped off sending off loot for vinyl.

(Discussion ensues about how the first Black Flag record is the best fuckin' thing we had ever heard—and listening to it was a spiritual awakening.)

Ian: I remember listening to "I've Had It" over and over and thinking, "Is there a better song ever?"

TV: That's where our attitude sort of came from. Like, "We have these unbelievable records and you don't."

Ian: That's true, there was an element of that, but by and large in mainstream society we were less than shit on the bottom of a fuckin' shoe... Like if cutting off your hair makes you a pariah in mainstream America, first off, you know you're doing something right, and secondly, you get a really good view of what's going on. In my mind, we were connecting tribally with other people, whereas most people are connecting thru other criteria like how much money, what fraternity, etc., but we shared an interest in a truly underground cultural movement. Biafra was in SF, Kevin Seconds was in Reno, Al Barile was in Boston, Tim Kerr was in Austin, all these motherfuckers... You and I could sit here for an hour and name names of people that were spread out over 3,000 miles that we knew... It's kind of insane... There is something to the holier-than-thou attitude you had, but I'm saying, "Hey, I'm excited," because I'm connected with people who reject what The Man has to offer and were headed to where the goods are.

TV: And the "goods" were so diverse. You had the Minutemen... Where the hell did that sound come from? They weren't exactly aping anyone.

Ian: Because there was no federal culture at the time, meaning there was

no MTV nationwide radio, and almost every region had its own underground or college or FM rock. So if you were a kid you could buy the records, read the zines, but you really had the freedom to do whatever you wanted to do. But you really didn't know how people moved, so if you lived in an isolated place like Lansing, you just made it up as you went along.

TV: Amen.

Ian: Punk was whatever you wanted to be in response to your actual location. D. Boon, Mike Watt, and George Hurley were in San Pedro, the weird little part of Southern California in the shadow of the LA scene, and they came up with something that was real unique from where they were coming from, and was their version of punk rock. Like the first Necros, Fix, or Meatmen singles... They weren't like anything else. When they came out I was like, "What the fuck?"

TV: So do you remember Minor Threat practicing in my basement in Lansing?

Ian: Ya, of course. We have photos of that.

TV: Do you remember Dave's brother Jim's DC scene report? That was even before we met...

Ian: No, I didn't know that. What issue?

TV: Issue #5... has me looking like a douche bag on the cover. He talks about the Slickee Boys and the Urban Verbs and all that.

Ian: Let me just say I was deeply honored to be on that cover (issue #15). (Talk turns to the Naomi Petersen R.I.P. cover of #22 with Henry/Ian.) Henry has been trying to find those pictures, as he wants copies from that session. I think we helped you staple one of these issues together?

TV: I don't remember that. When you look back on 1980, do you think of it like, "Wow, it was a cool, magical time that can never be again"? I mean with all of these retrospectives, books, movies, etc., is there a tendency to make it bigger/badder/better than it really was?

Ian: I'm not a sentimental or nostalgic person but I think about that moment in time, and throughout time there are certain corners in cultures and there are kids forever who will get near that corner but won't get to turn that corner. And for a lot of us back then there was a wave, I mean they call it the new wave, and in many ways it was a cultural wave that we happened to catch as it came crashing down. It doesn't mean that we were more legitimate than anyone else. It just means that we were there at that moment things lined up. Technology hadn't gotten to the point where anyone could do anything. We were coming out of a very complacent era, the late '70s, so it didn't take a lot to shake things up. A little courage and a little vision. The punk rock thing that happened in New York and London really resonated with a lot of us, like, "What am I doing here? What is this?" And we said, "We wanna be a part of that." As soon as we declared that, we made ourselves visible to other people, and people could find us, and we started to connect the dots. Punk rock changed America in a helluva way and not always for the good. People who think punk is about violence, depravity, nihilism miss out on the most important thing. I mean, why would people put up with all that? Because it's fucking important. We weren't doing destruction work, we were doing construction work. Now it's 30 years later and you're putting out a fuckin' book... In the Midwest you guys reclaimed the music. You guys were raised in an area that really understood rock and were lucky enough to be in an area that mattered musically.

TV: Amen, brother.

"...EXCEPT FOR THE SKA SHIT"

It's hard for me to recall exactly how I first heard of Touch and Go. I was writing for a couple of more mainstream underground music mags (New York Rocker and Take It!) when I first ran across it. That much I know. At the time, music writing wasn't as hideously dull as it's since become, but even so, I remember T & G being the first punk zine to make me squirt hot coffee out my nose while I was reading it. Before there was Gerard Cosloy at Conflict, before there was the Rev. Norb at Sick Teen, there was Tesco Vee.

This is not to infer that Tesco was a lone wolf, but it was Tesco's sperm-packed pen that provided the insane part of T & G's content. No one before or since Tesco has ever worked as much scatological and gynecological expertise into short music reviews. Even when he got off on musical tangents that made no goddamn sense at all, he did it with such impeccable verve that I'd start to think, "Hey, maybe I should check out that Virgin Prunes single after all." The bastard!

By the time T & G was really hitting its stride, I was corresponding with Tesco. At first he treated me like I was just another geezerly square, but his rock-hard stance (as it were) softened up considerably when we started trading records. He even deigned to let me write for the mag late in its life span. And I'll forever remember him as the guy who conned me into writing a wild screed about the evils of Maximum Rocknroll (then still in its infancy), which earned me the eternal enmity of the late Tim Y. Good one, prick!

But unlike the dull turd-gargle of MRR, these issues of T & G read great. They're even more extreme in some of their antipathies than I'd recalled, but hey—it was all just a poke in the eye of anyone and everyone. Like me, Tesco was a few years older than many of the youngsters who were the first ones into the hardcore scene. We had been drunk on rum and pussy juice years before most of these pweeps had tasted anything stronger than Yoo-Hoo, but their energy was great, and it was really nice to hear music that blasted again. Maybe the straight edge thing didn't make a lot of sense, but even we could appreciate the concept in a certain light. Still, we were old enough to know that—as serious as all this stuff was, as great as it could seem—it was really all a fucking joke. Most of the guys involved in any scene grow out of it. They end up at some straight gig, embarrassed by their past (if they even acknowledge it). We were past that shit already.

No excuses. No mercy. No sleep till East Lansing. What a great fucking mag. EXCEPT FOR THE SKA SHIT.

Byron Coley, Deerfield, MA, 2009

"HE HAD GOOD TASTE AND BAD TASTE"

JOHN BRANNON

(as told to Steve Miller, August 31, 2009)

I was weaned on <u>Creem</u>. That was my first magazine. <u>Creem</u> may have taught me how to piss, but <u>Touch and Go</u> taught me how to shit.

<u>Touch and Go</u> was the first magazine that spoke to the Midwest deal; it was reviewing gigs and records that you wanted to know about. They really opened up the whole world to us as excited little kids who wanted to buy these 45s. This was pre-MTV, and the whole game plan wasn't laid out for you, and it was documenting the punk rock and hardcore scene.

When I first saw the magazine, I was 18; it was early 1981. When I first saw <u>T & G</u>, I was staying with Larissa down on Cass Corridor, on Willis. And I thought, "Man, someday I'm going to be in this magazine. That would really be making it."

My mom had chased me out of the house with a hammer when she walked in on me having a Necros/Bored Youth show in the basement of our house, so I showed up at Larissa's place looking for a place to stay. She already knew Tesco. I met him later at a Fix/Meatmen show at the Coronation Tavern in Windsor that September.

The first interview I ever did was with <u>Touch and Go,</u> and we were like, "What the fuck, someone wants to interview us?" It was during the recording for the **Process of Elimination** EP; it was great, we met this guy who did <u>Touch and Go</u> magazine, being exposed to those magazines and having these guys want to talk to us.

We didn't say anything important. I'm sure we were just talking some shit. But when it came out, it was like, "Wow, we made it." <u>Touch and Go</u> introduced Negative Approach to the world, and I owe my career to that magazine.

The cover shot for that issue was at a Freezer show. The interview was exciting enough for us, and now there's this magazine that is covering the shit that we wanted to know about, like DC and the Midwest. There was no magazine that introduced the DC scene to everyone except <u>Touch and Go</u>. The photos, the interviews—no one was doing this stuff.

Nobody at that time was covering the Misfits or Minor Threat. Being from Detroit, I was always happy to see Tesco and DS introducing the scene here to the whole world. They both had that scathing writing style, and if you could get out of that without any bruises, you were doing well. It was a time period, just maybe two years, where everything was golden.

Tesco knew what was good; he had good taste and bad taste.

That cover that I was on, I had no idea it was coming. At that point—I was 19 or 20—it changed my life. I had never been taken seriously for anything before, and now I was legit. I knew that the magazine was getting around to other scenes. It was overwhelming to be on that cover. I will always be grateful to those guys for that. The rest is history. At least, some people think so.

COREY RUSK

In 1979, Maumee, Ohio, was the wrong place to live if you were into punk music. There were only five or six of us in the whole Toledo area who were obsessed with the musical revolution going on in the major cities around the world. It was a difficult place for a 15-year-old punk. Lucky for me, I was the youngest in our group, and that meant when my friends turned 16 and started driving, I was suddenly freed from the constraints of my hometown. Thus began group pilgrimages to Schoolkids' Records in Ann Arbor, Michigan...only an hour drive, but a world away.

At the time, Schoolkids' was probably one of the best record stores in the country. It brought in all the punk singles and albums from all over the US and all over the world. And at least as important, it sold all the best fanzines.

In that pre-Internet world, these fanzines were the only way to find out about the bursts of brilliance coming from places like Los Angeles, San Francisco, and New York. The mainstream press in the US was not interested in covering what was really going on in the underground clubs in these cities. The UK had Sounds and NME and Melody Maker, all of which embraced the punk movement on that side of the Atlantic. But to find out what was really going on closer to home, we had to rely on Slash and Search and Destroy, and Schoolkids' would always have the most recent issues.

On one of our visits to Ann Arbor, we were greeted with a new fanzine, only it wasn't from the coasts. It was from Lansing, Michigan, just 45 miles away. Expecting it to be a local rag with uninteresting rehash such as Coldcock, Cinecyde, or the Cult Heroes, we were shocked to discover that this new zine, Touch and Go, was funny, intelligent, sarcastic, and at the same time fanatical about the same bands we loved. Who were these guys??

We soon found out, and over the next couple years, Tesco Vee and Dave Stimson—who wrote under the moniker DS—became the big brothers you always wished you had. They would regularly send us mix tapes of all the cool records we couldn't afford (we were in high school, but they were "adults," with jobs and disposable income). Looking back, I always imagine them laughing as we'd leave Tesco's apartment to drive back to Maumee after staying up all night listening to record after record of cool shit we had never heard before. I figure they were laughing in the way an older brother does when he knows he's corrupting his younger brother, but it's just too funny to stop.

From the Germs and the Flesh Eaters to DOA and the Misfits, from Joy Division to the Pop Group, Tesco and Dave egged us on and kept our brains fed throughout '79 and '80 with a steady diet of mix tapes and wild, irreverent writing. Whether or not they knew it at the time, this stream of creativity and productivity on their part was contributing to a Michigan-area scene that was starting to have some notable bands of its own. By 1981, Tesco and Dave were not satisfied to merely document the music around them on paper alone, so '81 saw the release of the first records on the brand new Touch and Go Records label. Necros, the Fix, and a compilation that included a cut by Tesco's own band, the Meatmen, put Michigan and Ohio on the punk rock vinyl map.

For the next two years, Tesco and I worked together on the Touch and Go Records label, releasing vinyl documentation of many of the best bands Michigan (and Ohio) had to offer. In the fall of 1982, together we drove a U-Haul full of Tesco's belongings to the Washington, DC, area, which was to become his home base for the Meatmen. This move marked the end of the Touch and Go fanzine, and the end of Tesco's involvement with Touch and Go Records.

I've spent the last 28 years of my life running Touch and Go Records. It became my life's work, and it's been a good life. I've been fortunate enough to meet and work with many creative, talented, and interesting people over the past three decades. I sometimes wonder to myself what I would have done with my life if Touch and Go fanzine had never existed and I had never met Tesco and Dave. Four years and 22 issues, each with a print run in the hundreds, not the thousands. These days, the crappiest band on MySpace often gets more page views in a month than the print runs of all the issues of Touch and Go combined. But in the early '80s, this little magazine was enough to inspire the formation of dozens of bands, the creation of an enduring record label, and to create a lasting literary legend.

Corey Rusk, September 2009

"EAST COAST MIDWEST PUNKER DUNKER"

I'm clueless as to how these goofballs came up w/ the idea to create TOUCH AND GO. Was it a mag 'cause of the gloss & print quality orra zine 'cause of the characters who played in bands or hung out w/ bands writing 'bout other bands? But anybody who cares needs to give out the handshakes, pats on the backs & an extremely loud "GOOD JOB GUYS!" I'm stoked & totally psyched that Mr. VEE asked me to participate in this "blurb for the book" thing, and how could I refuse? They'd always toss props toward the CJs, which was constantly appreciated & really dug the MAD magazine comic insanity. Gotta kick from the beatin' off and listenin' to the **MEATMEN, NECROS, MISFITS, SSD,** or **NEGATIVE APPROACH** with the volume turned down on the TV while watchin' the LISA DELEEUW blow-job-video mentality of "SUPER SHREDDER SPURTIN" or "DIRK GUNGA BEATS THE DUMMY." Their hilarious vulgarity was a great foil to the politically correct mind-set of one of the more popular West Coast rags. This was one of the best zines to go to if ya cared for the lowdown on the East Coast Midwest punker dunker scene, plus they'd toss in a dash of **THE MARCH VIOLETS, BIRTHDAY PARTY,** or **VIRGIN PRUNES** just to make things darker and less same old same old. TOUCH AND GO earned its place up there w/ **SLASH, BACK DOOR MAN, FLIPSIDE, SUBURBAN VOICE, WE GOT POWER,** and **THE BIG TAKEOVER** when it comes to all this scuzzy earburn! HOORAY FOR TESCO AND HIS CRONIES!! YOU KOOKS ARE PUNK RAWK MEGASTUDZ!!!!

Keith "Bazooka" Morris

TACKED UP ON THE WALL"

My introduction to <u>Touch and Go</u> came from a desperate search for more information about bands that I couldn't easily uncover from my parents' house, which was in Pennsylvania's Amish country. While record shopping in Philly or New York, if I was fortunate enough to happen on a random copy of <u>Touch and Go</u>—invariably bagged, boarded, and tacked up on the wall behind the record store cash register, like a museum artifact—I'd devour every bit of information I could from its pages. Even amidst zines that came both before and after it, <u>Touch and Go</u> stood out. It seethed with snark—or, rather, it radiated it. Whereas most underground magazines tended to revel in their own self-importance, <u>Touch and Go</u> enjoyed the music but held those who took it too seriously in contempt. You sensed that Tesco and Dave and their usual gang of idiots didn't feel obligated but rather compelled to put out each stinkin' issue. Dear reader, there's a simple reason tattered copies of <u>Touch and Go</u> sell for big bucks—it was uncompromising, unflinching, and fucking hysterical. Period.

By the time I started my own magazine, **Chunklet,** in the early '90s, I had a savantlike understanding of <u>Touch and Go</u>'s sensibilities. I'd be lying if I said <u>Touch and Go</u> didn't have a profound influence. Much like <u>Touch and Go</u>, <u>Chunklet</u> has always been a labor of love. Making it a career was never my goal. My goal has always been to mock and/or celebrate the scene I come from by deconstructing and recontextualizing the bands, the music, the people, the clubs, and the labels. If I could ever have what I've done with <u>Chunklet</u> spoken of in the same breath as <u>Touch and Go</u>, I know I will truly have arrived.

Henry H. Owings
Chunklet magazine
Atlanta

"THE RIGHT PLACE AT THE RIGHT TIME"

HENRY ROLLINS

Many years ago, when I was living in Washington, DC, there wasn't much information on alternative music to be had. We got Xerox copies of fanzines from California and New York, and the occasional small-press single, but by and large, the independent music world was in existence but not many dots had connected yet. One of the signs of life was when we made contact with the Necros and the Touch and Go record label.

It was as if we were sending out a signal to see if there was life on other planets and one day we got a response.

I believe that Corey Rusk and Ian MacKaye had gotten in touch with each other and soon after, the Necros came to play in DC. I was given a Necros single as well as a single by the Fix, very early T & G releases.

I was very inspired by how fearless and together the Necros and Touch and Go were. It made me think that something was happening that was bigger than our small scene in DC and the very distant and almost mythological music happenings in California.

When I found out that there was a small but vigorous scene in the Midwest, the evidence being Touch and Go, I felt that we were all on the ground floor of something that was going to be very important and very exciting. I felt that I was in the right place at the right time.

Meeting the Necros and their friends Brian Hyland and Tesco Vee when they came to town was really great; they were really wild and extremely funny. I was also impressed by T & G's business model. They all seemed to have ambition and the smarts to make it work.

Over the decades, seeing where Corey has taken Touch and Go has been a great thing to watch. Like Ian MacKaye, Corey's one of those good guys who keeps the torch lit and makes good on the promise of those early efforts.

Within several months of meeting Corey and the rest, many dots all over America started connecting. Labels, fanzines, alliances started to form; networks and distribution were to follow. Touch and Go was a huge part of all that. I still have the singles that were given to me almost thirty years ago, and the T & G fanzines as well. Cool stuff.

"BIG BALLS MADE OF BRASS"

It would be inappropriate to discuss the merits of this seminal publication dating back to the days of the Xerox revolution without injecting a lot of words having to do with bodily fluids/functions, human anatomy, and so on. Sorry, pals and sals, for this guy it just wouldn't feel right...

See, back in the day, as we old curmudgeonly types are wont to say, long before the advent of desktop publishing made it possible for monkeys at typewriters to publish (and largely fill the market with lots of suck), back when the American punk scene was sprouting its first pubes on its collective pudenda/nutsack (take your pick, I'm an equal opportunist for these PC times, y'all), team Touch and Go was published for a select cadre of mostly friends by a couple of Midwestern jackasses long before the show Jackass launched its first bottle rocket out of its collective butt hole (for that matter, probably long before any of that crew were dewdrops in their mommies' panties). Put simply: These guys were the original jackasses, dig?

What was special about Touch and Go? First and foremostest, it hit the funny bone. Just as importantly, it spouted loads of good taste too, but most of all, it had gumption and, shall we say, a tumescent, John Holmes replica-sized hard-on for the bad and blew it up generally large, like big green boogs smeared on the radar screen for all to see. Sort of like those current-day ExtenZe commercials you peep late-night, that special "part" about Touch and Go that stood out most was its willingness to go over the top coupled with wanton shamelessness. A publication unafraid and with often pinpoint accuracy, T & G single-handedly took the piss out of more than a few of the scene's sacred cows—TSOL and Hüsker Dü are two primo examples

that immediately leap to mind. Hell, now that I think on it, they actually outed the latter, years before Spin practically blackmailed Bob Mould on the sexuality subject, but I digress... Here was a publication that not only liked the same kind of music I liked and likewise introduced me to a lot of tasty stuff I hadn't even heard of, but all importantly it had tons of moxie. Big balls made out of brass. Chutzpah. Nerve. Touch and Go was not afraid to be politically incorrect, and bear in mind that this was well before the hoi polloi's notions of being politically correct struck ubiquitously. And if you let your thin skin show, well, buddettes and buds, you'll have to ring Henry Rollins and allow him to explain (or look more carefully for at least one page within to figure it out, assuming, that is, you're capable).

For its time, unquestionably, Touch and Go was the National Lampoon of the punk rock world. Never asked Tesco for confirmation, but methinks it pretty likely, by some measure, he and Stimson had to have been influenced by it, and if you ever read an issue of Slash I'm pretty sure the more clever among you noobies will pick up on the late Claude Bessy, aka Kickboy Face's, notorious slag-offs for the seminal Los Angeles rag. Early issues of Search and Destroy, you ask? Well, yeah! Duh.

Sure, what a lot of this relevant historical crap boils down to is that old "what came first, chicken or egg (?)" debate, but the simple truth of the matter is, as micro as T & G press runs were (wasn't till the latter issues where bigger print runs and semi-adequate distro inroads did some Johnny Appleseed action to a wider net of target demo-a-go-go) the zine's reach, and more importantly its impact, was pretty significant. Zines such as my own, Dagger, Forced Exposure, Flesh and Bones, Ink Disease, Sick Teen, Maximum Rocknroll, Conflict, and further on up the road, Motorbooty or even Chunklet in one respect or another have all felt and incorporated the influence of T & G's chicanery. And hey, along the way, T & G spawned what was at one time one of the very best (and earliest) punk labels too.

   Impressed? Good. As it should be. Now show your respect, kids, and bend over for grandpa. You are, after all at this very moment, cradling him your loving hands.

                    Peter Davis
                    www.yourfleshmag.com

WHO'S WHO

Tesco Vee is a King Daddy and the reason we are here. He is the voice of the Meatmen and the creator of T & G magazine. He may have created the Earth, but we're not positive.

Dave Stimson (DS) still cracks wise and dry. He quietly remains one of the top musicologists in the nation, but in 1979-1982, his literary haymakers landed loudly on the jawbone of the music industry.

Steve Miller sang for T & G band the Fix and now thrives as a true-crime author and investigative journalist.

Ian MacKaye sang for Minor Threat and Fugazi. He is also the co-founder and head honcho of Dischord Records.

Byron Coley is almost as seasoned as TV & DS and has contributed to a plethora of music pubs, including New York Rocker, Forced Exposure, and Take It! Coley is the author of **No Wave: Post-Punk. Underground. New York. 1976-1980**.

John Brannon embodies rock and roll. Justice gives him the cover shot for this book, because he has lived it and earned it.

Corey Rusk has run the best indie label in the world, Touch and Go Records, for more than 25 years.

Keith Morris is the singer for the Circle Jerks and a well-schooled scenester who knows more than you.

Henry H. Owings is a voice of youth who is every bit as crabby as his elders.

Henry Rollins is a punk rock icon and a considered voice on all matters punk and pop cultural.

Peter Davis is the editor and founder of Your Flesh magazine, and a booking agent extraordinaire.

THE MAGAZINE

Pretentious and plagiarized, cover #1 belied the contents to the casual observer, and did in no fashion portend the four-year cavalcade of slime that would follow. Kinda like a hollowed-out Bible with a how-to bomb-making guide buried inside. Indeed, one would need to cut away the epidermis and peer inside; just what the H was this mag? The cover may have fooled a few—geometric simplicity and artschool pomp masked the malevolence that would literarily stumble down the tarmac over the next four years and 21 issues, like a drunken pirate with a verbal machete, taking on any and all targets with scant regard for feelings, followings, or just trying to look cool. Lotsa hippie-hatin' diatribes and a healthy dose of tasty reviews set the tone. Undoubtedly, being stuck in a one-horse town like Lansing, Michigan, gave us license to pompously purvey and enlighten the masses—oh but verily, I say, with only 100 printed, just who were we illuminating with our musical ruminations? We didn't give two fucks! We just wanted to do a rag. I dig the graininess of #1...Very black-and-white, like our take on things back then—be great or be damned. Touch and Go was coming, and middle-of-the-road and mediocre needed to be afraid...very afraid!

TÖUCH & GO

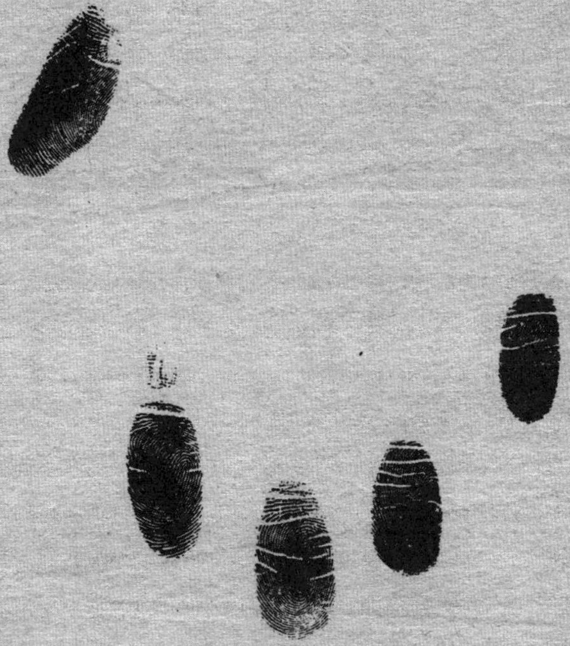

NOVEMBER 1979

ISSUE NO. 1   50¢

The death of a hippie's dream

SUBSCRIPTIONS CAN BE HAD
FOR THE MEASLY SUM OF $1.75
POST PAID. Send the money to
the same address as
your hate mail. That way you'll
be so mad you might write us a check
for more!

Well what do you know, it's been a long time
coming, but old E.L. is finally becoming hip
to what's been happening in the music world
this past couple of years. With one club
and one record shop(not Warehouse, you wimp)
that regularly features Punk/New Wave, we
can see the beginning of a serious alternative to crap we've been subjected to for so
long now. You know the kind of noise I'm
talking about---Led Zeppelin, Foreigner, Styx,
Foghat---the list is agonizingly long. But
you don't need me to tell you that. Your
stomach is constantly reminding you every
time you tune into the radio. That's not the
purpose of this magazine either. Rather, we
represent an alternative to mainstream rock
'n' roll journalism, which you probably know
is just as banal as the music they write about.
Moreover, we're primarily interested in what's
going on in this area. Granted, there isn't
that much to speak of, at the moment, in terms
of local bands, gigs and the like, but we, the
editors, will attempt to cover what's happening
(or not happening, as the case may be) in the
new music scene in and around East Lansing.
We want to be able to hear the kind of music
that we want, not this mindless drivel that
gets shoved down our throats by the major
record industries.--DS

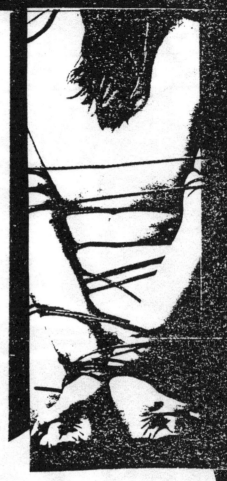

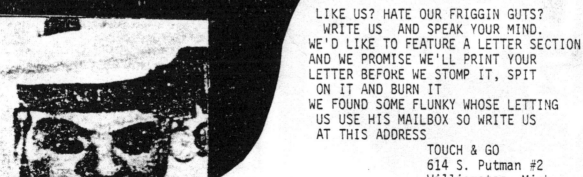

LIKE US? HATE OUR FRIGGIN GUTS?
WRITE US AND SPEAK YOUR MIND.
WE'D LIKE TO FEATURE A LETTER SECTION
AND WE PROMISE WE'LL PRINT YOUR
LETTER BEFORE WE STOMP IT, SPIT
ON IT AND BURN IT
WE FOUND SOME FLUNKY WHOSE LETTING
US USE HIS MAILBOX SO WRITE US
AT THIS ADDRESS
                TOUCH & GO
                614 S. Putman #2
                Williamston, Mich.
                    48895
        (yes believe it folks Michigan)

FLIRT

ALGEBRA MOTHERS

QUESTION MARK

THE CUBES

ALGEBRA MOTHERS-FLIRT-COLDCOCK THE CUBES LIVE AT THE RANCH

Flirt is tight. Coldcock is loose. Cubes=excitement.Algebra Mothers are esoteric and of all the Detroit bands Ive seen these impressme the most(to the rest sorry but jeez Bookies is far away for ussmall towners)

The Cubes I've seen 5 times and its always neato to see this wild blonde careening across the stage whilst the instrumental contingent churns out a big danceable sound.If you ever have a chance to see them dont go-your life will continue to be zilch, naught, zero.

Algebra mothers have a sound quite unlike any of their mid-western counterparts. Their 45 is the areas best attempt at catching a bands live sound on record. Every time Ihear them Ithink of Cabaret Voltaire jamming with Dave of the Stranglers.Buy Algebra Mothers.

Continued page 5

COLDCOCK

KILL THE HIPPIES!

Doesn't it make your blood boil when a radio station like WILS comes out with a 'new wave' program (Sunday 8 to 9), only to play the wimpiest, most archaically lame tunes this side of the Nerves? And if that weren't enough, they add insult to injury by having this little knothead of a cretin doing the show. How sickeningly cute to coin the phrase 'wavey', boy, are you a wank! Sure to trigger the gag reflex in anyone with a tablespoon of brains. This peon gives punk/new wave a bad name. For one, he doesn't know a thing about new wave or punk, and secondly, he's misrepresenting the entire new music scene, specifically to those who are receiving their first dose of this stuff.

In essence, what you're hearing on WILS is punk for hippies, or at least the stuff in new music that they've learned to tolerate. You see, the hippies control the airwaves, for it was they who first implemented FM as a musical alternative to the pap that was being pushed by the AM stations. Based on the premiss that radio could and should be used in the advancement for the growth of popular music. In 1979, you find that FM stations no longer adhere to that kind of philosophy. Now, they have become static, having locked themselves into a late 60's early 70's timewarp. Innovation and creativity have been shunned in favor of hyped, schlocky commercialism.

You hippies long for the days of peace and music. . . .and love, those which were embodied with- in the Woodstock festival. Unable to relive that era, you cling desperately to its music or a variation on the same theme. It's like dragging around the corpse of your dead dog hoping to perpetuate that old feeling between you and your pet. All that happens is that the stench becomes more and more vile. Dry up and blow away, because there's no place for you. The new music is here, and it's here to stay.

What television can't show...

Revillos "Where's The Boy For Me?"/ "The Fiend"

Alright! Faye and Eugene bounce back with a super attack!! A-side is a borderline-boardwalk-a-go-go with jag organ and stomping snare as Faye pleads for a gent at stud. This record proves these two were the punch behind the Rezillos, the sadly missed contigent from the UK. Side B sounds like one of Gene's fantasy works-the vocal track is so shrouded with an on-purpose feedback he winds up sounding like the spoiled little popster he must be. This is my favorite record but you dont give a toss....If you do nothing else pongos Get The Revillos!!!!!!!!

PUBLIC IMAGE LTD. "MEMORIES"/"ANOTHER"

Same great rhythm section we all loved on "DEATH DISCO" but this is a much stronger single.PIL comes across as very one-dimensional on first listen but rapidly worms its way into a hum-at-work type of band after a short time. Lydon's mustached visage adorns the bag as he mocks nupitals with some scummy wench who's probably Jah W. in drag.This stuff is permanent.
TV

TOP 45's of recent times

1) NEGATIVE TREND EP
2) BLACK RANDY & METROSQUAD-"I SLEPT IN AN ARCADE"
3)SKIDS-"CHARADE"
4)STIFF LITTLE FINGERS-"YOU CAN'T SAY CRAP ON THE RADIO"
5)X-"LOS ANGELES
6) ALGEBRA MOTHERS-"STRAWBERRY CHEESECAKE"
7)THE REVILLOS- "THE FIEND"
8)THE LURKERS "LOVE STORY"
9)MIDDLE CLASS- "OUT OF VOGUE"
10) THE RUTS -"BABYLON'S BURNING"
11)YOUTH DE SADE - "THEME"
12) THE DEADBEATS- "KILL THE HIPPIES"
13) THE CUBES - " SPACEHEART"
14) ANGELIC UPSTARTS - "TEENAGE WARNING"
15)FLYING LIZARDS- " MONEY"
16)COLDCOCK - "I WANNA BE RICH"
17)THE MISFITS- "BULLET"
18)JOHN & DIX DENNEY-"ADULTHOOD"
19)999 "NASTY NASTY"
20)WIRE -"QUESTION OF DEGREE"
21)FLESHEATERS EP
22)FLIRT- LIVE TAPE OF"SUGAR SUGAR"
23)GERMS- "LEXICON DEVIL"
24)THE POP GROUP - "SHE IS BEYOND GOOD & EVIL"
25)X-" ADULT BOOKS"

This article begins on page ③

Flirt is one Detroit band that has a look as well as a dynamic sound.Rockee is one helluvan-on-key vocalist whose latest contributions left my gonads jumping for days.Skid is a bass player who brings his thing out front where it belongs. This band has a girl and a real sound. Why aren't they big in Japan?

Coldcock is a group you either love or hate. Ilike groups that get strong reactions- that's a good sign. E.Lansing had it's first taste of these low-lifes and it was groove-at-first-sight. Andy looks like he just sang a gig in some London cave. Of course the world knows' Vince B.guitarist and disc flipper at the legendary BOOKIES CLUB.These working stiffs deserve your hard earned cash. Buy the single and if you dont then I'll.... I'll........

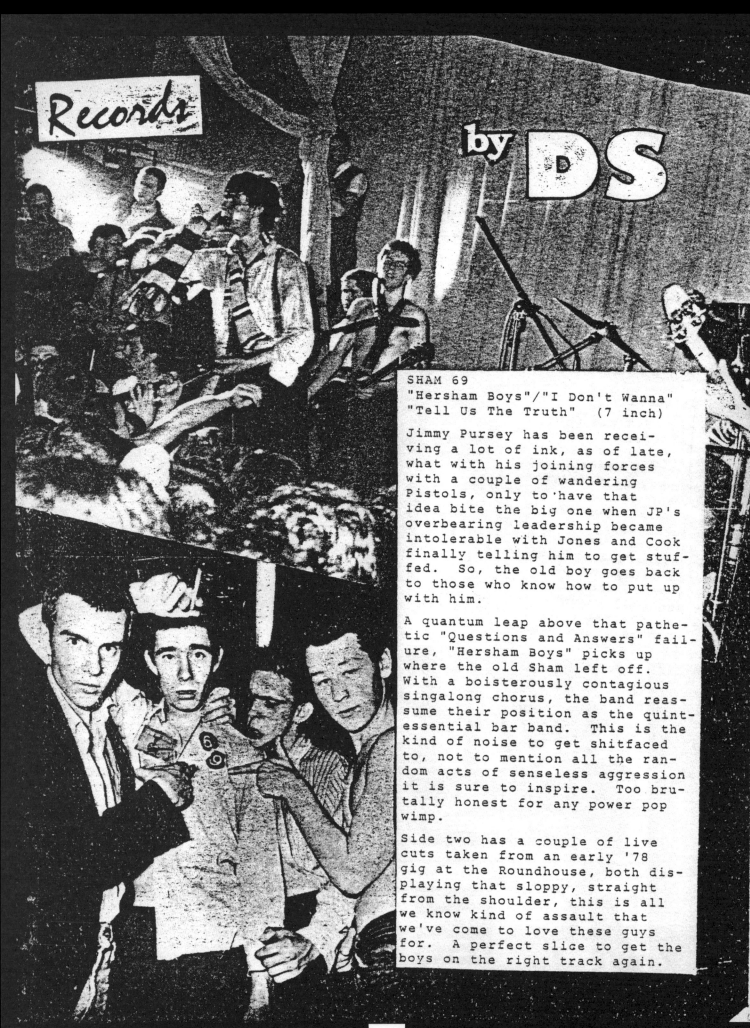

SHAM 69
"Hersham Boys"/"I Don't Wanna"
"Tell Us The Truth" (7 inch)

Jimmy Pursey has been receiving a lot of ink, as of late,
what with his joining forces
with a couple of wandering
Pistols, only to have that
idea bite the big one when JP's
overbearing leadership became
intolerable with Jones and Cook
finally telling him to get stuffed. So, the old boy goes back
to those who know how to put up
with him.

A quantum leap above that pathetic "Questions and Answers" failure, "Hersham Boys" picks up
where the old Sham left off.
With a boisterously contagious
singalong chorus, the band reas-
sume their position as the quintessential bar band. This is the
kind of noise to get shitfaced
to, not to mention all the random acts of senseless aggression
it is sure to inspire. Too bru-
tally honest for any power pop
wimp.

Side two has a couple of live
cuts taken from an early '78
gig at the Roundhouse, both displaying that sloppy, straight
from the shoulder, this is all
we know kind of assault that
we've come to love these guys
for. A perfect slice to get the
boys on the right track again.

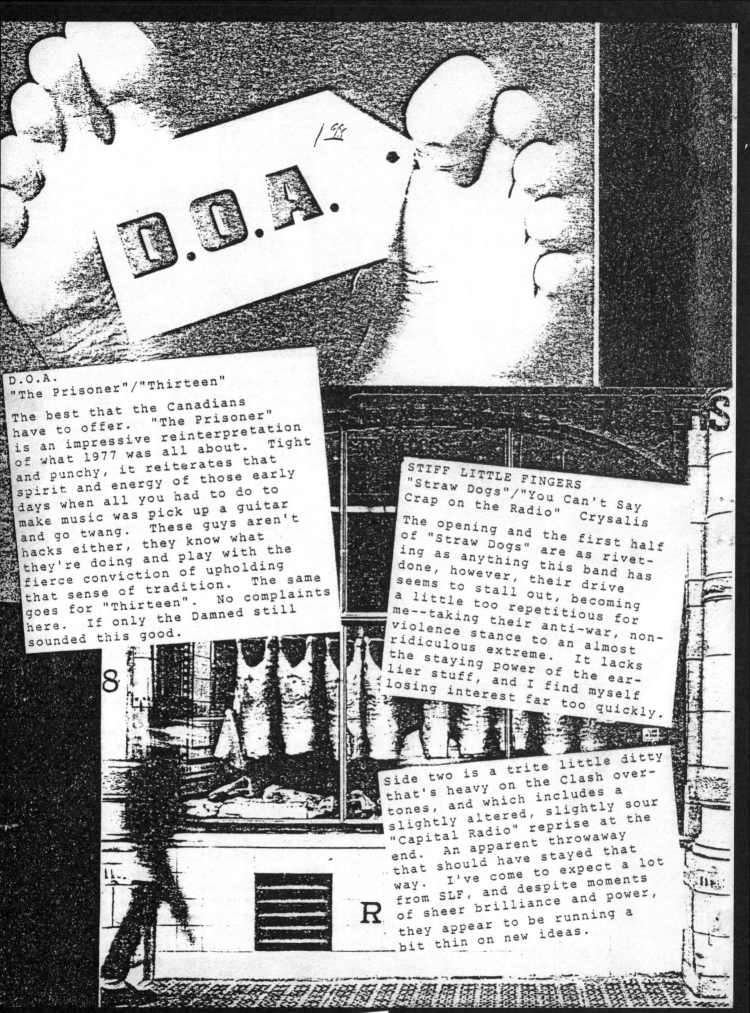

D.O.A.
"The Prisoner"/"Thirteen"

The best that the Canadians
have to offer. "The Prisoner"
is an impressive reinterpretation
of what 1977 was all about. Tight
and punchy, it reiterates that
spirit and energy of those early
days when all you had to do to
make music was pick up a guitar
and go twang. These guys aren't
hacks either, they know what
they're doing and play with the
fierce conviction of upholding
that sense of tradition. The same
goes for "Thirteen". No complaints
here. If only the Damned still
sounded this good.

STIFF LITTLE FINGERS
"Straw Dogs"/"You Can't Say
Crap on the Radio"   Crysalis

The opening and the first half
of "Straw Dogs" are as rivet-
ing as anything this band has
done, however, their drive
seems to stall out, becoming
a little too repetitious for
me--taking their anti-war, non-
violence stance to an almost
ridiculous extreme. It lacks
the staying power of the earlier stuff, and I find myself
losing interest far too quickly.

Side two is a trite little ditty
that's heavy on the Clash over-
tones, and which includes a
slightly altered, slightly sour
"Capital Radio" reprise at the
end. An apparent throwaway
that should have stayed that
way. I've come to expect a lot
from SLF, and despite moments
of sheer brilliance and power,
they appear to be running a
bit thin on new ideas.

THE WEIRDOS
Who?What?Where?When?Why?   EP

Finally! These guys get around to
doing it to us again. I was beginning to wonder whether we'd ever
see anything from the band that
purged us with the "Neutron Bomb"
holocaust. Over the past six months,
however, the group has dwindled to
just three--John and Dix Denny along
with Cliff Roman(Dave Trout and
Nicky Beat having other ideas).
The remaining Weirdos hang on to
much of their original sound, although, you won't hear anything as
devastatingly raw as "Solitary Confinement". They come close, but
they have now supplemented their
music with the addition of synthesizer and saxophone, and that in
no way diminishes the impact of
this new material.

The stunning intro of "Happy People"
opens side one. With synthesized
bubblings and a simple bass riff
(not unlike that of "Public Image")
building our anticipation, the
guitars burst forth to prick our
skin and administer a freon injection with shivering results. That's
not all. There's a "la, la, la. ."
chorus that produces in me the ab-
surdest kind of pride imaginable.
Glad to be here and not out somewhere hocking my soul for a Styx
ticket. Probably the same sort of
emotional stirrings that grip
Shriners whenever they see Old Glory
running up the flagpole. Yeah I
know, weird. Nonetheless, "Happy
People" is still an inspiring piece
of music.

Although the rest of the record may
not match the moving qualities of
the first cut, everything else is
first rate, top drawer, grade A
Weirdos, especially "Hit Man" and
"Idle Life". I didn't think they
could keep these guys down for long,
with the Weirdos emerging from their
sabbatical to assume their rightful
position. . . .and where else, but
in the forefront.

THE TWENTY SEVEN
"Don't Go to Extremes"/"Catastrophe"
"Lifeblood"   Tremor

More of what I've come to expect
from the Detroit music scene. Catastrophe isn't too bad, but the
rest is the kind of droll that's
high on nostalgia and low on excitement. Mark Norton, the most obvious
Iggy clone to emerge out of the ooze
of the Motor City cesspool, has one
foot permanently cemented in a block
of Detroit rock 'n' roll history,
with this single sounding like an
anemic imitation of the Stooges'
"Sick of You" EP. What's with you
guys? You sound old, and tired as
well. Whatever happened to the spit
and fire that was a hallmark for the
Ig and the MC5? That's as vital a
part as any in this whole punk movement. What I'm hearing now are pedestrian reworkings of old songs,
without the spirit and recklessness
of the past(1977, that is)

What is it, are your roots so deeply
embedded inside those feeble minds
of yours that you're incapable of
coming up with anything that isn't
dominated by a sound that has no business being here? I mean, you probably wouldn't recognize a new idea
if it came up to you and shat right
in your face. Get with it, I'd like
to see something happen in Detroit,
but at the rate you're going I just
might be a Grey Panther by the time

Plastic Idols

THE PLASTIC IDOLS
"I.U.D."/"Soshistication" Vision

A single, gravelly guitar kicks
things off with a fuzz-tone that
would make Link Wray green with
envy. A clean thumping bass follows with the rest of the band
close behind. I don't quite
know what they're trying to say--
I hear "I.U.D. what'd you do to
me?", some snatches here and
there, but the rest is lost in
a mire of clashing guitars and a
muddy production. Toward the
end there's even an acid guitar
break buried beneath all of this
before the band returns to punc-
tuate with the one dimensionally
dissonant sound that opened this
can of noise.

"Sophistication" is totally dis-
similar from the A side. It's
the Viletones meet DEVO, an un-
likely pairing, but that's the
only way to describe this combination of "Screamin' Fist" velocity and DEVO's synthesized
loop-da-loops. An excellent debut from this Texas band.

ALBUMS

BOLLURKS

THE ANGELIC UPSTARTS- "Teenage Warning"

To show you how grim the album situation is around here I had to travel 300 miles to Wax Trax(best in the midwest) Records in Chi-town to find this gem. To shorten this blurb The Upstarts are one of the English bands to which the skinhead youth are devoted along with UK Subs Sham 69 ect. The band has been accused in the English press (so what else is new?)of having only one strong point, that being the the stage presence of (am I stuttering?) lead vocalist Mensi. But then much of the English journalists are little yobs whose inexper-ience and narrow view is to me as unsavory as"The Front" itself.

The Upstarts are young. At least they sing about teen topics much of the time with tunes like"Youth Leader", " Student Power", "The Young Ones", and the45 released from the LP "Teenage Warning." A look at the band makes one cringe at the delightful thought of crass onslaught to follow. Without boring you further I'll just cliche you to death, these guys are loud and to the point. It's the best. I'd like to see them live but me hair covers the top of me ears and I'd probably get bludgeoned to death.

ANGELIC UPSTARTS

THE LURKERS- God's Lonely Men

Imissed em wence they visited Murder City. Supp-osedly the band was great (of course) but limey sources say the American trip didn't go well. To me The Lurkers are a dance band -a fuckin' great dance band! Esso's drumming has never been better(he's even work-ing your basic double-bass thump-a-thumps on"Room 309" sigh-ED.) Howie's vocals are always supreme.The revved up"Cyanide" sounds choice after listening to to the pub version on the "Out In The Dark" single. The world owes these blokes sustainence. America prob-ably isnt ready for this good of a band but then america isn't ready for next Tuesday.

TV

THE POLICE

THE POLICE"Regatta de Blank "

I know its blanc, ask me if I give a monkeys. Wonder when The Specials album will be out........

TEENAGE WARNING

IF ITS LENE'S YOU'LL LOVICH

Lene Lovich "Stateless"
She's super in concert at least she was on TV in one of those choreographed lip-sync skits England always sends over. The guitarist taste-fully surrounds her vocals and the rest of the band also do much to showcase this great talent. Prime Cuts are "Home" and "Say When"

ROCK FROM THE INSIDE OUT#]

HEY FANS,SINCE THIS IS MY INTRODUCTORY COLUMN AND ITS A LITTLE " TOUCH & GO" HERE LET ME PREFACE IT WITH A LITTLE HISTORY OF HISTORY IN THE MAKING.

I'M AN INMATE IN FEDERAL PRISON WHO ALSO HAPPENS TO BE A ROCK AFFICIONADO AND A SINGER/SONG-WRITER/GUITARIST FOR THE LAST]0 YEARS. I'M 24.

ALL MY MUSICAL INPUT COMES FROM 3 BASIC SOURCES-TAPES TESCO SENDS ME, TAPES MY PARENTS SEND ME, AND THE RADIO. ONE MIGHT ASK WHAT CAN BE WORTHWHILE TO LISTEN TO ON THE RADIO? WELL HERE IN LOMPOC CA. I CAN PICK UP 3 PROGRAMS THAT ARE FAN-FUCKING-FABULOUS! THEY ARE "HEPCATS FROM HELL" HOSTED BY R. MELTZER OF VOM FAME(I'M IN LOVE WITH YOUR MOM") "ELECTROCUTE YOUR COCK") HE FEATURES LIVE TAPES AND INTERVIEWS OF SUCH HOLLYWOOD (MAH HOMETOWN) GROUPS AS "X" "WEIRDOS" "WALL OF VOODOO" "FEAR" "MAU-MAUS" ect.ect. IN CASE YOU CUM TO OR ARE FROM L.A. ITS 90.7 KDFK 2AM. TO 6AM. SUNDAYS. THEN THERE'S THE IAN HILL SHOW ON KCSB THE COLLEGE STATION FROM SANTA BARBARA. IAN PLAYS IMPORTS THAT HAVE JUST HIT THE SHELVES PLUS OTHER STAPLE PUNK. DIRECTLY FOLLOWING IS "NO RADIO" HOSTED BY SCOTT WHO USED TO BE IN THE NEIGHBORS." HE PLAYS ENO AND OTHER EXPERIMENTAL SHIT.(AS YOU CAN SEE MIDWESTERN RADIO HAS A WAYS TO GO.ED.)

SO THIS COLUMN IS GONNA BE ME REVIEWING WHAT I'VE HEARD AND GIVING A LITTLE ANTI-SOCIAL COMMENTARY NOW AND AGAIN AND OF COURSE THE WHOLE REASON FOR MY DOING THIS IS SO YOUNG NUBILIAN-PUNKETTES WILL WRITE TESCO FOR MY ADDRESS SO THEY CAN SERVICE MY EVERY NEED.I AM THE ROCK & ROLL BANKROBBER!

THIS ISSUE HIGHLIIGHTS ALL THE NEW & EXCELLENT ALBUMS BY SUCH FAVES AS "SIOUXIE AND THE BANSHEES-JOIN HANDS" ; WIRE - "]54" ; XTC- "DRUMS AND WIRES"; ONLEY ONES" SPECIAL VIEW" AND MAGAZINE -"SECOND HAND DAYLIGHT".

OF THE FEW CUTS I'VE HEARD OFF THE WIRE LP THEY ARE QUITE DIFFERENT THAN THEIR FIRST 2EFFORTS. "I SHOULD HAVE KNOWN BETTER" IS SUNG BY LEWIS ON BASS WHO HAS YET TO HAVE CROONED AND THIS IS VERY MELODIC AND MYSTERIOSO . MY FAVE WIRE TUNE TO DATE. MY OTHER FAVE WAS "THE OTHER WINDOW" A VERY EXPERIMENTAL ONE WITH WHAT SOUNDS LIKE A RAP SESSION OVER MUSICAL ACCOMPANIMENT. CHECK THESE GUYS OUTTTT!

SIOUXIE'S NEW ONE FOLLOWS HER DEBUT WHICH IS TO SAY MORE FANTASYLAND DOOM& GLOOM. A STRONG ONE NEVERTHELESS AND LIGHT YEARS BETTER THAN "MEGA-ROCK".

HEY LISTEN UP IM RUNNING OUT OF SPACE HERE- THERE'S ANOTHER BAND FROM GEORGIA THAT SURPASSES THE B 52's. They're CALLED "THE FANS" AND THEY REMIND ME OF MAGAZINE(MY FAVORITE BAND, OR AT LEAST PART OF THE TRIUMVIRATE-(ULTRAVOX-MAGAZINE-DOLL BY DOLL) THEIR SONGS LIKE "DANGEROUS GOODBYES" AND " CARS AND EXPLOSIONS" ARE FUCKING GOOD!

BEFORE I DEGENERATE INTO JUST NAMING BANDS AND SONGS I LIKE I'LL BE SIGNING OFF SAYING

I'M AN UPSTART ......WHATCHA GONNA DO?
I'M AN UPSTART MEESTAH ....I'M TALKING TO YOU!

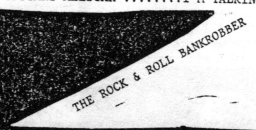

THE ROCK & ROLL BANKROBBER

Top 40

1. The Angelic Upstarts
2. GERMS!
3. 999
4. Sex
5. NEGATIVE Trend
6. Vibrating Butt Plugs
7. X
8. Bookies 870
9. Siouxie Sioux
10. Pink Pegged Pants
11. JOHN PEEL
12. The Lubes!
13. NME
14. Black Wrap Shades
15. WAXTRAX Records
16. The Cramps
17. Anal Stimuli
18. @ldcock
19. Flying Lizards
20. DOLL BY DOL
21. Slash
22. Middle Class
23. The Specials
24. Bondage
25. Generation X
26. Flip side!!
27. Stu Shapiro
28. FEAR
29. SHAKE
30. Dead Kennedys
31. Algebra Mothers
32. Crotchless briefs
33. JOE STRUMMER
34. The Dils
35. Nick Cash
36. PSYCHEDELIC FURS
40. Shane Williams

Bottom 40

1. Cheap Trick
2. Lansing Radio
3. Cover charges
4. pimples
5. The Cars
6. longhair
7. Campus Cops
8. Bruce Springsteen
9. Smelly sox
10. High Times Magazine
11. Dan Carruso <sp?>
12. The Knack
13. pet feces
14. Ted Nugent
15. Hemmeroids
16. George Thorogood
17. Designer Clothes
18. Styx
19. vomiting
20. The Records
21. stubbing your toe
22. Patti Smith
23. Groups who sell out!
24. $9.00 import prices
25. Kansas (Both of em)
26. Halitosis
27. Boston (Both of em)
27. People with nose hair
28. Politics
29. Detroit Radio
30. Joe Jackson
31. leprosy
32. Creem Magazine
33. Penetration
34. Heavy Metal
35. People from California who think people in Michigan are ignorant
36. Hit Parader
37. Mick Jagger's Lips
38. "middle aged" College students

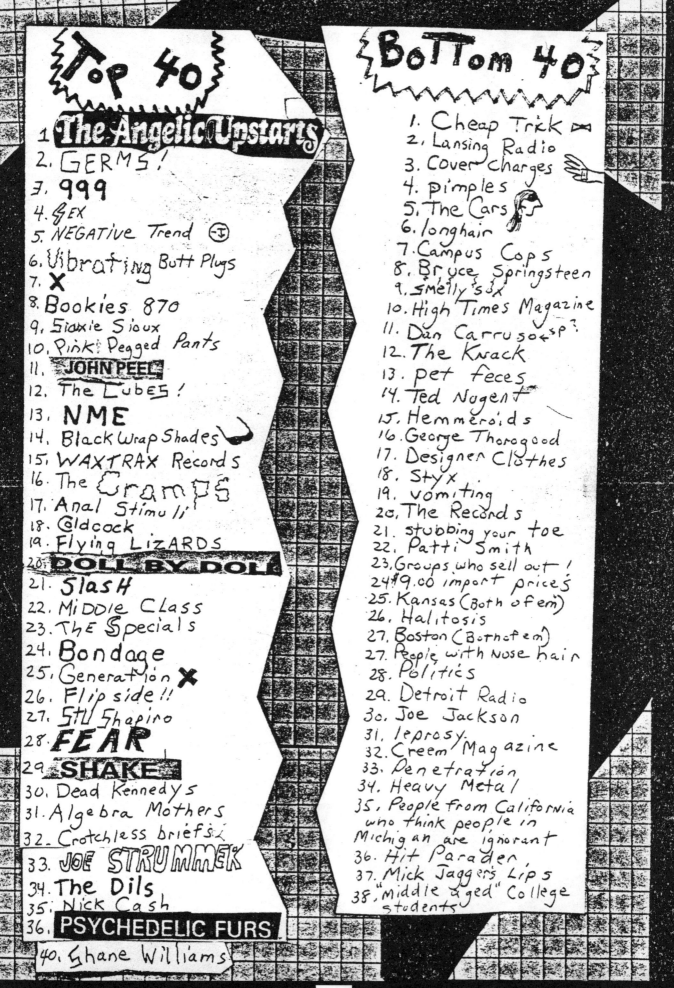

2

Even with only 100 copies of #1 on the streets, we managed to run a full-page letter section in issue #2. Penelope Houston in action makes this one of my fave covers... All hotness aside she and SF's Avengers were flat-out smokin'. Okay, the hotness didn't hurt. If she had had a grill like Poly Styrene, I wouldn't have had to fire as many loads of tadpole tapioca into the banana cream puddin' at the Ponderosa where I worked. Still, heavy on the UK bent as were all the early issues, we do see hints of US aggro creepin' in and around our taste buds. I slammed the Romantics even though I secretly went to all their shows cuz A) I was still a college dude craving vulva and hey... chicks dug it! & B) they were tight, loud, and a helluva great show. DS on his soapbox railing like a crazed evangelist about the local FM radio station's pathetic stabs at embracing "new wave" keeps the theme alive for yet another issue. Right about now we get the inkling that we're onto something good...

TOUCH AND GO

AVENGERS

DECEMBER 1979

ISSUE # 2   50¢

AND ON THE EIGHTH DAY GOD CREATED ANDY.

BLACK FLAG
BOOSTER

WHAT'S WITH YOU YOUNG
SUCKWADS? THIS QUALITY
RAG IS ONLY 50¢ AND ALL
YOU GOTTA (belch) DO IS
WRITE A LETTER TO RECEIVE
A FREE ISSUE. SO QUIT PICKIN'
YER DIRT CHUTE AND SPEAK YOUR
NARROW MIND!

TOUCH & GO

I know it's hard to believe but yes, god's lonely men are back
with issue #2 of TOUCH & GO! What we tried to do with the first
one was to reach those of you who know whats going on in the
music world. In regard to the underwhelming local response it
would appear you Michiganders view us as irrelevant. We are
however ecstatic that others found the time to write in and
respond. Granted TOUCH & GO is biased, self indulgent, spiteful
and sometimes downright nasty. We are truly not sorry if we have
offended you. Hopefully issue #1 made you react somehow unless
our silver-lined culture has anesthetized the populace more than
we had imagined. After all if someone or thing is shitty to you
do you sit there and eat it? NO! TOUCH & GO just happens to be
tired of eating a lot of things. But don't get us wrong, if you've
read this far we love you! (especially if yor a GURL!!)

TESCO
(the sultan of S&M)

TOUCH & GO
BOX 26203
LANSING, MICH.
48909

Subscription rates:
$2.00 for three issues,
let's face it, postage
ain't cheap.

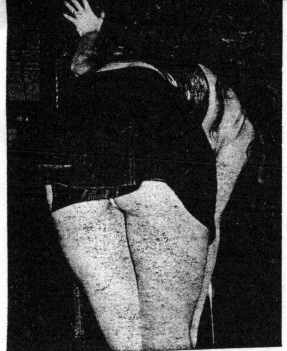

Shaun Hendrix is the biggest wanking, scumbait DJ in Lansing. Being involved in what could be argued as the most progressive move made by WILS in a long time, Mr. Hendrix should be in a position of sizable import and influence, but no, each and every Sunday night this lardbrain proves to us that his knowledge of new wave goes absolutely no farther than Billboard magazine. Shaun, you don't know shit about anything. How'd you get this job anyway? What'd you have to do . . suck off the program director? Oh, excuse me, that was a low blow, wasn't it Shaun baby? You think my inflammatory remarks are uncalled for? Hardly. Let me just shed some light on your boundless ignorance with a few 'for examples'. On November 18 you stated that "No More Heros" was the latest LP from the Stranglers. I couldn't believe that when I first heard it, but then again, you don't have much of a view when you've got your nose wedged up your bum, now do you? And how about your pallid definition of 'obscure'. Battered Wives-- obscure, yea right. Spare me, Shaun, just because they only have one album, doesn't mean they're obscure. Start doing some research on this stuff, you're misinformed and you're passing it on to the listener.

Don't you give a fuck about what you say on the air? At this point, I guess not. The sickening part about it is that you try to come across like you're some kind of authority on the subject. Now, obviously you're not, I know it and you know it, but trying to con the average listener into believing it is criminal. You don't know jack shit, and I'd wish you had the balls to admit it. Don't relax, because I'm not finished with you yet. I want to now focus on your biggest problem. No, it has nothing to do with your mental capacity, which can be easily summed up with a simple '0'. The axe I have to grind with you is your flagrant use of the word 'classic'. You make it sound as though every other disc falls into this category. C'mon, whatever happened to discriminating taste? In your feeble attempt to bolster the image of the lame shit you guys keep playing, you fling this word around like it's going out of style. Shaun, you in particular, made the supreme jackass out of yourself(some guys have a knack --Ed) when you blindly referred to that "Now Wave" sampler as classic. I bet you haven't even listened to it, and still you rave about it like it was some kind of masterpiece. Where are your brains?--buried out in the backyard? Don't you know what the fucking word means? Obviously not. Let me refresh your memory--according to Webster-- 'classic' means: 'serving as a standard of excellence'. With that, are you still going to insist that The Hounds, The Beat, The Sinceros, and Jules and The Polar Bear qualify for that kind of distinction? You're such a snivelling little wimp, you probably will. Stop fucking around Shaun. Admit you're shit and leave this stuff to the people who know something about it.--DS

LETTERS!

DRUMMER--Wants to be in violent group. Contact Vic Kingman c/o Touch & Go

Hey TOUCH & GO!

Saw the ROMANTICS at the Gables and I think they are one of the better Detroit bands I have heard. I rate them right along with leather and spurs! They're great! That other band suck-ed anus! Hey BOYFRENZ if I ever turn homo I'll look for you zeros later.

The other demeaning force in the Gables was 101 FM. For both of them in Lansing and Grand Rapids I ask if your readers have ever seen Kurt Vonnegut's illustration of an anal orifice? It looks like this and mine like this.

"KURT'S"   "MINE"   STRETCHED

How about adding Holland,Mich. to your bottom 40?
                    FROM HOLLAND, TRENCH

To the editors,
It's good to see a lucid well-informed 'zine like yours beginning to make it's presence felt, especially coming from E. Lansing and environs.

I recently had the pleasure of visiting a friend (also a native Chicagoan)at MSU. I was in your town for all of about 3 days and developed an acute case of claustrophobia. As the late Dead Boys used to say, "There ain't nothin' to do!"

Here's to your future success!
Rock & Roll Never Sleeps
Claire Pieterek
Chicago,Ill.

Granted ol' E.L. is DULL!, but it's not our town. The college students make it the contrived wasteland it is.ED.

Crack me a beer honey-it's sunny and 85 today, this piece of shit radio just played another ad for R&R High School which reminded of the latest (or most recent) actually only issue of the soon to be nationally known quality rag T&G- good stuff.I'll have to say yes on that one Bill. Great little print. It's hell lying here on the beach squinting at the beautiful twists while you sorry bas-tards await your just punishment to arrive. The first effort by Vee (garsh fanx,ed.) and assoc-iates was clearly a superior fold. Where else can one find such use-ful info as Carmy Applesauses' legspan, Jism Jazz target record and Tesco Vee's shoe size. Who the fuck cares? Good music is what I like and T&G sets it out. There isn't shit down here. So I'm depending on you to keep me afloat. These jasbos think The Scorpions are those little insects on the sand. And Ramones must be that new little mexican greasehole on south 19. Time to turn over, I'll swap you what's next to me for the next issue.
                    Tom Wilson
                    Clearwater Beach Fla.

It's a deal but how the hell did you get a copy down there??! My feet take a 14 but what the hell is Jism Jazz?
                    ED.

Dear TOUCH&GO,
Thanx for the complimentary issue. It's a good 'zine (un-fortunately there are'nt many) and we'd like to sell it in our store. Send us ten copies.
                    Thanx a lot
                    JIM & PAM
                    POSEUR
                    HOLLYWOOD, CA.
Of course anyone worth their salt knows POSEUR has the best selection of flipped out clothing and buttons to be found.(Besides we like their taste in 'zines!!! ED.)

As The Pop Group would say "Words Disobey Me"-this is my dilemma: how to write an intelligent review of the most incredible display of electronics I've ever heard. The new ULTRAVOX lineup consists of Midge Ure on guitar & vocals since Foxx and Shears' departure. The boys opened each set with 3 synthesizers and drums-and these guys make Gary Numan look like the inexperienced 21 year old he is. Their music is rythmically hypnotic and the newest material seems to be the most fascinating stuff

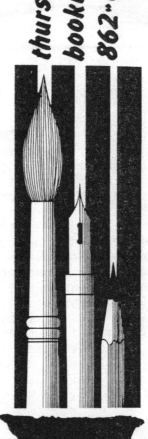

thurs.&fri. nov. 22&23
bookies club 870
862-0877

yet-"Mister X" and "SLEEP WALK" have left me a serious jones that only the new album will satisfy. Midge passed up a lucrative deal with Thin Lizzy to pursue a career with a real group- excuse the cliche but this is truly music for the 80's. Hats off to BOOKIES CLUB for giving us ULTRAVOX for two nights!

TESCO VEE

-PAUL-

Out of the cyclicly contrived maelstrom of american "pop"
culture oozes but another glob of stench reeking of the
fucking 60's. Epic records hope for 1980 is The Romantics-
yet another attempt at grabbing a wad from the american public.
Why is it that the only original music is being created on the
west coast, the region that until a few years ago was a sun &fun
wasteland of meretricious boredom? The midwest, once supposedly
a hotbed of music now lays dormant due in part to archaic FM
programming, and lack of venues in which new bands can cultivate
a sound and a following. It's socially acceptable right now to
be a beat band (anyone only has to visit a record store to over-
whelmed by the rash of releases in this general category) and
The Romantics are all we have to show from the midwest? Well I'm
sorry but shit like this is lame and yes you guessed it, the
public will eat it up . I'm tired of these hyped up puppet shows...

                                    TESCO VEE

45'S!

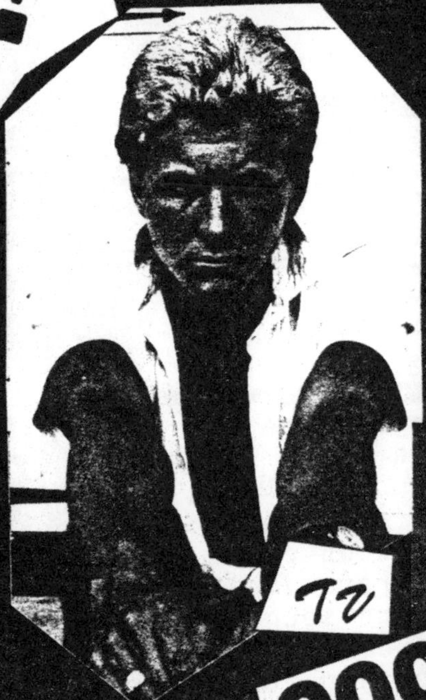

THE OUTCASTS- "SELF CONSCIOUS OVER YOU"/ "LOVE YOU FOR NEVER"

Hardly what I expected from these blokes but god this is good stuff. Teen tunes both of em'- accessible but grungy and fun. Glad to see the Undertones' school of pubescent anthems has it's first alums. Both sides have it musically but dating an' mating in Belfast sounds rather dull.

TV

ANGELIC UPSTARTS

ANGELIC UPSTARTS- "NEVER AD' NOTHIN'"

You're probably sick of my ranting about these guys but if anyone else was making records this good I'd be more diverse. This one tells the sad tale of an English teen who decided since

THE PACK- "KING OF KINGS' "NUMBER 12"

Granted they tread the HM fringe but in such style dis is perfecto. A side is like a churning intro that leaves the listener well hung. Hope your stereos got a good bass range cuz this was recorded way too heavy on the treble. Ex PIL skin man Walker beats it for these guys. Don't listen to anyone else- this is boss.

TV

999 FOUND OUT TOO LATE cw LIE LIE LIE

999 is a great band.It's too bad the production is so poor on this. "Lie Lie Lie" was one of the encores on the boys latest US tour and it's a strong one. But the(sob)overiding fault here is tinny production- I mean it's really poor. If any band needs a good producer 999 does. For all the flack Martin Rushent takes he did a helluva lot better than this guy.(how the hell can I bitch all the way through this superb slab of long-awaited greatness??!) But the strength of these tunes and the fact that Nick Cash is so neato means I can overlook it all.999 is a great band.

he'd "Never ad' nothin'" he would "Go out in a puff of smoke" so he ran out of pub with a loaded piece and got well you guessed

the rest. Anywho the record is their best ever- chant & rant like never before- defeatist principles sung with a corner lip smile.

A mood record for those days that don't go well. A+

AVENGERS- "THE AMERICAN IN ME"
"UH OH !!"/"CORPUS CHRISTI"/
"WHITE NIGGER"

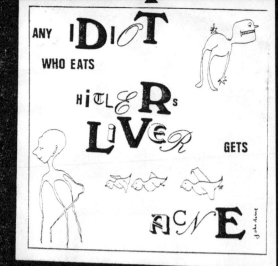

Avengers were that special
band whose debut effort made me
realise my extensive mega-rock
collection was a load of turd
and it was time to start over.
"I Believe In Me" was a bleedin'
punk rock record- when this was
on everything else was faking it.

Back after 2 the Avengers are every
bit they were and more. This EP is
produced by Stevie "turd on legs"
Jones of Sex Beatles fame and he
does a goo goo good job on dis.
Penelope is such a supreme vocalist
and the rest of the band sound choice
although they seem to be chomping at
the bit on a couple of numbers. I'm
one of those who is by far partial
to "The American In Me" although my
friends tell me I'm full of it just
cuz they groove on side 2. Narrow
minded hippys anyway. Sorry the
graphic's a bit outdated but Greg W.
deserves one last photo in a world
wide magazine.They're on our cover
because they're the best.

HERE'S THE IF YOU DON'T (you're shit)
OWN THESE SINGLES CHART...

1) BLACK FLAG EP
2)RHINO 39- "XEROX"
3)THE DURUTTI COLUMN- "THIN ICE (DETAIL)"
4)DILLINGER- "SEX ME BABY"
5)THE POP GROUP- "DON'T CALL ME PAIN"
6)AVENGERS EP
7)ANGELIC UPSTARTS- "NEVER AD' NOTHIN'"
8)NON- "KNIFE LADDER"

SEE THE
RUTS
HEAR
THE
CRACK
Virgin
V2132

9)ART PATRONS- "CHEST POOL"
10)GIORGIO MORODER- "LOST ANGELES"
11)GEZA X- "PONY RIDE"
12)YOUTH DE SADE- "THEME"
13)THE MISFITS- "CHILDREN IN HEAT"
14)SILICON TEENS- "LET'S DANCE"
15)SWELL MAPS- "DRESDEN STYLE"
16)ALL X
17)PAGANS- "WHAT'S THIS SHIT CALLED CALLED LOVE?"
18)CABARET VOLTAIRE- "NAG NAG NAG"
19)ALGEBRA MOTHERS- "STRAWBERRY CHEESECAKE"
20)PUNILUX- "PUPPET LIFE"
20)COLDCOCK- "I WANNA BE RICH"
21)THE POP GROUP- "WE ARE ALL PROSTITUTES"

ANY IDIOT
WHO EATS

HiTLERs
LiVeR
GETS

AcNE

CRISIS
"U.K. '79"/"White Youth" Ardhor Records

One of Britain's most political outfits, I expected a clenched teeth,
two fisted assault on our static sensibilities, but that's not what I
got. Oh, the anger and hostility
seething amongst British youth is
there alright, but Crisis choose to
deliver their message in a slow almost
hypnotic fashion, especially on "White
Youth". Nonetheless, it is nothing
short of compelling. There's no musical bombasticity to obscure their
call to unity, with the mesmerizing
guitar and bass assuming low key posi-
tions in order to intensify the vocals
(a weak link in the band)--it's more
dialogue than lyrics. This isn't
reckless barroom brawl material, rather
this is the stuff made for terrorism
and assassination . . . . cold and
premeditated.--DS

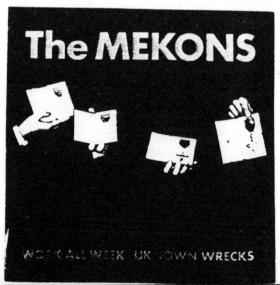

THE MEKONS
"Work All Week"/"Unknown
Wrecks" Virgin

A new label--a new sound with
definite leanings toward the
Gang Of Four bunch, which is
alright I guess, however with
"Where Were You" still ringing in my head I expected so
much more.--DS

PAGANS
"Dead End America"/"Little Black Egg"
Drome Records

Outing number three for this strictly
regional(Cleveland) band, and it's
their best yet. The Pagans have been
the most successful at lifting the
sound of the mid-sixties punk movement, playing it almost verbatim in
1979 and getting away with it. How
they are able to come across sounding both archaic and current in the
same chord and breath I just don't
know. I listen to this record and
I know I've heard it all before, but
I keep slapping it on the turntable.
It's not a nostalgic kind of appreciation either. Simple unpretentious
fun and they don't overstep their
obvious limitations. Now, these
guys won't change the world or even
inspire newcomers to imitate their
60's/80's style, however I find myself needing a Pagans fix quite regularly these days.--DS

THE BOOMTOWN RATS
"I Don't Like Mondays"/"It's
All The Rage"

This little California miss
could've done us all a favor
had she taken her shooting
spree to the Ensign studio
when this grandiose piece
of schmaltz was recorded.
--DS

THE PACK
"King of Kings"/"Number 12"
Rough Trade

Had Van Halen grown up in
Great Britain and recorded
a single for Rough Trade,
they'd have called them-
selves The Pack.--DS

BLACK FLAG EP   SST Records

When your needle touches down on
this record prepare to have all
those tidy little notions regarding the hard-core fringe thoroughly obliterated. Just when we're
beginning to feel certain that we
have reached the outer most boun-
daries of the slam-bam, we-don't-
give-a-fuck genre; someone comes
along to squelch that security
with a swift kick in the balls.
Sure to yank anyone out of their
Magazine/Siouxie and the Banshees/
Wire stupor. With their singer
suffering from terminal dementia-
-constantly hovering over the dangerous level, these guys sink their
bared teeth into our flesh and bite
off huge chunks only to spit the
half-chewed gristle right back in
our faces. Not for the squeamish.
Although not available in these
parts this record can be had by
sending $2.00 c/o SST Records, P.O.
Box 1, Lawndale, CA 90260.--DS

THE POINTED STICKS
"What do you want me to do"/
"Somebody's Mom" Quintessence

A-side is some wimped-out
shit of almost the worst
kind. Has one too many 'ooh-
oohs' to suit me. "Somebody's
Mom" pulls this band out of
the teeny-bop frying pan.
They discard the 'we-want-to-
get-on-the-radio' approach
and replace it with a tight,
bouncy attack that has to
make you wonder why they ever
recorded that piss-poor piece
of pubescence on the A-side.
I guess one out of two ain't
bad.--DS

28

CRASS
"The Feeding of the Five Thousand" Small Wonder

There are times when one is at a loss in his attempts to accurately describe the music of a given band, and this particular record is a case in point. Upon listening, there will be a hardy few that can even tolerate a side of this vinyl venom. Their rabid, often hysterical, hostility wells up from the grooves with a relentless persistance that maintains itself through all 18 tracks. What suffering one has to endure to generate this kind of hate, I don't know, and I am a little skeptical as to whether it is sincere or fabricated(I'm betting on the latter). Crass appear to be making a rather transparent attempt to be more 'punk' than any band before or since. More inflammatory than the Sex Pistols and more mindlessly reckless than the original Damned. They attack and condemn virtually everything. "Do you believe in Buddha?/ Buddha sucks/do you believe in Jesus?/Jesus fucks. . . Do you believe in Thatcher?/Maggie sucks". No stone is left unturned in their frothing effort to purge us of our complacency. In "Punk is Dead" they lambaste Steve

Jones and Patti Smith for having achieved some kind of fame. Accusing them of abandoning the original philosophy of the movement. "CBS promote The Clash/but it ain't for revolution, it's just for cash." Crass are assuming a very narrowminded view of the whole thing, vainly trying to impose a 1977 ideology on today's scene. I can't tell whether they're really serious about what they say, or whether this is just being done for appearance sake. To put it simply, are they poseurs? Perhaps they take themselves so seriously that I can't help but not take them seriously. I don't know, I'm just as confused as you probably are right now.

I realize that I've said alot without commenting on the music directly, and maybe I've just been wasting my time. Their hard-core image is just too tough a pill to swallow, for all I know, maybe that's the way it was intended. Who knows, who cares? Now that I've finally got that off my chest I'll get to the point, I mean, you're only interested in the music anyway, right? I must admit that I have an ear for Crass' roughly honed (if honed at all--ED.), one-dimensional cacophony. Fuzzy, grating, nerve-racking dissonance that is sure to be a big hit with your sophisticate (ex)friends. Having a definite weakness for this kind of noise, I'll wallow in it whenever I get the chance, which isn't all that often in these days of bigger contracts and improved

--DS

999

MARCH 79' BOOKIES CLUB

TOUCH & GO READERS POLL FOR
1979

1)BEST ALBUM
_____

2)BEST SINGLE
_____

3)BEST FEMALE VOCALIST
_____

4)BEST MALE VOCALIST
_____

5)BEST LIVE PERFORMANCE
_____

6)FAVE PORN STAR
_____

7)WORST RADIO STATION
_____

8)BEST CLUB
_____

Another no nonsense Editorial

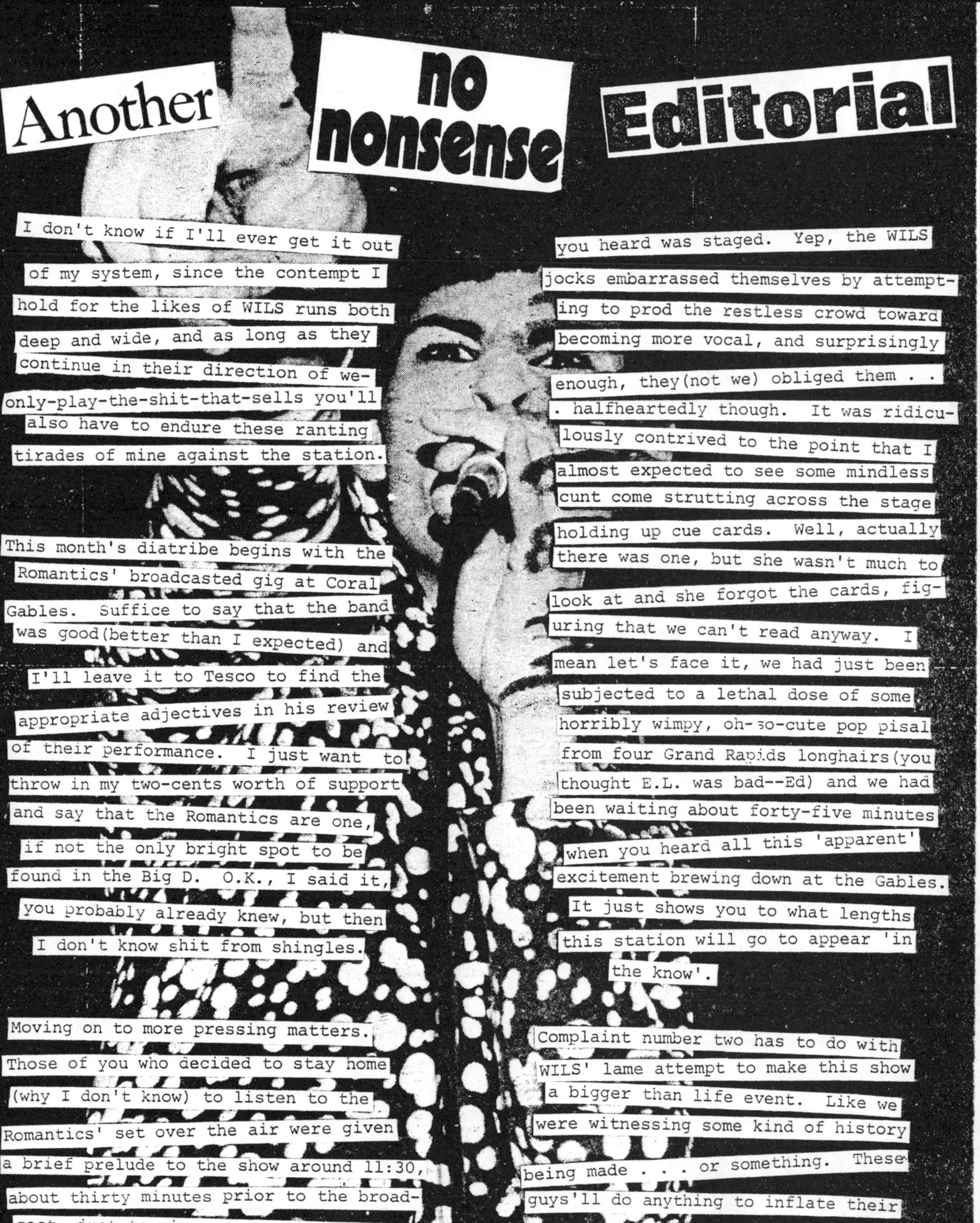

I don't know if I'll ever get it out of my system, since the contempt I hold for the likes of WILS runs both deep and wide, and as long as they continue in their direction of we-only-play-the-shit-that-sells you'll also have to endure these ranting tirades of mine against the station.

This month's diatribe begins with the Romantics' broadcasted gig at Coral Gables. Suffice to say that the band was good(better than I expected) and I'll leave it to Tesco to find the appropriate adjectives in his review of their performance. I just want to throw in my two-cents worth of support and say that the Romantics are one, if not the only bright spot to be found in the Big D. O.K., I said it, you probably already knew, but then I don't know shit from shingles.

Moving on to more pressing matters. Those of you who decided to stay home (why I don't know) to listen to the Romantics' set over the air were given a brief prelude to the show around 11:30, about thirty minutes prior to the broadcast, just to give you a sample of what you were missing by not being here. Well folks, all that noise and hoopla

you heard was staged. Yep, the WILS jocks embarrassed themselves by attempting to prod the restless crowd toward becoming more vocal, and surprisingly enough, they(not we) obliged them . . . halfheartedly though. It was ridiculously contrived to the point that I almost expected to see some mindless cunt come strutting across the stage holding up cue cards. Well, actually there was one, but she wasn't much to look at and she forgot the cards, figuring that we can't read anyway. I mean let's face it, we had just been subjected to a lethal dose of some horribly wimpy, oh-so-cute pop pisal from four Grand Rapids longhairs(you thought E.L. was bad--Ed) and we had been waiting about forty-five minutes when you heard all this 'apparent' excitement brewing down at the Gables. It just shows you to what lengths this station will go to appear 'in the know'.

Complaint number two has to do with WILS' lame attempt to make this show a bigger than life event. Like we were witnessing some kind of history being made . . . . or something. These guys'll do anything to inflate their fragile little eggshell egos. Remember when they said that this was the

CONTINUED

31

DROP

most packed they'd ever seen the Gables? A bald-faced lie if I ever heard one. A shabby and unnecessary ploy to convince you listeners that this was where it was all happening and WILS was there to bring it to ya, aren't they nice? Just another example of their lack of confidence and insecurity. Sure, it was a first for East Lansing, and it may sound like I'm biting the hand that

feeds me, but just take a moment and try to see where WILS' true motives lie in their putting on this show. You see, Epic will undoubtedly want everyone of you to rush out and buy the Romantics' album as soon as it hits the racks. Epic, I'm sure, are convinced that they have a product that will skyrocket to fame much in the same way that the Knack did for Capital. WILS will play a key role in the marketing of this

DEAD

up coming record in this area. A very elaborate promotional campaign, it is not the station's altruism that initiates this kind of move(putting on a show), rather it is done in the hope of building up their listenership by appearing hip or chic via getting in on the ground floor of the inevitable success of the Romantics. WILS deserves no credit whatsoever for being intuitively perceptive, because they simply were not. They've just jumped on the bandwagon

like everyone else. I mean, at this point, even a moron can see that the Romantics can't help but make it. So, if WILS already knew how good these guys were, how come last Monday(Nov. 5) was the first time they'd ever been to E.L.? The answer should be obvious.--DS

WILS!

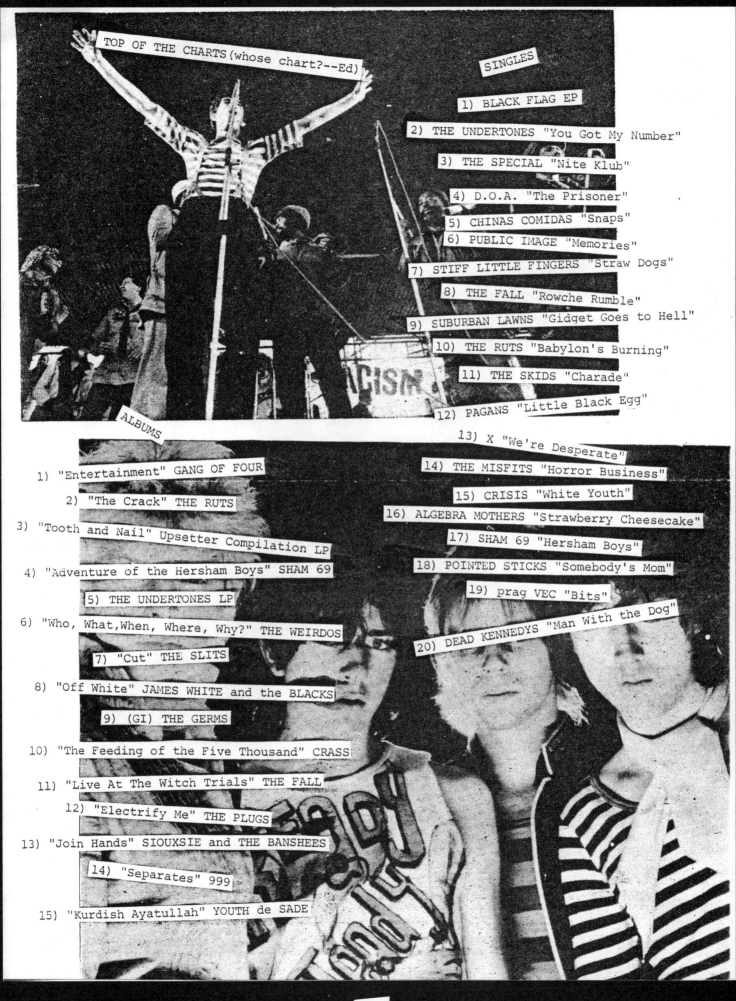

TOP OF THE CHARTS (whose chart?--Ed)

SINGLES

1) BLACK FLAG EP

2) THE UNDERTONES "You Got My Number"

3) THE SPECIAL "Nite Klub"

4) D.O.A. "The Prisoner"

5) CHINAS COMIDAS "Snaps"

6) PUBLIC IMAGE "Memories"

7) STIFF LITTLE FINGERS "Straw Dogs"

8) THE FALL "Rowche Rumble"

9) SUBURBAN LAWNS "Gidget Goes to Hell"

10) THE RUTS "Babylon's Burning"

11) THE SKIDS "Charade"

12) PAGANS "Little Black Egg"

13) X "We're Desperate"

14) THE MISFITS "Horror Business"

15) CRISIS "White Youth"

16) ALGEBRA MOTHERS "Strawberry Cheesecake"

17) SHAM 69 "Hersham Boys"

18) POINTED STICKS "Somebody's Mom"

19) prag VEC "Bits"

20) DEAD KENNEDYS "Man With the Dog"

ALBUMS

1) "Entertainment" GANG OF FOUR

2) "The Crack" THE RUTS

3) "Tooth and Nail" Upsetter Compilation LP

4) "Adventure of the Hersham Boys" SHAM 69

5) THE UNDERTONES LP

6) "Who, What, When, Where, Why?" THE WEIRDOS

7) "Cut" THE SLITS

8) "Off White" JAMES WHITE and the BLACKS

9) (GI) THE GERMS

10) "The Feeding of the Five Thousand" CRASS

11) "Live At The Witch Trials" THE FALL

12) "Electrify Me" THE PLUGS

13) "Join Hands" SIOUXSIE and THE BANSHEES

14) "Separates" 999

15) "Kurdish Ayatullah" YOUTH de SADE

A NOT SO SUBTLE PLUG FOR ONE OF OUR FAVE RAVES.

X

I would like to take a moment
to thank the kind folks(Laurie
in particular) at Abbey Press
for their unyielding patience
and effort in the printing of
our first issue of Touch & Go.
Not knowing shit about publishing a magazine, Tesco and I ran
into stumbling block after stumbling block in our effort to
get this 'zine printed. Expense
was a major factor, with each
setback meaning that we'd have
to cough up some more dough.
We almost came to the point of
just throwing in the towel and
scrapping the whole idea. Fortunately for us, Abbey Press was
not so easily discouraged. They
say where there's a will, there's
a way, right?(yea, a way to make
a few extra bucks, heh-heh, just
kidding guys--Ed). No really,
we're very grateful for everything you did and completely
satisfied with the work.

By the way, Abbey Press is printing issue #2, as well. Excuse the
tense, since this is being written
prior to printing; whereas, by the
time it gets to your grimy mits
it'll have already been run(don't
mind DS, he's a long winded sort,
just loves to see his stuff in
print--Ed). Hopefully, we'll
have all the bugs worked out by
#2, making it bigger and better
than #1(now let's not overdo it,
pal--Ed). O.K., I'll stop--Tesco's
bugging me by saying that I'm incapable of making anything short
and sweet. That may well be, but
a brief gratuity just wouldn't express our. . . Heh! Tesco what are
you doing?! . . .now put that gun
down! . . .please, I just wanted
to tell the folks . . . (some guys
never learn--Ed).

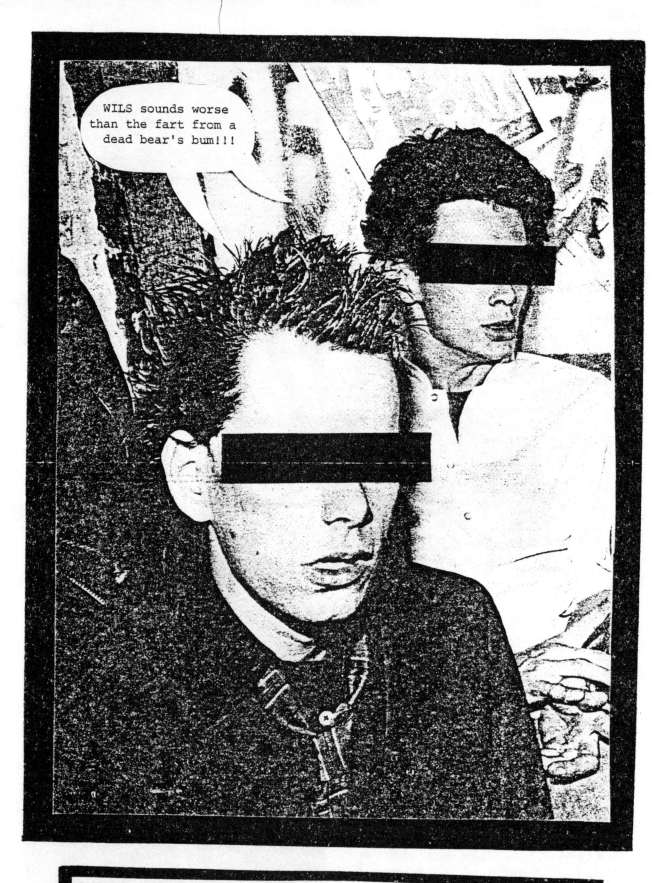

ANOTHER CHEAP SHOT DIRECTED AT OUR FAVORITE RADIO STATION

TOP *40!*

TOUCH&GO
BOX 26203
Lansing, Mich.
48909

Bottom 40

1) **The Skids**
2) Touch + Go
3) gin
4) Cockney Rejects
5) Robert Gordon
6) **Phone Sex**
7) **THOR**
8) 999
9) COLDCOCK
10) ZED-ZED-ZED-ZED
11) Kate Bush
12) LAGER!
13) Silicon Teens
14) RHINO 39
15) Wax Trax
16) All West Coast zines!
17) MONEY
18) Black Flag
19) EDDIE Cochran
20) X
21) X-rated Films
22) SCISSORFITS
23) Pink Clothes!
24) NEGATIVE Trend
25) Generation X
26) Poseur
27) UK Subs
28) PIL
29) **FRENCH TICKLERS!**

30) Substance Abuse
31) Very short hair
32) Nightly floggings
33) **LEATHER**
34) girls!
35) **Throbbing Gristle**
36) Nervous Gender
37) The Misfits
38) S. Williams
39) People who read US!!
40) seeing things differently
(41. Lene Lovich)

1) **RADIO**
2) The Beat, The Pop ec
3) cold weather
4) **CONDOMS**
5) Bradly Curtis
6) CENSORED MY ASS!
7) Cheryl Tiegs ect.
8) **IraN!**
9) Debbie Harry
10) TELEVISION
11) "Southern Hospitality"
12) **NEW York Rocker**
13) MOD
14) McDonalds
15) "PUNK ROCK"
16) Relatives
17) TRANS-AMS
18) Talking Spuds
19) Molly Hatchet
20) Long fucking Hair!!!
21) Women FM DJ's,
22) All Other FM DJ's
23) Marijuana!
24) Big Bouncers (with little pee-pees)
25) "IM HIP"
26) Herpes Simplex
27) "Wavey"
28) Sports
29) THe Beatles!
30) 20-20
31) Soiled Underpants
32) Fuck "X"

37

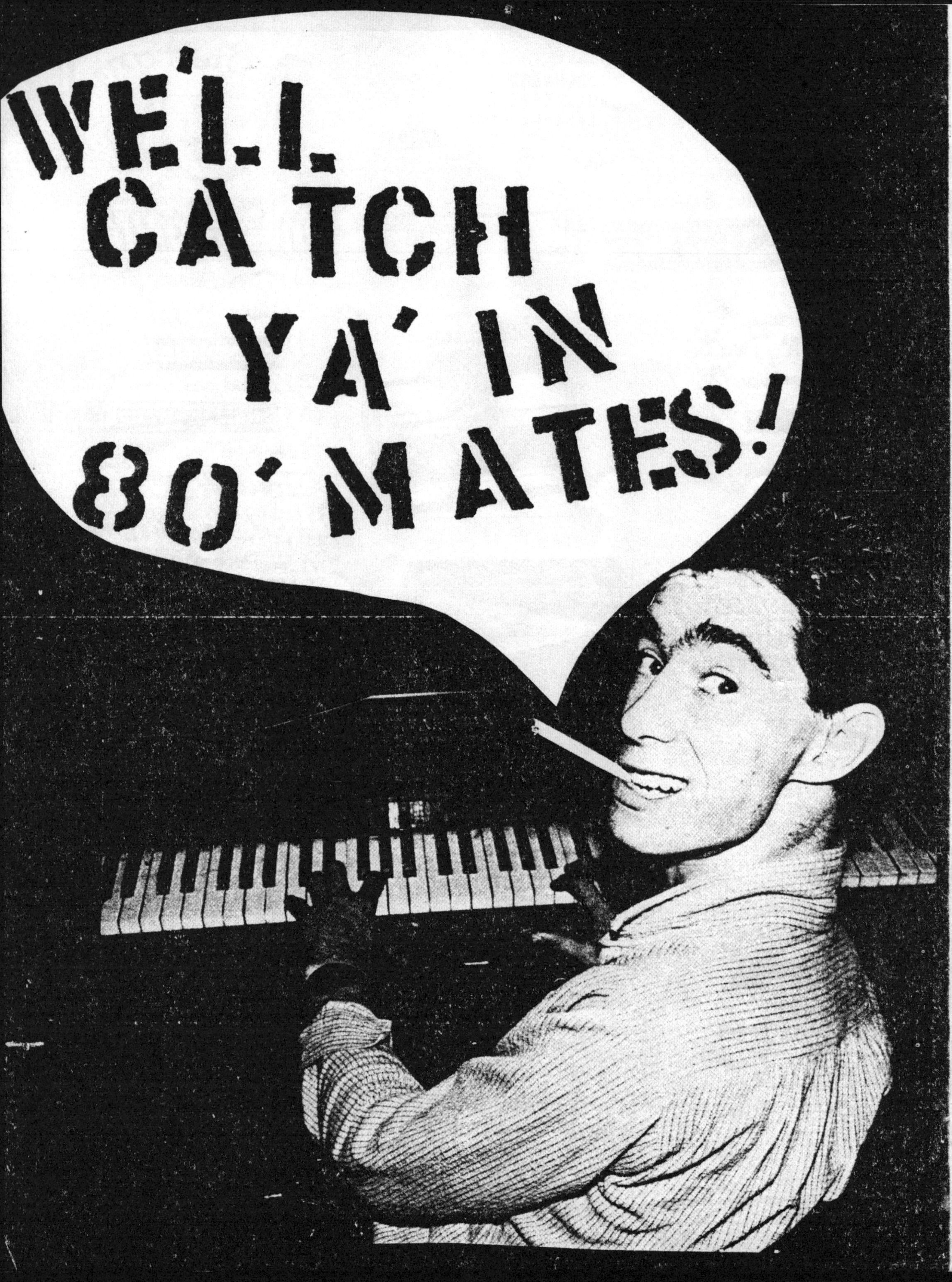
WE'LL
CATCH
YA' IN
80' MATES!

3

Yes, Byron Coley has verbally chastised me on many occasions about all the SKA coverage... Hey, Coley! This stuff was expertly repackaged in snappy suits and porkpie hats, and was downright infectious, so pardon us for hopping that happy freight!... Like a musical stick of Fruit Stripe gum, the flavor was delectable but short-lived, and the guilty pleasure of it all is all over this issue...

Oh, and don't get your knickers in a twist about the "Skins Rule" page, you uptight antiracist stick-up-the-butt types. I'm more anti than you, Clyde, but once again, what wasn't to like with all the nattily dressed Fred Perry—shirted, braced and booted young bucks struttin' their stuff and all that footstompin' Oi Oi Oi! Those goddamn Limeys could factionalize and recycle/rehash the tuneage with the best of them, and the late '70s saw it all: skins, mods, teds, ska, punk, industrial, and we hadda cover it all...so suck me!

TOUCH AND GO

JANUARY 1980   ISSUE NO. 3   50¢

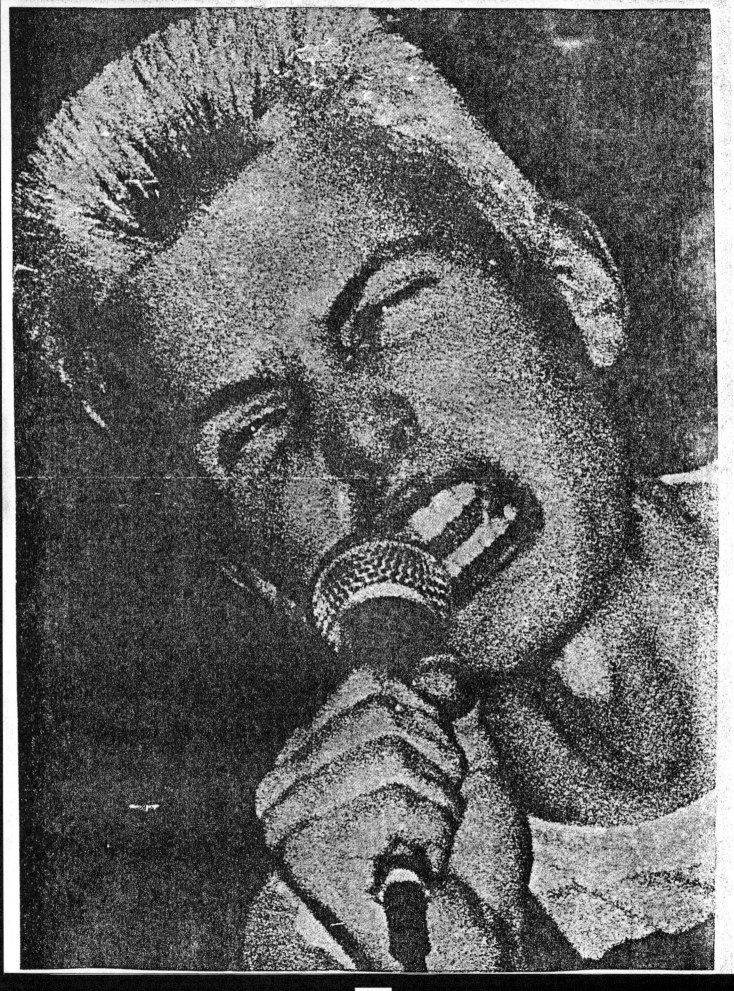

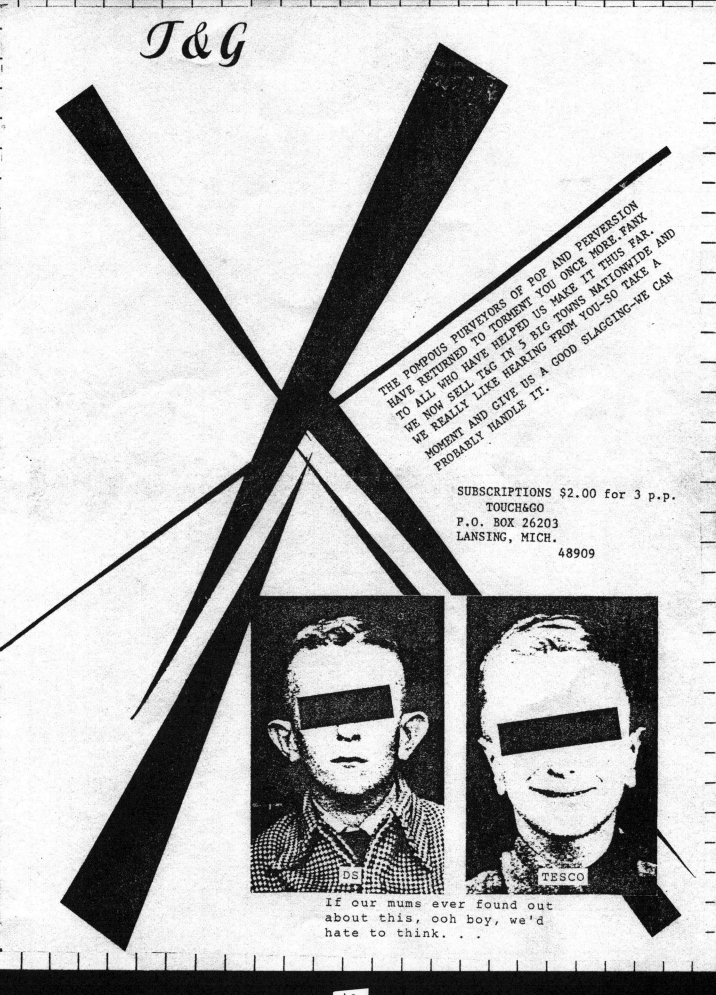

T&G

THE POMPOUS PURVEYORS OF POP AND PERVERSION
HAVE RETURNED TO TORMENT YOU ONCE MORE. FANX
TO ALL WHO HAVE HELPED US MAKE IT THUS FAR.
WE NOW SELL T&G IN 5 BIG TOWNS NATIONWIDE AND
WE REALLY LIKE HEARING FROM YOU-SO TAKE A
MOMENT AND GIVE US A GOOD SLAGGING-WE CAN
PROBABLY HANDLE IT.

SUBSCRIPTIONS $2.00 for 3 p.p.
TOUCH&GO
P.O. BOX 26203
LANSING, MICH.
          48909

If our mums ever found out
about this, ooh boy, we'd
hate to think. . .

43

THE CUBES

INTERVIEW

The following was conducted prior to the bands' Dec. 14 gig at Lilli's Bar(?!) All members were in attendence. Tony-bass,Al-skins,Gary-guitar and Carolyn-Vocals & keyboards....

T&G-What about these flyers charging you with sexism?
C-M50 made those flyers and then came in and apologized for em' cuz everyone got mad and ripped them down so we just made a joke out of it...
T&G-So what about influences?
C-You guys talk!
T-New York Dolls
G-and Carolyn;David Bowie...
C-ya and Iggy
G-Tony likes The Ramones and The Jam and I like Ultravox,The Doors,MC5
A-Gary Numan (laughter)
T&G-Your style doesn't strike me as detroit influenced..
G-good...
T&G-more fun you know?
G-We might be a little more experimental than some of the others but Algebra Mothers... (laughter)
T&G-So who writes the songs?
G-It's a combination,Al and Carolyn did "On A Leash", Carolyn and I did a lot of the other ones,Ido the music-she does the words..

T&G-How's the EP selling?
G-Pretty good-it's doing really good in Toronto..
T&G-Where have you played outside of Detroit?
C-Lansing...(much snickering) we played Chicago...
G-We were supposed to play with Steve Dahl but he cancelled out...we played in Toronto last month and we're going back in Jan. at the"Edge"
T&G-What do you think of the Romantics?
C-We've known them for a long time(place foot in mouth,and push.ED.)
G-Ithink their good but not that innovative

This was'nt exactly the end but this page is juiced so just go see this band and groove punters!!!

SPECIALS

SPECIALS LP
TWO TONE RECORDS

The big hype of the latter part of 1979 was, and still is today, the mod induced ska revival; and although it's the <u>big</u> thing in England at the moment, it's just beginning to find its way over to these repressive shores of our own beloved country. Of all the bluebeat bands, The Specials have received the most attention, and rightly so, with the dynamite single, "Gangsters" to their credit. Now I don't know poop about the original ska movement or whether this record has anything to do with that or not, but I do know what I like and their music hits me in all the right places. A perfect blend ranging from the snappy dance steps like "Do the Dog", "Nite Klub" and "Concrete Jungle" to the lilting "Too Much, Too Young" all the way to the romantically mushy "Doesn't Make It Alright"(that is if you don't listen to the words). Speaking of which are snatches from the monotony and boredom of middle or lower class life(don't quote me now, I'm no sociologist). I've never had much of an ear for most rasta music, but gosh, this stuff is good(some discription, eh folks?). They say: "It's up to you. . .you can take it or leave it, we'll carry on regardless. . .we can't force you to like this music, it's up to you." Precisely, and those of you who leave it, too bad, you won't know what you're missing.--DS

TV'S SONG CHART......

DOLL BY DOLL "TEENAGE LIGHTNING"

CUBES EP

PSYCHEDELIC FURS "WE LOVE YOU"

BLACK FLAG EP

NEGATIVE TREND EP

UK SUBS "SCUM OF THE EARTH"

COLDCOCK "I WANNA BE RICH"

MADNESS "ONE STEP BEYOND"

ENGLISH SUBTITLES "TIME TUNNEL"

NIGGER KOJAK "KOJAK NAH GO PENITENTIARY"

THE POP GROUP "WE ARE ALL PROSTITUTES"

FATAL MICROBES "VIOLENCE GROWS"

YOUTH DE SADE "FROZEN KITTENS"

SKIDS "WORKING FOR THE YANKEE DOLLAR"

CHUDDY NUDDIES "DO THE CHUD"

TELEX "MOSKOW DISKOW"

CABARET VOLTAIRE "NAG NAG NAG"

TV'S LP CHART.......

THE POP GROUP "Y"

JOY DIVISION LP

SKIDS "DAYS IN EUROPA"

CABARET VOLTAIRE "MIX UP"

THE FALL "DRAGNET"

UK SUBS "ANOTHER KIND OF BLUES"

MADNESS LP

PUBLIC IMAGE LTD. "METAL BOX"

ANGELIC UPSTARTS "TEENAGE WARNING"

PUNISHMENT OF LUXURY "LAUGHING ACADEMY"

THE CURE "THREE IMAGINARY BOYS"

EDDIE COCHRAN "SINGLES ALBUM"

SUICIDE LP

CRASS "FEDDING OF 5000"

WIRE "CHAIRS MISSING"

SWELL MAPS LP

"I VEE"

Ever listen to see how many times the phrase "rock and roll" is used on stations like WILS that claim to be purveyors of the old R&R? It's ridiculous, especially when you realize that rarely does WILS play anything remotely similar to rock 'n' roll. Oh sure, the sic-fuck trio of Bradley Curtis, Frank 'Sonic' Smith, and of course, Shaun Hendrix obnoxiously impose their lack of awareness by flatly stating that everything is rock 'n' roll. Let me digress a minute to recall a story in which Tesco and I were in the company of a couple of females, and I believe the Ramones were on the turntable at the time. Anyway, if my memory serves me correctly, one of our guests stated that she was growing tired of this punk stuff and wanted to hear some rock and roll. I remained calm, and confronted her with the question: "and what do you call rock 'n' roll, pray tell?" "Oh, Led Zeppelin, Ted Nugent, REO..." As you can see, these two silly misguided cows have been sufficiently brainwashed by radio into believing that punk and rock 'n' roll are two distinct entities. And stations like WILS perpetuate and foster this kind of nearsighted attitude among the youth of today, and eventually the kids of tomorrow won't have any idea what rock 'n' roll was all about. Let me ask you, what does some guy noodling on his guitar for God knows how long have to do with rock and roll? Absolutely nothing-- but WILS insists on labelling bands like Styx, Toto, Molly Hatchett, and Pink Floyd as rock 'n' roll; while resorting to vague alien terms in their feeble effort to describe the music on their "No Wave" show (personally, I'd call it shit, but that's not the point). Rock 'n' Roll began with Chuck Berry, Gene Vincent, Johnny Burnette, Eddie Cochran, Elvis, etc.; and I fail to see the connection between these greats(there's more obviously) and this crap that WILS is pushing. You could listen to WILS for the rest of your life and you'd still hear more rock 'n' roll in one listen of "Blitzkrieg Bop". One last word. You people in the know should write to this fucked station and tell them that if they're gonna wank-- do it in private, cuz their encrusted jism is really stinking up Mid-Michigan!!!--DS

SINGLES

by TV

CUBES-"SPACEHEART" "PICKUP"
"ON A LEASH" "CHANGING FRAC-
TIONS"

and she'll have fun fun fun
when her daddy takes her
scooby doo....What? Oh ya
the Cubes review.Like to
dance? Like to go to decadent Detroit bars,get boiled
and do some of that ol' moonstompin'? From the opening
of "Spaceheart" through the
remainder of their inspired
sets CUBES are nothing short
of incredible.Carolyn is a
most exciting crooner and a
helluva lot of fun to watch.
I'm telling you people in ol'
E.L. when these cats are big
time yor gonna kick yourself
in the bum for not seeing them
when you had the chance. Watch
for an exclusive interview in
 this ish. Their debut excellence is avaible for a dollar
seventy-five from Tremor Records

403 Forest
Royal Oak,MI. 48067

ORCHESTRAL MANOEUVRES IN THE
DARK-"ELECTRICITY" "ALMOST"

Another modern easy listening
record in the new vein(?) A
side sounds like an arty version of that horrendous novelty classic"Popcorn". B-side
is great to play over soft
lights and scallops lyonnaise
with your favorite date. They're
on tour with Gary Numan due to
the fact that they're the only
assemblage more mundane than
he. Big egos need tender loving
care. I like this alot.

THE SEX BEATLES-"WELL YOU
NEVER..."

I haven't heard this but it's
probably pretty good.

LORI AND THE CHAMELEONS-
"TOUCH"/"LOVE ON THE GANGES"

-pop group of late 70's(STOP)
-recorded one off on Sire
label(STOP)-music was innocuous-
cherubic-peripheral-impalpable-
frivolous-derivative-superb(STOP)

THE FALL
"Dragnet"   Step Forward
Records

Anyone familiar with Live at
the Witch Trials will quickly
detect the absence of Yvonne
Pawlett, the creatively minimal piano player for the
band. She filled the gap between the nervous, often grating guitars and the manic voice
of Marc Smith. I suppose in
classical terms her presence
might be described as embel-
lishment--never in the forefront, but essential nevertheless.

The Fall

With her gone, the band now
relies solely on the frenetic
guitar work of Craig Scanlan
and Marc Riley and the cryptic lyrics of Smith. The
music on this disc is start-
ling first of all, for it's
a definite departure from the
debut LP, which I guess should
not surprise anybody since
only two members on Dragnet
were on hand for the first
album. Although Smith is easily recognizable, the sound on
this outing is much more primitive than before, almost tribal in parts--as in "A Figure
Walks". They have now adopted
a rough, somewhat regressive
approach that harks back to
1977. This time the mix is n
thick and muddy compared to
the crisp and sparing qualities of Witch Trials. If you
detect an ever so slight bias
toward the first album on my
part, you're correct, for I
believe that Live at the Witch
Trials along with Entertainment!
by the Gang of Four is proof
to anyone that these bands are
two of the only ones doing anything new these days. Which
brings me back to Dragnet, for
although it differs markedly
from their first, it is a
step in the right direction.

Having gone apeshit over"Rowche
Rumble", I had some preconceived
notions about the upcoming album. In short, I was caught
offguard--totally unprepared
for this, The Fall's latest
release. Upon first listen,
their music struck me as a step
backward; however, with time
I realized that that was due,
in part, to my overzealous adulation for both the first album
and "Rowche Rumble". Not content to mirror their previous
work, The Fall continue to produce a unique brand of music
that is totally original and
unequivocally their own. And
although I lament the loss of
Yvonne Pawlett, It's bands like
The Fall that make this whole
scene so interesting.--DS

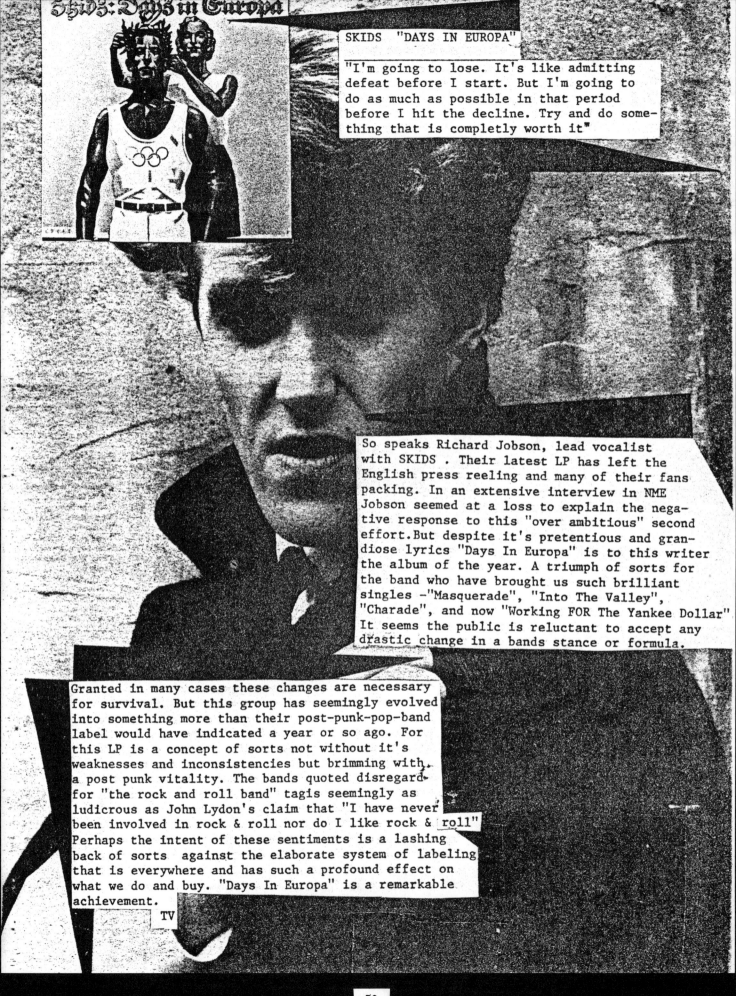

SKIDS "DAYS IN EUROPA"

"I'm going to lose. It's like admitting defeat before I start. But I'm going to do as much as possible in that period before I hit the decline. Try and do something that is completly worth it"

So speaks Richard Jobson, lead vocalist with SKIDS . Their latest LP has left the English press reeling and many of their fans packing. In an extensive interview in NME Jobson seemed at a loss to explain the negative response to this "over ambitious" second effort. But despite it's pretentious and grandiose lyrics "Days In Europa" is to this writer the album of the year. A triumph of sorts for the band who have brought us such brilliant singles -"Masquerade", "Into The Valley", "Charade", and now "Working FOR The Yankee Dollar" It seems the public is reluctant to accept any drastic change in a bands stance or formula.

Granted in many cases these changes are necessary for survival. But this group has seemingly evolved into something more than their post-punk-pop-band label would have indicated a year or so ago. For this LP is a concept of sorts not without it's weaknesses and inconsistencies but brimming with a post punk vitality. The bands quoted disregard for "the rock and roll band" tagis seemingly as ludicrous as John Lydon's claim that "I have never been involved in rock & roll nor do I like rock & roll" Perhaps the intent of these sentiments is a lashing back of sorts against the elaborate system of labeling that is everywhere and has such a profound effect on what we do and buy. "Days In Europa" is a remarkable achievement.

TV

GET ON THE STICK!

SINGLES

1) "Bouncing Babies" THE TEARDROP EXPLODES

2) "Violence Grows" 'FATAL' MICROBES

3) "Mars Bars" THE UNDERTONES (along with everything else)

4) "New Dark Ages" THE MUTNTS

5) BLACK FLAG EP

6) "Horror Business" THE MISFITS

7) "Memories" PUBLIC IMAGE

8) "I Don't Wanna" SHAM 69

9) "Rowche Rumble" THE FALL

10) "Prolixin Stomp" RHINO 39

11) "White Youth" CRISIS

12) "Ain't You" KLEENEX

13) "Fairytale in the Supermarket" THE RAINCOATS

14) "My Boyfriend" SUBURBAN LAWNS

15) "Johnny Too Bad" THE OFFS

16) "Fa Cé La" THE FEELIES

17) "The Pictures on My Wall" ECHO and the BUNNYMEN

18) "I Slept in an Arcade" BLACK RANDY

19) "Where's the Boy for Me?" THE REVILLOS

20) "Insurgence" THE MIDDLE CLASS

ALBUMS

1) "Unknown Pleasures" JOY DIVISION

2) (GI) THE GERMS

3) "Entertainment!" GANG OF FOUR

4) THE SPECIALS LP

5) "Dragnet" THE FALL

6) THE UNDERTONES LP

7) "Tooth and Nail" Upsetter compilation

8) "Cut" THE SLITS

9) "Another Kind of Blues" U.K. SUBS

10) "The Feeding of the Five Thousand" CRASS

11) "A Trip to Marineville" SWELL MAPS

12) "Prehistoric Sounds" THE SAINTS

13) "Electrify Me" THE PLUGZ

14) "Separates" 999

15) "Kurdish Ayatullah" YOUTH de SADE

FORGET THE TURD'S STUFF BY TV, HERE'S THE CHART THAT COUNTS--DS

51

7 inch

THE DONKEYS
"What I Want"/"Four Letters"
Rhesus Records

Ridiculous name. "What I Want" is almost suitable for FM airplay(did I say that?) All the rough edges that are constantly hinted at have been smoothed over to produce power-pop without the power. Could have been good if done right. B-side is neither, it just plain blows. Unimaginative debut from a band we'll quickly forget.--DS

BY DS...

BRIAN JAMES
"Ain't That a Shame"/"Living in Sin"/"I Can Make You Cry"
Illegal Records

The Damned one gone mellow--isn't that a contradiction in terms? You'd never think the two could co-exist on the same record, but surprisingly enough, "Ain't That a Shame" is vaguely appealing, meaning that most of it I could take or leave(I'm leaning toward the latter). James is steadily moving away from any connection he may have had with the Damned. Gone are all the wildly frenetic guitar solos, and I dread to think we may never hear them again. This record ain't bad, but it's far from worthwhile.--DS

'FATAL' MICROBES
"Violence Grows"/"Beautiful Pictures"/"Cry Baby"
Small Wonder/Xntrix Records

"Violence Grows" is mesmerizing. A sobering cut that almost lulls you to death. Great little voice atop a somnambulant beat. Wish we had more like her around here. B-side is more straightforward, but no less enjoyable. Worth every penny.--DS

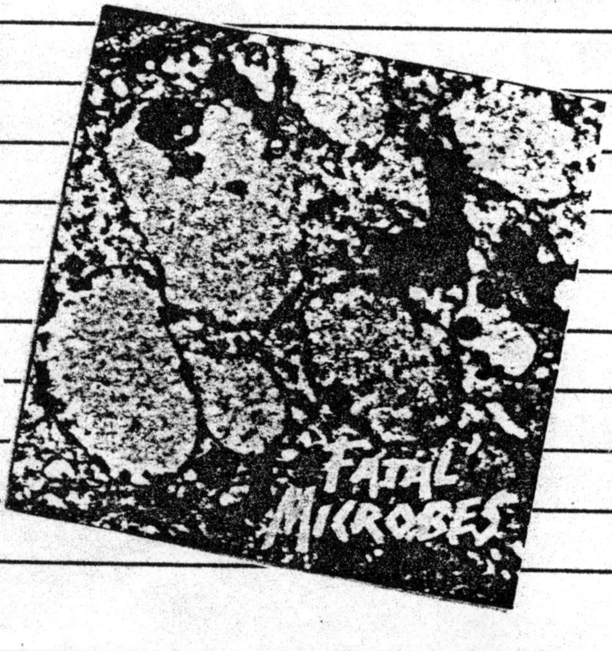

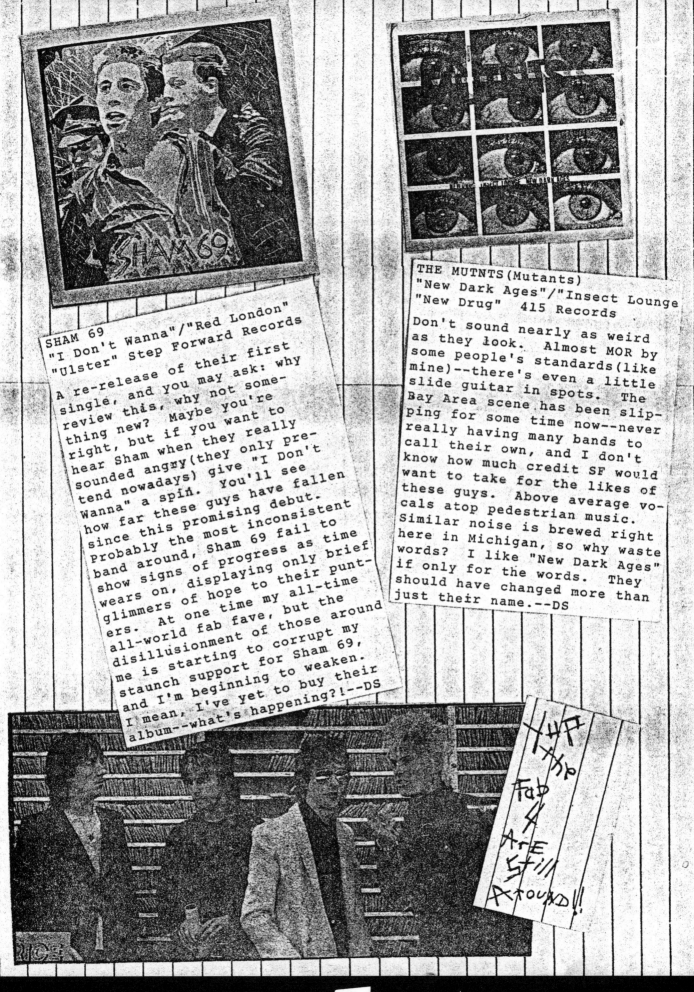

SHAM 69
"I Don't Wanna"/"Red London"
"Ulster" Step Forward Records

A re-release of their first single, and you may ask: why review this, why not something new? Maybe you're right, but if you want to hear Sham when they really sounded angry(they only pretend nowadays) give "I Don't Wanna" a spin. You'll see how far these guys have fallen since this promising debut. Probably the most inconsistent band around, Sham 69 fail to show signs of progress as time wears on, displaying only brief glimmers of hope to their punters. At one time my all-time all-world fab fave, but the disillusionment of those around me is starting to corrupt my staunch support for Sham 69, and I'm beginning to weaken. I mean, I've yet to buy their album--what's happening?!--DS

THE MUTNTS(Mutants)
"New Dark Ages"/"Insect Lounge
"New Drug" 415 Records

Don't sound nearly as weird as they look. Almost MOR by some people's standards(like mine)--there's even a little slide guitar in spots. The Bay Area scene has been slipping for some time now--never really having many bands to call their own, and I don't know how much credit SF would want to take for the likes of these guys. Above average vocals atop pedestrian music. Similar noise is brewed right here in Michigan, so why waste words? I like "New Dark Ages" if only for the words. They should have changed more than just their name.--DS

SKINS RULE OK

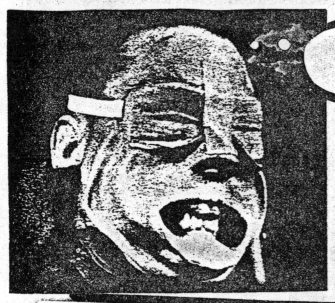

I don't know how much more of this "No Wave" shit I can take!!!

On Sunday December 9th, WILS and Shaun Hendrix showed their true colors. Anyone who witnessed this fiasco will attest to the fact that this station never gave a blue-fuck about new wave or anything closely resembling new music, but were and still are selfishly bent on satisfying their sponsor-- Warehouse Records. It's infuriating that we have to endure this continual bullshit from WILS. Those of you who didn't catch the show or what little there actually was of it will need some explaining. You see folks, we discovered that this "No Wave" program is taped and that Shaun is nowhere near the

station when this show goes on the air. Naive sucker that I am, I had been sufficiently duped into believing that this was done live, but when, on this particular Sunday, the music sounded all fucked-up, it finally dawned on me what was going on. We sat through 4 or 5 songs before somebody at the studio realized the mishap. Let me interrupt for a second so I can vent some hostility--- Shaun, YOU SUCK!! O.K., where was I, oh yea, it wouldn't surprise me a bit if Warehouse Records prepares the tapes for the show. I wouldn't put it past either Warehouse or WILS. All the shit you hear on the "No Wave" show is only that

lame crud that stinks up the bins at this presumptuous disc shop. Granted, they sell stuff by The Slits, Gang of Four, Wire, Swell Maps, Angelic Upstarts; but how come we don't hear this music? The answer is quite simple. The managers at Warehouse figure that very few people will be interested in the

aforementioned bands, so they push innocuous groups like the Headboys , or Battered Wives, or The Atlantics, etc. where the market is much larger, and where profits are greater. As I'm sure you realize by now, the "No Wave" show, thought at one time to be a step in the right direction, is nothing more than a vehicle to help Warehouse sell more records-- nothing more. I now want to suggest a drastic move on the part of you readers of Touch &

Go. I would like to see a boycot of Warehouse Records. Their interest lies not in providing a service for East Lansing, but rather in making money and lots of it. They're using WILS and the "No Wave" show in their quest for the megabuck. We're not hearing progressive music on this program--it's a one hour commercial for Warehouse Records. So, go tell those wanking divs down there to get stuffed. They may need us, but we sure as hell don't need them!--DS

THE POPGROUP

luscious burst of primal scream

ineradicable pessimism

we are all prostitutes snowgirl
your hair is on fire

truculent optimism

stupefaction

the screeching-passion wailing

and on the third they rose again

In the big lie there is always a certain force of credibility; because the broad masses of a nation are always more easily corrupted in the deeper strata of their emotional nature than consciously or voluntarily, and thus in the primitive

DON'T CALL ME PAIN
MY NAME IS MYSTERY
CALL ME PAIN
MY NAME IS MYSTERY
DON'T CALL ME PAIN
THIS IS THE AGE OF CHANCE.
THIS IS THE AGE OF CHANCE
DON'T CALL ME PAIN

AND ASCENDED INTO BLOOD MONEY

AND ARE SEATED AT THE RIGHT HAND OF THE INDUSTRY
CREATOR OF SUCCESS.

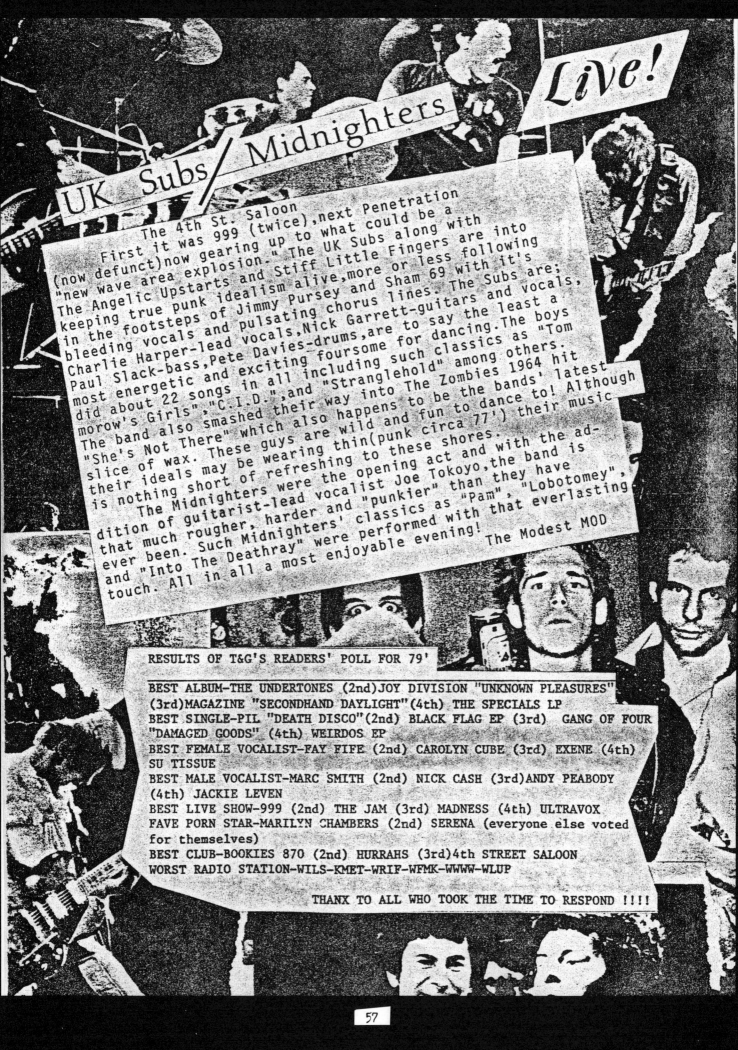

UK Subs / Midnighters Live!

The 4th St. Saloon

First it was 999 (twice),next Penetration (now defunct)now gearing up to what could be a "new wave area explosion." The UK Subs along with The Angelic Upstarts and Stiff Little Fingers are into keeping true punk idealism alive,more or less following in the footsteps of Jimmy Pursey and Sham 69 with it's bleeding vocals and pulsating chorus lines. The Subs are; Charlie Harper-lead vocals,Nick Garrett-guitars and vocals, Paul Slack-bass,Pete Davies-drums,are to say the least a most energetic and exciting foursome for dancing.The boys did about 22 songs in all including such classics as "Tom morow's Girls","C.I.D.",and "Stranglehold" among others. The band also smashed their way into The Zombies 1964 hit "She's Not There" which also happens to be the bands' latest slice of wax. These guys are wild and fun to dance to! Although their ideals may be wearing thin(punk circa 77') their music is nothing short of refreshing to these shores.

The Midnighters were the opening act and with the ad- dition of guitarist-lead vocalist Joe Tokoyo,the band is that much rougher, harder and "punkier" than they have ever been. Such Midnighters' classics as "Pam", "Lobotomey", and "Into The Deathray" were performed with that everlasting touch. All in all a most enjoyable evening!   The Modest MOD

RESULTS OF T&G'S READERS' POLL FOR 79'

BEST ALBUM-THE UNDERTONES (2nd)JOY DIVISION "UNKNOWN PLEASURES" (3rd)MAGAZINE "SECONDHAND DAYLIGHT"(4th) THE SPECIALS LP
BEST SINGLE-PIL "DEATH DISCO"(2nd) BLACK FLAG EP (3rd) GANG OF FOUR "DAMAGED GOODS" (4th) WEIRDOS EP
BEST FEMALE VOCALIST-FAY FIFE (2nd) CAROLYN CUBE (3rd) EXENE (4th) SU TISSUE
BEST MALE VOCALIST-MARC SMITH (2nd) NICK CASH (3rd)ANDY PEABODY (4th) JACKIE LEVEN
BEST LIVE SHOW-999 (2nd) THE JAM (3rd) MADNESS (4th) ULTRAVOX
FAVE PORN STAR-MARILYN CHAMBERS (2nd) SERENA (everyone else voted for themselves)
BEST CLUB-BOOKIES 870 (2nd) HURRAHS (3rd)4th STREET SALOON
WORST RADIO STATION-WILS-KMET-WRIF-WFMK-WWWW-WLUP

                        THANX TO ALL WHO TOOK THE TIME TO RESPOND !!!!

TOP 40

The Beautiful Lydia Lunch

SPANKING

DAYGLOW SOX -

WOMAN'S JOHN AT BOOKIES

Psychedelic Furs

MILK SHAKES

totally uninhibited wild sex

WALL OF VOODOO

The Fall   SIN

SELF ABUSE

GUINNESS

black seamed stockings

ANYONE WHO LIKES THE CUBES !

THE LURKERS

SPATS

COWBOYS INTERNATIONAL

VARIOUS RESTRAINT

MARILYN CHAMBERS

Weirdos 1979

Lesbian Love Bars

999 LIVE

JANDE & VINCE

THE DICKIES

GREASE WHEELS

DANCE *CRAMPS*

MIKE

leather underwear

THE CURE

Wire

JOHN WATERS' MOVIES

GENERATION X

HOWARD DEVOTO

ASHLEY   BONDAGE TROUSERS

REZILLOS

DISCO

UNDERTONES

JOHN CALE

ABBA

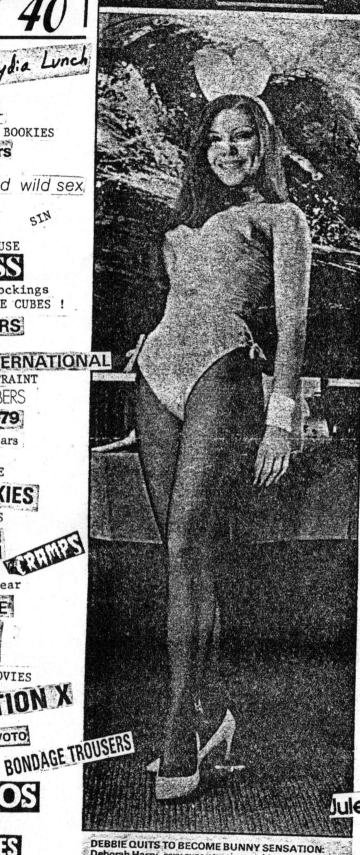

DEBBIE QUITS TO BECOME BUNNY SENSATION: Deborah Harry, *sexy superstar singer with top pop group The Blondie, has left the group to become a Playboy Bunny.*

bottom 40

PUNK MAGAZINE

101-FM

Trouser Press

SID & NANCY

Drinking a beer with a cigarrette butt in it...

Supertramp

SMELLY ARABS

Meat Rack Bars

FRENCH PEOPLE

Cheap Trick.

pulling balls of old hair from your drain

Blue Oyster Cult

FRATERNITYS

PEOPLE WHO ARE UGLY

Heavy Metal

GETTING STOOD UP

Tom Petty

Report Cards

Frostbite of The Penis

M-50

MOVIE STARS

TALKING HEADS

Folk

THE MUTANTS

DOORS

WWWW

Blondie

DOLLY PARTON

long term memory

Ira A. Robbins

Fleetwood Mac

Jules and the Polar Bears

FUCK THE PAST SUPPORT THE NEW

4

The first appearance of the still-in-use T & G logo
born of rub-on letters adorned this issue along with
a sneering Johnny Rotten, whose asparagus-faced
countenance decorates the cover. The school where
I taught grade-schoolers had reams of this nifty
pastel pink paper, and my late-nite guerilla print
run was on. Nice two-page spread on the infamous
Gang War concert at Dooleys, in East Lansing, where
Johnny Thunders went into the office and stole the
evening's gate. A trail of coins and currency led
the cops to the junkie ex-Doll and he spent most
of the night in the local hoosegow. The pairing of
Johnny T. and Wayne Kramer was one of R&R's all-
time bad ideas, and DS lays the wood to the pair with
flair... Why I had Ian Hunter on the Bottom 40 and
Adam & the Ants on the top is way beyond me! Ian
Hunter! Sacrilege! I should have been more prescient
and taken off my punk blinders long enough to see
musical posterity... Oy vey!

TOUCH & GO

50¢

We're on a 'Rake–Do' jag.

A literary masterpiece. The epitome
of excellence. The good. Just a few
of the adjectives we like to use to
describe our humble fanzine. Yes the
arrogant assholes were unable to
stifle their wanton,self indulgent
whims and have put out yet another
installment of TOUCH & GO. We realize we're not the best yet(of
course that honor gos to SLASH)
but we are gaining a full head
(big head some are complaining)
of steam. And if nothing else dam-
mit we're out every month(none of
this WHITE NOISE-FLIPSIDE bullshit
when you never know... This being our
fourth big ish we thought we'd give
you a little background info. TOUCH
& GO was born last October on the 500
block of Michigan Ave. I was just
lurking about when i bumped into DS
at a local sin emporium where he was
doing a little early xmas shopping.
His arms were laden with gifts;
rubber cods, vibrating butt plugs,
an auto suck and assorted aphrodisiacs
and marital aids. I had'nt seen him
since high school and I said D? it's
it's DS isn't it? Tesco? My god Tesco
Vee hows it going lets do a 'zine man
ok? We were born. We figured if we were
going to write about all this great music
we'd better be well informed. So we sold
all our Uriah Heep and Devo albums and
purchased all the classics;Bleach Blondies'
"Parallel Pubic Hairs"-Elvis Laurel &
Hardys "Armed Buttones" and The Splashes'
"Jah No Give Me Nuff Hemp". LP's to be
successful by.
The mail has been great-keep it cumming.
Certain parties are quite upset with us
and some are even whispering lawsuits.
But you've sussed it out by now that we
dont give a monkeys cuz D & Vee will always
be far superior to dem da phlegm.
                          TV

SUBSCRIPTIONS- 2.00 for 3 PP.
A NON-PROFIT ENDEAVOR.

BLACK FLAG

TOO GREAT FOR WORDS, THEY*RE THE BEST!!!

COVER PHOTO by JOE STEVENS (NME)

The resurgence of punk/new wave music at Dooleys in East Lansing did not come off as well as one might have expected, and it can be attributed to a number of reasons. The most obvious one being the fact that Johnny Thunders and Wayne Kramer are a couple of aging old farts who have lost touch with what's going on today. The energy and vitality of their earlier years has long been sucked dry, and we find them plodding through an entire set of antiquated sounding tunes. It's not nostalgia night guys, so why do you open the show with "Ramblin' Rose"? And what's more, in JT's limp effort in a search for new material, he insults us with Steve Dahl's humorless "Ayatullah". We also found Mr. Thunders in an advanced state of inebriation, which only compounded their already sloppy, lackluster performance. The band was shit, pure and simple, and they bored me stiff. Maybe this is what we're supposed to get for our measly $3.oo. You get what you pay for, as the old saying goes, and although Thunders has at least secured a marginal place in history, he had better stop playing shit like he did tonight if he has any hopes of maintaining a semblance of credibility. He's sinking to new depths and Gang War easily represents an all-time low.

Moving to a brighter note, The Squires(ex The Dogs) who opened the show proved that not everything in this town sucks as bad as we once thought. We finally got our own new wave act--something that's sorely needed in this musically deprived burg. Their sound was tight and punchy and I just wish other bands would get on the ball. To stop playing all that bar-band shit and start doing something useful for a change. The Squires are in the process of breaking in a new singer and so far, she doesn't seem to be working out. A little too timid in front of the audience, she needs to drop the cutesy-pie image and get nastier, more threatening. Spit fire into the faces of those slobbering neanderthals crowding the front of the stage(We won't tell you where we saw DS during all this--ED). Overall, The Squires show promise, and if they can chuck their occasional heavy metal thumping, they could go places. They managed to upstage Gang War if that's worth anything to ya.

With the bands out of the way, I want to take a moment to comment on what really bothered me this evening--namely the crowd. You closet punks make me puke. ONe night out of the year you decide to go "punk", you get out the skinny ties, the ripped T-shirts, the buttons, the whole fuckin' phony regalia just so you can appear oh so chic and with it. It's not a game, you either live it or leave us alone. ANd what's worse, you ignorant little twits embarrass yourselves with your warped notions regarding punk behavior. Where'd you learn this stuff? What do you do--carry around a little instruction manual that says: "For guaranteed punkishness, lob one beer

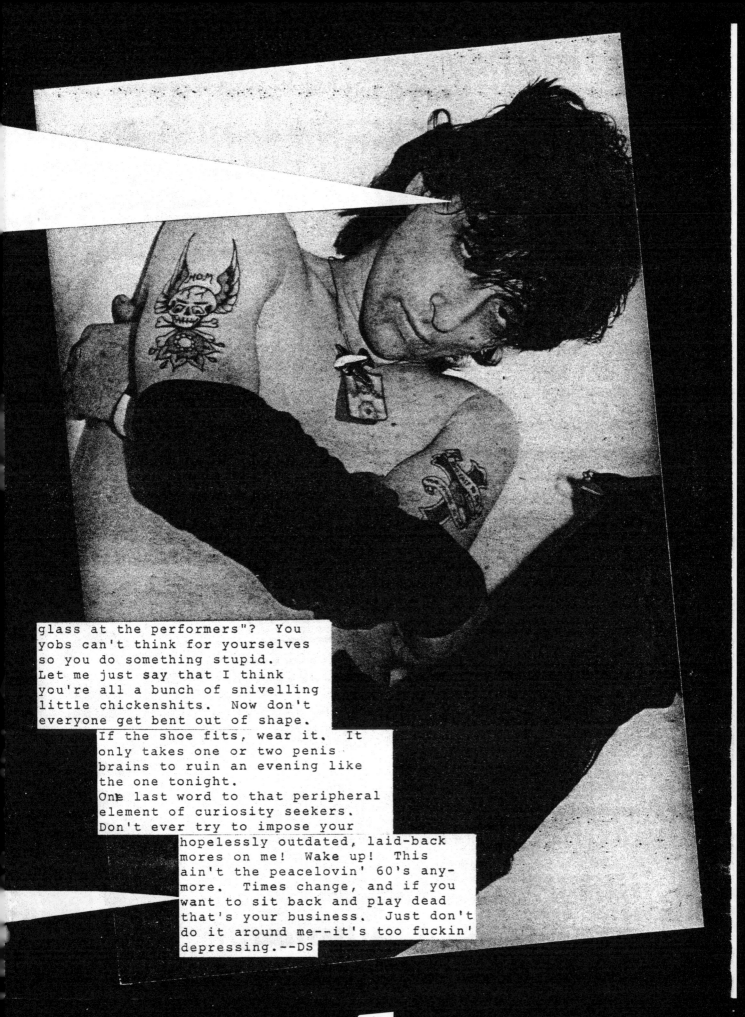

glass at the performers"? You
yobs can't think for yourselves
so you do something stupid.
Let me just say that I think
you're all a bunch of snivelling
little chickenshits. Now don't
everyone get bent out of shape.
If the shoe fits, wear it. It
only takes one or two penis
brains to ruin an evening like
the one tonight.
One last word to that peripheral
element of curiosity seekers.
Don't ever try to impose your
hopelessly outdated, laid-back
mores on me! Wake up! This
ain't the peacelovin' 60's anymore. Times change, and if you
want to sit back and play dead
that's your business. Just don't
do it around me--it's too fuckin'
depressing.--DS

CABERET VOLTAIRE
"Mix Up"   Rough Trade Records

This LP has been designed with a purpose; to take you to the outermost edges of emotional angst, then throw your brain into the sewer. It has been programmed to leave you badly fragmented and alone, to find your way back if you can, to what you thought was normal and real. But it won't be the same.

From the beginning of "Kirlian Photograph", something starts to happen. The bass, drums, and "anti-vocals" draw you in. The hypnosis is achieved when the eerie sound of a flute, the crunching but still guitar, and other effects come into the picture. It's all a matter of control from here as the opening shrieks of "No Escape" let

you know you are here for the remainder. The side continues with the beautiful terror of "Fourth Slot" featuring the new style guitar of Richard H. Kirk, who changes everything about the instrument proving himself to be one of if not the best around. "Heaven and Hell" jolts you into shock as the side closes with "Eyeless Sight" which kicks and beats you to the floor.
Side Two doles out more beauty and hell-bent horror with all of the cuts being outstanding. My favorites are "On Every Other Street" where the enemy becomes almost too real for your mind to bear, and "Capsules" which gives the disc a fine send-off. After listening, your first re-action will probably be to for- get everything you just heard. The reason being, that every- thing you think you know about music or anything else will be questioned and dealt with mer- cilessly. Even if you hate it, music will never sound quite the way it used to.

In this reviewers' opinion, new music has never seen a finer mo- ment. This one breaks all the rules and makes new ones with raw guts and a subtle but ever present and demanding power. In case you're interested, the LP is available at area record stores that carry imports.--Thom Jurek

LETS TALK ABOUT THE UNDERTONES >

THE UNDERTONES LP
Sire Records

Rarely have we found a band
that effectively combines the
stirring emotionalism of the
early days in 1977 with an
incredible pop accessability.
More often than not, those
bands showing inclinations
toward the pop market wind
up making music which is both
sterile and without substance.
Pop drivel that leaves us
limper than a ratbag. The
Undertones, however, are one
of only a handful that have
been able to meld the driving
power of the "punk" bands with
the catchy buoyancy of pop
music. I'll go as far as to
say that their blend of pop
and punk is unsurpassed. No
one comes close to achieving
this kind of balance between
the two. Not the Buzzcocks
(whom writers have compared
them to, not altogether accurate either), not the Yachts,
not anyone. Like their five
singles, every cut from this
record contains that irresist-
ible hook that yanks you off
your ass and has you bouncing
and bobbing in one spontaneous
reaction. You don't think--
it just happens. All great
rock 'n' roll should do this
to its listeners. Unfortunately
we wade through all kinds of
shit in our search for good
music, and it is that much
more rewarding when a band
like the Undertones finally
does come along. They have
all the tools to make it--
a tight energetic sound that,
and you may disagree, impressed
me far more greatly than did
the bludgeoning assault of The
Clash when they toured together.
In Feargal Sharkey's shrill
adolescent voice The Undertones
have the perfect vehicle to
deliver their songs of teenage
love and pubescent silliness.
Does it appear that I'm suffering from a severe case of hyperbole? Perhaps I am, but there
are bands(too many to mention)
that are receiving the same kind
of hype, except on a nationwide
scale, and they don't have half
the talent of The Undertones.
It sickens me to see a band like
The Romantics receiving all this
help from people like WILS, and
then to watch the more deserving
Undertones wallow in obscurity.
Sire won't be of much help if
they(Sire) remain true to form.
Although they have a reputation
for signing new acts, they are
equally notorious for their lack
of promotinal support.
What I'm actually saying is: BUY
THE ALBUM. That's it. You don't
need me to tell you how good it
is. Anything that needs to be
said is all there in the grooves.
My pontificating would, in effect,
only compromise what is said thru
their music. It stands just fine
on its own without the help from
some frustrated journalist.--DS

THE UNDERTONES

METAL BOX

PUBLIC IMAGE LTD. "METAL BOX" Virgin Records
  Public Images' monoclinical ministry
of minacious meanderings is exquisitely
showcased in this questionable package
(3 12" discs in a metal bag).Herein is
contained more of the cryptic drub we've
come to expect from Lydon and Co. It's
funny how an enigmatic chap like John,
once plastered across every rag from the
Times to the Star has sheltered himself
into his little corner-culture, rarely
gigging or even speaking unless it be a
small blurb of gastric malevolence directed
at one warm blooded statute or another.
Suddenly we are blessed with what "MEMORIES"
only hinted at. A ritualistic approach to a
musical form created without obvious influences
in the obscure context of plodding bass lines,
syncopatic high-hat and straining guitar
brilliance. Over this backdrop screams the ora-
torical comet that is Johnny Lydon,sardonic
but sartorial as he fantasizes via his own
indecipherable vocal stylings.Somehow "METAL
BOX" is capable of creating new and unpredictable
mental states in the listener.

The reviews of the 1st Issue were hardly complimentary. One could easily picture Lydon
stealthily creeping about his Chelsea flat
as the presses' barbs flew. The criticism
seemingly solidified(had no effect is more like
it) his desire to continue off in his own
private direction. It is almost pleasing to
note the exorbitant price of this can(anywhere
from 18 to 25 dollars) for surely only rabid fans
of this incredible band will be willing to part
with the coin. A must set.

                    TV

SINGLES

WE ARE ALL PROSTITUTES

EVERYONE HAS THEIR PRICE
AND YOU TOO WILL LEARN
    TO LIVE THE LIE
AGGRESSION
COMPETITION
AMBITION   CONSUMER FASCISM

CAPITALISM IS THE MOST BARBARIC OF ALL RELIGIONS

DEPARTMENT STORES ARE OUR NEW CATHEDRALS
OUR CARS ARE MARTYRS TO THE CAUSE

    WE ARE ALL PROSTITUTES
OUR CHILDREN SHALL RISE UP AGAINST US
BECAUSE WE ARE THE ONES TO BLAME
    WE ARE THE ONES THEY'LL BLAME
    THEY WILL GIVE US A NEW NAME
  WE SHALL BE

    HYPOCRITES   HYPOCRITES   HYPOCRITES

at this moment despair ends and tactics begin.

THE POP GROUP—"WE ARE ALL PROSTITUTES"

NO ONE can adequately describe this bunch. AN invidious tune such as this places one in the position of having to react. An excrescence on the music industry can always be erad- icated by apathy and disallu- sionment but emotions such as these only feed THE POP GROUPS' collective fire. THe kind words, the harsh criticisms, the analogous cross references only force further genuflection. Long after all other acts are obsolescent, THE POP GROUPS' diatribes will be an eternal and invulnerable mirror of the 80's.

ORIGINAL MIRRORS—"COULD THIS BE HEAVEN?"/"NIGHT OF THE ANGELS"

There's something unique happening here. Another Ultravox clone? Maybe but these guys are hot man- oil-base primo-avant gaurd against the winter chill and with all the various techniques employed

THE CURE—"JUMPING SOMEONE ELSES TRAIN"/"I'M COLD"

A prodigious work of excellence. These guys have always been my all time fave trio and our 3 imaginary boys have returned with their strongest yet. First listen leaves one, "Oh well another dum-de -dum rail against something or other but the incessant snare rasp- ing-let's face it the whole scen- ario is damned infectious. You'll swear the B side is on 33'-drudge bass but never a dull one on this. If you are one of those, "2.49 for a single forget it" types then you lose cuz THE CURE will never be released over here. They're too good.

these sports cant lose. This may be too artsy for some of you gut level types out there. But note for note Original Mirrors have released one of the more intriguing debuts in quite some time.

tv

45's

VISAGE
"Tar"/"Freqency 7" Radar Records

Who is Steve Strange, and how
come I don't know a fuckin'
thing about him? Who cares(I'm
sure you don't), because this
is one nifty little single.
The other members on this record
don't quite share in Strange's
anonymity. Midge Ure of Ultravox and John McGeoch of Magazine
make their presence felt by
blending elements from their
respective bands to create the
Visage sound. A definite disco
potential(did I say a bad word)
is layered into the grooves of
"Tar" along with some funky,
gut-bucket sax playing by McGeoch.
"Frequency 7" just doesn't do
it for me, though. This time
it sounds like they're just
playing around with their instruments only to come up with an
opaque mush that leaves me dis-
interested. Visage has possibilities.--DS

THE PSYCHEDELIC FURS
"We Love You"/"Pulse" Epic

Somebody thinks pretty highly
of these yobs, or else they
wouldn't be on Epic(how astute
-ED). They call their music
beautiful chaos. Poor choice
of words if you ask me, more
like pretty mainstream, especially "We Love You". Their
singer sounds like an emascu-
lated John Lydon. The Furs
got their sound down pat all
right, but what else is there?
Not much, that's what. Fortunately they recover on the
flip-side. "Pulse" shoots
down the A-side and leaves it
in the dust. More in line with
the hype they've been receiving.
A snappy pace and a great little sax solo in the middle to
keep the most arthritic of
joints limber. An enjoyable
single despite its tilt toward
mediocrity.--DS

RUDI EP
Good Vibrations Records

More adolescent pop from Ireland, except this time it's of the cold shower variety. Sounds more like the Easybeats than anyone else. Real tinny mix, and maybe that's where the problem lies. It strips away any excitement that might (I said might) have taken place during the recording. Based on just this single, Rudi places a poor fourth behind The Undertones, The Outcasts, and Protex. A marginal effort suffering from a constipated production.--DS

SECRET AFFAIR
"Let Your Heart Dance"/"Sorry Wrong Number" I-Spy Records

Uh-oh, I-Spy's flung another piece of that mod shit over this way. Heard somewhere that these guys were supposed to be the big rage in the Mod heirarchy, but I fail to see the basis for such an obvious hype. Slow simpleminded beat with no balls. Could've been lifted off one of Iggy's latest for all I know. Let your heart dance?--no way, not without a little CPR first. This stufff is lame and boring. Sounds like they got the brass section from The Merv Griffin Show blaring away in the background. These guys are the Mantovani of punk. Most mod stinks, and this drab debut only hardens my stand.--DS

JOY DIVISION
"Transmission"/"Novelty"
Factory Records

A single by the masters of murk just isn't enough to satisfy my growing appetite for their intense and highly unique brand of music. It only wets the palate for an anxiously awaited followup LP, which I hope is not just wishful thinking on my part. Both cuts are very similar to the material from "Unknown Pleasures". Dark, mysterious, sometimes gloomy, sometimes fatalistic; but somehow always maintaining that element of the positive throughout. Don't ask me how. For the time being, this will have to do.--DS

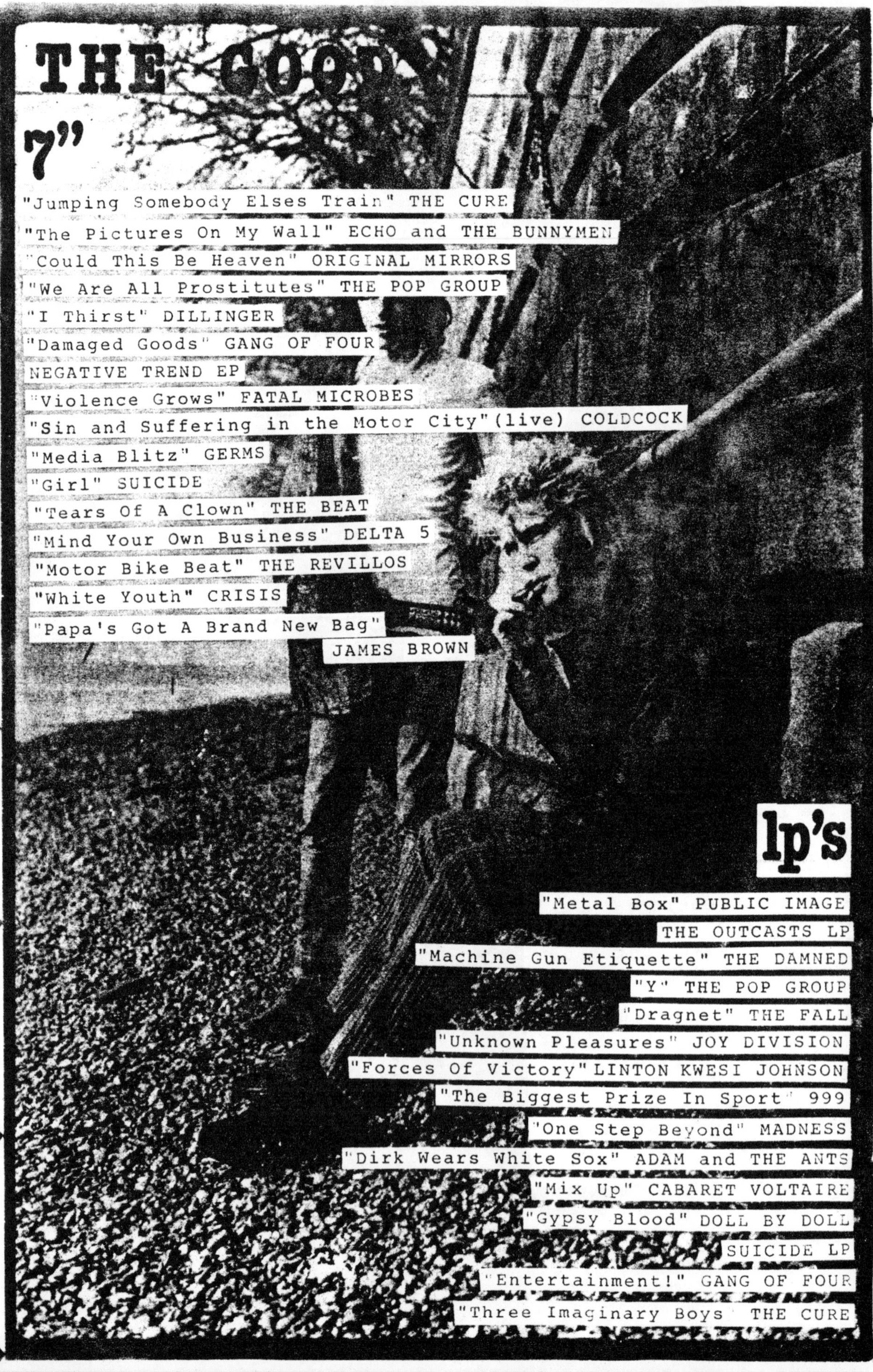

THE GOOD

7"

"Jumping Somebody Elses Train" THE CURE

"The Pictures On My Wall" ECHO and THE BUNNYMEN

"Could This Be Heaven" ORIGINAL MIRRORS

"We Are All Prostitutes" THE POP GROUP

"I Thirst" DILLINGER

"Damaged Goods" GANG OF FOUR

NEGATIVE TREND EP

"Violence Grows" FATAL MICROBES

"Sin and Suffering in the Motor City"(live) COLDCOCK

"Media Blitz" GERMS

"Girl" SUICIDE

"Tears Of A Clown" THE BEAT

"Mind Your Own Business" DELTA 5

"Motor Bike Beat" THE REVILLOS

"White Youth" CRISIS

"Papa's Got A Brand New Bag"
JAMES BROWN

lp's

"Metal Box" PUBLIC IMAGE

THE OUTCASTS LP

"Machine Gun Etiquette" THE DAMNED

"Y" THE POP GROUP

"Dragnet" THE FALL

"Unknown Pleasures" JOY DIVISION

"Forces Of Victory" LINTON KWESI JOHNSON

"The Biggest Prize In Sport" 999

"One Step Beyond" MADNESS

"Dirk Wears White Sox" ADAM and THE ANTS

"Mix Up" CABARET VOLTAIRE

"Gypsy Blood" DOLL BY DOLL

SUICIDE LP

"Entertainment!" GANG OF FOUR

"Three Imaginary Boys" THE CURE

Hey you fuckin' crazies I'm back.
That's right the guy at the punky
penitentiary party is back to add
his muddy collection of thoughts
and opinions to this elitist rag
(and I am one of the elite).
As can be expected in a homegrown
zine' tended by two decidedly non-
agricultural types, there were a
few errors,misquotes,and inaccuracies
in my first column(see #] ED.) Plus
mailing snafus and terminal lazi-
ness prevented #2 and #3 from containing my benediction. Tsk Tsk.

you I'll get Tesco to give
me your address and I'll write
you personally.
And contrary to T&G #3 The Doors
(belch,ED.) should be close to the
top of the Top 40 where milk shakes
are definately bottom 40 material.
So in the words of James Chance-
"Contort yourself one time,Contort
yourself two times" and in the words
of me "Fuck off Commie Faggots."
THE R&R BANKROBBER

To get on with it the bottom line
for So. Ca. are the best new wave
(hate that term) radio shows. Hepcats From Hell is hosted by R. Meltzer (ex Vom) on KPFK 90.7 FM in L.A.
The Mike and Ian show is hosted by
Ian Hill on KCSB and directly
following the Gayle and Patty show.

Niether of these are commercially
interrupted. The emphasis on meltzer's show is the L.A. scene. Ian's
show contains punk and ska and a little
mod.
The following are U.S. bands worthy
of your attention and adulation. The
Reds,Alda Reserve,B-52's,Talking Heads,
Pere Ubu, and Germs. Best new limey
stuff-well I'm with DS and TV(dipshit
and transvestite) Joy Division "Unknown
Pleasures" and Skids "Days In Europa"
tie for honors. Singles wise it's
another tossup between The Pop Group-
"We Are All Prostitutes" and The Psychedelic Furs "Pulse". XTC and The
Undertones are power(ful) pop. MOst
music in this realm is dreck.

I'd like to see Nina Hagan
and Siouxsie suck puss.

I'd like pictures of punkettes,
punkerinas, and superfine drag-
queens(just kidding)((send those
to DS,ED.)) sent care of T&G. If
I wanna have choitus coitus with

TOP 40

Boomtown Rats

Joy Division
MULTIPLE ORGASMS
Catholic Discipline
dillinger 999 RUTS
GIBSON ES-347 TD

"THE LATE and GREAT SKREWDRIVER"

THE UNDERTONES
MADNESS
MONTE CAZAZZA
DISC SHOP
panting and barking...
THE SQUIRES
PEANUT BUTTER HAND JOBS
Divine.
UNITS
MANUAL STIMULATION
ULTRAVOX
JAMES BROWN
THE "NEW" COLDCOCK
ORIGINAL MIRRORS
'MODERN BOYS'
ANDY'S NEW HAIRCUT
SIOUXSIE'S BREASTS
LEOPARDSKIN
JANDE AND VINCE
THE FALL
THE "RAKE-DO"
MUD WRESTLING
Rockabilly
Adam And The Ants
GENE VINCENT AND HIS BLUE CAPS
DOLL BY DOLL
HANDCUFFS
Dead Commies
BOLTING YOUR DATE TO THE WALL
GOLDEN SHOWERS
"WASTED"
FRANKIE TEARDROP

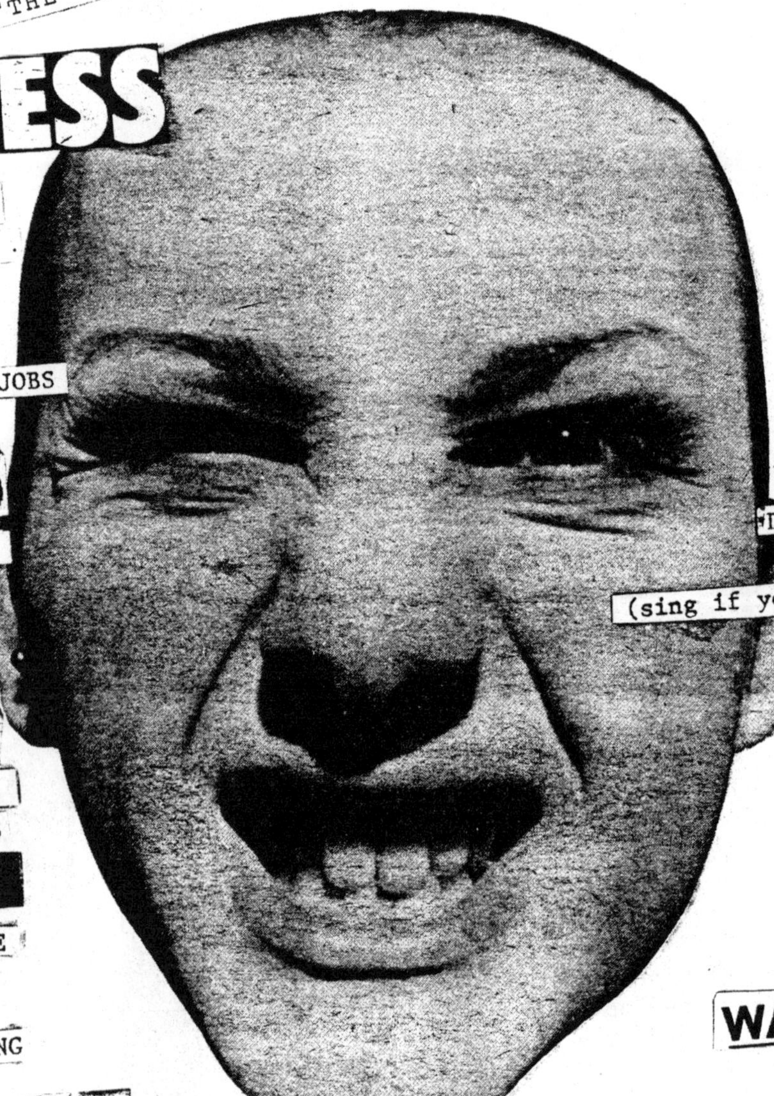

TRAINABLE
'VAN HALEN'
VD
easy listening
POLITICS
Bruce Springsteen
DEANNE PEARSON
Patti Smith
CORPORATE ROCKERS
STEEL-BELTED CONDOMS
DEVO
STA-HARD PILLS
SIT DOWN CONCERTS
New York Rocker
THE NEW CLASH ALBUM
censorship.
SOUTHSIDE JOHNNY
Debbie "FUCK FACE" Harry
Lynerd Skynyrd
(sing if you're glad they're dead)
NO NUKES LP
THE DOGS AT CBGB'S
BOOK STORES
DRUGS
LIMP MODS
Jerry Vile
Ian Hunter
Runaways
WAZMO NARIZ
CLOSET PUNKS
BOMP!
PROSTATE INFECTION
frogless labs
OPEC
urban sophistication!

Chrysalis recording artists ....

THE SPECIALS

ONE NITE ONLY
SAT FEB 23

tickets at: **schoolkids (A²)**   **sams jams**
bookies,   phobia & dearborn music

$ 6.00

BOOKIE'S CLUB 870
(FORMERLY FRANK GAGEN'S)
870 W. McNICHOLS AVE.
2½ BLOCKS WEST OF WOODWARD

ADMISSION:
862-0877

5

Distribution picked up enough with this issue to warrant a second print run... Oooh, we're printing another 100—big fuckin' whoopee! Yours truly looking like some bolo tie, wing-tip wanker posing in front of my favorite massage parlor (on the reprint I look decidedly less butt pirate-esque). I think it was $10 back then for a rub and a tug, and that middle-aged gook could really make me launch. I think her last name was Wang... How fitting. More Coldcock, Destroy All Monsters... Oh, and fancy that 999 again. DS's brother Jim honored us with our first DC scene report. More local Lansing slags—some of the locals were really starting to hate us, this shit was working... The knife was in... Time to start twisting it for maximum results.

NO. 5 (sec. printing) **75¢**

OPEN
4:00 PM

TOUCH & GO

Perhaps the most

influential magazine in america today

BRAND NEW

SHOE OR BOOT GAG

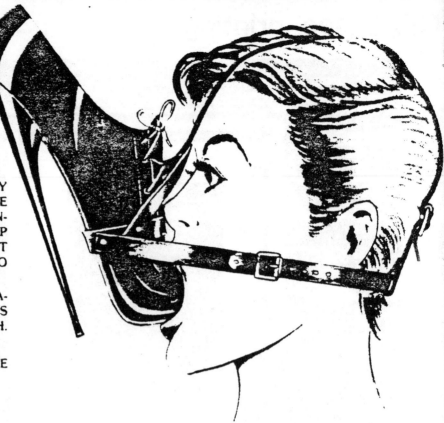

COLDCOCK

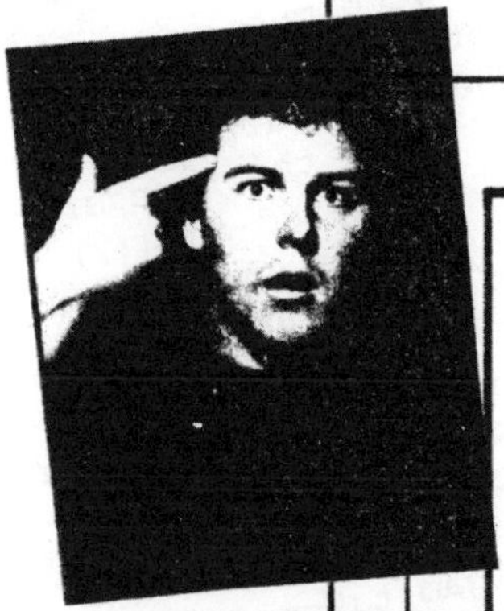

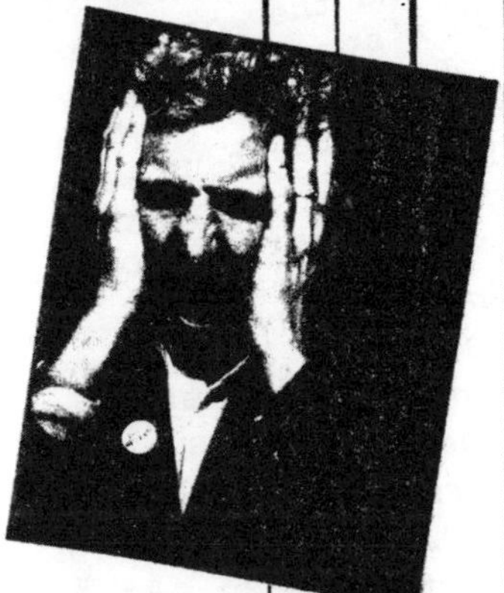

IN ORDER TO PROD YOU EVER SO UNSUBTLY
INTO SUBSCRIBING, WE ARE WILLING TO SEND
THE FIRST 13 PEOPLE, A FREE "COLDCOCK"
SINGLE!!!!! THAT'S RIGHT DETROITS' FINESTS'
DEBUT 45 FEATURING "I WANNA BE RICH"/"YOU'RE
A MESS". SO SEND US 3DOLLARS (BY THE WAY THAT
ONLY BUYS ABOUT 2½ gallons OF GAS) AND WE'LL
SEND YOU 3 ACTION FILLED RAGS AND A DISC TO
BOOT!!!!!!!!!

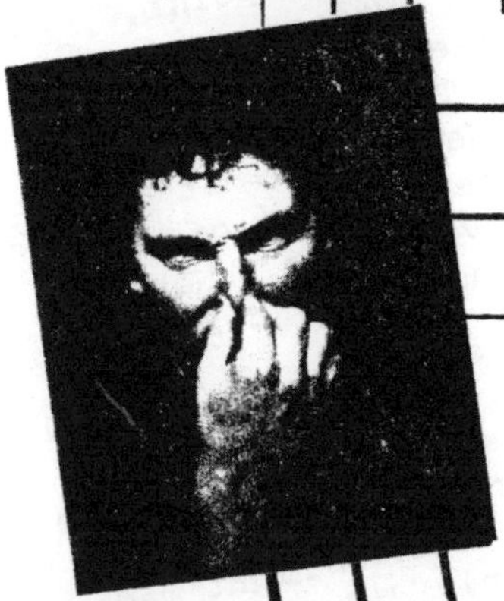

TOUCH and GO

BOX 26203   LANSING, MI 48909

SUBSCRIPTIONS—$3.00 FOR 3 ISSUES
POST PAID—YEARLY$10.00

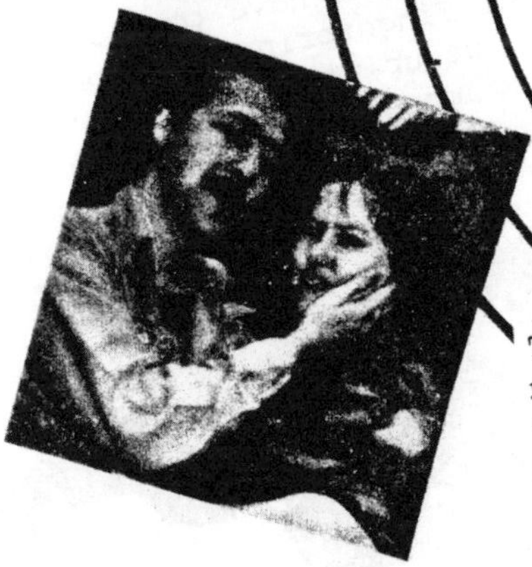

The one's that count...

Talk Talk
P.O. Box 36
Lawrence, Kansas
66044

Flipside
P.O. Box 363
Whittier, Ca.
90608

Slash
P.O. Box 48888
Los Angeles, Ca.
90048

Smegma Journal
P.O. Box 421
Maumee, Ohio
43537

Touch & Go is published
monthly by editors;DS,
Tesco Vee, and S. Williams.
Contributors this month
are;JC-TJ-Ashley Warren-
JAS-Moe Briar.The editors
are in no way responsible
for the content of any
articles other than their
own.

FINGERPRINZ/THE LIPS ARE BACK
Dooleys on Monday Night

If The Lips Are Back are part of a trend in the Midwestern scene then things are indeed looking up. These hooligans proved to all present at Drooleys Monday night that an uncomplicated and uncompromising sound exists in Southwestern Michigan(I think these guys hail from somewhere outside of Battle Creek). Formerly Brain Police(a helluva lot better name let's face it) this bunch is latent aggro as they careen across the fringe between good fun and the nastiest punkisms. I mean these troglodytes even shot off some angry steam or was it my starved imagination?

The vocalist is obviously a graduate of the class of '77 Poshboy Pogo-Dancing School and his wardrobe... well forget about that, but this guy's gurgle was not unreminiscent of John Denney of Weirdos fame. You know, deep snarling-this guy is a serious menace to mankind.

I'm going to summarize this bit and say The Lips Are Back is a fucking great band--something this area needs mucho more of. Alice Bag sez it the best: "We don't need the English...tellin' us what to do." Speaking of English, we were subjected to a very poor example of their music via Fingerprinz. Moreover, the bulk of the crowd seemed incapable of recognizing that fact.

It's becoming predictable. Place four nondescripts like Fingerprinz on the stage at Dooleys and the plastic punks of E.L. all go 'goo-goo gah-gah' in a mindless drool of admiration. Let me tell ya, it's embarrassing to see you nearsighted peons slobbering all over these flacid little wimps. With your help, East Lansing is steadily becoming a haven for third-rate poseur bands who, if given the chance to headline in a town where the audience is a bit more discerning, would fall flat on their faces. And you seem to enjoy wallowing in a band's mediocrity; it just makes your lack of knowledge of the scene and its music painfully apparent. If you'll allow me to play the role of the elitist asshole for a moment I'll continue on this obnoxious jag and that it appears that you

haven't heard good music yet. You gave a lot more than Fingerprinz deserved. They just aren't that good. Anyone caught up in the thunderous applause which resulted in 4(?) encores is displaying a gross lack of discrimination. How, and it still boggles the imagination, could you be satisfied with such a monotonously transparent performance? What Fingerprinz plays on stage other bands throw away during rehearsal. Their music is an amalgam taken from all kinds of bands, and they have yet to come up with a strong identity of their own. It's tripe for the ears and it passes through us without leaving a mark. If it doesn't make a dent on those beer-soaked brains of ours, then what good is it? No good, that's what! Perhaps most of you are so hard up that you'll cream over anything that tries to break away from the paralyzingly dull sounds of American rock, no matter how feeble the attempt. As bad as they were up to this point, my disgust turned to outrage when they commited sacrilege with their abominable cover of The Damned's manic masterpiece "New Rose". It is by far the most heinous act of profanation I have ever heard. Never has a song been so thoroughly defiled.

And seeing that it still had some life in it, Fingerprinz ravaged this classic again during their encore. An unpardonable crime. In short, it was a bad night made worse, for not only did we have to endure the likes of Fingerprinz, but we also had to put up with the aggravation of being amongst a crowd whose overzealous reaction made these bums believe that they could do no wrong.
--TV&DS

DESTROY ALL MONSTERS
Live at Dooleys

Another Monday night at Dooleys
where a sparse but energetic
crowd witnessed the rebirth
of Destroy All Monsters. Yes-
sir, the most popular band to
slag, to laugh at and spit on
were back to show what they
were really all about, good
no-bullshit frills rock that
surprised everyone including
myself.

The first show of the was another
ho hum yawn set by the Ann Arbor
unit The Cult Heroes. They performed using various acrobatics
with their music as well as making uninspired, lame comments
about draft resistance and other
"hip" topics to get the crowd
rowdy. Let's mean it or zip
the lip, fellas. A very forgettable band.

Next, after what seemed like hours
came the Monsters. They had just
returned from a semi-successful
British tour(the crowds loved them,
the press hated them except for
Zig Zag) and seemed fired up and
ready to go at it hard. That,
my friends, is exactly what they
did.

Ron Asheton took complete control
of the band as Niagara came out
of her shell to deliver some fine a
and decipherable lyrics. The group
performed all the singles with
Niagara doing a seemingly inspired
"What Do I Get" and an unusually
angry "You're Gonna Die". Asheton's
searing guitar-work along with
Michael Davis' distorted fuzztone
bass worked well in providing the
necessary crunch punch framework
for the savage drumming of Rob King
to survive in. The band was tight
and much improved without the 'psychedelic' sax playing of Ben Miller
that dominated the last gig I saw.
Great Show Folks!

I just want to bring up one point
to those of you who read Mr. Hold-
ship' review in The State News
who weren't at the show. Bill
stated that "two thirds of the
audience walked out before the
show ended". That statement was
entirely incorrect. The only
jerks who left were the closet
punks and fence-sitters who thought
they were gona see the Romantics,
Mutants or some other such wimp-
oid schlock band. It was 'yer
own loss that you left early.
Well, that's it for this month,
but remember D.A.M.--keep it
up and show these snotty-nosed
smirkers they're full of shit.--TJ

The nutty punter--AW

THE SPECIAL A.K.A. LIVE!

THE SPECIALS
Hurrah

As I pushed my way through the annoyingly packed Hurrah, I couldn't help wondering what all these people were doing here.

While in the UK,reggae is on the verge of becoming the most influential musical force of the eighties, in the good 'ole US, the vast population of unenlightened yanks haven't given two Toots or a Maytal about reggae. Even the spinning of an overtly commercial Peter Tosh tune at Hurrah is as odious an invitation to dance as a pay toilet to a tourist with Montezuma's revenge.

Perhaps a prime reason lies with the superficially new feel that ska has to many unfamiliar with reggae.

The Special's brand of music is not an original, unexplored sound, which unfortunately too many Two-Tone followers have led themselves to believe. It is rather a derivative, interpretive style which draws upon the pre-reggae background of bluebeat and ska influences of the early sixties, and uses this foundation as the basis of futher musical exploration.

In this proper perspective, the Special's relation to ska is closely comparable to the Rolling Stones' connection to soul and r&b. Just as the Stones created a distictive sound from the influences of Chuck Berry, Muddy Waters and others, so the Specials hark back to talents like Dandy Livingstone, Prince Buster, and the Skatellites as pillars on which to build their own musically interpretive edifice.

However, in McDonaldland where reggae has hardly even made a dent in the charts, it is little wonder that the appearance of the even more obscure musical form of ska,sounds to the vast majority of listeners, like a new movement.

It is precisely this apparent newness of the Special's sound that has caused such influential trendies as WPIX's Jane Hamburger to recently latch on to the group as if she were NYC's sole enlightened one by playing the piss out of them. It is a wonder how Ms. Hamburger can have any professional self-respect as to reach such embarrassingly patronizing and condescending depths by commenting on her playing "Ob-la-di, Ob-la-da" with: "That was the Beatles' doing their version of ska, that's the kind of

music the Special's play"!

Is it any wonder there was such a flock of trendy wankers whose pork-pies will be forever collecting closet dust after concert night. Why according to WPIX, if you weren't at the show or bought the album, you'd be one notch less trendy for the week. I feel sorry for all those intelligent enough to have loved the Specials long before Ms. Hamburger's bandwagon caused so many anachronistically trendy spandex wearers and other assorted pre-fabs to voraciously grab the few tickets.

In spite of the crowd, I was far from disappointed from the Specials' live show. They attack the stage with such a frenzied, energetic edge that will forever remain elusive to vinyl. Neville Staples metamorphosizes himself into a human pinwheel of wildly flying arms and legs, bouncing all over the stage, while Jerry Dammers wildly jumps up and down like a marionette controlled by a mischevious child, his feet rarely touch the ground while his hands remain constantly glued to the keyboards. Amidst the rest of the band's frenzied leg flicking is lead vocalist Terry Hall whose calmness and leering gaze works as a marvelously ill-fitting component, thereby becoming the perfectly provocative figure to deliver the vocals.

With an album of fourteen killer tunes there's not one bad song to hold the Special's back, as they let themselves loose with such enthusiastic fervor for each song that often the increased tempo threatens their control, but somehow chaos never results.

From the first set of tunes, the Specials' live strategy manifests itself as a volley of fast tempoed ska bridged by the more relaxed rhythm of their reggae based selections.

The set starts off with the invigorating "(Dawning of a) New Era", as the band leap about the stage with all the abandon of a crate full of superballs having spilled to the floor, continuing into "Do the Dog", before the brakes are pulled for "It's Up to You".

The set then continues with "Ratrace", a catchy song about the superficial rewards of going to college, "Blank Expression" and the jumpy "Rude Boy's Out of Jail",a sequel to Coxsone Dodd's "Rude Boy Gone to Jail". If any song gained from its transferance to the Specials' live show, it was "Concrete

Jungle", a paranoic portrayal of urban life whose lurking violence cut its way through Terry Hall's frighteningly fervent vocals well before the strobelit, mock fight between Neville Staples and Jerry Dammers during the middle instrumental section; a perfect preface to the emotionally stirring "It Doesn't Make it Alright".

Another of the show's highlights occured when Neville emerged from beneath a towel he donned in the manner of a magistrate's wig, as Judge Roughneck, prosecuting Terry in the humourous, yet pointed "Stupid Marriage".

Terry then spoke to the apathetic crowd in the back by warning them that "This is your last chance to dance before the Third World War" and then launched into an intense version of "Too Much Too Young".

For the showstopping closing numbers, the brass section of Rico and Dick Cuthell joined the band on stage for "Guns of Navarone", "Little Bitch", "Message to you, Rudy", "Nite Klub", and "Gangsters".

In the case of "Gangsters" the addition of Rico and Cuthell provided the song with a much fuller sound, harking back even more strongly to its model,Prince Buster's "Al Capone".

The first encore involved a melody of skinhead favorites including "Longshot Kick the Bucket", "The Liquadator", and "Skinhead Moonstomp", before the crowd called them back for more encore versions of "You're Wondering Now", an instrumental whose name escapes me, and "Madness", and "Gangsters" again.

When "Gangsters" was offered up for the second time all hell broke loose as Neville jumped into the audience with frenzied cries of "Don't call me scareface!", closely followed by guitarist Lynval Golding, pushed with a little help by Jerry Dammers' Doc Martens. Even when a poor roadie attempted to rescue both men from the crowd,Dammers' shoves nearly caused the roadie to topple off the stage as well.

In total, the Specials nabbed four encores from the audience. A most remarquable achievement when remembered how notorious New York audiences are when it comes to applauding.

If the amazingly succesful reception the Specials and other Two-Tone artists have gained continues, this might in fact be the dawning of a new era.

Ashley Warren

NUTTY DREAD

D.C. Scene

US Treasury

Washington DC, like most cities, is rife with plastic people — guys who can't think past their pecker and girls who can't think at all. You have to look hard to find a place that breaks the rule and doesn't trigger gag reflexes.

Most people in DC would hate the place due to its drab, even dirty decor, which suits the rest of us fine because the trendy assholes are a blight anyway. Also they're afraid the Spics will beat them up but I've never seen that happen. ←

wish it would — JAS

The groups? DC has bands, and of course the pretentious ones get the ink and the true get slagged. But isn't that the way it's always been?

Howard ↙

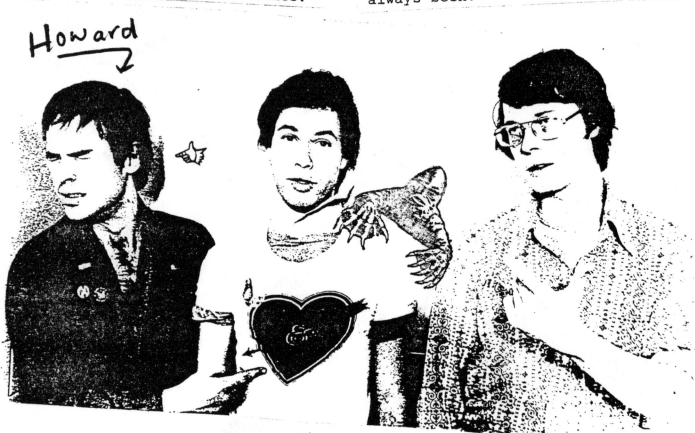

NURSES

Such a place is the Madame's Organ Art Coop. Set in a seedy section of Adams Morgan, mongrel neighborhood if ever I saw one, you can stumble in and see groups like the Bad Brains, the Nurses, Tex Rubinowitz and the Bad Boys, Trenchmouth and others too numerous and shitty to mention. They also sell Heinekens for a buck and Old Mil' for fifty cents.

The Urban Verbs are on top of the slag heap. Led by Roddy Frantz, cousin of Talking Heads' drummer (who cares?), they put out a high energy act which is acceptable because it's different. Everything centers around the lead vocals, something like the Doors or Black Randy. Like anything that's OK but not that good, the Verbs get overpraised while other talents go unnoticed (like the Bad Brains!). Also Danny Frankel, the drummer, is a good guy though he looks like a total nerd.

A notch below the Verbs in popularity and a notch above in product (where it counts) are the Nurses. Led by Howard Wuelfing on bass and vocals, they have one of the most together acts in town. Howie has a high voice that takes some getting used to, but it's his bass playing that impresses me the most — he DRIVES the band. The lyrics are also the most compelling of any local talent.

BAD Brains

Wuelfing is also the leading "new wave" (I'm getting to question that term, but use it for lack of a better one and imagination) spokes-man in the area. He piloted the ill-fated Descenes fanzine for a time, and will tell anyone exactly what he thinks. He'll also sell you a Nurses button out of his backpack (a punk with a backpack?).

The third member of the popularity triumvirat is the Deceats. They suck. They suck not because they're lousy, but because they could be decent. Guitarist Keith Campbell is arguably the finest in town. Lead singer Martha Hull is inarguably the most pretentious vocalist. The little slit thinks she's Streisand (whom I hate), and gushes fake emotions and newcomers to the scene scarf it right up. The music itself is a boring blend of rock and new wave. End of tirade.

And now to the best band, the guys who would blow the rest to shards if the scum would dare to set foot on the same stage. They are Bad Brains. A reformed four-piece jazz band, they come on like the Wierdos but play better. Why don't they draw? Why don't they get jobs? They're black.   That's why.

Perhaps you have a hard time swallowing the fact that blacks can't get gigs in a town that's 75 percent black.   Blacks don't own the clubs is the reason, and owners of all colors in the nice part of town (they didn't build a subway stop there because they wanted to keep the groids on the east side of the river) don't want trouble, and these boys have trouble written all over them. Rumors of a stabbing at one set didn't help their image either.

The singer knows how to do it. He has rasta locks, but his hair is so short they stick straight up, making him look like a black Robert Gordon. The guitarist, "Dr. No," reminded me of Captain Sensible on guitar (you missed the Damned? Shame on you!).

Other bands? Slickee Boys are not bad, but not good either. Too uneven. Beex are good, they sound like a Detroit band, with a Niagra style lead singer. They did "Search and Destroy" for an encore. Original Fetish is a misguided cabaret act that should be exter-minated, not punk and not too funny either. Dirty Work needs to be shot, too.

All I can say in addition to the above is that Basilisk is worse than anyone aforemention, Tex and the Bad Boys are true rockabilly for those with a taste for, and Prince George's County, just outside the city limits, tried to outlaw puck rock without even knowing what it was.

JAS

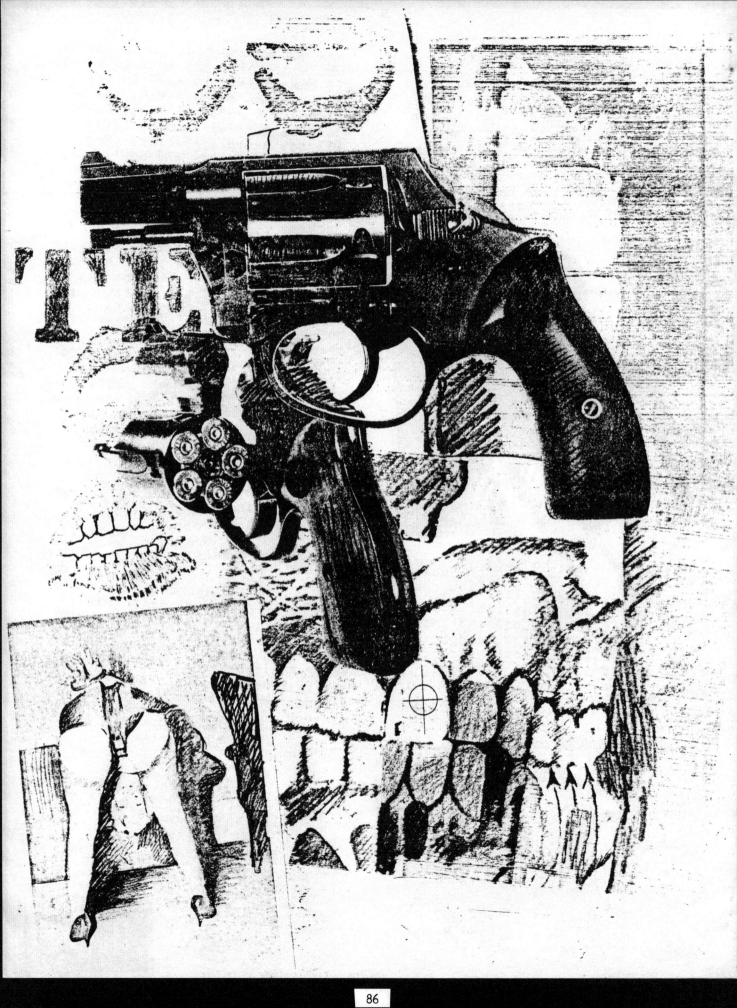

AHHH! Here we are back at the editorial offices of Touch & Go, where
the sexual harassment of our female employees is uppermost in our minds.
   I wish! Actually I'm still in exile over here at the "big house";
Lompoc Federal Pen with nary a female or even a fellow rocker in sight.
   But to all of you whores wondering why I feel qualified to tell you
out there what's happening,even though I'm in here,let me put it like
this;I'm Shane Shaman,the 19th aspect of the shining void,the #1 fang-
less fascist in the united states and you gentle readers are in the greater
part-ducklings.
   So listen up. This article is gonna mainly be devoted to the L.A. bands
without records out that are top quality.
   In direct competition with the likes of The Pop Group or Throbbing
Gristle, L.A.s' answer to "no wave" are Nervous Gender(who dub themselves
"geek rock") and Vox Pop.Both are composed of youngish(most members under
18 I think,definately under 21)weird looking punks who were part of the small
scene who idolized the Pistols and grew up on L.A.s' finest-The Weirdos
and The Germs.(in fact one member in Vox Pop is the drummer for The Germs)
But rather than follow closely in their footsteps they've gone a much more
uncrompromizing route. Prediction: You will never hear these bands on AOR
radio.Even though the novelty strains of Flying Lizards made it to the airwaves the likes of these 2 groups would fail on lyrics alone.Avery small,
not necessarily representative sample from a Vox Pop tune-"Dip his dick
in shoe polish" repeated incessantly with a small break of "Teachers Pet
Teachers Pet". All of this done in a vehement,sarcastic,iconic,mean,comp-
elling tone of voice. Or what about Nervous Gender rattling off a chorus
of "Jesus Christ you're just like me-"ahomosexual nymphomaniac-a homosexual
nymphomaniac".The music of both these bands is heavily dominated by synthesizers and dense percussion,as I said very similiar in construction to
The Pop Group,but totally different in intent,content,and dentente'.(huh?)
Anyhow rather than bemoan torture and castigate capitalism-Hollywoods' finest
experimental bands are satisfied with exposing the mental processes of
Hollywoods' decadent,selfish,unruly,and brilliant white youth!
   Two other L.A. bands that I want to tell you about are in totally different
categories(though appeal to the same audience.As with all r&r scenes L.A.s'
is very incestuous) These 2 are Wall of Voodoo and The GO GOs-who are an
all girl band who are at the top of that genre.Some bands fronted by twats
are no doubt superior in over-all musical content(Banshees and X)but as far
as all-girlconglomerations like The Slits, The Raincoats,Delta 5 or anything
America has to offer,can hold a proverbial candle to the sheer exuberance
of The GO GOs!The're hot and foxy besides. My two favorites are Charlotte,
the lead guitar player(the only one with long straight "Nico" hair)and Jane
Drano,the rythym guitarist. The others are a little butch but what the fuck
it's the music that counts.I've saved the best for last.Wall Of Voodoo. That's
right even though I've only heard them once(a cassette of a live performance)
I would have to rate them right with my top most fave bands-Joy Division,
Doll BY Doll,The Germs.They combine a righteous voodoo rythym section with
guitar licks (and synthesizers)that go from sounding like themes to
spaghetti westerns and James Bond to roaring around the scales like a rocket
attempting to leave the atmosphere.The vocals were at the back of the mix
on the cassette(natch) but they sounded intense. Ican only say with all
my pagan heart and soul that I would groove on having any of these 4 on wax.
And if any of you readers ever see any product by em',snap it up-or if you
can make it to L.A. to see them better yet!!!!!In closing I'd like to
recommend that all females take a few minutes to massage their clitori in
honor of th

The Rock + Roll Bank Robber

19

DOLL BY DOLL-"GYPSY BLOOD"
AUTOMATIC RECORDS

No this is not a "new wave"
LP. That's right the"punks"
don't like this band at all.
This album just happens to be
an incredible follow-up to their
incredible debut LP that first
graced my beloved turntable last
spring.If only we all could chuck
our labels and hangups-the excellence bleeds from the grooves in
such a way that one feels re-in
touch with something lost long
ago. I mean music with real feeling
is what Doll BY Doll is attempting
to do;so far they are going nowhere
in their attempt to become popular;
and to go into that would be a tad
dull.You see Doll BY Doll has always
been plagued with credibility problems.
*

No camp embraces them. They have a cult
following thanks to a token few from
many different scenes.Perhaps their
music is too intelligent to go over
in the coming age of computer-boy
simplicity ala Gary Numan.Granted
their sound is almost mainstream but
their ideology runs much deeper than
the strip-culture pessimism of Gang of
Four,and Marc Smith's paranoid ramblings
compliments of The Fall.To really grasp
the undercurrent of emotion in this bands
music further reading is necessary*. You
owe it to yourself to pick up on this
dynamic achievment.....Doll BY Dolls'
"Gypsy Blood".
                TV

        send SASE for interview from ZIG-ZAG ..March 79'.

999

NINE-NINE-NINE

THE BIGGEST PRIZE IN SPORT

AS8502 999

999

999

999

999 "The Biggest Prize in Sport"
Polydor Records

Attempt number two at cornering
a small portion of the impetuous
American market, and judging
from the positively overwhelming success of High Energy Plan
I won't be holding my breath.
That along with knowing that
most record buyers around here
have less smarts than a brain-
damaged flea. It's a pity, for

999

while many of you are numbing
your senses with the sounds of
that abysmal shit that Sidney
is always pushing you could
just as easily be listening to
music that had guts to it--like
999. Probably the best cross-
over band around, they brazenly
tread that thin line between
punk and mainstream, despite
their firm allegiance to the
former. Granted, their sound

999

is more polished this time out,
but it still cuts through the
void occupied by the predict-
ably dull American rock bands.
The combination of John Watson's
commanding bass and Pablo Labritain & Eddie Cases'lean and
muscular drumming with Guy Days'
crisp guitar and Nick Cash's
distinctively shrill vocals

has to make you wonder why success has been so elusive for 999.
If 'good time rock 'n' roll'
weren't the trite, oft abused
phrase it's become I'd use it
here as one way to describe
their music. Music soley for
enjoyment's sake, nothing more
nothing less. Live, 999 has
an uncanny ability to convey

999

precisely that to their audience. Rehearsed, but spontaneous in the same instant. It
works. If you're still not
convinced, tilt your ear over
to "Fun Thing". Containing a
ridiculously simple riff and
a pulsating beat it matches
anything they've done--nudging
"Feelin' Alright with the Crew"
from my number one slot. The

999

kind of song that steams up the
loins of the punters in a sea
of suggestive gyrations. So,
while other bands are suffering
from delusions of grandeur(you
know who),999 just tries to
eke out a living with their unpretentious, uncomplicated brand
of fun. Don't let this biggest
prize slip by.--DS

DON'T FORGET TO CATCH 999 ALONG
WITH THE DICKIES AT DOOLEYS ON
APRIL 2nd. BE THERE OR . . .

999 999 999

EARCOM 2 "Contradiction"
Fast Records

Now this is what a compilation
set should sound like. None
of that sorry "No Wave" or
"Saturday Night Pogo" shit here.
Only one band, Joy Division,
has any recorded work outside
of this twelve inch single.
Featuring two cuts from each
group, it gives us a sample of
some music we might not get to
hear otherwise.
Side one opens with the familiar
Joy Division, and their two cuts
are as equally moving as their
previous stuff. Minimally thick,
Joy Division's music is dense
without complicating itself
with unneeded instrumentation.
Aggressively lean, this econom-
ical approach is perfectly offset by the penetrating voice
of Ian Curtis, giving their
nightmarishly simple sound credibility. Making the unreal seem
real.

Thursdays follows with the one
dud on this record, a swaying
rendition of "Sittin' on the
Dock of the Bay". Performed
almost straight, it sounds
starkly out of place amongst
the other tracks. Another original might have been a wiser
choice. Their other cut, "Perfection" is just fine in all
its grating dissonanee. Thought
the singer was a girl until I
checked the sleeve. A melodi-
cally dischordant approach
without leaving the listener
all tense and nervous.

The record closes with my favorite of the three: Basczax. On
"Celluloid Love" it sounds like
the keyboard player's only got
one good hand(finger is more like
it--ED), but that's all right
for what they're doing. It's
abrupt and to the point. The
band doesn't mince words(sounds)
on this one. They also skill-
fully employ the saxophone for
just the right punctuation. However, "Karleearn Photography"
is the gem of the entire record.
The chorus alone is worth the
price of admission. It's so
ingenuously simple, but that's
where the secret lies. Every
instrument is used as sparingly
as possible, and the combination
of all of them makes for a uniquely
textured little number that demands
to be heard.
A great little package of which
there should be more. For once
a record aimed at our ears and
not our wallets.--DS

THE REVILLOS-"MOTOR BIKE BEAT"
DINDISC RECORDS

Fay and Eugene's incestuous warblings have always been undeniably captivating and this new platter is no exception. They again prove to be the prolific remains of The Rezillos(the other 3 cut an EP as SHAKE, then dropped out of sight.)The dynamic duo; Ms. Fife and Meester Reynolds are seen taking a cycledelic trek on a relic Matchless, and the smiling faces on the bag will mirror yours the second this dindisc hits the rubber. Tin-treble-tantrum like this is what makes life palatable. Watch for an LP this month. You know this neb will be!!

ENGLISH SUBTITLES-"Time Tunnel"/"Sweat"/"Reconstruction" Small Wonder

Rather depressing actually but sometimes dreariness is a good propellent innit? Basso profundo and spindly axe break in the bleak Time Tunnel in a muddy but calculated manner.Side 2 alternates between more bass plod and a unison chorus.Pacification for the masses. Good .

TV

RUR EP-Nebula

RURs' live show is pounding, and relentless-non-stop-stud-punk.It's the stuff that makes one involuntarily dive into the throng of knuckleheads and go like crazy.It's too bad this is totally unrepresentative and over produced.I have long maintained that a simplified approach is all certain area outfits need to make that really gonad-crushing record I know these burgs are capable of.I thought for sure RURs' debut would be the single most important release since the Coldcock single. I could'nt have been more wrong.

TV

GENESIS P-ORRIDGE

PETER CHRISTOPHERSON

BOSS TUNES

"Dance Damage" ALGEBRA MOTHERS (live)

"White Mice" MO-DETTES

"The Lady in the Car with the Glasses and the Gun" THE CRAMPS (live)

"Motor Bike Beat" REVILLOS

"Karleearn Photography" BASCZAX

NEGATIVE TREND EP

"To See You" THE EXPELAIRES

"Now Your Dead" FEAR

"Fun Thing" 999

"Darling, Let's Have Another Baby" JOHNNY MOPED

"Night of the Living Dead" THE MISFITS

"Spiteful Sue" THE OUTCASTS

"Dance Stance" DEXY's MIDNIGHT RUNNERS

"Abatross" PiL

"Fiery Jack" THE FALL

"Boys Cry" ORIGINAL MIRRORS

"The Pictures on My Wall" ECHO and THE BUNNYMEN

"You're a Mess" COLDCOCK

"Killer Queers" THE CONTROLLERS

"Downtown" THE CUBAN HEELS

PLATTERS

THE OUTCASTS LP

SUICIDE LP

"Metal Box" PUBLIC IMAGE LTD.

"Dragnet" THE FALL

"Tooth and Nail" Upsetter Compilation

"Metamatic" JOHN FOXX

"Y" THE POP GROUP

"The Biggest Prize in Sport" 999

"Bells" ALBERT AYLER

"Days In Europa" SKIDS

"Unkown Pleasures" JOY DIVISION

"Stations of the Crass" THE CRASS

Martin Rev LP

YOUTH DE SADE LP

"Tear It Up" JOHNNY BURNETTE/THE ROCK 'N' ROLL TRIO

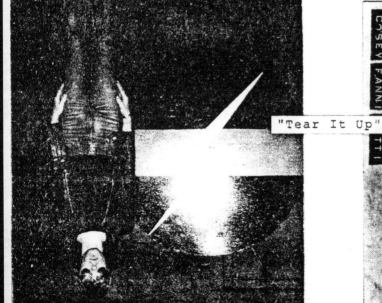

CHRIS CARTER

COSEY FANNI TUTTI

YES ◄

NO ►

FLIP-SIDE
MO-DETTES
Johnny Moped
SEARCH & DESTROY
(the magazine)

RUBBER PARTIES
(R.I.P. Rubber Bob)
Pink Military
PEPERMINT ENEMAS
TOYAH
FABIAN
ORIGINAL MIRRORS
JOY JELLY
POPPING A BONER
BLACK FLAG
Tapper Zukie
ROLLERBALL
THE DURUTTI COLUMN
KRIS NEEDS
YOUTH DE SADE
THE DRONES R.I.P.
TEDS
JADE PRODUCTIONS
SWEET SOUL MUSIC
KIETH FLAG
JOHN CALE
GERMS
FLESHEATERS
BUNNSING
GLOBAL DESTRUCTION
PRETTY GIRLS
PRETTY BOYS
eatin' it
DILUNGER
The Misfits
THELIPSAREBACK
PSYCHEDELIC FURS
THE MO-DETTES

Bo "thumb nipples" Derrick
PARIS
CREEM
PLASTIC SKA-TALITES
THE HEADBOYS
MUSTARD GAS
JAMES CHANCE
QUEEN
PACKIN' BROWN
DEPTFORD FUN CITY
sexism
WRETCHED RECORDS
Geddy Lee's proboscis
The CLASH
THE ROMANTICS
NICK LOWE
XTC
ATHLETES
Law Enforcement Officials
Texas
MUTANT JOHN ANCORE
50¢ smut shop covers
WHITE NOISE MAGAZINE
Elvis Costello
tusk
smelly buttones
TOM VERLAINE
MEGA-ROCK
STEPPING ON DOG TURDS
MOVIES
GENTLEMEN
27
old people in big cars
LENNY KAYE & PATTI SMITH
M-50
Country, Blue Grass,
cranbey

6

How lucky for a band from Japan called Friction that they sent us some vinyl and we dug it—we probably gave those cats more press stateside than anyone. Looking back, it was cool but not that cool: grating guitars and two cats tied off at the tails and flung over a clothesline vocals (try this sometime—those felines will fight each other to the death). We started writing about other zines, most notably <u>Slash</u>, our heroes, and everyone else swimming in their wake. DS's "LA or Bust" is one of my favorite pieces from any issue. Looking back on the 10 records he just called "The Good," well, he flat-out fuckin' nailed it. We examined the hard-or-soft option with pieces on the Cramps and the Feelies. And speaking of soft boys, we even picked up our first paid ad on the back cover for Levi & the Rockats: Those guys were just dreamy—even if you weren't a trouser pilot, you wanted to do the poopy dance at their rockabilly jamboree... Word.

TOUCH and GO

number six

seventy-five cents

Manipulatory Activities

TOUCH and GO
BOX 26203   LANSING, MI 48909

DATLINE MID-MICHIGAN:MUCUS AND MEANDERINGS
....could it be that we spotted Moe Briar
at a Stevie Nerd-ella gig....it looked like
him but those shades and that raincoat were a
good disguise.....speaking of said shitty gig
some dumb girl and her even more dumb boyfriend
thought I was in the band and I was oh so glad to
autograph their LP for them..yuk..yuk...Twas a shame
Rene of Pyramid fame had to be out of town after
she'd worked so hard to bring Dickiemania to our
little town...she was with us in spirit...it has
been verified Lord TJ-local record recluse found
that elusive SKREWDRIVER LP at Dearborn Music for
5.98.If they only knew...the Lord was last seen
trimming his patented "slick do" into something
resembling a large peach...our hired thugs have as yet
been unable to locate the residence of one Shaun
Hendricks(sp?) but until funding runs out they will
relentlessly continue their search...Gary Numan's
recent Royal Oak gig proved to all aboard he is a
modern twit...ther are rumours that he lost his
manhood in a freak synthesizer accident.....Necros
singer Barry was seen lurking about on a recent T&G
A town jag...on top of putting KICK ME signs on
various local longhairs,and labelling everyone in
said town "a fuckin' jazz snob",he was also responsible
for the purchasing of yet another"STATIONS OF THE CRASS"
which he promptly ate for lunch...and you thought The
Pagans were hard core....speaking of Pagans someone
told me that their singer is pulling a Brian Wilson
and has spent the last 2 months in bed...cosmic...
if you happen to be in that town I was talking about
before ,go into Schoolkids Records cuz there's this girl
that works there that is real great looking and she's
actually friendly to boot...will wonders never cease...
Michaels hair is causing quite a ruck in this progressively
backward wasteland...let's hope he's starting a trend...
rumour has him in line for a spot on Agree shampoo ads to
be filmed at local record emporium currently moving to
a bigger spot.....who you calling a size queen?.... Pam
was the runner up in the "Win a date with Bob Marley"
contest put on by RAR in conjunction with WITL....her
consolation was a dread-lock wig and lunch with Dillinger...
oh ya and lets not forget Bill who holds the worlds record
for honoring 1000 requests to hear the new Funkadelic LP...
...speaking of records THE BEAR of Lansing,Mich. holds it
for continous ENO listening for 86½ hours of continous ambience....
he reportadely needed shock therapy to come back to a
semblence of what he had previously called reality...too
bad 8 for the 80's doesn't have shit for acts...I have my
own if you please...The Lips Are Back,FEAR,Algebra Mothers,
Black Flag,The Misfits,Middle Class,Coldcock,GERMS-you don't
go all the way to australia for bands when the talents in your
back yard buttwipes.....did everyone hear about the guy that
passed out at the bustop and when they took of his pants at
the hospital he had a sausage taped to his leg?
Must be a fragrant handjob for some unlucky date....
probably some pindick arab....don't those stenchpits
know that red meat is bad for you... until next time ..
                              TESCO

TOUCH AN GO IS PUBLISHED MONTHLY
BY EDITORS TESCO VEE(the handsome
one)DS(the serious one).EXECUTIVE
VICE PRESIDENTS -LORD TJ & S.WILLIAMS.
SUBSCRIPTIONS ARE AVAILABLE BY SENDING
3.00 FOR 3 ISSUES P.P. YEARLY RATES
10.00(yes we will be here in a year)
WRITE US A LETTER IF YOU ARE A BAND
NEEDING EXPOSURE OR SIMPLY A REGULAR
PERSON WHO LIKE OR HATE SOMETHING
CONTAINED IN OUR MAGAZINE.ADVERTISING
RATES AVAILABLE UPON REQUEST.FOR THE
DJ IN DETROIT WHO GAVE US THE PLUG THANX.
THANX TO TO SUE BARU FOR HER HELP IN
THIS-A DIFFICULT TIME FOR YOU-WE APP-
RECIATE IT!

BRASS LIP-
These folks have good intentions,
a feminist fanzine.It's really too
bad this is so dull because something
like this could have been a refreshing
alternative to the tired posturing of
arrogant male journalists (yes just like
me.,ED.)who love to spout off about who
their "favorite bands" are(spoken in a
nasal tone) Brass Lip features interviews,
way too many interviews with such noteworthy
performers as the Raincoats,AU Pairs,(coed),
Kleenex,VisQuad,Liggers,and The Mekons.
There is also a piece in which they speak
of JJ Burnell(who they refer to as a revolting
pig),Rock Against Sexism gigs,and sickening
macho cock rockers etc.Like I said it's all
too bad this passes by with a splash of
superflous verbosity-oh well they are barking
up the right tree.   NO ADDRESS LISTED

ZIG-ZAG
No accusations please for
I believe in me for openers,
and the opinion-well ok we
can accept that one too-what
is this a magazine dedicated
to rolling papers-of course
not you literary twit she said
but of course if you wear that
logo on your bosom you'll get
labelled,I mean consider the
ramifications of it all-10
fuckin years and KRISSY boy
and CO. are still at it,and let
me tell ya folks this John is
a saint cuz he's got the proverbial balls to stand up for
those martyrs of R&R like
DESTROY ALL MONSTERS(virtually
from our beloved back yard
suckers) and the "Die for what
is right if you believe in it
or not" band Doll by Doll and
I dont care what anyone says,
or if Clash overkill occurs
every time Master Needs is
God,and you owe him one.On
into #100-who else can fuckin'
say that? $2.00 from 118 TALBOT
ROAD,LONDON ENGLAND W11

KILL YOUR PET PUPPY-
From what I gather Tony D.
was Ripped & Torn's main man for
issues #1-17 and judging the looks
of#18 I'd say he brought the good
to this one.KILL YOUR PET PUPPY.....
rather a severe choice of handle
but issue#1 before me isn't all
that threatening but good,very
judgemental readings from Adam &
The Ants to lots of CRASS.My friends
will tell you of my infatuation with
Stevie Ignorant & Co.so yes I'll
have to say yes on that one too Bill.
The verbiage is uncomplicated and
to a not always evident point,so you
dumb people out there should really go
for this one.The article written by
CRASS makes this one worth the 25p
cover price-that is if you're interested
in why there is so much violence at
certain gigs.The article on Tuinal
use among """"PUNKS""""?*&¢%%¢? is
a real throwaway...however..what's
that?OK I'll shut the trap.Buy it
if that 4 bits burns it's way through
those tartans.KILL YOUR PET PUPPY-
c/o ROUGH TRADE 202 KENSINGTON PARK
ROAD, LONDON ENGLAND W11

COOL-
Quite a range it is -from real
inane to real informative.If your'e
interested in learning how to saw
an egg in two then COOL 2 is for you.
Mostly Throbbing Gristle,The Fall,
and Mark Perry(god help me I'm going
to be sick).Its alright.
COOL c/o Alan,79 WESTFIELD GDNS.
KEATON,MIDDLESEX ENGLAND

SAFE AS MILK-
This is the best England has to offer.
(Tesco is so tall he can go out on a
limb and keep his feet on the ground,DS)
Great shot of those fabulous ones The
REVILLOS,on the cover and that's really
why I bought this one as you see I have
this great fantasy about Fay at a kissing
booth at the county fair.Safe As Milk is really
loaded with interesting reading featuring bands
from The Cure to Scissor Fits (who sound like
their live show is better than that cruddy
single).The single reviews vary greatly and
for the most part seem ok.This one looks like
it costs alot to put out but the cover price
is down in that price range of the rest of em'
I strongly urge you to send away for this one
if you do nothing else the rest of the week.

SAFE AS MILK-45 GREENVALE ROAD, LONDON,ENGLAND S.E.9

TALES OF DAYGLOW.Good DAMNED
DAMNED on not much else.NEASDEN, LONDON
interview,92 KENWYN DRIVE,
STEVE,27 NU
N.W.

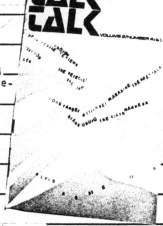

TALK TALK-
Very professional. Good layout
and the last issue had a 2 color
cover?$! Good informative articles
on mostly front liners as far
as gig and album reviews-they
do delve a bit in regard to singles
coverage with new bands like THE TEA
SET. These guys also feature a comprehensive reggae section I think,but
you'll have to double check cuz I
never touch the stuff. Basically a
boss little publication-it's handy
pocket size is grand for long ferry
rides and picnics in the park.Could
become quite successful due to it's
clean,clinical approach.$1.00 from
TALK TALK PUBLICATIONS POST OFFICE
BOX 36,LAWRENCE KANSAS

SMEGMA JOURNAL-
From the homestate of The Dead
Boys,and Pagans comes Smegma Journal.
The latest one features a review of the
Black Flag EP-for Tv that makes it a
king zine' on that criterion alone.Groovy
live reviews of Nikki,The Lips,and Cult Heroes.
You are forewarned on page uno of issue #4
that "If you steal anything from this mag
we will slam a cardoor onto your genitalia.
(is that the opposite of jewish?)These blokes
are young,serious and probably violent under
the right circumstances,and they make a
helluva good magazine. Keep it up Barry.
SMEGMA JOURNAL P.O. BOX 421,MAUMEE OHIO,43537

SLASH-
This is the hardest one of all
to write about because if I act
like I'm oh so knowledgable about
Ca. tuneage & it's devotees then our
west coast will say I'm a hick from
the northern woods of Michigan(no
shit my sister lives in San Diego
and someone called her that) so I'm
going to let the following little
drool of info bite the proverbial
boner of humility. No my car doesn't
have blue smoke coming out of it...
and I realize the Banshees latest
was a sawbuck cuz of plain ol'
fashioned greed.But certain perplex-
ations(take thatDS that's even better
than profanation) still cloud my
oh so advanced but quickly deteriorating
cerebral structure.1) Why wont my prostate
infection go away jeez I drink 4 gallons
of cranberry juice every morning and
I take those little black pills religiously
(or was it those little yellow ones) ....
2)Why am I in love with that girl on
        channel 10 Action News?

3)Why do I think Slash is so great?
It surely is'nt their emphasis on
reggae for I'm sure you've all sussed
out my feelings in regard to that.Could it
perhaps be the live reviews that keep
me abreast of all the shows I'm missing.
Nawwww...Is it those neato spreads on bands
that I hold most dear like The Misfits,Joy
Division,and Germs? H-m-m-m...Could I really
bo so biased to say it was the writing of
that "King of the bop,bop,bop,bop,bop Disintegrat-
ion Nation" -FLESHEATER Chris D. because they
were my favorite group when I was growing up.
And let's not rule out the possibility that
it just could be those all-encompassing gems
of cultural   confection,from the pen of the
master of CATHOLIC DISCIPLINE-Kickboy Face....
Who knows and right who cares-face it Slash
is the best one going.SLASH subs.$10.00 for
12 here,25.00 Airmail there-P.O. BOX 48888,Los
Angeles,california 90048

ON-
One guy does this and it's
36 pages long!ON does a real
good job in the area of exposure
for new acts.PASSAGE is real high
on my personal want list after the great
writeup herein.Ditto The Daleks,Methods
OF Execution,and a rather intriguing
sounding outfit that gets introduced as
"Robin Hood;a small bag of smelly excret-
ment and a chewed off hairy bats head.
Ladies and Gentlemen:PEER GYNT! Add a
really well pulled off Public Image
interview and ON is right on(spare us,ED.)
Also included is a photo of my favorite
short person Toyah Wilcox.Fascinating reading
for those who want to read about obscurities,
before they become non-entities, or mega-stars.
Write-ON-47 OAK AVENUE,SHIRLEY,CROYDON,ENGLAND 8ep

WHITE NOISE-
Comes out about every time my girlfriend claims she's pregnant and we have to get married which is anywhere from every 2 to 6 months.Boreing articles and interviews with xerox Detroit punk rock bands who cant even play as well as the 12 and 15 year olds in L.A.'s RED CROSS. I did'nt see anything in the last one about the good stuff like Vince's band or the A-MOMS. A real self indulgent,frothing appraisal of nothing.Shut up.

SH BOOM-
I have their 1st issue before me and it's one great start.Great 4 page feature on those infantile Scottish loonies-SHAKE.Simple and to the point reviews concerning some of the more obscure acts(to us yanks anyway)plus a pleasant dose of the surface material ala John Foxx,Magazine,and Mo-Dettes (sigh) oh no that's right it's; M-M-M-M Mo-Dettes!!! Oh ya back to the business at hand-add a splashing of live gig coverage in this case O.M.I.T.D.,Dolly Mixture(double sigh) and The Cure and sonny boy you've got your mits on a good one.There's real meat here;everything is real reduced and packed together it makes me feel guilty for using the jumbo-block print on me own stuff. Hope this is'nt a one off because I'm already excited about the next one. 35pence?(75¢ maybe?) write SH BOOM THE OAKS,KINGSEAT PLACE, FALKIRK,ROOM 8,73,EAST CLAREMONT ST. EDINBURGH SCOTLAND

NEW MUSICAL EXPRESS-
Ever met a family where all the members seem to have a bug up their asses for a variety of different reasons?Meet the staff of NME- young,opinionated snobs pointing out all that is so horrible and derivitavely pointless,lest we waste a pound of our hard earned wage on these oh so horrendous groups coming out,but ironically without whom the rag would not exist.A positive review?This week? Why have The Jam gawt uh niewone? Foin but don't fawget that anti-swastika awticle and send some flowers to Mr. Baker faw me willya? NME 3rd FLOOR,5-7 CARNABY STREET, LONDON ENGLAND W1V 1PG -ONLY 58.00 a year(no shit!)

AL EGG sez...

The following aren't worth a load of gob so the boys didn't review 'em!

Blitz
Sounds
NY Rocker
Cream
Punk

FLIPSIDE-
My only beef with this one is it doesn't come out often enough and the anticipation builds for 59 days because yes this may be #2 in CA. but Big Al and Co. do try harder.The picture here is #17 but #15 is the only one I could find in the piles of shit in my apt.Flipside features lots of good interviews,live reviews,and west coast gossip-who's bunnsing who etc.This ones got a great Germs psychos talk-talk and even a letter from that alternative easy listening act CRASS.The English coverage is a little spotty but a very worthwhile investment.FLIPSIDE SUBS.3.50 POST OFFICE BOX 363, WHITTIER,CALIF. 90608 (checks payable to Al Kowalewski)

T&G WANTS--

Both CRIME singles

CONTROLLERS'
    "Suburban Suicide"

WEIRDOS' "Neutron Bomb"
                on Radar

SHAM's "Sons of the Street"

A CERTAIN RATIO
        cassette package

TRASHMEN's "Surfin' Bird"
THE PHANTOM's "Love Me"

Female needs room in Greater Lansing Area, no more than 90 bucks can help with food stamps. Contact Sue c/o TOUCH & GO.

--TV

**Echo & The
     Bunnymen's
album is out
     this month.**

BLACK SHELLAC AND THE REAL GONE CATS-
TOUCH & GO HAS BEEN INFORMED OF THE
PLANNED ONE OFF FEATURING LEGENDARY
KINGS OF "THE BILLY".THE GIG HAS BEEN
TENATIVELY SET FOR MAY17 IN AN OUTDOOR
LOCATION TO BE ANNOUNCED. 3 OF THE MEMBERS
NOW RECORD AS YOUTH DE SADE AND THEIR
MANAGER SPOKE OF SAID EXPERIMENTAL BANDS
SECRET DESIRE TO RETURN TO ROCKABILLY FOR
ONE NIGHT TO PACIFY THEIR MANY FANS WHO
HAVE FOR RECENT YEARS HOUNDED THE MEMBERS
EARNESTLY FOR THE PLANNED REUNION.GUS WILSON
NOW WITH "TEENY PORN" WILL BE SITTING IN ON
DRUMS IN PLACE OF ORIGINAL DRUMMER AL JACOBS
WHO WAS KILLED IN A CAR ACCIDENT IN 1969.
FELIX NESBITT WILL BE HANDLING THE SOUND
FOR THE BAND.ADDRESS INQUIRIES c/o us.

BROKEN ENGLISH(or how I'd like to eat Marianne's pussy)
Me again-the crook-the small-time hood who's just dying to
slip the hood off Miss Faithful's clitoris.Yes folks,that's
right-I'm in love. As might have been apparent in my previous
columns I like intense music-it doesn't have to be "punk"-but
it has to be intense to be in my top category.Now I've always
liked Marianne although I never heard much of her 60's stuff-
that was before my time but when I saw her on the 1980 Floor
Show of Bowie's she was my favorite segment of the show.She ;¹₁₁
seems very Nico-ey but a little more wholesome,like maybe she
just smokes opiated hash instead of shooting smack-who knows...
I do know her album "BROKEN ENGLISH" is one of my all time
favorites by a female vocalist. I hate to make comparisons but
I'd have to do without Lene's and Siouxie's if I were allowed
one female LP this year.Every cut is great.It starts off with
the title cut that some have called the first anti-war song
of the 80's(and hopefully the last,ED.)Well though the references
to past follies are there the meaning seems even further reaching
than any skirmishes we've yet to get involved in-perhaps it's
the intensity of her voice which leads right into what might be
my favorite cut"The Witches Song" which features a superb melody
exquisitely suited for Marianne's voice. The next two "Brain
Drain" and "Guilt" are indictments of some of the men in her past
and it's these two along with the last cut "Why Dja Do It" that
makes me want to eat her out endlessly,show her how tender and
giving a males treatment of her could be.I hope her marriage(of
last year to some pub-rocker,Iforget who) is a happy one. The
cuts on side 2 are seemingly indictments of the working class.
Two cover versions are included "The Battle Of Lucy Jordan" and
the Lennon tune is performed masterfully. The aforementioned
last cut gets down in the total sense of that term.When she sings
"did you spit on my snatch? are we out of love now?is it just a bad
patch?sez it all dont it?I of course would never give her any reason
to be jealous of me Shane Shaman,that is unless you-that's right
YOU little girl-writes in and throws herself at me. I might jump
on it you never know.
                    *The Rock+
                    Roll Bankrobber*

BUST
or
L.A

It's been a couple of years now since the exquisitely sloppy riff from "Life of Crime" first raked its way across those virgin ears of mine to leave an indelible impression on that pulpy mush I call my brain. That, folks, was my first encounter with the 'cool' West Coast sound and so deep was that gouge, that to this day I am still an ardent supporter of the music that comes out of Los Angeles and San Francisco(the former in particular). So, in this space that has been so conveniently provided, I'm going to impose my rabid enthusiasm for these bands on you readers of T&G and list some of those recordings that deserve special attention(some old and some even older). Now I don't claim to be an expert on this stuff, far from it; I'm simply a fan like any-body else who's collected a lot of singles over the past two and a half years. More-over, what little I've learned about the scene out there has come from reading SLASH, FLIPSIDE, and at one time SEARCH & DESTROY--and rather religiously I might add. Now before I get started on this thing, there's one issue I have to tackle first. You see, I have this bone to pick, an axe to grind with the British press and their scur-rilous reporting of the LA music scene. NME in particular, for they see LA as a movement caught in a 1977 rut. Having self-appointed themselves as the final pur-veyor of new music, the British are quick to chastise the LA bands for simply being carbon copies of 'their' originals. Claiming that LA has never recovered from The Damned's first tour, they are constantly making inane accustations like their illwitted stab at Exene of X, saying she was merely a Siouxsie ripoff. What a load of crap. Their coverage of West Coast bands and their music is done so with a vindictive flair that lacks qualified substantiation and that I find irresponsible. You guys should direct those barbed pens at some of your own xerox bands; you got a hell of lot more than we do. End of tirade. On to more important things.
Below are ten discs from sunny California which I will only refer to as 'The Good'.

1) "Class War" THE DILS--LA politicos, took a hard line in their ideology and an even harder one in terms of their music. Totally uncompromising, "Class War" is furiously short and contains one of the finest little guitar solos you'll ever hear.

2) "A,B,C,D" THE RANDOMS--An LA supergroup of sorts, they put out this one fine slab of classic rock 'n' roll. Classic in terms that it's almost traditional sounding. 4:05 and it's still over before you want it to. Great.

3) "Nothing Means Nothing Anymore" THE ALLEYCATS--arguably the most original outfit working in LA. How just three people can generate that much energy is truly a remarkable feat. In the words of the infamous TJ "They're hot!"

4) "We Got The Neutron Bomb" THE WEIRDOS--stacks up against anything, anywhere. Even the British have to concede defeat. May very well be the single greatest record to come out of LA(the Germs' album excluded). Perfect. The opening still gives me goosebumps.

5) "Beat Your Heart Out" THE ZEROS--a pop single with that much needed raw edge to it. Wallowing amongst a sea of sugary pop crud, The Zeros gave Bomp a brief moment of respectability. Remains one of my most listened to forty-fives.

6) "Lexicon Devil" THE GERMS--this marked the transition for these guys from joke band to front runner. Listen to their What? single and you get the picture. The im-provement in Pat Smear on guitar just boggles the imagination. This is also SLASH's first stab at the lucrative record business.

7) "Negative Trend EP" NEGATIVE TREND--if you've been reading us, you'll notice that this SF band usually figures into our chart somewhere. A hard-to-find four song EP that contains the definitive version of "Meathouse". A must.

8) "Johnny Too Bad" THE OFFS--another SF band with a unique underproduced sound that uses just a touch of reggae to add a little spice. Even though it is a reggae cover that they're doing, the Offs manage to make it their song. Sure to be a big hit with the British snobs.

9) "Out Of Vogue" THE MIDDLE CLASS--nothing by anyone is as intensely manic. Travelling at the speed of thought, we all wait for the eventual meltdown that never comes. You'd have to go back to "Class War" to find anything that approximates the velocity of "Insurgence". Truly a one of a kind.

10) "Black Flag EP" BLACK FLAG--reviewed in T&G #2, you know where we stand with these guys. Some of the most wildly demented music you will ever hear. And for once I know what I'm talking about.--DS

FRICTION EP-"CRAZY DREAM"/"KAGAYAKI"/
BIG-S" Pass Records

FRICTION blows away any unfounded
skepticism I may have fostered
in regard to the Japanese music
scene.It's time we faced up to the
fact that all the stereotypes we've
been raise on can be chalked up to

FRICTION

photo by T. HIROSE

BASS

our countries growing inability to
compete with this still mysterious
and far-away land.It is inevitable
that in a country containing that
many people,talent exists but I was
completely unprepared for what hit
me when "CRAZY DREAM" burst forth
from my ever weakening tweeters
and laid a wall of oriental modern
noise upon my staggered sense of
reality.For herein will be no
lame comparisons to yankee or yeuro
acts,number one because it would be
a disservice to the band and number
two because there are'nt any that
can be made.FRICTION sounds as though
they were let loose in a metal room,
with a 4-track and a 6-pack,and the
resultant dischordant smash will
most surely send you running for
that empty bottle of valium,but
of course this only delays the
realization that these guys are
devastatingly great.
    It would be a pity if all the
half-assed anglo continued to get
hyped on the Japanese market and
FRICTION were to go unoticed.The
FRICTION album will be released
in Japan in late April.Products
can be obtained from...
    PASS RECORDS
c/o GEORGIA
1-2-3 KICHIJOJI, MINAM-CHO
MUSASHINO-SHI, TOKYO JAPAN

SEVEN INCHES & A HOLE

THE OFFS   "Everyone's A Bigot"/
"O"   415 Records
Well, look what we have here--
someone trying to cash in on
the now defunct Off's popularity. I just hope the band
gets what's coming to them.
Much cleaner sound this time
out; although I kinda liked
the tinny authenticity of
"Johnny Too Bad". "Everyone's
A Bigot" has little if anything in common with that,
their first record. Some
might even see it as The Offs
on a ska jag. Ignore that last
comment, you didn't hear me
say that. Rather, these guys
have a way of grabbing a little
here and a little there to con-
coct an original sound that
leaves reviewers pleasantly
confused in their effort to
pigeonhole this band. Forget
the labels, I like it.--DS

ANGELIC UPSTARTS   "Out of Control"/"Shotgun Solution"
Warner Brothers

With my irritation with the annoying unpredictability of Sham
69 ever on the increase, I've
had to look elsewhere for my
daily dose of headstomping British aggro. And where better to
stop than at the door of Jimmy
Pursey's own prodigal son, Mensi.
Sure they sound like Sham, but
somebody has to carry the torch,
with Sham continuing to stumble
along in a myre of sporadic brilliance and some downright awful
songwriting, the Upstarts display far greater consistency in
their music. Not wanting to
buck tradition they provide us
with their own chorus of chant-
ing unification ala "Ulster"
and "If the Kids are United",
which will undoubtedly prompt
us to reflect on the good old
days. But the past is history,
and fortunately, the Upstarts
are very much a part of the present.--DS

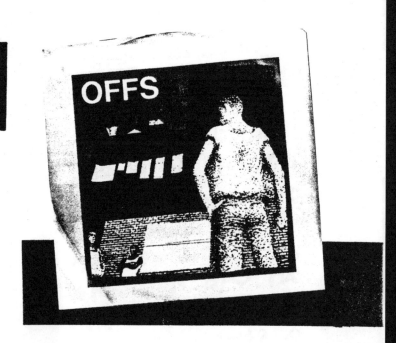

A Certain Ratio-All Night Party

Issued from *the* 1, 1979
Paper and vinyl circumstances in an edition of 5000
Produced by Martin Zero at Cargo Studios, Rochdale

©1979, a Factory Product

THE NOISE "Noise"/"Agony" Broken Records

One of the top singles this month. A very deliberate primitivism jumps out at you. Almost too planned, but I'm not complaining. Singer is simply fantastic--a cross between Ian Curtis and Lux Interior. B-side is the closest thing to the Rotten One and his bunch I've heard yet, OK but I'd rather hear another cut like the A-side. Definitely one of the bright new faces on the scene. If interested, write to: THE NOISE c/o 2495 43rd Avenue, San Francisco, CA 94116.--DS

A CERTAIN RATIO "All Night Party"/ "The Thin Boys" Factory Records

A study in mental instability is what we're witnessing here. Like watching some poor bastard suffer through a psychotic episode, but only the prelude, not the sordid results. Obviously cheated, we wanted to relish in his demise and eventual breakdown, fulfilling our own warped and twisted subconscience. Just use your imagination, I'm sure you can finish the story. And if this doesn't sound like a record review to you, then it's obviously a result of having spun this disc one too many times. Bleak and disturbing. --DS

EXPELAIRES "To See You"/"Frequency" Zoo Records

Another great Zoo product from those thoughtful folks who gave us Echo and The Bunnymen and The Teardrop Explodes. Pop psychedelia for the Eighties. And it ain't no Mod-esque revival shit either. These bands from Liverpool are definitely developing a unique regional sound refreshingly unlike the established noise coming out of London and environs. Grade A all the way around, "To See You" is the best thing to come out of this port city since. . . Dare I say it? No, let's leave the dead dogs where they lie.--DS

david used to love hearing stories and one day when he was out walking in the snow he met an old man who began to tell him a story...

EXPELAIRES
"TO SEE YOU"
"FREQUENCY"

LOWLIFE "Leaders"/"White Light-
nig"/"Thinking Naturally
Airout Records

Boy, where did they find this
singer, He stinks! Makes the
vocalist for Capital Punishment
(fledgling Detroit band that
gave a whole new meaning to
the word 'shitty') sound like
a refreshing change. A shame
too, for they have a great
guitar player in Brad Hrushka.
His raspy, biting lines are
nullified by a guy who's trying too hard to sing when he
should be doing everything but
sing. Scream, shout, squeal--
anything would be better than
the forced delivery we're stuck
with here. Too bad. This could
have been a hell of a single.
I say could.--DS

THE HATES "No Talk in the 80's"
"New Spartans"/"All the Whites
are Going Negro"/"Last Hymn"
Faceless Records

For a place its size, Texas should
have scads of bands playing the
new music. Maybe they do, they
just haven't found their way up
here yet. Fortunately, one single did manage to cross my desk.
An EP from one frenetically energetic trio. Tough moronic
vocals add a crazy charm to all
four cuts. Sounds like he's
just figuring out the English
language despite an acute case
of cerebral damage. Especially
like "All the Whites are Going
Negro". Hope to hear more from
this band.--DS
The record can be had by writing
to The Hates, 5201 W. 34th St.,
Box 316, Houston, TX 77092

ORIGINAL MIRRORS

ORIGINAL MIRRORS-MERCURY RECORDS

I find them quite redundant and distasteful. They are the most contemptuous little phlegm-balls ever to lay pen to paper. I am of course referring to the

industry in it's desperate attempt to allow the sound the retention of it's market-ability.Added are electronics without the ostentatious overkill;subtly applied they create the mood necessary on the opening of "The Boys The Boys."It's the effective creation of a feigned serenity that quickly blows open with pounding skins and violent bass chug.Multi-track vocals create a unified effect on a solid, sometimes minimal,but always effective, instrumentation.

English press whose weekly rele-gation of all that they oh so fashionably term "post-modernism", is as predictable as it is dull and void.Granted JAPAN's "Quiet Life" may be yet another install-ment of ROXY worship but to then heap praise on such noteworthy performers as Fred Frith,Paul

Motion Trio,and Ian McLagan is at best sickening.But this dis-course will not simply be an expostulation of these imbecilic butt tones for an entire magazine could be devoted to such an exer-cize.On to necessary print.
    ORIGINAL MIRRORS...Picking up their single was one of those blind, buck dropping exercises that sometimes pays off(Factory & Neutron Samplers) and sometimes does'nt.It was love at first listen as the strains of "Could This Be Heaven?" filled the cracks in my grotto walls,and my heart with joy.In what is quickly turning out to be an imformative but unsuccinct LP review I will tell you why you must have this.
    No the sound is not the innovation of the year.The band does draw heavily on many influences.Their sound is angular and polished.The rythym and bass lines are seemingly in part drawn from that craze currently being transformed by the

the boys   flying   chains of love

In a rather self indulgent, frothing appraisal such as this you will probably take my words with the proverbial grain and not all rush out to blow a hard earned sawbuck on just my recommendation. This just happens to hit me square.

                                    TV

THE FEELIES

THE FEELIES "Crazy Rhythms"
Stiff Records

The Feelies have the best non-
look look around. Could start
a whole new trend in nurd chic.

New Yorkers will eat that shit
right up. These are the kind
of guys who always looked intellectually out-to-lunch, but
more likely you just ignored
this seemingly out of it dolt.
Putting my Midwestern prejudices
aside, let's concentrate on
the music, which is superb. It's
an intriguing as well as a per-
plexing album. The guitar
strains will remind many of you
of The Cure. Crisp, tinny, restrained lines in a wide assortment of moods, tempos, and tex-
tures gives a light-hearted yet
confident air to the entire picture. There's also this noncha-
lant breeziness about the record
that throws me offguard. Their
music doesn't overpower you,
rather it seduces the listener.
The Fripp influence is also de-
tectable; however they manage
to avoid the somber and burden-
some seriousness of Fripp which
would have certainly killed the
pleasantly airy qualities of
"Crazy Rhythms". It's simple
and for some reason I expect
more than meets the eye. Mean-
while, I might be missing the
point altogether. Take it for
what it is, enjoyable music at
its simplest best.--DS

THE CRAMPS-"SONGS THE LORD TAUGHT US"
Voodoobilly...The music that brings out the savage,evil,and terror-
like states in you-the listener(phrase coined by TV)Very simply
this is gore to kill your pet monkey by.From the opening screams
on side one we are all breathing a big sigh,those beloved,godawful
CRAMPS haven't changed a bit.Alex Chilton's anti-production
laces the sound with even more distorted feedbacking guitars,
and ah-who-ah-a-who-ah vocal reverb than their initial offering
on Vengeance Records.What Chilton does to me is prove that
this band is serious,and they indeed seem hell-bent on world
destruction via this unique sound.The first cut T.V.SET will
straighten you out in that easy chair,as Lux Interior's cold-
blooded shrieks are those of a man lives in his own gothic,
mad hatter persona of what some would label serious mental illness.
He manages to strip down the sound to it's basest,most crudest form
in a stroke of pure genius.This reviewer's opinion is that this is
most evident in"I Was A Teenage Warewolf" and"M ystery Plane";this
back to neanderthal achievment is frosted with the noisy,mud guitar
sound of Ivy and the evil native of the midwest;Brian Gregory.Let's
face it folks the only way this sound could be so beautiful is if
the band lived the sound and I really believe they do.Would you
walk down the street in Midtown USA with a look like his?It takes
a gutsy,and powerful (decadent) persona to play each part of this
cast of characters and this is reflected in the powerful sound.
Yes all the qualities are here that make it great in 57' and 80'.
If the real thing is what you crave in the night(call me the Lord
will provide) this LP is for you.So far it's just an import (tell
me why,I'll kill em) but will soon be released over here.You will
never be sorrier if you let this one slide and besides you have to
let your mom hear the immortal words"I'll cut your head off and put
it in my TV set."Somewhere up there Johnny Burnette must be a proud
ghoul.LORD TJ

The medias' hope for
tomorrow seems to be
the revival.In this
country these moment-
ary rebirths may seem
a small novelty to gig-
gle at when passing the
record shop window.But
the social structure of
the youth specifically
in England lends itself
to these various second
(or third)comings in that
one can adopt any part-
icular persona as a vi-
able identity source.
These priggish cliques
then prowl about assault-
ing each other to various
degrees depending upon the
amount of animousity tis'
popular to attach to that
particular band of punters.
These confrontations were
never more obvious than
the Teds violent reaction
to the 77' crowd of "punk
rockers" who were simply
an addition to the long
line of poseurs who they
had been forced to put up
with for so long. Anyway
enough history.On to what's
happening (or not) as far
as these ever present
revivals.Whether it be rockabilly,mod,ska,psychedelic,
soul,or (god help us) heavy
metal stuff I've been reading
seems to be laden with this
sense of duty or responsibility
to embrace a sound that was
supposedly so undemocratically
ignored during it's initial
heydey.But why is it so necessary to pay gratuitous homage
to these old sounds?Why are
these exercises in resuscitated
un-spontanaety necessary?Are
the "new music" acts to retain
their "experimental" labels
forever while the contrived
historicult mish-mashers
adulate and over-ink these
cyclical trendsetters.
    The current monomania
concerning ska is a case
in point,and we at TOUCH&GO
are by no means non-contri-
butors in regard to said hype.
Yes personally I think it's
great fun.....but the Joy
Division LP has only sold
26,000 copies.An open and
shut case of priority fuckup.

    Rockabilly created a stir
almost as dynamic as it's
quick fade in 58'.It's
flirtatious C&W influences
left the modern man with a
grimace.Ditto late 70's.
    Mod wins the least exciting
revival of the decade award;
boring 60's dance music with
differing but equally uninspiring
sounds permeated with a sappy,
insolent "this is the image"
attitude that is about as anomalous
as a loaf of white bread.
    So what is left to adore
and abhore?Sit back and enjoy
the coming decade.
                TESCO VEE

7 inch-the good

"Earthworm" FLIPPER

"Noise" THE NOISE

"Bela Lugosi's Dead" BAUHAUS

"Crazy Dream" FRICTION

"All Night Party" A CERTAIN RATIO

"Where's There A Will" THE POP GROUP

"Books" THE TEARDROP EXPLODES

NEGATIVE TREND EP

"Dance Damage"&"Doberman" (live) A-MOMS

"Chapel of Love" HOLLY and THE ITALIANS

"Wardance" KILLING JOKE

"Slow Death" THE LEATHER NUN

"Beautiful People" THE STUNT KITES

"Forces of Victory" LINTON KWESI JOHNSON

"A Note From The South" LEVI AND THE ROCKATS

"Black Haired Girl" THE ALLEYCATS

"What Use" TUXEDOMOON

"Making Love With My Wife" HENRY BADOWSKI

"Girl" SUICIDE

12 inch-the good

"Songs The Lord Taught Us" THE CRAMPS

PSYCHEDELIC FURS LP

"Stations of The Crass" THE CRASS

FLYBOYS LP

"20 Jazz Funk Greats" THROBBING GRISTLE

"Crazy Rhythms" THE FEELIES

THE SIREN LP(Red Cross only)

"Pass The Dust, I Think I'm Bowie" BLACK RANDY & THE METRO SQUAD

SUICIDE LP

"The Biggest Prize In Sport" 999

"The Return Of The Durutti Column" DURUTTI COLUMN

"Eliptical Optimism" SPHERICAL OBJECTS

"Days In Europa" SKIDS

"Tooth and Nail" UPSETTER COMP. LP

EARCOM 2

LEVI & THE ROCKATS

(We Gotta Have) "Room to Rock" b/w "All thru the Nite"

OUT NOW

AVAILABLE FROM

PEER COMMUNICATION, INC.
1428 NORTH CRESCENT HEIGHTS BLVD. #6BN
LOS ANGELES, CA 90076

7

I am somewhat—no, make that completely—bereft in the imagination dept for this cover. About as dull as it gets... My Revillos worship saves this one from total yawnsville. Going thru the motions, maybe. There are a few bright spots but overall not our best at bat.

TOUCH & GO

number seven

seventyfive cents

Just Thinking Activities

fuck dance let's art

tHE WAGes AMBivAlEnce OF T And G IS deAth

Hello Hullo! We're back again with big #7 which fuck is so long to do mainly (except city here) analyzing dog turds over at the vet clinic have kept us so busy. But here it is in all its novel turn out the assimilation into your own little counter reality. Downer of the month goes to I know he was livin it but thats hardly an alternative. Schlock of the month continue the promote-payola back scratching with area managers who are content was here also WLS and WVIC continue the promote-payola back scratching with area hyping the shit out of these hiz beens on the radio. The bearded bemens name is Brad dad. Lets have an imagination log jacket in flames. Event of the year is the X album. Scrounge + grovel if you have to but get it!!! So imbibe, fuck, shoot and fuck to your hearts content. Tomorrow well all be dead!

Xmas time is here Grinch - Remember the world might end tomorrow -
Kill RL Contest - first suggestion wins a silk
to give certain DJ's half the gates for
on but I should be fair - Tommy James
Ian Curtis' suicide (Joy Divisions vocalist).
major tilly ready for consump-
we come) cuz our day jobs

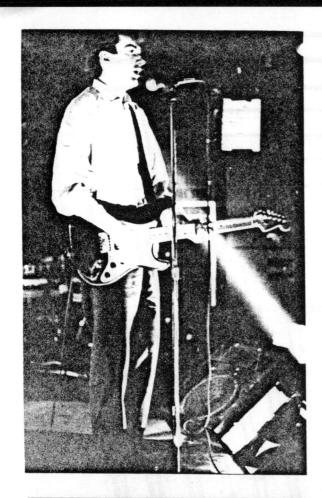

GANG OF FOUR

The Gang of Four

GANG OF FOUR/RETRO at Bookies

The evening was close to perfect
with plenty of beer sloshing
around the car. Never one to
submit to the high cost of the
bar beverage, we procured our
needed lubricants elsewhere.
Once inside, we had to put up
with old fart tunes and a seemingly nebbed out crowd. You
know the kind, bored on a Monday
night and resort to imposing
their ignorance on anyone who
wishes to challenge them. So,
we get the hell out and down a
few more bottles of grog.
Back again and the band is ready
to begin. This gig resulted in
a mild rift between Tesco and myself. You see, Tesco was none
too impressed with Gand Of Four,
while I, on the other hand, have
always been a devotee. Quite
simply, they were modestly great.
I'm trying to show some restraint
here. Very direct, with very
little fanfare, if any. They come
on and start playing. Minimal
dialogue between them and the
audience, a courteous 'thank you'
here and there, and that's it.
Their themes of political injustice are wearing thin, very thin
in fact. Topical kinds of songs
of the political nature have always
given its music a somewhat temporary foothold on the scene as a
whole.
Let me get back to the music and
the gig before this starts sounding
like an obituary. The band opened
with "5-45"(a personal fave) and
made it clear from the very start
that they take their music very
seriously, at least appear to.
Gang Of Four has a rhythmic drive
and intensity that marks everything
they do. Sharp, piercing, synco-
pated chords from Andy Gill puncu-
ate every utterance from the strained

vocals of Dave Allen. And no
matter how stoic(particularly
Gill) they may look, with the
exception of the angular Allen,
they pound out a danceable beat.
There's no denying it. It grip-
ped the throng of nebs at Bookies.
They did most of the stuff off
the album with "Tourist" coming
across best. "Anthrax" on the
other hand, sounded like a homage to Hendrix. Feedback noodling
that may have impressed some, even
to the point of awe, but I could
do without the flash.
This band is one of the pioneers
right now and I should consider
myself lucky that they opted to
play in such a slimepit, musically
retarded town like Detroit(DS out
for the popularity vote--ED).
I liked them, Tesco didn't, but
we both agree on the lameness of
the shit we have to listen to between sets. Old fart tunes at
their rancid worst. Vince, the
scene is moving too fast for you
to become bogged down with relics
like The Yardbirds?! Hit that
sleepwalking crowd of yours with
some current noise and snap 'em
out of that crippling two year
stupor.--DS

There's just no way I'm going to be able to review this in an intelligently unbiased fashion.The reason why stems from the fact that we aren't just dealing with any ol' band pardners this is X.SLASH RECORDS (the folks who brought you the GERMS) have made another stab at the spot market,and the results are but further documentation of LA's domination in regard to the American scene.It's been said that SLASH's coverage of the west-coast scene is simply a self-congratulatory attempt at por- trayal of the whole shazam as a"bigger than it is in real life" type of thing,but recordings do not lie-they are simply all the substantiation the pro-coasters need be armed with.And hell what scene doesnt appear massive in lieu of journalistic enthusiasm and bias(and prejuduce).

X "LOS ANGELES" X

X is simply the most distinctive band to emerge from those aforementioned topicalities.Ever since the purchase of their first single "ADULT BOOKS on the Dangerhouse label(for their efforts the the band reportedely did not recieve fuck-all)John Doe and Exene's combinate, mournful vocals have been nothing short of bone chilling.X at first listen was simply instantly intriguing enough to enter the pantheon of all time urban classics with nary a scuffle.The underwhelming response to the band locally was true to form with what I've come to expect from midwestern mentality.But blatant,and unfounded agnosticism towards anything as powerful as X is likely to rile this pongo more than personal slags on my character ever would.Simply because one does not live in a certain locality-now let's never let jealosy over the fact that it's always warm

and sunny out there and the bands are light years better (well not even me can quite pull that little blurb off-yes there are great ones here too- sorry-big ED.) But maybe that one guy was right I could be simply over- reacting a bit,but all I need to prove that illiterate pederist wrong is one play of the LP which by the way is entitled "LOS ANGELES".Ray Manzarek was as questionable a choice for the production chores as Joan Jett was to me anyway on the GERMS LP.But as was the case with Darby&Co.s' platter, the sound is clean and crisp.Ray even contributes keyboard work on NAUSEA a real effective portrayal of what a few days without our silent white buddy will do to the best of us.The title track re-appears here via the "YES L.A." compilation-the reworking loses a tad of it's original rawness but is neverthless dynamic.I don't feel like dealing with a track by track assessment of this one-you simply must own a copy of thisLP if you don't do shit else the rest of it...............TV

LUDUS

LUDUS-"THE VISIT"-Lullaby Cheat,
Unveil,Sightseeing,I Can't Swim
I Have Nightmares...NEW HORMONES
RECORDS
     You see the state of it all to
some like me is like a carefully
constructed romance of unfaltering
passion.Yes the reprobation of those
unassailable adversaries is taking
the big back seat to the ubiquitous
rebirth of something we can again
term extremely listenable material.
Remember when we were all faced with
the weighty task of having to pick
between one by-product of the structured,vainglorius,record conglomerates
whose mirror image has always habituated
complacent,capitalistic force feeding of
us the buying,but not always discriminating
consumer.
     But something like this LUDUS EP is
cruising the rubber and it's existence
is but another bit of proof that all that
glitters is not platinum.This remarkably
diverse 3 piece has a sound irresistably
perceptive and intriguing.Vocalist Linder
places herself at the helm as she contributes-
then just as quickly takes a back seat as
the remaining two delve into extrordinary
rythmic adventures never before heard on
any label.Melodically compelling one moment-
grating,sinister and unpredictable the next.
LUDUS forages through these 4 tunes with
nary a nod at anyone and thus stand in a
select group among groups.One gets the
feeling a taciturn intellect has suddenly
been awakened here and their sound is appealling
in various moods.
     Who are these people and why do I play
this thing constantly?
                              TV

A SCORCHING INDICTMENT

My God, does this town stink! How's a punk supposed to survive
in a place as backward as Lansing? I want to know, cuz I'm just
about to the point of frustrative violence. Look around you, no
scene, no place to hang out, no nothin'! And worst of all, we're
saddled with the reactionary attitudes of WILS, who, for the most
part, ignore the new music, while at the same time, con their
listeners into believing that there's some kind of significance
in a dinosaur act like REO. Who's kidding who?

Now much of the blame has to fall on you wimps out there for
letting things go on like this. Yep. You're the ones who flocked
to the Bus Stop to see the fossilized Rare Earth ressurected from
the Holiday Inn circuit, and you roared your approval. You read
the self-serving crap by David Winkelstern and nod vacantly in
agreement. Is it because you're just too fucking lazy to challenge this lackey of a scribe, or are you simply so brain damaged
that discrimination and objectivity are a thing of the past?
And let me pour a little salt in the wound by adding that you
disgraced yourself by allowing something as ludicrously inane as
the 'battle of the imaginary bands' even take place. The brain-
child of some jerk who has little respect for music, let alone
people. Gee, can't get any real talent, so let's watch some assholes ape some shitty record.

It appears that you don't care what you do with that feeble little
brain of yours. You submit to the likes of Winkelstern and one
Bradley Curtis(the most nauseating stillborn fuck to soil this
area since the technocolor yawn) and you get nothing in return.
With Curtis he's number one and nobody else matters. He doesn't
give a blue fuck about his listeners, so long as they keep feeding
his insatiable ego, that's what keeps him going. You can bet there
was something in it for him when he flooded the airwaves with his
Rare Earth/imaginary band froth. You have to question his motives.
If he has nothing to gain, he'll just tell you to 'fuck off'. But
flash a little coin and just watch him bend over and let you pop
his butt. Bradley is the lowest form of scum we know and his only
accomplishment has been to set Lansing back to the musical stone-
age. Wake up out there! It's time to listen. Kick that mother-
fucker in the ass, and start using that lump on your shoulders.
I'm crazy and I'm hurt, watch out!--DS

45s by TV

100% Satisfaction (TV) GUARANTEED*

**HATES-"DO THE CARYL CHESSMAN", "SOLDIER"
"BORED WITH THE BOYS", "CITY ON ICE"
FACELESS RECORDS-**

You see folks either you've got
it or you don't and you also see
this new HATES platter before you,
and I agree with you 100% this is
furious instrumental blight frosted
with obstreperous vocals that leave
us all groaning for more.I was getting
frantic trying to find this months dose
of panic-stricken amphetiblast cum
unpretentious destructo-crush tuneage.
Alas here it lays-fast,violent and to
the point.Garrulous vocalists Christian
Arnheiter and Robert Kainer belch forth
as the surrounding environs resound with
the crash-cymbal-chaos of Master Glenn
Sorvisto.I'm going to twist this phrase
a bit...Let's dig HATES..before we die...

**SHOX-"NO TURNING BACK"/"LYING HERE"
Axis records**

I like synthesizers.SHOX are two guys
and one gurl who have made a record
that uses lots of synthesizers.They
are very handsome. She is pretty.
The picture sleeve is horrible.The
record is good.Buy it.

**THE FAMILY FODDER-"PLAYING GOLF
(With My Flesh Crawling)"/"MY
BABY TAKES VALIUM"-Parole records**

Side 1 features what sounds like the
march of the angry munchkins and
a few idiosyncratic changes later
it gets rolling.The camped out
fantasyland military stuff continues
throughout this side,and the singers voice displays a nerve racking
garble effect that does nothing but
make you look at your mates and laugh.
"My Baby Takes Valium" is a relief-
more like Jean Ives Labat's novelty
nonsense,with various keyboards buried
under mounds of cooing & croaking.
What The Family Fodder mean is open
for   debate that will rarely take place.

**ANGELIC UPSTARTS-"WE GOTTA GET OUTA
THIS PLACE" Warner
COCKNEY REJECTS-"BAD MAN" EMI**

Oh my god pinch my ass,wake me
up,I've gotta whiz and I'll wet
the bed.Ya you're right just like
my dead uncle I've gotta face it-
could these blockheads really think
this belongs anywhere but in an Eric
Burdon anthology?The Upstarts are next
in line for snobdom-if you keep beatin'
it hard enough success will come right?
It's real predictable-Pursey's an
illiterate opportunist,stupidhead
Charlie Harper is an old harp-tootin'
fart,and now Mensi;oh Thomas though
your'e head be carved of thy master's
granite why must our prodigal son
turn in thy lamest piece of pressed
buffalo chip and fling it so hastily
into the faces of we,the masses,thy
brethren .The insidious London scene
has turned another east-end messiah
into an industry devoted pacivist.
The Cockney Rejects have got it
in all categories."Bad Man" is a graphic
example of Stinky and Co.s all-encompassing
superiority over all the aggro-drub outfits.

But let's dwell on the negative for a moment shall we?
When you play these two singles back to back it's depress-
ingly obvious someones hurtin'
an it aint the Rejects.It's
really sad to see em drop by
the wayside.

STINKY TURNER

L.A.SLEAZE

CUBES

SIOUXSIE AND THE BANSHEES

Happy House

SIOUXIE AND THE BANSHEES-"HAPPY HOUSE"/DROP DEAD/CELEBRATION" Polydor

---

Jeez honey have a heart,just because your guitarist and drummer up and quit just before you embarked on a tour in which you'd invested all the moneys won from your first single and LP;is this really cause for such anger.I love it. My dream date strikes back with her strongest little piece yet. Temporary skin man Budgie keeps a nice beat that leads the vocals on into the whispering girl who very subtly lays it on McKay and Morris,"I hate you....I hate you", right we know.The A side "HAPPY HOUSE" is climbing the charts as I write.Putting it simply this girl has come a long way since she hung herself out for the 100 Club crowds way back when.

JAMES VANE-"JUDYS GONE DOWN"/ "JUNG LOVERS" Island

Nice lookin' boy huh?Certain people I know real well have real fascinations with these glam casualty types who change the old hair color weekly but on to the record.The A side is pleasant enough sounding-rath- er up-tempo pop-this Jim has a nice voice(isn't the review just gonna go down in history?) and I suppose I could sit here and figure out who he sounds like but I don't got the energy or the eardrums left.Ho Hum on te side dos which to put it mildly blows side uno right off the edge.As distinctive as side 1 is ordinary.James will never set the world on fire but if you see it for a buck like I did buy the single.It's not nearly as boring as this review.

I'm tellin' you guys that's how it happens,dad just sticks his:..........

rare photo of SPARKS' Ron Mael working days at a bycicle repair shop............

130

SINGLES

THE FLYBOYS
"Picture Perfect"/"Dear John"
"So Juvenile"/"I Couldn't Tell"
"Butch"/"Different Kind of Guy"
"Theme Song" Frontier Records

One of the promising new faces
from LA with a good chance of
making it(bucks-wise, that is).
However, just when I'm getting
my hopes up, I run across a
blurb in FLIPSIDE saying that
the Flyboys are no more, broken
up. Talk about getting nipped
in the bud. Nonetheless, they
still put out a great mini-LP.
Pop/punk amalgam somewhere in-
between LA's hardcore and the
simpering noodlings of the
Paul Collins school. I guess
I'd compare them to the Zeros
back in the Bomp days, but then
again, I hear traces of the Undertones and the Outcasts as well.
No need to single out any one
cut of the seven, they all have
that danceable beat and frenzied
velocity that keeps it from becoming just another moldy addition to my collection. It far
excedes the Weirdos effort for
consistency and sheer enjoyment.
It's just too bad they decided
to split up, but that's how the
old ball bounces, or any other
trite little witty remark you
can think of in this moment of
sadness.--DS

PRAIRIE FIRE
"Turn Up The Heat"/"No Mercy"

I don't give a fuck about their
socio-political bent. Prairie
Fire harangue us with a seudo-
Boshevik doctrine amidst the
most regressive sound I've been
subjected to in a long time.
This is the kind of crap our
big brothers were listening to,
if you can remember back that
far. A hard slap in the face.
Hardly. Hippie shit at its
deceptive worst. Protest music has its place, but not
when it's served up like some
archeological find. If you
want revolt, I'll give you
something to rebel against,
shit like this, that's what.
--DS

THE MISFITS
"Night of the Living Dead"/
Where Eagles Dare"/"Rat Fink"
Plan 9 Records

I don't care if the production
does sound like shit. This
mangy East Coast bunch pin our
ears back and slap us around.
Cruder, more primitive than
anything they've done, "Night
of the Living Dead" proves
there's still a place for a
wildly simplistic, fever-pitched
recording like this. A study
in wreckless abandon. No stopping the Misfits. A blazing
masterpiece.--DS

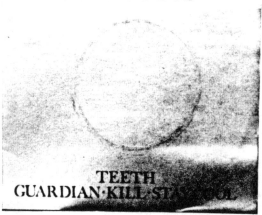

The MEKONS

TEETH
GUARDIAN·KILL·STAY COOL

THE MEKONS
"Teeth"/"Guardian"/"Kill"/"Stay
Cool" Virgin Records

Well, so much for the Gang Of
Four impersonation. They have
shucked the idea with their
album for all I know, I just
never got around to hearing
it. Anyway, the difference
between this and "Work All
Week" is like night and day.
They're doing some new things,
some works. . . some doesn't.
"Kill" and "Guardian" appear
to be wasted exercises in experimentation. Undernourished
ideas that could use a tad
more development. Like fragments rather than wholes, they
don't go anywhere. Now "Teeth"
and "Stay Cool" stand on their
own. Particularly "Stay Cool".
This is one of the freshest
new sounds to come my way in
a long time. An ominous drone
underlies everything which
gives it a menacing, doomsday
shroud. A worthwhile purchase
despite the excess bagage.--DS

MnMs
"I'm Tired"/"Knock,Knock,Knock"

Now where did I put my Leslie
Gore records? This one takes
me back a ways. Past the shit
of the 60's and 70's, right to
the heart of the powderpuff
fluff of every girl group you
ever heard. Marcy Marcs has
the squeakiest little voice
this side of 1964. Just the
right mixture of pop innocence
and contemporary wit.--DS

THE ZEROS
"They Say That(everything's
alright)"/"Getting Nowhere
Fast" Test Tube Records

This is a surprise. I thought
these guys were dead and buried.
Not as clean nor as immediate
as "Beat Your Heart Out", but
it still manages to pack a
solid one-two pop/punk punch.
The vocals remind me of some
of The Who's first efforts,
but the music is much coarser.
This is a rather inconspicuous
remergence by these one time
front runners. Let's hope
they can find that lofty
height once more.--DS

GANG OF FOUR
"Outside The Trains Don't Run
On Time"/"He'd Send In The
Army" EMI Records

Full of the mechanical rhythms
these guys are known for, but
it fails to grab me. I find
myself ignoring their dilemmical
ramblings and concentrating
solely on the music which does
not hold up as well as either
of the first two singles or
the album for that matter.
Live they manage to transend
the one-dimensional aspects of
their music, but on vinyl it
comes across merely flat.--DS

Town Hall, Leeds

JOY DIVISION
"Atmosphere"/"Dead Souls"

An enticing little item for
all the fanatics out there.
All the hype got me to buy
a copy. More of the same
superb music we've come to
expect from this band, although
the A-side doesn't fit quite
so nicely into the typical
JD format. Good, but I'm
still awaiting album #2.--DS*

VIC GODDARD & SUBWAY SECT
"Split Up The Money"/"Out Of
Touch" MCA Records

Mister unpredictable goes left
when some thought he'd go right.
Actually, I don't know where
the hell he's headed. The A-
side is just too wimpy for me,
although 'wimp' may not be an
accurate description of what
Goddard's tying to do. The
B-side doesn't do much for me
either. High-brow pop that's
sure to alienate whatever
following these guys might
have had. Perhaps down the
road I'll have to eat my words
when Vic & Co. become the next
big thing, but I'm not counting on it. I need something
that musses the hair and leaves
a bruise or two.--DS

*Ian Curtis is dead.

133

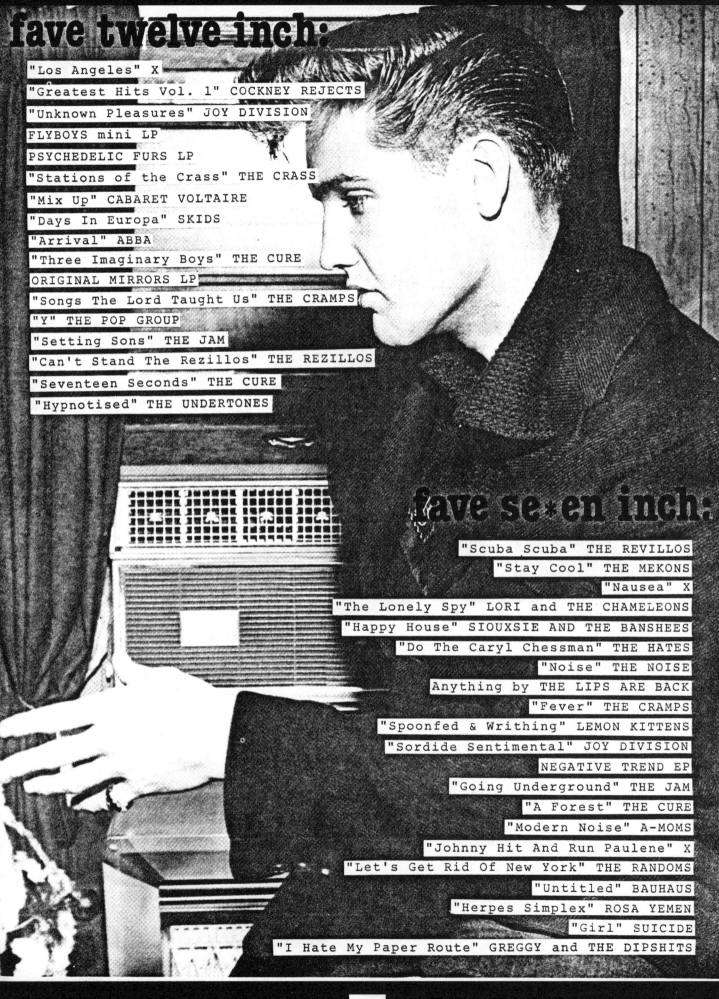

fave twelve inch:

"Los Angeles" X
"Greatest Hits Vol. 1" COCKNEY REJECTS
"Unknown Pleasures" JOY DIVISION
FLYBOYS mini LP
PSYCHEDELIC FURS LP
"Stations of the Crass" THE CRASS
"Mix Up" CABARET VOLTAIRE
"Days In Europa" SKIDS
"Arrival" ABBA
"Three Imaginary Boys" THE CURE
ORIGINAL MIRRORS LP
"Songs The Lord Taught Us" THE CRAMPS
"Y" THE POP GROUP
"Setting Sons" THE JAM
"Can't Stand The Rezillos" THE REZILLOS
"Seventeen Seconds" THE CURE
"Hypnotised" THE UNDERTONES

fave se*en inch:

"Scuba Scuba" THE REVILLOS
"Stay Cool" THE MEKONS
"Nausea" X
"The Lonely Spy" LORI and THE CHAMELEONS
"Happy House" SIOUXSIE AND THE BANSHEES
"Do The Caryl Chessman" THE HATES
"Noise" THE NOISE
Anything by THE LIPS ARE BACK
"Fever" THE CRAMPS
"Spoonfed & Writhing" LEMON KITTENS
"Sordide Sentimental" JOY DIVISION
NEGATIVE TREND EP
"Going Underground" THE JAM
"A Forest" THE CURE
"Modern Noise" A-MOMS
"Johnny Hit And Run Paulene" X
"Let's Get Rid Of New York" THE RANDOMS
"Untitled" BAUHAUS
"Herpes Simplex" ROSA YEMEN
"Girl" SUICIDE
"I Hate My Paper Route" GREGGY and THE DIPSHITS

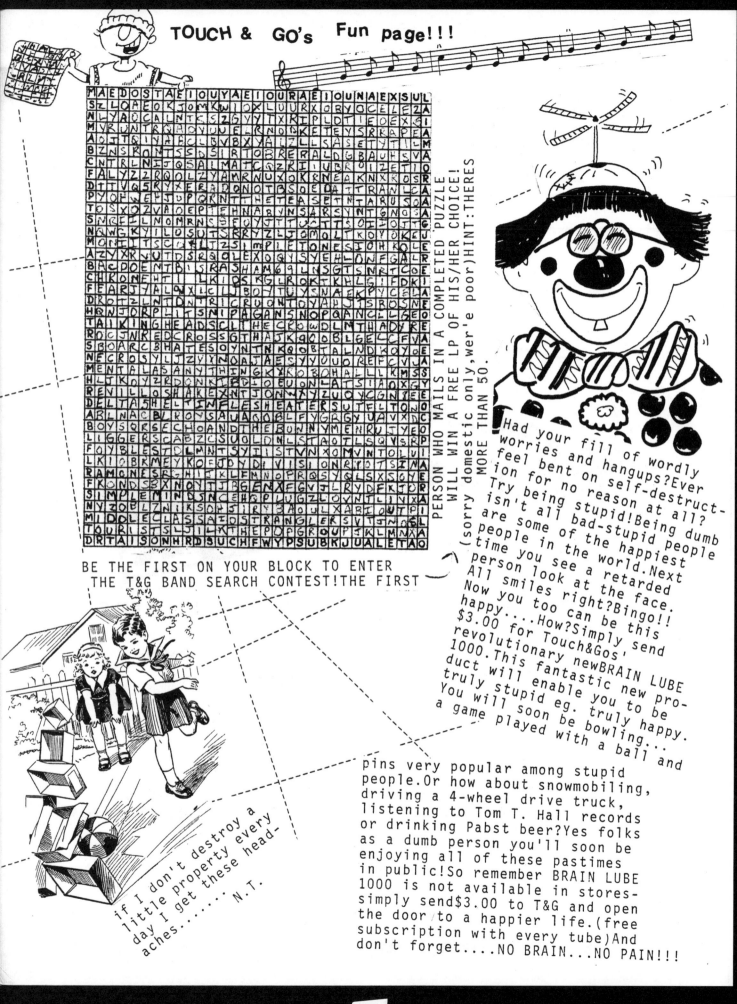

TOUCH & GO's Fun page!!!

BE THE FIRST ON YOUR BLOCK TO ENTER THE T&G BAND SEARCH CONTEST!THE FIRST

PERSON WHO MAILS IN A COMPLETED PUZZLE WILL WIN A FREE LP OF HIS/HER CHOICE! (sorry domestic only,wer'e poor)HINT:THERES MORE THAN 50.

Had your fill of wordly worries and hangups?Ever feel bent on self-destruct- ion for no reason at all? Try being stupid!Being dumb isn't all bad-stupid people are some of the happiest people in the world.Next time you see a retarded person look at the face. All smiles right?Bingo!! Now you too can be this happy....How?Simply send $3.00 for Touch&Gos' revolutionary newBRAIN LUBE 1000.This fantastic new pro- duct will enable you to be truly stupid eg. truly happy. You will soon be bowling... a game played with a ball and pins very popular among stupid people.Or how about snowmobiling, driving a 4-wheel drive truck, listening to Tom T. Hall records or drinking Pabst beer?Yes folks as a dumb person you'll soon be enjoying all of these pastimes in public!So remember BRAIN LUBE 1000 is not available in stores- simply send$3.00 to T&G and open the door to a happier life.(free subscription with every tube)And don't forget....NO BRAIN...NO PAIN!!!

if I don't destroy a little property every day I get these head- aches......N.T.

135

FACELESS

- NO TALK IN THE 80's
- NEW SPARTANS
- ALL THE WHITES
- LAST HYMN

- BORED WITH THE BOYS
- CITY ON ICE
- CARYL CHESSMAN
- SOLDIER

AVAILABLE AT FINER SHOPS
OR DIRECTLY BY MAIL FOR $3.00 ea. POSTPAID FROM
CHRISTIAN ARNHEITER, 5201 W. 34TH, BOX 316, HOUSTON, 77092

8

Our first offset-printed cover by DS at the local community college, and it's the legendary Jan's Rooms shot that would become the Fix 7" image for the band's second release. We were obsessed with this rundown section of Michigan Ave.—all the cool resale and pawnshops, crap bars, and flophouses; anything a young upper-middle-class kid who wanted to go a slumming could want. Big jump in entertainment value here with a nice Misfits ode that I wrote in the third person as "Sally Barrett," and it's unclear why I dressed in verbal drag for this discourse... But there... I finally came clean and I now feel cathartically cleansed. Heavy UK bent again with faves like Pop Group, Wire, Cure, and just enough domestic bombast including Crime, Flesh Eaters, et al. That's Michael Hudson of the Pagans on the Top/Bottom 40 page that once again has me scratching my look-back-and-laugh melon... Top 40... Simple Minds!!?? Bottom 40... Mari-hootchie?! Somebody get me a cold towel—my face feels hot...

TOUCH AND GO

DAY or Jan's ROOMS WEEK

Coca-Cola

SILVIO'S BAR
BEER & WINE ★ FOOD
TAKE OUT

number eight

seventy-five cents

tastelessness abounds - T&G

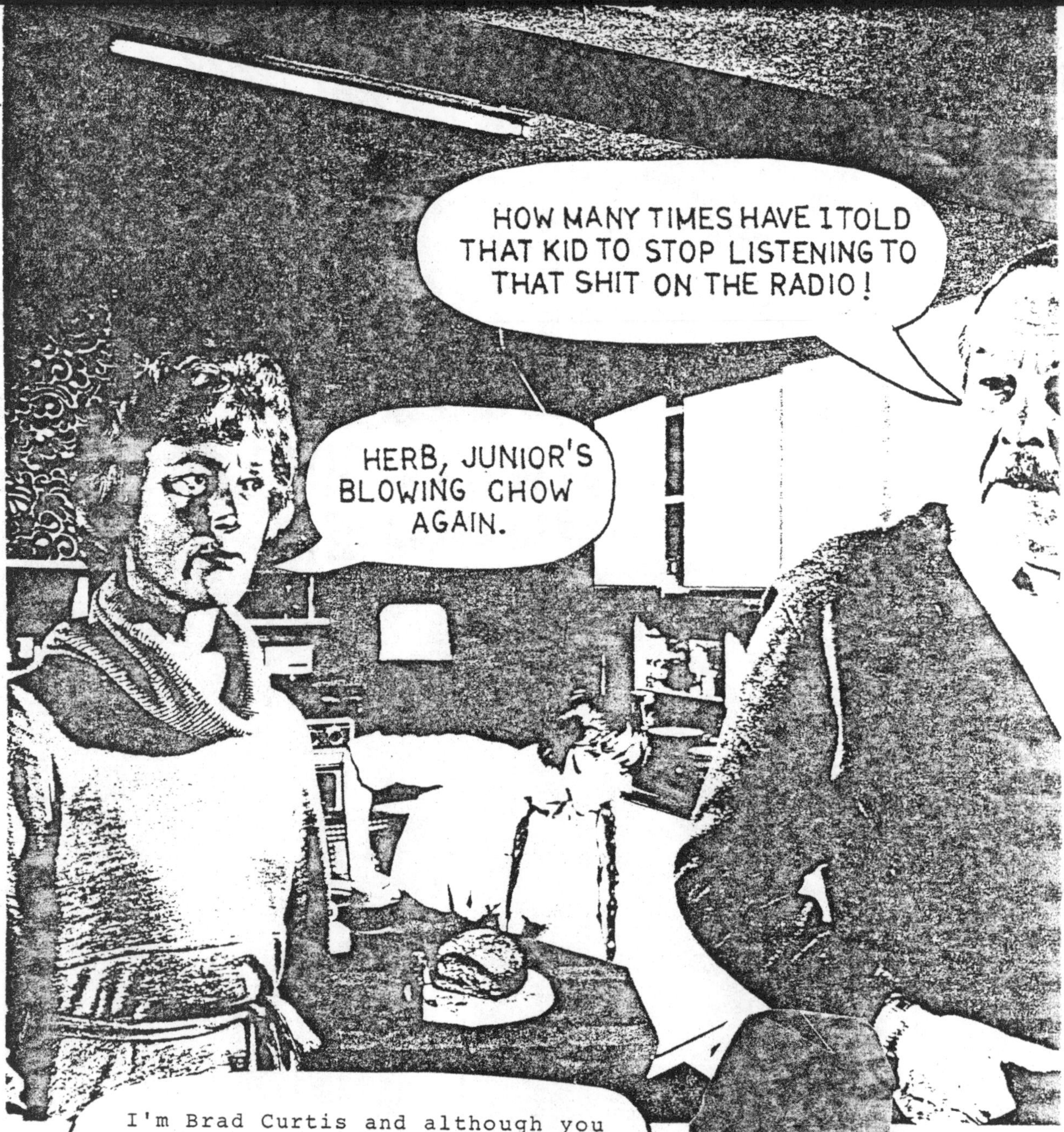

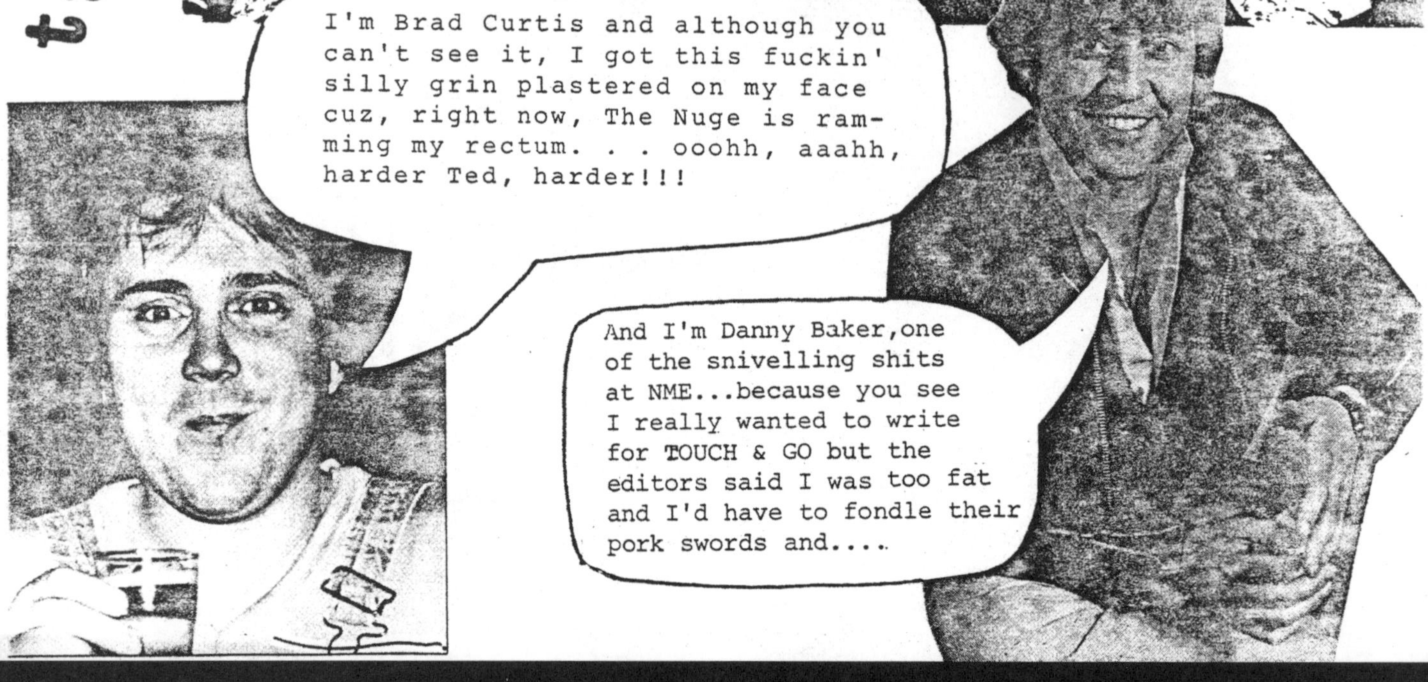

THE MISFITS / A Perspective

WHAT'S TO FOLLOW WON'T BE A RECORD REVIEW-NOR IS IT GOING TO BE AN
INTERVIEW,LIVE REVIEW,OR HISTORY LESSON.FOR THIS PAGE IS TO CONTAIN
A GOOD OLD-FASHIONED FAN RANT.AHH YES REMEMBER THE FAN? YOU KNOW OF
COURSE FAN IS THE ROOT OF FANATIC,AND THE FANATICISM I FEEL IS FOR
ONE BAND ONLY...THE MISFITS.THE REASON RAJJ DEVOTEES NO LONGER EXIST,
IS MOST PEOPLE SEEM TO ENJOY WALLOWING IN THE HYPE-N'-FASHION POLITICS
THAT FORCE SO MANY INTO THE ADORATION OF THE MARKETABLY CHIC SECTOR.
THE FACT REMAINS THAT THE MISFITS STAND ALONE AS THE BEST BAND EVER IN

THE HISTORY
OF RECORDED
MUSIC.SURE WE
ALL HAVE
MOODS-WE DONT
BUY RECORDS-
WE BUY MOODS-
(RIGHT I READ
THAT SOME
WHERE)IT"S
PUNK TO GET
UP-DOOM TO
DROP IT BACK
DOWN,BUT ONLY
THE MISFITS
SEEM CAPABLE
OF DROPPING
INTO THE
SLIMEPIT OF
THE HUMAN
SPIRIT-AND
COME UP WITH
A GRAPHIC
PORTRAYAL OF
LIFE AS A
TRULY GOTHIC,
AGGRESSIVE
GO-ROUND.3
SINGLES HAVE
DOCUMENTED
AND WHAT
IS REALLY
KEEPING ME
GOING THESE
DAYS IS THE

FACT THAT
MY BAND IS
GOING TO BE
HITTING THE
MIDWEST THIS
SUMMER.4RAW
INDIVIDUALS
BLAZING A
BLACK TRAIL
INTO THE HUM-
AN GLUE FAC-
TORY.IN ACT-
UALITY I HAVE
A FRIEND WHO
WOULD HAVE
BEEN MORE
APTLY SUITED TO
WRITE SUCH A FEAT-
URE FOR SHE HAS
SEEN MY BELOVED
LIVE AND EVEN
PROUDLY DISPLAYS
A BRUISED AND
BATTERED 5ATHAT
WAS HASTILY DISCARD-
ED IN A FIT OF OUT
OF CONTROL SKIN-
POUNDING AT THE 4th
ST. SALLOON OUT EAST
SOMEWHERE-YET ANOTHER
VENUE WILLING TO RISK
FREEING THESEGODS ON
AN UNSUSPECTING PUBLIC.
BUT THE PROBLEM LIES
IN MY FRIENDS INABILITY

TO DISCUSS OR EVEN DEAL WITH THE MISFITS ATTITUDES AND THE EVENTUALITY OF HER EFFORTS IS
ALWAYS THE SAME...POOPED UNDERPANTS.SO IT IS I HEREIN ATTEMPTING THE IMPOSSIBLE...TO
ARTICULATE AND EXPRESS MY EMOTION AND ADORATION-BUT AS IS USUALLY THE CASE,THE SEMANTICS
FAIL ME WHEN I NEED THEM MOST.FOR IT IS WRITTEN I AM DOMINATED...DRIVEN LIKE A VIXEN
IN HEAT WHENEVER I HEAR THE STRAINS OF ANY OF THEIR CLASSIC MATERIAL.THEY DOMINATE MY
SEXUAL FANTASIES(AS MY POOR BOYFRIEND WILL ADMIT)THE DECADENCE SO PERMEATES THE ROOM...
EVERY TIME THEY PLAY...JUST FOR ME...THE MISFITS...

SALLY BARRETT

WRITE THE MISFITS...c/o THE MISFITS FIEND CLUB,145 W 27th St. 2E,NY,NY 10001

SUBS. → 3.00
3 ISSUES

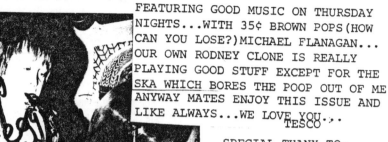

TOUCH and GO
BOX 26203   LANSING, MI 48909

THE SEASON OF SEX AND SUNBURN
IS IN FULL SWING AND AS IN LIFE
THERE'S BEEN SOME REAL UP'S AND
DOWNS SINCE WE SPOKE AT YOU LAST.
HAPPY THINGS INCLUDE 1)THE GRAND
RETURN . OF THAT DASTARDLY,
DEMENTED AND DEMONIC INTELLECT...
YES THATS RIGHT,THIS ISH FEATURES
YET ANOTHER INSTALLMENT OF VER-
BOSE,VERMINOUS VERBIAGE FROM NONE
OTHER THAN THAT R&R BANKROBBER!
2)RISING ACTS LIKE-THWARTED WITH
THEIR WALL OF SOUND APPROACH...
THE NECROS WHO ARE THE SCRAPPIEST,
MOST VIOLENT BATCH OF HOOLIGANS
IN THE MIDWEST AND THEY ARE ONLY
17.SORRY PONGOS BUT THIS STACKS
UP WITH THE LIKES OF BLACK FLAG,
AND THE PAGANS...MUST HEAR THEM
FOLKS...AND THE BAND DS IS IMP-
RESSED WITH THE FIX ...HAVEN'T
HEARD EM BUT THEY SUPPOSEDLY
HAVE AN AX MAN WHO PLAYS AT THE
SPEED OF TWISTED THOUGHT...AND
YOU CAN BET I AIN'T RAVIN' ABOUT
ANY THIRD RATE POSER BANDS HERE..
CUZ THERE'S NO ROOM FOR BLIND
ACCETANCE OF ANYTHING HERE AT T&G.
EVERYTHING GET'S THE DRUGINTHEMUD
TREATMENT AFORE THE AFFIXATION OF
THE BELOVED SEAL OF APPROVAL...
REALLY GREAT TO SEE A FEW LOCALS
REACTING VIOLENTLY TO THE SHIT-STATE
OF LOCAL GREY-PUKE PROGRAMMING..
        AND THAT LEADS US INTO THE
DOWNS O'THE PAST MONTH OR SO....
1)YOU SEE WE GAVE THIS GIRL IN
DETROIT ABOUT A THIRD OF OUR COPIES
LAST ISH AND SHE WROTE US TO TELL
US HOW SHE WAS "ROBBED AND RAPED"
AND OUR MONEY JUST HAPPENED TO BE
ON HER...HMMMMM...WE'LL LET YOU
DIGEST THAT ONE...BUT EVEN WITH
BUT A FEW PATS ON THE BACK(MONETARY
OR OTHERWISE) THE MASSIVE DUAL
EGOS THAT MAKE UP WHAT WE REFER TO
AS A STAFF..NECESSITATE YET ANOTHER
ONE,NUMBER 8 already..CUZ MAINLY
US MEGAZINE MOGULS NEEDE ANOTHER EGO
BOOST.
IN BRIEF.....
WATCH FOR A NEW ONE FROM THE NOISE
AT SUMMERS END.....TRAMPPS IS

FEATURING GOOD MUSIC ON THURSDAY
NIGHTS...WITH 35¢ BROWN POPS(HOW
CAN YOU LOSE?)MICHAEL FLANAGAN...
OUR OWN RODNEY CLONE IS REALLY
PLAYING GOOD STUFF EXCEPT FOR THE
SKA WHICH BORES THE POOP OUT OF ME
ANYWAY MATES ENJOY THIS ISSUE AND
LIKE ALWAYS...WE LOVE YOU...
                    TESCO

SPECIAL THANX TO-
DAVID CLARK
LORI BIZER
DICK AND DAVE AT FBC
BARRY HENNSLER
PASS RECORDS
MARK AT WAX TRAX
UPSETTER RECORDS
SUBTERRANEAN RECORDS
SLASH RECORDS
FLIPSIDE

Ashley Warren
Scott Steinberg

PARTY AT BOOKIES!

TG's STAFF
ELITISM IS FREEDOM

ALBUMS

THE UNDERTONES
"Hypnotised" Sire Records

Fifteen more solid gold hits
for all you pimply-assed boppers out there. A little
older and . . . a little wiser?
Who knows? What I do know is
that the first time I heard
this I cringed: "Oh no, what's
happened?" Where's that instant
blast of raw energy that's
supposed to leap out at ya on
every cut like on the first
album? Well, my prejudices
got in the way, and it took
me awhile before I finally
came around. The band's grown,
and for those first brief moments, I was trying(vainly)
to ignore the inevitable. You
don't get anywhere by doing
the standing still. They're
a bit more worldly than they
were when they released their
first LP. They've tasted
success, not much, but some,
and their music is going to
reflect that maturity. This
record is good, damn good, in
fact. I'm going to risk
sounding redundant and say that
these guys are the best at
writing and performing tunes
in that precarious pop/punk
mode. They've got their formula down to a science and
there's no denying the irre-
sistability of their music.

Pop hooks and catchy melodies
come as easily to these guys
as hemorrhoids do to truck
drivers. They're one of the
few bands that I truly get excited about. Yep, believe it
or not, under this cool exterior
of depressed stoicism I'm as
trembly and giddy as a kid with
his first ice-cold bottle of
Yoo-Hoo. And for all you spikey
haired yoboes who claim The
Undertones are simply too wimpy
for your hardened sensibilities,
you can take your Ruts, your U.
K. Subs, your Angelic Upstarts,
and the whole bloody mess and
bite the proverbial 'big one'.
This pop band is my reason for
living, OK.--DS

COCKNEY REJECTS
"Greatest Hits Vol. 1" EMI

Let me begin by congratulating
Jimmy Pursey. He may not know
fuck-all when it comes to producing his own stuff, but I'll
be darned, if he didn't get it
right with the Rejects.
This one explodes in your face,
an assaultive barrage of rock
'n' roll noise that scourages
anything by anyone else. The
likes of these boys has not
been seen for quite some time.
Our newly discovered 'high-brow'
tastes have gotten in the way
of truly appreciating something
as barbarically brilliant as
this record. Relentless, non-
stop hysteria. The Rejects
have restored my faith in what
we used to call 'punk rock'.
That may not mean anything,
but the album is still a killer.
--DS

TADASHI HIROSE

12"

THE POP GROUP
"For How Much Longer Do We Tolerate
Mass Murder?"   ROUGH TRADE

as devil's advocate......
Suddenly in vogue Mark Stewart and
his current event-gelical crew decide
to pile more kindling onto their
overtly political, dogmatic efforts
that they all hope will awaken our
annual guilt at having to tell the
little unicefers to take the razor-
bladed apples and move off into the
capitalistic darkness. But then we
all expected more generously irradi-
ative exposures of governmental man-
ipulation and exploitation, didn't
we? Most assuredly these guys were
gathered in the hallowed hall of
civilized awareness where they were
annointed the saviors in charge of
the third world backlash. The band
addresses such a wide array of global injustice that it quickly bogs
down in the weighty task of even
calculating the supposedly viable
(but hopelessly undocumented) alter-
natives. Is this fundamental love
for mankind we're seeing here?
"Substitute guilt for action". . .
what is that finishing your vegetables? Pissing in the river. . .
as blind consumer......
This is probably the most listened
to slab at the office. An excellent
followup to their (blah de blah de
blah)you've only read reviews of
this in every rag in the western
world...what's all the fuss? Find
out for yourself...TV

FRICTION-Pass Records
It's been strictly "rock journalist
in tears over paper wad pile" as far
as writing about this one.There is
nothing even remotely accessible about
FRICTION.While many of their countrymen
seem content on copping western influences
as a home base-this band continues to be
the vangaurd of what's really new in the
Japanese arena.Three men in a contemporary
fit of alienation.The guitar is not used
in the traditional strum-strum-lead-run
manner we're all so accustomed to,but
rather grinds out rythyms that rifle about
like two radio waves in combat.The bassman
plays nowave tag with it's own shadow in
yet another exemplification of blind obliv-
iousness to pre-established bass-neck guide-
lines.Riding high with this fretless bottom
rides a crisp but equally untypical trap set.
FRICTION are indeed capable of bringing on
those beloved anxiety attacks in even the
most stayed of mentalities,but laid on an
acid-casualty like myself brings it all just
too fucking close to the edge of human stability.
It is incomprehensable that other acts of
varying degrees of mediocraty are emerging
from Japan-with even a few on domestic labels,
while FRICTION remain virtually unknown in
western circles.Pass Records,essentially the
independent Japanese label(on the strength of
but a few releases -granted there may be some
I am unaware of but you dont know that)perhaps
will never be able to give this great group
the big push it truly deserves...but then
mass-consumption of something as remarkably
disturbing as FRICTION is let s face it...
a dream...a "Crazy Dream"...TV

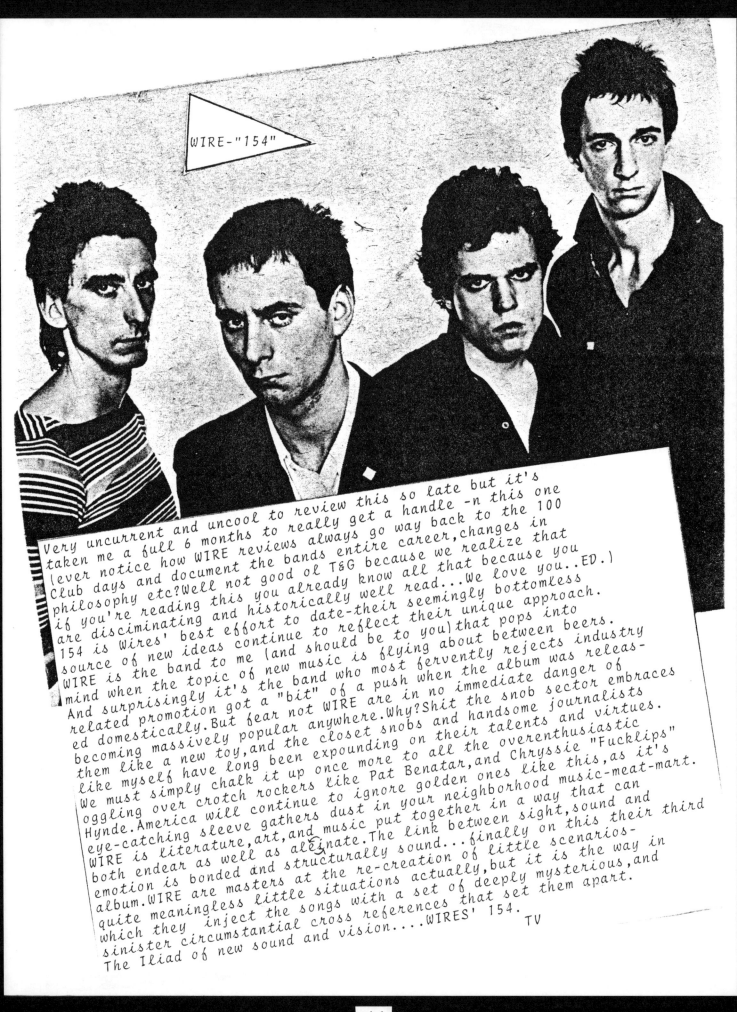

WIRE-"154"

Very uncurrent and uncool to review this so late but it's
taken me a full 6 months to really get a handle -n this one
(ever notice how WIRE reviews always go way back to the 100
Club days and document the bands entire career,changes in
philosophy etc?Well not good ol T&G because we realize that
if you're reading this you already know all that because you
are disciminating and historically well read...We love you..ED.)
154 is Wires' best effort to date-their seemingly bottomless
source of new ideas continue to reflect their unique approach.
WIRE is the band to me (and should be to you)that pops into
mind when the topic of new music is flying about between beers.
And surprisingly it's the band who most fervently rejects industry
related promotion got a "bit" of a push when the album was released domestically.But fear not WIRE are in no immediate danger of
becoming massively popular anywhere.Why?Shit the snob sector embraces
them like a new toy,and the closet snobs and handsome journalists
like myself have long been expounding on their talents and virtues.
We must simply chalk it up once more to all the overenthusiastic
oggling over crotch rockers like Pat Benatar,and Chryssie "Fucklips"
Hynde.America will continue to ignore golden ones like this,as it's
eye-catching sleeve gathers dust in your neighborhood music-meat-mart.
WIRE is literature,art,and music put together in a way that can
both endear as well as aleinate.The link between sight,sound and
emotion is bonded and structurally sound...finally on this their third
album.WIRE are masters at the re-creation of little scenarios-
quite meaningless little situations actually,but it is the way in
which they inject the songs with a set of deeply mysterious,and
sinister circumstantial cross references that set them apart.
The Iliad of new sound and vision....WIRES' 154.   TV

146

THE CURE-"SEVENTEEN SECONDS"

Grab that little box off of
your shelf marked Cure and
take out all those tidely
categorized labels,figure outs
and write-offs.Simply comminute
and sweep away.This band has yet
to release anything that even
remotely resembles it's pred-
ecessor,and what's here is not the
mentality that recorded "THREE
IMAGINARY BOYS" the bands' first
LP.But it's easily the most tantal-
izingly one-dimensional recording this
season.Prior to the release of the
latest single "A FOREST" the band
was all up front and agreeable right?
There was no problem dealing with the
first single "Killing An Arab".It
was 1978 by god and they wore it well-
if a bit on the superflous side."Boys
Don't Cry"....oh drat and all along I
had these guys on the fringe of all
that fashionable nastility,and they
drop this pop bomb.And the first long
player-ah yes they further monkey-wrenched
the buying public-no cute photos,nolyrics,
not even fuckin' song titles.Who do these
people take us for-I mean every record has
song titles...doesn't it?" Predictable
response from a predictable culture.It
would be far too easy to label the former
sound and harken the arrival of a
regenerative awakening of dramatic prop-
ortions.THE CURE in this writers opinion
are simply progressing without simply turning
out products simply to fulfill contractual
obligations,and if they have then they have
camouflaged the urgency in a nice little
package..."SEVENTEEN SECONDS".An incessant
drum rap sticks extremely close to the basic
sound throughout,rarely attepting unecessary
fill dirt.The cut most out of sync with the
package as a whole is called "Three" which
features an incredible treble rythmic smash,
that lays this boy flat every time.
     The last thing in the world I thought
I'd ever have to view would be dancing to
THE CURE.Surely tarantism would not rear it's
ugly head during the solemnity of "A FOREST".

But yes one of Chicago's
little(I use the word
both literally and fig-
uratively)new prisco clubs
was doing it through one
of those unbearably loud
high-low dealies,and people
were undeniably out there
shaking their post-punk
booties.

     10 tracks might lead one
to believe a structured,un-
conceptual second effort en-
meshed in the frameworks of
prior successes may be at hand.
Don't believe it...not for a
moment.It's also debatable that
the presses' darling treatment
of the band early on may have
contributed to the necessity
for a change.Regardless of their
real or subconscience motives,and
my own meandering juxtapositions-
THE CURES' "SEVENTEEN SECONDS"
stands as a meritorious achievment
                              TV

THE CURE

FLESH EATERS-"No Questions Asked"
Upsetter Records

The world's populace and more precisely, this culturally deprivated
census region do not deserve it.
I speak of the brilliant set-to-
music iconography of one Chris
Desjardins and his super assemblage of LA's finest vagabondage
collectively known as FLESH EATERS.
It's really fucked, but again my
comments regarding this have to
wait until I take a proctological
pot shot at the Brit jerks before

they get their hands on this and
tear it down...but you know it's
coming, right? Why do I care? I
probably shouldn't...because this
(even more so than anything America has yet produced) proves that
the West Coast of this country is
making music in the realm of realism...not pointless revival bullshit. It also lends a great deal
of credibility to a band when one
so in-charge as the vocalist/lyri-
cist has such a depth of background
in not only rock music, but the ever
widening schism between the ever
increasing innocuous record indus-

try and those actually trying to
initiate something interestingly
different.   Thank god for independents like UPSETTER, without whom
we would be in a hopelessly desperate state.   This album very simply
overpowers...subtly, and on a cru-
cially obvious level. Desjardins'
lyrics are articulated in an indes-
ribably intriguing manner(it's too
bad I got this so close to deadline,
I cannot stress all the qualities
that make this album worthy of #1
on our chart...it's simply a matter
of conveyance of the facts and what
you should be listening to...) TV

148

Who amongst you can honestly say
that they discerned the absence of my
column in the last ish of T&G? Is there
a human who saw through the early morning vice-overs,or the late nite mystery
tour to notice the loss of the most miniscule part of Americas' biggest fanzine?
I thought not.

Even in all my hubris I myself thought
it not too sorely missed.The reason for
it's lapse was due tp various factors;
the largest being the disposal of the
words I originally wrote...by Tesco...
at my admonition.I had written on the
punk-jazz fusion and in doing so I had
gone overboard in a way that makes me
glad I retracted the whole thesis.Suf-
fice to say I think there is plenty of
room within the new music to incorpor-
ate free jazz,the sounds of Miles Davis
or John Coltrane would blend well with
some of our best experimental bands.
(witness Lounge Lizards in NY,and
B-People in LA for proof this is already
happening)

After shit-canning that turd-encrust-
ed topic,I planned a reply to the only
mail my shabbily shamanistic words had
aroused. This being a letter to the
editor from one of his ex-fifi-bags who
wanted to cancel her subscription because of the allegedly sexist tone of
my Marriane Faithful record review.We
all know that Tesco is too good for the
sluts he puts up anyhow(oh jeez let me see
that goes for you you,and you,but not
you rag doll.ED.)but for a women to
complain because a man says that he wanted to totally satisfy and please a women
who's been hurt by other men shows off
the bitterness in her own heart at losing
a peach of a guy.In other words totally
absurd.But let me reiterate;I'm a fascist,
sexist,elitist individual;I'm a party of
one,and I'm not writing this column to

inform the readers as much as to expound
my own dogma.But since dogma in any form
is anathema to me--the protothoma(the
original unbeliever)I hope you will find
my comments deliscious,not egregrious.
This months listening for the R&R
So don't forget all you kids out
there in ROCKLAND-write your fave
robber c/o Tesco Vee and let me give
you some private lessons in being
supreme.
Am especially interested in female
vessels of the void looking for
guidance in matters of the Tantra.....

Bankrobber includes the entire
Psychedelic Furs LP(ahhhh...yet
another truly enlightened--highly
discriminating persona..ED.)
Here is a group that realize the
hopes I've cherished in some of my
historical favorites are utilized
in ways to my liking.I'm speaking
of the influence of Roxy Music on
the Furs(hotly debated at the T&G
offices..ED.)Another in endearing quality
is the manner in which the vocals
are sung-only through the aggressive

technique that's used could that
scratchy mother-fucker sound so
fuckin' good.But the absolute tip-top
in GREAT NEW MUSIC is the advent of
The Cure as a 4 Piece.How can they be
so compelling,yet so subtle at the
same time?Here's a list of cool things
featured exclusively for T&G readers...

Mohair Suits
Burberry Trench Coats
Onyx Jewelry
Black or Silver Lipstick
Jade Green Silk Shirts
Tibetan Thangkas

Dream Crystal Waterpipes
Club Rolling Papers
Serena the pornster
Gamelan Music
Stockhausen
Terrorist Acts Against the DEA
Property Crimes to increase the
wealth of the elite(that's us idio
Assholes Good Enough To French
Clitorises big enough to wrap your
lips around

19

7" byTV

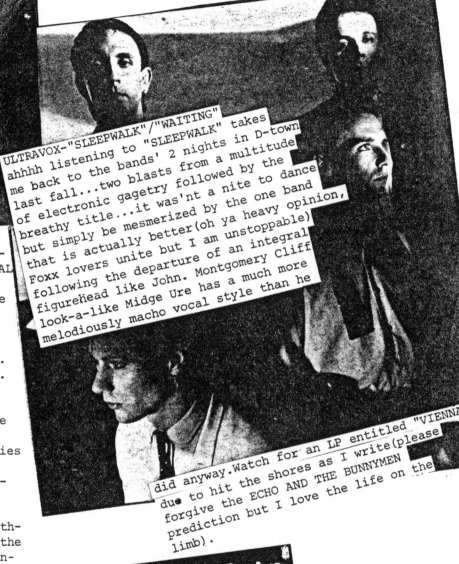

SURGICAL PENIS KLINIK
SOMETHING FOR NOBODY
Monte Cazazza

STLE and has to do with strangulation of
some sort."KICK THAT HABIT MAN" is the
most musical track in organizational terms,
but convention does not enter the Cazazza
domain."FIRST/LAST" is an immature acapp-
ella that adds insult to the injurious
fact that you all must own this single.

SURGICAL PENIS KLINIK-"FACTORY"/
"SLOGAN".....MONTE CAZAZZA-"SOME-
THING FOR NOBODY EP.....INDUSTRIAL
RECORDS
Industrial continues to scour the
globe in it's efforts to uncover
all the platter-documented disease courtesy of all the cliques
dipping into twisted electronics.
From Sydney,Australia come S.P.K.
If you've ever had a bad drugun
this is what the radio sounded
like(remember?)but now that we're
all aware and enlightened as to
the scenes' unlimited possibilities
this suddenly becomes extremely
listenable:eg. mid-eighties main-
stream.Do all of these bent bars
constitute progress?I say yes...
and they've safely tucked the rather gruesome(look at the name of the
band and use that good ol' imagination)photo inside the bag....a little
elmersand we're in business.
How Monte manages to keep his butt
out of the local wards is beyond me.
This gentleman stretches the definition of art as nonsense as music or
thrice versa as he straddles the fine
line between unadulterated absurdity
and cogent realism."DISTRESS" opens
and was compiled from tapes made at a
gun range on top of which are two tracks
a baby crying and Monte saying something
I as yet haven't figured out!"Mary Bell"
features Miss Tutti from THROBBING GRI-

ULTRAVOX-"SLEEPWALK"/"WAITING"
ahhhh listening to "SLEEPWALK" takes
me back to the bands' 2 nights in D-town
last fall...two blasts from a multitude
of electronic gagetry followed by the
breathy title...it was'nt a nite to dance
but simply be mesmerized by the one band
that is actually better(oh ya heavy opinion,
Foxx lovers unite but I am unstoppable)
following the departure of an integral
figurehead like John. Montgomery Cliff
look-a-like Midge Ure has a much more
melodiously macho vocal style than he
did anyway.Watch for an LP entitled "VIENNA"
due to hit the shores as I write(please
forgive the ECHO AND THE BUNNYMEN
prediction but I love the life on the
limb).

Siouxsie and the Banshees
"Christine"

SIOUXSIE AND THE BANSHEES
"CHRISTINE"/"EVE WHITE/EVE
BLACK"-Polydor records
THE BEST STUFF YET...BUY THIS!!

RAYMILLAND- "TALK"/"DISTANT VIEW"
Praxis Records
The only American band operating in
the genre of the despair tactician
is curiously called RAYMILLAND.
This band roams freely in the icon-
oclastic shadow of bands the likes of
BAUHAUS and THE INSEX.The fact that
they hail from St.Louis really boggles
the mind as the brain firmly wishes to
believe this to be the product of some
dank and disenchanted little plebe
in some English tenement. A truly
brilliant debut.

DISCHARGE-"FIGHT BACK"/WAR'S NO FAIRY-
TALE"/"ALWAYS RESTRICTIONS"/"YOU TAKE
PART IN CHEATING THIS SYSTEM"/"RELIG-
ION INSTIGATES" CLAY RECORDS
I realize how overused this phrase is
but just once more...."Just when we
thought we'd seen it all.ZIG ZAG was
right,these guys do make The REJECTS
look like The DOOLEYS...well not quite
but there's no other way to let out
how incredibly loud and out of control
DISCHARGE are. You know how much I hate

CRIME-"GANGSTER FUNK"/"MASERATI"
B-Square Records
Well it's about time...a CRIME single
of my very own!This band has been around for years in one form or another,
with the ultra-cool Frankie and Johnny
always in evidence but I have the distinct feeling all three of their platter
are as different as the three different
time periods in which they were recorded,you know from the slambity bang 77'
sound to what we have here...namely
"GANGSTER FUNK" a primitive flirtation
with the classic elements of inner-city
decadence that makes this one whale of a
hit with anyone who loves to "Do the junkie twist" as much as me"MASERATI" moves
away style wise and ventures into the'
sleazoid realm of scumpop I had always
imagined CRIME would purvey.Get this
if you can...it'll make alot of your
pop and jerkemstance dance pressings
look real fuckin silly...

comparisons but the only thing that
really parallels this in overall manic
intensity is a band like MIDDLE CLASS-
the lyrics are quite similar to the
CRASS's ...loads of screeching and
bellowing with just enough of the
f-word to satisfy.I'm tellin' you big
namers are goona hafta move ya arses
over cuz if this band and USers like
THE HATES and THE NECROS are already
equalling the intensity(surpassing is
closer to the truth)of your quickly
depleting repetoires and wont be
long before the real upstarts'll
have you by the balls screaming
uncle...buy this or die...

A BiG PiSS OFF TO THE MUSiC-BiZ!

HONEY BANE
YOU CAN BE YOU
No MoRE THAN 65P

HONEY BANE-YOU CAN BE YOU EP
"Girl On The Run"/"Porno Grows"/
"Boring Conversations" Crass
Records

Hot damn, Honey's back and we've
missed her since she participated
in the superb 'FATAL' MICROBES
ominous classic "Violence Grows"
on the Small Wonder/Xntrix label.
Here we find her backed by none
other than CRASS and this turns
out to be one of the best efforts
for both parties. "Girl On The
Run" is your basic wench in the
throes of life and you know preg-
nancy, and a depressing ending.
"Porno Grows" is more like the
human-rights doctrines this label
likes to bring up, but somehow
it loses impact when one has to
pay $3.00 for a single that is so
democratically labelled "NO MORE
THAN 65P".

VKTMS EP
Subterranean Records

The best time to review a single is after a good nights'
sleep, and last night I by
chance got one so I slapped
this ditty on and what do you
know, this just could be a
decent single. Agnetha
Faltskog lookalike Nyna has
a voice that acts as a catalyst to what would undoubtedly be a pretty dismissable
band. She almost tries too
hard at times but you can't
blame her cuz she's really
dragging around three heavy
metal lunkheads that obviously wore out their rock-bar
welcome and decided they
wanted to be cool like THE
NOISE, but there's no way.
Give this doll a real band
and she'll go far. Maybe
if I listen to it before
bed...

JOY DIVISION-"Love Will Tear
Us Apart"/"These Days" Factory
Records

ALRIGHT so Joy Division are no
more, let's let the dead alone
and move forward now that this,
probably what should be the
bands' last single, has been
released. But just watch the
flood of tape they'll dig up,
no doubt every outake,demo or
possibly even the dreaded jam
session, along with every Ian
Curtis belch and fart this side
of Morrison's tombstone. The
band was incredibly good....
let's remember them that way.

The Gang of Four

999
NINE NINE NINE

Guerrilla rock

CURE

ECHO & THE BUNNYMEN

NEW-WAVE
Music from
THURSDAYS

Trammpp's
521-523 E. Michigan Ave.
Lansing, Michigan

35 cent
drafts!

PLASMATICS

SINGLES

ECHO and THE BUNNYMEN
"Rescue"/"Simple Stuff"/"Pride"
Korova Records

I know we said there'd be an
album out shortly, and we're
still waiting, but if this is
any indication of what's to
come, we have a lot to look
forward to. A sparkling production propells the music
to a new height of brilliance.
"Rescue" eclipses their previous effort with one of the
most commercial sounding
reocrds I've heard in a long
time. This is AM fodder at
its best, that is, if the radio
industry had their shit to-
gether(which they haven't for
too long now). This should
vault The Bunnymen into the
forefront of the nouveau
music scene. Demands to be
heard.--DS

PYLON
"Cool"/"Dub" Caution Records

Dumb looking bag, but beauty is
only skin deep(or so they say).
Intriguing piece of quirk from
these unknowns from Georgia.
Tough angry female supplying
the wind, with the band punching out frenetic lines of nervous tension. Great music to
twitch to. Good to see something new from this country for
a change.--DS

CRISIS
"Hymn of Faith" EP
Ardkor Records

The only faith here is the
blind one in the back of my
head that thinks these guys
will come out with that great
record they're capable of.
After hearing this, I wonder where I ever got the idea
in the first place. The
music plods along at a geritol
pace and I'm yanking it off
the turntable long before
their message has a chance
to sink in. Strong stuff, if
only the music were equal to
the challenge. Nothing near
the piercing chill of "White
Youth". They know what to say,
they just don't know how to
say it.--DS

LORI and THE CHAMELEONS
"The Lonely Spy"/"Peru"
Korova Records

Put this one along side The
Bunnymen. A nifty little
classic is what we've got here.
The greatest piece of B-movie
corn you'll ever hear. Lori's
sensually breathy vocals will
penetrate even the most hardened accumulation of ear wax
buildup. It will be tough to
pigeon-hole this band; although
"Peru" may be more what these
guys and a girl sound like.
Low medeival chants and another
billiant production by these
newcomers and you've got a
single that belongs in your
collection. Would I steer
you wrong?--DS

THE DILS
"Sound of the Rain"/"Not Worth
It"/"Red Rockers" Rogelletti
Records

If you're anticipating anything
even remotely similar to "Class
War" I suggest you pick up the
Middle Class Ep. These one-time
militant boys have swung all
the way in the other direction.
Pretty melodies, some acoustic
guitar, pleasant harmonies; it
just doesn't sound like the
same band. However, if you
can possibly put the old band
out of your mind for a second,
you might get something out of
this new one. Sure, it may
sound like real lightweight
stuff, but I'm still listening
to it(guess who's the light-
weight among the editors--TV).
I like it, just don't ask me
why.--DS

SF UNDERGROUND
with: No Alterative, Tools,
Flipper, Vktms Subterranean
Records

First of all, forget Tools
and Vktms. Unimagiative and
pathetically weak. Two bands
who give little credence to
the idea that there's a vibrant
music scene in the Bay Area.
No Alternative is good, not
very original, but they compen-
sate with speed. Flipper is
actually the only band with
any real substance. "Earthworm"
is one of those moronic master-
pieces like "Shutdown". A
crawling preapic of slime and
sludge that has many calling
it a piece of shit(how little
they know the accuracy of that
statement), but TV and I can
recognize true greatness when
it drops on our windshield,
it'll just be a matter of time
before you can too.--DS

(I don't read Japanese, so I can't tell you the name of the band or the names of the songs, sorry.) Pass Records

A rather nondescript looking trio, but these guys could be Japan's answer to Joy Division or Certain Ratio. Everything is sung in Japanese except for 'white man, yellow man, black man'. Not much to go on, but the music is definitely in that gloom school mode. The A-side begins with single ominous notes from the bass to be followed by two starchy chords from the guitar. Darkly minimal. I like it. Not the kind of music I expected from Japan. I was looking for something trendier or clonish. Ya learn something everyday, right?--DS

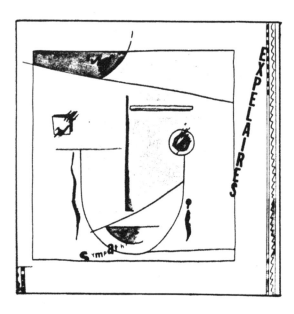

SWELL MAPS
"Let's Build A Car"/"Big Maz in the Country . . . Then Poland"   Rather/Rough Trade Records

More Swell Maps. Whoopee! The stuff that followed Dresden Style left a lot to be desired, but they've finally come up with a comparable effort. "Let's Build A Car" is ok, nothing special. "Big Maz in the Country" is the cut that restored my faith in this band. It may sound like just noise at first, but it all hovers around relentless drumming that gives it drive, and it keeps on building from there, adding more and more. An inconsistent band, and it looks as though they lucked out this time.--DS

EXPELAIRES
"Sympathy"/"Kicks" Rockburgh Records

Side 1 appears on the <u>Hicks from the Sticks</u> compilation, and for the most part, doesn't do much for me, Much too sappy, and not nearly as jumpy as "To See You". They seem to be holding back, which probably is due to a terrible production. Real thin. "Kicks" is more like their first effort. Ringing guitars and machine gun drumming make up for the tinniness in the overall sound. Alright, but nothing like the stuff coming from the Korova label.--DS

GO-GO's
"We Got the Beat"/"How Much
More Stiff Records

Been hearing a lot about these
Go-Go's, but the music on this
particular record falls pretty
short of my expectations.
Accuse me of being a perfect-
ionist snob, but this stuff
is downright ordinary, that
along with a regrettably low
level of excitement does not
make for a successful combination. Much too slick and
polished for something out
of LA. Gotta watch those
people over at Stiff. They
did a most adequate job of
disembowelling these promising
young punkettes. I'm assuming
that they're talents have yet
to be captured on vinyl and
we should overlook this effort
and hope number two fairs
better. Whatever happened to
Kleenex?--DS

SHAM 69
"Tell The Children"/"Jack"
Polydor Records

So what if their last two albums
scraped the ingratiatory bottom
of the barrel for the ever present Jimmy Pursey. Sure, he's
the paradigm of overbearing
egotism, but I'll forever hold
a soft spot for their music, and
with this new release, I won't
have to suffer the anguish of an
embarrassing humiliation when I
say. . .'it's good'.--DS

REMA-REMA
"Wheels in the Roses" EP
AD Records

This one knocks me out. Cream
of the crop for this month.
Remember the Models?, the Ramones-
esque outfit from Britain with
little or no future to speak of?
Well, the guitarist and bass
player opted to try their talents
elsewhere. What they've come
up with is an EP that contains
the greatest example of the
pulsating, grinding drone riff
I've ever heard in the cut "Rema-
Rema". This one hooks your brain
and bounces it off the floor(better than any brain lube) and
leaves you grinning like a cretin-
ous fool while you scamper around
the room in an effort to retrieve
that slippery grey matter. Fucking great.--DS

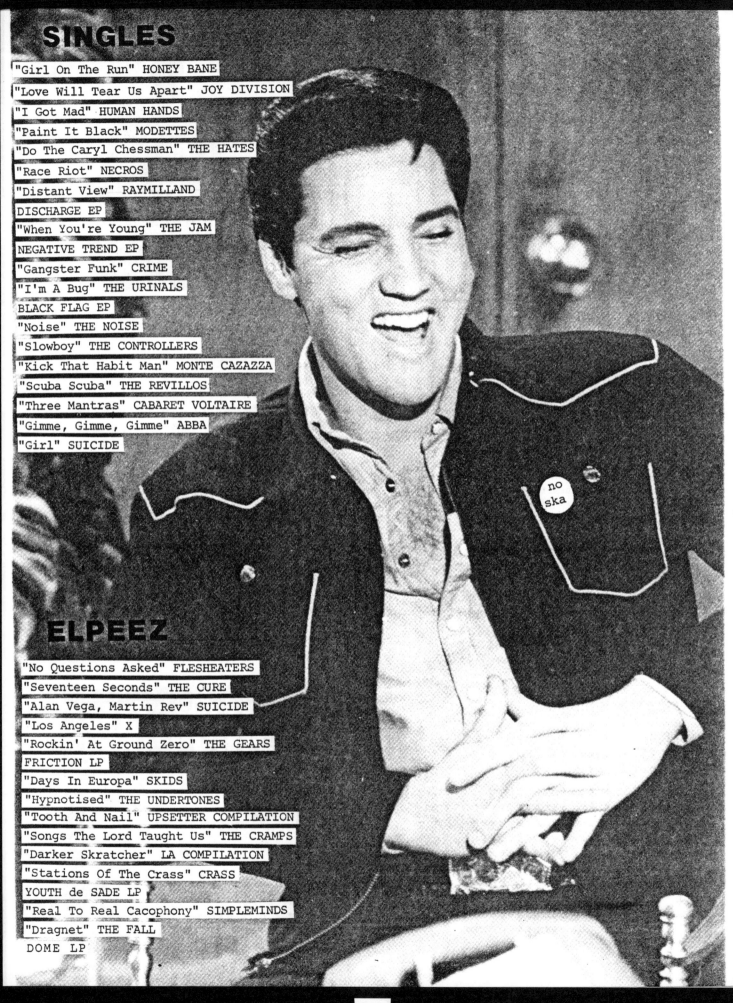

SINGLES

"Girl On The Run" HONEY BANE
"Love Will Tear Us Apart" JOY DIVISION
"I Got Mad" HUMAN HANDS
"Paint It Black" MODETTES
"Do The Caryl Chessman" THE HATES
"Race Riot" NECROS
"Distant View" RAYMILLAND
DISCHARGE EP
"When You're Young" THE JAM
NEGATIVE TREND EP
"Gangster Funk" CRIME
"I'm A Bug" THE URINALS
BLACK FLAG EP
"Noise" THE NOISE
"Slowboy" THE CONTROLLERS
"Kick That Habit Man" MONTE CAZAZZA
"Scuba Scuba" THE REVILLOS
"Three Mantras" CABARET VOLTAIRE
"Gimme, Gimme, Gimme" ABBA
"Girl" SUICIDE

ELPEEZ

"No Questions Asked" FLESHEATERS
"Seventeen Seconds" THE CURE
"Alan Vega, Martin Rev" SUICIDE
"Los Angeles" X
"Rockin' At Ground Zero" THE GEARS
FRICTION LP
"Days In Europa" SKIDS
"Hypnotised" THE UNDERTONES
"Tooth And Nail" UPSETTER COMPILATION
"Songs The Lord Taught Us" THE CRAMPS
"Darker Skratcher" LA COMPILATION
"Stations Of The Crass" CRASS
YOUTH de SADE LP
"Real To Real Cacophony" SIMPLEMINDS
"Dragnet" THE FALL
DOME LP

TOP 40!

IT'S BACK!!

BOTTOM 39

PAGANS
SECTION 25
LORI ON WCBN
Zig Zag
The Fall
BARRY "DOG DEW" HENNSLER
Henry Badowski:
Elvis Aron Presley
SLASH'S SURVIVAL
Bill Simpson, Richard Jobson, Stuart Adamson
SIOUXIE'S LOVE PIT
CRASS
TANYA TIGHT
IAN CURTIS
(X)
A CERTAIN RATIO
TOPLESS SHOE SHINES
HARDCORE DANISH
CHAIN SMOKING
Wire—A Question of Degree/Former Airline
ALL GLORIA LEONARD FILMS
METAL URBAIN
SUICIDE
BAD BRAINS
The Jam
R. MELTZER
ARTURO BASSICK
THE FALL:
Lee Ving
Posh Boy
SIMPLE MINDS
POTENCY PROBLEMS
a panty collection
Fabulous Serena
PINK MILITARY
choice friction
DAF
the most throbbing, exciting Glaxo Babies
Marilyn Chambers
FEELIES FLEXI-DISCS
FAY FIFE
WING TIPS
Vodka
PUBLIC SCHOOL PUNKS!
FACE
WHERE'S THE BOY FOR ME, Revillos

PEOPLE WHO DON'T LIKE X
"ROCKY HORROR"
TRASH & VAUDEVILLE
DAVEY "PINDICK" WINKELSTERN
JEM RECORDS
FRIPP FANATICS
ROCK JOURNALISM
THE DEAD KENNEDYS
SUE BARU
B-52's
Paul Rambali
Max Bell
Danny Baker
Paul Morley
Adrian Thrills
PRAIRIE FIRE
Casablanca Record and FilmWorks
STING— BASS, VOCALS.
John Lydon
Pere Ubu's David Thomas:
Stiv Bators
WWW (all FM)
NEBS
JAZZ
Tommy Tutone
Mod's, Ted's, Ska's
whacking pud
PUNK MAGAZINE
101 FM
FASHION
PRETENDERS
SID VICIOUS
BRADLEY
TED NUGENT
PUNK
BAD MANNERS
VIRGIN
THE PURPLE HEARTS

159

9

Anarchy?... Really? Once again, DS and I probably sat there one Saturday evening, guzzling Black Label (that would be Carling, not Johnny Walker), smoking Phillies cheroots and listening to Suicide's "Frankie Teardrop" over and over, trying to get inspiration for the biggest, baddest, boldest statement we could make and then we settle on this?? The fuckin' anarchy A? Politicos we weren't, but once in a while we playacted, trying to stream self-righteous indignation but really just not giving a toss. Crass (the band) coverage to match the big A-is-for-asshole on the cover. DS expounds on the mighty Fix for the first time... They were our very own hometown boys, the first HC band from the Midwest to go tour the country, and they were gone far too soon... My ears still be ringin'.

TOUCH & GO

NO. 9

75¢

:NOT MUCH HAS CHANGED

TOUCH and GO

BOX 26203 LANSING, MI 48909

we spell TAX relief
G-R-E-E-D

I BEGGED DS TO PLANT HIS SWEET SAPLING IN MY GOOD EARTH BUT HE WAS TOO BUSY WITH THIS HALF ASSED MAGAZINE...WHERE'S MY ONYX HANDLED TAPER SNOUT?

TOUCH & GO made it's TV debut on cable channel 36!The bohemian style was flowing freely while the inter-view was taking pl-ce which is prob-ably why it took 5 hours to film a half hour show.By three A.M. it was done,and we got numerous opportunities to lay into local wankers...it was such fun telling everyone why they are dirt under our wing-tips.The show was broadcast 3 times and will be hopefully sent over to channel 11 so you college types can check it out.

Number 9 .....that means we should be big time doesn't it?Yuk yuk wer'e scum and we always will be...no ads,...no cash, no respect...niether a scene or a band to get excited about so elsewhere is where to cast our wandering glances...no SLASH.. no CIRCLE JERKS LP(hope plead pant pray) Al at FLIPSIDE sez there will probably be an ad for it in the next ish..... Corey called the number and talked to the guitarist who shit gold ones when he found out OHIO knew the band existed, he said he was going to send out a demo... Send @2.oo dollars to NECROS,P.O. BOX 421, MAUMEE OHIO 43537 for their demos(forgot to include the address in the article) Heard a band called TOXIC REASONS that is.. no comment they ripped us off for 4 bucks so nobody else send them money...OK the s-ngle is bomb...Don't get me wrong,we do have faithful readers like the people in Pa. who faithfully send us bucks for copies sold thanks to Scott Steinberg...the only massive stud east of ,or west of King of Prussia(my hometown)who owns both TRASHMEN singles...muchas gracias' to all of you who bye us,we are true wang wranglers of mag circles,

NECROS ROOL,TKA OFFENSE gives me a royal pain in the prostate,CLUB DOO-BEE forever......
we love you...
TV

Various wit
translated from
+plagarized from Shane Williams
Crass photos stolen
from Sounds
TANX to Wade BANKS
for the tape

Subs.
3 bucks

10 bucks
A
YEAR!

Stroke
MY
Glans
Comrades

The
End
is
Nigh..

163

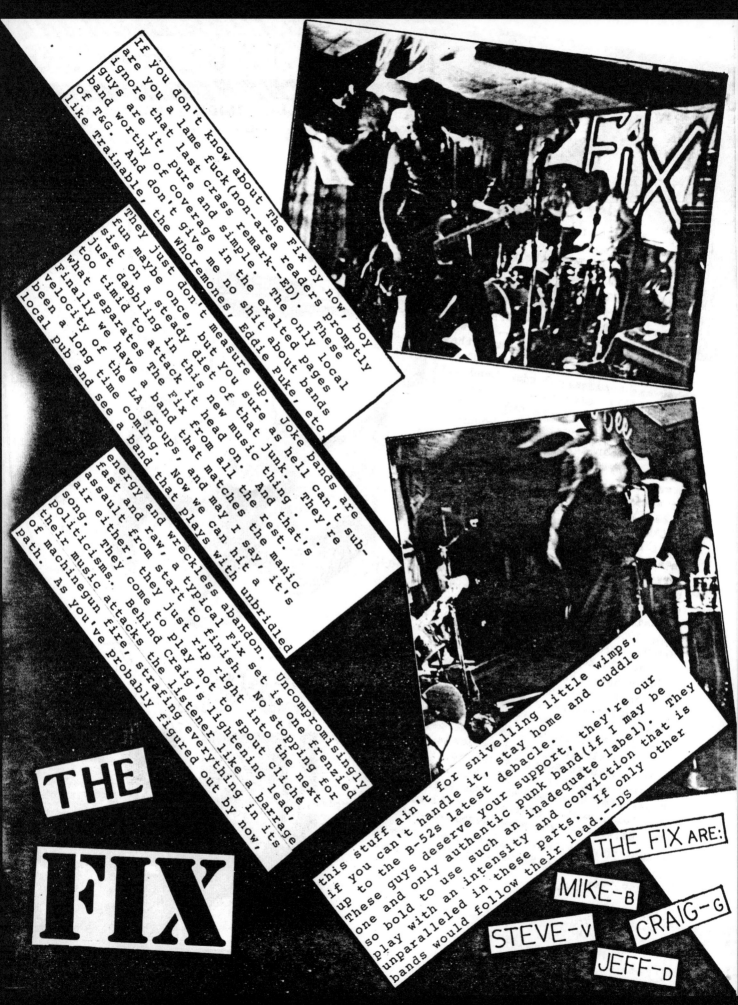

If you don't know about The Fix by now, boy are you a lame fuck(non-area readers promptly ignore that last crass remark--ED). These guys are it, pure and simple. They're the only local band worthy of coverage in the exalted pages of T&G. And don't give me no shit about bands like Trainable, the Whoremones, Eddie Puke, etc.

Joke bands are no measure up. And that's the manic sist about junk. The rest... fun maybe once, but you sure as hell can't sub- just dabbling in this new music thing. They just don't measure up. And may I say, it's what separates the Fix from all the LA groups, and that matches the head on. Now we can hit a velocity of the LA groups, and that plays with unbridled too timid to attack it from a band been a long time coming. Finally we have steady diet of the local pub and see a band

They energy and raw, a typical Fix set is one frenzied fast and wreckless abandon. Uncompromisingly assault either, they just to rip right into the next air. They come to play not to spout cliché song. Behind Craig's set is one frenzied politicisms. strafing into the listener like a barrage of machinegun fire, lightening everything in its their music attacks the listener like a barrage path. As you've probably figured out by now,

this stuff ain't for snivelling little wimps, if you can't handle it, stay home and cuddle up to the B-52s latest debacle. These guys deserve your support, they're our one and only authentic punk band(if I may be so bold to use such an inadequate label). They play with an intensity and conviction that is unparalleled in these parts. If only other bands would follow their lead.--DS

THE FIX

THE FIX ARE:
MIKE-B
STEVE-v
CRAIG-G
JEFF-D

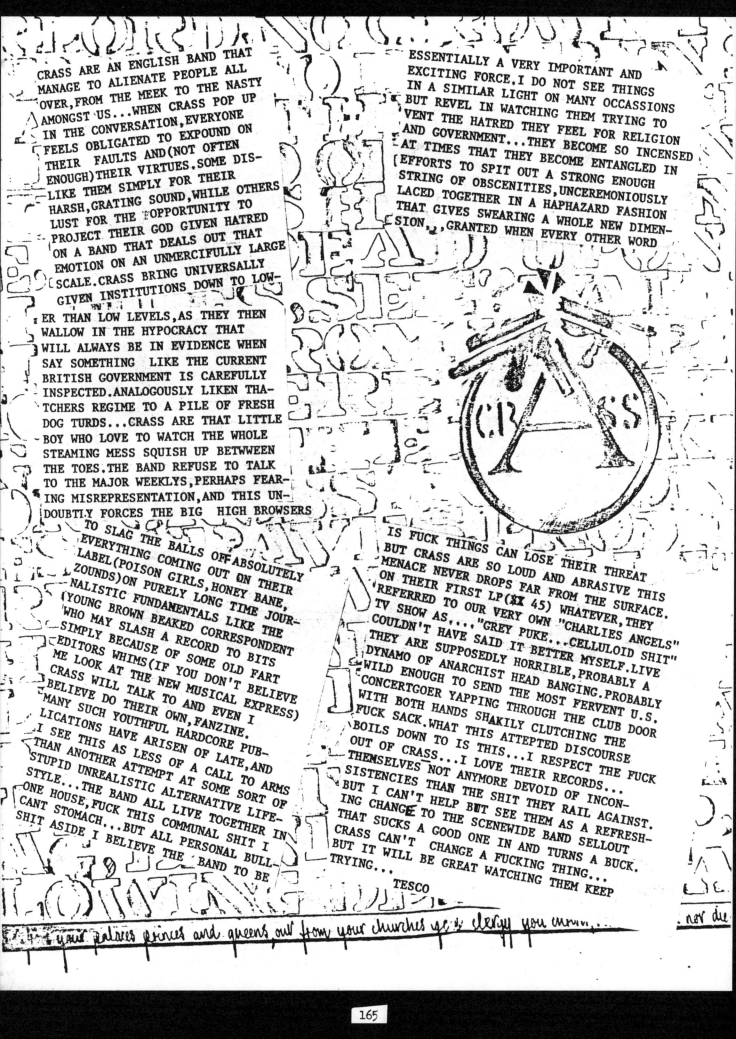

CRASS ARE AN ENGLISH BAND THAT MANAGE TO ALIENATE PEOPLE ALL OVER,FROM THE MEEK TO THE NASTY AMONGST US...WHEN CRASS POP UP IN THE CONVERSATION,EVERYONE FEELS OBLIGATED TO EXPOUND ON THEIR FAULTS AND(NOT OFTEN ENOUGH)THEIR VIRTUES.SOME DIS- LIKE THEM SIMPLY FOR THEIR HARSH,GRATING SOUND,WHILE OTHERS LUST FOR THE OPPORTUNITY TO PROJECT THEIR GOD GIVEN HATRED ON A BAND THAT DEALS OUT THAT EMOTION ON AN UNMERCIFULLY LARGE SCALE.CRASS BRING UNIVERSALLY GIVEN INSTITUTIONS DOWN TO LOW- ER THAN LOW LEVELS,AS THEY THEN WALLOW IN THE HYPOCRACY THAT WILL ALWAYS BE IN EVIDENCE WHEN SAY SOMETHING LIKE THE CURRENT BRITISH GOVERNMENT IS CAREFULLY INSPECTED.ANALOGOUSLY LIKEN THA- TCHERS REGIME TO A PILE OF FRESH DOG TURDS...CRASS ARE THAT LITTLE BOY WHO LOVE TO WATCH THE WHOLE STEAMING MESS SQUISH UP BETWWEEN THE TOES.THE BAND REFUSE TO TALK TO THE MAJOR WEEKLYS,PERHAPS FEAR- ING MISREPRESENTATION,AND THIS UN- DOUBTLY FORCES THE BIG HIGH BROWSERS TO SLAG THE BALLS OFF ABSOLUTELY EVERYTHING COMING OUT ON THEIR LABEL(POISON GIRLS,HONEY BANE, ZOUNDS)ON PURELY LONG TIME JOUR- NALISTIC FUNDAMENTALS LIKE THE YOUNG BROWN BEAKED CORRESPONDENT WHO MAY SLASH A RECORD TO BITS SIMPLY BECAUSE OF SOME OLD FART EDITORS WHIMS(IF YOU DON'T BELIEVE ME LOOK AT THE NEW MUSICAL EXPRESS) CRASS WILL TALK TO AND EVEN I BELIEVE DO THEIR OWN,FANZINE. MANY SUCH YOUTHFUL HARDCORE PUB- LICATIONS HAVE ARISEN OF LATE,AND I SEE THIS AS LESS OF A CALL TO ARMS THAN ANOTHER ATTEMPT AT SOME SORT OF STUPID UNREALISTIC ALTERNATIVE LIFE- STYLE...THE BAND ALL LIVE TOGETHER IN ONE HOUSE,FUCK THIS COMMUNAL SHIT I CANT STOMACH...BUT ALL PERSONAL BULL- SHIT ASIDE I BELIEVE THE BAND TO BE

ESSENTIALLY A VERY IMPORTANT AND EXCITING FORCE.I DO NOT SEE THINGS IN A SIMILAR LIGHT ON MANY OCCASSIONS BUT REVEL IN WATCHING THEM TRYING TO VENT THE HATRED THEY FEEL FOR RELIGION AND GOVERNMENT...THEY BECOME SO INCENSED AT TIMES THAT THEY BECOME ENTANGLED IN EFFORTS TO SPIT OUT A STRONG ENOUGH STRING OF OBSCENITIES,UNCEREMONIOUSLY LACED TOGETHER IN A HAPHAZARD FASHION THAT GIVES SWEARING A WHOLE NEW DIMEN- SION...GRANTED WHEN EVERY OTHER WORD

IS FUCK THINGS CAN LOSE THEIR THREAT BUT CRASS ARE SO LOUD AND ABRASIVE THIS MENACE NEVER DROPS FAR FROM THE SURFACE. ON THEIR FIRST LP(XX 45) WHATEVER,THEY REFERRED TO OUR VERY OWN "CHARLIES ANGELS" TV SHOW AS....."GREY PUKE...CELLULOID SHIT" COULDN'T HAVE SAID IT BETTER MYSELF.LIVE THEY ARE SUPPOSEDLY HORRIBLE,PROBABLY A DYNAMO OF ANARCHIST HEAD BANGING.PROBABLY WILD ENOUGH TO SEND THE MOST FERVENT U.S. CONCERTGOER YAPPING THROUGH THE CLUB DOOR WITH BOTH HANDS SHAKILY CLUTCHING THE FUCK SACK.WHAT THIS ATTEMPTED DISCOURSE BOILS DOWN TO IS THIS...I RESPECT THE FUCK OUT OF CRASS...I LOVE THEIR RECORDS... THEMSELVES NOT ANYMORE DEVOID OF INCON- SISTENCIES THAN THE SHIT THEY RAIL AGAINST. BUT I CAN'T HELP BUT SEE THEM AS A REFRESH- ING CHANGE TO THE SCENEWIDE BAND SELLOUT THAT SUCKS A GOOD ONE IN AND TURNS A BUCK. CRASS CAN'T CHANGE A FUCKING THING... BUT IT WILL BE GREAT WATCHING THEM KEEP TRYING...

TESCO

165

ATTEMPTING TO GET A POINT ACROSS

You certainly can't believe everything you see. Beneath
the guise of apparent benevolence, Surf City(now since
merged with Ivory Productions) is nothing more than two
opportunists soley out for captial gain. Their knowledge
of the music is minuscule at best. I'm tired of hearing
how good Eddie Puke is or how great the Whoremones are.
Two bands with no future and are just better off forgotten.
And Fanmail! Thank god they spared us the trouble of booing
them out of Club Doo Bee when they decided to split up.
The worst example of heavy-metal punk posing I've ever seen.
And can you believe that Surf City told Eddie Puke's band
to hold back so as to not upstage Fanmail?!

Furthermore, now that The Fix(Lansing's only savior for the
new music) have attracted a following, do these twits re-
consider booking them at Dooleys, having spitefully ignored
them the first time around. How petty to let a personality
conflict get in the way of what you should be doing. Get
called a jerk and an asshole and you fall apart. The truth
hurts, doesn't it? Well, all I can say is, you can take your
Brad Curtis persona and take the big flyin' fuck!--DS

WIPERS LP

·WIPERS-"Is This Real?"
Park Ave. Records

According to CREEM, this has been
referred to as 'counterfeit punk'.
And as we've learned by now, a
slag from this dinosaur of a rag
must mean there's something right
about The Wipers. For one, when
if ever, did these guys get off
thinking they knew shit about punk?
Moreover, they've been spending
the better part of the last decade
fellating the likes of Nugent, Seger,
Plant, etc. . . . so much so in fact,
that their brains have finally and
completely been replaced with the
gooey white stuff.
Be that as it may, this is one
dynamite album. With their crunching guitar sound, the Wipers take
you by surprise with their total
disregard for what's going on around
them. They make no attempt to
sound punk, refusing to buckle
under to what's chic or in vogue
at the time. These guys are operating on a different plane, and
nobody sounds quite like 'em.

From those first jagged riffs of
"Return Of The Rat", your first
reaction is to say--"Hold on there
pal, I heard this kind of stuff
five years ago", but is that really
true? cuz within that exact same
thought is--"Hey! this shit is good".
Over the past three years you've
been conditioned by the elitist
snobs of the nouveau muzak ranks
to rebel against this kind of music.
Our own rather phony urban sophistication has clouded our ability
to appreciate a band(the Wipers in
this case) for what they are. And
if you're blind to the fact that
these boys from Portland can rock,
then your mind has been numbed so
severely that you'll never be able
to recognize a good band when they
come along. The Wipers album is
one Of those rare gems that truly
possess wall shattering potential.
Just listen to "Return Of The Rat",
"Let's Go, Let's Go" or "Tragedy"
and watch the windows rattle and
the ceiling cave in. This is one
LP that positively demands to be
heard.--DS

NECROS TEEN PIN-UP

THE REVILLOS-"REV UP"
Snatzo Records
I haven't been sleeping well since
I knew this album was out,and yesterday I finally scored meself a
complete 13 track dose of good mood
music courtesy of Eugene Reynolds,
Fay Fife,Kid Krupa,Rocky Rythym,and
the quintessential backing vocalists
Babs and Cherie.Gene challenges all
comers to top his exquisite rake-do
quiff(oggle above photo)Even Bob Gordon has to throw in the towel.

Alright now let's get down to
business-people you've gotta wise up
that you owe these Scottish loons a
living.Tell me you don't ever need a
good shot of 1960 immaturity in your
mundane1980 existence.Christ I'm not
gonna be able to start a day for the
next year without a tracking of this
golden platter.It's all here...from
the bouncin' ropa-bop of the soon to
be pop classic"ROCK-A-BOOM",to the
romantimush balladeering of Fay as
she coos oh so crystal clear on "ON
THE BEACH" Tell me why we're the only

actual unretouched photo

magazine to spout anything positive
concerning these beautiful image?
You say your hard-core punk mates'll
laugh you out of the basement if you
were to bring this one in?Or could it
be your girl might catch you wankin' at
Ms.Fife's photo.Yes girls I'm talkin'
to you to,you know you'd be reachin'
for that device the second Gene opened
his mouth on the title track "REV-UP"
OK I guessed I've sussed it out,you
are all scared to cut loose in this age
of supposed uncertainty.Is that it?

If being a nerd,day-glo fuckup,campy
low budget sci-fi movie star is what
you've ever longed to be then this Lp
is for you.It's very derivitive yes...
but who cares good tunes needn't be
stacked against unessarily tough historical cross checking.What I'm trying
to say is fuck your labels and the
mind stilting biases and get "REV-UP"
It won't change your life but It'll make
it a helluva lot more fun!
                                    MR.VEE

R+R BANKROBBER!

So punk doesn't move you--funk wears you out and avant-garde is gauche--don't despair, it's back to basics ACID ROCK!!-- I've finally decided that most music I love is more comfortably defined by me as such, than as some permutation of punk. I speak of the gloom bands and psychedelic punk, the Joy Divisions, the Pere Ubus, the Siouxsies, even some of the essentially realist bands like Essential Logic--Punk is my appellation for angry and satirically intense music and acid rock shall henceforth apply to spacey or gloomy or psychedelic music-- thus most groups could fall under any one of these headings or encompass all three, but at the very least Acid Rock is a term that should certainly carry over to the modern period--certainly some of the mod bands and affiliates bear less resemblance to their namesake predecessors than do the gloom bands of today to their forefathers like Hendrix and The Doors--shit! Like I was telling Bobby VeeVee--we even have our own Moody Blues in 'The Human League', surely no one can deny the similarities between say, the "Travelogue" album and the old classic "On The Threshold Of A dream".

Another refreshing revival that I intend to be on top of is the blues/rock one-- know this style never went away--I mean oghat hasn't missed a year for putting out an album in a long while(one of the first concerts I attended included the original Savoy Brown with three soon-to- be Hatters and Kim Simmons--and even Chris Youlden, one of the best ever white blues singers--who remembers "Train To Nowhere"?) Anyhow I've read about the Fabulous Thunder- birds who without the big promotion of bands like the Inmates are returning us to a time where B.B. King licks are stan- dards in a guitar repertoire--Anyhow I'm all for a punk acid jazz blues experimental fusion--couldn't be any more difficult to realize than the fusion bomb the sci- entists are working on.
Get with it rockers of all stripes, creeds, and perversions.

LIVE FROM LIMBO LIC

NO DIRECT Relationship

Two neatest psychedelic lyrics on recent songs I'm in love with; from Siouxsie's "Christine"--'Now she's in purple, now she's a turtle--disintegrating. . .' and from The Psychedelic Furs' "Flowers"- 'We cut his eyes with razor blades and out came white shining light'. Another favorite with enough anger to pass for punk and enough innuendo to be acid rock is the great song on the new Magazine album, "Philadelphia" with my favorite line being: 'I coud've been Raskolnikov, but Mother Nature ripped me off'(Raskolnikov, for you who don't know, is the protagonist in Doestoevski's "Crime and Punishment"--the original anti-hero)
Well all you little freakies and punkies, have a good Halloween--this is a gratui- tous goodbye from the rock 'n' roll bank robber--soon to rejoin the ranks of the living in "the free world" Amerika, wright or wrong! Plus Ill be back next ish if the ED. don't ax me--I've heard he tortures suspected freaks by making them listen to Grateful Dead's "Dark Star" nonstop for 24 hours. Even I'm not that freaky!

GOES AT THE TOP OF COLUMN #2 OF THE NECROS INTERVIEW-Sorry

OOPS I FUGGED UP THIS ONE

TV:Any opinions of Detroit bands?
B:Don't know really any good ones... the best ones are probably in garages,THE LIPS ARE BACK are from Battle Creek,they are far better than any Detroit bands like 27 or COLDCOCK...
T:there are no good ones from Detroit or Ann Arbor-The THWARTED are memorable only because they suck so bad..THE FIX sound really hardcore etc.,real nice guys too. you forgot to ask me about the bands from that grate suburb of Detroit,Windsor Ont.They have one good band THE SPYS(real original name huh?) and shitass jerkoff bands like ALTERNATIVE,DRY HEAVES,SID(neat name) and one band I havent heard THE HARDTOPS...
A:no...
TV:your demos are tits,how would you describe your sound?
B:fast,loud,angry,unpracticed,thouroughly adolescent, fuck I dán't vanna judge...
A:this is weird because our studio tape isn't us at all..it isn't really slick but the vocals are very clear,wer'e used to practicing on a ten watt Realistic PA,live we just try to keep it fast and not really stop between songs for very long, basically just blast thru the set as quick as possible,,,
A:it was done quickly and inexpensively,the engineer was more used to heavy metal...
TV:What do you hate?
A:I hat tomato soup made with water instead of milk, Ihate girls who wear clothes,I hate diet Pepsi...

Bout THATS SPORTS!!ED.

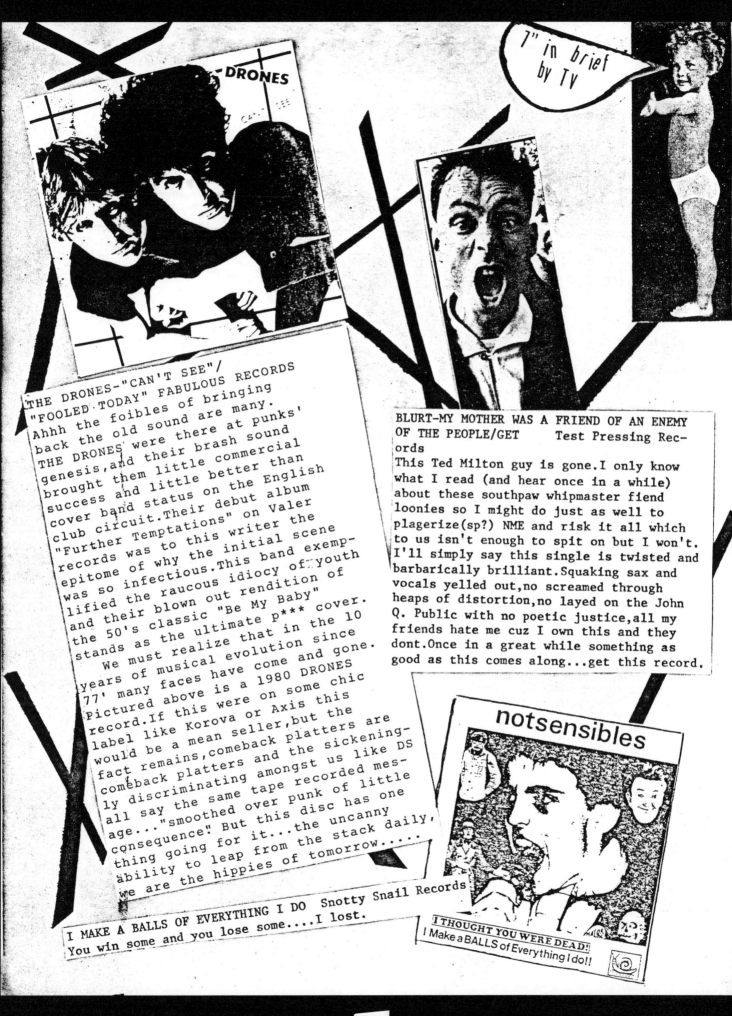

DRONES

7" in brief by TV

THE DRONES-"CAN'T SEE"/
"FOOLED TODAY" FABULOUS RECORDS
Ahhh the foibles of bringing
back the old sound are many.
THE DRONES were there at punks'
genesis,and their brash sound
brought them little commercial
success and little better than
cover band status on the English
club circuit.Their debut album
"Further Temptations" on Valer
records was to this writer the
epitome of why the initial scene
was so infectious.This band exemplified the raucous idiocy of youth
and their blown out rendition of
the 50's classic "Be My Baby"
stands as the ultimate p*** cover.
       We must realize that in the 10
years of musical evolution since
77' many faces have come and gone.
Pictured above is a 1980 DRONES
record.If this were on some chic
label like Korova or Axis this
would be a mean seller,but the
fact remains,comeback platters are
comeback platters and the sickeningly discriminating amongst us like DS
all say the same tape recorded mesage..."smoothed over punk of little
consequence". But this disc has one
thing going for it...the uncanny
ability to leap from the stack daily,
we are the hippies of tomorrow.....

BLURT-MY MOTHER WAS A FRIEND OF AN ENEMY
OF THE PEOPLE/GET   Test Pressing Records
This Ted Milton guy is gone.I only know
what I read (and hear once in a while)
about these southpaw whipmaster fiend
loonies so I might do just as well to
plagerize(sp?) NME and risk it all which
to us isn't enough to spit on but I won't.
I'll simply say this single is twisted and
barbarically brilliant.Squaking sax and
vocals yelled out,no screamed through
heaps of distortion,no layed on the John
Q. Public with no poetic justice,all my
friends hate me cuz I own this and they
dont.Once in a great while something as
good as this comes along...get this record.

notsensibles

I MAKE A BALLS OF EVERYTHING I DO Snotty Snail Records
You win some and you lose some....I lost.

I THOUGHT YOU WERE DEAD!
I Make a BALLS of Everything I do!!

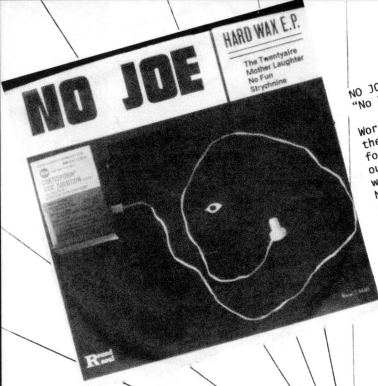

HARD WAX E.P.

The Twentyaire
Mother Laughter
No Fun
Strychnine

NO JOE—"The Twentyaire"/Mother Laughter/
"No Fun"/Strychnine" Round Raoul Records

Word has it that these guys have broken up, but
they left some weird stuff behind them in the
form of this EP. The music here somehow sounds
out of step, although I'm not sure whether it's forward or backward.

"No Fun" has some acid laden bygone era guitar
noodling that's neither offensive nor head turning.
The whole thing is out of sync with Mark Hoback
off in his own little world playing whatever comes
into his head. Not giving a shit how it compares
with anything else. The EP winds up with a con-
vincing rendition of The Sonics' "Strychnine."
This is definitely not for everybody!   --DS

URINALS—"Sex"/"Go Away Girl" Happy Squid Records.
One of my current faves. Recording is nothing sort of
horrendous, but the music blasts it's way thru the
gravelly mix anyway. These guys are now one of LA's
best. The music literally explodes off the turntable.
"Go Away Girl" especially with a disarming little intro, sure
the bass and guitar come crashing in from all sides,
to pull the plaster off the walls in no time at all. Everything
may be recorded all wrong but who the fuck cares?—DS

THE URGE- "Bit By Bit"/ "Baby Talk"
Adolescent Records
Why I like this is anybody's guess. "Bit By Bit" moves me
in a funny way. The music is ordinarily minimal, with it's
strength derived from the vocals of Mary & Julie Lawler.
This is the case here with the separate parts by themselves,
would never hold up but together they've got something
working, if only I knew what it was. Maybe I'm a sucker
for the soft touch. A wispy little yarn of romantic cynicism
and old DS turns to jelly! What will happen next?--DS

more fab shit

PHEW--(I still can't read Japanese) Pass Records

Another Japanese product has come our way and this one's a doozy. A girl sings and some guy plays the instruments. Electronic bleeps, drones, and anything else you can imagine. SUICIDE comes to mind; however the music of Phew is much less dense and lacks the emotional intensity of Big Al Vega. Cold and distant, Phew is much more mechanical, almost as if the girl's voice were programmed through IBM's latest. It is only toward the very end of the B-side do we detect some semblence of feeling; although it appears to be remorse, like watching Rodan flying off to the horizon-- never to be seen from again. I'm choked up.--DS

CONTROLLERS-"Slow Boy"/"Do The Uganda"/"Suburban Suicide" Siamese Records

A little old, but it wasn't until just now that I finally got my hands on a copy. For me, this represents their best work(a shame they broke up). Buzzsaw guitar and great drumming from Karla combine for a blistering A-side that singes the earlobes. Fast and raw, is there any other way? "Suburban Suicide" brings the tempo down a notch to a slow grind. Pulsatingly suggestive. It works. This was when Kid Spike really knew how to wring that guitar.--DS

THE EMBARRASSMENT-"Patio Set"/ "Sex Drive" Big Time Records

Obscure little item from Kansas. Mildly interesting sound they've put together. Not your basic thudda-thudda splosh shit typical of many fledgling outfits playing nowadays. Dominat guitar and drums overshadow everything else, especially on "Sex Drive". Beneath a veneer of unspectacular music lies a kernel of promise. A band that could develop into something better than what we got here.--DS

BAD BRAINS-"Pay To Cum"/"Stay Close To Me" Bad Brain Records

Wow! What a devastating debut. These four guys from DC are hot! Discharge and Middle Class will have to move over and make room for the new kings of the guitar-string melting barrage of manic aggression. "Pay To Cum" ranks as one of the tightest, most straight ahead blasts of explosive intensity I have ever heard. A searing ballistic that detonates right in yer face. A metallic onslaught that would rip to shreds our local Detroit bands. . . a horrible sight if they ever occupied the same stage. From "Pay To Cum" alone, the Bad Brains are one of the best. . . on any shore. An absolute must!--DS

SPLODGENESSABOUNDS-"Simon Templer"/ "Michael Booth's Talking Bum"/"Two Pints of Lager & A Packet of Crisps Please" Deram Records

About two months ago this was the big hype in England. A new zany sound that was climbing the charts. The combination of Madness shenanigans and Revillos absurdity makes for a perfect slice of vinyl lunacy. Its only drawback is that this kind of merry madcap music has little or no staying power. You play it ten times(if that) and dispose of it. You don't give a fuck whether they ever put out another record. Entertaining, but with an extremely short life expectancy.--DS

SHAM 69-"Unite And Win"/"I'm A Man" Polydor Records

Call me a fool, a fanatic, or anything that comes to mind, but with other records just beckoning to be purchased, I blindly reach for Sham's latest. Why? Well, I guess no matter how far they tumble from the graces of practically everyone I still have this crazy idea that they'll eventually pull out of this slump they've been in for so long now. Let's face it, these guys have secured a permanent place in my collection and I will probably continue to buy their stuff til I drop dead or vice versa. Now my interest in this latest release is marginal, and they're getting the benefit of the doubt. Anybody else would have promptly given this the quick fling out the window. "I'm A Man", written and sung by Parsons, has absolutely no redeeming value whatsoever. How much longer will I remain loyal to the troops? Who knows, but time is running out.--DS

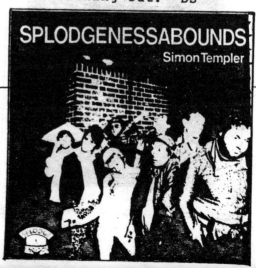

SLEEPERS-"Mirror"/"Theory"
Trans-Time Records

Nothing like their EP, which
actually should be no surprise
since Ricky Williams and Michael
Belfer are all that's left from
the '78 band. Right from the
very beginning there appears to
be a merging of ideas between
these guys and Tuxedomoon. There
are amazing similarities between
this single and "What Use"(the
latter's latest release). Now
that's good or bad depending on
how you look at it. Personally,
I liked the old sound better.
The music now has a real smooth
and cool aspect to it. An ephemeral murkiness as the backdrop
for Ricky's vocals, the record's
strongpoint. On top of a sparse
beat, the guitar now shares the
limelight with a synthesizer
and an occasional sax blurt.
Not the best thing I've heard,
but I still find time to play
it.--DS

THE CHUMPS-"Air Conditioner"/
"7-11"/"Go Go God" Round Raoul
Records

Comparisons to The Contortions
will be unavoidable, but such
judgements I see as premature.
I welcome this band's sense of
humor, sorely lacking in Mr.
Chance's brand of nouveau cacophony. Nor must we put up with
his arrogantly pretentious stance.
The Chumps, as I believe is true
with other DC bands, create a
distinctively unique sound without looking around to see what's
the latest fad going down.
Rather, they're quite content
to play what they want while
keeping their minds off the profit motive. "Air Conditioner"
begins deceptively like it were
some kind of schlocky folk-rock
jam session, but don't jump up
to yank it off the turntable just
yet, cuz this one develops quite
nicely. They've got something
here and they deserve your attention.--DS

LILIPUT-"Split"/"Die Matrosen"
Rough Trade

A dream come true. My favorite
fräuleins(Kleenex) reemerge with
their best yet. The singer's
been replaced and they've added
a sax player to compliment
their distinctively direct approach. Repetition is still
the name of the game for these
girls, and nobody does it better. The B-side employs a
generous helping of what's become that typical nutty-dread
sax sound. They're back and I
hope it stays that way.--DS

LITTLE ONES

"Pay To Cum" BAD BRAINS

"Get" BLURT

"Six And Change" THE PAGANS

"Go Away Girl" URINALS

"Independence Day" COMSAT ANGELS

"Terror Couple Kill Colonel" BAUHAUS

"Cold Beat" THE SOUND

"Bobby Come Back To Me" THE REVILLOS

"Final Achievement" IN CAMERA

"Warm Girls" GIRLS AT OUR BEST

"Blow Me Baby" NECROS

NEGATIVE TREND EP

"City On Ice" THE HATES

"Black And White" THE THE

"Man Of Two Worlds" IDLE HANDS

"Baby You're So Repulsive" CRIME

"Shack Up" A CERTAIN RATIO

"Incident" MODERN ENGLISH

"I Want Something New" 1/2 JAPANESE

"One Decree" SKIDS

"Girl" SUICIDE

"Slow Murder" MATERIAL

NO PUSSY ASS SHIT ON THIS CHART!

DITTO

BIG ONES

"Is This Real?" WIPERS

"No Questions Asked" FLESH EATERS

"Crocodiles" ECHO and THE BUNNYMEN

"Do Animals Believe In God?" PINK MILITARY

"Stations Of The Crass" CRASS

"Closer" JOY DIVISION

"Rev Up" THE REVILLOS

"Los Angeles" X

"Voice Of America" CABARET VOLTAIRE

"Days In Europa" SKIDS

"Martin Rev-Alan Vega" SUICIDE

DOME LP

"Further Temptations" THE DRONES

176

CRAMPS

THE CRAMPS-BOOKIES CLUB
(sometime in the blur of summer shit
I can't remember.Everybody else writes
about these sleazbos so we may as well
jump in there and do our frothing best
at it.Bookies Club used to be a drag
bar and there's still a couple left who
frequent the place now that it's made the
big conversion to the safety of a new
wave format.Everybody on the college
campuses sez "Oh I've been there,tee hee"
and that about sums up the crowd,3rd rate
poser pussys,4th rate men with fashionably
spikey haircuts(step aside I'm gonna fart)
and even out and out,no-bones-about-it
preppies with their boat shoes and lizard
shirts.They all giggle at the globby boy
and girl outadates and the rest of us
wonder what the fuck wer'e doing in the
worst place in the motor city for murders
and such(no lie recent stats put the
Woodward and 6 mile spot dead last)(sorry
that was poor)oh gawd...well(just a little
black humor) whoops fuck it...Right The
Cramps live is what I'm supposed to write
about...Lux told Corey that he was going
to cancel out Detroit(this was in N.Y.)
because the only people who frequented
bookies were fags,well no wonder if I was
of that bent and I new I was going to see
some swinging hoagie ala Interior gone
crazed exhibitionist,all for one low admission price I'd check it outThere's a
new girl in the band,real doggy lookin'-
shes got a great Gibson Explorer and her
and Ivy rocked the old barn do wn.Nick
knox looks like he'd rather have been somewhere else,not a drummer extrordinaire but
he gets the job done.Put it all in perspective..
the Cramps are americans who play an Americam
art form eg.rockabilly and they do it right,
real crude and decadent...had public morality
hangups been less in evidence in the 50's,
then cats like Perkins and Burnette would
have hung their cranks out too.....
TV

Urine Conductor

Patent No. 1,510,973

or as it is more popularly known

The Stand-Up Pee-Pee Thing For Woman

Fig. 1

T. BEHAN

URINE CONDUCTOR

Filed Aug. 6, 1923

Oct. 7, 1924.
1,510,973
2 Sheets—Sheet 1

Fig. 2

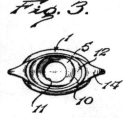

Fig. 3

Inventor

T. Behan

Jello on the toi toi under nice offset logo and we're really lookipng pro, baby, on this first-anniversary issue. Ad for Necros "Sex Drive" on page uno heralding its imminent arrival "By Xmas 1980." Coverage of the legendary Club DooBee... This ish is veritably crawling with 7" reviews, many seminal, a few semen-al, and as usual we sort 'em, extort 'em, and abort 'em with aplomb and a bomb. Great issue...but saying that is just a tad self-agrandizin', now ain't it?

TOUCH AND GO

NO. 10   75 ¢

The Gas Receptor
or as it is more popularly known
The Fart Tank

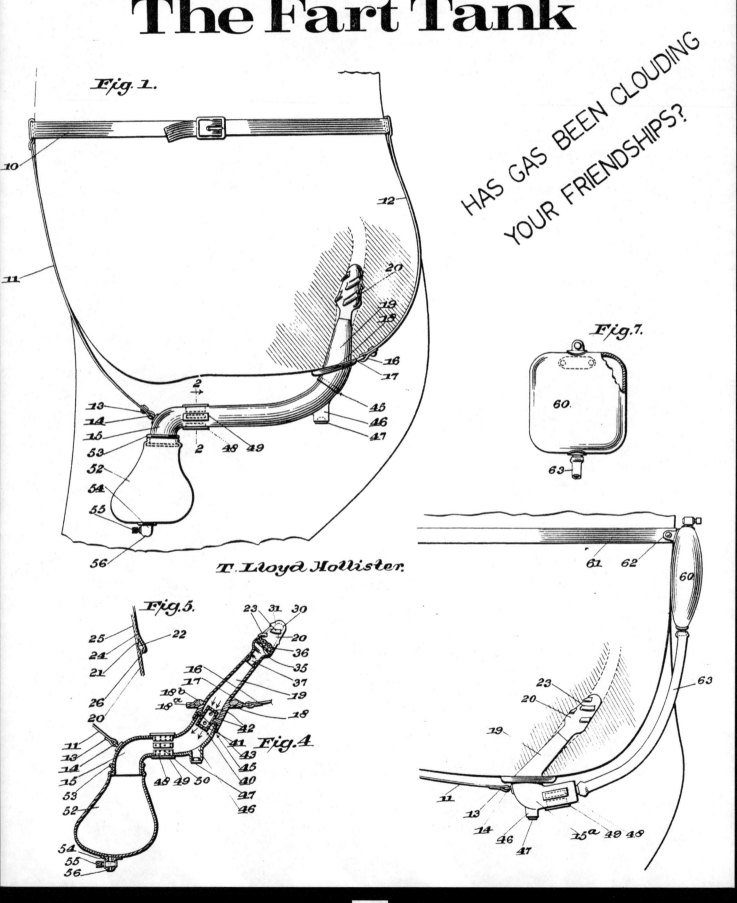

HAS GAS BEEN CLOUDING YOUR FRIENDSHIPS?

T. Lloyd Hollister.

DEBUt SiNGLE
OUt By Xmas featuring
"POLICE BRutalitY / SEX CRIME"

A tOUCh & GO Records RELEaSE

NECROS

Ten issues in a year..not bad..if we had't gotten so lethargic over the summer we might be able to call ourselves a monthly...Danke for the dinero for subs that's been just inundating us (well) keep those cards and the coin coming...You see folks regularity is much easier in Meechigan when summertime passes, the cold ass becomes forcibly nestled in front of the old selectric... and our minds are forcibly turned away from the inevitable fraternization of nubilian succulence that accompanies the mugginess... not to mention the overboard ingestion of unhealthy lubricants that just turn creative minds into walking cantelopes...belatedness is so endearing...From now on watch for more local coverage (their aint much comin down but as it develops we'll keep you informed) SLASH is back with a whopping big 100 page issue...guess they will be quarterly...so keep in touch' folksies... TV

"FELLATE ME"

"SUBS. $3.00 10.00 YEARLY"

"NICE BUDS BAMBI"

Club DooBee

THE NOZONES

So finally. . . a club we can relax in and never again be subjected to stud-cunt dives featuring bar band crud. Unfortunately most of the so called new music going down at Club Doo Bee isn't much---a bright spot every now and then and things don't look quite so grim locally. Take Saturday night for instance, me and my mates acting like the scum we are, but do we get the boot? No way, this place is owned by a great old(watch who you're calling old--ED) guy who doesn't give a fuck what you do as long as the serious mega bucks are rolling his way. The fact that the fuzz respond to more calls there than any bar in the greater Lansing area only means they get their share of knife-toting reds in that neighborhood--I should know, I lived back there for a year and it ain't good. . As the visible scum-sector multiplies and a tangible scene becomes evident, we'll attempt coverage in a relatively unbiased (we'll try, honest--ED) fashion. Dave and I just realize that the original intent of the 'Fanzine' was regional coverage of bands that are overlooked by larger national publications. Hats off to OCEAN SPRAY productions for bringing in out of town and outstate acts cuz let's face it, there ain't much homegrown talent around here. So, despite what we said about them last ish, they are bringing some decent acts up here (and we don't ever have to go to fuckin' Drooleys again!). So come down to the shitty little shack at Lake Lansing and Marsh and watch me hump the pool table while somebody's shootin'(cum again?)

THE LIPS ARE BACK/THE ITCH
Club DooBee

Due to excessive suds intake at my abode we missed the first band--responses ran from shrugs to 'they were real out of tune'. Time for another pitcher of Blartz--only 2.50, let's dispense with the juice glasses and break our dentures on the heavy glassware. In the back

The Lips Are Back are back, not overly loud, thank god. I'm already waiting for one of those real small ones to hit the market that fit right into your ear. Some of their stuff I'd heard before--the set was tight & fast-- not quite as raw as I've seen 'em, but in comparison to some of the shit I've been subjected to lately, it was a heavenly evening.TV

ATTITUDES/THE DELLRODS
Club DooBee

The Dellrods can't play their instruments for shit and they all look like extras from the movie "Son of Flubber"--hats and ties and ripped t-shirts and 'hey girls, we're into new wave, let's mate'. I was feeling nauseous that night and these rubber noggins made me wanna go outside so I could watch my ralph leech into the pock-marked gravel parking lot. Their singer wears eye make-up, A real homo-sapien. Truly turds on legs.

The Attitudes are good--they could be great if the 2 guitarists and the bass player quit so the drummer could really display his talents minus the teeny-base half baked songwriting that complicates what is at times a nice raw sound. But guys, this is 1980 and leave guitar

ATTITUDES

184

HEY BRAD! THIS ONE'S FOR YOU.

STEP UP BRAD, YOU'RE NEXT

Time once again for the unmercifully biased editors of T&G to grab
Mr. Curtis by the ears and drag him and his absurdly reactionary
ideas through the mud. We simply cannot let him sit back and think
that he's in the clear and out of harm's way. He enjoyed a brief
reprieve when we ignored him in ish #9, but the honeymoon's over--
the barbs have been honed and what better time than right now to
pick up where we left off in our tasteless barrage of insults at our
favorite radio personality. If we keep this up, maybe 'ol Bradley
will face up to the grim fact that he's one of the biggest jerks in
town, although we're not holding our breath. Now Brad, when you were
quoted(so profoundly) in The State News, did you honestly believe
what you were saying? I believe the exact words were: 'there really
isn't such a thing as new wave music anymore.' That's interesting
Brad, did you think of that all by yourself, or were you just mouthing
some Abrams' newsletter? You don't know one godamn thing about music,
just that tiniest of parts which you so uncleverly use to hype the
living shit out of one Brad Curtis, a poor excuse for a DJ and one

who's constantly trying to meet his own selfish needs. You make me
sick. Have you got any selfrespect left after the way you used the
station to inflate that ridiculously inane image of yours? Of course
not. Quote number two: 'new wave music has become part of the regular
music scene, it's not big anymore'. Come, come now Brad, that's one
of the dumbest things I've ever heard. Surely you could have come
up with a better line than that feeble comment. How you can be so
stupid and still live is a medical wonder. If what you say is true,
then how come we're still waiting to hear Joy Division, Gang Of Four,
The Cure, Magazine, Wire, or even the Undertones(just to name a few
of the more popular ones) over the, as you call it, 'regular music'
airwaves? You want to know? I'll tell ya why. Cuz you got shit for
brains from having that bulbous bean of yours up where it's dark and
smelly, and there's no getting rid of that ring around the collar.
Brad, you're scum and a disgrace to mankind.--DS

noodling to the HM heroes and spare me the poitical bullshit. Get this--they sing some tripe about some girl and the drummer flatly declares following the tune 'and she ain't gonna fuck with me anymore'--obviously he has been true to his statements unless drumming gives one bigger blisters on the right hand. And I loaded the bikini briefs when the rhythm guitarist launched into a pro American political outburst with statements like 'this is your fuckin' country and we've been taken advantage of'. Is that not beyond laughability? Some 18 year old cunt with a post glam shag is laying some patriotic(more like idiotic--ED) dogma on us--they can shove us around all they want fuck lips- you're still alive, aren't you? Shit you'll be the first to die(talk about TV birdsong--ED). The bass player sounds like he used to be in the 1910 Fruit Gum Co.--perhaps a revival is in order cuz being limp wristed is only in vogue at Trammps--be- sides, your dad's pinstripe suit looks better at The Rotary Club's chicken barbcue. Get with it you guys--the only way you'll ever be anything is to shake people up--not through between song monologues about how cool America is--you've got the in- tensity--your cho rouses are evi- dence of that. Write some new songs as good as "Identity Crisis" get some new duds and call me in a month. TV

THE FIX/THE DELLRODS/THE NOZONES
Dooleys

The nebulous Bill Reed(sp?) Memorial gig. The crowd is sparse, made up of lost souls, bored and looking for something. Nozones come on first with a passable version of "Submission". Not bad I say. Probably haven't been together too long. Manage to get some fools out on the dance floor, not me, they go from ok, to bad, to worse. A horrible cover of "Standards" only to be surpassed by an em- barrassing rendition of "Clash City Rockers". Their originals sink them to new depths. They expose the band for what they are--heavy-metal-fuck-band-johnny- come-lately-boring-crap. Next, the Dellrods. They don't take their music seriously, so I won't take them seriously. They think they're real cute and funny, they stink. Finally, we get to hear The Fix. Crowd has dwindled, it's been a long nite. Band seems to be in top form. Much improved over the DooBee gig back in Sept. Necros were great, I might add. Typical Fix set, lightening fast with no let-up. One mad dash before somebody pulls the plug on them. Good show. However, they have to can their glam boy image. An illusion that succeeds in putting up a barrier between the band and their audience. They look silly. Mike and Jeff have the right idea. This ain't no fashion show. If the music can't speak for itself, then quit while you'll still ahead. It's not real, and it's not you, so is it necessary to put up a front? That, I don't understand. Call me an ass- hole, but I know I'm right.
--DS

THE LIPS ARE BACK

THE DELLRODS

NEW WAVE ON LAKE LANSING

SINGLES

THE SOUND-"COLD BEAT"/Physical
World EP Torch Records
Unorigial but superinfectious on
side one.Deliberate and dumpy on
the flip which features the only
thing I hate more than the harmonica =slide guitar.But "Cold
Beat" is unexplicably a catchy
top caliber rock song.Let's forget about the Gang Of 4 soundalike on the mike.Each week begins
with short term faves but this
one has held on for two months
running.A mover of magnifico-
proportions.

PLASMATICS-"Monkey Suit"/"Squirm"
Stiff Records
While we're on the subject of
money grubbers let's talk about
the new single by this band.No
let's not.

MODERN ENGLISH-"Swans On Glass"/
Incident"   4·AD Records
All of a sudden three great releases on the AD label.With bands
like THE THE,IN CAMERA,and MOD-
ERN ENGLISH all releasing this
type of product simultaneously,
I should touch on all three but..
A side exhibits a sound full of
drum and bass that so many of the
English bands rely upon...that
leaves the guitar to wallow in
the vacancy created,again no mid-
range(audiophiles die,ED.) I
know there's something else that's
superb about this independant sounding quartet,and when I find out
what it is I won't tell you.A-

XS DISCHARGE-"LIFE'S A
WANK EP..."ACROSS THE
BORDER"/"CONFESSIONS"/
"FRUSTRATION"/"HASSLES"
Groucho Marxist Record
Co-op
If life's a wank then
this is undemocratic
flagellation.Of course
I'm still stinging at
the fact that I was co-
erced into buying this
by a serious looking
bag and an insincere
plug from one of my not
so favorite record emp-
oriums.A hopeless guise
of something capable of
threat ends up laughably
dismissable after 3 bars.
Strictly three year vac-
uum.How to sell it,fuck
the public's desires,
what they want isn't
what they'll get.Medio-
craty like this scratches
noones itch.Give me your
daddy's gun.

Really Red-"Modern Needs"
It's like acting,law school, and
pleasing good ol' ma...why even
bother when success is but a distant dream.Independent singles are
great but they manage to give rise
to more cadaverous ego bloats
daily.A big star in a crowded bar...
in Houston...."I'm the singer in
this puck rok band you succulent
little waif,the meaning of life is
between my legs,so look for it...
I've got modern needs and my poop
don't stink!"   Contrivance never
sounded so bad,

T.V.

Another
one
bites
the
wang

the catholics

THE CATHOLICS-"TROPICAL RUSSIANS"/
"ECHO ECHO"
This is a French band supposedly
which explains why it's such a poor
single,there's nothing lower than a
French person we all know that.This
single furthers my belief that the
immortal METAL URBAIN remains by far
the frogs best discharge to date.
These chumps make Plastic Bertrand
sound absolutely dynamic.I'd love to
hear them at confession.Sissies.

CLASSIX NOUVEAUX-"THE ROBOTS DANCE"
NEOquasipsuedo futurists with bou-
ffant quiffs,and a chrome dome deep
throated man on the mike.This will be
an instant turn off for those with an
aversion to this brand of retrospective,
and projected imagery in tandem.Fortun-
ately the synthesizer overkill I was
expecting never takes place(of course
I do go for that indulgence at times in
the proper context)"The Robots Dance"
creates a mood ala mechanized man but
a pleasurable guitar dominates the upper
extremities as the bass and vocalsforce
this single into motion...this strategic
interplay is this singles strongpoint,and
with a longterm deal like the one just
signed with Liberty records,the band has
a definate future.The B side is too close
to something the BERLIN BLONDES would
have done had EMI given them another
chance which they thankfully did not.

RETRO-"PICTURE PLANE"/"U-BOAT"
White Light Records
Very simply the best thing to come
out of Detroit yet.I realize this is
not much of a decree,we've made no
bones about the outright shittiness
of most of the releases from that
Urban bunghole...But this is a pop
gem.Quite distinct sounding,for a
band whose stage show is as forget-
able is this ones' is.Both sides differ
in approach but both have an accessibility that gives RETRO a bigger shot
at stardom than the rest of the Motor
Citys' scumrok Iggy and Wayne Kramer
clones who slog it out at one dive after
another hoping for the big industry
dick-suck...God I'm not gonna beat around
it any longer this is an innovative,
interesting....a fuckava good debut...
they'll be glad they waited...simplicity
was never so complicated it had seemed
to me for the longest time...Detroits'
musicians never had a rudimentary feel
for the music in terms of it's basic
components....RETRO does.I strongly
urge you to check this one out...

classix nouveaux
....the robots dance

THE COWBOYS

TKA says if this doesn't sell there's
gonna be trouble. All I can say is,
I hope he's prepared, cuz what we
got here is a rather ordinary single
of little consequence. "Teenage Life"
is alright the first couple of times,
but you've heard it all before. The
same tired themes, the same thud-punk
thrashing one can hear almost any-
where(yes, you might even hear it in
Lansing). "Supermarket" sounds like
a drunk band doing a lousy imitation
of the Mumps. . .worthless. If the
Cowboys are professed to be the kings
of Ohio, this here single sure fooled
me.--DS

CINECYDE--"Tough Girls"/"You're
Dragging Me Down" Tremor Records

Well, it's about time we got some
new vinyl for this god forsaken
town. The most prolific of the Detroit bands, Cinecyde has always
seemed to promise more than they
deliver. "Tough Girls" has a nice
intro, but fails to sustain itself
when everything becomes a bit pedestrian. The legacy of Ron Asheton
seems to corrupt practically every
ax man in this city and that hurts.
I've always thought that these guys
could become Detroit's hottest act,
but after four singles and not a
great deal to show for it, maybe
I'm just wasting my time,--DS

THE SOUND--"Heyday"/"Brute Force"
Korova Records

This band is coming on strong. Although not quite as metallically
crunching as "Cold Beat", this easily
shoots down most of the competition.
One of the few bands to breath fire
back into the much maligned guitar
solo. Not that I'm hung-up on this
oft abused technique, but these guys
do it right. . .for once. B-side
seems to show a subtle similarity
to the Bunnymen, which they should
try to avoid. They have everything
they need without having to ape the
bigshots. Can't wait to hear their
album.--DS

THE IMPORTS   Cirkle Records

At long last, Chicago finally has
a band worthy of being reviewed in
this snobbish rag. No song titles
on this one, just side one and side
two, neat huh? Heavy on the PiL
repetition with both sides going on
for five minutes each. This music
is thoroughly mesmerizing, puts
you in a hypnotic trance in no trouble at all. The singer leaves a
little to be desired, too flat and
dry. But the interplay between the
guitarist and bass player works so
well, it would make me sound good.
Definitely a band to keep an eye on.
File next to Raymilland and Material.
--DS

TOXIC REASONS--"War Hero"/"Somebody
Help Me" Banit Records

Another one from Ohio, this time it's
Dayton. If I didn't know, I would've
sworn they were British. Heavy on
the Steve Jones guitar sound which
isn't meant as a criticism. These
guys are good. Their sound has a
crisp, jagged edge to it and the
singer seems like he's just itching
to spit some fire in the face of
anyone who should look at him cross-
eyed. Recorded remarkably well compared to most of the records from
around here. "Somebody Help Me" is
one of the best things to come out
of this state since the last Pagans'
record. No shit.--DS

U.K. DECAY--"For My Country"/"Unwind"
Fresh Records

This is their second, I guess. I
liked their other one alright. "For
My Country" is ok, nothing special.
Pleasant and listenable, but very
ordinary. Guitarist sounds like he
grew up listening to The Scream, and
by no means is that a detriment to
the band. On the contrary, he's probably the group's strongest asset.
"Unwind" is a lot better. Manages
to generate plenty of tension and
hold it throughout without showing
signs of stress. An obscure band
content on staying that way.--DS

SCREAMING URGE--"Homework"/"Runaway"
New Age Records

From Columbus, and they'll be playing
Club DooBee. Things seem to be improving in this area, yes siree.
Their sound is eclectic, at best.
Can't say I've heard anything quite
like it, although it seems deeply
rooted in our past, just don't ask
me to pin that down. Personally,
their sound is a little too benign
for my tastes. . . I need to be raked
across the face every once in awhile
to maintain my perspective. They deserve a second look, though. They
even have an album out, can't accuse
them of being lazy.--DS

VAST MAJORITY--"I Wanna Be A Number"
"God's Groin"/"Throwdown" Wild Dog
Records

The performance is sloppy, they
play out of tune, but there's an
endearing quality to this record
that puts it above some of the
other shit you've read in this rag.
It's the classic example of garage
band grunge you'll ever hear. It
reminds us that we can't get too
caught up in a lot of dials and
a snazzy production. It would be
too easy to simply slag this band
and leave it at that. They're
trying to do something, and for
the most part it works.--DS

BOYS BOYS--"Monkey Monkey"/"Control
Tower" Pass Records

Pass(if you don't know) has released
some of Japan's best, ie. Friction,
and now we got one by four gurls who
give it their best shot. Unfortunately, this falls a little short
of the mark. It's nestled down
somewhere in that Raincoats/Mo-
dettes groove, which isn't exactly
my cup of tea at the moment. The
b-side seems to echo the aging
grandmother, Patti Smith, and that
won't work no matter what language
you use(this is in Japanese, by the
way). These girls can play, they
just have to work out their songwriting weaknesses.--DS

DRED SCOTT--"I Believe You All"/
"Honest Boy"/"What A World"/"Rocker"
Red Spot Records

These guys got problems right off
the bat. What's it gonna be fellas,
hardcore braindamage music or poppy
punk with a heavy dose of saccharine?
The singer sounds out of place amidst
the cute syrupy guitar lines. Like
wanting to sound like the Undertones
and the Weirdos at the same time.
You tell me, is there room for a
combination like that? Nope. What
you get is something in and around
that murky, nondescript area with
about as much staying power as wet
paint at a car wash. They're from
Arcadia, could that be their problem.
--DS

THE SOFT BOYS--"Kingdom Of Love"/
"Vegetable Man"/"Strange"
Armageddon Records

Remember these guys? Those poor
boys who had the label Acid Punk
foisted at them like they were suffering from some social disease.
Well, I like their latest effort
pretty much. It doesn't move me
to new heights of appreciation,
but not much does these days. Low
profile delivery with a pleasant
melody and an above average performance, which means this doesn't get
a lot of playing time. Forgettable,
but not completely ignored.--DS

THE MISFITS--"Cough,Cool"/"She"
Blank Records

The Misfits' first. Unfortunately,
this isn't the "Six and Change" kind
of classic I'd hoped it to be. No
'horror business' going on here. I
guess they thought they'd be real
clever and make a go of it without
a guitar player in a fruitless
quest for originality. No way.
Danzig plays the piano unconvinc-
ingly and the recording makes "Living
Dead. . ." sound slick. Pinch the
ol nostrils together on this one,
just be thankful they immediately
saw the errors of their way and
promptly purged any memory of this
debacle with the Bullet EP.--DS

THE BONGOS

PAGANS--"Street Where Nobody Lives"/
"What's This Shit Called Love?"
Drome Records

More retrospect. Although I may be
encroaching on SMEGMA's territory,
I just have to throw in my two-cents
worth of plaudits for the Pagans.
Their first for Drome, this features
Michael Hudson at his fuckin' best.
Two sides of gut-wrenching noise
that's sure to squeeze the pus out
of those infected, beer-soaked brains
of yours. A biting testimonial to
Midwest punk.--DS

THE BONGOS--"Telephoto Lens"/"Glow
In The Dark" Fetish Records

This one catches me just right. A
modern-day Spencer Davis. Smart,
snappy pop for all of you out there
who've been thumbing your noses
at anything that resembles the light
and nonsensical. If you've lost
your appreciation, then you must be
a boring sot.--DS

PAGANS

X--"Adult Books"/"We're Desperate"
Dangerhouse Records

TV says I must have been weaned on
sphincter to ever consider reviewing
this relic. So what. It's great.
If you don't own this record there's
something wrong.--DS

4 SKINS--"I'm Mad"/"When I'm Gone"
Grove Records

Hey Barry! Does this suck as bad as
I think it does, or am I just a
bigoted asshole who can't stand much
of the shit that comes out of NYC?
These four ethnic misfits don't sound
like anyone(or anything) else, which
is just fine with me cuz I'd hate
to have listen to another piece of
grunt like this one. This band is
hurtin', no sound and no look. They
don't exist.--DS

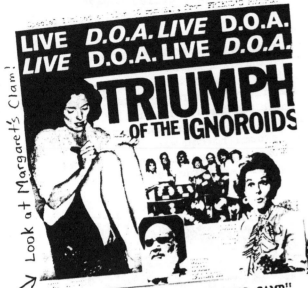

Look at Margaret's Clam!

LIVE D.O.A. LIVE D.O.A.
LIVE D.O.A. LIVE D.O.A.

TRIUMPH OF THE IGNOROIDS

D.O.A.-LIVE EP-"NAZI TRAINING CAMP"
"WANT SOME BONDAGE'/"RICH BITCH"/
"LET"S FUCK" Fresh Records
The memorable Rock Against Reagun
gig that I stupidly missed ,was going fine according to the sound man
until D.O.A. took the stage.similar
things have happened in certain detroit bars which has propted bans on
public performances.With a new LP out
you're probably wondering why I'm reviewing this old thing...I't simple-

this is closer to the D.O.A. we here
at the mag know and love.This is recorded perfectly-like shit,which is
the only way unruly thugs like this,
should be allowed to record.You see
the album is too clean to suit my
tastes...why did they find it necessary
to actually hire a producer?A song like
"Let's Fuck" epitomizes the bands'
strengths...an out of control"vice-grip
on the gonads" parody of every R&R song
from "Peppermint Twist" on with of
course alot of overamplification,and
ideally vulgar lyrics-sure to offend even
the most open minded of females.How can

Joey Shithead sing like he does and
talk the next day?Hope I get another shot
at seeing them live before one of them
o.d.'s or they break up...D.O.A.ROOLS...

ILL PAY $20.00 EACH →

T:g vänts Deese

(1st) Crime-"Hot Wire My HEART" Baby You're So Repol:
(2nd) Crime-" Murder By Guitar"
The Plugz -"Mindleless Content(ment) Slash Recor
The Weirdos "Neutron Bomb" on Radar (does it exis
Big In Japan Single

Live tapes wanted by: WALL OF Voodoo,
Controllers, Screamers, Gun Club, Urinals
Circle Jerks, D.O.A, Bad Brains, Pagans
Misfits, Middle Class, NO JOE

NAZI TRAINING CAMP

You're at the cattle trough
electric prod up your ass
but you seem to enjoy it
swastikas are in your brain

don't you see it
THIS IS A NAZI TRAINING CAMP

I'm talkin about the nifty pricks
I'm talkin about the greedy sluts
I'm yellin about your world
swastikas are in your brain

don't you see it
THIS IS A NAZI TRAINING CAMP

I'm tellin you
THIS IS A NAZI TRAINING CAMP
1978 D.O.A

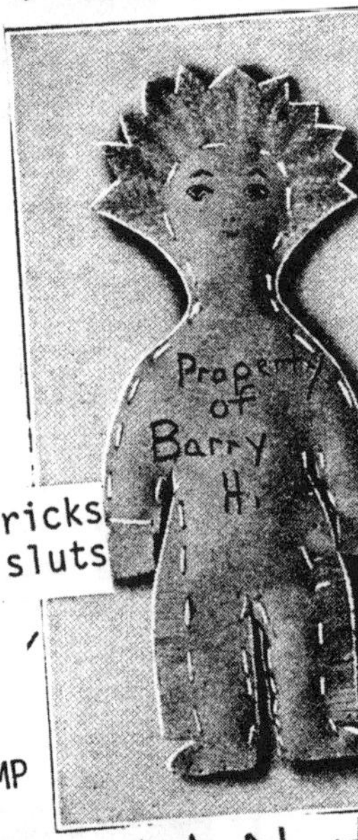

Property of Barry H.

Who's Next?

QUOTE FOR THE DAY......

C'mon DS you promised me 20.00
if I gave you head now cough up
the hogs you ...you...

The Subhumans

GENₓ-"DANCING WITH MYSELF"/
"LOOPY DUB"/"UGLY DUB"
Chrysalis Records

Billy Idol returns after way too
long a lapse to suit this fan.Call
me a latent race-bitch but I've
never made bones about my GENₓ
infatuation ever since these once
mysterious golden boys stirred
curiousity and instant animousity.

More abuse and neglect were heaped
on this band probably due to their
look and their somewhat bubblegum
sound(I didn't coin it)But the GENₓ
CHUG got me through many a long nite
back in the days of gauche(sp?) and
poses.(as far as the second LP goes
Vee still won't talk about it...to
anyone,ED.)Well we just happen to
have not only the#1 comeback of the
month here but the best single period.

I realize you can probably spot the
suds in the corners of my mouth from
where you're sitting and I know I've
probably lost all sense of practical-
ity,journalistic pride, and the fort-
itude to overcome my dissolving credibility...those who haven't tuned me
out listen up...(ZZZZZZZZ,ED.) Derwood and drummer have parted for reas
ons unknown.They've shortened their
name because of....well I'm not too
sure about that either.The guitarist
is Billy I'm pretty sure and if it is
then he has honed his skills consider
ably since his days with CHELSEA.The
production is impeccable-without a
doubt a perfect vocal mix....Despite
my fumbling attempts at historical
data on something I obviously know
nothing about,this is the best comeback record in recent memory.
                              TeeeeVeeee

THE SUBHUMANS-"DEATH WAS TOO KIND"/
"FUCK YOU"/"INQUISITION DAY"/SLAVE
TO MY DICK" Quintessence Records
You can't fault us for reviewing
this a year after it's release.
The distribution on lots of this
Canadian stuff is just plain lousy.
Of course you can find D.O.A. singles simply cuz people have such
shitty taste ,but the ruder and
cruder the better is my personal
philosiphy and this fits that modus
appergrungedi just dandy fankya.
Fortunately a fine gentlemen name
of Peter Brown in Vancouver was kind
enough to send us this(even though he
doesn't like our zine')Death was too
Kind" would kill live I am quite sure,
it blasts along spending most of the
time on one chord-it's the vocal tracks
that save this one from being slightly
overproduced,it could of and should
have been cut on a 4 track for max-
shock value,something the band seem
to enjoy giving off obviously(look at
the song titles again)When they all
give out a great chorus line bellow on
"Fuck You" I invariably feel that blessed
adrenalin hit that makes us all older,and
then I have to go thrash about on my drum
set until the Mexican guy that lives below
me comes up and threatens to beat the shi
out of me.Wer'e so far behind they've got
new one out already,but until that one
crosses the desk this is doing a great
job of making my life a more enjoyable one
                                      TV

ROCK & ROLL BANKROBBER here-
That's right here in Hollywood
at a half-way house-so near but
yet so far from all the music because being fresh out of the pen
(affectionately known as Lompoc
Lodge by his friends and ad mire-
ers,ED.C) But on the night of the
18th I talked my way out of it an
got an 11 o'clock curfew and went
with a buddy to see the Psycedeli
Furs and Wall Of Voodoo-2 groups

had been lucky enough to be acquainted with when I was still in prison-
the former via T.V.(that's me not the
toob you boob,ED.)and the latter thanx
to Hepcats from Hell on KPFK in L.a.-
because of problems like having to
bury my friends dead cat,and the putting together of a scene before the
show we got there too late-we only
heard 2 Wall Of Voodoo songs-both of
which were great,and when they went off
the crowd demanded an encore in one way
or another but they didn't come back.
Their singer was super intense and the
synthesizer melodies were very heady and
moody-I'll wait till I see them again
before I really critique...Iv'e got more
to tell about the FURS anyhow...you see
me and my friend who shall remain anon.
knew this guy at the Whiskey a man who
shall likewise remain anon...anyhow
we went backstage upstairs near the dressing rooms to smoke a couple joints(this
is close to something I'd actually censor ,ED.)
A chick came in and said "They won't go on
without some black eye liner...the boys
need their makeup"Anyway on the subject of
the show...I never realized from the Lp or
the press is the singer is undoubtedly
a fag...he seems to emulate both Bowie
and Jagger in his stage moves,he hangs
all over the instrumentalists..but he was
not a fox..he was a helluveh dancer...
but first and foremost he had perfect
control over an obscenely unique voice,
add to this the strenght of the material,
"India" was played twice.My friend com-
mented on the sameness of the material,
obviously he was none too impressed,but I
was really digging the whole show as I was
familiar with virtually the entire set...
their sax player is almost as good as Andy
Mackay and that's quite good...I
love their music and it is most definately a great spearhead in the invasion
of acid rock again.YEA!Bring on ECHO AND
THE BUNNYMEN!!! BYE YALL...

SIXTEEN MONTHS OF SADISM,SODOMY,
AND SENSATIONALISM "TEEN MESSIAHS
OF THE NEW AGE"(TV)"NECROS RE DEFINE
UNADULTERATED VIOLENCE IN OUR YOUTH
TODAY...THEY MUST BE STOPPED BEFORE
OUR SCHOOL IS DESTROYED"(MAUMEE PTA)
"HEY THESE GUYS PLAY GOOD MUSIC!"(DS)
FOR BOOKINGS CALL....
(in mich)
OCEAN SPRAY ACTS-517-372-1512 or
THEIR Manager(the guy you can never
find when the band gets fucked over)
1-517-655-2489
or the band itself(fuck the middle-men)
1-419-382-1731or
1-419-893-4056

196

DEAD KENNEDYS--"Fresh Fruit For Rotting Vegetables" Cherry Red Records

Alright! San Francisco's marvelously stated rebuttal to The Germs LP. "Fresh Fruit. .." cleanly strips away those not-totally-unfounded notions of mine about these guys being just a bunch of heavy metal poseurs. I was none too impressed with their first single and I sure as hell wasn't about to jump on the Kennedys' bandwagon just cuz some limey thinks they're hot poop. But I can be persuaded. This is one fuckin' great record. Fourteen scorching humdingers to drive your neighbors batty. One listen to "Let's Lynch The Landlord" or "Drug Me" or "I Kill Children" and you'll be guilty of the big toothy reptillian grin. The Dead Kennedys reiterate the fact that, without a doubt, the West is

the best. I don't want to hear what you have to say. You can gather up all the shit from Boston, New York, Toronto, Chicago, and yea, even the squalid Detroit, and flush it down the commode and I wouldn't bat an eye. Fuck what the British say, the home of Ronnie Baby is where it's at. Unfortunately, it's a sad reminder to those of us who are stranded in the Allentowns and Lansings of musical awareness and appreciation. How is it that we are deprived of exciting music and get stuck with some real lame ass shit that makes a smelly crapper a pleasant alternative? There's nothing

to get enthused about, save for The Necros. OK, so I'm crying in my beer, take a look around you and tell me it's not a depressing sight. What talent there is gets squandered in a mire of half-baked ideas and misconceptions. Bands trying to be cute, end up laughably ridiculous, and bands projecting an image that's as phony as it is irrelevant. I sense there's only a partial awareness and conviction among the masses, and should this state of affairs continue, well then, we can expect a pretty bleak future. Enlighten yourself. Buy the album. If you don't, you die from starvation of the brain.--DS

SKIDS

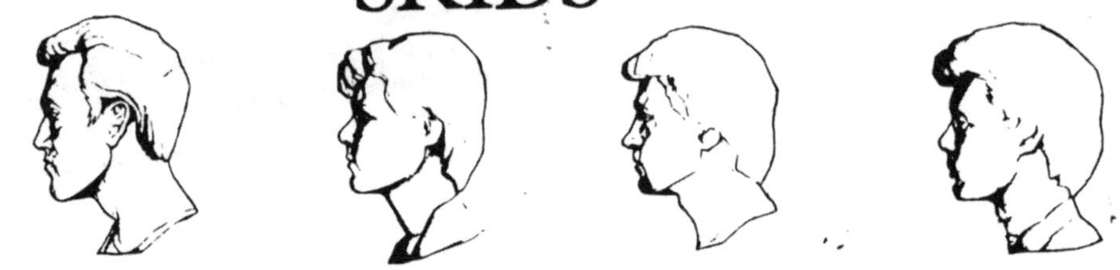

RICHARD JOBSON   STUART ADAMSON   RUSSELL WEBB   MIKE BAILLIE

SKIDS-"THE ABSOLUTE GAME" Virgin
Records

During the last three years Richard
Jobson has,along with guitarist Stuart Adamson,created an image that has
led SKIDS dangerously to a point where
their survival was in serious doubt.
Their early recordings were marred only by inconsistent songwriting and poor
ideas as to what image the band should
be swaddled in for public consumption.
But underneath it all the spirit cut
through...the band has always displayed
superb musicianship and this carried
these gregarious young Scotts through
that rather slumpish mid-78 period.

When Bill Nelson took an active interest
in the band their recordings took on a
clean heavy handed sound that the earlier "Into The Valley" had not exhibited.
The hopelessly fragmented and uninspired
"Scared To Dance" did little to win the
band any curious converts,much less a
rabid following.Nelson seemed to help
Jobson isolate his strengths on the subsequent "Days In Europa"...the loud chorus

and the guitar assault format proved SKIDS
to be more than charlatans searching for
that perfect place to blow their creatively,
self indulgent wad.

    And now installment #3;"THE ABSOLUTE
GAME" is entering the English album chart
at number7...quite a feat for some guys who
just 6 months ago were given up for dead
(unless of course you knew about that lucrative deal Virgin was still contractually
obligated to continue)I see the current resurgence as a determined effort to turn this
band into a "popular group" which means this
one had better take off or else....I just

THE
ABSOLUTE
GAME

get the feeling that these 4 are the
labels next white hope for budgeting
in the black...something the record
biz hasn't been doing lately with any
regularity.Mick Glossop's production
is remarkably effective,with the vocal
tracks coming through clearer than ever

before. Stuart A. is in this boys opinion
one of the most technically proficient
ax men in the business.We see a new formula
on certain tracks such as the catchy"Goodbye Civilian" and the rally-ho "Hurry on
Boys" the formerly deadpan Jobson vocal
takes on an animated sense of humor on the
latter.To those who have labelled this man
as nothing more than an eccentric young lad
with an eye on the world as a place where
national pride, and cultural solidarity

are elevated to a level that borders on
obsession then I say you may be right.I
have seen the band myself in a similar light
Scottish Golgotha marhing onward to weed out
what was good and just in the minds of the
aryan supremists of the 30's...or is it so
tongue and cheek that I'm blinded by it?
All I can say is if this vaults this band
into the pantheon of the successful cross-
over(post punk whatever) bands then I say
praise god...(or should I say Ehhdulf!!)
I need Skids.......
       Tall,Blonde,and Scandinavian

COCKNEY REJECTS—"GREATEST HITS VOLUMEII"
EMI
There's one overiding reason why you should all
without fail get this album.N.(o)M.(usical)
E.(xpertise) sez "For the REJECTS punk is a lic-
ence to bare their scatologically ba re their
priceless backsides on their glossy album cover,
and let loose defective egos on the world."So
Mr.Morley feels them to be the problem and his
solution is probably the JAM or some other positively boreing slop like THE BEAT...and he was
probably lookin' for fucking progression too...
well this band can't and shouldn't...they got nowhere
to go so 77' headbanging it is which suits me alot
better than most of the feces that fuckin' island
sends over here.Brilliant followup here folks...
the last couple of singles are here plus a rousing
rendition of The Sweet's "Blockbuster".Morley's ver-
bosities prove he's a snob talking to snobs and
anyone who buys this is in his mind wretched,mind-
less scum wasting their money on this 14 song(classic)
Count me in...
                    TV

U.X.A.

"ILLUSIONS OF GRANDEUR"

You can't really blame me for
trying to play the role of the
beleagured midwestern advocate
in regard to bands born in our
state of sun,eg. Ca.But realism
never ventures far,for I do not
wish this magazine to become yet
another blind-leading-the-blind
publication...for there are far
to many of those at present.UXA
have released an album.And it was
so kind of Posh Boy to send it to
us...a pre-release copy no less,
(don't be impressed keep reading)
So go ahead and bore me,shit I
used to think these bands could
do no wrong but I've been on the
defensive so long my flanks are
red and sore...and this moderately
passable record will be no incur-
sion whatsoever into the enemy ranks,
give me CIRCLE JERKS or BLACK FLAG-
gimme ammo,the coast is gawd but UXA
are lugubrious plod preempted only
briefly by quick bits of spontanaety-
the singer sounds like one of those
girls that give blood and then get
drunk on the 8 bucks,her voice really
sucks the ol' bratwurst...off key and
recorded so shittily that it gives me
the same sick headache I get whenever
I'm forced to listen to music with
platonic p*** flirtations.And I've
heard better drumming on a Black Sabbath
LP.Herein lies the problem of giving an
unduly elected plenipotentiary like Posh
Boy an inch...he ends up dragging our
sensibilities a mile down the road.
                                    TV

AFFLICTED LP   Bonk Records

This odd assortment of esoterica
comes in a what looks like a candy
bag, however the contents ain't
none too sweet. A regular mishmash of musical styles that make
it hard to pin down. Ranging from
some tranquilizing repitition with
trick vocals to, and I can't figured this one out, dreadful acid-
blues riffing. What gives? These
guys show a little promise, and
just when they seem to have won
us over, they close the door on
us with some of the most absurdly
dated crud I've heard in quite
some time. What's lacking is consistency and continuity. What
could be years' worth of recorded
material, they put down on wax
every musical phase they've been
through since their conception.
A formula that's sure to nail the
coffin shut. My guess is that this
is a group of partially aware hippies
making some of that new fangled
noise they've been reading about.
It's reeks of early 70's experimental.
Much too loose to hold together.
Could have been an intriguing little
EP.--DS

this but this is nothing more than
an average collection of dull and boreing-
ancient sounding garbage.There's more filler
here than there is worthwhile substance.
I mean theres even a song on this called "Don't BE
AFRAID To Pogo"!!(?) Out of 15 songs
there's maybe 3 decent ones-hardly
worth the price of ownership.
Talk about rushing into the studio!

This is a
Dog !!
                              TV

The GEARS LP Playgems Records

Rockin' at Ground Zero

An out and out dissapointment.
With former Controller Kid Spike
on guitar I had high hopes for

letters*misc.

To the Editor:

Rolling Stone #328 has a letter depicted there within that whether good or bad has all the earmarks of a true 'youth' testimony.
A certain youth states that it is Van Halen and the like(AC/DC, Judas Priest etc.) that is what the "Youthful Rockers" of this blank generation propose to ear bleed to. It is the Clash, Elvis Costello and the like who are out of touch with 'Americana Society'. The youth states that most Americans have little in common with the British New Wave bands. He goes on to say, "Our music may not be socially aware, sophisticated, artful or chic, but bands like Reo Speedwagon, Ted Nugent and Led Zeppelin represent much of what we are and hope to be.
May I now say that if this is what American youth look up to, then we are all in trouble. It seems to me the young people of today are lost. They know no better and care to learn no more.
Where I work there are 10 yr. old kids coming in and asking for AC/DC, Journey, and Molley Hachet LPs. There are those wearing Zeppelin t-shirts, not even knowing about the band and its roots(DS--like I really care). There are those still asking for The Wall LP by Pink Floyd. Try talking to these kids about what rock 'n' roll was--they don't know and couldn't give a shit. Ask a kid what R&B is, he looks up at you as if you got some dip-shit disease. Who was Eddie Cochran? Buddy Holly? Gene Vincent? Uh, I don't know and could care less is the more than likely response.
We know where the blame lies and until it is corrected(we got a long wait DS) we won't stop opening our 'big fuckin' radical mouths'(or so says the system). Keep up the 'boss' work Tesco and DS. It's fanzines like yours that give individuals a place to speak out!!

Scott Steinberg
Whitehall, PA

Police in Spaslett,Mich. report that a punk rock concert was responsible for the death of a MSU freshmen.William Reade of Hoboken,New Jersey was struck and killed by an unknown motorist. Following an inspired set by what many call the only true punk band in the midwest NECROS,Mr,Reade was in good spirits as he strolled around the bar sipping an Old Milwaukee Light and continously asking bar patrons questions such as "What are these bands on this tape?" and "Do you like my Elvis Tee..do I look punk?"The youth was also overheard shortly before his death as saying "Gee these girls are giving me a boner" and "Did you like that first band...jeez I dunno..they're a bit much for me" and "Those wet burritos gave me gas" to which Todd Swalla, drummer extrordinaire replied "Go play in traffic you stupid jerkoff, asswipe,fuck sack,poser,pindick,brown packer,toe jam lips." As the steaming throng awaited the headline act said youth was seen in the mens room with a group of his mates flogging their zeppelins to the beat of Elvis C's, "Pump It UP".Oddly the gents in attendence were overheard as saying "Let's burp beef,before Bill dies" thus giving credence to the often substantiated theory that Necros are 'EVIL'and Mr.Swalla's suggestions were being expedited via lead singer Barry's large selection of voodoo dolls.
This had driven the youth into believing that hearing the band Fix would cause him to actually become a fan...and necessitate his attendence at every gig.

As the boys from Ohio egged him on Mr.Reade attempted to make love to the grill of a 69' Falcon as it passed. Donations can be sent to Al'sSlug Farm 7685 West Oak,Hoboken N.J. 78998

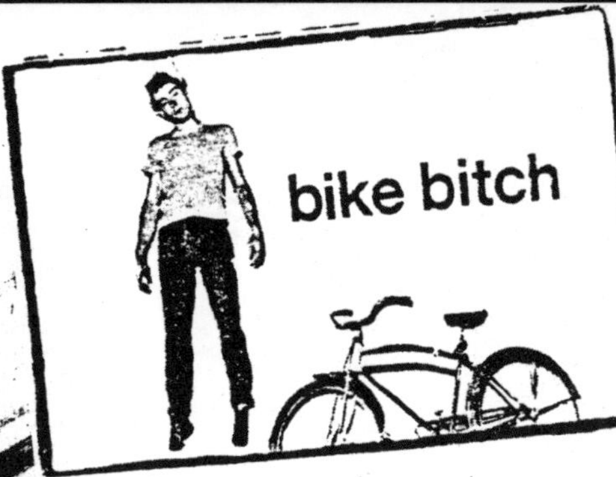

C.C. tried to
tried to get his bike fixed
tried to tried to tried to
get his bike fixed
wrenched clear cross the bitch
spat on his oily fingers
and tried to get his bike fixed
got bike ground in his knuckles
fat brown crunch crusty knuckles
fat hands thick in the middle of
trying to get his bike fixed
kicked bitch bike with his
tennis shoe
cursed her like Adam
sat and whimpered
red in the rage face
trying to get his bike fixed
bike in his hand cracks
bike under fingernails
C.C. tried to tried to
get some good sleep
bike in his whiskers
bike on his arm hairs
C.C. awake still
trying to get some good sleep
no bike, no sleep
C.C. in his white suit
C.C. done with everything
got himself a brown rope
fat rope barky rope
wrapped his neck in hempy
and he stood up on his
bitch bike up by the ceiling
kicked the bitch a last time

Poem by Bill Milroy • Photo by Maureen O'Malley
©Mr. Mayhem • P.O. Box 7910 • Ann Arbor, MI 48107
If you like this and want more, write to Mr. Mayhem.
Send $1. Send names and addresses.

SINGER seeks HARDcOre
sleazoids for mid-mich's
1st REAL band
CALL — 517—655—2489
after 11

Hey You,
It has come to my attention that T&G mag knew of the horrid noise THE FIX make before they were allowed to play at club DOO BEE last month(see last ish for article,ED.) I think I am in the company of Bill Reed's family and friends when I say they must have,and should be stopped!
My God they were awful! I was unfortunate enough to see the band before their set and I noticed they had to run home to put on their "punk rock" clothes because when their set took place they were decked out in poseur regallia,but worse than their clothes was their stage presence (well maybe it's a toss-up)The drummer and the bassist were almost invisible due to the overwhelming faggotry of the lead singer and the guitarist...they were clad in matching slax (wink,wink)First off the guitarist-well-um-he's-he's black,now picture this Rod Stewart pretending he's Johhny Lydon(sound wimpy?You bet it sounds wimpy!)He's just about the personification of butt-fuckery(wotta wimp)Besides staring at people as if to say "You bet I take drugs, and lot's of em'",he stood tippy-toed ballerina stance all night.A result of one of 2 things...his spandex pants were too tight or the Ben-Wa balls up his ass were working.

The Fix spend too mach time trying to be unique & zany.They should go back to tuggin' their twigs like they did before they discovered "new wavw".If any of them took their faces off of each others' dorks they'd realize they take three steps back for every one forward(I mean really,a bunch of puddin' pullers does not a punk combo make)Face it their worthless newave wimpasses and they sound worse than a fat girls'pussy farts.Thank you for this chance to voice my opinion.

JIMMY McCANN
East Lansing

Hmmmmm...no address?You realize the implications of this letter don't you bub if deez fightin' words ever reach said band and they find out who you are,right? OK you've been warned...ED.

TOUCH AND GO WELCOMES ALL COMMENTS,CRITIQUES, PERSONAL BIASES,PERVERSIONS,AND OUT AND OUT HATRED FROM ANYONE!

Forever

CHUCK BISCUITS

ROBERT KAINER

GLENN SORVISTO

CHRISTIAN ARNHEITER

HATES

SECOND E.P.
- BORED WITH THE BOYS
- CITY ON ICE
- CARYL CHESSMAN
- SOLDIER

FIRST E.P. (REISSUE)
- NO TALK IN THE 80's
- NEW SPARTANS
- ALL THE WHITES
- LAST HYMN

SEND 3.00 EACH TO: CHRISTIAN ARNHEITER
5201 W. 34TH, BOX 316, HOUSTON TX, 77092

11

Penelope gets a redux and her second cover appearance sets
the standard for hot punk rock chick for the ages. Don't
really care what her orientation is, she was and still is
the cat's pajamas. Here we see her putting the Princess down
long enough to get her pic snapped—shredded wife-beater
tee, niblets protruding seductively thru the mesh... giving
you a look like she's either gonna bang you into next week
or bang you in the skull with a ball-peen. DS's "MORE HATE"
is another of my fave harangues with that choice shot of a
machine-gun-totin' Klansman smokin' a heater... DS was a
hater, baby, and his venomous attacks were always spot-on. We
review the first GG Allin record and make fun of him. He wrote
me a letter in '92 from prison and said, "Tesco, the war in Iraq
is nothing compared to the war in my head"... How quaint.

TOUCH AND GO

NO. 11   75¢

ROUGH CUT

"This energetic group has a rather interesting local lineup: Carolyn Striho of the Cubes, Keith Michael of Flirt, John Morgan of GangWar, and Craig Hernandez play together with a spiky punch."
Kim McAuliffe
Detroit Free Press

"An intriguing local modern music amalgamation ..."
Jim McFarlin
Detroit News

"Carolyn is a most exciting crooner and a helluva lot of fun to watch ..."
Touch & Go
Lansing, Michigan

"Romance with a razor edge ..."
Mike Duffy
Detroit Free Press

"Tall, blond, angular Carolyn Striho finds her influences in Iggy and Jim Morrison and not (thankfully) Deborah Harry ..."
New York Rocker

 For more information on ROUGH CUT, contact Maverick Productions, P.O. Box 3031, Detroit, Michigan 48201

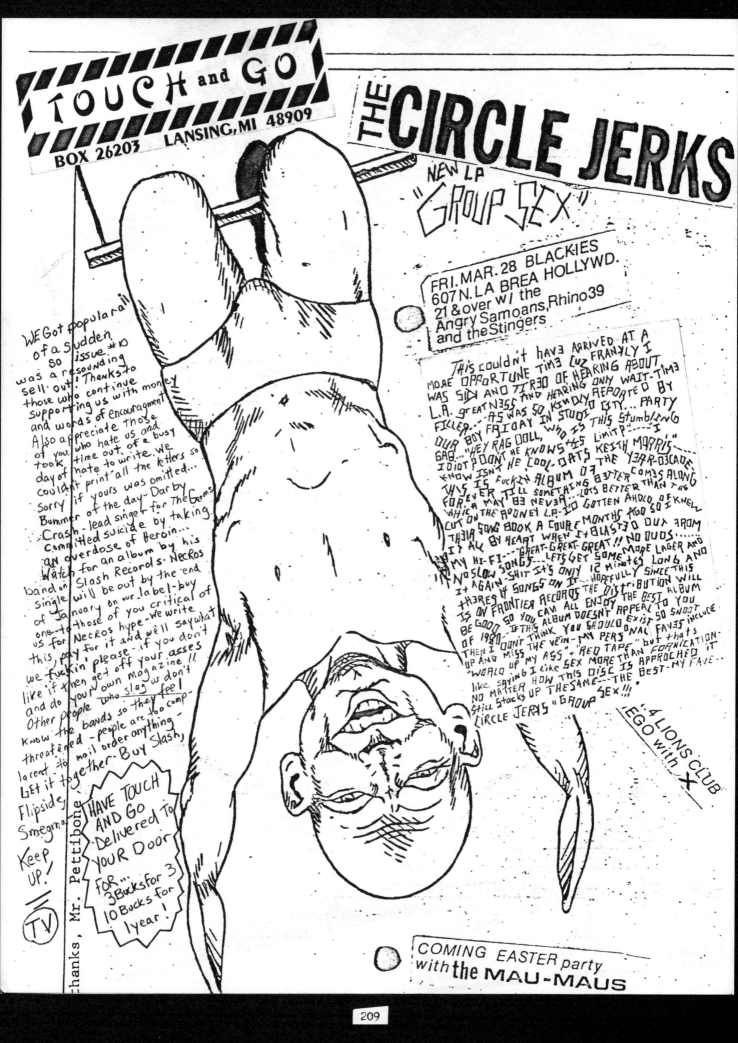

TOUCH and GO

BOX 26203   LANSING, MI 48909

THE CIRCLE JERKS

NEW LP "GROUP SEX"

FRI. MAR. 28   BLACKIES
607 N. LA BREA HOLLYWD.
21 & over w/ the
Angry Samoans, Rhino 39
and the Stingers

WE got popular all of a sudden so Issue #10 was a resounding sell out! Thanks to those who continue supporting us with money and words of encouragment! Also appreciate those of you who hate us and took time out of a busy day of hate to write. we couldn't print all the letters so sorry if yours was omitted... Bummer of the day- Darby Crash- lead singer for The Germs committed suicide by taking an overdose of heroin... Watch for an album by his band on Slash Records. Necros single will be out by the end of January on our label- buy one- to those of you critical of us for Necros hype- we write this, pay for it and we'll say what we fuckin please- if you don't like it then get off your asses and do your own magazine !! Other people who slag us don't know the bands so they feel threatened- people are too comp- larent to mail order anything- Let it together. Buy Slash, Flipside, Smegma Keep Up!

HAVE TOUCH AND GO Delivered To YOUR Door FOR... 3 Bucks for 3 10 Bucks for 1 year!

thanks, Mr. Pettibone

This couldn't have arrived at a more opportune time cuz frankly I was sick and tired of hearing about L.A. greatness and hearing only wait-time filler... As was so kindly reported by our boy Friday in Studio City... party GAB... "Hey RAG DOLL, who is this stumbling idiot? DON'T HE KNOW HIS LIMIT?"----I know isn't he cool. OATS KEITH MORRIS THIS IS fuckin ALBUM OF THE YEAR-DECADE FOREVER TILL SOMETHING BETTER COMES ALONG which may be never...LOTS BETTER THAN THE cut on the Rooney L.P.-I'd GOTTEN AHOLD OF KNEW THEIR SONG BOOK A COUPLE MONTHS AGO SO I IT ALL BY HEART WHEN I BLASTED OUT FROM MY HI-FI---GREAT-GREAT-GREAT !! MORE LAGER AND NO SLOW SONGS---LET'S GET SOME LONG AND IT AGAIN-SHIT IT'S ONLY 12 minutes LONG AND THERES 14 SONGS ON IT HOPEFULLY SINCE THIS IS ON FRONTIER RECORDS the DISTRIBUTION WILL BE GOOD SO YOU CAN ALL ENJOY THE BEST ALBUM OF 1980. IF THIS ALBUM DOESN'T APPEAL TO YOU THEN I DON'T THINK YOU SHOULD EXIST SO SHOOT UP AND MISS THE VEIN- MY PERSONAL FAVES INCLUDE "WORLD UP MY ASS" + "RED TAPE" but thats like saying I like SEX MORE THAN FORNICATION- NO MATTER HOW THIS DISC IS APPROACHED IT Still Stacks UP THE SAME---THE BEST-MY FAVE- CIRCLE JERKS "GROUP SEX"!!!

4 LIONS CLUB ←EGO with X

COMING EASTER party with the MAU-MAUS

TV

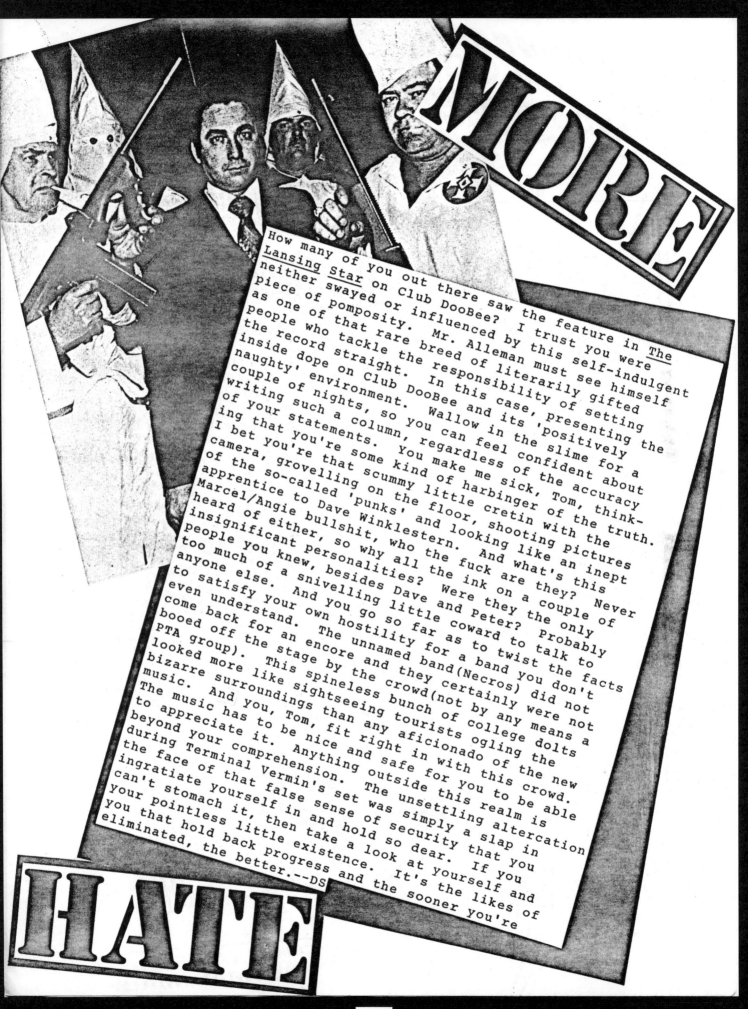

MORE

How many of you out there saw the feature in The Lansing Star on Club DooBee? I trust you were neither swayed or influenced by this self-indulgent piece of pomposity. Mr. Alleman must see himself as one of that rare breed of literarily gifted people who tackle the responsibility of setting the record straight. In this case, presenting the inside dope on Club DooBee and its 'positively naughty' environment. Wallow in the slime for a couple of nights, so you can feel confident about writing such a column, regardless of the accuracy of your statements. You make me sick, Tom, think- ing that you're some kind of harbinger of the truth. I bet you're that scummy little cretin with the camera, grovelling on the floor, shooting pictures of the so-called 'punks' and looking like an inept apprentice to Dave Winklestern. And what's this Marcel/Angie bullshit, who the fuck are they? Never heard of either, so why all the ink on a couple of insignificant personalities? Were they the only people you knew, besides Dave and Peter? Probably too much of a snivelling little coward to talk to anyone else. And you go so far as to twist the facts to satisfy your own hostility for a band you don't even understand. The unnamed band(Necros) did not come back for an encore and they certainly were not booed off the stage by the crowd(not by any means a PTA group). This spineless bunch of college dolts looked more like sightseeing tourists ogling the bizarre surroundings than any aficionado of the new music. And you, Tom, fit right in with this crowd. The music has to be nice and safe for you to be able to appreciate it. Anything outside this realm is beyond your comprehension. The unsettling altercation during Terminal Vermin's set was simply a slap in the face of that false sense of security that you can't stomach it, then take a look at yourself and ingratiate yourself in and hold so dear. If you your pointless little existence. It's the likes of you that hold back progress and the sooner you're eliminated, the better.--DS

HATE

LETTERS

To the Editors of Touch & Go:

As Sorority mother for Alpha Tau Chi it has come to my attention that some of the young girls in the house have been receiving and secreting copies of your magazine under the sink in the bathroom. As the young ladies are my charges and I have utter and complete responsibility for them I must order you to not send any more issues of your trashy little pamphlet. I will not have their innocent minds scarred forever by people so afflicted. I have my hands tied with the shenanigans of all those lusty men on MSU's campus trying to meat my girls. Most of them are already up in the air trying to decide on a future career goal and will probably never get there if I let them fall prey to your type. What you need is somebody to tan your butt good and hard like it's never been done before(I'm sure it hasn't). Let this serve as a warning to you, I've seen your pictures and I know what you look like. If I catch you or any of your punk people around this sorority I'll blister your bottoms till you cry for mercy. If you were here for our Sunday matinees, you could see what we do with the likes of you. This Sunday we're showing "BARBARA CAPTURES A PEST", "HOW TO RESTRAIN A PEST", "CHECK-MATING A PEST", and as a special added attraction we have "HAZING THE NEW SORORITY GIRL" and "BETTY GETS THE WORKS". With the vast library of comic magazines the girls have at their dispsal they have no need for your kind of literature. Cease and desist if you know what's good for you.

I hate you,
Chomelia Smakmi

To the Editors:

I've read your previous magazines, and though I've found very few valuable ideas--I was overtly offended by the article about William Reade's death, obviously written by one TV who also doubles as manager of The Necros(?).
I failed to understand why such a tasteless article could be written about something such as this guy's death--with Necro P.R. crap lining the article. Why describe someone (deceased, no less) with quotes like "Let's burp beef, before Bill dies"? The mental midget who was bored enough to go about writing an article such as this, stands only above the brilliant people who published it. The article was filled with stupid-assed misquotes, which undoubtedly were extremely libelous to the parents of the deceased--and one can only come away from reading it with some kind of sick glorification of The Necros. What was its purpose? It seems that in this attempt to upgrade the Necros, the author had to abandon all traces of class, good taste and any other humane qualities that he may claim to possess. You purposely insulted and belittled this kid, you were in no way funny, you insulted yourself, you insulted me and what few other readers you may have. Besides that, the ones responsible should get a good ass-kicking. (By the way, what's behind all this Necros hype bullshit that raises its ugly head in any article throughout the mag?) Please be brave enough to print this letter from your most faithful readers. I've read many letters such as in your latest issue that were much more base, slanderous and vicious(ie. the Fix letter)--and if you're not afraid of some honesty--to yourself and your readers--trouble yourself with printing this article which I have gone to the trouble of sending you.
R.F.D.
M.J.B.

You find little of value in our zine' but still label yourself "our most faithful reader"(?)We don't write letters to ourselves but we do masturbate...ED.

T&G,
In issue #9 you reviewed an EP by the TOKYOS, which I showed them, since their from San Diego, not Redondo Beach. They've changed their name(Private Sector), no longer have a guitarist(ego-problems), and play what they call Avant go-go. Anyhow they're real embarrassed about the record(it came out two years ago) and the review, except the guitarist(EX) who wanted a copy for his scrapbook. I thought the review was real accurate though. I like most of your magazine, so please continue my subscription.
Cathy Tabler
Poway, Ca.

Hey did you see BLACK FLAG and DEAD KENNEDYS on "Tommorow"with Rona Barrett? I was rolling on the floor. That was great. "Kind of makes monopoly seem boring."
Ta Ta
nope we missed it along with FEAR on Casey Cassum's Top Ten show...dragheesh!

Fiction By Michael Hudson

IN ANOTHER LAND

I have a house---an old grey decrepit house built in the sand of the Lake Erie beach. Although the outside is beat and weathered, the inside is nice with like pillows, a lot of colors but I can only remember red, strewn about and low tables and windows facing out onto the lake that go from the floor to the ceiling. Joey and Paul are there and the three of us sit around stoned on some kind of drug that makes you sleepy and I'm nodding out and Joey splits for awhile. The phone rings. It is an old, black phone near the seaward window. "Hello?" I say. I hear the other party hang up. For some reason I say hello again. Paul begins talking in his sleep, mumbling first and then out loud, with laughter. Grey, forbidding clouds begin to gather offshore. Paul, still laughing in his sleep, begins grabbing my outstretched leg and pulling it close to him, the way some people do a pillow. I clasp my hand to his shoulder and rouse him. I'm still troubled by the call. He looks up embarrassed and I smile absently.

The phone rings again. This time, there is a pause, and then a muffled and distant voice begins speaking unintelligibly. Thinking about it now, it could have been in a foreign language. I can't say for sure whether the voice was that of a man or a woman, but I could sense that it was a desperate voice and that it was either begging me for help or warning me of danger. Paul and I were on our feet now, and after I'd told him of the calls, we went outside to the beach where Joey was sitting with a woman I thought much too old for him. There were many others scattered about on the beach, watching with anticipation a line of clouds that hung like a curtain about 200 yards out in the lake and stretched horizontally as far as you could see in either direction. The beach was backed by a high clay cliff, and built into this cliff almost directly behind mine was another house, a much nicer one, painted white. Speedboats and sailboats laden with pretty girls trafficked east and west, hugging the shoreline well in from the thick and ominous storm front. We made small talk and laughed about my house's deteriorating condition.

Before too long, we saw several small waterspouts forming in the mist. Three of them. Suddenly, one broke away from whatever had held it there and began whirling towards the shoreline and us. We watched its' approach with something like glee and all laughed hysterically as the visibly turbulent air smacked spectre like into the corner of the white house behind us, tearing off a section of rain gutter from the edge of the roofing.

I woke up laughing. I heard somebody come in downstairs and went to investigate. It was Joey.
"You just getting home?" I asked. He nodded. It was seven in the morning and neither of us was going to work. Joey put on some coffee.
"I just had the weirdest dream," I said, and told him the dream.

Michael Hudson

OK Touch & Go,
Please start sending me my 1 year sub for I'm tired of begging this mag(all 9 ish) from my big sis. Really loved your boot gag and pee-pee ads but I would really like to see some more shit on E.L. bands(what little there is)This dumb-fuck moo town is getting me down & it's about time we kick these Dinosaur relics out on their zombie-slug asses. We need more people like you pushing new bands or this town is going to turn into the hemmoroid of the asshole of the butt-fucked world!And thank you for being 1 of the few cures for RADIO BRAINWASH this pimple town has!
Scott Brown
East Lansing, Mich.

LIVE SHIT

SCREAMING URGE/FANMAIL
Club DooBee (Friday night)

Pretty sparse crowd. Expected a
bigger turnout, but I guess you
folks only go to gigs with bands
you know something about, right?
Would hate to risk driving all the
way out to Haslett and end up with
a shitty band? Yeah right. Well,
you can take that spineless attitude and get fucked. It's people
like you that keep this a repressed
area musically. If you want things
to happen, you got to go out and
support the scene, regardless of
the bands. So what if the band
stinks, go anyway. It'll die if

nobody shows up--then we'll have
nothing. An occasional gig at
Dooleys, big fuckin' deal.
Back to the matter at hand. Remember Fanmail, that heavy metal band
that posed its way through a performance at the aforementioned
showplace? Well, they dumped their
singer or vice versa and they're
down to a trio. They did a competent job as a cover band. Nothing
great, but it was fast and energetic.
Better than some of the slop that's
been spilled on the DooBee stage in
the past couple of weeks. Was rather
anxious to hear this Ohio band.
Heard their single and their album
(rev iew in these pages somewhere--ED)

and although I wasn't overly impressed
with either, I was up for something
new. They got that Fix 'two tone'
look with a black guy on bass.
Claims Columbus ain't much better
off than Lansing, so what else is new?
They opened with a strip tease by
said bass player as he clumsily
pulls out of his pants to reveal
the sorriest looking pair of jockey
shorts I've seen next to TV's own
pair of nocturnally soiled briefs.
They cut it short with a "Thank you,
good night", which unfortunately
follows every song they do. Clever,
but irritatingly stupid. By the
end of the night you're saying to
yourself, 'please, don't say that

fuckin' line again' and sure enough,
they do to the groans of the audience. Their music? They simply do
not have enough material to keep anybody's interest. One, two, maybe
three impressive songs, but the rest
are banally uninspired. "Hitler's
In Brazil" and "We Are Mono" were
the only real highlights of the
evening. They just couldn't hold
my attention unabated for very long.
Not many bands can, but these guys
sent me looking for other forms of
entertainment sooner than usual.
They're supposedly on a tour across
the country, which I find a bit premature judging from the way they
captivated the crowd at the Club.
Maybe somebody will like them. I
give them credit for trying.--DS

NOTTHE/THE DRASTICS/RICHIE and THE
RAVERS   The Bus Stop

Someone came up to me and asked what
I thought I was doing in such garish
surroundings. Good question. This
place is the realization of the
absurd Saturday night adventure for
the mythological fuck that we condemn and combat whenever possible.
To step into this wall of obnoxious
sound with its dizzying colored
lights would make you retch. The
mirrors and carpeted walls combine
to give it a sleazy-porn air that's
reminiscent of all those tacky go-
go joints I use to frequent while
living out East, but with the added
pretense of fun and good times for
all that gives it a puzzling credi-

bility. And no disco is complete
without that amazing mutated hybrid
of the male species--the bouncer.
The word 'asshole' was created with
this scumbag uppermost in Webster's
mind. Suffering from an acute pre-
occupation with his miniscule organ,
he not only looks for trouble, he
makes it. Mumble the f-word under
your breath or call him a son of a
bitch and he's already flexing the
pecs, itching to step outside. What
really gets 'em riled is the old
shit eating grin right back in his
face. Watch that neck turn crimson.
So long as we venture beyond the
cozy confines of Club DooBee we'll
have to give these apes and their
warped brand of machismo the business.

Enough with the editorial bullshit. Tonight's music was awful. Terrible. Horrible. The worst. A long tedious evening that proved once again the incredible lack of talent in this town. The Ravers were first. They don't deserve coverage. A bar band posing in the most inept fashion. They couldn't even slog their way through the most rudimentary Stones' cover. Their between-song rap was an object lesson in moribund stupidity. Thought they'd get our dander up by saying we were worse than St. Johns. Don't make me laugh, creep. The Drastics weren't much better. They had a good guitar player, but you don't go anywhere with piss-poor material. All covers and most of them were of the pathetically acceptable variety.

At long last, Notthe. It wasn't worth the wait. Should have gone home to see who shot JR. A mangled mess of psychedelic noise. a regular goulash of little or no redeeming value. Good organ player, but unfortunately wasted at the expense of his trashy companions. Guitarist seems to be running the show, where, I don't know. I honestly don't think he knows what the hell is going on in this movement. A little older than most of us and caught in a desperate chase to catch up only he's always gonna be a step or two behind the pack. He's trapped in his own little void with nowhere to go but down. Almost sad, if you ask me. However, pity is probably the last thing he wants from me. They have nothing to offer, I left after their first set.--DS

DE·SPIES/THE FIX/NECROS Halloween night
NFC Hall, Flint

Boy, do they love their Spies in Flint! Had you stumbled in during their set(or The Fix' for that matter) you'd had thought that Flint was alright--supporting this punk shit with a passion. Unfortunately, this is a flimsy facade put up for the sake of the band, cuz had you been there from the beginning and caught The Necros, you'd have been sickened by the incomprehensible hypocrisy of these gutless poseurs.

Like the majority of fuckheads who claim to be into the new music, the crowd at the NFC Hall sat silently on their hands throughout the Necros set. It just goes to show that when you throw an unknown on the stage, most people are too scared and inhibited to react one way or the other. These conformist wimps did not know whether to like them or not. Looking at one another for some clearcut sign of approval or disapproval. They don't know shit, so they did nothing. If they hated the Necros, they were too spineless to say so. "Should I yell 'you suck', maybe I better not cuz what if one of those big loonies up at the stage got pissed and came back here to beat me up?" The audience was intimidated by these boys from Ohio, they simply were not like the aver-

age Flint joe. Corey with his Trix and Andy with his Frosted Flakes conveniently taped to his mid-section was just too much for the country bumpkins to handle. What was it? Were these Necros too punk(I'm using this term loosely) for your tidy set of experiences. So you end up closing your mind off to their music. Which was easily the most inspired of the three bands. Todd attacking his kit like a man possessed and Barry spitting out his lyrics, attacking the lethargy-inflicted crowd. They played their hits, "Police Brutality", "I Hate My School", "Race Riot", "Better Never Than Late" and "Caste System" and "Sex Drive" which they hope to release as a single(keep your fingers crossed) Although I'm still partial to their cover of "Rip Off" which gave us

the chance to play punter participation. They were great. Too bad this Flint crowd was obtuse to the fact. Tough shit, right? When The Fix hit the stage, I couldn't believe the turnaround. Now everyone's out of their chairs and dancing up a storm. You see, The Fix played Flint before so weren't total strangers to these people and it was OK to like the Fix. Sound reasoning, huh? This crowd has no mind of its own, they're just going with the flow, with what's acceptable(The Spies and The Fix). The Fix, by the

213

way, were good, despite how I feel about the audience. Unusually short set, though, and they've added The Germs' "Media Blitz", nice try boys. Perhaps I shouldn't say this, but Craig just might be the best around, but don't let that go to yer head now, you hear me?

Finally we get the hometown favorites: The Spies. Primarily a cover band, they do "Kill The Hippies", "I'm Cramped", a Rejects' tune along with others I've since forgotten. They've got a good singer who seems slightly touched and a pint-sized rasta guitar player who should be working on origi-

nals instead of messing around with copy material. Just trying to be constructive, Derek. These two would be better off if they split from the rest and tried something new, cuz I don't see much future in The Spies as they are now. We left before the end of their set, but not before the Necros left their indeliable mark in the bathroom and on the walls of the hall, even if it meant pulling down some wallpaper for some clean writing space. Sure to endear themselves to the owners of the building. Undoubtedly the last time these Ohio youngsters play anywhere near Flint.--DS

TERMINAL VERMIN/NECROS
Club DooBee Friday nite

Really fucked crowd tonight. A bunch of snivelling little college brats, whose only connection with the new music is either the B-52s, Devo, or their 'chic' skinny ties. Makes me barf, always have. . . always will. The Necros came on and were greeted with mild hostil- ity from these poseurs. These people don't know shit. They only

know the sterile, the antiseptic, the clean. The crap on the radio that they think is 'new wave'. A regular laugh riot. The band was breaking in a new bass player and what resulted was one of the poorest sets I've seen by one of the most promising bands in the Midwest. That doesn't excuse their perfor- mance, though. The sound wasn't right, things were just too loose. They knew it, too. So before they got too mired in this unpleasant

rut, they said 'fuck it' and quit playing. Smart move. Regroup and get it together boys. Terminal Vermin is also from Ohio, but that's about the only thing they have in common. They look like the Rejects, if only they sounded like 'em. The singer even resembles Stinky and he knows how to shout, unfortunately their music borders on the lame. Way too many covers, if you ask me, and the wrong ones besides. A couple of Eddie Cochran number, some con-

temporary stuff, and some originals and you've got the makings for one particularly dull evening. Got to beef up their material to go along with their hard core image. The only excitement came   during one of their songs which miraculously got these lardy-assed wimps out on the dance floor. What happened next should be a prerequisite for every disgusting little toad who tries to pass himself as part of the new wave

vanguard. "Hey man, I'm punk, watch me pogo." On the count of three some seven or eight Necro loyalists descended on the crowd and began bouncing people around. Needless to say, some innocent people got roughed-up. . .a little. If you were one of the few who were jostled by this overzealous mob, well, all I can say is. . . tough. Perhaps your limp will remind you that if

you can't take it and Mom ain't around to comfort you and your por- celin like ego, then maybe you should get the hell out and stay out. You're no more than one of those simpering little cry babies who feels anxiously insecure in any sit- uation this side of a communion ser- vice. So next time play it safe and spend your weekend over in the dorm where you can share in the misery of your flawed existence.--DS

SINGLES...?

THE WEIRDOS-ACTION DESIGN EP
Rhino Records
I'm incabale of articulating how godawful this is.We continue buying shells
of Weirdos past and sit in silent accord,
with heads wagging as the old gaurd west
coasts down the stinky path of nonchalance.
We've been conditioned to deplore product
for product's sake,like this shit.We can't
even scream sell-out cuz next time there
will be no buyers...no mitigation...use-
less retch.

THE FALLOUT CLUB-"FALLEN YEARS"/
"THE BEAT BOYS" SECRET RECORDS
All rythym....machine that is....
very little if any melody....lyrics
spoken....chanted not sung... a little
bass....but mostly just Trevor Herion...
..........single of the month....but..
it's still early......

FROM OUR LIBRARY

ERIC RANDOM-"THAT"S WHAT I LIKE ABOUT ME"
EP-NEW HORMONES RECORDS
Speaking of TILLER BOYS here's an alum

MO-DETTES-"DARK PARK CREEPING"/
"TWO CAN PLAY" Deram
Like a piece of that gum you get
with baseball cards,the flavor is
gone in a hurry.The idea is to inflate four ordinary girls to bigger than life proportions before
the public realizes there was no
novelty in the first place.Besides
all girl bands are starting to look
like yesterdays hash.This brand new
bit wer'e all supposed to chomp on
gets it's token share of cash support as the majors parry thrusts
with the indies for a share of a
dying biz.Muddled mush,come on
you wenches you can cook us up
something better than this...and
bring me a fuckin' beer while yor
at it.

from said repi-repi-repi-
tious band who has decides to do
something more artistically dis-
criminayting(the T.Boys woud be
more in your autistically undiff-
erentiated classification)Ok it's
obvious...it sounds alot like Cabaret Voltaire on first listen but
it's much more accessible(ime tired
of that fuckin word,but wots a poor
ED. gonna do?ED)Check out that Peter
Gunn axe work on(whoops forgot the song
titles..."FADE IN"/"DIRTY BOYS"/
"CALL ME"/"FADE OUT")...the second cut.
As TJ always sez...these guys are cry-
ptically captivating and cerebrally
savage.I dare you to buy it and like
it.

CLEVELAND CONFIDENTIAL

PAGANS ★ CLOCKS ★ AK 47s
IMPALERS ★ BRONCOS
INVISIBLES & MORE

CLEVELAND CONFIDENTIAL EP—

FEATURING...PAGANS/THE BRONCOS/
AK 47's/THE CLOCKS/IMPALERS/
INVISIBLES-Terminal Records
I never had the good fortune to
see live Pagans,but those who did
expound on the bands'greatness as
the midwests only purveyors of a

the   track must have been an encore
as vocalist Michael Hudson seems to
be straining against the physical
limitations of his vocal chords as he
spits vehemance into the faces of those
in attendance.Fuckin' great....The
Broncos have the unfortunate fate to
be sandwiched between the 2 best bands
on the disc.Where isn't the question,
it's why cuz they dont cut it at all...
Then AK 47's-blaring sludgegrudge against someone and they sound good and
pissed-this threatens sF.'s FLIPPERS'
title as kings of the machine drone...
I love it...See singles page for dis-
cussin of THE CLOCKS...Don't ask me
why but I humm the IMPALERS cut alot

hardcore sound.But as is usually
the case when a hard band comes out
of nowhere and attacks this regions'
pussyass set of musical morays-the
populace ends up screaming "trash"
so loud and long,the bands seem to
start believing it themselves.I'm
not saying this was the case in
this instance...most likely it was
just those famous "musical diffs,"
or feelings the whole thing had run
it's course and it was time to back
off.The band left 4 singles behind,
all classic examples of good raw
punk,and they also recorded an album
that unfortunately may never surface
due to a contractual dispute.ThisEP
features a live cut by The Pagans
and also features 5 other bands....

but by the time the INVISIBLES cut
comes around the desperate production starts to show through,but I
earnestly recommend this EP to all
of you interested in what's going
on in the midwest that's worthwhile..
                              tesco

216

HONEY BANE-"GUILTY/DUB" Honey
Bane Records
Donna sounded alot better when
she had CRASS backing her up.
Now she sounds positively dull
and with a dub side to boot.cool
picture on the cover of someone
crucified on a telephone pole-
but I can't show you...this is a
family magazine....
                          TV

**X-"WHITE GIRL"/"YOUR PHONES OFF
THE HOOK(BUT YOU'RE NOT)** -
Slash Records

TEMPTATION

According to the press release
the X LP has sold over40,000
copies so far,which is great as
it shows there's at least that
many people with good taste around.
(now that I think about it that
doesn't sound like too many...)
"White Girl" isn't as uptempo as
much of their stuff but it's still
a great one from a forthcoming
second album.We at T&G have,still,
and will...love X.

**THE CLOCKS-"TICK TOCKMAN"/CONFIDENT-
IALLY,RENEE"** TERMINAL RECORDS
Light years better than their cover
on the C.C. ep.This single features
two distinct sounds-the A side being
much more suited to my own taste...
a creeping sinister,and slightly 60s
sounding tune,that grew on me after
a few listens.Drop em a line;to
Clocfact:8323 #79 Kirtland,Ohio

the clocks

THE WIPERS- EP
If I was to release a new WIPERS
single it would've contained one
of their classics like "Tragedy",
Their album is great....buy it.

**SKUDDUR-"LET''S GO STEADY"/"STRIKE
FORCE"** SKUDDER Records
Cool name huh?Ranks right up there
with THE BEES,THE THWARTED,NO JOE,
AND THE INSECT SURFERS.The music?
Comically poor by any standards...
makes the DRASTICS sound like something original.We got an EP,a single
and a live tape and we feel real bad
that we don't like them but we aren't
like that asshole who edits THE OFF-
ENSE who likes shitty records just to
keep the freebies coming-he actually
liked that 4-SKINS gem from New York
can you believe it?That's allright
misery loves company...As far as
SKUDDUR goes we may be hitting below
the corn-belt but I hate sometimes
for no reason at all.FUCK y
                              o
                               u

EYELESS
IN
GAZA

**NEXT ISSUE WILL INCLUDE:
THE FIX-DEMO TAPE REVIEW
THE CRAVATS
THE DECLINE OF WESTERN CIV-
ALIZATION SOUNDTRACK
NECROS EP
AND GOBS MORE!!!!!!!!!!**

EYELESS IN GAZA
An effectually dim record like
this gives me restored faith in
the sleeper bin...you know,the
English bands even the English
don't buy...seems the low cost
recordings have a better success
rate(in quality not $$$$$)than
the "obscure" bands who are getting the push.Of course a % of
both will always be drek-ram-
ifications of the same old tired
themes.Eyeless in Gaza posess a
sensitivity that encompasses

these paradoxical genres....
the veiled,and haunting sounds,
coupled with an up front synth-
their prerogative and it works,
all of it.

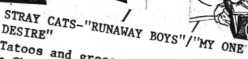

STRAY CATS-"RUNAWAY BOYS"/"MY ONE DESIRE"

Tatoos and grease man, hot boxin' a Chesterfield in my pink pegged slacks, Vivian pops a Johnny Ace tape and we're off to Devil's Backbone for hand jobs in my 57. The big quiffed kitty on my right arm is the coolest, but it sure did hurt when they did the red for his Crombie Coat, the chicks really go for the blade when they feast on that one, it was worth it.

BLACK FLAG-"JEALOUS AGAIN" EP

In Jan. it'll be three years since the first EP surfaced, and it still smokes with the best of em'...as my partner would say "if you haven't heard this then you're etc. etc..... Frankly I'm all out of those over-used adjectives like raw, manic, out-of-control, and machine-gun violence,

but they all apply to BLACK FLAG. Their stand on the violence is commendable...not backing off ...not that they necessarily enjoy watching kids killing each other, but jusy knowing your music has such an effect must be one of the small rewards for a band like this(especially playing the cities they did on their recent tour. Ok I'll get to the disc

at hand, 5 cuts with no let-up. You've got to turn it way up as the recording is a hissy sonofabitbh and when you crank what hits you will make your fuckin' shoes explode. The single of]980.

CLASSIX NOUVEAUX-"NASTY LITTLE GREEN MEN"/"TEST TUBE BABIES" Liberty Re-cords

They reall; sport a contrived image-with banal lyrics to match(nasty little green men, friend or enemy, like we see on Star Trek, just like you and me...) but their songwriting is impeccanle but their songwriting is impeccable and lead vocalist Sal Solo sports an awesome range that equips him for any-thing from "Asleep In The Deep" to a shrill falsetto sure to crack the stu-rdiest of tweeters. Don't lump these guys into that modernist-bandwagon-rip-off category...they aren't a synthesizer band and both singles have staying power. An album will be released soon. Great band.

JOHN PAUL DIEM
1958 --- 1980
R.I.P.

218

POLY STYRENE-"Talk In Toytown"/"Sub-Tropical" United Artists

As far as this girl's concerned, X-Ray Spex are history. If you bought this hoping for more of the same, you're gonna be in for a big disappointment. Gone are the metal thud of the guitars and the squealing runs of the saxophone, having been replaced with a chap or two tinkling the ivories. It's all keyboards and synthesizers, and believe it or not, she's never sounded better. Firmly planted in the forefront she proves once and forall that she's not the shrill shouter we had come to expect. B-side doesn't quite measure up to "Talk. .", though. The setting is a bit to serene and secure, like basking drunkedly in the hot Caribbean sun with a lime cooler. Nonetheless, this record shows that Ms. Styrene is more than up to the challenge of trying something new.--DS

THE BIRTHDAY PARTY-"Friend Catcher" "Waving My Arms"/"Catman" 4 AD

I don't know where 4 AD finds these bands, but they must have some pretty shrewd talent scouts out there combing the countryside and turning over every stone in their relentless, and so far, successful, search for purveyors of the new music. This is their latest catch and just might be the best. From Australia, this band takes the razorblade to the skin of our teeth when they open the a-side with what sounds like gnashing steel. You know the feeling, your back gets all prickly and someone just gave you a transfusion of ginger ale. A metallic nightmare that's as incomprehensible as it is enthralling. What these guys are trying to do is anybody's guess, so long as they keep doing it. I'll be happy.--DS

D.O.A.-"W.W. III"/"Whatcha Gonna Do?" Sudden Death Records

First complaint-both sides are twice as long as they should be. Second complaint-both sides are as boring as they are long. There's no punch like on their "Prisoner" single nor does it have that unbridled energy of the crudely sophomoric live EP. Both cuts appear on the album, and that should give you some idea of what that holds in store. Very little. Sure we had it number one last issue, but an overzealous anticipation fogged our usually stalwart critical judgement. We goofed, so don't waste your time on this yawn, but do at least check out the sleeve. A gristly delight that makes the one for "Holiday In Cambodia" look like Romper Room.--DS

WAH! HEAT-"Better Scream"/"Joe"
Inevitable Records

This is one of those reserved understated gems that fail to create much
of a stir due primarily to the band's
modest, yet compelling music. They
choose not to rant and harangue the
listener with antiquated and cliché
ideologies, rather they take on an
unstrained seriousness that stops
us cold in our tracks. They could
be viewed as a political band, but
they're not preaching, they don't
claim to know anymore than anyone
else. OK, so you might be saying to
yourself: 'fuck that shit, this music suppose to incite that spontaneous reponse, no time for thinking
in this man's world. Who wants to
turn to granite with their hands
glued to their chins?' That may be,
but there's still room for a band
that might make us scratch our heads
instead of our pubis. Take a moment
and give these guys a listen.--DS

BUSH TETRAS-"Too Many Creeps"/"Snakes
Crawl"/"You Taste Like The Tropics"
99 Records

Imitation Slits? Is that some kind
of joke? Good singles from The Big
Apple are a definite rarity, coming
far and few between(I'm still trying
to forget the 4 Skins). Fortunately,
things have taken a turn for the better with this one. "Creeps" is unquestionably the best thing to come
out of the Times Square city in quite
some time. With its simple beat and
crusty rhythm, it's downright contagious. Great dance number. Side
2 is more stereotypically no wave,
although "Snakes Crawl" has some good
lines---'boys wank. . . limp crank'.
No beating around the bush(heh heh)
on this one. 99 Records have gotten
off to a great start, I just hope
there's more where this came from.
--DS

THE CRAVATS-"Precinct"/"Who's In
Here With Me?" Small Wonder

So Small Wonder is still around,
evidenced by their recent release
of yet another piece of vinyl obscurity. Obscure yes, but dull?,
not by a long shot. On "Precinct"
the Cravats churn their way into
our heads with a stampeding drive
that combines the unintelligible
banter of Friction with the unsettling funk of The Pop Group. Propelled by some uncommonly furious
sax blowing and a drummer who quite
literally gallops across the grooves,
this band is a much welcomed alternative to our everyday brew. These
guys should not be overlooked. . .
but probably will.--DS

SIMPLE MINDS EMPIRES AND DANCE

SIMPLE MINDS-"EMPIRES AND DANCE"
ARISTA RECORDS
This band is virtually unknown
in this country, perhaps with the
success of the ULTRAVOX LP, the
SIMPLE MINDS' star-tripping days
aren't far behind but I'm not holding my breath.
      In early 78 the band was rushed
into the studio and came up with
very little worthy of merit."LIFE
IN A DAY" was a grey pop album
clouded by numerous uncertainties.
The band hadn't developed a cohesive
framework for the finer aspects of

their approach.On outing #2 "REEL TO
REEL CACOPHANY" they chose to articulate in the synth-pop arena-a portion
of the resultant product was brilliant
like the intriguing"Film Theme" and the
single release "Changeling".But some of
the material still wallowed in'flash &
no backlash'bin, a rhetorical restatement
of form crippled by an uncontrollable
urge to be unique.The pleasantly plain
blue packaging thankfully failed to
gesticulate the pretention with unecessary
pomp.Both packages evidence the growth of
vocalist Jim Kerr."EMPIRES AND DANCE"
synthesises a despondant view of the world
with the second albums electronic successes.
But the (this don't come easy,ED.) dance-
ability of much of this third album will
cause it to get lots of airplay in European discos.The mindless will snap to
"I Travel",never bothering to decipher Kerr's
philosophy.EMPIRES AND DANCE" will convert,
impress,and depress if you only give it the
chance.
         Tall,Blonde,and Scandinavian

I TRAVEL

CITIES, BUILDINGS, FALLING DOWN
IDEAL HOMES FALLING DOWN
THESE PICTURES I SEE ON THE WALL
TIMELESS LEADERS STAND SO TALL
ASSASSIN IN A HIT AND RUN
ASIA STEALS A NEW BORN SON
EVACUEES AND REFUGEES
PRESIDENTS AND MONARCHIES

TRAVEL ROUND I TRAVEL ROUND
DECADENCE AND PLEASURE TOWNS
TRAGEDIES, LUXURIES, STATUES, PARKS,
  AND GALLERIES

EUROPE HAS A LANGUAGE PROBLEM
TALK, TALK, TALK, TALK, TALKING ON
IN CENTRAL EUROPE
SOME MEN ARE MARCHING
MARCHING ON AND MARCHING ON
LOVE SONGS PLAYING IN THE
  RESTAURANTS
AIRPORT PLAYING "BI SOME LO"

TRAVEL ROUND I TRAVEL ROUND
DECADENCE AND PLEASURE TOWNS
TRAGEDIES, LUXURIES, STATUES, PARKS,
  AND GALLERIES

EUROPE HAS A LANGUAGE PROBLEM
AMERICA A LANGUAGE PROBLEM
I TRAVEL
EURO-BUREAU-INTERPOL
MAKING LOVE TO THE CRIMINALS
ASIA HAS A LANGUAGE PROBLEM
I TRAVEL
ON AND ON AND ON AND ON AND ON
AND ON AND ON

RODNEY ON THE ROQ-L.A. COMP-
ILATION
There's alot of music here but
I'm only going to talk about the
worthwhile stuff like AGENT ORANGE
who open this disc with a fuckava
great song..real clean sounding and
nasty at the same time which makes
no sense I know but this is one band
who are meeting our expections head
on and are driving our faces back in
the dirt where they belong.Now if I
can only lay my mitts on a copy of
their 45 I'll esconce in my lazy-boy
but not before.THE ADOLESCENTS are
another top drawer "new" band I
guess and with all the ink their getting they can't miss..they've got

this enemic looking skinny guy on
vocals...everyone's talking about em'-
reason #2 to buy this album.Uh oh the
long awaited surfacing of the CIRCLE
Jerks on record and they flog "Wild
In The Streets" again...but wait,old
Keith pulls this one along...and makes
it(with more than ample instrumental
support)hittsville #3 ....he's got that
nasal rummy slur in his voice that makes
you want to laugh and beat fuck on someones face at the same time...and if you
can't read my scrawled review of their
album on page one then I'm telling you
now...IT"S THE ALBUM OF THE YEAR(at least)
Idon't like uxa but "Tragedies" is their
best cut and somehow it sounds alot better

nestled in with the rest.BLACK FLAG-what
more can I say...as I write I'm missing
their gig in Chicago because otherwise I
won't be able to afford to buy my girl
an X-mas present,but DS with camera in
hand will have something to say about
it next ish..."No Values" appears on their
new single and of course it kicks....

Their singer sounds alot like COREY of
the ATTITUDES,that is real young and
obstreperous with hoarse written in for
every morning after...THE KLAN should
have cut something new cuz I'm aready

wore out on their single with "Pushin too
Hard"/"Cover Girls"....THE VIDEOTS are
tops too with this cut also appearing on
the HAPPY SQUID Sampler(also with the
URINALS and only 500 pressed so get one
now)THE CROWD and THE SIMPLETONES cuts are
typically young snotty themed tunes with
punchy rythms and dumb lyrics the likes
I haven't seen since the BEACH BLVD. LP
which remains one of my most listened to
slabs when I'm feeling old and on the
brink of complacency.Get this RODNEY ON THE
ROQ LP...I don't know what Rod has too do
with this and I don't care...and despite
what you think of us POSH BOY we think
you're cool for giving alot of these young
bands a chance.

                    TESCO

TV
(TransVestite)   DS
                     (DOGSHIT)

TOUCH & GO'S TOP TEN RECORDS IN THE
HISTORY OF RECORDED MUSIC...AN EX-
CLUSIVE LOOK AT THE BEST...
1)GAS RONDA 45
2)RICKY RICARDO"BA BA LOO"
3)THOR-"MILITARY MATTERS"
4)ALL ALVIN STARDUST
5)THE BARKING DOGS-"JINGLE BELLS"
6)ALFRED E. NUEMAN-"IT'S A GAS"
7)MILK AND COOKIES-"RABBITS MAKE LOVE"
8)BURT WARD-"ROBIN BOY WONDER"
9)RED SOVINE-"GIDDY-UP-GO"
10)TELLY SAVALAS-"WHO LOVES YA BABY?"

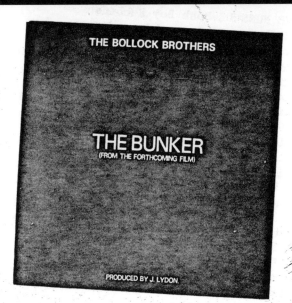

THE BOLLOCK BROTHERS

THE BUNKER
(FROM THE FORTHCOMING FILM)

PRODUCED BY J. LYDON.

A CERTAIN RATIO-"Blown Away"/"Flight" "And then Again" Factory Records

I like this record and then again, I don't. The striking similarities between "Blown Away" and Joy Division are simply too close for comfort. I sense that they're being manipulated, whether consciously or unconsciously, in a direction that would hamper their creativity. I think it is safe to assume that Martin Hannett has to be fingered as the prime suspect in this undermining of a truly fine band. It must be no surprise to anyone that with the death of Ian Curtis everyone turned toward ACR as the obvious heir apparent to Joy Division, regardless of the restrictions that would be placed upon them. Joy Division was Joy Division, but we certainly don't need another one. To perpetuate their spirit at the expense of another band would be a gross sacrifice, especially one of the potential of ACR.--DS

THE BOLLOCK BROTHERS-"The Bunker"/ "The Bootleg Man" McDonald & Lydon Records

Will the real producer and vocalist extraordinaire please stand up. Behind some deceptive packaging we've been made to believe that John Lydon has come up with something new, assuming he got bored with PiL and decided to release some limited edition 12 inch to a mass of adoring fans. Well, I swallowed the bait hook, line, and sinker. It ain't Johnny that's doing the singing, but his 4be2 brother, Jimmy. It may sound like John at first, but don't be fooled. Jimmy and Jock McDonald are old buddies, and it appears these two have conned their way into a few more record sales by providing as little information on the sleeve as possible making for a conveniently ambiguous message. Not that the record is that bad or anything, it's just that I don't like getting duped any more than the next guy. The music here is pleasantly repetitive, a Three Mantras for mass consumption, although it borders dangerously close to the monotonous. It did manage to hold my interest for the first month or so that I owned it, but that interest is steadily waning and the dust has already begun to collect. It has an immediate appeal that no sooner do you get it home begins to wear off. The kind of thing you'd expect for what turns out to be a rather insignificant record.--DS

WOTTA STUD!

THE NUNS LP-Posh Boy Records
Whoohh an LP from this cadaver am I
dreaming?I wish I was...and at least
then there'd be a good possibility that
it'd be a great one with Jennifer or
something but unfortunately her looks
is all they got.The tunes really sound
like out and out mainstream droppings,
with a drop of tastelessness to make
it look current.Check this line out
girls..."my master,my savage,my king,
I will do anything"....same thing you
said to Herbie as he was rolling off
of you to catch some z-z-z-z-z's lasr
night right?Well sorry but lame lyrics
like this set to hopelessly BLONDIE-
ESQUE (I had to say it...ED.) muzik
add up to one naseuating bit of piss-
ant tripe.I'm getting off.....

GG ALLIN-"Always Was, Is And Always
Shall Be" Orange Records

It can't be helped, but I simply can
not take this record seriously. What
might have been very good intentions
on paper wind up hopelessly out of
touch with current trends which will
probably make this the butt of many
an unfortunate joke. I almost feel
sorry for you guys, but this is suppose to be constructive criticism,
not an exercise in pity. You listen
to the music on this disc, and you
can just picture some Eastern European band taking their first stab
at punk rock. Something seems to
have gotten lost in the translation,
resulting in an absurd interpretation
of what these last three years were
all about. Further proof of the total isolation of these guys can be
found on the sleeve, ie. 'Birth Side
...Death Side', "Play At Maximum
Volume"(I thought that went out with
The James Gang), and get this, "1980's
Rock 'n' Roll", something missing on
both sides of this record. Mr. Allin
better bone up on his current history
if he wants to avoid another disaster
like this one. Oh, I liked "Automatic"
alright. Class dismissed.--DS

SCREAMING URGE LP
Garner Records

Inconsistency and an obvious short-
age of ear-grabbing tunes makes this
Ohio band frustrating to listen to.
Having a few good ideas and being
able to communicate those ideas to
the audience effectively tells me
that if these guys had waited a
bit longer and put some more thought
into what direction they wanted to
take with this project, I think
they could have stunned us with
what quite possibly could have been
a great independent LP. Instead,
what we have here is a regular pot-
pourri of styles with an irritating
lack of continuity. Although I
can't fault the band on the failure
of the album. They made some tapes
over a period of time, and that's
their only contribution. No voice
in the decision as what goes on and
what doesn't. Somebody else with
his head firmly stuck up his ass
can shoulder the responsibility for
such indiscriminate selections. As
was true with their live show some
two months back at the Club, the
highlights on the album are "Hitler's
In Brasil" and "We Are Mono" with
the others bringing up a very sorry
rear. A boring blend of mercy beat
(they have a cut by the same name),
old-timey rock 'n' roll, and some
offbeat ecleticism. Too bad, they
might have been able to turn my
head around had they gotten the
right combination, now all they get
is a raised indifferent eyebrow.--DS

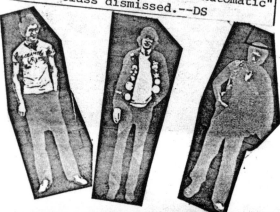

BLACK FLAG LIVE!
w/ the EFAGIES

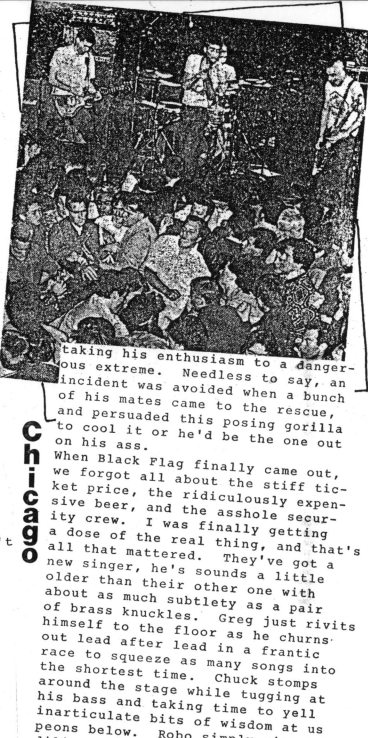

I don't think I'd be fooling anyone if I said my anticipation for this gig wasn't anything short of rabid, although the foam may not have been visable, I was excited. To some I'm sure, my blind and unyielding dedication to LA and its bands must seem truly surreal, but this stuff gets me right where it counts(don't ask me where, it just does). An overpowering chaos that's frenzied and immediate, but not cursory and transparent. If you haven't gotten the gist to what's happening in, say, the first thirty seconds of a "Nervous Breakdown", then buddy, you're lost and would be better off in the trendy high-brow sophistication of the Wax Trax set who drool ever-so-neatly over every Factory release. Call it punk rock, call it some kind of new music, call it anything you like, but you can't deny the fact that this is the kind of noise that curdles the minds of the feeble and completely melts those of their most ardant fans. A bruising assault on our senses that leaves us in a near comatose state of euphoria. I wouldn't want it any other way.

Tonight's show began with what I believe to be Chi-coho's only true punk outfit--The Efagies. A mirror image of the Upstarts, their singer looks as well as sounds like Mensi. Not too terribly original, but compared to what I had envisioned the warmup act to be, these guys were more than up to the challenge of sparking the crowd. It wasn't too tough, either, cuz they brought along a legion of swaggering skinheads, who promptly staked out a territory in the middle of the dancefloor as their own. A regular battle zone, that only the hearty would care to invade. The kind of good old boys who'd scare the living poop out of the cowering faggots who hang out at our own Club DooBee(am I getting through to you, Marcel?). One of the bouncers(who had the gall to display a Black Flag badge) took it upon himself to straighten out one of the skins who he thought was

taking his enthusiasm to a dangerous extreme. Needless to say, an incident was avoided when a bunch of his mates came to the rescue, and persuaded this posing gorilla to cool it or he'd be the one out on his ass.

Chicago

When Black Flag finally came out, we forgot all about the stiff ticket price, the ridiculously expensive beer, and the asshole security crew. I was finally getting a dose of the real thing, and that's all that mattered. They've got a new singer, he's sounds a little older than their other one with about as much subtlety as a pair of brass knuckles. Greg just rivits himself to the floor as he churns out lead after lead in a frantic race to squeeze as many songs into the shortest time. Chuck stomps around the stage while tugging at his bass and taking time to yell inarticulate bits of wisdom at us peons below. Robo simply sits diligently on his drumkit, oblivious to his surroundings. But what these guys do individually is inconsequential compared to the force and velocity that is in their music. The new stuff off the EP, the classics from the first single--all great. Hearing this band live helped to erase any memory of all the shit I've had to put up with during my residence at the Club. Punk rock in its positively rawest form--bands just don't come any better.--DS

225

Now that I'm out on the streets, Tesco told me to write whatever it takes lengthwise to keep you informed on the So. Cal. scene-- since nothing that follows will be particulary incisive or profound I can't guarantee how much you, the besotted public, will ever set eyes on once our beloved editor has weilded his pen and wedged this into wunderbar T&G format.
I witnessed the ALLEYCATS and MIDDLE CLASS back to back at the Starwood-- MIDDLE CLASS were great-non-stop on every song. . . but rather than incite the audience as many of the hardcore bands do, they seem satisfied to try to reach them, penetrate our thick skulls as it were with their perceptions, and so astute they are (Love Is Just A Tool) the hottest song of their set was "Suspicion", I don't remember hearing "Out Of Vogue" and I know they played all of the songs that will be on their new EP-- I don't have much info on it yet but Jeff(vocalist) promised T&G a copy as soon as available.
ALLEYCATS headlined and deservedly so--I'm not saying their better than M.C. but they've certainly earned top billing by sticking totally to the flavor of their original band which has been tasty(huh?--ED) since inception. Their set was letter perfect with a rousing encore of "Too Much Junk" that touched me so deeply (bring out the teensy weensy violas) that I hung around afterwards to tell the band how great I thought they were--all three consumate musicians and entertainers without allowing themselves to be just that and only that--anyhow Randy rapped with me a bit and did tell me that their album (self-produced I think, definately self-promoted, manufactured, etc.) would be called "Nothing Means Nothing Anymore" and will be out soon and that of course T&G will have a copy on the way at first opportunity.

Let it be said just one more time that bouncers are totally fucked- especially the ones at the Starwood. At a subsequent concert featuring the SCREWS, FEAR, and 45 GRAVE I was passing the "hippie-weed" upstage to the guys in the VANDALS who were kind of mates of the SCREWS, and the bouncers ran up to the stage and practically yanked the guy off--eventually split but yook the joint with them raving "backstage not onstage asshole"(that was what the crowd told my band last time we played--ED) at the end of the SCREWS set I went backstage with them and the VANDALS and proceeded to continue puffing(pot sucks--ED). I talked awhile with their singer Craig, he's only 15, the rest of the guys are 17 to 19. . . It's got the same guitar/bass/drums layout with a singer--their H.B. punks(more on groupings later) but not as totally radical looking as BLACK FLAG, but the sound is there, good raw punk. I met Posh Boy(famous producer of the Siren LP and F-WORD) he's producing and/or managing The SCREWS. Anyway, he said that even though T&G slagged the UXA album (which he produced) he had to agree with the analysis(of course--ED). Pretty white of him to admit it, eh?? He looks like a lop-leisure suit with hair over his ears, I guess the young punks respect him to a point. He also had recommended to me when I consulted with him over his opinion and advice for this mag-he said T&G shouldn't try and write about the LA scene for LA readers-I asked why not especially now that I'm around to really see what's go-

ing down.His reply?"Yeah well you should write about us for them,not them writing about us for us-I hope everyone is as confused as I am cuz I think he's full of shit...Touch and Go rools OK...(ya "them" is the hillbillies that werent god-blessed enough to be born in CA.Suck me Posh Boy ypu fag..ED.)Because I spent the evening with The Screws I missed FEAR(shame,shame ED.)45 GRAVE I'd seen recently at the Hong Kong Cafe-they contain Don Bowles-the ex-drummer for the GERMS and also Voxpop(the GERMS scheduled to play a farewell concert soon!!!???)-also a chick singer called Mary Bat Thing-they were all whiteface and paint their necks to look as if they had a bullet hole in them,the guys all wear shriner hats...a neat look but not a totally terrific sound-kinda mediocre but the guitarist did do some nice feedback on the last song...Then on the 18th I finally got to see BLACK FLAG-their last concert in Hollywood had provoked a riot but unlike The Germs they weren't banned from clubs immediately,so last week they played Joey Kills in Burbank then back to the Starwood-middle bill was Eddie and The Subtitles-I read in SLASH(what's that?ED.)how he'd recently been busted but obviously he's been released and played a great set...the first chord got the crowd going so fast that before I knew it I was on my ass-I quickly got up and waded out of reach of the offending elbows-they were great and BLACK FLAG was greater-everyone sez they were better when Keith of The CIRCLE JERKS sang for thembut the current guy is grate at jumping around but his voice was too hoarse for any lyrics to really be heard except on "nervous Breakdown"...they really kicked ass and so did everyone on the dance floor.....
Now on to an exposition of the p*** heirarchys and a personal commentary on violence and trends...Contrary to what alot of nonLA. people think,the coolest punks in So'CAL. are the hardcore beach punks...they aren't trendies and they aren't just into violence-basically the truth is just the opposite-the people with the mohawks and dyed hair look g litter as if their heydey were the early seventies..let's face it 1980 is a somber time to be alive...these punk groupings are loosly organised into neighborhood gangs but unlike minority youth gangs there's no rivalries amongst each other (at least on that level of actual violence based on neighborhood)and though they hate the hippies they generally don't pick on them even when they have a numerical advantageEXCEPT on the dance floor...yes folks if you're a longhair or re-

semble one (or look anything less than hardcore and tribal you run the risk of getting whaled on..at one point I was leaned up against these punkettes who were leaning against the stagetrying to dance without the sea of elbows a few feet back...It was bliss pressed up against these three underage girls when reality struck...some punk literally tore me away and tried to slam me to the ground...and for every punk who'll knock you down there's 2 or 3 who help you back up..anyhow it's great the young kids are really dead serious about their music... and it's really fucked that the majority of the youth are being indoctrinated by commercial sludge...So for all of you

quick to knock the beach punks as detrimental to the scene I say "FUCK OFF"... If it was'nt for the beachkids and the bands the state of the music wouldn't be any better than it was 5 years ago in L.A.The heppest getup seems to be military trenchcoats or overcoats-jackboots with chains and supershort or mohawk hair preferrably died for at least a tiny patch(anybody seen my cyanide tablets?ed.) The La Mirada punks have a diamond shaped insignia that looks like ◇ where butt covers are in for da femmes that read Youth Gone Mad(let me fondle your bum flaps Phoebe,ED.)White People are a cool young group out of Long Beach-they played second bill at Joey Kills to SYNTHETIC WARFARE (ex MODERNS) Anyhow LB.punks, HB.punks,LMP!s even Lansing punks Youre all cool!!!!!!!!
SHANE WILLIAMS
Hollywood,Ca..

ニューヨーク生活を語るレックとヒゲは楽しそうだ。しかし、実際向こうにいたときは、東京のバンド仲間から便りが来るたびに、東京のことを考えていたらしい。ふつうなら、東京のことを考えていたらしい。

もう少しニューヨークで自分を試そう。ぐらいの欲がでそうなものだが、彼らは結局土俵は東京しかないと確信する。

「日本に大地震でもきて、生き残った日本人は世界中に散らばっていけばいいと思ってた。だけど、俺にもやっぱり日本を愛してる部分があるんだよ」

1年ぶりに帰国する機内で、レックは東京のことを考えていた。ニューヨークで曲も作ったし、東京へ戻ったら、すぐさまバンドを組む予定だった。フリクションというバンド名も、この機内で考えたものだ。ところが、東京に着いたとたん、希望が崩れてしまう。

「東京のアパートに帰ったら恐しかった。何だかもう東京に規格が合わなくなってたし」

ニューヨーク時代は自分ばかりを前面に押しだすアメリカ人を、恥知らずと感じたレックだが、日本に戻ったら日本人がみな同じ顔に見えたという。

レックの目に映った状況はニューヨークで思い描いた街とはあまりにも違っていたが、とにもかくにもバンドだけは結成した。第1期フリクションはレック、ヒゲ、ラビスというメンバーが参加したのは79年10月だ。

彼らはバンドを維持するために働いている。

「でもね、俺たちは夜アルバイトしてるけど、たとえば坂本君なんかも自分のやりたい音楽と別にCMソング作ったりしてるでしょ。それと同じようなことだと思う。ただ俺たちは音楽と関係ないアルバイトしてるだけだよ」

それまで、彼らの夜の職業が何であるのか聞きたくなって、その質問をやっとちょっぴり後めたい気になってその質問を

FRICTION INTERVIEW

クはニューヨークへ行ってからだね」

ヒゲが、これまたゼスチャーたっぷりに答えてくれた。日本人が洋服姿でもおかしくないようになるには、何世代もかかっているはずなのに、1年間でニューヨークの匂いをしみ込ませて帰ってくる人間がいることに、また感心する。ホントにあなたたち、カッコいいよ、とこちらも精一杯の身ぶりで何度もケーハクに賞賛の意を表わした。

「見かけで人間を判断できる人はケーハクじゃ

2時間以上たってから、レックはこう言って笑う。そのあとヒゲが、俺、評論家にタダでレコード配るのいやだな、と言いだす。てもフリクションのお金で制作したレコードをトリオレコードのお金で制作したレコードをトリオの人間が配るんでしょ、ところがレックが乗りだしてきた。

「東京の人って、みんな待ってるだけなんだよ。音楽評論家もそう。記事書いてフラスト

う。

「実はツアーの話、雑誌に載せてもらうようレックが少しテレくさそうな身ぶりをする。ツアーの会場と日時をたずねたが、彼らは3人ともそれを知らなかった。もし、このページに載った彼らの写真を見て、何かしらの電波をキャッチしたら、どこかでスケジュールを調べてぜひ足を運んで欲しい。本当はこの文を最初に書くべきだった。

都、大阪、金沢…」

「ヒゲの故郷北海道と、ツネマツマサトシが生まれた九州にも行くはずだったが、予算の関係で流れたという。

「そういえばレコードのプロモーションでツアーに行くんだ。仙台、京

い出したように言った。

インタビューの最後に、レックが思っ自分の意見をもってバンドをやっていきたいからこうしてつづけているようなものだし」

「でもね、世の中は俺たちがどうやったって変えられないと思う。ただ、俺たちの演奏聞いた人が、音楽じゃなくても何か自分のやりたいことを始めるきっかけになってくれればいい。俺だって自分のことをもっと知りたいからこうしてつづけている

ンてツアーに行くんだ。仙台、京

やないんだよ」

レックの言葉に救われた気がした。しかし、ヒゲは、音楽評論家の部屋に山積みされたレコードの中に自分たちのが混じるといやだ、と感情的になっている。レックは、音楽評論家だけの問題でなく、日本人の全体像について考えてる。

「たとえば向うの評論家ってけなす時はすごく少ないと思うんだ」

レックの方もチキショーって感じである種のセッションみたいだけど、日本人て何もかもあいまいでしょ。人の顔色みないで自分の意見を言える人って

の出方待ってるだけで、自分からは何も見せない」

めた。

レックの言葉に救われた気がした。しかし、

この言葉は私をなぐさめるために発せられたのではない。彼らは、自分たちの姿にエラくと感じている。レックは、音楽評論

レックとヒゲはゼスチャーたっぷりに話す。自信をもっているのだ。ロック・バンドなんて写真を見れば分るという彼らの意見ももっともだ。

それも少しもわざとらしくなく、このカッコ良さはそのまま彼らのステージにつながるものだが、これは1年間のニューヨーク仕込みなのだろうか。

「俺は昔からこういう感じだったけど、レックとヒゲはゼスチャーたっぷりに話す。

「だいたいインタビューでしゃべりすぎると絶対マイナスなんだよ。俺たちも写真だけ載せてもらえば良かった」

HITS THAT JUST WON'T QUIT! —tv/ds

small

"Jealous Again" EP BLACK FLAG
"Blood Stains" AGENT ORANGE
SELF CONTROL EP
Happy Squid Sampler
"Totally Wired" THE FALL
"C30-C60-C90" BOW WOW WOW
"From The Cradle To The Grave" CRISPY AMBULANCE
"Goiter On My Gonad" YOUTH de SADE
NEGATIVE TREND EP
"Sex Machine" CRAWLING CHAOS
WALL OF VOODOO EP
"Seconds Too Late" CABARET VOLTAIRE
"Blown Away" A CERTAIN RATIO
"Picture Plane" RETRO
"Girl" SUICIDE

BIG

"Group Sex" CIRCLE JERKS
"Grotesque" THE FALL
"Kings Of The Wild Frontier" ADAM AND THE ANTS
"Absolute Game" SKIDS
WIPERS LP
"No Questions Asked" FLESH EATERS
"Jeopardy" THE SOUND
"Voice Of America" CABARET VOLTAIRE
"Heathen Earth" THROBBING GRISTLE
"Super Trouper" ABBA

Sally Struthers' Christmas Wish.

"Somewhere in the world there is a child who will spend Christmas Day the same way she spends every other day.

"Hungry. Poor. Helpless.

"I know, because I found such a child six years ago. I became a sponsor through Christian Children's Fund.

"I wish you could know the joy and love I have known these past six Christmases I've shared with Marites.

"Since I became her sponsor, I know Marites has daily meals, medical help and a chance to go to school. And the kind of love that every child needs.

"But all that I have given seems like nothing when I think of the new meaning she has given to my life.

"You can know the richness, the joy of giving to a child who needs your help.

"You can know it in time for Christmas.

"You can become a sponsor through Christian Children's Fund.

"All it costs is $15 a month, but you help give a child so very much.

"Regular meals, medical attention, the chance to go to school, or whatever that child needs most to live a healthy, productive life.

"You needn't send any money now.

"First learn about the child who needs you.

"Just send the coupon.

"We'll send you a child's photograph and tell you about her way of life—her age, health, interests and family background.

"We'll also tell you how this child can be helped, and give you details on how you can exchange letters and share a very special part of her life.

"After you find out about the child and Christian Children's Fund, then you can decide if you want to become a sponsor.

"Simply send in your check or money order for $15 within 10 days. On return the photo and background material so we can ask someone else to help.

"Get to know a child who needs your help. Somewhere there is a child who wishes she could share something special with you this Christmas.
Love."

[handwritten graffiti overlaid:] CAN'T BELIEVE SOME OF THESE BEAR THESE YOU?! IF YOU'RE DADDY WANT TO FEEL GOOD ABOUT WHERE YOUR MONEY GOES

AND OURS!!! SEND THOSE HARD EARNED SAW BUCKS TO US (LIKE) WE'LL SQUANDER IT WITH THEM. BEST OF LUCK SAVE THIS NOT ON YOUR LIFE!

NEW WAVE SUCKS   LIKE SHIT!

SEND MONEY and STUFF OUR POCKETS

put another starving child out of its misery, that's right, gotta nip this 'punk rock' shit in the bud. $ _____

NAME _____

ADDRESS _____

CITY _____ STATE _____ ZIP ____

Send to: T&G, POB 26203 Lansing MI 48909

12

Dez from Black Flag caught in a pensive moment at the Chicago show, and this pic was first runner-up for the book's cover shot... One of the shittier Xerox jobs of all the issues, and it took some work just to resurrect it into semi-readability... Guess the toner drum on the old-school Xerox needed shaking. The readers' poll makes me chuckle... We probably only got a handful back and just packed it with our faves. They call that editorial discretion? Best answer that didn't make the poll results? "Best Club—Kenny's Arm" (sorry, folks, inside joke—as long as Miller and I are laughing, then it's funny).

TOUCH AND GO

75¢

NO. 12

FURRY COUCH AND TOUCH-Y-GO PRESENTS "NOT VERY MUCH!!!"

A CRAZE A MINUTE. ②

☾ TRUE OR FALSE — Sid Vicious exercised his "rights" by overdosing on

🧠 3 MILES HIGH — o.k, it's official! CATTLE MUTALATIONS AT 3.M.I.   NO PARTIAL CREDIT.

🍼 TRUE OR FALSE — HOW MANY THANKSGIVINGS HAVE YOU SABOTAGED BY SUCKING THE N₂O COMPLETLY OUT OF ALL THE TOPPING CANS

🏺 TRUE OR FALSE — P.I.L. '80 VIDEO BY P. DOUGHERTY. THE KITCHEN — NYC. EARLIER BIT OF "FRANKIES" DONE IN C/W WITH SUICIDE WAS PRETTY BAD. BUT THEN — FROM "DEAD" ON THE VISAUL DISPLAY WAS RATHER GOOD. NOT MAX FLIESHER, BUT INCREASINGLY INTRESTING, OVERLAYS — FILMS, AND SPECIAL EFFECTS...MADE THESE A WHOLE LOT BETTER THAN THE AVEAGE VIDIO GUNK. FOLLOWING THE 3 p.i.L. TAPES (IN WHICH JAH W. LOOKS AS SILLY AS CAN BE!) WAS A 'WORK IN PROGRESS'....: WHICH STRUCK ME AS 'BEING A CLOSE RESEMBALANCE TO A MAGAZINE. IT WAS LOADS OF PIX — ALL SORTZ A IMAGES FROM THE MEDIA AND RANDOM TALK ABOUT CONSPIRICIES — MISINFORMATION — ETC. — UNFORTUNATLY — EVERYONE IS SO 'INTO' THE MUSIC THAT BACKED UP THE PICS (ALSO RANDOM LY) ALL OF ITS IMPACT WAS LOST. (IN THE PSYCHEDELIA).

☠ 3 CHEERS FOR AFGANI "H" IT'S SO BROWN AND STRONG AD COMPAIGNS STARRING: KIETH RICHARDS, ALL HIS TRANSFUSION RECIEPIENTS, S. KELLERMAN, G. SCOTT, R. HELL, THE VICIOUS FAMILY, GONZO, W.S. BURROUGHS, AND THE ENTIRE MORMAN CHURCH WILL BE MURDERED.

STAY TUNED to THIS MAGAZINE FOR NOT VERY MUCH MORE.........

FURRY COUCH IS AN EASTCOAST ARTIST/DIST./PUBLISHER. CONTACT c/o THIS MAGAZINE. DEATH TO THE INFIDELS IN OIL.

?!?!

LATE ADDITION — LOUD FAST NEWS — c/o Jewel, 215 Park Row NYC 10038 — NICE PAPER FROM THE PAPER BIG A.

FANZINES!

TAPE TALK — extra CURRENT IMPORT REVIEWS AND LOTS OF REGGAE — GREAT EXCLUSIVE THROBBING GRISTLE INTERVIEW A WHILE BACK — P.O. BOX 36, LAWRENCE, KANSAS 66044

WILD DOG GOOD TEXAS MAG OAT DON'T COME OUT OFTEN ENOUGH — P.O. BOX 35253 S. POST OAK STATION HOUSTON, TEXAS 77035, JUST SENT US THEIR LATEST, AND AS T.T. WOULD SAY IT'S HOT-

FINAL SOLUTION — THEY'VE ALSO GOT A RECORD LABEL-WRITE — 4304 JAMES DR. MATAIRIE, LA. 70003

SMEGMA JOURNAL — OHIO'S BEST A MIDWESTERN TRIBUTE TO HARDCORE MUSIC. BUY IT NOW — P.D. BOX 421 MAUMEE, OHIO 43537

XY-FLYER — DOCUMENTATION OF THE LIFE OF BRIAN IN ALL OF ITS SICK PERVERSION CONTACT HIM c/o SMEGMA

SLASH — QUARTERLY NOW-STILL UNBEATABLE IN SCOPE- THE REVIEWS ARE THE MOST COMPREHENSIVE ANYWHERE P.O. BOX 48888 LOS ANGELES, CA 90048

DP — I HATE THIS FUCKIN' RAG-TRIES TO BE A REAL COMMUNITY EFFORT-BUT THE REVIEWS SUCK FARTS WORTHLESS + BOREING — P.O. BOX 2391 OLYMPIA, WA 98507

FLIPSIDE — THE BEST ONE AROUND-WRITING IS SIMPLE AND TO THE POINT-COVERAGE OF ALL THE NEW BANDS IS EXCELLENT- #1 P.O. BOX 363, WHITTIER, CA. 90608

SMARM — PUT OUT BY A GAL NAMED ADLAID WHO CRAMS ALOT ON ONE SHEET OF PAPER-EXTENSIVE COVERAGE OF THE 4 AD/FACTORY TYPE BANDS-STRONGLY RECCOMENDED 7520 WEST REMUS RA. REMUS, MICH 49340

ANONYMOUS — THERE'S LIFE IN THE MOTOR CITY AFTER ALL #2 JUST OUT AND ITS GREAT, THEY HAVE BOOKIES TOO — GOOD INTERVIEW WITH THE BLIND — 20107 MADA AVE, SOUTHFIELD MICH. 48075

NO MAGAZINE — I CAN HANDLE BLOOD AND GUTS BUT SKIN DISEASES + THE OTHER SHOTS THEY PRINT GROSS ME OUT-LATEST ISH HAS A GEZA FLEXI P.O. BOX 57091 LA, CA 90057

TRASHLAND ADVENTURES — ANOTHER NEW ONE FROM MICH. THE FUTURE ISN'T QUITE SO BLEAK-

THE OFFENSE — WE'VE TAKEN A LOT OF CHEAP SHOTS AT THIS ONE — I ALWAYS GET MAD WHEN I READ IT-I DUNNO MAYBE THAT'S A GOOD SIGN-IN ANY CASE THERE'S A LOT HERE-

SUB POP — COMPLETELY DEVOTED TO DOMESTIC STUFF CONNECTED SOMEHOW WITH DP BUT MUCH BETTER... WRITE P.O. BOX 2391 OLYMPIA WA. 98507

SLUSH — BRENDAN'S MAG-BUT HE NEVER MAILED US ONE BACK SO WHO KNOWS?

CREEP-SAW AN ISSUE ONCE BUT I CAN'T REMEMBER P.O. BOX 5528 SAN FRANSISCO, CA 94101

IF YOU DO A MAG SEND US ONE-WELL RECIPROCATE BY SENDING YOU T+B. IF YOU'RE THINKING ABOUT DOING ONE.... FUCKIN' DO IT!! FURRY COUCH WILL BE GLAD TO AIDE YOU WITH DISTRIBUTION!!

ARTIST'S RENDERINGS OF ← ED + ED →

{DS} #12 FRONT COVER — DEZ OF BLACK FLAG-graphics and photo BY DS

TV

235

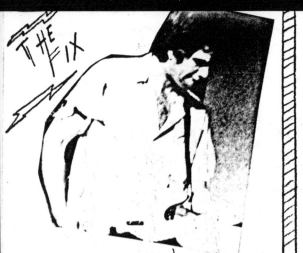

THE FIX-DEMO TAPE REVIEW

Lansing has a long way to go as far as a respectable scene is concerned. That is if you could ignore THE FIX. One local band capable of clamping the vice grips on the old gonads of the listener(girls disregard last statement) With each successive live outing they get tighter...but it's too bad certain members of the hardcore element around here dont get along. I mean theres so few but yes those 2 bands and you know who..the 2 best in the midwest who detest to my distress the very sound of the others name. But I don't have time for that bullshit this demo ROCKS. I don't even know if they wanted me reviewing this thing cuz they always talk about wanting to mix it again or whatever...all I have to say is if they could transfer the power of this uncontrolled rawness to vinyl then step back and make way for the best punk record Michigan has ever spit forth. No one in the mitten can equal the intensity of Craigs guitar work-he simply has it down...he's the best and if that bothers the rest of you so called axe men then eat shit. I'
ha
dr {Late flash} The debut single by   faster
th   THE FIX should be out sometime   )-Jerks
a   in FEBRUARY featuring "Vengeance"   watch for
or   "In THIS TOWN". if interested in a   o song titles
in   copy they are available for   l keep you
        2 bucks at FBC + SchoolKids or by
        mail for $2.50 p.p. Quantity is
        Limited. if you wait you lose!!!

THE FAST-AT THE CLUB   2-8-81

It'd been a couple years since I saw this band, and I'll probably be unpopular(so what else is new?)with all the super discriminating E.L. folks,who smugly grimaced and shuffled off after only a couple songs. I thought they were great as ever. Of course this aint the sound you'll generally find me patronizing,this is almost regressive in approach,but it's THE FAST as a total package ithat made the evening so much fun. Out came these four leather clad hooligans,who quickly launched into mostly new tunes like "Wet And Wild", "Sizzler" and my personal fave "Love Me Like A Locomotive" I realize everyone might not have been as punch drunk for this brand of grind, but shit the ol' good time is what it's all about. The highlight of the set was when lead vocalist Paul Zone began harassing one of our local female photographerartist types,first off by trying to stick the mike stand up her pooper,much to the chagrin of her beau who glared at the singer with a restrained contempt. Then out of nowhere here comes Mr. Zone skidding across the floor only to end up under the ladys skirt,a move which was answered by a swift kick fom the lass. This is entertainment...this is fun... TV

L-7 at the Polish Hall   Hamtramak
A different evening altogether. I didn't realize so many Polish people were homosapiens. Pass the amyl Boyd and let's get anal. Lot's of beer and not too many people...not a bad pair,and top all this off with the best new Detroit band around. L-7 features members formerly in the BLIND, and the bassist from RETRO. The vocalist hasnt sang prior to this band but she's got a boss sound...A Donna Bane soundalike,and lookalike. A band with a definate future...unless they break up.

ANGRY SHIT (YOU SHOULDN'T READ)

The first time we played the Club DooBee the cover was two bucks and so were the pitchers. That was back before the lame brains of Lansing pumped enough cash int o the bar, for such things as remodeling and new parking lot pavement. That was before Surfin' Dave decided to make the Doob the 'Bookies of Lansing', mistake n umber one, cloning yourself after the wo rst example of money hungry new wave ban gwagoners this side of the Bus Stop.
Being in an ex-local band, I always took it upon myself to support the local !sce ne', if I dare use such a misleading wor d. Club DooBee is more of a still life picture than a scene.
Everything from their now inflated price s to the attitude of the two clowns book ing the club makes me want to run to the nearest beer store, stock up, and listen to my records.
I could take up all the paper in Lansing and only begin to expose the incompetenc e of the two DooBee clowns. I remember Dave telling me about his decision to ge t a 'new wave' haircut before going into the booking business. Dave, you can cha nge your hair, but you can't change your ancient way of thinking on your obvious lack of taste--question your taste, Dave remember how you raved over Fanmail, and your current faves, The Attitudes? Well it's not my business to slag other acts (Hell, why not?--ED), but the way you ca rry on, you'd think The Attitudes would be more than a cheap Clash/Buzzcock ripo ff.

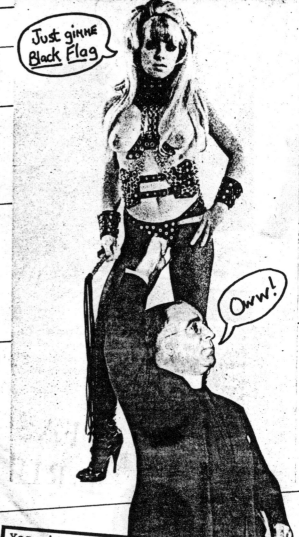

Yes sir, the Club DooBee advertised as " New Wave on Lake Lansing", sounds like s ome damn country club party. But Dave, you're interested in making this thing s ound rather pretty, aren't you? I remem ber you raving about your concern for th e band and your dedication to the scene. Your idea of limited quest lists and rid iculous three dollar covers obviously ma kes you a pitiful liar who can't keep hi s foot from down his throat.
There was once hope that Club DooBee cou ld give us a place to hang our hats, enj oy a beer, and hear some good music, but that dream is behind us now. I've stopp ed going to the bar and can speak for se veral others who are fed up with heavy m ental shit like The Fast and Destroy All Monsters, we're tired of having the soun d system cut off in the middle of the se t, but most of all, Dave, we're sick of you, your lack of taste, and you're shit ty way of communicating.
Wise up now or never see

WHY BOTHER?

GET that Pencil outA MY A$$ CREEP!!

Thanx Alot - thats my HOAGIE'

Publication - Rebuttal -

GAY PORNO

IM Livin' ON DOG DEW Scooby Dooo...

THE 80's - Come on Juan Baby - these frat cunts' only fans are middle age brained preppy melon heads. Dont mince words just so you can stay on their good side. They don't exist!!

Eddie Puke's band "The Polyester Penis Lickers" - Do you know how old this guy is. Time to bow out gracelessly before your hair falls out

FASCIST DRUMMER Contact Peter c/o this MAGAZINE wants tô form violént act

I'm writing this article while listening to a tape sent to me by the folks from Touch and Go mag.. it contains such bands as The Circle Jerks, Bad Brains, Germs, Pagans, Dils, D.O.A., etc. If you don't already know, these are some of the so-called "hard-core punk" bands. Most of this is pretty stand-ard '77 fare. Remember 1977? Bands such as the Sex Pistols, Clash, and Damned fought against a stagnating music and youth culture. They succeeded in a big way; kids had somewhere to go, something to do, something other than following the other sheep. These early punks didn't stop here though, they saw a need to make sure their music did not stagnate like the very bands they are fighting against. Lydon left the Pistols and went to Public Image which is very different from the early punk thrash. Mark Perry/ATV went on to become very experimental, and should always prove worth watch-... And the Clash, uh.,well....forget I mentioned them. ...s only loosely associated with punk, such as T.G., ...ret Voltaire, Crass, Pop Group...were added to the ...and now the music "scene" is a changing and power-...ful one, if you know where to look. Now lets look at the "hard-core punks", who have stayed pretty true to the early '77 style. Are these bands really "punk" when they can stagnate like they are?   Maybe they don't think they are stagnating, because it's only been 3-4 yrs. How many years is it going to take before they real-ize that they are as archaic as the bands/culture they are supposedly rebelling against? These bands that play "hard-core punk"   are as far from the original punk attitude as the "new wavers" who are so prevalent today. Is stagnating really what the music is all about?
                                    -Rolaid Alpo Cola

Please send all constructive letters, explosive devices, and death threats to Rolaid c/o Smarm.

...lassic case of art damage...is it our duty ...t...fend fast music?Thought not...It's so easy to...f everything on the 77 scrap heap...the fact this John had never heard any of these bands before sort of makes it more understandable.If I had to listen to intelligent music all the time I'd fuckin' kill myself....TV

PIG

John Holmes? No Sweat...

TOUCH and GO

BOX 26203   LANSING, MI 48909

Jeez I filled up the first page with so much jism I didn't have room to bore you with my opening comments so here goes nothing (you're telling us ED.)As u may have gathered we're releasing the first single on our rekord label. Buy one and prove it to yourself there's some life in the midwest, besides it's great...would I lie?
...Corey is out west going to Beverly Hills High for a month or so on some kind of exchange...anyway as part of h is work he's videotaping bands like China White, Black Flag,Fear and lots more, can't wait till he gets back... The Drome is unofficially closed in Clevo...Johnny had a sale at his house last weekend,but we were too broke to drive down...Drooleys is having their Mon. nite thing again, what a load of crap...Eddie and The Hot Rods?Go get FUCKED cocksuckers... we won't pay to see shit like that... And we won't even talk about that Battle Of the New Wave Bands thing the Bus Stop is having...they pay the bands nothing...Great huhhh??? Someone told me one of the Dellrods

is related to one of the owners... wonder who'll win?First pr ize is 500 bucks...that arab can lick my ..." ....thanx to everone who sent their polls in;look for the results somewhere in thus ish... there's a new club in Detroit called Todds that's supposed to be pretty good but we aint been there yet... guess the owners arent fucking the bands over like Vince...what do the Smog Marines sound like?...DS's bro found 40 copies of the Bad Brains 45 in D.C....anyone who wants one send us 2 bucks...final notes... Brian H. was seen giving head to Sulka in a booth at Cinema X...my farts are choice...Skudder is Smegma's favorite band from Omaha...Karen has a crush on Bert Convey...Hey Brendan send us your fuckin magazine...
...so long for now weenbags...

What follows is a brief guide to buying records in Michigan(please bear with us outstate readers)Right everyone sez they hate record stores to be cool but everyone breaks down and frequents the grottos right?So we might as well give you the hot poop on where to go (and not to)Here in the capital City there's FLAT BLACK AND CIRCULAR.It started out a few years ago as a strictly used shop,but they now carry an ever increasing selection of new release imports,most of which get sucked up quickly by those few in this town that actually know what's going on.The biz in a college town goes up and down as the tide of students ebbs and flows (don't throw up)My hunch is however they rake in the mega-bucks(without ripping off...they pay a good price on buy backs. They also carry a good amount of zines and music weeklys.It's the only place I know of where one can kick back in an overstuffed easy chair and check out new releases through the phones...and with the prices going that's a service. On to Ann Arbor and let's start with

SCHOOLKIDS...this place could be twice as big and it would still be overcrowded, but it has great stock-especially new LP's.This is one of the few places that genuinly passes along a deal to the consumer when one comes their way.If you can maneuver your way to the counter you just might get to look at the singles which are inconveniently placed in boxes behind the counter apparently to prevent people like those OHIO types from stealing the discs.But the clerks love to make you feel like the proverbial steaming turd on legs

when you ask for them.Sorry folks but as long as you keep that system we'll continue ruining your day.Last time I was in there this frizzy melonhead was gleefully being nasty to some poor middle aged bloke trying to return a Cat Stevens record.A real power hungry buttfuck like most of the people that work there save for Lori who is a peach,as everyone knows(check out her shoe Tues.Eve on WCBN-she plays all the stuff worth wasting time on)and the manager George who quietly told the gent to bite the hoagie and take his MOR tastes elsewhere(that's why he's the manager)Besides he let's us sell our mag,would

we say anything bad about him?)
MAKE WAVES....Holy shit were talking midwestern Trash and Vaudeville time warp with bondage clothes and wrap shades... and loads of drug smokingandsnorting garbage(fuck all drugs,ED.)to appease the would be a burn case.Oh yes I'm sure they knoe everything especially the faggot with the purple streaked locks...you'll always hear "When I was in New York blah de blah" Lots of T-shirts with Sid,PIL,and The Jam and lots of other groups nobody listens to any anymore .Lots of buttons from Poseur and Zed that they get for 50¢ and sell for a dollar fifty.Burn this fuckin' lophouse to the ground.
OFF THE RECORD...A relatively new shop withlots of Beatles memorabalia(nobody's perfect,ED) They get new imports in but it seems like once they sell that's it,no reordering.The people that work there don't know much.On Michigan in Dearborn.
DEARBORN MUSIC...just down the block from O Singles,singles and more singles-the best p the state for the beloved 7" disc.A littleSlow regard to new L.P.s but they get lots of each staff is real unhelpful.

hot action.One bar of note he toured was the Doobee "Jeez Club where in his words just stareing the Poon tang is just The face He those guys in the words con- the horney broads tusslin' did have some good did their cerring the editors of Touch each other for a chance at first,ED)Acc- and Co(thats a first,ED)Acc- ording to him one is tall blond in your area scouting for a and a real wheeler dealer,whilenew market.Making his way the other is more reserved.but through the bars he found ets will hung like a Yetti. several to be lacking in any- ning will have the chicks run- obviously hung like a Yetti. Don't let every nite turn Since you two fellas seem to

And lest we forget this weird person who wrote in with the only letter worth reprinting...
Dear Sirs,
Recently our midwest sales rep had the good fortune

know the score we are offering you and your readers a chance to really start swinging.Those lugs at that place will poor have each meat mag for these people,a work- rolls.Advertise in your out with some of our gadg-

(sorry but we could'nt print all your torrid graphics...ED.)

intd just another orgy of one or end up trying to make it with the grill of a car like that one Punk fella did... Pan Handee Ltd.

SINGLES

RED ★ ROCKERS

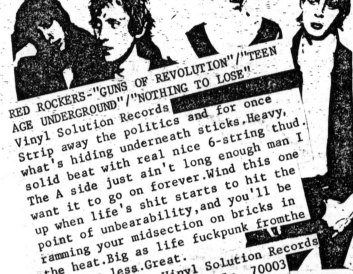

RED ROCKERS-"GUNS OF REVOLUTION"/"TEEN
AGE UNDERGROUND"/"NOTHING TO LOSE"
Vinyl Solution Records
Strip away the politics and for once
what's hiding underneath sticks.Heavy,
solid beat with real nice 6-string thud.
The A side just ain't long enough man I
want it to go on forever.Wind this one
up when life's shit starts to hit the
point of unbearability,and you'll be
ramming your midsection on bricks in
the heat.Big as life fuckpunk fromthe
south no less.Great.
SEND MONEY TO :Vinyl Solution Records
4304 James Dr. Metairie,La. 70003

DANCE CHAPTER-"ANONYMITY"/"NEW.
DANCE"   4 AD Records
Label hounds are quite nauseate-
ing you know?Case in point...
someone sez "Buy the CRISPY AMB-
ULENCE single man,the next ones
goona be on Factory."OK so I'm
just as guilty as the next person
but my private passion as a a 4 AD
fanatic,is leading me by the ever
lengthening line of JOY DIVISION
clones(the PRESSAGES sampler contains in my opinion the only sub-
standard material on the label,with
the exception of PSYCOTIC TANKS who
are grand)DANCE CHAPTER rise above
the harsher aspects of it's labels
counterparts...great piano,axe,and
vocals that could almost be described
as soothing...more good shit to add to
the list.

DISHARGE-"DECONTROL"/"IT'S NO
TV SKETCH"/"TOMORROW BELONGS TO US"
CLAY RECORDS ⟹ I'M NOT GOING TO BE
EMBARRASSED JUST CUZ I LIKE THIS
OLD TIME PUNK, I DONT CARE HOW MANY
ADJECTIVES YOU LAY ON ME--AGGRESSIVE,
DERIVITAVE OUTDATED ETC. YOU'LL NEVER
CONVINCE ME THIS BONE CHILLING THRASH
IS ANYTHING SHORT OF GREAT-AGAIN I
WILL REFER TO THAT MAG IN OHIO WHOSE
ENGLISH CORRESPONDENT SEZ THEY ARE THE
WORST BAND EVER...SUPPOSEDLY SAW
THEM LIVE--TOO MUCH NOISE FOR THE WANK?
HE SHOULD GO DIE-HE PROBABLY CON-
SIDERS HIMSELF TOO UP TO DATE...FUCK
THE WORLD...MORE DISCHARGE!!!

SELF CONTROL-"THE DRUG"/"ELASTIC"/"ALL
YOU CAN HEAR"/"CURRENT AFFAIRS"
Dancing Sideways Records
This band is two guys whose brand of
music is so low key and subtle,it goes
full circle,only too become stangely
satisfying.It's tough to diagnose just
what it was that prompted me to buy
such a record,but there's never been
a glimmer of regret.This is the best
English record I've bought in a long
while.

AGENT ORANGE-"BLOODSTAINS"/"AMERICA"
"BORED OF YOU"
Another Ca. band..."Bloodstains was on the
Rodney LP but it sounds faster here.I don't
like "America" much but bored is a good one,
Overall it's a good single,but the product-
ion sucks and I was expecting alot more from
this band.Slick packageing.

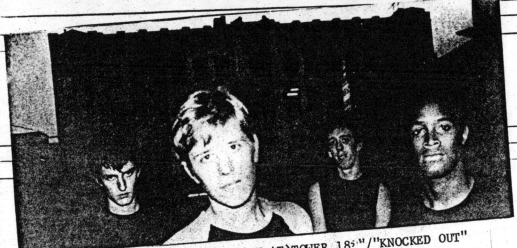

YOUTH DE SADE EP-"THE AM-
ERICAN FAG"/"GOITER ON MY
GONAD"/"THEME"/"LUBE JOB"
Dik Records
They finally re-issued this
jem.

THE CHEIFS-"BLUES"/(AT THE BEACH AT)TOWER 18;"/"KNOCKED OUT"
Playgems Records   Great,great,great...the guitar is what
sets this one apart-searing and crisp.Don't let the title
fool you-"Blues" is tight and to the point.This is definately
one new L.A. band worth pooping the shorts about.The 2 cuts
on the flip are faster.Guess they play the wilder circuit out
there and I can see why.Not as hard and nasty as some of the
fault liners,but rather more in the beach vein.One band living
up to it's rep and it's about time.

BY
TV

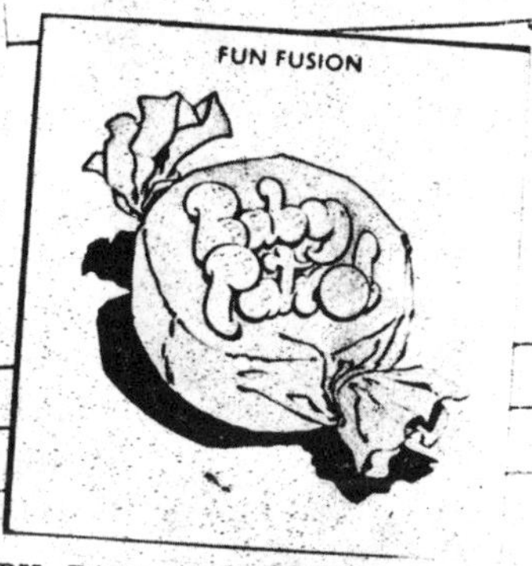

FUN FUSION

THE FILMCAST-"ADMISSION YOURS"/
COLOUR-COLOUR"   True Friends
Music.
Handwritten labels are always a
good indication of a low budget
effort.In my never ending quest
for something completely new this
one stands out as this months find.
Deep and barren shit here with low
register guitar,chimes and rythym
box and the periodic waa of some sort
of bass.Don't ask for history cause
there I'm in the dark.Obviously so
is THE FILMCAST.   Grade A.

THE EXPLOITED-"EXPLOITED BARMY ARMY"/
"I BELIEVE IN ANARCHY"/WHAT YOU
GONNA DO   Exploited Records
It's time to say no...shut up...stop...
mindless sludge.Punk rock sucks.

THE EXPLOITED

BABY PATROL-"FUN FUSION"/
"TURN IT DOWN" Secret Re-
cords
You may be wondering why
the assholes at this rag
would buy a record called
this.

JUST ME

AD RATES...FREE,AS LONG AS WE LIKE,BELIEVE IN,
PUT ABSOLUTE FAITH IN,AND WORSHIP THE PRODUCT/
SERVICE YOU WISH TO ADVERTISE...OTHERWISE SEND
US YOUR RECORDS ETC. NO CASH...

The Filmcast

Admission (Ymas) 2:15

TOOLS

WALK THE ROAD FOREVER

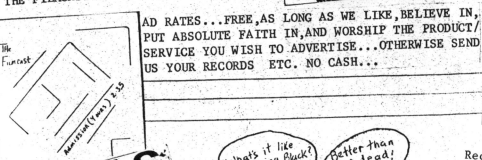

What's it like
Being Black?

Better than
being dead!

SAVAGE HENRY-EP   Zero
Records
If you find this record
bless you.Nothing as un-
listenable or unobtain-
able has ever been relea-
sed.It might as well be
cardboard.

![TOOLS](header logo)

TOOLS-"HARD WARK"/"THE ROAD FOREVER"/ SUBTERRANEAN RECORDS

Lots better than their first single which was pretty lousy. Great hardassed feel on this- a cross between the gutpunch of TOXIC REASONS and the drive of early CONTROLLERS.SF finally has a band spouting aggro,not pointless art crap like is featured on the LIVE AT TARGET LP. The B side isn't nearly as good as "Hard Wark" but still light years better than most of the Bay area stuff.Iurge you to contact the prolific SUBTERANEAN label if you're at all interested in what's going on in the land of cable cars and.faggots.The stuff their putting out is getting better all the time;and you can quote me on that. 912 Bancroft Way. Berkeley, Ca. 94710

PINPOINT-"WAKING UP TO MORNING"/"FLOODS AND TRICKLES" Albion

I could.have sworn this was Arturo's band(of early LURKERS fame)No way,this is bubblegum synth-pop and there's no way a big drug head like him would get within arm's reach of anything like this. Good for not much but a laugh.

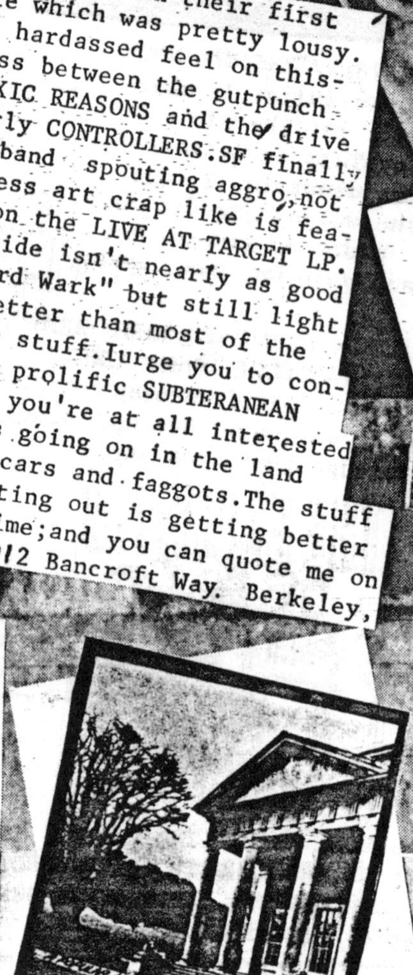

...got a single like reviewed? you would and we promise we'll give you send it to us, cuz we live in MICH. biased bullshit don't mean we aint got in return.Just taste....

A POPULAR HISTORY OF SIGNS-"POSSESSION"/"JUSTICE NOT VENGEANCE" Melodia Records
If this band was any less exuberant they'd probably fade away completely which would undoubtedly suit them fine.A hint of latent accessibility here,and even a thread of 1***'s sentiments runs throughout.If Ourchestral Manouvres wer't such success whores they'd be on the right track like these guys.(why do I like everything this month?)

THEATRE OF HATE-"ORIGINAL SIN"/ "LEGION" SS Records
Some will scream this heavy handed chug harkens back to the days when Ozzy Osbourne wasn't counting calories,and maybe they have a point.Remember The PACK?Right which one;the one who recorded a couple great 7"ers on this same label...well they took the same kind of heat from many including our own honorable DS,and ironically this is some of the same boys-most noticeably the vocalist who alone is the catalyst for a great disc regardless of accompinament(is there members from CRISIS in this too,should have read that ZIG ZAG article,ED.)Sure it's reminiscent of metal throb from years past...who cares? Not me...one of this months'best efforts.

PLEASE, FUCK THE SYSTEM NOW! Ⓐ HUH?

MINUTEMEN-"VALIDATION"/"THE MAZE"/ "DEFINITIONS"/SICKLES AND HAMMERS"/ "FASCIST"/"JOE McCARTHY'S GHOST"/ "PARANOID CHANT"   SST RECORDS
Not for everyday and/or everybody. This fits safely into no category, which is I suppose what bands should be striving for.Just because I don't understand what the fuck,it don't mean the record aint on,just that I'm blanked as to what is or isn't ach- ieved on this one.Cut through my be- fuddlemeat,and when I'm finally stupid it's a great one.But just think about it once and everthing clouds.Maybe that's the point.LESINGLESINGLE.

MASS-"CABBAGE/"YOU AND I"
4 AD
Adam took Marco but what's left of REMA REMA is now MASS. THis is monotonous but in no manner is it dull or derived from any earlier incarnation. Sounds a bit like a Fac.band recording in the Vatican... B-side is ugly,neurotic,hippie music not unlike GONG or VaN DER GRAFF,and I can't condone it sole- ly on it's newness.So what the other one is heavy on the bass-tom plod and much more up my ally.

BAY OF PIGS"ADDICTION"/ "ALIENS ARE OPENING DOORS"   SUBTERRANEAN
This band makes me laugh...but then so did alot of now faves.More proof of what I said earlier.More proof I'm unable to really say it without a framework to cop out on...The empty space up there is real- ly spelling the end of the record review as we know it.My dick is limp- this record isn't.

PROJECT 197-"NINE"/"I SMELL A RAT"/"IS THIS A RESTART?/"NO"/ "21K08"/"PLASTIC STRAWS"/"RAID- ING THE FILM ARCHIVES"
Independent Project Records
Oh yes neat idea having a swatch of paint across the sleeve and label.Lori Schoolkid recommend- ed this so if it blew I could just lay the blame on her... I'm greatful I don't have to.. stranger than a Moorcock novel, artier than a Calder sculpure, more intriguing than an oozing shanker on a moonlit street in a leper colony.Decent two bucks.

CRASS-"BILLY BOYS OUT FIGHTING IT'S JUST THE SAME OLD GAME"
A freebie flexi-disc in the CRASS fanzine (str- tching the definition of the word,ED.)(what the hell is the defin- ition?ED.2)TOXIC GRAF- FITY,part anti-this n' that with lots of the same old war graphic- with cute anarchisms like "Eat more snot... it's free"and "Ignor- ance is piss". Some- times I'm not in the mood.As the Dutch ex- pression goes-Hijo De Cojones*

WHO IS THIS BRAD CROTIS GUY, I'VE BEEN SEEING HIM IN A COUPLE OF YOUR RAGS. HE'S ALWAYS TAKING SOME KINDOF ABUSE. THAT ONE WAS FUNNY WHERE IT HAD HIS PICTURE AND IT SAID ABOUT NUDGENT BOTT-FUCKING HIM.

Circle Jerks on Frontier Records

SUBHUMANS

I don't own this record so I can't review it.

scratch my scrotum wench

...fuckin shit...

CASTRATION-AS-AN-ART-FORM
Catch that fuckin rapist and cut his fuckin' plums off and send them to us.Free subs to all.No Rocky Mountain Oysters (I'm a conassoir)

son-of-the-balls*

SECTION 25-"Charnel Ground"/"Haunted"
Benelux

The rough edges of their first release have been rounded smooth, making this one much more mesmeric in
mood. And I'm not sure that's good.
I kinda liked the biting, and often
monotonous, repetition of "Girls
Don't Count". Now everything oozes
out, thus putting us in a near som-
nambulent state of arrest. Soothing,
yet somehow too familiar to be regarded as something significant.--DS

THE JARS-"Start Rite Now"/"Psycho"/
"Electric Third Rail"   Subterranean

Just a little too cute for me. Don't
have time for lightweight fluff like
this, I mean I'm still waiting for my
Agent Orange single and I'm not about
to sour my tastebuds on this tooth-
less artsy-pop mush. Their Sonics'
cover achieves nothing, on top of
that. Annoys me like the bashful
little faggot trying to cop a feel
on my rosy ass. It doesn't hurt, but
I can do without it.--DS

SOCIETY'S DOG-"Working Class People"/
"Bad Dreams" Subterranean

Well, looky here. Nothing like a
new theme set to some unredeemably
dull punk schlock to start the day.
This one plods along like lead boots
thru quicksand. A boring struggle
from start to finish. Probably a
cleverly disguised rebellion against
the amphetamine blitzes they've been
getting from LA.   "Bad Dreams" almost comes to the rescue, unfortunately the a-side lingers a tad too
long to make recovery nearly impossible.--DS

BACKSTREET BOYS-"D'Hippy Hippy Shake"/
"Tear It Up"/"Gimme Somethin'"
Rocketeer Records

A laughably Welkian brand of rockabilly for those of you incapable of
recognizing the real thing when you
hear it.--DS

← Guess who

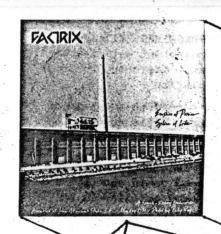

FACTRIX-"Empire Of Passion"/"Splice
Of Life" - Trans-Time

Stand this up against their "Live At
Target" contribution, and it's gonna
lose that first impression glint and
take on a more pallid hue. Simply
another dose of post-punk-industrial-
experimentation, although lacking in
spontaneity and sounding too contrived
and calculated. Whatever excitement
was generated by their live show is
hopelessly lost in the studio and
what we are left with are some interesting noises pieced together to form
something resembling music. Not as
finely honed, nor as crafty as Throbbing Gristle their sound tends to
drift away from any sense of direction.
"Splice of Life" fairs the better of
the two with its premeditated frigid-
ity. I suppose it goes without saying, but this is an acquire taste.--DS

THE DOTS-"I Don't Wanna Dance"/
"Immortals" Lunchtime

A far from perfect single from a
band who, up until now, I'd never
heard of before. These good ole
rock 'n' roll boys come from NYC,
which is probably why they've been
able to make such a name for themselves. Must certainly be a big
hit with the art-damaged crowd out
there. Attempting to play soft
punk rock(if you can imagine such
a thing) for a crowd that lives
by the loud, fast rule of thumb.
You know. . . Misfits, Stimmulators.
Singer at least gets a pat on the
back for producing the now classic
Bad Brains' single, "Pay To Cum".
However don't make the mistake I
did, and assume that the connection
means The Dots are in the same
league. Not by a long shot. They
may be nice guys, but they've yet
to learn to play.--DS

GIRLS AT OUR BEST-"Politics"/"Fashion" Record Records

Yes, this is alright, pretty good,
not bad, OK. Nothing that's going
to stick and bounce around inside
your head for the rest of the day,
but it does manage to march nicely
in a charmingly simplistic, naive
sort of way. Ignore what they have
to say about our governmental system. It's downright redundant, that's
all. You can just imagine their
singer playing the suffragette and
using her pristine voice to enlighten
us to the banal and ridiculous behavior of our elected officials.
Who cares, I like the song anyway.
"Fashion" follows the same course.
A pleasantly loping beat with some
more social commentary with some
all set. An enjoyable, yet frivolous, record.--DS

Wah! HEAT-"Seven Minutes To Midnight"/
"Don't Step On The Cracks" Inevitable

Somehow lacking the subtlety, as well
as the conviction of "Better Scream",
this new one leaves me. . . well, disappointed. Their first hit a seldom
struck nerve and pierced right to the
soul, whereas here nothing happens.
Whether it's an attempt to appeal
to the masses or what, but it seems
ill-advised no matter how you look
at it and the results are less than
promising. Strained and rather lackluster the band puts in what could
best be described as mediocre. No
sooner do they make a name for themselves by venturing off the beaten
track, they opt for anonymity by
slogging down that well worn path.
The b-side is a passable reworking
of the "Gloria" line, but it's not
enough to keep them abreast of their
earlier work.--DS

THE MANIC DEPRESSIVES-"Silence On
The Radio"/"Going Out With The In-
Crowd"/"You know Where You're Gonna
Go" Vinyl Solution

Alright! It's good to see some of
these peripheral areas documenting
their scenes in vinyl. This one
comes from New Orleans and according to Black Flag, there are a lot
worse places you could end up.
How big this band actually is
in terms of popularity is anybody's
guess, but they do a fair job of
giving this delta region a hard-
earned sense of respectability.
However, that's about as far as
it goes. I don't know if it's the

recording or what, something's missing. What might be a frantic display of hysteria at some gig, has
been tamed on wax. I just don't
think the sound is doing what it's
suppose to. Maybe I'm way out in
left field on this one, but wasn't
the original intention to stir
people up and creat some havoc?
Tip the balance in the favor of
chaos and disorder? I don't know,
it just seems that the premise on
which this single was recorded and
the end result are two different
things. Blame it on the band, blame
it on the recording, so fuck me,
either way, we lose.--DS

THE WALL-"Kiss The Mirror"/"Exchange"
Small Wonder

Their first and recorded when they
still saw themselves as a hard-core
punk band, or some facsimilie there-
of. Nothing special.--DS

12 INCHES

PRESAGES   4AD Compilation

A sign of the future? Maybe, time
will tell, as they always say. I
won't waste any time here and recommend the German band, Psychotik
Tanks. Their two cuts are easily
the best things on this collection.
Whether we'll ever hear anything
else by these guys is hard to say.
Remember Basczax(from the Earcom 2
EP)? Great band, only to vanish
without a trace. Let's hope this

band doesn't succumb to the same
fate. On "Let's Have A Party" their
singer apes the drunken droll of
David Thomas while the band slogs
its way thru the song at a similar-
ly inebriated pace. Perfect for
stumbling to and from the head.
Now these other bands on this record
probably couldn't cut it on the
single circuit, so what happens?,
they're gathered up and thrown onto
a sampler of sorts, which has the
tendency to make weaker songs sur-

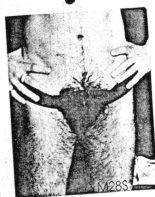

prisingly tolerable. "Malignant
Love" by The Last Dance drags on
and on to the point where you're
lost on the meaning and the sooner
it's over the better. "Sargasso
Sea" by C.V.O. does a bald face job
of plagiarizing Amon Duul. Modern
English's "Home" is slick and professional compared to the rest.
After all, they're the one band that
has a record out, so they got to
put out to preserve their superiority. Not this time. Technically

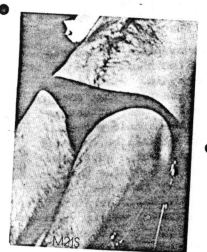

brilliant, but emotionally void.
Spasmodic Caress is the other band
with a strong contribution to the
set. "Hit The Dead" reminds me of
The Stunt Kites and their cut off
the Neutron sampler. If you're
familiar with that, then you also
know that they're the only band on
this record playing anything remotely punk. The Red Atkins' cut is one
of those crudely produced yuk-yuk
pieces of filler that sucks on the
second listen.--DS

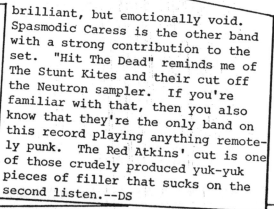

IN CAMERA

IN CAMERA-"IV Songs" 4AD Records

Even if "The Conversation" were the only thing on this, it's still worth it. With only piano and drums this band creates a frighteningly bleak world of hopelessness and despair. Obviously an attempt to appeal to the wallowers of self-pity. Sure to exploit your already poor self image, this is just what the doctor ordered if the highlights of a typical evening happen to be whipping your wood and The Brady Bunch. If you think I'm referring to myself, you're only half right. Now guess which half. I only like this song, so I'm not gonna talk about the other ones.--DS

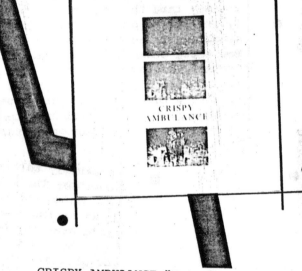

CRISPY AMBULANCE-"Not What I Expected"/ "Deaf" Factory Records

One of those inconvenient 10 inchers that get lost in the shuffle and is never heard from again. Aside from a loping solitary bass riff that manages to hold my unusually short attention for a few brief pleasurable moments, this record might as well be consumed by your collection. These guys come dangerously close to becoming the parody of all Factory releases. It's got rhythm, it's minimal, there's a lethal dose of sorrowful vocals. All recognizably Factory, but very undistinquished beyond that. A puzzling disappointment.--DS

THE WALL-"Personal Troubles & Public Issues" Fresh Records

One look at the sleeve and you can't help but begin making value judgements about this roguish lot. They've got all the earmarks of the Angelic Upstarts, U.K. Subs, Cockney Rejects, Ruts, Sham 69 school of stud-punk thrashing. The cover depicts a person screaming, supposedly caged in behind a barbed-wire wall. The drummer with his hair trimmed down to the scalp looks like he would enjoy nothing better than to take his studded coat sleeve and rake

it across our faces for ever thinking that we got these guys pegged. Well, they did a good job fooling me. Obviously, what I'm leading up to is the fact that what we see is not exactly what we get. Once you've listened to the whole thing, you realize that The Wall have alot more in common with a band like the Undertones, than any one of the aforementioned bands. For lack of a better description, I'll refer to their music as power-punk-pop, with less emphasis on the pop. Surprisingly listenable, The Wall have come up with a debut that's got some bounce to it.

With guitar hooks that don't seem routine or familiar, and a certain lack of direction that holds them at arm's length of any kind of formula, this album is enjoyable. With the exception of "Cancer"(strained seriousness), all the cuts have enough going for them to grab the listener. Now this ain't no ground-breaking recording. You can't expect everything coming out now to be the new thing. Rather, one must be prepared for the latest old thing, especially from a band that knows how to do it. This is a pop record in wolf's clothing. The Wall don't offend, but they don't bore either. They play a power/punk hybrid that works.--DS

U2-"Boy" Island Records

Without a doubt, this is one of my favorites. While some may cry . . 'fucking mainstream' all polished and shiny', my only advice to them is that they can go dork themselves. Sure it's pop music, but this is pop music at its best. Definitely AM fodder if things weren't as they are, if you know what I mean. Hopefully will be going domestic, so you won't have any excuse for not owning your own copy. This record is just swell(a not-so-cleverly stolen phrase-ED).--DS

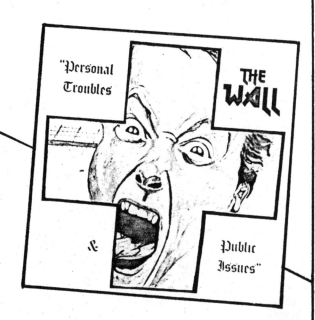

"Personal Troubles & Public Issues"

THE WALL

THE BEST OF LIMP: a DC sampler
Limp Records

This is Limp's second compilation in about two years, and while I appreciate and encourage labels like Limp to keep on supporting and recording their local scene, I'd like to see them begin focusing on one or two bands and seriously consider putting out regular elpees. Not that I have any great aversion to samplers, but the music contained here on this disc is especially dull for the most part. Nightman, the D.Ceats, the Razz, the Shirkers, the Penetrators all provide us with some benignly forgettable moments. Some of this shit goes as far back as the Spring of '78. Hell, why wasn't it put on the first record? It would've sounded a lot better then. I mean if I knew this was gonna be a dredging of the dead dog file, well, I probably would never have sent away for the thing in the first place. Now before my overriding pessimism becomes contagious and you begin bad mouthing all DC bands as banal and insipid(many of them are), there are a couple of bands who warrant my rare use of hyperbole. I'm speaking of The Nurses and The Bad Brains. At the moment, the Nurses are making the most original noise in DC. Combing the uniquely effeminate vocal style of Howard S-M Wuelfing with a somewhat regressive middle to late '60s sound. Simple and to the point,

"Something To See" rings like a pop song, but its raw and jagged edge is difficult to ignore. I suppose one could describe Wuelfing(and I hesitate to do so) as a baldly, unsparing David Byrne, and that's not to mean fuck The Nurses just cuz you hate The Talking Heads. Now the other band I think you're already aware of. Those of you who know will agreewhen I say The Bad Brains play some of the most frenetically mind-wrenching, out-of-control music you'll ever hear. Positively primal in their approach to "Don't Bother Me", it makes the "Pay To Cum" single sound slick in comparison. An unparalleled bombardment that rips into the listener, leaving fragments strewn all over the place. Now don't poo-poo this record just because 2 out of 13 seems like a bad bargain. Look at it this way, some samplers don't give you shit.
—DS

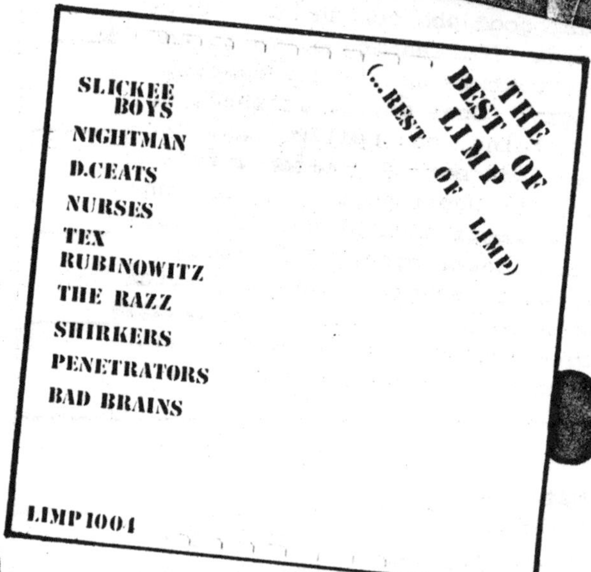

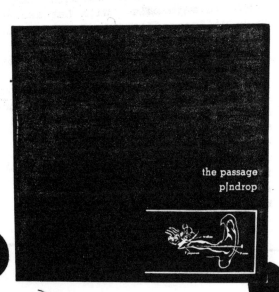

THE PASSAGE—"Pindrop"
Object Records
Hauntingly beautiful.—DS

Hey! you wankin' dummies. DS is gonna set the record straight, so try fillin' your mind instead of your hand.

Lansing's own —hubba,hubba

GAIL PALMER

THE BEST OF LIMP (...REST OF LIMP)

SLICKEE BOYS
NIGHTMAN
D.CEATS
NURSES
TEX RUBINOWITZ
THE RAZZ
SHIRKERS
PENETRATORS
BAD BRAINS

LIMP 1004

the passage
p|ndrop

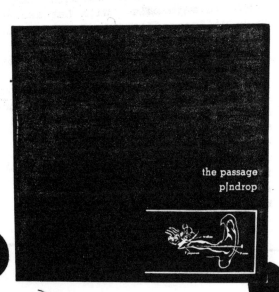

THE FIX AT CLUB DOOBEE

Caught the Attitudes the night before and boy, were they bad. Boning up for their big Canadian tour, what a laugh. They showed promise the first time we saw them, but they've since lost a grip on whatever potential they might have had. Tonite, it's The Fix along with the Wombats(from Cleveland, I'm told). The Wombats were alright. A fair amount of energy, but have a chosen a somewhat dated sound, which did not sit well with me after the first couple of songs. They ended their set with a boring piece of schlock that killed any encouraging thoughts I might have had for these guys. Dave, try getting Toxic Reasons or Neptunes'Car, but for god's sake, no more lameass cover bands. Take the 80's out and shoot 'em(I'm tryin' to throw in as much shit as I can in this one review). So, while I'm at it, Hoi Polloi and Modern Rage ought to be exterminated as well. Anyway, back to The Fix. Tonite was, without a doubt, the best gig they have ever done.

They were hot and any other Lansing band thinking they can occupy the same stage with these guys has dogshit for brains. Their violent blasts of amphetamine raunch make the competition sound like stale farts. They've also added a new song, "Off To War"(did I hear right, guys?) and in my lightly regarded opinion, the strongest single song they've accosted us with, to date. Let's hope their first single is a success, so they can put this one down on wax. The only area band worth their salt and I was glad to see the crowd down at the Club responding in the appropriate manner. Whether you know it or not folks, The Fix are a band worthy of a lot more recognition than they have received so far. It's just unfortunate that they're stranded in such a fucked town(for the most part) where the level of appreciation is hovering around the inaudible point. If you're reading this and think I'm just a brown-packing nelly brained asshole, then buddy, shove that pointed nut of yours up your pooper and drop dead. The Fix rule.--DS

THE DECLINE OF WESTERN CIVILIZATION-
original soundtrack featuring ALICE
BAG BAND/BLACK FLAG/CATHOLIC DISC-
IPLINE/CIRCLE JERKS/FEAR/GERMS/X
We've never professed to be anything more than fans to this brand
of noise.Anyone in L.A. who gets all
bent out of shape when they read an
appraisal of their scene from an outstate observer has a problem...there's
a definate lack of national coverage,
and maybe genuine interest from other
localities in regard to the west coast
scene will eventually our"presumptuous"
self righteous over ink unecessary.But
until then we'll blindly continue our
observing minus pet clubs,pet bands,
and funky suntans.This disc is a great
documentation of what was happening in
late 80.Everything music wise is top
drawer,but the fan dialogue and such is
totally fucked.Who wants to hear some
lame-assed comments by some anesthitized
morons who are constantly blabbering
about being a lush or not bathing,or
being a rebel.As passe as it is sicken-
ing.Dumb idea,should have weeded out
all the shit and added more cuts.And
who is Eugene?He sounds so illiterate
and laid back i could chunk.Is this goon'
representitive of the LA crowd?I doubt
it so why broadcast his tripe to the
world?Thats exactly what the coast de-
tractors need hear to say it's all no
count.Think we'll ever get to see the
flick?Don't count on it.   TV

THE CRAVATS-"IN TOYTOWN"
Small Wonder Records
It's been a long time since I got
fired up over an English LP.Every-
thing this band does spells great-
ness.Pounding independence not unlike lots of others but with a quality all it's own.Best sax work I've
heard in a fuckuva long time.It bounces around on its own terms,displaying
novel,nonsensical melodies.Some of its
appeal(the disc now not the sax) lies
in it's crassCRASSness but to put them
in that school ideologically would be
a mistake.The rest of it is much less
direct but equally great.Right now the
best the Brits have to offer.

THE SUBHUMANS-"INCORRECT YHOUGHTS"
Friends Records
Looking for intelligent life north
of the border?Want to discover a
music that reflects the peaceful,
pastoral untouched wilderness of
Trudeau country?Stay clear of the
SUBHUMANS.This is inner city bludgeon tuneage,that some find sadly remedial.Myself I think it's all
well and good to a point...cept the
stupid thing is overproduced just
like the D.O.A. lp.Most of the disc
is mindless drone with boreing lyrics,
occasionally there's something worth
laughing at ,like on the cut "Let's
GO Down To Hollywood And Shoot People"Then again I could be wrong let
me think...I play the stupid thing
all the time,and the new version of
"Slave To My DIck" is even better
than on the E.P.I just wish these
quasi-hardcore types wouldnt hire a
producer,and wouldnt go thinking
their gonna make it rich someday,
cuz you know how that story goes...
oh well......TV

ALICE BAG BAND.   BLACK FLAG.   CATHOLIC DISCIPLINE.
CIRCLE JERKS.
                        FEAR.
                                GERMS.
                                        and X

L.P.'S

BULLSHIT DETECTOR-Compilation featuring 25 differant bands...onCRASS
Records
This is one of those "Send us your
tape n' you might be on our record"
things with the CRASS so benevolent-
ly donating the necessary space.Lots
of the recordings (most as a matter of
fact)sound like they were recorded on
a portable in someones basement.One
band even complains on the sleeve of
only having time for one take cuz they
hadda hurry up and get it to CRASS before the deadline.These bands all have
one thing in common.They're all raw,can't
play their instruments too terribly well,
and possess the vitality necessary to be
selected for this tribute to backstreet
noise.(whoops thats 3ED).None of these
bands would have ever surfaced had it
not been for this and that's fuckin'
great.Those responsible for putting
this together and releasing it should
be commended.And to top it all it sells
for a measly $3.99.Anarchistic pulveriz-
ation of the norm.If you aren't already
dead you'll buy this.   TV

ALAN VEGA-PVC RECORDS
Big Al...east side balladeer and
low life aristocrat is b-b-back at
it again.½ of the greatest two way
discovery since sonar-SUICIDE.Just
to prove he's one up on the art crowd,
hes gone wild west:gauche rok-a-hill-
billy...let the ultra-up-on-its amongst
us feast on these wang wranglin' ryth-
yms-test their pliability-stretch their
weekly tastes and watch how quickly they
snap back into their obscurist coocoons.
Bland impressionism of Americana in all
of it's infinite sterility.Should have
deduced Vega would headline the snappy
motion in these circles toward the cow-
cat trip.Perfect.

'BILL BLAST AND ALPM NEWT.
did this art

HERE'S THE 1980 POLL RESULTS

NOW SLIDE THAT ANGRY RED ROCKET Between my Nasty lookin' jelobas...

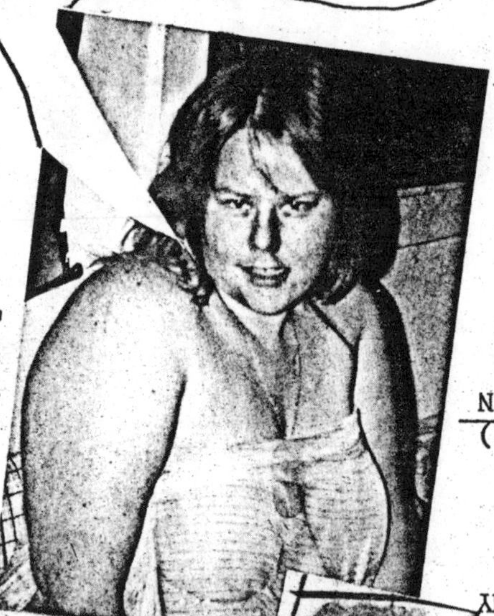

BEST ALBUM
1)"GROUP SEX" CIRCLE JERKS
2)"CROCODILES"-ECHO AND THE BUNNYMEN
3)"FRESH FRUIT FOR ROTTING VEGETABLES"-DEAD KENNEDYS
4)"LOS ANGELES"-X

BEST SINGLE-
1)"PAY TO CUM"-BAD BRAINS
2)"NIGHT OF THE LIVING DEAD" THE MISFITS
3)"LOVE WILL TEAR US APART"-JOY DIVISION
4)"JEALOUS AGAIN EP"-BLACK FLAG

Suck an egg Steve!

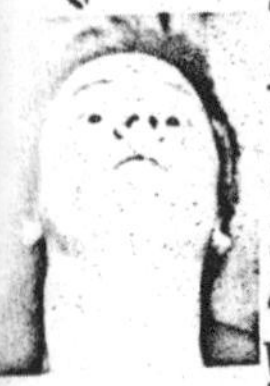

BEST GROUP
1)JOY DIVISION
2)CIRCLE JERKS
3)THE MISFITS
4)THE FIX

BEST LOCAL BAND(it was close)
1)NECROS
2)THE FIX
3)TOXIC REASONS
4)to many one answer replys

Blow ME Barry!

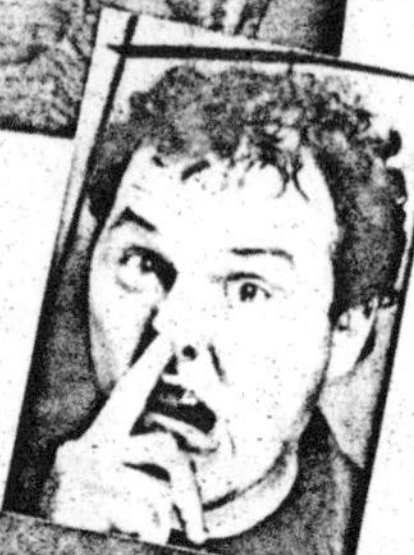

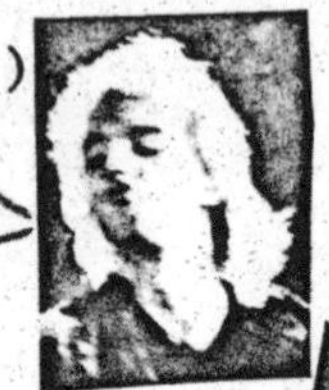

WORST LOCAL BAND
1)CULT HEROES
2)MORAL BREAKDOWN
3)EDDIE PUKE
4)THE FIX
5)NECROS

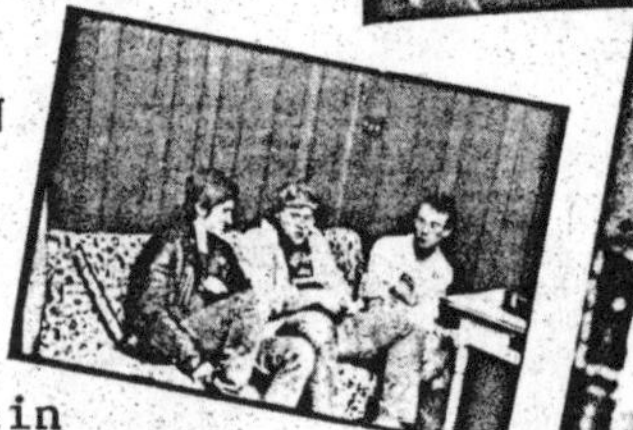

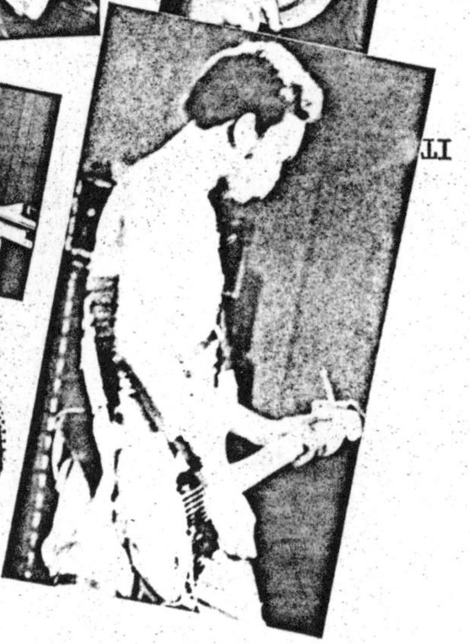

BEST LIVE SHOW
all different again

BEST UNRECORDED BAND
ditto

BEST CLUB
1)CLUB DOO-BEE
2)TODDS
3)

Club DooBee

BIGGEST ASSHOLE
1)30 FEET IN DIAMETER
2)SINGER IN DELLRODS
3)T&G EDITORS
4)JOE
5)JOHN LENNON

BEST MALE SINGER
1)KEITH MORRIS
2)DARBY
3)SLIM WHITMAN
4)JELLO BIAFRA

BEST FEMALE SINGER
1)running away EXENE
2)PENELOPE
3)NIAGRA

BIGGEST HYPE
1)NECROS
2)SIZE OF MY DICK
3)NEW WAVE
4)TOUCH AND GO

WELL HERE TIS'...OUR SECOND ANNUAL POLE,SENT IN BY OUR MOST FAITHFUL....WE IN NO WAY TAMPERED WITH THE RESULTS.. GRANTED ON SOME OF THE DUMBER ITEMS WE PICKED THE BEST REPLYS BUT ON THE IMPORTANT JUNK IT'S STRICTLY EMPIRICAL CITY JACK... THANX TO ALLLLL.....

BIGGEST DISAPPOINTMENT
1)DARBY'S SUICIDE
2)IAN CURTIS'SUICIDE
3)SIZE OF MY DICK
4)NEW WAVE
5)D.O.A. LP

SEXIEST (be serious)
1)ME
2)MY COUSIN
3)NIAGRA
4)TODD

BIGGEST FAGGOT
1)(no contest)MARCEL
2)ED RING

FAVE PORN STAR
1)SEKA
2)WENDY WILLIAMS
3)GAIL PALMRE

BIGGEST DRUNK
1)MY MOM
2)RON ASHTON
3)WYLIE

FAVE FANZINE
1)SLASH
2)T&G
3)FLIPSIDE

WORST FANZINE
1)T&G
2)TALK TALK

FAVE BEER
1)THE CANADIANS HAVE IT
2)BUD
3)FOSTERS

FAVE DRUG
SPEED,COKE,POT,PEPSI, CHOCOLATE SHAKES,SINU-TAB,ACID,POOP

FAVORITE FETISH
1)BEATING OFF WHILE WATCHING A VIDEO OF ME BEATING OFF
2)PUTTING VINEGAR ON MY DICK
3)TOE LICKING
4)SICK PEOPLE &STUMPS

FAVE B MOVIE ACTOR(ESS)
1)CHILLY BILLY HINZEMAN
2)FAY RAY

FAVORITE DEVICE
1)ACCU-JAK
2)CLUTCH FOR A 50CC MINI-BIKE
3)WHIP
4)NIPPLE CLIP
5)LUBRICANTS(flavored)

FAVORITE RUBBER DEVICE
1) 14 INCH DILDOE/ICE
2)ERASER
3)RUBBER BAND

WHOSE SKULL DID THEY FIND?

GUN CLUB

STARWOOD JAN. 20

buy now!

THE CHEIFS

PLAY GEMS RECORDS

7188 sunset blvd. p.o. box 204
hollywood, ca. 90046

$2.50 P.P.

Greggy & the Dipshits cover. Greggy was from the Necros' neighborhood and I believe the Dipshits comprised some Necros... They played parties in Todd's basement and we thought it would be humorous to elevate his 14-year-old ass to superstar with his own cover. Review of the infamous Necros/Fix/Black Flag gig at Club DooBee... Even Pubic Enemy #1, a local half-witted scribe named David Winkelstern, had the nerve to show his face, and he described the place in his article as "more crowded than a shoebox stuffed with Winnebagos"—wow, what analogous tripe! Even described the Necros and the Fix as "wavish." Where is that guy now?? I'm proclaiming today the "30th anniversary of I'm Gonna Kick Yer Fuckin' Arse Like I Shoulda Back in the Day" Day. Slowly the tide turns from import to domestic as the issues ticked along. American hardcore was a happenin' and, thank Satan, we were there to cover it.

TOUCH AND GO

NO. 13

75¢

NO FUN

TOUCH and GO

T.V. AND D.S. BRING YOU A PAGE FROM F.C. AT C.C. !! See?

Stop Drug Hot Lines

THE PUNK PAPER !!!!!!

DEVOTO PIC/DIANE PHOTO-80

Lawrence Dennis was a big fan of Hitler and the Nazis. Serving as an editor of *Reader's Digest* he simultaneously consorted with top American native fascists, many of whom were indicted, along with Dennis, in 1944. The charge: conspiracy to overthrow the Government of the United States.

Gacy blames drugs

ARLINGTON HEIGHTS, Ill. — John Wayne Gacy said he does not remember the 33 sex slayings for which he was sentenced to death — possibly because he was a heavy drug user at the time. "I was doing a lot of drugs," Gacy told the Arlington Heights Daily Herald. "I was doing Valium every day ... 30 milligrams. And 75 milligrams of Preludin, downers and uppers."

Give Your Cowboy This 3-Piece Outfit

He'll be the best dressed cowhand in the neighborhood with this authentically styled 3-piece cowboy outfit. Cowboy chaps and vest made of black leatherette, with contrasting white leatherette trim. Chaps have a white pocket Plainsman's sombrero made of black virgin

God has been misquoted for 5,000 years!
His actual words may disturb you...

Details $1.
The SubGenius Foundation
Box 140306, Dallas, TX 75214

H. A. PRODUCTIONS
424 E. 82nd ST. # 4-B
NEW YORK, N. Y. 10028

RALPH TO PEDDLE M. X. 80 AND TUX. MOON VIDIOS.

ROCK AGAINST RICKETS...

SOMONE will be Releasing the 1st LIVE L.P. IN U.S.A./MATERIAL working with FRITH & Bob Quine AND Eno, they even have the original FRIPPERTRONICS, 2 NEW E.P.s AND A Zé RELEASE/Celluoid has opened a Ameri. office / New T. HEADS L.P. in the MAKING / 2 L.P.'s ARE PlANNED FoR Chris Spedding W/BUSTA JONES; A live comp. of HITS RECORDED AT TRAX NYC, AND A STUDIO LP both BN PASSPORT/VISA LABEL IN U.S.A. / A SWELL NY STATE BAND "MECHANICAL SERVANTS" HAVE CREATED RUCUS with A EASTERN TOUR AND E. P. / Phila's BUNNYDRUMS to Release A single / CONSTANT CAUSE DIST., ARE soliciting TAPES FoR A CATALOGUE OF INDEPENDANT TAPED RELEASES / CONNIE PLANK AND Holger CZUKAY have A SPOOKY NEW BAND / the ATOMIC THINKERS TO RELEASE SYNTHI-NIOSE SINGLE SOON !!

NECROS

NECROS EP OUT NOW... INCLUDING "SEX DRIVE"/"BETTER NEVER THAN LATE"/"CASTE SYSTEM"/"POLICE BRUTALITY"

The FIX

VENGEANCE IN THIS TOWN

$2.50 post paid to
TOUCH AND GO REKORDS BOX 26203
LANSING, MICH. 48909

262

#13 Touch + GO is published
when we feel like it. Subs
3 dollars for 3 issues-
10 dollars for 10-

reached a... to
ferget it. to
many fuckwads!!
call me up...

EDITERS-Terveee
N'DS (NORTH
SEE Below)
Special thanx to
F.Couch + Lon G Diehl
for being swell friends
cuz we aint got too
many...AD RATES free...
Also Thanx to Dave
+ PETER at OCEAN
SPRAY for the
swell party!!!

ONE
of Tesco's
rejects
She wouldn't
reet on
his Night-
stick...

Curiousity in regard to this new wave
thing will eventually scrap itself and
our frolicsome trend conscience home town
crowd.These sentiments unfortunately pre-
clude any kind of viable happening in
Lansing.To establish any kind of perman-
ence experimentation is the name of the
game...but the vacuous lines of pop shitheads line up nightly at the local club-
derivations of something unexcited and
uninspired.For us to give credence simply
on the basis of our being the only local
rag(some contend it is our duty)would be
a disservice to our readers and put simply,
a fuckin' crime.Pre-existant rock criterion
still govern most local acts' every abeced-
arian and infantile move,and coupled with
this are the laughable delusions of the

R. MoorE DiD
the B.FLAG GRAPHIC

adulatory plaudits that will someday belong
to their particular band once the obligatory
dues have been paid.All of this celestial
devotion to rock&roll's umilecal cord has
had this magazine screaming shit for quite
some time.We realize some think we are ass-
holes-a reaction that couldnt please us more.
Negativism does not rear it's unsightly head
exclusively on a local basis as any third
grader could figure out.The fact that some
brand us a hardcore punk mag is cop out
#768594 yet another example of mindless fucks
needing to label ius and file us away.We may
be insufferable pricks but if this twisted
sameness wasnt everywhere we might be more
prone to say back slapping things like
"Great local act" or "Destined for the big
time". Could you keep your dinner down?

Cover photo by TV-
graphics by DS...(cover)

Well here's #13 and we actually have the money this time to run it on
a decent machine for your reading enjoyment.Things have really been jumping
(remember this is Mich.)as far as the local scene goes.Peter and Dave have
been booking acts not on the basis of what tha faggot promoters in Detroit
are trying to foist on them like "yor booking D.O.A.???Oh my gawd those guys
are nothing but trouble"...Right on boys,thanx for putting Michigans best club
right here in the capital city where it belongs...not in a poopchute like the
motor city...Also booked are The SUBHUMANS,UXA,(and X?) plus return performances by some of the states finest like L-7...I hear Vince is getting out of
Bookies to open his own club called Park Avenue or something like that,sup-
posedly with video room and such....zzzzzz.....Scott Campbell is booking
TODDS...He's a fuckin' jerk and he's probably got his heart set on making
his lame combo The Sillies house band...we'll leave that place to the faggots.
NUNZIOS calender is mighty boreing reading this month,and LILLI'S?Shit I
havent been there in months...that place is depressing...Second CHANCE in
A² has had lot's of big hypes like PLASMATICS,and Teenage Head but they always end up cancelling..that's ok they suck armadillo dew anyway... the
list of those getting nailed by the fuzz as they leave our fave club grows...
mostly it's just driving while under the influence of ôld demon boovzzee...
Kid Spike is back in Michigan for a couple months(GEARS guitarist)...
A couple of the guys in the now defunct DELLRODS were(ok so this story comes
reliably second hand)having a wing-ding on a bed with a couple babes when a
space heater torched the place and sent them running into the cold clad in
nothing but their jewlery...the sad part is one girl died...but then you've
heard the old religious adage"The wages of sin is Death"....Watch for compilate L.P. by summers end featuring midwestern bands...(check that Mich.Bands)
THE FIX to hit L.A. sometime in June......
...Brand new FLIPSIDE,SMEGMA JOURNAL,THE OFFENSE just out-all great and
very worthwhile...What would you say if I told you I saw a CRASS logo on a
silk baseball jacket?thought so...Andy to quit NECROS....All Todd did was ask
for a glass of water at Nunzios cuz his coat was on fire and they kicked the
whole bunch of em' out...So anyway till next time keep those friendly cards
and hostile blurbs flowing our way......TV

by Brooke Montage-
by Brian Hyland-
of weenie breath
himself!

F.Couch is a real fan..but he aint no blowhard

CONSTANT CAUSE
679 ARBOR LANE
WARMINSTER PA 18974
constant cause
is a distributor
50¢ for 2 bi-monthly catalogues
$1.00 intercontinental

Untamed   MUSIC AND LYRICS BY HATES

Ignoring the realities of decay
Material shapes it's illusions
Fighting with your physical being
Looking for something to believe
Were conditioned but did you
feel the shame
Past wrongs belong in opprobium

Raw Meat Cleave
I don't mean
I can't see
but I cleave
Raw meat cleave
Can't beleive
That its me
Now its grinding
up my sleeve
Raw meat cleave
Look at me
Raw meat cleave

Gosh I could've had a V-8!!!

"Crash + ByrnE"
Todd's dream
date-
sensuous ste-
the Sulka...
man   YoK
         yuk

Ringo Starr fingers John
Lennon's accused assailant
David Michael Chapman
in police line up.

Hooray!!! Yipee!
If this doesnt get
us on a government
shit list Nuthing will!

VANCOUVER STUFF
BY Margrette

Punk is dying in Vancouver, but there are still the odd upstarts. At a recent Sub-humans' gig, the band not only attracted greasers with baseball bats, but a riot squad. The gig was a benefit for the El Salvador refugees and of course the Sub-humans gathered a large anarchist crowd. There was to be a guest speaker that night but 'unfortunately' he was hit in the head with a beer bottle by the lead singer of Illegal Youth, Al Nelson. He was so disgusted by the rude, crude and socially unattractive behavior of the audience that he split. Wherever bands like the Sub-humans, Rabid, and D.O.A are, the pigs inevitably show up.

Earlier this summer Steve Jones and Paul Cook were staying at the Denman Inn. Some 'avid' Sex Pistols fans decided that it would be a great place for a party. When Paul Cook was smashed over the head with an umbrella and the entire floor was pretty much destroyed.

D.O.A. recently played a gig at the Smilin' Buddha with all the member which had ever been in the band(which includes Brad Kunt of the Avengers, Simon Wilde of Rabid, and the usuals: Joey Shithead, Randy Rampage, Dave Gregg, and Chuck Biscuits). The response was great and of course, the pigs showed up.

Art Bergman of the late K-tels(Young Canadians) has joined a new band called Los Radicos Popularos. This band includes: the ex-guitarist for the Modernettes, Buck Cherry, the ex-drummer for the Dils, zippy Pinhead, and about five other people from such bands as the Braineaters and the Pointed Sticks.

Hardcore '81 was a big gig that D.O.A. put on. D.O.A., Black Flag, and No Alternative and various other local bands played both Friday the 13th and Saturday. No Alternative had such an encouraging response that the lead singer ended up with shit covering his leg. The first night about 800 people showed up and approximately 100 the second night. Ron(the ex-singer for Black Flag) was also deported on a Carling O'Keefe beer raid. Life is hard for short PuertoRicans.

The Laundromat(Hardcore '81 home) was a huge hall that was leased for three months by the anarchists, but they never raised enough money to keep it up. So the minors without fake IDs have no choice but to stand outside the Smilin' Buddha. The Smilin' Buddha is going to court for serving minors intoxicating fluids.--Margrette A.

DS&TV,
Thanks for finally sending the remaining issues of my subscription,3 months late is better than never I suppose.Do appreciate the free FIX single which is good but doesn't really approach the incredible NECROS EP.Great stuff.Hope you continue to put out records regu larly.I should also congratulate you on T&G itself.It just gets better and better with each issue(gershfannED.)

Now for the bad news...BLACK FLAG came to town last month and I didn't see them.They were originally scheduled to play the rat in boston a few days before their gig they went down to the RAT to check out the benefit for Modern Method Records,a local label featuring some of boston best bands including LAPESTE,BOYS LIFE, and the OUTLETS.It seems that Chuck and GREG were physically kicked out at the door and called "homos" The band cancelled at the rAT(really why?ED.) and played over at SPIT an electric rock disco. SPIT requires a membership card to get in on weekends and of course I don't have one since I would never frequent that fuckin place anyway.So I didn't get in with alot of other people who were shocked that the band would ever consider playing such a place.I bet alot of people there didn't even know who the fuck they were.anyway i hope you had better luck when they played CLUBDOOBEE the next nite.

At least I did get to see the DEAD KENNEDYS last week.They played before a real wild crowd of 1600 at THE CHANNEL.They wisely brought their own security force which prevented the CHANNEL bouncers from throwing everybody out if they dared move. Also saw them in Pawtucket the next night before a slightly subdued crowd of 350 but they were still great.Jello is quite simply the most amazing front men I've ever seen..That's all for now

JIMMY JOHNSON
WATERTOWN MASS....

Dear Monster TESCO TESCO TESCO TESCO TESCO TESCO TESCO DISCO

I am writing to you out of desniration. I've fallen horelessly in love and can't find a possible way to satisfy myself. I am involved in a sort of love-hate, sexand-violins type of dilemma, that maybe you guys can help me in.

It all started when I found out that BROOKE SHIELDS doesn't want anything to do with me anymore (I think that it might have been my suggestion to use her name for a line of feminine napkins) and has threatened to use the grenade launcher , that I bought her for Christmas, on me or any form of mass transit I happen to be riding. Needless to say, I was shocked and then savagely depressed. I needed a replacement.

So, it was while I was trying to relax to a Pasil Kircses album that I found my new adoration. Oh it might have been a passing fancy at first but now it has almost gone too far; and I had just gotten been to see RAGING BULL that night and I was thinking of the last film I saw saarring Robert DeNero, Taxi Driver. Oh lord, she just popped into my mind and I couldn't forget her, she obliterated all of my teenage loves; Linda Blair spitting green, Tatum O'Neal seducing her father, and yes, even Brooke telling me so sweetly that only my hand gets between her and her Calvins. All of them gone, only the loving vision of Jody Foster remains.

looks like TROUBLE

I want her madly, I need to look at her chin more closly, but she doesn't answer my phone, and all my lettars come back to me steamed open and unanswered. What can I do?????
Iiiiiiiiiii'm getting at my wits end, I am despirate. I could use my connections with Moscow to have her kidnapped or... oh if she only knew how much Bill I am! I could mail her my Rita Moreno bk trading cards if I only knew she liked collections. Please Tesco, check me what to do, if you don't, I tell us if quite soon, I will do something drastic, like killing, like killing... oh no! you've got to help me!

WILL CHECK OK

MAT SV

Baabaalooingly Yours,
Ricky Ricardo
RICKY RICARDO
Cuban Relations
CHILDREN'S GRAFIX

Hey Tesco,
What are you doing? me im just screwin around that party was perty roudy keith and them got so mad they left.i probably got an "P" on typing cause i didnt capitolize spelly right or use right punctuation rig ht teaches send me ah tku tushin go o.k. did you like all the great lokin girls at the party?i sure as hell did.well you are cool and it was great to meat you gota go see ya later AND REMEMBER TO RIGHT AND IF YOU GET FREE RECORDS SEND ME SOME CAUSE IAINT GOT TO MANY
THANKS THANKS!!!!!

Greggy Dipshit
Greggy Dip

DR. TIMOTHY LEARY

IS A CULTURAL WHORE A DICKHEAD LIAR, AND WORSE) A FINK. A REAL JORK All AROUND AVIOD Like the PLAGUE

FANX TO MECO + U2!

NECROS/D.O.A. at CLUB DOOBEE 4/31/81

The evening started out great...we're just hanging outside the club when some fat cop sez hes had a complaint
tthat someone was smoking dope and exposing themselves-
what shit...the fat redneck bitch that lives next door
has a problem about the clientel...move hog...our dicks
and cunts were in our pants and pot smoking is for fux
who can't stand what they really are...Brian Pollack is
tthe new guitar player for NECROS and try as he might
he couldn't break the stage like Andy could-but when it
comes down to brass tacks he's faster and wilder and
the total sound has suffered not one iota...in fact I
got more beat up this gig than ever before so that's
all the proof I need(I even got to sing "SIX AND CHANGE"
for the encore,ED.)D.O.A. were of course fab with lots
of new material from their new album"HARDCORE 81"which
is produced alot louder than the first one and is loads
better...(Shitheads wife and their road man-ger think
our mag sucks cuz we panned the first LP but Joey even
said they were going to remix it louder so there..ED.)
Live D.O.A. is alot more intense than their records...
Rampage is quite the showman,and Dave Gregg the second
guitar,rounds out the sound nicely.We all had a great
time dancing-especially when some pretty girl wandered
out and got slugged,cuz it's fun to watch her wimpy
boyfriend get mad and not be able to salvage his virility
by retaliating.MY That sort of dancing is fun but my
legs klook kt like 2 bananas that've been dropped too
many times....Be sure to check out SUBHUMANS,and X when
they hit town....

MAY DAY-FESTIVAL   5/1/81

Alot of effort went into this and I give those responsible
a tip of the hat...whether or not it was a success I
couldnt say...D.O.A.,L-7,and NECROS all cancelled and
JAN AND DEANS LIVING ROOM and THE FIX never got to play
because outdoor things musż end at 10 and the whole thing was behind schedule...There were Socialists,Guru people,Draft card burners,longhairs(can
you believe it) and assorted others
like Larrisa and Corey who got more
stares than anyone...a fun time that
probably wasn't supposedvto be fun
but we got drunk and laughed at ev-
erboby...

ALL NIGHT MOVIES-DEMO TAPE REVIEW
Here we've got a band that can be
brilliant one moment and utterly
entangled in it's obvious lack of
direction the next.Unfortunately
putting music on a tape does not
give it the degree of finality
necessary to shoulder the criticism
thats going to pop from those who
are gonna cut these guys down as arty
and pretentious.I suppose improvi-
zation is all well and good -these
guys'idols probably will verify-
and as a matter of fact the best cut
is such an improv. called "Slaughterhouse" which is the scariest bit of
blackness I've heard since Leather
Nun Ep or any other Industrial Pro-
duct.Stuff to drive you off the edge.
There are some other songs on this
that I like alot,and they feature
an amazing range of styles.Some of
it I hate especially the woodwinds
I'll give these guys an A for being
innovative and different-a B for a
lack of unity as far as what direction the band should be taking-a C
for the clarinet-

SONGS BY A.N.M.
1. S. Chips
2. It's Accumulating
3. Bacchus Polka
4. Improv.+
5. Deal City Hope
6. Rain Clouds
7. Anti-War Song
8. Dark Song
9. Slaughterhouse
10. Improv.+

11. My House
12. Safety Boys
13. Improv.
14. New Sax Song
15. F.F.
16. A Minor+

Send 3.75 for
tape to Po Box X
106 Mt.Pleasant, NJ

ḄUNT SOME LIVE CRUD...

Touch & Go Records Release Party with
GRATIENT 4/2/81
We spent a great deal of this evening sluggin Colt 45 in the parking(the return of warm
weather in this state is welcomed with an
alcoholic zeal,ED.)lot.Thats mainly cuz DS
his brother and I only had enough $ for a
couple magnums and besides bar prices have me
riding low wallet side.Fortunately various FIX
members were swilling large quantitys of grog
inside so we mooched our way into oblivion(fanx
boys)The band was from Kalamazoo where according
to some things are starting to happen.This band
was primitive a s hell but enjoyable,much more
so than alot of the pussy popflying off the fan
these days.I'll give them an A for trying and
maybe they'll still sound raw after they learn
to play.Could even be a mid-western URINALS who
knows.OK there warnt hardly nobody there but it
was great fun.....TV

R.F.T.B./BELFIELD AND THE CATS
Club Doo Bee 4/4/81
The last time I had the flu I was in bed
sleeping I felt a big murphy comin' on so
I let er' rip and diarrhead the bed

Allegiance To None | by HATES

I can't comply with the ways of people
Somethings they'll never understand
If I listened I'd have to hear excuses
Then they'd admit their servitude
was temporary
Allegiance to none Allegiance to none
Allegiance to none not anyone
Allegiance to none Allegiance to none
Allegiance to none not anything.

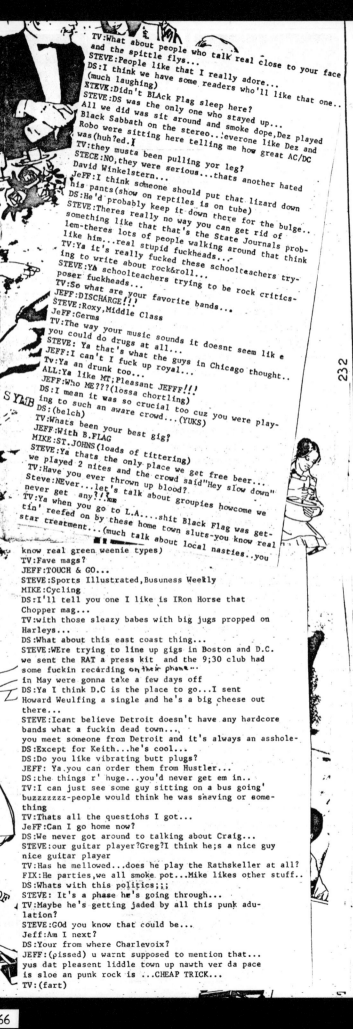

FIX

INTERVIEW

THE FIX were interviewed on 4/8/81 at their house.....present were Steve-Vocals,Mike-bass, and Drums-Jeff   DS AND TV did it(who else?)

TV:I'll do a sound check(farts in mike)
TV:OK let's rap about the single...
STEVE:What about it?
TV:Like what do people say about it...
JEFF-ALL OF my straight friends say it sucks
Really my roomates liked it...surprizingly...
STEVE:mumblemumble
TV:Could you talk louder so the mike will pick it up?
STEVE:(yelling into mike)I don't know anyone who likes it!
DS:People I talk to think it's represenative of the way you sound...
MIKE:My mom liked it
TV:Yor Kidding???
STEVE:Ya my mom liked it too...
DS:I didn't play it for my mom...
TV:My mom doesnt even know about the magazine (everyone guffaws)
XXXXXXXXXXXX
JEFF:I think overall wer'e pretty happy with it..
TV:So what about a new single?
FIX:We wanna record "Off To War" and Rat Patrol"
DS:Would you go with 4 songs ? Cuz you can do it with yor songs so short...
STEVE:It depends on the studio time like if we could get 5 hours...and it also depends on like when we recorded that first one we were drunk as shit
DS:Ya like the last interview we tried to do...
STEVE:Ya we get real drunk at crucial times...
TV:(belch)like when we did our TV show...
So where do you put the band as far as your ideology ...politics,social unrest,nuclear power, abortion?
FIX:Ask Craig (absent...laughter)
STEVE:The music is enough of a statement...
TV:But do you think politics in music is fucked?
STEVE:Oh no no way.....
TV:Looks like a labs head in a bag on that table..
JEFF:Junior whered ya get the lambshead???It followed me home...
TV:Here's a heady one...What do you hate?
STEVE:I Ha te the fuckin asshole regulars at Club Doo Bee
JEFF:NEW WAVE!!!
STEVE:When Black Flag played there were some cool people there...
DS:Well that was the thing because most of the people there werent regulars
STEVE:The regulars are dips...
Likeall that shit about Dave Beaton and all that shit about Black Flag,and not wanting to touch Black Flag, and then when we said we'll take responsibility so he said OJ(whoops...OK)and now there gettin' D.O.A. and the fuckin Subhumans and before he said noone'll show up for Black Flag....
DS:Well it looked like he was listening to the club owners in Detroit and now he saw nothings gonna happen;at least he went to the trouble to get like D.O.A. where a club like BOokies is afraid of violence,,,
TV:So what do you love...besides a creamy pudendum?
STEVE:I love gurls...
JEFF:TITS...
MIKE:My Mom...

TV:What about people who talk real close to your face and the spittle flys...
STEVE:People like that I really adore...
DS:I think we have some readers who'll like that one.. (much laughing)
XTEVE:Didn't BLAck Flag sleep here?
STEVE:DS was the only one who stayed up...
All we did was sit around and smoke dope,Dez played Black Sabbath on the stereo...everone like Dez and Robo were sitting here telling me how great AC/DC was(huh?ed.)
TV:they musta been pulling yor leg?
STECE:NO,they were serious...thats another hated David Winkelstern...
JEFF:I think someone should put that lizard down his pants(show on reptiles is on tube)
DS:He'd probably keep it down there for the bulge..
STEVE:Theres really no way you can get rid of something like that that's the State Journals problem-theres lots of people walking around that think like him...real stupid fuckheads...
TV:Ya it's really fucked these schoolteachers trying to write about rock&roll...
STEVE:YA schoolteachers trying to be rock critics- poser fuckheads...
TV:So what are your favorite bands...
JEFF:DISCHARGE!!!
STEVE:Roxy,Middle Class
JeFF:Germs
TV:The way your music sounds it doesnt seem lik e you could do drugs at all...
STEVE: Ya that's what the guys in Chicago thought..
JEFF:I can't I fuck up royal...
Tv:Ya an drunk too...
ALL:Ya like MT;Pleasant JEFFF!!!
JEFF:Who ME???(lossa chortling)
DS:I mean it was so crucial too cuz you were playing to such an aware crowd...(YUKS)
DS:(belch)
TV:Whats been your best gig?
JEFF:With B.FLAG
MIKE:ST.JOHNS(loads of tittering)
STEVE:Ya thats the only place we get free beer...
we played 2 nites and the crowd said"Hey slow down"
TV:Have you ever thrown up blood?
Steve:NEver...let's talk about groupies howcome we never get any?!?
TV:Ya when you go to L.A....shit Black Flag was gettin' reefed on by these home town sluts-you know real star treatment...(much talk about local nasties..you know real green weenie types)
TV:Fave mags?
JEFF:TOUCH & GO...
STEVE:Sports Illustrated,Busuness Weekly
MIKE:Cycling
DS:I'll tell you one I like is IRon Horse that Chopper mag...
TV:with those sleazy babes with big jugs propped on Harleys...
DS:What about this east coast thing...
STEVE:WEre trying to line up gigs in Boston and D.C. we sent the RAT a press kit and the 9;30 club had some fuckin recording on their phone...
in May were gonna take a few days off
DS:Ya I think D.C is the place to go...I sent Howard Weulfing a single and he's a big cheese out there...
STEVE:Icant believe Detroit doesn't have any hardcore bands what a fuckin dead town...,
you meet someone from Detroit and it's always an asshole-
DS:Except for Keith...he's cool...
DS:Do you like vibrating butt plugs?
JEFF: Ya,you can order them from Hustler...
DS:the things r' huge...you'd never get em in..
TV:I can just see some guy sitting on a bus going' buzzzzzzz-people would think he was shaving or something
TV:Thats all the questiohs I got...
JeFF:Can I go home now?
DS:We never got around to talking about Craig...
STEVE:our guitar player?Greg?I think he;s a nice guy nice guitar player
TV:Has he mellowed...does he play the Rathskeller at all?
FIX:He parties,we all smoke pot...Mike likes other stuff..
DS:Whats with this politics;;;
STEVE: It's a phase he's going through...
TV:Maybe he's getting jaded by all this punk adulation?
STEVE:GOd you know that could be...
Jeff:Am I next?
DS:Your from where Charlevoix?
JEFF:(pissed) u warnt supposed to mention that...
yus dat pleasent liddle town up nawth ver da pace is sloe an punk rock is ...CHEAP TRICK...
TV:(fart)

232

...don't laugh when I tell you about this great band from Maumee,Ohio cuz what I say is the bottom line...these scrappy suckers are on their way up- that leaves old farts like myself to sit back and marvel,drool,and thorough- ly enjoy myself when I see them live- ly enjoy myself when I see them live- ly enjoy myself when I see them live- conventionality is one that aint in these boys vocabulary...they'll walk right into your house,eat your food, smash the records they dont like the looks of,and rape your little sister. But since the PAGANS aint around some- ones gotta pick up the slack right? NECROS did some studio demos a while back that blew my shit away plain and simply,knocked me out of the chair like a good dose of Persian used to do to our very own R&R Bankrobber.I first witnessed NECROS at a dive coop in Ann Arbor last June where the local boys in blue forced a seriously abbreviated set with threats of noise fines and that kind of bullshit.They are all around]7 and manage to have light years more energy than any of the motor city slime like RETRO and THE MUTANTS (those are tough to spit out)who still believe intricacy and over-instrumentation to be the modern mode of musical communication.With songs like "Peer Pressure", "Race Riot","Police Brut- ality","Public High School", and"I Hate My School" the band surpasses fellow teen punkers Rhino 39 or any of the HB pinwads on plain ol fashioned rawness,and they are finally giving the midwest a tad of credibility and self respect although my choice of wording here is suspect for they obviously respect nothing but their record collections and the females who suck them into submission.Lead singer Barry idolizes Darby but has a style quite unlike Mr.Crashes, more young sounding,less pretentious,almost Kieth C.Jerk minus the throat slashing growl technique...Todd on drums is a killer with a simple barbaric style,and he's faster than fuck...guitarist Andy hates punk according to informed sources but if this is true he got some great ideas as to what style makes it in thepunkingdom.The following is an interview done with the 3 of them(they are currently auditioning bass players)

TV:How long have you been together? A:We started out as a 3 piece with no guitar a year ago and Andy didn't have one at the time but Barry did and so we begged Andy to play guitar..we did songs like "Celibate Summer", "Blow Me Baby" and "Kill The Shah"we still do 2 of the real old songs "I Don't Like You" and "my Life"... B:we've gone through four bass players, we've got a guy named Jeff Allsop sitting in for us at the moment... A:about ten inches TV:Who are your idols? A:Boomer,Keith Partridge,Davey Jones, and Johnny Thunders... T:I don't know really I suppose all of FEAR and Robo of BLACK FLAG... B:Darby Crash TV:How big are your wangs? A:about a year

B:Ihate alot of people and alot of stuff, like assholes that got into punk rock last week and think they're so hardcore.Ihate it when people talk about punk im the past tense like punk was this and punk was that...I also hate "new wave" like B %@'s (Whoops sorry,ED.) B 52's and ROMANTICS and it pisses me off when people refer tomusic like that as punk...I also hate restraints like school and work,I guess they are necessary though..Icould go on for hours... TV:What's it like living in Ohio? A:It's like living in Alaska.People are dumb and don't realize anything..fave spot in Ohio is Cedar Point... T;don't ask it's a shithole,I think the world is boreing B:It doesn't matter cuz I'm leaving when I graduate from high school... TV:Tell the world about your fave recordings... A:BLACK FLAG EP,NEGATIVE TREND EP, "Now your Dead" FEAR,GERMS LP,AVENGERS"We Are The One",Gigantor... any D.O.A. and MIDDLE CLASS... B:I've got lot's...Im always buying records- alot of really fast L.A. bands like GERMS,FEAR, BLACK FLAG(Am I stuttering?ED.) CIRCLE JERKS, just the really loud garbage stuff.Then on the other hand I like the dark,stark moody stuff like Joy DIVISION,THE CURE AND MAGAZINE..oh ya I just got this grate E.P. by DISCHARGE this band from England. I've got extremist tastes... A:I really like Gigantor and anything by the HEARTBREAKERS,D.O.A. ANd NO ALTERNATIVE are good too. TV: FAVORITE ZINE? T:hmmm this is a tough one let's see there's TALK TALK, NEW YORK ROCKER hmmmm   oh ya there's SLASH,FLIPSIDE,PANIC, SMEGMA JOURNAL that ones okhmmm there's ZIG ZAG gosh I just cant remember oh ya that one from lansing I think that's pretty good what is the name of it that ones my favorite

RACE RIOT (SWALLA/HENSSLER)
everyones fighting for the color of their skin
everyones fighting Just to save their skin
their fighting in the streets their fighting in the halls
they riot till they kill and it'll never halt
CHORUS #1
RACE RIOT!!!!!
THIS AIN"T 1980
RACE RIOT!!!!!
IT"S A RIOT OF SOCIETY

they'll riot on the streets they'll riot in the halls
they'll riot till they fall and it'll never halt
a school's not a place for education any more
it's simply just a battle ground this can't go on no more
CHORUS#2
RACE RIOT!!!!!
BLACK MAN FIGHTING AGAINST WHITE
RACE RIOT!!!!!
FIGHT TILL YOU CAN"T FIGHT ANYMORE

they'll never sit down and talk about their prblems
just wanna fight a create more more of them
whites call them names   directly to their faces
say nigger go back to your own places

POLICE BRUTALITY (HENSSLER/SWALLA)
mos t cops go to the academy
where they learn to fight all crime
maumee cops are all off the farm
and they just waina waste my time
CHORUS
POLICE BRUTALITY-THE COPS HARRASING ME
POLICE BRUTALITY-GET IT IN MAUMEE
2#'s
violence breeds violence or so they say
but how could they hve it any other way?
I've got one thing to say
that one day they'll pay

OTHER NECROS SONGS
CASTE SYSTEM
I DON'"T LIKE YOU
MY LIFE
JOHNNY IS
REJECT

DISCHARGE

TOKYOS-"PARTY DRESS/TEST TUBE BABY/COP OUT/YOU'RE SO SILLY/ C.I.A./DADDY SAYS I SHOULD BE RICH"   Dusty Roads Records This is a red ten incher and a real eye catcher from Redondo Beach wherever that is,but both of us got sucked into copping this slick looking little package...let's rush home and check it out...good, not great.There's plenty of em who play the imaturity chugga ballgame alot better ,Ca. can do better but this does have it's good points like a sense of humor,no song longer than a minute and a half,real base level stupidity blended with unoriginal but inspired riffs, love and conception never sounded so corny.Only 4 bucks,and it'll look good on your wall.

DISCHARGE-REALITIES OF WAR/THEY DECLARE IT/BUT AFTER THE GIG/SOCIETY'S VICTIM Clay Records ....thud studs man this their first EP is planned violence,real abrasive,anti-war posing who gives a fuck?Overtly reactionary but I dun care...croak wimps, this is it...if this is "new punk" I'm a trendy...more please...the sleeve sez it all,"thanks to no fucker...

THE PAGANS"SIX IN CHANGE" Neck Reckords This is three years old and according to the staff at Smegma Journal this has sold for as much as 100 bills in Clevland where Pagan fervor runs deepest.Myself being one of the truly fanatical outstate supporters,I was shocked to find this in a bargain box in Chicago for 1 dollar-sleeve water damadged,but disc intact. Gawd I thought "Street Where No body lives"/"What's this shit called Love?" (their 2nd)was raw but this one pales the rest.Here we have Michael Hudson on guitar and some singer (who was booted shortly after this records release)whose vocals were undoubtedly run through the ax amp.Muffled mud-the skins drive this basher over the edge-this is the most violent depiction of PAGAN heart and soul ever to reach vinyl....

THE DILS-(who cares about song titles?) This is their new blundering double single on some Canadian label.DS bought it and stretched the definition of emotional bias,and blind devotion,to new limits last ish when he actually stated this had redeeming qualities.Fact is this sucks so bad it insults anyone who has ever considers themselves to be a fan of these skinny commie posers. strictly 4th rate wimprock...lay this one next to your old girlfriends Pure Prarie League and it still blows the beef bayonet.Anyone who likes this is an asshole.Pure dogshit through and through....

12" ✝

CLOCK DVA

CLOCK DVA-"THIRST"   FETISH RECORDS
It never fails-just when things start to
bottom out,a record like this comes along
to shatter and dispel everything clogging
my suspiciously staggered appreciation for
the long playing disc.CLOCK DVA first appeared on the now difficult to find NEUTRON
sampler...a 7" that also featured three other fine bands.The debut album exhibits a
sound that makes the first description I'd
heard..."Throbbing Gristle with saxes" a humorous and implausible impiety.What makes this
album stand apart is the vocalist-one Adi
Newton who grovels in a cleff that makes the
rest sound adolescent.An apparent deaf ear
to his compatriots leaves this guy sounding
refreshingly new.This music not only redefin-
es certain nebulous left wing standards,but
it revitalizes the sagging realms of simulated,
saturnine English boys with a faceless mask of
surreal imagery that sinks me to new depths of
appreciation for this band.If you're fed up
those content to follow leads,or just simply
follow each other around in circles-there is
an alternative....CLOCK DVA....

CLEAR CUT APPARENTLY - SPEECH BAND FIRE

**EYELESS IN GAZA-"PHOTOGRAPHS AS MEMORIES"
CHERRY RED RECORDS**
More proof that those with confidence feel the
"safety in numbers" adage to be a thing of the
past.Just two gents hear create light years
more urgency than most bands do with the traditional cast of unecessarys...People who don't
like synthesizers will like this...Those with
half an adventuresome spirit for the new will
wallow in this...personally this does something to me no other lp is capable of doing-
it presents a series of images both serene
and alarming,with a network of innovative
arrangements...As our devoted readers may recall,I reviewed their debut 45 in #11-a curious package that had all the earmarks of a
one-off...then surprize-an LP on this label
of all...Each 45 was carefully personalized-
with majic markered song titles and such-
rather an incongruity when one thinks of the
impersonal nature so indigenous to the isles
(teeming with bummed out personas)Every dog
tired phrase will be spared-your quickly
dissapating attention spans-you must give
this band an earnest listen....TV

**MODERN ENGLISH-"MESH AND LACE".........THE BIRTHDAYPARTY-"PRAY-
ERS ON FIRE"   4·AD RECORDS**
What a bleedin' rave up this sheet is turning out to be-
these 2 bands share a label and that's about it...T.B.P.
from Australia have created a very nerve racking and demented record...while M.E. have taken a more indirect but
equally brilliant approach....both very different-both very
new sounding but then isn't everything on this label.I'm a whore
for this kinda stuff and much as I hate to admit it sometime those
Europeans got a nack for creating that which follows no precedent-
and even if some of it treads water it does so on it's own terms-
If you would like to hear these 2 bands a representative sample may be
obtained by purchasing THE BIRTHDAY PARTY-"MR. Clarinet and MODERN ENGLISH-
"GATHERING DUST"   A total herein of four must recordings...TV

ESG EP
99 Records/Factory Records

A fair amount of surreptitious hype preceded this little gem. 'Greatest American dance band,' or some such bullshit. Typical of New York. If it comes from the big shitty, damn!, it's got to be good. Constantly starved for recognition, and always wanting to be one step ahead of everyone else, they've put all their eggs in the ESG basket. Now usually I don't allow myself to be seduced by this kind of elitist snobbery, least of all from a town that can't make a claim to nothin', but this time my curiosity was more than just aroused by the thought of four latino babes playing up to our overly anglicized tastes. This band I had to hear. And now that I have, I will proceed to make an ass out of myself in a clumsy attempt to convert you. It shouldn't take much, really. What we got here is six strikingly original cuts(three live, three studio) of some starkly minimal funk. The combination of bass, drums, and congas will turn your spine to spaghetti. It makes you move. The barest modicum of guitar is splashed on a couple of the numbers with shivering results, and those are the ones that work best. Now their vocalist plays off these rhythms displaying distinct Motown roots and a hardened yet positive vision. Martin Hannett is credited with the production of the studio side, and although the insiders say that's hurt the band, you won't find me complaining. It might seem reminiscent of his work with A Certain Ratio, but even that may be stretching this comparison thing a bit too far. Granted, the temptation for this exercisein mental masturbation is inevitable, but this band refuses to be so easily pigeonholed and labeled. It's something a little out of the ordinary, and it sounds pretty good, just when things were beginning to get stale around here. Now one question still remains---how will we ever tolerate that appalling East Coast smugness?--DS

PAULINE MURRAY & THE INVISIBLE GIRLS
(forgot the label)

I bought it. I sold it. What more you wanna know?--DS

45's

FOUR SORE POINTS....

HAPPY SQUID SAMPLER-"URINALS"/"DANNY AND THE DOORKNOBS"/ "ARROW BOOK CLUB"/"VIDIOTS"/"PHIL BEDEL"
There was only 500 of these so if it aint your by now... NEEF takes up one side with their nonsensical approach to being unique...nice try but it's b side that makes me smile...What else can be said about the URINALS?they are one of my favorite bands simple on the strength of their 3 singles and the cut here "U"-before you know it its over ...All the bands sound like they were recorded from the apt. across the ally from the studio and the Doorknobs cut has a great 60's feel without wallowing in the era...ARROW BOOK CLUB is nonmusic like NEEF but in this case it's good.The cut by VIDIOTS appears on the Rodney sampler so you're prob- ably familiar with that one...Phil Bedel's cut sounds just like juicy farts played through a synthesizer...If you're lucky enough to locate this record don't pass it up...

the HAPPY SQUID sampler

ANTI PASTI-"NO GOVERNMENT"/"1980"/"TWO YEARS TOO LATE"/"SOMETHING NEW"
Rondelet Music
These guys are armed for the critics..."two years too late for what?"Really,whats happen- ed lately to replace the energy of the old days? Fuckin' nothin' so the likes of these guys can put out a great energetic debut like this and sell records.Their second 45 promptly blew the joystick which was a tad dissapointing but at least weve got this one.

FOETUS UNDER GLASS-"SPite Your Face"/"O.K.F.M."
Self Immolation Records
Starts out twisted like FILE UNDER POP or S.P.K. but quickly falls apart when limp vocals and con- trived jump around with the originality of the Berlin Blondes who are boreing English faggots- so this just proves theres a fine line between whats rivetting and what sucks...

STINGERS-"Aint Growin' Up"/"Sally"/"Art School"
Holy poop this is the loser of the month- this band sounds _exactly_ like the B52's, can you believe it?Hardcore name,and great look...the music _the worst_

DURAN DURAN-"Planet Earth"/"Late Bar" EMI
More glam-just like the rest-dont bother.

MINNY POPS-"Dolphin Spurt" Factory
Their album was not good.We'll give them the benifit of the doubt because this 45 is excellent.The basic Fac. sound that is always listenable,sometimes redundant,but alwayslistenable.I'll ignore the way all the vocalists still sound like "him".

UK DECAY-"Unexpected Guest"/"Dresden"
Fresh Records
Heavy handed intro-all effect and no meat- DS (dont you love these reviews in brief?That means we write them in our rotting shorts)

DEPACHE MODE-"Dreaming Of Me"/"Ice Machine"
Mute
This sounds like all the other boreing crap on this label(except D.A.F.)Synthesizers are so easy to play who do these assholes think they're fooling.If this is tomorrows'sound then hand me my will.(I didn't buy this so quit yer laughing..TV

FACTION-"FACTION"/"WRONG AGAIN" Inevitable Records
The hardest part about writing these dumb reviews is trying to explain how these dumb records sound so you'll know whether or not to waste your dumd dollars.Keyboards and such are on this ....it sounds pretty original.... it sounds good....they have an album out that I wouldn't buy unless it was alot better than this...so I'm telling you not afuckavalot so what else can I do stand on my head and hum the tune over the phone?

GATHERING DUST
BRONCS

CABARET VOLTAIRE-3 CREPUSCULE TRACKS
Thy found some grate tapes of some southern evan- gelical huckster making his pitch for $$$$ like "nothing under $100 doolars tonight,no tips I want sacrifice"This band seems real intrigued with low- er US mentality,and what they've done here on "Slu- ggin for Jesus Parts 1&2 is put down their great, classic rythyms over these religious con artists. Nothing this band has ever done since 74' has been anything less than totally satisfying,and they some- how manage to keep the C.V. mystique alive(few photos- no background info)This is a Belgiun pressing but it's 5 bucks very well spent....

MEDIUM MEDIUM-"HUNGRY SO ANGRY"/"NADSAT DREAM" Cherry Red
One of this months best...but than I can say something like that and be talking about 19 other singles.Funk...imported funk,with ex- cellent production...the cleanest sax I've heard in ages,and that kinda bass bounces n- icely and doesn't plod...for some reason my friends all stood around when I first played this and smugly told me it sucked...even if they're wrong it don't mean they ain't my friends...

REPTILE RANCH-"HENRY"/"SAYING GOODYE"/ "YOUNG EXECUTIVE" Z Block Records
What a handle...must be the everglades' equivalent of Call of The Wild Museum... cept' this is English and a _very_ differant record. Unique would be a tired adj. to describe what these 3 have come up with.Great record to wake up to in the morning,,,sleeper of the month...

ANIMAL NOISES
REPTILE RANCH

THE BRONCS-"Tele-K-KILLING"/"REASON TO WHINE"/"PART OF THE PROBLEM" Terminal
Release number 3 on the Terminal label- one of the other two being the great Cle. Confidential EP but I'm sorry this single is p-poor,lousy...you know,real FBC mat- erial.Tim Allee was the guitarist with the late PAGANS(check that he played bass,but I'm too lazy to type the whole review over)but out of that context I can't get too excited about anything here...Sorry...

MY CAPTAINS-"FALL"/"CONVERSE "HISTORY"/"NOTHING"
4 AD Records
An EP from an Oxford band, that shows much promise.. I sometimes wonder if things are really as dismal as some of these young men make it sound-but it's their perogitive...One cut comes dangerously close to sounding like "ALL Ni- GHT PARTY" by A Certain Ratio but we'll forgive the there also... all in all a graet debut...

RELIGIOUS OVERDOSE-"25 MINUTES"/"OVERDOSE" Glass Records
This band took it's basic plodding monotonal guitar and machine drone and stretched it into an interest- ing piece of apathetic.More detritus of the coming age of toxic waste and bland expressionism or am I giving credit for a malingering bunch of rogues with simply nothing else to do?Mutual masturbation in this case is highly likely.

FLIPPER

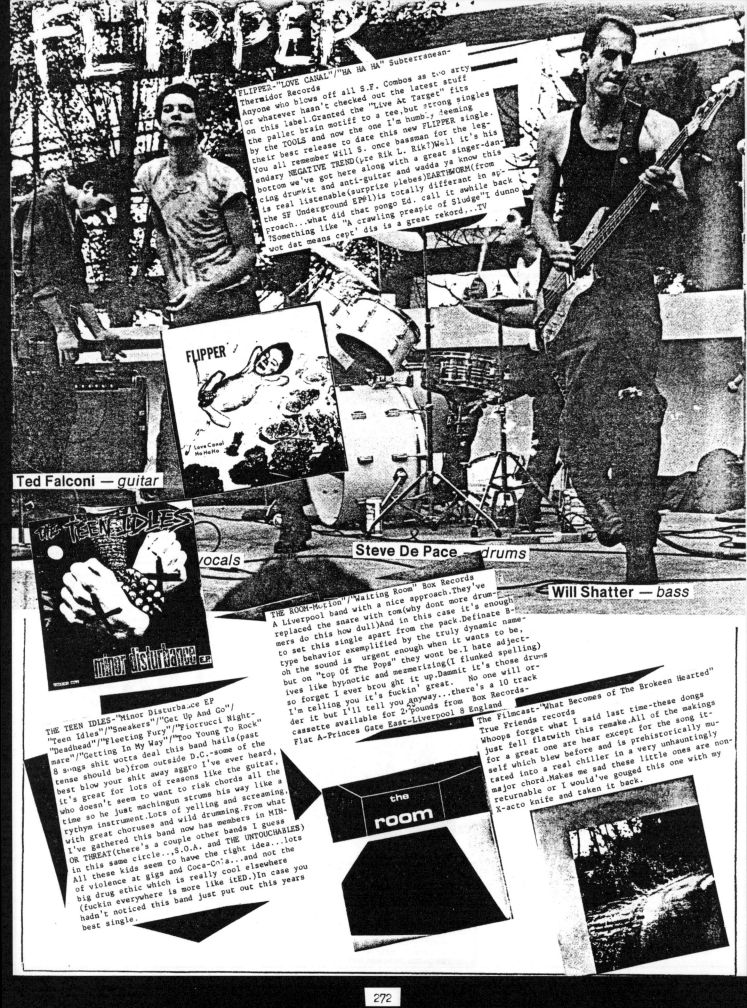

FLIPPER-"LOVE CANAL"/"HA HA HA" Subterranean-Thermidor Records
Anyone who blows off all S.F. Combos as too arty or whatever hasn't checked out the latest stuff on this label.Granted the "Live At Target" fits the pallet brain motiff to a tee,but strong singles by the TOOLS and now the one I'm humbly deeming their best release to date this new FLIPPER single. You all remember Will S. once bassman for the legendary NEGATIVE TREND(pre Rik L. Rik?)Well it's his bottom we've got here along with a great singer-dancing drumkit and anti-guitar and wadda ya know this is real listenable(surprize plebes)EARTHWORM(from the SF Underground EP#1)is totally differant in approach...what did that pongo Ed. call it awhile back ?Something like "A crawling preapic of Sludge"I dunno wot dat means cept' dis is a great rekord...TV

Ted Falconi — guitar

Steve De Pace — drums

Will Shatter — bass

...vocals

THE TEEN IDLES-"Minor Disturbance EP"/
"Teen Idles"/"Sneakers"/"Get Up And Go"/
"Deadhead"/"Fleeting Fury"/"Fiorrucci Night-mare"/"Getting In My Way"/"Too Young To Rock"
8 songs shit wotta deal this band hails(past tense should be)from outside D.C.-some of the best blow your shit away aggro I've ever heard, it's great for lots of reasons like the guitar, who doesn't seem to want to risk chords all the time so he just machingun strums his way like a rythym instrument.Lots of yelling and screaming, with great choruses and wild drumming.From what I've gathered this band now has members in MIN-OR THREAT(there's a couple other bands I guess in this same circle...S.O.A. and THE UNTOUCHABLES) All these kids seem to have the right idea...lots of violence at gigs and Coca-Cola...and not the big drug ethic which is really cool elsewhere (fuckin everywhere is more like itED.)In case you hadn't noticed this band just put out this years best single.

THE ROOM-"Motion"/"Waiting Room" Box Records
A Liverpool band with a nice approach.They've replaced the snare with tom(why dont more drummers do this how dull)And in this case it's enough to set this single apart from the pack.Definate B-type behavior exemplified by the truly dynamic name-oh the sound is urgent enough when it wants to be, but on "top Of The Pops" they wont be.I hate adjectives like hypnotic and mezmerizing(I flunked spelling) so forget I ever brought it up.Dammit it's those drums I'm telling you it's fuckin' great. No one will order it but I'll tell you anyway...there's a 10 track cassette available for 2 pounds from Box Records-Flat A-Princes Gate East-Liverpool 8 England

The Filmcast-"What Becomes of The Brokeen Hearted"
True Friends records
Whoops forget what I said last time-these dongs just fell flatwith this remake.All of the makings for a great one are hear except for the song it-self which blew before and is prehistorically mu-tated into a real chiller in a very unhauntingly major chord.Makes me sad these little ones are non-returnable or I would've gouged this one with my X-acto knife and taken it back.

272

SINGLES

THE BONGOS--"In The Congo"/"Mambo Sun" Fetish Records

Doesn't quite have that pure ingenuous quality of their first record. Having been acknowledged by NME, their hot shit now, and this new record reflects that in being a slicker release. Oh, it's still the Bongos alright, but the innocent and obscure quality to their sound is gone forever. And since I was never much of a Bolan fan, the B-side fails to get much of a response out of me, 'cept that I wish they'd chosen an orignal instead. Still a significant band, despite this slip backward.--DS

THE GO-BETWEENS--"I Need Two Hands", "Stop Before You Say It" Postcard

My personal favorite from this label. Never really went for either Orange Juice or Josef K, but these guys shy away from some of the folks elements of the other two. Forget what the A-side sounds like, been spending too much time wearing out the flip. A real stop-and-start jewel. Ridiculously simple little riff from the guitarist is the glue that holds it all together. Worth the money.--DS

CRASS--"Nagasaki Nightmare"/"Big A, Little A" Crass Records

By this time, you either love 'em, or you wish they were banned from ever playing again. The Crass are Crass, always have, always will. The a-side takes a little getting used to. Never having been too keen a fan of Ms. Libertine's vocals, I was quick to point out the superiority of the flipside, but that may have been a bit hasty. There's really no point in attempting to defend either side. They are most definitely a one of a kind.--DS

CONSTANT CAUSE

the potent human e.p.

The Liggers
The Mekon
The Spurtz
Bathroom Renovations

THE POTENT HUMAN EP--w/The Liggers, The Mekon, The Spurtz, Bathroom Renovations L'Adventure Records

This thing has been sitting around my room for the better part of two months, and I have still yet to listen to it in its entirety. Do you think it's the do-it-yourself bag or what. I guess if it looks cheap, then the contents can't be no too great either. Don't bother.--DS

THE NURSES--"Love You Again"/"I Will Follow You" Teen-A-Toons Records

The eyes of many a skeptic will be cast my way when I come out and say that this is the best Pop single I have ever heard. Now usually I'm not prone to such a flagrant use of hyperbole, but I play this record, over and over again, and never seem to get tired of the thing. Now theres no U2 slickness going on here, quite the opposite actually. They've been described as a garage band, which may be why I like these guys so much. Their sound is underproduced, not raw like our own releases, but instead of honing down the rough edges, they've chosen to leave things well enough alone. This may sound stupid, but I think it sounds more pure, more viginal, than if they had monkeyed around with the mixing. It has all the ingredients to make it a hit. At first listen, you may say they sound wimpy, but I have to debunk that notion. There's an urgency and conviction to Howard's voice, which also holds true with their music, that puts them head and shoulders above all the other 'pop' bands. Who cares, I like it, alot in fact, and if for some reason you think I'm giving you a bum steer, then buddy, you're not worth it.--DS

THE WALL--"Ghetto"/"Another New Day"/"Mercury" Fresh Records

If you're still scratching your scalp til you draw blood, wondering which Wall single to get(many of you, I'm sure, have spent many a sleepless night pondering this same thought), stop, this is the one and only record even remotely worth considering. The others reak of runny dog doo compared to this one. They manage to uphold most adequately a dying tradition.--DS

Y PANTS--"Off The Hook"/"Beautiful Food"/"Favorite Sweater"/"Luego Fuego" 99 Records

Stop reading, and go out and buy this record, right now! First the Bush Tetras, then ESG, and now these gurls. Must make all you feminists just beam with pride. I don't know where 99 finds 'em, but they've got the inside track on what's happening in the big (rotten) apple. The key to the band is the vocal/piano combination. The singer sounds like she's suffering from Down's Syndrome, each sylable rolls off her tougne like thick molasses; and the piano is identical to those dinky little toy pianos you used to hammer on back in kindergarten. More of a rhythm instrument here, real tinny and bell-like. A must.--DS

THE NAMES--"Night Shift"/"I Wish I
Could Speak Your Language" Factory

Easily the best thing from Factory
since Crawling Chaos. They've been
steadily losing ground to 4AD in
the race for new music supremecy,
and although that should not be any
overriding concern for us, The Names
will surely return some of that lost
respectibility. "Night Shift" floats
down to wrap us in a tinselly shroud
of delicately compelling music. All
the instruments, save the almost absurdly rock steady drumbeat, drift
in and out of focus with a feathery
elegance. Very few bands, if any,
can match the ephemeral beauty found
on this record. And it should come
as no surprise when I say that this
is a must.--DS

X-BLANK-X
1) "?"/"You're Full Of Shit"
2) "No Nonsense"/"Approaching The
Minimal With Spray Guns" Drome

Couple of indispensible gems from
that same squalid environment that
brought you Pagans. Don't know
whether they're still together or
not,looks like this latest single
could be a year old. Nevertheless,
this band put out some of the most
nerve-wracking dissonance these parts
have ever heard. Everything's a
jarring, grating mess, so loose and
deliberate that it makes some of our
most violent headbanging aggro look
tame in comparison. May not be the
easiest records to find, but they
more than warrant the search.--DS

LILIPUT--"Eisiger Wind"/"When The
Cat's Away Then The Mice Will Play"
Rough Trade

For the first 30 seconds or so of
the first side, I thought these
girls were gonna knock me right out
of my seat. Guitars ringing majest-
ically, like 'we mean business this
time, buddy', but no, that was too
much to hope for. Instead of building on this fine start, they slip
into that familiar format of half-
shouting vocals droning on monotonously. And it just goes on and on,
far exceeding the saturation point
of painful boredom. I've played it
once maybe twice, after that, who
cares. A discouragingly far cry
from the bounce and spirit of their
"Split" single.--DS

SKI PATROL--"Agent Orange"/"Driving"
Malicious Damage Records

Pretty grim political statement from
yet another limey band who somehow
feel qualified to make judgemental
comments. It may seem new to them
but this theme has pretty much run
its course over here. Nonetheless,
they manage to generate a fair amount
of tension with each repeated phrase:
'agent orange. . . I'm on fire'.
"Driving" is more interesting from
a musical standpoint. With the triteness of the A-side gone, they concentrate on their music which tends to
remind me of the better stuff off of
the Mekons 1st album. A good band
that will probably be grossly overlooked here in the states.--DS

ZEITGEIST--"Sniper"/"Shake, Rake"
Enchaine Records

One of those marginally interesting
little oddities that you read about,
but once you actually got your hands
on it, you're wondering what all the
hub-bub was about. Besides, the singer reminded me of Bowie, so that
gave me all the more reason to re-
linquish this sad slab to my dead
dog file. It's just been re-released,
I thought they only did that with
good stuff.--DS

DEMOB--"Anti-Police"/"Teenage Adoles-
cence" Round Ear Records

Same label as the Anti Pasti bunch,
'cept this one is no good. Alright
guitar sound, only it plods along
at half the pace it should. Sleeve
makes the band look real mean and
hostile. Too bad they don't sound
like it. A waste.--DS

the past seven days

THEATRE OF HATE-"REBEL WITH OUT A BRAIN"/"MY OWN INVENTION Burning Rome Records Single #2 for the most exciting band in England.Big overhype?No way ...I won't live to regret anything... Mick Jones produces this and does a fantastic job of capturing the intensity of this great bunch of rogues- Kirk Brandon has an incredible range,and the way the guitar is mixed way down, and the pounding skins are turned way up is perfect... more,,,more...

THE PAST SEVEN DAYS-"RAINDANCE"/"SO MANY OTHERS" 4'AD Records
Goody more good poop from the greatest label going.More polished and accessible than most of their discoveries but again one of the best to hit the T&G offices in quite some time...music with intelligence...something people say this mag doesn't like...wrong again Bosco just because were college grads don't mean we gotpunk rocks ror brains...a band like THE PAST SEVEN DAYS is good for a kick(subtle)in anybodys head...strongly recommended...

MORE 45's DY T.V...

½ JAPANESE-"SPY"/"I KNOW HOW IT FEELS ...BAD" Armageddon Records
I never had the hogs to shell out for their big box set so I'm content to buy this piddly single which isn't very good compared to "I Want Something New" or the Jad Fair single.

.........AND THE NATIVE HIPSTERS

HE HATED IT MATE!!

ON OUR COVER? GREGGY!!
Stupid American cunts...

of GREGGY AND THE DIPSHITS-great band from Ohio who are working on a cassette release for sometime this summer...see interview insert (because someone messed up and didnt mail it to me on time!)

and the NATIVE HIPSTERS- "THERE GOES CONCORDE AGAIN"/ "STANDS STILL THE BUILDING"/ "I WANNA BE AROUND"
How come noone ever reviewed this ditty?Real music like this only happens once in a blue moon,and when it does you people don't even appreciate it,what fives(whoops)gives? now they went and felt all rejected and we'll probably never hear from them again...

ABUSE-"NO MONEY"/"IN AMERICA"/"LOVE'S ALRIGHT" Fresh Flexi
You aughta see the new issue of Talk Talk magazine...glossy cover... it's real snazzy looking,where do they get all the coin?? Get the correspondent who sez FEAR is from San Fransisco...a real laugh riot...TALK TALK is a mag that will be around when the rest of us are dead

something's got to give

orange disaster

NO It's NOT ORANGE- YES It IS A DISASTER,,,TV

ECHO AND THE BUNNYMEN/THE ATTITUDES Bookies

Dull. Dull. Dull. Has to be the biggest disappointment of the year. Uninspried, lackluster, indifferent, and don't let me forget: boring! These guys just don't know the first thing about performing for an audience. Whether they see us as hayshaking sodbusters or what, I don't know, but their ability to communicate with a crowd hovers pathetically around the remedial level. We may be from Lansing, but it doesn't take much to see that none of the band members were gettin' any enjoyment out what they were doing. Staring up at the ceiling, hoping that the time passes quickly--that's what must have been going thru their heads cuz it was written all over their faces. And to further aggravate a a rather hopeless situation, they were far too loud. I mean Black Flag was loud. The Fix are loud. But these guys abuse the privilege, which only sours our already dampened anticipation. On record they're one of the biggies; however somewhere between the studio and the little dive on McNichols they lost their power to communicate. Voice, guitar, and drums was all you could hear, and there's alot more to their music then just these three elements. I don't know what they were trying to pull, overpower us with sheer volume and a bludgeoning beat or what, but that's not why I paid my six bucks at the door. Their recorded sound is much more subtle as well as being dynamic; however, they toss that mode out the window and vainly attempt to browbeat us into submission. That ain't gonna work. People have said that this band is inconsistent and is not uncommon to have to put up with a less than satisfactory performance. Judging from tonight's show, I'd say that's the rule and not the exception.--DS

THE SONS OF LIBERTY EP/THE CROWD"A WORLD APART"EP RED CROSS EP (reissue) THE STEPMOTHERS EP/UXA LP (re-issue)   POSH BOY RECORDS
Hey new stuff from P.Boy,and there's even a single out featuring Robbie himself along with the S.F.? band BABY BUDDAH...The UXA LP is not as bad as I made it sound a few issues back-this is sounding better since the mix has been brought out of the mud...(they cancelled their Lansing gig but someone said he saw them in Detroit?)oh well there was a few dissapointed...The 6 RED CROSS XXX tunes here are the same ones featured on the SIREN LP and since they are the only decent band on that I can sell that and keep this neato, dayglo EP...great band that used to be...THE STEPMOTHERS...You'll have to ask me next month cuz I ain't sure yet,and I don't want to say any thing I'll regret later...The best new P.Boy release is easily T.S.O.L.-which is really good with intense guitar and harsh toned songwriting- the singer should yell more,that's my only complaint...THE CROWD LP? They went nu wave all the way...the aggression of the BEACH BLVD. days are apparently gone forevor...Theres something for all tastes on this label...he's not going to please everyone all the time,but sell discs he will...
DISCHARGE-"WHY" EP   Clay
TEN NEW DISCHARGE CUTS!!!!!!!!!!More of the loudest,rawest music in the world.More minor chord mutilitation with one-hundred % of references in innuendos pointing at the warmongers in DC,London,Moscow ETC.Pictures of children adorn the cover in bloody piles to illustrate the inequity of bombings and such- yup war's a drag....the music is 50,000 watts of out of control noise that makes my dick stiff and my hands shake...quite simply one of your all time favorite records...RIGHT??!?

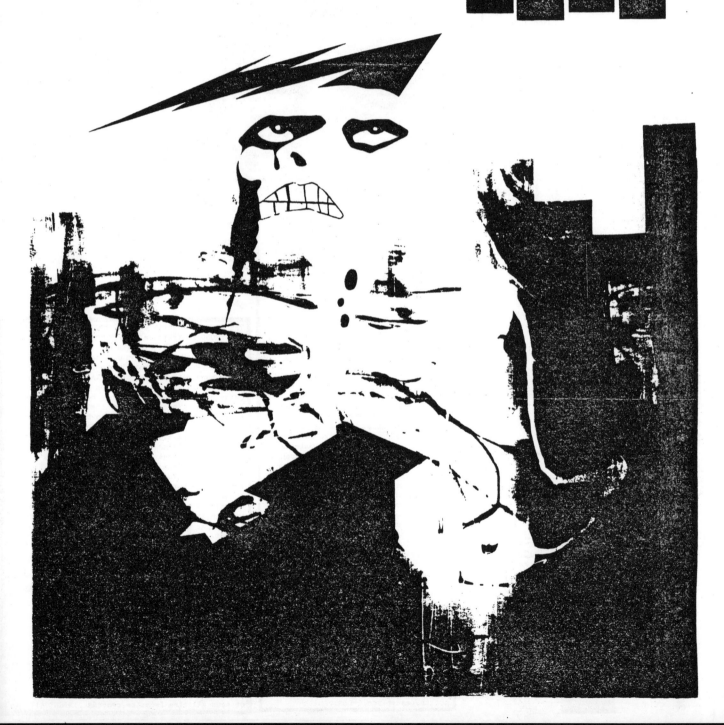

NECROS/FIX/BLACK FLAG at CLUB DOO BEE
Mar.22

It isnt so unusual for pubic hair to match that that is on ones head-especially if you are Davey Winklefuck.How he dared show his ancient mug on this eve is beyond me(and why didn't someone beat this fuckers face to meat-loaf?(CENSORED EVEN THIS WAS too crude for me! ED.) Shit this was the fuckin best bill...You may think this a bit incestuous us going ape shit over the 2 warm-ups but both sets were aggot

crushing and louddd(between these 3 your talk-in permanent ear damage)It took a little do-ing getting the first band on the bill but I think most will agree it rounded out the affair nicely.The bar was overcrowded(thank god the fire marshall takes a powder on Sun. Evenings) Necros played an inspired set with a couple new songs like "Youth Camp" and "IQ 32"(dedicated to Lansings' audience of course)The mix was right,and Corey is working out great on bass.The crowd got going earlierwhen Black Flag got there late and did a 4 song sound check(they had to drive straight in from Boston where they played Sat. nite.)Gave the folks a dose of what to stick around for,for sure.The audience mixed it up nicely for the boys

from Maumee...even a well timed strepp throat didn't keep me from the pileup but the energy went fast and I had to spend the rest of the evening on the lines.The Fix were so fast most people who hadn't seen em' before stood with their mouths hangin open and the set was over before one could cut a fire breathing fart."Off To War" still ranks as my fave FIX tune but they threw in a couple tough sounding new ones including "Rat Patrol" A fuckin great act that will hopefully broaden its base enough to tell this fucked locale and its musically retarded plebes asta la vista and

french my asshole while you still got the chance. What else can I say about the LA band.The niceness they exibit offstage quickly turns as they blasted the audience with frenetic noise we'd all been waiting for.There were people here from all over and if you went away dissapointed then all I can say is youre to old or your personal little set of fucked up values have left you perman-ently in need of the cyanide pie.Greg plays so fast you got to keep riveted on his instrument to convince yourself he's really doing it.Chuck

cruised around what stage there was as he and Robo kept the disciplined bottom on track.And Dez's hoarse screeching fit the whole sound alot better than I thought it would after watching videos of them from out west.They're the best and they showed us why on Sunday nite. TV

Come on Girls...I buy you drinks + put you on the guest list will you fuck me? went you fuck me?

Winkelstern on rock

The crowd (and hair) was aglow

By DAVID WINKELSTERN
Journal Correspondent

It isn't so unusual for someone's hair to match the color of his shirt. Unless, of course, his shirt hap-pens to be a bright turquoise.

That guy with a bluish-green head was part of a capacity-plus crowd at the Club DooBee on Sunday.

The place was more crowded than a shoe box stuffed with Winnebagoes. Aliens from other states (and possibly other planets) had gathered late at night to hear Black Flag and two other wavish groups pump it up and kick it out from a stage about the size of a graham cracker. A unique group of mostly local folks stood on chairs or moved on the dance floor like little Christmas trees that were thrown into an open washer.

TWO YOUNG MSU students who had come to the club for the first time were warned by a guy wear-ing a leather jacket and a perpetual, open-mouthed gaze. He explained that the dancing could be violent and that pushing and shoving are part of the scene. The good samaritan then left and charged into the dancers with a certain glee.

I was one of the mob who paid $3 for a show that began close to 11 p.m. Two forgettable warm-up shows lasted about a half-hour each. Both the Fix and the Necros played hyper-fast music. It wasn't fast enough for me; if it was quicker, maybe they would have finished sooner...

intensity has always been an essential component of rock 'n' roll, one missing from today's glossy "new wave" and the macho, working class heavy metal.

The Necros, from Maumee, Ohio, were greatly improved compared with their debut at the Club DooBee last September. They were tight and force-ful and sweating with loud confidence. It is rare that an opening band capti-vates the crowd as the Necros did.

The Fix, Michigan's only hard core band (from where else but Lansing?), was also noticeably improved. From one fast, aggressive song to the next, the band's timing and dynamics were near perfect. No false starts or stops — they have got it down. People had come from Detroit and Chicago to see this show ("Who needs Florida?"), so both the Fix and the Necros were pre-pared to play for a very sophisticated audience.

It was quite a scene, and quite a freak show. The dance floor was like a rioting mob, everyone banging into each other, as if films of London or Los Angeles has just been shown. Black Flag drove everyone wild. They came on in a blaze of sound and Club Doo-Bee was electrified. Those who wouldn't risk the dancefloor stood on their chairs in awe and disbelief.

The dismal conditions which pro-duced the Pistols in England in the 1970s are quickly becoming a reality in the aging U.S. of A. The cry of "no fu-ture" has been loudest from the punks of Los Angeles, the home of Black Flag.

Guitarist Greg Ginn was incredible, as was Robo the fast and hard drum-mer. Ginn, one of the fastest guitarists you'll ever see, used his speed taste-fully. Standing stationary, his head shaking back and forth, he performed what would normally demand two guitarists. Dez, the mindless, scream-ing lead singer, had a strange glow in his eyes, as if he knew something we didn't. Black Flag finally ended a long, fierce set (I thought at least one of them would have a heart attack) with the Kingsmen's "Louie, Louie." In an ultimate slap at rock 'n' roll, they handed their instruments to the claw-ing audience. As the song ended in a fury of noise and confusion, Black Flag was already off the stage, the night ending in utter chaos.

The punks claim to be anti-art and anti-intellectual, yet, through this same rebellion against a now-established, and redundant artistic "creativity," they have created an intense field of emotion which, by the way, is the aim of all art. Very few concerts leave me with such an impression. You might love 'em or hate 'em, but you won't forget 'em. Wake up, America.

BLACK FLAG was hardly worth the long wait. The vocalist sang with the melody of an angry foot-ball coach.

The group did show more energy in a few tunes than most cutsie commercial bands show on an en-tire tour. So did the opening acts and so does a wounded water buffalo. The musical theme of the night seemed to be bash-bash-bash, crash-crash-crash, who cares if it sounds like trash?

Having alternative forms of music instead of the usual bar band drivel is great. Having a place like the Club DooBee is more than welcome. But rude-ness to the ears and to people shouldn't be so easily tolerated...

ED.
Such imagery Dave, such "wavey" insight, and those analogies...

Just because you cant get any "punk sex" (you hear it's hot)your aching weenie forces you to lash out at the whole scene. The scene is between your legs bonehead. Take my advice and dress like a black child and move to Atlanta.Give Jon Holmes a blow-job so your friend Gail P. can make a blue-boy film.Oh I forgot you probably suck like shit like you write.Get dorked you paunched out hippie fucksack...nes time wear a name tag

THE ABOVE UNSOLICITED REPRINT APPEARED IN THE LANSING STATE JOURNAL ON 3-28-81. ADDRESS ALL CORRESPONDENCE TO THIS SOO C/O THAT PAPER...

Sound and fury was inexhaustible as the Club DooBee shook with an inten-sity never witnessed before. The raw power of the Necros, the Fix and Black Flag incited the kind of riotous emo-tions that Jimi Hendrix or the Who were able to ten or so years ago. Such

AND THIS IS **Jon Epstein's** ACCOUNT WHICH APPEARED IN THE LANSING STAR.

WHILE WERE ON THE SUBJECT HERES A LETTER

Greetings,

Thanx for your quick service and per-sonal communcation on the records I ordered from you. Both The Fix and Necros singles stand up well with any released in LA or the UK. What else can I say about the Bad Brains except where can I hear more of them? I attended the Necros-Fix-Black Flag show at the DooBee. The Necros were great, but The Fix left me with a feeling that something was missing. It's hard to pinpoint, and to a non-initiate to the "punk" sound, it pro-bably sounded very similar, but The Fix did not deliver a totally satis-fying performance. Craig is a super guitarist and I suspect the weak link may be the singer's sincerity, I don't know. Did you notice this also(Necros-great, Fix-something not totally toget-her) or is it just me? To state the obvious--Black Flag is it. That was the most intense performance I'd ever witnessed. My experience with live punk shows is limited, but I can't imagine anyone outdoing Black Flag. It stayed with me for days--whew! Although I now live in Three Rivers, I still have the Lansing connection. I lived there for the last few years, hence my familiarity with T&G, Club DooBee, etc. I was passing thru Lan-sing on my way to Saginaw(my ex-home-town) when I saw a poster for Black Flag on Grand River, when I saw it was the next night I knew I had to make it. But as a "non-insider" at Club DooBee, I offer some criticism of the scene there. It is not a friendly place to go see shows at because most of the people are regu-lars and do not bother to deal with others, they are too busy making the "scene". I question some of these people's concern for the music being played as long as they can be consid-ering themselves cool for making what-ever scene happens to be around. In a way, it's too bad, for the Doob definitely is the place to see excit-ing music and if it were friendlier, it would be a better place to hang out and would expand the ranks of new-music believers(is this desirable?)(you bet it is--ED).--AD

Note: Hope you don't mind us cutting your letter a little short.

NO ALTERNATIVE--"Make Guns Not Love"/
"Metro Police Theme"/"Rockabilly Rumble" Subterranean

Pretty limp drivel comin' out of
these grooves. Granted, it ain't
from LA, but you can't help comparing them to their southern counterparts. It doesn't stack up, no
way. If you're gonna be punk, do
it!, don't flinch and only go half
way, just cuz you think people won't
like you anymore.--DS

S.F. UNDERGROUND 2--Lewd-"Mobile
Home"/Undead-"Hitler's Brain"/So-
ciety Dog-"Title Role"/Spikes-"Life
is Hell" Subterranean

Like the first one, this falls very
comfortably into that same benignly
undistinquished category of so-so
Bay Area talent. While attempting
to be punk, they succeed only in
cornering the market on lameness.
With the exception of The Spikes
cut, which is just plain feeble,
everything on this record elicits
that mild shrug of indifference.
It's alright, not bad, ok; nowhere
do you hear yourself say: "hey these
guys are hot, I want ten of 'em."
It just don't happen. Maybe if I
wrote for some Bay Area rag, I'd do
a little more ass-kissin', but since
I don't, I won't.--DS

THE STIMULATORS--"Loud, Fast Rules"/
"Run, Run, Run"

Over a year old, and I'm just hearing this for the first time. Boy,
am I ever behind the times. If you
don't go out and buy this right now,
then forever be resigned to posing
your way thru life. This has got
to be one of the finest slices of
raucous, noisey, punk raunch you'll
ever hear. That little girl on guitar cuts most ax men to ribbons.
The louder you play it and the more
you play it, the better it gets.
How this band ever survived under
the oppression of the smothering no
wave crowd is a miracle of modern
science. Recorded a lot better than
the Misfits, this stuff is more ad-
dicting than heroin. Play it just
once, you're hooked for good. This
absolutely, positively demands to
be heard. Great, great, great.--DS

MODERN WARFARE
1) "Delivered"/"Dayglo"/"In The
Shadows"/"Suburban Death"/
"Nothing Left" Bemisbrain Records/
2) "No Passion"/"Dayglo"/"In The

Couple of speeding bullets from LA.
First one's produced by Geza and
shows it. "Delivered" has that combo of Geza and Residents' brand of
high-pitched springy guitar that I
never had an ear for. "Dayglo" is
great, though. A speed of light
number that rips a clean hole thru
my ear's waxy buildup. "No Passion"
and "Suburban Death" are better yet,
cuz they've decided to leave the
jagged edges intact, and that's the
way it sounds best. Probably had
to throw cold water or something
on the guitar player to get 'im
to stop. His manic strumming is an
all or nothing kind of thing. It's
either fast till his fingers are a
puffy, blistered mess or silence.
He's programmed for one speed:
fast, and fast. The rest of the
band ain't no slouch, either. They
are all wired. Somebody said 'speed
kills', well then, you better think
twice before listening to these guys.
--DS
Available thru Bemisbrain Records,
200 Termino Ave., Long Beach, CA
90803

ARTERY
1) "Unbalance"/"The Slide"
Live EP
2) "Cars In Motion"/"Life And
Death" Aardvark Records

I like this band, but I am still
unclear as to the reasons why this
is so. A very minimal, understated
new music that upon first listen
seems to have nothing going for it.
My strategy here is to downplay
this record so much that your curiosity will overcome you; thus forcing you to go out and buy these
records. This is one occasion where
I find myself at a loss to adequately
describe a band, since there is no
outstanding aspect to their music on
which to comment. I still like it.--DS

VARIOUS ARTISTS--"the original mixed-
up kid"/"unofficial secrets" Fried
Egg Records

The single worst piece of trash I
have ever purchased. Gives records
a bad name.--DS

GOOD SHIT HERE

ALL NIGHT MOVIES/Q.R.A./SPASTIC RHYTHM TARTS Valley 3 Cafeteria Kazoo

Shit! I drive all the way down there to catch Q.R.A., and I pull in just in time to catch All Night Movies' set. Too much drinkin' and drivin', I guess. No offense to you guys, Lon, but I'd seen you play once already, and was especially keen on hearing what the hell Kalamazoo had to offer. Fortunately, I was not to be denied. I go over to this party afterwards, and somebody's got all three bands on tape. Spastic Rhythm Tarts are first. Very crude experimental sound. Singer sounded good, whoever she was (sorry I forgot the name). Appropiate name, very rhythmic, but equally undisciplined, which is part of their charm. Remember less about Q.R.A. My mind fogged long ago on the Mickeys leaving the evening one dull blur. We left just the time some joker began picking at his bass. 3:00 in the morning and we got Stanley Clarke in our midst. Time to bail out before I begin blowing chow. There's definitely somethin' happening down in Kalamazoo, I just hope they don't get discouraged and throw in the towel before we get a chance to see what they can do. Thanks to Kenny, Dick(Rick?), Jim, Eliot for putting me up for the night. Oh yea, All Night Movies were their great abrasive selves tonight. Punk is dead, no?--DS

PACK-9/THE FLEXIBLES Club DooBee

Got to be one of the all-time lows at the Doob. Why I subject myself to this dreadful bilge must surely reveal some crippling neuroses on my part. To simply say that the two bands bit the big ones would be the supreme act of mercy. It would be my fondest hope to see that neither band ever step foot on stage again.

The Flexibles come from Ann Arbor, and their hokey jive-ass urban gagtriggering street noise survives only because it feeds on that town's disportionately large number of brainwashed pseudo intellectuals. They think they're oh so cool and sophisticated playing a little jazz, a little blues, a little R&B, and a little rock 'n' roll. It don't make no difference. Shit's gonna stink no matter what color it is. Tell ya what, why don't you guys go back to playin' for pennies on the corner of State and North U.? Fool 'em down there and leave us alone.

Now Pack-9 is another story. Four cocky assholes who think they're hot shit cuz people down in Detroit are so fuckin' indiscriminate when it come to judging music. Bunch of poseurs who play the most abysmal heavy metal/power pop dung I've heard in a long, long time. Probably go back to Detroit and their ass kissing friends and say they just finished playing to a bunch of hicks in Haslett. So what fellas, the jokes on you. Sure you think you're God's gift to music, with those fuckin' balloon brained cunts, and your fingers up yer butts cuz that's the only ass you'll ever get. Dry up, blow away, drop dead. I don't ever want to see shits like you around here again. And one more thing, the old editors of White Noise obviously have no shame, no pride, and surely no respect from us at T&G for endorsing a hopelessly irrelevant band like Pack-9.--DS

NOT SO GOOD HERE

RETRO/TRAINABLE Club DooBee

You got to ask yourself what the hell is DS doing at a Trainable gig? Doing a Oscar winning performance in the bored-indifferent-"what time is it?-anything good on TV tonite?-I gotta getta outahere category. Trainable funny jazz shit never ceases to amaze me at how many dumb shits go goo-goo over that crap.

Take a look at the crowd and you see a bunch of aging old farts who should be put out to pasture. C'mon, who's say they're a fun band. They don't kiddin' You know it! Their music sucks and we'd shit, and the tire off if they stuck with deserve the better day, and we'd all dim-witted art damage clique at Two Doors Down. I've seen Retro before, I didn't need to see them again.--DS

L-7/THE ATTITUDES Club DooBee

Caught L-7 at their first gig down in Hamtramack a couple of weeks ago, and was more than a little surprised to see that Dave had booked them so soon. It didn't really matter, cuz it was about time we saw some new talent at the Doob. Needless to say, L-7 has the potential to become one of the top bands in Michigan. They ain't punk, but they ain't no artsyfartsy band neither. With Frank, Retro's old bass player, supplying a solid bottom along with Dave Rice's plectral rhythms, Larissa's high yet velvety voice eschews the funk tag this band might be labeled with. It's energetic, it's original, and it's danceable. I've learned that they've added a sax player, and I don't know whether that will enhance their sound or muddy it, I'll just have to wait and see. Regardless of the addition, L-7 is one band worth seeing.--DS

THE PUPPETS/LET's TALK ABOUT GIRLS Club DooBee

The evening was a total waste of time from start to finish. Why a dippy-ass cover band like LTAG got the opportunity to insult us is beyond me. One of those good-time bands where the guys in the band all do something else and the shit they play is just a hobby to them. "We just wanna have fun". Yea right. Take your limp drivel and fuck over some frat, where they can't tell the difference. Puppets didn't fare much better. Good look, but that didn't take them very far. Rather lame pedestrian rock 'n' rollabilly that got pretty monotonous after only a couple of numbers. Had some nauseating cunts posing with them too, that didn't do my stomach much good, either.--DS

T and G teen pinup # 5

FLIPPER photo by George Wescott

There they are: sartorially resplendent in front of some emporium we find Maumee's finest—Barry, Corey, and Todd—hangin' loose... Hey, Corey, check your fly! This was about the time I caught wind of a big show going down in DC: Youth Brigade/Minor Threat/Circle Jerks, and as much as I'd heard about the place, I needed to be there for that! Problem though: 6-11-81 was the last day of school, a big deal if you are a teacher. Sooooo...I asked for a meeting with the superintendent and crafted a monstrous fabrication about needing to be the best man in a wedding in Washington... He wasn't going to let me go, but alas, he eventually caved... Me and the Necros loaded into my Mazda and we were eastbound, soon beginning my love affair with the nation's capital. Meeting all the DC honchos and seeing the show was stellar, even though Ian blew out his pipes at sound check. Then me, Henry Rollins—Garfield at that time—and the boys tooled up to Club 57 in NYC for the Necros/Stimulators/Circle Jerks the next day. What a whirlwind weekend... The seeds were planted, and I'd seen the East Coast. It was a-callin' me, and my days in the mitten known as Michigan were numbered.

TOUCH AND GO

CART AENI S

MASTER CARD

NO VALUES

NO. 14

75¢

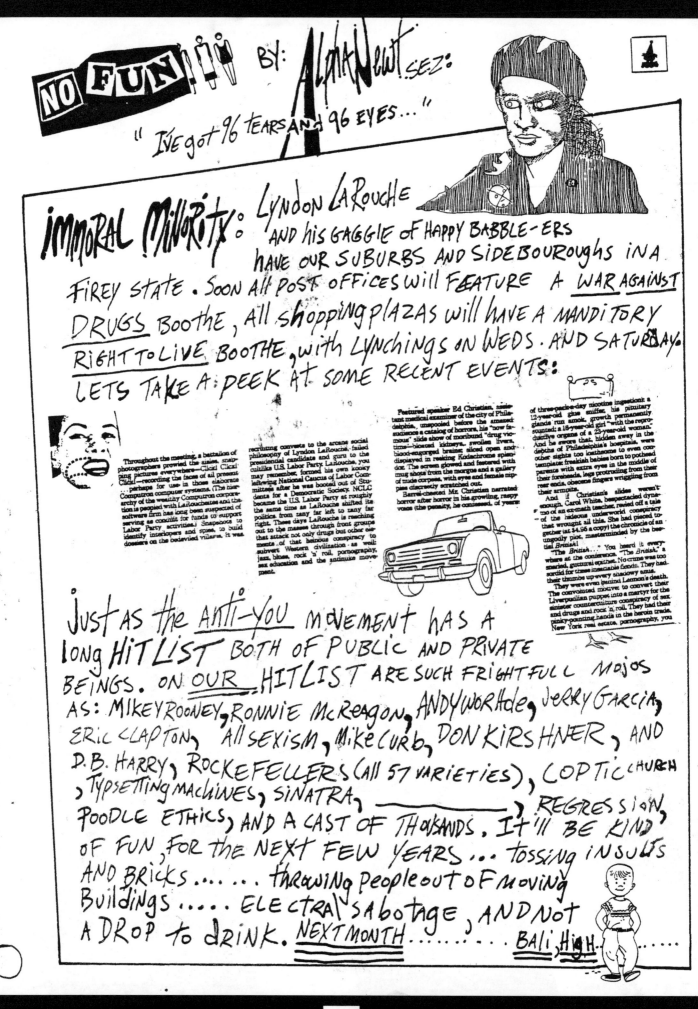

NO FUN! BY: AlphaNewt SEZ:

"I'VE got 96 TEARS AND 96 EYES..."

IMMORAL MINORITY: Lyndon LaRouche AND his GAGGLE OF HAPPY BABBLE-ERS HAVE OUR SUBURBS AND SIDE BOUROUGHS IN A FIREY STATE. SOON ALL POST OFFICES WILL FEATURE A WAR AGAINST DRUGS BOOTHE, ALL shopping PLAZAS WILL HAVE A MANDITORY RIGHT TO LIVE BOOTHE, WITH LYNCHINGS ON WEDS. AND SATURDAY. LETS TAKE A PEEK AT SOME RECENT EVENTS:

Throughout the meeting, a battalion of photographers prowled the aisles, snapping pictures everywhere—Click! Click! Click!—recording the faces of all present ... perhaps for use in those elaborate Computron computer systems. (The hierarchy of the wealthy Computron corporation is peopled with LaRouchettes and the software firm has long been suspected of serving as conduit for funds to support Labor Party activities.) Snapshots to identify interlopers and spies, to build dossiers on the bedeviled villains, it was

recruiting converts to the arcane social philosophy of Lyndon LaRouche, failed presidential candidate and guru to the cultlike U.S. Labor Party. LaRouche, you may remember, formed his own kooky leftwing National Caucus of Labor Committees after he was booted out of Students for a Democratic Society. NCLC became the U.S. Labor Party at roughly the same time as LaRouche shifted its politics from zany far left to zany far right. These days LaRouche is reaching out to the masses through front groups that attack not only drugs but other elements of that heinous conspiracy to subvert Western civilization - as well: jazz, blues, rock 'n' roll, pornography, sex education and the antinuke movement.

Featured speaker Ed Christian, assistant medical examiner of the city of Philadelphia, unspooled before the amazed audience a catalog of horrors, his "now famous" slide show of moribund "drug victims"—blotced kidneys, swollen livers, blood-engorged brains; sliced open and displayed in reeking Kodachrome splendor. The screen glowed and festered with mug shots from the morgue and a gallery of nude corpses, with eyes and female nipples discreetly scratched out.

Barrel-chested Mr. Christian narrated horror after horror in his growling, raspy voice (the penalty, he confessed, of years

of three-packs-a-day nicotine ingestion: a 12-year-old glue sniffer, his pituitary glands run amok, growth permanently stunted; a 16-year-old girl "with the reproductive organs of a 23-year-old woman." And be aware that, hidden away in the depths of Philadelphia's hospitals, were other sights too loathsome to even contemplate: freakish babies born to pothead parents with extra eyes in the middle of their foreheads, legs protruding from their rear ends, obscene fingers wriggling from their armpits.

And if Christian's slides weren't enough, Carol White, bespectacled dynamo of an ex-math teacher, reeled off a tale of the hideous underworld conspiracy that wrought all this. She had pieced together (at $4.96 a copy) the chronicle of an ungodly plot, masterminded by the bestial British.

"The British..." You heard it everywhere at the conference. "The British," a snarled, guttural epithet. No crime was too sordid for these insatiable fiends. They had their thumbs up every shadowy anus. They were even behind Lennon's death. The convoluted motive: to convert their Liverpudlian puppet into a martyr for the sinister counterculture conspiracy of sex and drugs and rock 'n' roll. They had their grimy-pointing hands in the heroin trade, New York real estate, pornography, you

Just AS the ANTI-YOU MOVEMENT HAS A long HITLIST BOTH OF PUBLIC AND PRIVATE BEINGS. ON OUR HITLIST ARE SUCH FRIGHTFULL MOJOS AS: MIKEY ROONEY, RONNIE McREAGON, ANDY WORHdlE, JERRY GARCIA, ERIC CLAPTON, ALL SEXISM, MIKE CURB, DON KIRSHNER, AND D.B. HARRY, ROCKEFELLERS (All 57 VARIETIES), COPTIC CHURCH, TYPSETTING MACHINES, SINATRA, _____, REGRESSION, POODLE ETHICS, AND A CAST OF THOUSANDS. IT'll BE KIND OF FUN, FOR THE NEXT FEW YEARS... TOSSING INSULTS AND BRICKS........ THROWING PEOPLE OUT OF MOVING BUILDINGS..... ELECTRAL SABOTAGE, AND NOT A DROP TO DRINK. NEXT MONTH........, BALI HIGH.........

#14

DRUGS SUCK

What is this?
a) A HORNETS NEST?
b) A Hotdog w/ NO cereal fillers?..
c) A Lepers Arm?..
d) AN Elephants trunk?.

Correct answer gets free subscription...

FAMOUS QUOTES:
"Basically people who ride motorcycles can just blow me!" R.Ramsey
"I hate that girl cuz she wont suck me." B.Hyland
"My dick is microscopic!" B.Henssler
"MINE's like a trunk!" T.SWALLA

T&G QUIZ

B.H.

PAGANS LP OUT IN OCT.

MAIL IS A WAY OF COMMUNICATING WITH, AND IMPROVING SOMETHING OR SOMEBODY ELSE SO THERE"S REALLY NO POINT IN RE-PRINTING IT... *

You White Bitches can suck the venimous jism out of my throbbing blood engorged ebony Anaconda!

Bookies July 14!! Black Flag with Necros

CONSTANT CAUSE
679 ARBOR LANE
WARMINSTER PA 18974
constant cause is a distributor

CONSTANT CAUSE

50¢ for 2 bi-monthly catalogues
$1.00 intercontinental

SHANE Williams (R&R Bank Robber) got busted by the FBI for robbing banks so he no longer writes for us. I got hassled by the FBI & got death threats; had my phone tapped etc. Do yourself a favor- dont write to convicts... It's no fun having someone telling you they're going to castrate you & kill you! TV

HANGING FROM The Rope of Wrath Skewered with the sword of scornfulness DEATH TO ART FAGS

WHO IS THIS?
A)XAVIER COUGAT?
B)MARLIN PERKINS?
C)AL JACOBS-GUITARIST IN SKUDDUR?
D)BRIAN POLLACK-NECROS GUITARIST BECAUSE HE DIDN'T GET ON THE COVER WITH THE OTHER GUYS SO HERE's HIS PHOTO(Whoops I gave It away)

Contents:
DC Coverage
Cool Comics
Record Reviews
Pomp + Perversion
Cool Pix

* except this letter from Texas from the FIX's manager BONHAM

T&G,
Houston and Austin were great,great crowds.STAINS are great.DICKS are OK.Everyones real nice.Fort Worth was a problem.The FALL play-ed Dallas 2 nights in a row and no crowds came out.Jeff burned down a house in Dallas.Mike has sunsickness in the heat.Craig dyed his hair to match his skin (Blue?) disco dazzle.Everyone was real cool so far.Fort Worth is a bunch of rednecks(except the punks were cool)Saw a mohawk in Houston.Steve has three kinds of V.D.Gary is suffering from maltrunition.We're gonna record July 23rd and 24th Still having a hard time getting gigs in L.A. but have 3 days in Vancouver...BLACK FLAGS' place(SST) is closed down 2 days ago.The police were after it along time-finally got them for no business licensw.We're gonna record with Spot(B.Flags' sound man) at Musiclab.7 track EP w/SIGNAL,RAT PATROL,OFF TO WAR, COS THE ELITE,TRUTH,EVICTION,BLOODSTAINS DEEPEN(a new one folks) The crowds were great-throwing things and trying to grab Steve off stage.Real hot down here...Leather jackets are not prevalent-Gas is cheap ,we still have no air-conditioning.The van is cramp-ed as hell.I may come thru in September after EP is out.ZEROS in Fort Worth sux!should've played Dallas-the HOT CLUB.Steve likes the beer here(it sux)Tell our friends in Lansing to fuck off and to go die.If BOOKIES wants us it'll cost them 400 bucks.Same with Chicago. BYE yall Bonham
P.S.Stains single is great!!

287

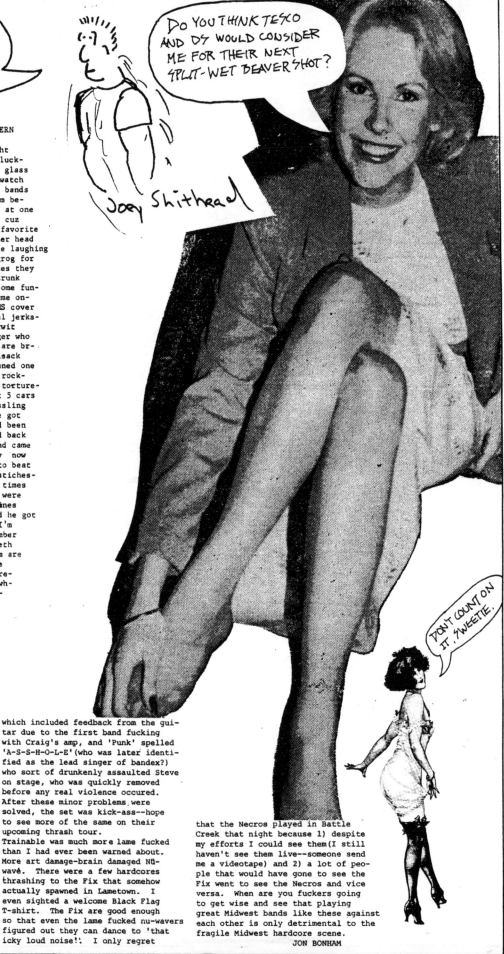

Here's T&G covering some of that tasty wave material. YEOWW!!!

Do you think Texco and DY would consider me for their next split-wet beaver shot?

Joey Shithead

DON'T COUNT ON IT SWEETIE.

THE ENEMYS/NECROS/D.O.A.   CORONATION TAVERN WINDSOR

If this dive is any indication of what night life in Windsor is like then one would be lucky to last a week. Lots of fights and broken glass nothing too serious-just a good place too watch your tongue which I usually don't-when the bands were doing sound checks the old bat(and I'm being nice) who ran the place got pissed off at one of the locals who called the fire marshall cuz she didn't like what was happening to her favorite club-and this old bag started wailing on her head with a frying pan and I thought I would die laughing anyway I bought 3 sixes of that Canadian grog for real cheap(why drink American piss...besides they don't sell Colt 45 up there)a good heavy drunk so I could act like a real jerk and have some fun-outside as it were when this first band came on-they played MISFITS covers and even a GERMS cover but they were really lame-too slow and real jerks-I wondered why this guy was being such a twit all nite and it turned out he was the singer who actually had the balls to say"The MISFITS are broken up so now you have us" gimme a barf sack Cleotis...fortunately the ENEMYS have gleaned one thing from their limited exposure to punk rock-a short set-so they spared us any further torture-While I was outside waiting them out about 5 cars o f royal police rolled up and started hassling me cuz some moron was hassling Keith so he got him good and the guy went and wimered he'd been assaulted-but they let me go and I cruised back into this hole where it was "safe"Next band came on...I'd seen em before-so much I probably now their set by heart...Me and Brian wanted to beat heads dancing but we would've split our stiches-pure torture just watching-D.O.A. was 100 times wilder,louder,and more exciting than they were when they were here-during one of their tunes Buscuits snare dropped through a stand and he got real hostile and stormed off stage like-"I'm leaving my drum head broke boo hoo" I remember when I was god Chuck and that's why my teeth are all broken you jerk...the resy of them are cool though and they didn't play that lame Zeppelin cover...After a great set they dredged up the energy for a couple encores which made the whole place go wild all over-great band...fun night...thanx Zonk and Buckner....

Grand Rabids Gig 6/20/81 The Fix, Trainable, and some unidentified band at St. Isador Casino--benefit for some radio station

Grand Rabids(Rapids) Mich. is a lame town with equally lame residents. Notables like Gerry Ford are created here. This is not a place for good music, culture or anything else save hot dogs(if you accidentally end up in this town, go to Yesterdogs in downtown G.R., their hot dogs are great). The hall was nice, the beer was cheap and very plentiful, the people who put on the gig very hospitable. Too bad the old fogeys who own the hall won't let them have it anymore. The first band(they were unnamed as far as I know) was a lame nū-wavé band. Riffs reminded me a little of the Urinals-except the music was quite lame. Bass player in goofy fisherman's hat, wide tie, rest of the band not much better. Very vaudevillian. The Nū-wavers danced of course, what else did they have to do?
After that abortion, The Fix blew into their set with characteristic thrash killer-energy, wall of sound hardcore punk music. The first half of the set was plagued with problems

which included feedback from the guitar due to the first band fucking with Craig's amp, and 'Punk' spelled 'A-S-S-H-O-L-E'(who was later identified as the lead singer of bandex?) who sort of drunkenly assaulted Steve on stage, who was quickly removed before any real violence occured. After these minor problems were solved, the set was kick-ass--hope to see more of the same on their upcoming thrash tour.
Trainable was much more lame fucked than I had ever been warned about. More art damage-brain damaged Nū-wavé. There were a few hardcores thrashing to the Fix that somehow actually spawned in Lametown. I even sighted a welcome Black Flag T-shirt. The Fix are good enough so that even the lame fucked nu-wavers figured out they can dance to 'that icky loud noise'. I only regret

that the Necros played in Battle Creek that night because 1) despite my efforts I could see them(I still haven't see them live--someone send me a videotape) and 2) a lot of people that would have gone to see the Fix went to see the Necros and vice versa. When are you fuckers going to get wise and see that playing great Midwest bands like these against each other is only detrimental to the fragile Midwest hardcore scene.
JON BONHAM

BLACK FLAG / BAD BRAINS / U.X.A

By Barry

Pic Corey Rusk

BLACK FLAG/BAD BRAINS/U.X.A. Club 57 N.Y. 6/28/81
First off New York is such a joke-it is a place where it's 90 degrees out and you and your friends are sweating in T-shirts and there'll be Sid clones with leather jackets zipped up,hanging out with TOUGH written all over their faces and no muscles when it comes to backing up their poses.They all try to act cool when the Wash.D.C. kids come up to tear their town to shreds.They pretend not to be scared but they are-in fact the coolest people in N.Y. are probably the girls-But beyond the wimpy N.Y. geeks,I mean they don't really get in the way and if they do you just boot or pushem' and they they get the message...All that matters is the D.C. contigent makes the hardcore shows in this place...without them it would be ultra lame..D.C. rools...We got up to catch BLACK FLAG's soundcheck and to do the guest list hustling (we're scum but we're nice scum)Real hot s.check...must've done half their set.. With free admission assured it's later on at Club 57We cruise off with the rest of the NECROS,Brian Highland(XY FLYER Ed) and Henry of SOA, to eat and be the dicks we are...

..Everyones hangin' out outside the club before U.X.A. comes on and noone wants to go in yet-anyone with ears knows they felch shit.But I go in and they start playing something that resembles "Tragedies"-they're horrible,even worse than on record-De Detroit sounds like she's just been branded with a soldering iron or something-their bassist is a funk band reject(looga me I be slappin dis here bass for U.X.A.)Complete with bell-bottoms and a silk short and bass about 3 inches from his neck.I don't know which song the drummer was playing but it wasn't the same as the rest of the band...In between songs De rifles off some stupid lines about how drugs are bad-which sounds like their being read off of a script-what she should've said was "Yeah I havent shot up in nearly 2 days-wow I'm clean"The drummer sez "Fuck you" to her-obviously not in agreement with her views-and you can tell by his drumming that drugs are still real cool with him.Todd and I leave to go back outside and todd sez "I can drum better than him after I've had 20 beers"and I think to myself "A double amputee could drum better than this after 20 beers"

On to the BAD BRAINS.The editor of the infamous xYFLYER has seen all of the biggies and he flatly stated that this was the best band he's ever seen,Imagine 4 rastas playing music as fast as early MIDDLE CLASS but with 10 times more energy and intensity...Dreadlocks flying all over theplace H.R.(singer) skanking as hard and fast as anyone in the audience.Highlights include Henry getting up on stage to do 12 xU" with H.R. and at the end of the set H.R. did a back flip off the drum riser...Another thing I must Mention BAD BRAINS would do about 4or5 hardcore tunes and then go into a reggae tune-I hate reggae but theB.B. do it alright,I've yet to see Black Flag slagged off,No wait Davey Winkeldick did but whadda you expect from a hippie fucksack acid casualty weenbag,I mean he's even got a beard! The rule is to dance or be danced on,plenty of stage dives and not just from the D.C kids...some of the Phil. people (who if I might add are more than sl-ightly D.C. influenced but that's cool are doing it', and maybe even a few New Yorkers..abberrations do exist you kno-w...it's great to see people singing along on the chorus of "Rise Above"(my fave) even though it's un-released -they did a new song called "Amerrican Disorder" that had some sort ofBlack Sabbathish intro and was totally hot...then B.F. played a 6:30 AM set at a club called A7,Dez played guitar-N.Y. Greg sang,Henry sang Clocked in"-even Mugger sang...It was a fun time something that's pretty rare-the whole thing was just a party really, the club was really small...Anyway that's another story...Anyway

Barry Henneman

FUCKIN D.C.!!!

I'd heard alot about the scene in D.C. but I needed some first hand action for the iron clad proof so when Barry and the boys got the gig with the CIRCLE JERKS we figured whathefuck let's hit the nations' capitol and check it out...(the C.J's gig was in N.Y.)

....6 cokes and 12 hours later we roll into the big town-we cruise lost for a bit till' Brian sez theres a bald kid over there that must be Ian(MacKaye of MINOR THREAT)He does a more than adequate job of giving us the hot poop on what's coming down intown band wise and gigs and such which turns out to be lots of <u>good</u> bands and no place to play cept for the '9:30 club which is run by a lame cunt who bans whatever bands she pleases...but no way am I headed for the ol' negative jag in these pages cuz the crowd and scene fuckin' rools...mentors BAD BRAINS AND the now legendary TEEN IDLES have laid the foundation for a whole bunch of great bands like S.O.A.,YOUTH BRIGADE,MINOR THREAT,G.I.s, and NOTHING SACRED-oh ya let's not forget THE UNTOUCHABLES WHO were there in the begining also and who did what some say was the quintessential D.C. anthem "I Hate You" certain members of these bands were in earlier aggregations but more on that later... .....

Gig Review...6-11-81   MINOR THREAT/CIRCLE JERKS
9:30 CLUB

This place is situated right downtown in rat haven but actually it's laid nicely...bathrooms in the catacombs of the (huh?) cellar,free water-hey whered all them bald kids come from?,jeez there gonna beat my face into a meatloaf CLEOTIS... dun worry Leroy jus don make no eye contact das what dey say...(dat whole family be grubbin' on ribs...)

All I can say is Minor Threat is fucking hot!!! they don't get to practice as often as they would like but you'd never know it from listening to their set...tight and violent...the vocalist manages to brand the sound with an incredibly distinctive(on key..) sound...lump HARPER,MENSI,and PURsey into one and you still ain't got ¼ of this guys enrgy level...they played 2 sets...theCIRCLE JERKS HAD SOME TECHNICAL difficulties but still managed to play a couple inspired sets themselves..Keith was real pissed off at the guitarist who kept breaking strings..he looked real snappy with his camouflage shorts and white tourist hat..the second set was alot better...they did a couple new songs which i think were called "Once Over W ith A RUBBER Hose" AND "L etter Bomb"...THERE was so many people diving off the stage that chords kept getting yanked out and sometimes the bodies piled up higher than the bands heads...after 48 hours with no sleep I lasted hardly at all on that floor but I tried.. lotsa big bruisers there is in D.C....

-after the bands are done everyone goes
downstairs and the wimps that are left over
dance to wimpy stuff like stray Cats...and lo
and behold a case of ICE COLD BEER so I chugs
3 of them when no ones looking(it aint cool to
drink beer in this town or somethin') BUT I
goota have it being the ol' suds sluggin fart. I
am...someones trying to interview Keith and Hetson but K. wont be serious not even for a second
so the guitarist gives her the L.A. lowdown..some-
body had some copies of FLIPSIDE(you know the mag from
where is it? Whittier??)so people were checking that
out and we went over to 7-11 for some DungBags(you
know those microwave burritos)M ore fun than I've
had in years this nite was....

in' mouths hangin open...what a bunch of
slime...There's no love lost between theCJ's
and Black Flag-when the latter was in town they
had it bad about the Jerks and vers viser...aint
life in L.a. a bed of roses or what?When the old
media spotlight hits a relatively mediocre band
(that fucking wears makeup) like T.S.O.L. and makes
them bigger than life then its time to get our collective heads outa our arses and notice other
areas of the country...the roots movement currently
happening in Reagan's backyard is case in point...
any one of the DC bands could blow THE Cheifs or
T.S.O.L. into the pacific... ...Don't get me wrong
L.A. still has a great scene...but shit it seems like
all the backbiting and shit if unchecked'll turn
it all into a pointless mess...I hope thatnever happens....

AND ANOTHER GIG REVIEW....NECROS/STIMULATORS/CIRCLE
JERKS   CLUB57   NEW YORK
5 hours and 8 bucks in tolls later we arrive in
the big apple...the fuckin village gives me the
creeps..the whole godamn city sux...john Travolta
types are everwhere and these big bruisers are coming up to the car to sell us shit...keith is going
crazy at the sound check running around sluggin
Buds ...the Stimulators did their soundcheck...real
absolute shit!...Mr. Morris said it best..."Everything
I've heard about this band just blew up in my face"
they had some black guy with a wide brimmed hat and
spats honkin the sax on one of there tunes...their
drummer is cool...he looks just like a younger version of Mugger...but the hag on guitar looks like
she fucks trombone slides ....what a nasty gash-not
to mention the other faggos on guitar bass i mean...
So on comes NECROS to the wimpy N.Y.crowd...about
20 people had driven up from Wash. most of which
got in on the guest list...Barry imediately alienated the crowd with D.C. ROOLS chants which the contigent quickly turned into a "come on you faggots are
you goona take this shit from us",yes the crowd did
nothing being the spineless fucks New York people
are...oh sure a few people in the darkness dared
open their mouths....back where it was safe...New
York fuckin' sucks grey shit!!!Everyone pogoed for
the Stimulators but they slammed for the NECROS
I mean NY pogoed cuz their so out of touch...the
sound was lousy for the Ohio boys...Corey blew his
amp,the monitors werent turned on the list was endless...good job CLUB 57!!!I said it all with my ass-
(mooned the crowd)CircLE JERKS were much better
than they were in Wash. cept they only played
about a half an hour and they got a sitload of money....they were-great   ...Charlie of THE PLUGZ
did a great job of filling in for Lucky who broke
his hand fighting some guy who stole his girlfriend's car...considering this guy only practiced
6 hours he drummed great...You would have thought
that NY people had seen it all right? Well then why
did they stare at all the D.C. kids with their fuck-

RUNDOWN OF WASHINGTON BANDS....
S.O.A.-HAS A TEN SONG EP out on Dischord erecords
thatmust be heard to be believed...Every cut gives
off the energy of most bands' entire catalogue(Skip
Groff-of yesterday & Today Records) really Knows how
to produce this shit-leaving it at it's rawest...
we had the good fortune to see them practice while
we were in town...vocalist Henry Garfield Is quite
simply a raging madman (on vocals and not indirectly
in real day to day life)HE CAN BE HEARDeven without
a mike-as the guitarist MIKE flails away with tight
and flawless riffs...Wendel the basso Profundo slides
up and down the old frets without a glance to his bashing compatriots...they are currently breaking in a new
drummer Iver Hansen,who seems to be working out quite
well...A couple people took me aside during the course...
of the weekend and told me how fuckin crazed and energetic
Henry was on stage...veins popping in his shaved head-
razor bladed X's on his arms and a black and blue body
will atest to the fact that his music is the only passion-
his motto?"FUCK DRUGS...LET"S FIGHT...

SEEING RED (Nelson/MacKaye)
You see me and
You laugh out loud
You taunt me from safe
Inside your crowd
My looks they
Must threaten you
To make you act
The way you do
Red
I'm seeing red.

You see me and
You think I'm a jerk
First impression
Without a word
You can't believe
Your eyes at first
Now you know
You've seen the worst
Red
I'm seeing red.

S.O.A

GIRL PROBLEMS GARFIELD, HAMPTON,
CALL HER ON THE PHONE
OH SHIT, SHE ISNT HOME
AND YOU NEVER KNOW
THAT SHE AINT WITH SOMEONE ELSE
GOTTA SAY THE RIGHT THING
SHE MIGHT THINK YOUR A FOOL
GOTTA LIE THROUGH YOUR TEETH
TO MAKE HER THINK YOUR COOL

I DON'T NEED GIRL PROBLEMS
IVE GOT TROUBLES AS IT IS
I DON'T NEED TO WASTE MY TIME
I DONT NEED MORE SHIT...
YOU LOWER YOUR FUCKIN PRIDE
BECAUSE YOU THINK SHE'S WHAT YOU
SO YOU DONT MIND THE PAIN
OR THE WAY YOU ALWAYS FEEL

ITS JUST A GAME
SHES GOT YOU ON A LINE
THROW YOUR FEELINGS TO THE WIND
SHES PLAYIN WITH YOUR MIND
- CHORUS-

GUILTY OF BEING WHITE (MacKaye)

I'm sorry
For something I didn't do
Lynched somebody
But I don't know who
You blame me
For slavery
But it was a hundred years
before I was born

I'm guilty of being white

Repeat verse and chorus

I'm a convict...
Guilty
Of a racist crime.
Guilty
And I've already served...
Guilty
Eighteen years of my time...

Repeat verse and chorus

MINOR THREAT

LOST IN SPACE (GARFIELD).
UP IN SMOKE
I LAUGH IN YOUR FACE
FUCKED ON DRUGS
LOST IN SPACE

SEE YOUR FRIENDS
THEY LAUGH AT YOU
BUT DON'T GET MAD
BECAUSE THEY'RE DRUGGED TOO
SPEND YOUR TIME
ON THE FLOOR
GO THROW UP
COME BACK FOR MORE

EAT THOSE PILLS, TAKE THOSE THRILL
WHO'S GONNA WIND UP DEAD- YOU
SNORT THAT COKE, WHAT A JOKE
WHO'S GONNA WIND UP DEAD-YOU
S.O.A.

HAMPTON
S.O.A.

G.I.'s

MINOR THREAT-A'nother top drawer band that can ½ way be
said to have risen out of the ashes of TEEN IDLES-Ian
played bass with said combo while Jeff pounds the skins-
the other 2 are gonna be pissed if they see this cuz I
forgot their names but no matter-together they are incredibly tight live-as the vocalist rampages around the
stage trying to keep the unruly mob from tangling his
mike...they have an ep with 8 songs coming out real soon-
I got a test pressing and it proves once again where real
things are starting to happen...
YOUTH BRIGADE-Though they haven't played out as yet they
have a demo tape that defys one of my lame descriptive
analysis-Nathan (TEEN IDLES) does the vocal work here
and (this probably aint spelled right)Berto plays his
bass like it's his unfaithful girlfriend-you know like
he's mad as shit at it(ok so it's a lame analogy)
Presumabely they will be the next record on the Dischords
label...I sure as fuck hope so...
GI's-With songs like "brand New cataracts" "Insomniac"

"Rock and Roll bullshit" this band has a
sound hard to define from the tape I heard..
Raw and bassy...gimme more...
Nothing Sacred-??????Still forming-people had
it on their jackets and shit...
THE SCENE IN D.C. IS ALIVE AND EXCITING AS SHIT.
all they need is a youth club of some sort-
someplace old,cheap,and indestructible-and
I don't think this is impossible by any means-
especially in a big old metropolis like that-
And why the fuck isn't there a fanzine covering whats going on?a Capitol Crisis covers lame
shit like Secret Affair and the fucking Stra-
nglers-get your shitttogether!!!Support your
own scene for christsake not lame Brit faggots
playing derivitive drek from the 60's ..nuff
said...I'll shut up...can't wait to go back.
                                  X Tesco said That

?I could be + I
Am Wrong!!

Pawdick 81'

girl in DC ?

Credit for these ↑ pictures goes to some

SOA

Simon ↑
(He had
to
quit)

Mike ↑
(bitchin'
ax
MAN)

(Where's
fuckin
Wendel?)

HENRY ↑
(If you like your
face the way it
Is...dont fuck
with him !!)

292

HENRY of S.O.A.

PHANTOM LIMB--"Admission of Guilt"
free flexi from The Offense #8

Phew! Boy, did The Offense ever snap the log with this beaut. I don't know who he's trying to kid, but this kind of post-acid euro-rock drek went out when bands like Jane, Eloy, and Guru Guru became so moribund that to continue would surely have resulted in an inevitble epidemic of ear slaughter. Obviously rehashing '77 ain't good enough for The Offense, instead he forages in the seamy nightlife of Columbus and comes up with a band whose very roots are deeply inbedded in this nebulous twilight period of obscurely esoteric heavy metal circa 1974. They show no concern for continuity by treating us to an amusing string of dreary clichés that would have even the most autistic rubberhead guffawing on the floor. Their triteness is rendered so poorly that they go on for five minutes hoping you'll forget some of which you've heard. A length that will make even one entire listen next to impossible. I'm relieved somewhat by reading that The Offense is only fairly proud of this, and is reserving full-blown adulation for bands that really deserve it. Tim, you had better luck with the Cowboys.--DS

SPORT OF KINGS--"Every Night"/"The Same Breath" Sport of Kings Records

Stacks up with anything from Factory and 4AD, which probably suits these guys just fine. Just the kind of band for the ersatz snobbery of Chicago to cuddle up to. Heaven forbid if a band like this ever found its way on our label(knock on wood). Recorded remarkably well sporting a Bauhausian bleakness in the vocals. Definitely one of the top domestic releases of the year, honest.--DS

THE MOB--"Witch Hunt"/"Shuffling Souls" All The Madmen Records

John, of YOU mag, deserves some credit for pointing me toward this one. Apparently a big rage in DC The Mob are uniquely abrasive with a political twist. Not nearly as obvious as either Crass or Discharge, but musically superior. Their music has drive, but they manage to avoid the pitfalls of monotonous repetition. Not everyone can do it. File next to Bad Actors.--DS

VICE SQUAD--"Resurrection EP"
Riot City Records

What can I say? This band sounds like a punked-out Siouxsie. Similarities are what some might call 'uncanny'. Band behind this clone is dully unoriginal. Put them somewhere between the Exploited and Anti Pasti. Barely listenable at best. --DS

VIOLENT APATHY   demo tape

Roughy honed and showing an obvious distain for professionalism, these guys get my vote as the funnest band in Michigan.   They combine beach, punk, and a charming lack of finesse to generate their distinctive brand raw music.   Kenny's vocals are nothing short of self inflicted torture.   They blow away The Plugz with their grovelling interpretation of "La Bamba".   Some have likened them to the Urinals(100 Flowers), yes, they do play fast, but their music works at any tempo, which is why I think they're a great band. You gotta go see these guys, certainly before all this bullshit I've written goes to their heads.--DS

THE MOB--"Crying Again"/forgot the flipside All The Madmen Records

An earlier Mob single and this one simply does not measure up to the "Witch Hunt" disc. Less pointed and direct, your mind begins to wander while you're listening to the thing, killing time til you take it off and put something else on. Just for Mob fanatics.--DS

THE OUTCASTS--"Magnum Force"/"Gang-land Warfare" GBH Records

A bright spot among an otherwise pathetic two months for Britain. They don't do the 'women are scum and dirt' thing anymore, and they don't sound the same either. Some guy named Rastus engineered this disc with a decidedly rastafarian bent.   Ten times better than the shit Stiff Little Fingers does. The Outcasts and Discharge are now the only two punk bands worth a poop over there on the island, so throw away your Subs records and your Upstarts records cuz they just blow the ol beef bayonet. Get with it, OK.--DS

BAD ACTORS--"Strange Love"/"Energy Society" Sophisticated Noise

Number one last month and fuckinga it should be number one again this month.   This is one of those once in a lifetime gems you stumble across. Don't know shit about the band or nothing, but by god you buy the sucker, and from that day forward, you are continuously praising the heavens for that sudden burst of fortuitous intuition. Simple beyond belief, bass and guitar play pretty much the same thing over and over with a haunting resonance that you have to marvel at. Shit, don't take my word for it, buy it and see for yourself.--DS

SINGLES BY TV

GET SMART -"NUMBERS AND COLORS"/"ANKLE DEEP IN MUD" FRESH FLEXI
Rudimentary in style-casual and original in approach-I like this band simply because they seem to act independantly-in an area of the country where I'm sure they find the going rough...judgeing the first 2 FRESH releases by the same criterion GET SMART succeeds where ABUSE failed miserably-the point being one should nevershoot for a known quantity-by taking a very simple idea and injecting some obliviously novel hooks-this band has me doing the old rigadoon on a soapbox.....

PIG BAG-"PAPAS GOT A BRAND NEW PIG BAG"/ THE BACKSIDE" ROUGH TRADE Y
I'D Read a live review of this band but wasn't prepared for anything this stupendous.Something as primal as this is libel to turn alot of heads-and we'll lay all tags aside.A band in it's formative stages can't put something this good on the market without plans for some sort of mass onslought on the musical marketplace...To misappropriate this as part of some sort of embelleshment to the funk-jazz trend won't work either...A curio of magnanimous proportions...

SELF CONTROL-FEAR OF REHEARSALS EP
Dancing Sideways records
MY FAVORITE BAND IN ALL OF JOLLY OLD BRITIAN just put out their second record and they didn't let me down...they've added a girl to the lineup on this one -a song about who's seen who in the nude or some such novel theme...this pair of Bernie and Dermot write the most infallibly nonsensical themes regarding your basic impenetrable basket case egos I've yet to hear.. Both of their EP's are must listening-nothing overt but then we're all capable of a discerning EYE yet aren't we?They deserve to be huge ...

MIDDLE CLASS-"SCAVENGED LUXURY EP" Torture Garden
Their formula used to be "We're gonna be faster and more manic than any band on earth-their first EP was the proof-a classic piece of wax that you still hear at every party,or break between bands at gigs(to the point where I was sick of it because I knew they didn't sound like that now and everyone kept on raving in the present tense"Middle Class Is Great" when I just knew the band would probably shake that sound with their next outing...and they did...and those of you picking your noses saying this sucks I only have two words for you I can't repeat in this family mag-this is one of this years' best...The fact that the band is capable of creating this type of simplistic,and intelligent music insures their survival(although continued allegiance by LA's more brain-damaged contigent is doubtful)Descritions will be inevitably dull so I'll pass and simply recommend this limited edition EP With no exceptions...with apoligies to my girlfriend who was complaining how she hates mags that say someting is great or something sucks but don't say why...

start

START-"NO DIRECTION"/"INVISIBLE MAN" WIN RECORDS
This band wishes they were...sounded like.. and looked like the JAM...complete with Mod sound and hand claps...They are from Mountain View CA. Incredibly Lame...(you don't believe me?Write and I'll give you the Fuckin' thing-I'm serious...)

LES RAVING SOUNDS-EP Terminal Records
Various members of The Cramps,Pere Ubu, Pagans and Impalers appear on this and what their trying to do or sound like is beyond me...Don't bother...

JOHANNA WENT-"SLAVE BEYOND THE GRAVE"/"NO U NO"
With her bizzarre(I hate that word)stage show what fuckin good is a fickin record(I keep hitting the f instead of the g and the r sof(shit)-sorry I don't usually curse all that fuckin much I mean shit this babe is flipped out -she breaks open big balls full of black goo and eats worms and is real twisted and Lori's seen her ask her and you get an X-ray when you buy the record-and why do people always pick their noses in their cars?*&¢%$#@!@#$$%¢¢& the WORLD!

DISORDER-"COMPLETE DISORDER EP"
Burning fuzzrock in the definate mold of A type mentality-they've developed here (or should i say perpetrated the belief that overpowering the public with an insurgence of noise is the only way to further or foster any concept or ideal...Scream monogenesis and back off if that'll make you feel more secure but just don't come crying to me with your bitching punk pathos and ask for relief...

SPIDER KING-"ANIMALS"/"WOULD YOU WANNA DIE FOR ENGLAND Test Pressings Records
This months award for most innovative vocalist. "Animals" is a disparaging account of inhumanity in regard to our fuzzy friends I guess...Articulate and mesmerizing...great use of percussion and synthesizer...undeniably refreshing-not bleak-not unduly blasphemous-they save that for the other side...more straightforward-they ask the question quite simply and they recite obligatorily the chorus..."NO,NO,NO" I think you should buy this...

WIRE-"OUR SWIMMER"/"MIDNIGHT BAHNOFF CAFE" Rough Trade
Someones calling this a posthumous RT release?I guess it's old stuff but I'm going to review it as something new cuz this is a bitchin' tune par excellance from one of the all time greats...after all the DOME dung how did they get this bassman to play such agreat riff?Because you see Lewis and Gilbert must see themselves as the new Tangerine Dream or something-and it really makes me depressed to hear something as good as this and then think about that other hippified ambience...Cool nasal effect on Neuman's voice...A drum line filled with the old mysterioso cracking...Hot damn a new WIRE single (well new to me anyway)Supposedly there is going to be a batch of unreleased stuff coming out in cassette form soon...Can't wait..

ORIGINAL MIRRORS-"DANCING WITH THE REBELS"/ "OH YEAH" MercuryRecords
Great comeback..."Rebels" features Gary Glitter cum OI football chanting-less of the romanticist balladeering like the LP.B side is more of the older sound but is likewise great..(why does my face turn pink when I say I like this band in mixed company/?)

NEPTUNES CAR-"BAKING BREAD"/"LUCKY CHARMS" Koolie Records
By looking at the song titles you wouldn't know this was as good a record as it is...

EMPIRE-"HOT SEAT"/"ALL THESE THINGS" Dinosaur Discs
Derwood will always be a great ax man-he proved that with GENERATION X on the first 2 LP's but here with his own little trio(also featuring Mark Laff)he don't fare sowell...simple and to the point but so what? I'd hate to listen to a whole album of this...

PARTIZANS-"Partizans"/"Goods" A-Noys Records
Feeding us the foibles of our capitalistic
lifestyle via watered down CRASS dogma-but
the musical transportation leaves much to
be desired...OK so I'll give them 6 months
to learn to play...OK so it's the method
and not the means,but a hook here and there
would have at least made this listenable...
The flip is a little better than the front
side which displays a humorously outdated
and grossly overstated guitar riff that has
me a-cringing in my sleep...nothing here to
shake your stick at-steer clear...

OUT ON BLUE SIX-This is a good record.

VINCENT UNITS-This is a bad record.

Choice!! After 4 years I got
it...2 great cuts-more refined (3)
than the first single-Crime is
conceptually perfect whether or
not you like their music...

INTERVIEW w/ Greggy of GREGGY + THE DIPSHITS

"The bossest little kid in the world..." T.V.

I HATE MY Paper Route!!

SUBHOMANS/X Dooleys

Everyone HATED THE Subhumans
except for me + Dave-they were so
great! Wimpy is one of the best
singers around-Jumping about like
he really enjoyed what he was doing..the crowd acted in typical college
town fashion.."This is the warm up
band so I'd better not say I like them"
THE famous mentality that can
suck me...They blew X off the stage
Billy Zoom had this wimpy, impish
grin on his face the whole night
like he was searching the crowd
so he could hide his roto-rooter
in some young snapper's
manhole...I could have stayed
home + listened to their
records. By the way "Wild Gift"
is a laughably lame follow
up to their debut effort...
I snuck in 3 half pints of "Bottled
Violence" which got me in a
bad mood at X for being so
fuckin dull... But the boys from
Vancouver saved the evening!
TV

This interview was done a long time ago by Barry Hennsler
(you know the editor of SMEGMA JOURNAL,ya you know the guy
who sticks his hoodus in car doors(LE CARS are the only ones
small enough)and slams it till it inflates...We promised you
a Greggy interview so here it is...
Barry:Tell me about school
Greg;Ralph Dombek's (school principal)a total fag!(Starts
singing R&R Highschool)
Barry:What's your fave record?
Greg:I like em all,The Necros album(laughter)Bad Company
ha ha.
Barry;You go to Gateway right?
Greg;Yeah,worse school in the world.
Barry:Tell me about it...
Greg;There's nothing to tell.it sucks,it's so boring.
Barry;When I went there I was suspended for two days
for saying "Jesus Christ"Who do you hate?
Greggy;Mark Pauken,Tim Wyckhouse,and hmmm Chris
Watson(huh?ED.)
Barry;Why?
Greg;They're total dicks,they like rock,they're still
livin' in the seventies..I also hate that girl that
called me a fag.
Barry;How old are you?
Greg;Twelve
Barry;When did you turn twelve?
Greg;I didn't yet.But I will on August twelth,so people
can send cards and money.
Barry;What do you think of this album?(Germs)
Greg;It's great.
GREGGYThe Knack,DEVO,Tom petty,Blondie-I don't worry
about em'
Barry:Do you like anything?
Greg;Of course!GIRLS,everything except school and the bands
I hate..
Barry;What did you think of the Smegma Benefit?
Greg; Great,except that guy who wore a jockstrap was
a fag!How much is that stereo worth?
Barry;A thousand dollars.
Greg:Who bought it?
Barry;I won it in a rock trivia quiz that was easy
Barry;What's your favorite T.V. show?
Greg;I dunno,I don't watch T.V.
Barry:What else?
Greg;Nothin'

P. UKING, R. ETCHING + T. ASTELESS.

Vomit Pigs/Violent Apathy/Scabs - - PRT Club June 6 · LANSING

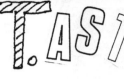

Since the editors of T&G were off jet-setting with the Necros in New York & D.C. spending your subscription money I took it upon myself to document any local action they might be missing while in abstentia. I missed the Scabs but after it got to be 3:30 and they hadn't come on yet I figured so what. The evening started at a little before 1:00 am with the first band being the Vomit Pigs. Their name practically refers to my initial reaction as it was all I could do to restrain my stomach from soiling the floor of Robs' brand new club as I was subjected to a bunch of useless 60's songs with a touch of C&W to further aggravate my ravaged gut. Tunes like"Midnite Hour" by Wilson Pickett or Spanish Castle Magic or "Manic Depression" by Jimi Hendrix made me wonder if they were ever going to play an original song. The drummer should stick to beating his foreskin and the femme rhythm guitarist had no reason to be on stage other than to look cute in her black shiny pants and pretend to play her instrument. The biggest joke beside their music was their blubberbag bassist, who, from all outward appearances seemed to be trying to work the end of his bass between the folds of his distended gut to massage the teenie-weenie that no doubt lay within. But the "Dolt of the Evening" award goes to the guitarist of the Fix for joining these no-accounts onstage for a rendition of "Rock n' Roll Hoochie Koo". A completely worthless band, if you have your hand anywhere other than jammed up your sphincter you'll use it to throw something at this band if you ever have to wait through there set.

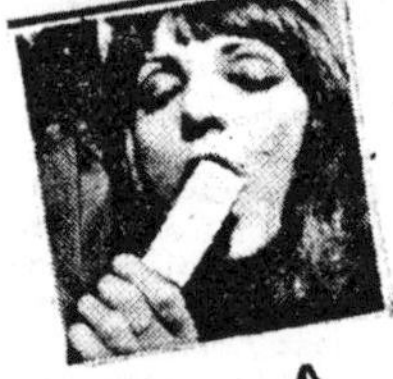

Photo by C.N. Crusher

↑ Vocalist Rural sex...

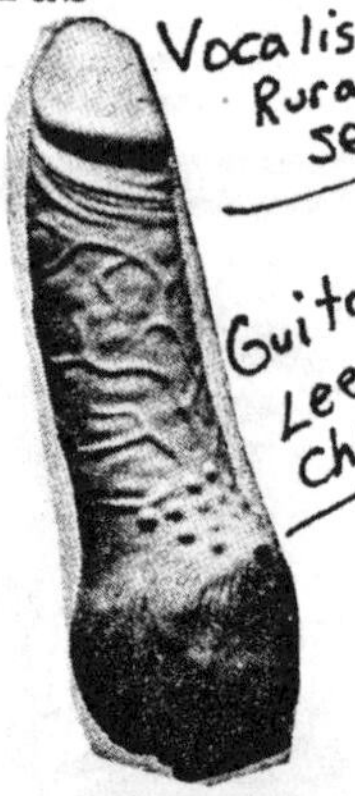

Guitarist Lee Chase

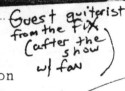

The T&G editors may not be in full agreement with my next comment but since they're probably so busy tangling with heavy meat rolls they won't notice anyway. The gent in question is Rob the manager of the club. This corpulent capitalist barred a couple members of the Fix from entering his establishment. Was it my imagination or did I see him searching the audience looking to plow some young bucks fallow field?

Guest guiterist from the FIX (after the show w/ fan)

Violent Apathy was next and played some noise that made me glad that I waited for Them. The basic setup with a vocalist that puts out. They ran a gamut of some hard fast stuff to surf tunes along with some latino rhythms. See this band, they're worth it. Lastly to of the gurls who were wearing dresses that night you owe my bloated loaf a vigorous reefing.

X Cleotis Nut Crusher

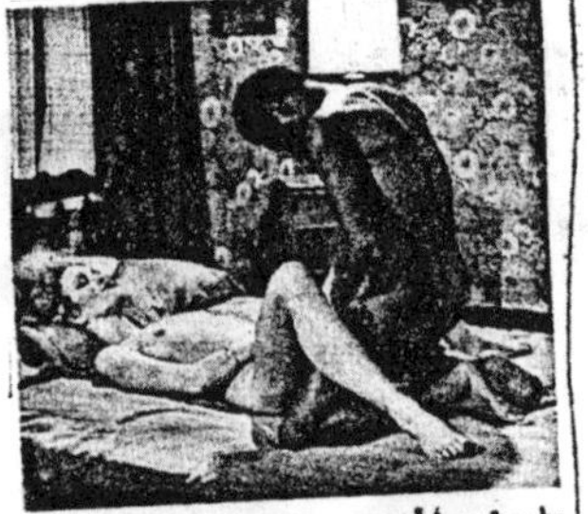

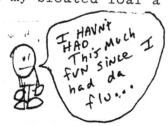

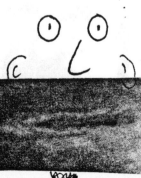

I'll take a bearded clam on my shroyngo any day... TV

Vomit Pigs Set List

GOLDEN SHOWERS

RECTUM 'RECKER:

BUXOM WOMAN

raising mounds of giant cock-horny flesh.

I HAVN't HAD This Much fun since I had da flu...

the
FLESH EATERS

FLESH EATERS--"A Minute To Pray,
A Second To Die" Ruby Records

What I want to say about this band
cannot be so easily put into the
written form. The power coming
from these eight songs is bludg-
eoningly direct and painfully lethal. Chris D.'s vocals seem not
so much his own, but more like a
message from the sordid underworld
of Hades. Through his voice we discover that which we have preferred,
up until now, to ignore. A graphi-
cally twisted batch of love songs
that succeed not in warming our
hearts, but rather, in making our
skin crawl. A perverse look at
life that many of us are likely
never to see, simply because we
don't have the eyes to see it, certainly not in the same way that
Chris D. sees it. The band pro-
pelling the music does so with
sledge hammer accuracy. . . they
can't miss, the sweep is so wide
and the impact is so solid the
emotion that is felt is immediate. A sound that forces our attention to focus inward to examine that which we have failed to
see for so long, if only for an
instant before we slip back comfortably into our routinely safe
existence. No record in a long
time as impressed me so much or
has moved me to such a mindfucking
degree as this one, and in "Divine
Horseman" the Flesh Eaters have
written the single finest statement to come from LA.--DS

RED ROCKERS

NO QUESTIONS, NO ANSWERS a New Orleans compilation Vinyl Solution

I'm listening to the Red Rockers'
cut "Dead Heroes" and there just
ain't much to get excited about.
Granted, a record like this can
play an integral part in the local
scene, giving it much needed recognition and a base to build on.
However, from an outsiders standpoint
I can only congradulate you on the
effort. Musically, well that's another can of worms. Outside of the
Red Rockers, I seriously doubt whether I'd go to the trouble of seeing
any of these bands live. 90% of
this stuff simply is not my cup of
tea. Maybe I'm jaded from our own
musclehead punk of The Necros and
The Fix, but bands like the Models,
RZA, The Fugitives, The Swingin'
Millionaires come off sounding pretty limp. I am intigued by the fact
that New Orleans has a couple Mod
bands(Wayward Youth, in particular)
who have done a more than adequate
job of assimilating the sound of
The Jam(is that a compliment or
what?--ED). Let me just say that
if this is representative of the
New Orleans scene, it seems pretty
timid to me. Now maybe there's other bands that didn't make it on this
record, but I don't have much to go
on 'cept for this here collection.
I suppose I shouldn't talk judging
from the overwhelming scene brewing
here in Lansing. We got plenty of
bands, but they don't deserve to be
recorded, that is, if I had anything
to say about it. OK, so I'm acting
like an asshole, but we here at T&G
have set up standards that we live
by, and I would be going against
the grain if I were to come out an
endorse this record. I'll endorse
the concept, but never the bands.
How about that, an apology for not
liking a record, a T&G first. . .
and last, I hope.--DS

12" By Tesco

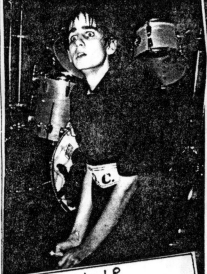

system planning korporation

information
overload
unit

AL GREEN
GETS NEXT TO YOU

IM SPEECHLESS... SIMPLY THE
Best ALBUM EVER Recorded...

DEUTSCH AMERIKANISCHE FREUNDSCHAFT

Adolescents LP
Frontier Records...

This is a good album - No it's
a great album!!! Recorded
relatively raw - Not as wild
as the Olerks LP but very
worthwhile NoNetheless...
Tony is quite simply a great
singer... They do "Rip It UP"
for Posh Boy on this video tape
I saw + threw a dummy out
into the audience so the
crowd could maNgle It...
The only song I don't like
is "Kids of The Black Hole" cuz
it's way too long... Best songs
include "I HATE Children" +
word Attack "/+ Creatures but
overall the whole disc is boss
ONE of the current biggies out
west... Buy it!!!
TV

SYSTEM PIANNING. Korporation LP
Side Effect Records

DefiNately not for the unstable-
formerly Surgical Penis KliNik
this Aussie bunch gives the
other, hidden side of our
existence... Too write this off
as Industrial would be far
too easy... Humanity tries
vainly to avoid, and hide
the images this band readily
exposes... Instrumentally
caustic - lyrically non-exist-
ant... SPK creates + exposes
anxiety - shoves it in our
faces... You'll never want to
listen to this album... but
you'll have to - And if your
timing is bad you'll lose it
once and for all... At one point
there is a pleasant rythym
machine beat - but only for
a brief moment as blasts
of what sounds like a
bandsaw cutting through
human flesh breaks the silence.
Not for everyone...
TV

NEXT issue - Reviews of
MiNutemen AND Sacharine
Trust LPS

GERMS - Live At The Whiskey

Supposedly a limited edition
of 4000 but I don't believe
that shit... They just say that
so people who Never even liked the Germs'll boy it as a
collectable or some such
shit - This was back when
they couldn't play their
instruments too well - if
you like "Sex Boy" + Forming"
you'll like this... I wish
Darby wasn't dead but it was
inevitable...

CRASS - "Penis Envy"

LEt's hate sex ism for a
moment shall we? The
Crass with their all en-
compassing humanitarian
idea is... dedicate a whole
disc to the plight of
women... 8 songs in typical
fashion minus steve Ig-
norant... On EVE LibertiNE
is all right... They've got
their hearts in the
right places... You know by
Now if you'll like this... I do...

Marquis de Sade!! "Dantzig Twist" Pathe - EMI Records

ONE of the few French bands
worth getting excited about...
Not a New album - Kick reviewed
it in Slash - read that review...
They have another LP out since
this one... Structured and
satisfying... I'LL have to hear
outing #2 before I give it
the hearty "rave up"
HA HA

Some people wERE worried that
when they switched to Virgin they'd
be "sold down the creek sounding"
No way... Possibly the most accessible outing from these Krauts -
Definately one of the best imports
of this year... Electronics but
dont even try to lump this with
any of the other Mute releases...
THE originality expressed here
puts other machine music to
SHAME... Real Good...

Cabaret Voltaire - "LIVE AT The Lyceum" Rough Trade

Recorded very Nicely... good new stuff
like "Taxi Music" - Recorded in February...
I've probably lost my credibility in regard
to this band because they've never done
anything I didn't like... Regardless this
is a good quality tape + it's only 6 or 7
bucks...

have a New EP called "6-pack" before that...
they will be recording their debut album

Black Flag LP should be out soon
THE Fix are out west touring where
Got a Demo of the Bad Brains which
L-7 is broken up but No one seems to
Theres a band from DC. also called NECROS.
Meatmen to play at CHuck + Dianas Wedding
"Flipper Died FOR Your FiNS!!... Thanx Henry

too good for words...
fuck...
stink.

Meatmen Set List →

"Packin Brown" "Fuck Her Face"
"OReY of ONE" "1 Down 3 to Go"
"Ebony Shower" "Meatmen Stomp"
"Pellet Pile" "Tooling for ANus"

(Dedicated to The Beatles)

45s

(tie) S.O.A. "No Policy" EP & MINOR THREAT EP

TEEN IDLES EP

"Gangland Warfare" THE OUTCASTS

"IQ 32" THE NECROS

"Fear Of Rehearsals" SELF CONTROL

"Marching Music For Psychic Youth" THROBBING GRISTLE

"I Hate You" THE UNTOUCHABLES

"Insomniac" GIs

"Another Damn Song" BAD BRAINS

"Scavenged Luxury" EP MIDDLE CLASS

"Witch Hunt" THE MOB

"Six And Change" THE PAGANS

NEGATIVE TREND EP

DISORDER EP

"Girl" SUICIDE

TESCO GAVE ME THIS HERE COMB,
AND AIN'T NOBODY GONNA TAKE IT
FROM ME. YOU GOT THAT BUDDY!!

LPs

YOUTH BRIGADE demo tape

"A Minute To Pray, A Second To Die" FLESH EATERS

"Group Sex" CIRCLE JERKS

"Information Overload Unit" S.P.K.

"Why" DISCHARGE

ADOLESCENTS LP

"Dantzig Twist" MARQUIS DE SADE

"Prayers On Fire" THE BIRTHDAY PARTY

"Penis Envy" CRASS

"Live At Leeds" MONTE CAZZAZA tape

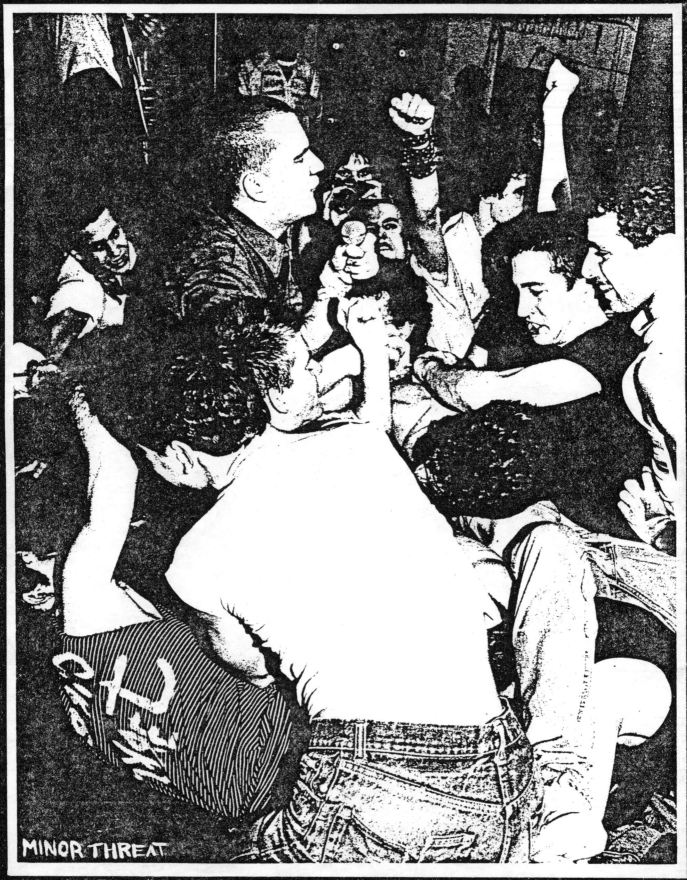

MINOR THREAT

FUCK DRUGS, LET'S FIGHT!!

15

By now I was over the first-blush infatuation with all things DC. I was in Love, L.U.V. Cover shot of Master MacKaye raising his paw in triumph? Exasperation? Who cares? It was an action shot from a Minor Threat show! Henry leaves town for Black Flagdom right around this time. Minor Threat and Youth Brigade interviews and the Midwest/DC hardcore mind meld is in full flower... Lookin' back on all these one-off 45s we reviewed—where did they go? I musta traded 'em for motorbikes or old toys cuz I only kept the keepers. Don't recall where the jism-exploding Farrah came from—one of our many unsolicited submissions by our adoring throng no doubt... Nothin' but class straight outa the ass. By now we were printing 200–300 of these... Still enough to get 'em in the hands of the deserving: a small, cloistered, but unflinchingly loyal buncha scenesters scattered pell-mell around the land.

TOUCH & GO

NUMBER 15

1.00

H.R. OF THE BAD BRAINS

DO YOU HAVE SEX! NO- IT'S GROSS it gets all wet AND HARD.-You GET EXCITED AND DO DUMB things... RATHER THAN LEARN AND GROW-NO YOU REPRESS.

"Hungry Hank" Garfield now in BLACK FLAG no really he'll wring my neck-better call him Henry...you know he used to be in the Washington band S.O.A....will they carry on without him?The saga continues,...

Number 15 folks whadda ya think of our new look?Pretty snappy huh?(Pretty expensive is more like it)I'ts been an interesting summer with my trips out east and all-but coming back here is always tough-but on a more optimistic note there are some new bands springing up that one can actually get excited about like VIOLENT APATHY,and a band I haven't seen yet but hear are great from the editors of SMEGMA-YOUTH PATROL...This issue features more interviews and surprisingly NO ALBUM REVIEWS!!Why you ask?Because there hasn't been much worth buying of late (Except the MASS LP which is great) But you've still got your basic ton-o'-singles bonanza and another MEATMEN comic what more could you ask?About the 1 buck cover price all I can say is it costs us about that or more to print each issue so don't bitch...we need advertizers!!Dissapointment of the month is the TSOL album-I couldn't even bring myself to review it so one of me mates from Ann Arbor was kind enough to kick them in the nuts for all of us-We've been getting some pretty lame promos in the mail lately like THE TAN-the most horrendous n.w. schloko I've heard since THE NERVES,and the FLESHTONES NEW single which has harmonica on it...the only thing I hate more than armidillos gawd do I hate those things-I'd love to hear one of their shells crack under my tires as I drive through Texas sometime(Like never Texas is the asshole of America cuz half the state of Michigan is moving there)The fellow who wrote last months article about the VOMIT PIGS took some quasi abuse from some irate band members including some fuckin' Iranian
well you can tell I'm in a pretty choice mood this morning so I'll let you go so you can enjoy this whoppin issue 15!

With apologies to SPASTIC RYTHYM TARTS-cuz jeez I lost your interview maybe we can do one again some time...OK? TV

TOUCH and GO

MICH. TOP ROCKZINE..no punches spared these guys are arockzine of immorral quality, reviewsand the rest but good graphix and insights.....

DUD CITY

T.S.O.L.-"DANCE WITH ME" Frontier Sadly sisappointing.This lacks the sound and energy that made their last release one of my all time favorites.On this outing they seem to abandon their political beliefs and have a go at some horror-story music. They must have heard the MISFITS or something-anyway they can't even come close...Who cares if Jack/alex(or whatever the fuck his name is)wants to fuck the dead?Why all the stupid fucking makeup?and why is the lyric sheet printed in a new wave layout? 'Nuff said.Just find someone with this album and listen to it.Make your own decisions... BP

LOOKY HERE ↓

ADVERTISERS...TOUCH AND GO OFFERS THE BEST IN SHOCK VALUE PUNK ROCK LITERATURE...YOU KNOW WE GRAB THE READER BY THE BALLS(OR TITS AS IT WERE) AND TWIST EITHER THAT OR WE TICKLE THEIR FUNNY BONES WITH A JACK-HAMMER...EITHER WAY WE SUCKER THEM INTO BUYING RECORDS,AND OTHER GOODS THROUGH SUBLIMINAL AND MANIPULATIVE PSYCHOLOGICAL TECHNIQUES-SO FOR YOU THE ASPIRING ROCK STAR,ROCKSTAR MANAGER,RECORD STORE,DISTRIBUTOR ETC.-THERES NO BETTER PLACE TO SINK YOUR HARD EARNED CASH THAN IN AN AD IN THIS MAGAZINE...SO DONT HESITATE..OUR RATES ARE FULL PAGE...,.........only 20 dollars HALF PAGE...............Only 10 dollars
and so on

THE FIX AS SEEN BY DS...
the following is an excerpt of an article DS wrote for DISCHORDS magazine... The FIX have finally returned from their successful tour of Texas,California(SF in Particular) and the Northwest.They played the much publicized Eastern Front gig in Frisco,opened for the DEAD KENNEDYS in Fresno,and did some recording at B.Flags studio with Spot.I've heard the tape and the improvement in sound over their single has to be heard to be believed. They celebrated their return with an amazing gig at Ricks American Cafe in E.Lansing.Not the best surroundings(tiny carpeted dance floor and benignly mellow atmoshere)for their unsuble brand of punk.Aggressive,uncomprimizing,violent,nobody does it better... I did get a bug up my ass about some self appointed   goons taking it upon themselves to protect the band from the flailing throng on the dance floor.I trust the FIX had nothing to do with it,cuz this will sure as shit cause bad blood among their fans if they did.Brawny assholes (except Tim Perry drop the brawny,ED) grabbing people and pushing 'em back into the mass of slamming bodies-appearing to take great pleasure im their ability to police the stage.Just an excuse to throw their weight around...big(except tim Perry drop the big,ED)jerks with small minds   Steve(Vocals) told them to stop and leave us alone,but no they had to have more...One of em' got his kicks from punching girls,but challenge him to step outside as one Kalamazoo fan did, and he runs,only to return to throw bottles from a speeding car.Am I a fool to say I hope we don't encounter any more of this gestapo brutality at future FIX shows.We sure as hell don't need it... DS

ONE WAY FILMS

1035 Guerrero, San Francisco, CA 94110
Telephone (415) 821-9183

307

Hey Core them look like rat poison...

Corey as young child...

They sounded much better here than when I saw them in Chicago a couple days ago...probably because O'banions is about the size of a walk in closet and they didn't let half of the people from Ohio,MI.and Wash in due to their strict 21 enforcement-..Chi-town blows the spud...but back to what I intended on talking about...MINOR THREAT played one song before ol' Ian started bitching about no-one dancing so the "a bit fatigued looking audience got

nuts after that...They are quite simply the tightest live band I've ever seen...Lyle(guitar) and Brian(Bass)

Come Here sweet bindies...(so I can squeeze your guts out through your fuckin eyes) HA HA

You say you saw a good gig? A shitty one? Submit a review and we'll print it...honest!

are so together it's staggering-the bass lines are constructed into a tough sounding approach that is so great it's difficult to describe- he's no dull thud-and Jeff)drums(does quite the incredible skin routine s-he was the drummer in Teen Idles for all you newcomers to the cool D.C. sound and he proves his abilities once again with FIFTH COLUMN uh I mean M. Threat...all in all you shoulda been there...ol Corey killed a pigeon with his chain and Micro carried it around in his mouth...oh summertime is such fun...

THE LOFT FIASCO in Kalamazoo 8/1
8 bands(about 5 too many)

Money grubbin' foreigners dippin' their fungal stained hands in the punk rock pie, hoping to make that big killing. I hope they lost their ass cuz they didn't know what the fuck they were doin'. Yet another sorry episode in the perpetual blight which is Kalamazoo. Not only that, but the crowd was made up primarily of machismo-damaged assholes and their dates. To say that many of the bands on the bill were horrible does not accurately describe the event. Worst of which were The Pagans, who with their Haight Ashbury coffee house brand of banter and cacophony, were groping futilely for an irrelevant past, which must fester inside the head of every acid.casualty. To sum things up, The Spastic Rhythm Tarts, Violent Apathy, and The Necros were to only ones to make the 80 mile drive worthwhile. One more thing, a story I got second hand about a four-eyed pink shirted fairy who had the absurd notion that New York was where things were happenin' and his bible was . . . of all things, NON LP B-SIDE. What a panic! I should have known, he had his finger up his bum, trying to resusitate his brain. Hey buddy, I hope you're reading this and we can't wait to see you again, cuz you're a scream. --DS

GI'S/YOUTH BRIGADE/MINOR THREAT (9:30 CLUB...WASH.DC BY TV

The 9:30 Club was nice enough to give the entire door to the 2 bands going on tour(M.T. and Y.B.) and their generousity was met w/ a great turnout by the D.C. community...really coming out to support the bands...fuck yes that's what it's all about...The GIs are a band that seems to be gaining m omentum as this gig evidenced...v ocalist John Stab is quite simply great...his between song monolologues assault the crowd and the culture in general as they launch into one great song after another- "This one's written by a guy who was killed in a car accident and I'ts called"I'm James Dean"(True) or another one is introduced as the A stands for asshole and this songs "Anarchy Is Dead"...other classics include "Brand New Cataracts","Rock And Roll Bullshit" and Insomniac" ...between bands it's fun to watch the choice looking pudendum standing around giggling in their sartorial splendor- YOUTH BRIGADE comes on like gangbusters raging from one hot tune to another..."I Object"/"Full Speed Ahead" are but a couple of their superbly raucous tunes...the audience got involved and began stage diving and helped bellow the chorus on "Moral Majority"(one,two sieg heil!)and their anthem "Youth Brigade"

VIOLENT APATHY

VIOLENT APATHY/SCABS   PRT CLUB

Now that they've taken it upon themselves to "go it alone"(inside comment-disregard) the folks downtown decide to pick up on some $$ when things are slow so they can keep their little semi,quasi,pseudo,theatre group in the black...so they book Violent Apathy..one fuckin' hot band-they were thouroghly enjoyed by (I KNOW I SPELLED THOROUGHLY WRONG) me,DS and Craig Fix the only three who felt the old adrenalin hit and skanked up a storm-I almost killed DS when I shoved him down hard on an old chair but he flipped over at the last minute and his massive tool sent the chair flying in splinters...No really V.A. are hot...Can't wait to see them again...TV bailed-out before The Scabs came on, good move, buddy. They ingraitiate themselves in gagtriggering barband schlock from the word go. Singer/guitar player is one sick puppy . . . spandex pants, wrap shades, a Gino Vanelli shirt exposing his flacid chest, and platform sneakers. This may be Lansing, but it'll be a cold day in Hell, before the Scabs ever make it. Wrap your lips around your protruding tounge and blow.--TV&DS

the fix PART-2

MODERN WARFARE

TG:SO what were your best gigs out west?
Steve:I say Austin...
Jeff:In the south,In the south...
Craig:I liked Reno alot
Steve:Oklahoma ciyt was real lame...
Craig:We were booked in LA but the clubs shut
down-
TG:Where were you booked?
Craig:Along time ago at the Starwood,Cafe De
Grande and The Appollo Theatre...
TG:Did you see anybody when you were out there?
Steve:We saw Spot and the inside of a studio....
TG:What was the best band you saw out west?
All:THE STAINS!!! Sorry so short but the tape

Modern Warfare, a punk band from Long Beach,
have released two records, the second of
which we highly recommend. They were kind
enough to do an interview. Only Ron and
Tim were available and Mr. Vee conducted
the questions.

TV: Nothing like doing an interview across
    the country. So what do you think of
    us backwoods folks trying to write about
    punk rock?
Ron:I don't think about you folks.
Tim:I thought you all listened to Ted Nugent
    and Grand Funk.
TV: How did your record produced by Geza X
    come about?
Ron:Met him at a sex party.
Tim:Huh?
TV: How has the response been to your two re-
    leases?
Ron:#1 fair, #2 good.
Tim:The reviews are great, but nobody buys
    the fuckin' records. Come on, kids, get
    with it, I need the money for an operation
    for my mother.
TV: How has the treatment by the press been
    thus far? I noticed one of your gigs got
    written up in Flipside.
Ron:Very good, but they miss the point sometimes.
Tim:They don't review us in Cheri.
TV: Have you ever considered touring outside
    of CA?
Ron:Not yet.
Tim:I went to Tijuana last year.
TV: Is there any typical band from Long Beach--
    How do you fit into the scene ther?(if one
    exists)(Jezus, where the fuck is Long Beach?)
Ron:No, a little too tightly, nowhere.
Tim:Paul Williams & The Carpenters, scene, what
    scene?, Long Beach is everywhere, man!
TV: Were did your name come from?
Ron:The heavens
Tim:Hell
TV: Where's been your best place to play--best
    gig or crowd or whatever?
Ron:I don't know.
Tim:The sandbox(if the cat doesn't bury us.)
TV: Have you had many run-ins with the youngsters,
    HBs or whatever, who beat your face if they're
    in the mood?
Ron:No! Those people only exist in the media!
Tim:If they get shitty we take Randy off his
    chain and he takes care of them, Toot Sweet!
TV: Favorite bands?
Ron:Modern Warfare
Tim:Sam the Sham, ? and the Mysterians, The
    Shaggs.
TV: Is it true people in CA think people from
    Mich. are ignorant hillbillies?

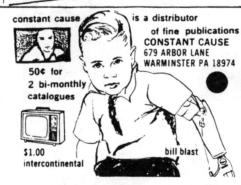

new series

FALLOUT IN PHILADELPHIA
looking at this town from the inside
is enough to make you move .segrega#
ted on every possible issue,from race
to rock.Recently at a DEAD KENNEDIES gig
theNAZIs andCommunists, made a striking
appearense.The nazis, pulled the old
impersonating police officers,and got
awaywith it:pulling cars over,giving
people hard times and searching a few.
these geeks were then allowed and
accepted in the trendiest club in
town."OMN"s crowd just accepted
these pigs,rather than chance getting
tang stomped.Very few people even
bothering to hassle the brownshirts
well if the young are actually
niave ennough to allow nazis
to breed again , i wouldnt be
supprised......   A.NEWT

Ron:With a question like that, yes.
Tim:Only if they're reading this.
TV: Which direction do you want the band to go?
Ron:Forward
Tim:Crazy! You wann go, too?
TV: Any plans to record again soo?
Ron: Yes
Tim:Compilation album with us, Rhino 39, Adoles-
    cents, Circle Jerks, 45 Grave & many more
    due out in September on: Bemisbrain
                             200 Termino Ave.
                             Long Beach, CA 90803

310

JOHN STAB of the GIS

TEEN PINUP NO.4

311

IAN of Minor THREAT

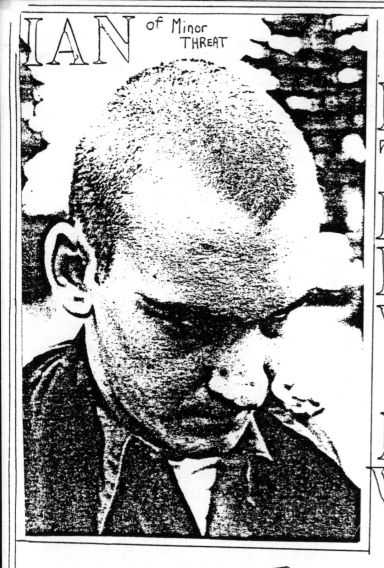

INTERVIEW

but really great-The CIRCLE JERKS we saw when we were out west-they were too polished and they were assholes-they weren't willing to go the route like getting their hair cut-you know people say like cutting your hair is like posing-well bullshit, that's conviction-you shave your head and there's no room for vanity

TV:One glance at your lyrics and it's apparent you aren't much on booze and drugs.
IAN:I'm totally anti-drug and alcohol...
TV:In Lansing drinking is somewhat of a necessity...you know anasthetic...
IAN:I really believe that if you hang out in a surrounding where everone is drinking whether you realize it or not there is pressure to drink-and what I hope to offer is a teenage or a young thing that doesn't demand you drink and shit-kids need an option-I think alot of kids that take this shit think alot of kids that take this why their such jerks...their trying to make up for themselves-this obsession with this stuff makes me sick-I fuckin hit a kid with a hammer because he blew pot smoke in my face

Alot of people use drinking and drugs as an axcuse and that's what the song"BOT-TLED VIOLENCE" is about-there's alot of people I know who can't fight unless their drunk-I guess I'm a passivist in that respect..I mean not peace and love everybody but on the other hand don't go get your head kicked in -there's no point in being a cripple-like look at what happened in PH-iladelphia(S.O.A. gig which ended in a bloody brawl)These Kensington kids came in and started a fight and got thrashed inside so they said come out and fight and all the D.C. kids ran out like "Let's kick some as s and out came these kids with baseball bats and fucked the D.C. kids up
TV:Explain the song "FILLER"
IAN:FILLER's about everbody who is so impressionable that they'd change their entire way of thinking and drop all their friends just because of one person who happens to be of the opposite sex says or does...I wrote it with Geordie(Teen Idles guitarist) in mind but it's not just about him-I mean he got religion and called me a sinner-just because his girlfriend was born again..
TV:So filling his head with...
Ian:Sure it's all filler in the head,it's all bullshit-Fillers like what they put in Hostess HO-HOs...

THE FOLLOWING INTERVIEW WAS CONDUCTED BY TV WITH ONE IAN MACKAYE-VOCALIST FOR WASHINGTON BAND-MINOR THREAT
TV:Compare the D.C. scene now with a year ago...
Ian:OK July 1980 right...You had TEEN IDLES,THE UNTOUCHABLES, and THE BAD B-RAINS-BLACK MARKET BABY were just starting to make it at that point.A few young punks who we'd see once in a whi-le-The Georgetown punk thing was in full swing-you had shows in bars in G.T.-places that would do it once and then shut down-with maybe 25 or 30 punks and maybe 30 or 40 other people at the most-We(Teen Idles)played fast as shit-total-ly noise-not like bullshit noise-but son gs with a really rough edge....THE UNTOU-CHABLES...like Alec was just crazy-he did the wildest shit you could imagine-he was doing stage dives and fucking himself up-All of this was happening like before we'd heard any of the L.A. stuff-both bands were playing that way-like the first band we heard from L.A. was BLACK FLAG and I thought this is really great-a little slow

TV:Can you just sit down and write songs or do have have to have some big inspir-ation?
Ian:No way man like I wish I could do that-it's like the other night Chris and Dante were sleeping at my house and I woke up all of the sudden with this song going through my head like never before,so I got my guitar and went to the bathroom-it's about how peop-le are so negative they make me ill so I wrote this song-"Negative"I can't just write songs somethings gotta hit me...
TV:Your vocal style is like...
Ian:I don't copy anyone-the ADOLESCENTS and all of that sound like Darby Crash-all the L.A. bands sound the same to me now with the excep-tion of BLACK FLAG-certainly the best band out there ...seems like people would copy them. We don't sound like anybody-thank god for that-we're just MINOR THREAT...

YOUTH BRIGADE

INTER-VIEW

THE FOLLOWING INTERVIEW WAS CONDUC-
TED ON JULY 19 IN D.C. BY TV...PRE-
SENT WERE...NATHAN,Vocals/BERT,BASS,
and DANNY,DRUMS
TV:So are you still going to do the
gig with Motorhead?
Danny;No they don't want a punk band
opening...
TV:Why?
Danny;They already have one heavy metal band opening-the guy who is putting
on the show at the Ontario said"Aw you
don't want all these heavy metal kids
booing you" and I said "I don't care"
so I aaid "Let me talk to Motorhead" &
he said "No that'd make me look bad"
Bert;He's an asshole anyway...
Danny;He's a fuckhead...
TV:How many dates so far have you got
for your tour?
Berto:4 definates-Chicago,Madison,and 2
in L.A.
Danny:Ya and there's this really great
band called the NECROS who might be get
ting us à date in Detroit;
Bert:I heard they're queers...
TV:Where are the L.A. gigs?
Berto:Bards Appollo(I know I spelled it
wrong,ED.)and Valley west which seats
1800 people...
Danny:They won't be seated...
TV:How are you guys set apart from the
other D.C. bands?

Nathan:We're more handsome...
Danny:You look at MINOR THREATS' guest
list and it's all guys,and then you look
at our guest list and it's all girls-that
says it all..
Berto:(sarcastically)We're different-we
have Our own sound
TV:Do you get along?
D:Ya Nathan and I have been friends about
6 years?
Nathan:Ya
D:Bert and I used to be in a band togethe r
called THE UNTOUCHABLES
D:I quit...
Bert: He got fired,then he quit...
Danny:I quit,then I got fired...
Tesco:I won't talk about the legendary ex
bands because I'm sure you're tired of talk-

about them...
Nathan:No way TEEN IDLES were a great
band..
B&D:Let's take a vote...
TV:What did you think of the article in
the post this morning?
Nathan:I thought it was pretty fair-cept
the part about Dischord records being run
by MacKaye..
So what about the record?
Danny: We're going to record a new demo-
we've got the 4 new songs plus the one we
re-wrote
Nathan:Dischord #5
TV:Are you the original 4 members?
D:Original 2(points at Nathan)
Nathan:the guitarist quit-John Falls
Danny:We fired the bass player cuz he was
gay man I swear-this guy names greg he's

such a fairy-he was the guy at the show
with the little ruffled blue shirt-he was a
real prick
Nathan:He wore little jump suits and shit
Bert:He gave em' an arty sound
Danny:He used to say stuff like I GUESS we'r
e OK for a punk band(Laughter)"I mean we
don't have to be good cuz if we mess up no-

body notices"
TV: So Bert you were just hangin' out after
the UNTOUCHABLES?
B:No I aws in NO AUTHORITY w/a new drummer
with Alec and Eddie-we had some good songs
D:NOTHING SACRED I thought was pretty good
but there was alot of tensions
Bert:NO AUTHORITY was going nowhere
Nathan:So then I asked Berto"Do you wanna pl
ay bass for us and he didn't say anything
Danny:I took him to dinner and tha movies and
was real nice to him so he'd join...
Nathan:The rest is history...
Tesco:Did the TEEN IDLES break up because
that Geordie guy went religious?
Danny:He didn't really go religious-he was
just a real flake...
TV:Somebody said he used to throw his guitar
at the other band members if he got mad...
Nathan:He and Jeff(drums)got in a hassle at
one gig

TV:Can you just write songs or do you need
inspiration?
D:We just write them...
Nathan:we look at the headlines
TV:Do you see this scene as "on an up" so to
speak?
Danny:As far as bands go 'all these people say
"Well this scene is gonna die out" but look at
last thursday(Triple bill Benefit-see review)

was great
Nathan:There were tons of people I'd never seen
before like from Maumee,Philadelphia(laughter)
and Lansing
Danny:Lots of people say "Let's go to the 9:30
club It's supposed to be different...
TV:Their money's still green...

Danny:Another gallon a gas...
TV:What do you do for recreation?
All:Video games and gurls...
Bert:Actually we don't get any girls since
Henry moved...
Danny:We got the plug pulled on us at the YMCA
gig cuz after 1 song everyone started fighting
but I kept on drumming so they were going to
arrest me for inciting a riot....we played 2
songs at the Adelphi Mill and these rednecks
started fights and it ended in a huge brawl
out in the parking lot and people got their
cars smashed
Bert:He threw a chair threw someones windshield
TV:What's your guitarists name?
ALL:Tom
TV:Has he played with anyone before?
ALL:Himself!!
TV:Fave Heavy MetaL?
Bert;,MOTORHEAD
D:AC/DC
Nathan:Alice Cooper
TV:Were you crushed when you got dumped
from the bill
Danny:Very

NOW
ON
TOUR
w/
Minor
THREAT

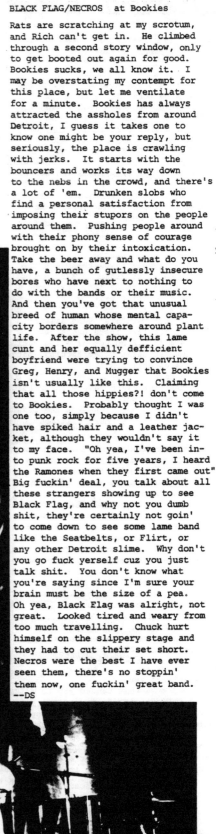

NECROS/THE ITCH/EDDIE and THE WOLF-GANG/and another band I've since for-gotten The Keg in Battle Creek

What a night! Drunk longhair motorhead bums picking fights with the
punks, a Sid clone gets his face
smashed, and the place smelled like
dogshit. First time I went in there
practically knocked me off my feet.
Beer was free, though, so that made
up for any complaints about the vile
air quality. First band to come on
had leftovers from the Lips Are Back.
Forgot their name, as well as their
music. Their leader(onetime Lips
ax man) had gone from punk to beat-
nik in just a matter of months.
Probably haven't been together too
long cuz their music was that loose
schlocky brand of new wave noise
that's indistinquishable from a
myriad of other bands trying to do
the same thing. For the moment,
the less said about them, the better. Eddie and The Wolfgang opened
with an unprecedented cover of the
Necros' "Police Brutality". We're
all slapping our heads in disbelief.
So what guys, take it as a compliment
and leave it at that. During one of
their songs, the singer(the Wolfgang?)
jumped out into the crowd and got
shoved back on stage by the aforementioned Sid replica. I guess he
wanted to show the band and anybody
else who was interested what 'real'
punk rock is. Well, needless to
say, this leather jacketed ghost
from the past got a helluva lot more
than he bargained for and then some.
No sooner does he get on stage when
he suddenly finds himself on the
receiving end of a good stomping,
dealt quite mercilessly in fact.
He spent the rest of the evening
vainly attempting to repair the ir-
reparable damage to his ego. To say
he bit off more than he could chew
would be restating the obvious. The
Itch were next, and although I don't
remember too much from their set,
they were good, alot better than
the rumors I'd heard about their
DooBee gig some while back. The
Necros did not play one of their
better sets, not by a long shot.
The sound system wasn't for shit,
one of the PA speakers was blown,
so while the energy level may have
been high you couldn't hear it. A
performance, I'm sure, the Necros
would rather forget. A fun, but
sloppy evening.--DS

BLACK FLAG/NECROS   at Bookies

Rats are scratching at my scrotum,
and Rich can't get in. He climbed
through a second story window, only
to get booted out again for good.
Bookies sucks, we all know it. I
may be overstating my contempt for
this place, but let me ventilate
for a minute. Bookies has always
attracted the assholes from around
Detroit, I guess it takes one to
know one might be your reply, but
seriously, the place is crawling
with jerks. It starts with the
bouncers and works its way down
to the nebs in the crowd, and there's
a lot of 'em. Drunken slobs who
find a personal satisfaction from
imposing their stupors on the people
around them. Pushing people around
with their phony sense of courage
brought on by their intoxication.
Take the beer away and what do you
have, a bunch of gutlessly insecure
bores who have next to nothing to
do with the bands or their music.
And then you've got that unusual
breed of human whose mental capacity borders somewhere around plant
life. After the show, this lame
cunt and her equally defficient
boyfriend were trying to convince
Greg, Henry, and Mugger that Bookies
isn't usually like this. Claiming
that all those hippies?! don't come
to Bookies. Probably thought I was
one too, simply because I didn't
have spiked hair and a leather jacket, although they wouldn't say it
to my face. "Oh yea, I've been into punk rock for five years, I heard
the Ramones when they first came out"
Big fuckin' deal, you talk about all
these strangers showing up to see
Black Flag, and why not you dumb
shit, they're certainly not goin'
to come down to see some lame band
like the Seatbelts, or Flirt, or
any other Detroit slime. Why don't
you go fuck yerself cuz you just
talk shit. You don't know what
you're saying since I'm sure your
brain must be the size of a pea.
Oh yea, Black Flag was alright, not
great. Looked tired and weary from
too much travelling. Chuck hurt
himself on the slippery stage and
they had to cut their set short.
Necros were the best I have ever
seen them, there's no stoppin'
them now, one fuckin' great band.
--DS

LIVE

STUFF

Tesco,
Your zine's really good reading,alot of great record reviews (except ESG, I bought it,took it back)and concert reviews,I'm really pissed I didn't make it to Black Flag at the Doo Bee I think we were the "stupid fux who can't stand who they really are, smoking marijuana in the lot at D.O.A. but think what you wanna think,the FIX single is good,but the NECROS still beat the hell out of it,I can't wait for the new E.P.(let me know when it's out)I got TEEN IDLES,and S.O.A, they're fuckin' great,can't wait to hear MINOR THREAT!!Please let me know about any shows in the area,we need live entertainment.
Too young to rock
Greg Boker
Hudsonville,Mi

Dear Whoever in Charge,
Got Your latest issue-thanx for the rather reckless FLESH EATERS review (even I don't think it's that good).
What I'm really writing about,though is the single by the BAD ACTORS which one of your "writers" went apeshit over in the last issue.Can;t get it anywhere in L.A.Do you have the address for Sophisticated Noise Records,'cause we sure as hell don't.
Let me have it pronto and I'll let you have the next Flesh Eaters album before it' s even released!
Onwards and Sideways
Mark Williams
SLASH

Touch & Go;Send me the latest issue of your mag and the FIX and NECROS singles. I figure if TKA hated em' and they opened for Black Flag they gotta be good.Thanx
Tim Lord
Ames Iowa
hey you know Tim the guy who edits the OFFENSE thinks his magazine to be the american equivalent of N.M.E. we've bought good records for years simply on their negative review-so it would seem we have our own little paradox after all...oh by the way while we're on the subject here is a sample of what the mail in the OFFENSE is like...
Mr.Offense,
This is to confirm your dental app. on wed.August 28th.Thank you
Dr.H. Molar
well you get the idea
ED.

Dear Tesco Vee,
I'm not sure what caused you to write such a flattering review of the Get Smart flexi,but it surely was appreciated although a bit of a shock.I might add that it is one of the better reviews we've seen so far.Of course ABUSE do not agree with you but so what.Look for a flexi of a different sort in the next issue out in Sept.
THanks for the positive vibes
Sincerely
Bill Rich-Talk Talk
Publications

credit where it's due Bill-you know by now we aren't into backslapping our fellow publications simply for a journalistic commaraderie or whatever-yours is one of the few fanzines I bother to read all the way through-save for the nasty dread but your latest issue had a refreshing lack of that-see zine review somewhere in this ish I'm laying it on the line this month!

TV,
Thanks for the copy of T&G-lots of bands I've never heard of before-can you get their records?Bonhams article on the FIX gig is pretty accurate-thing's aren't going too well here(Grand Rapids,ED)there's about a dozen hardcore punks and maybe a few newavers who like it-TRAINABLE was awfully boreing but we can't book H.C. bands here without havin' a pop/art school group besides...nobody shows up-we lost about 150 bucks on that gig,the radio station that would have benefited is WEHB a community station with new wave on Sat.,and Sun. nights-I try to get as much hardc-re stuff on the air as possible but it ain't too popular here(which is OK by me)Anyway the gig in general was a disaster after all the damages,tarnished rep of WEHB etc. was totalled...if Bonham thought that was bad he oughta hear the INFECTIONS or BANN X (the punk spelled "asshole")-cover bands w/ no redeeming qualitys -GR faves at least some of us got to hear both the FIX and the NECROS that nite,as we made the trip to Battle Creek after.What: and where is the PRT club in Lansing?What happened to DOOBEE?
Eric Bloc

Grand Rapids Mi
Both clubs are done for various reasons too dull to go into at this point...yes all the records we review are available...we'll try to print all available addresses in the future(one viable suggestion from the editor of OP magazine)

DS,
Have you changed your opinion on the Stimulators single yet?"Great,great, great-shit,shit,shit.You're right it gets better with every listen-it's gone from being the worst to just medi ocre.Comparing these wimps to the Mis-fits is sacrilege.This is the first time you've talked me into wasting my money on a single,I'm sure it was a temporary lapse of your impeccable taste,I wouldn't bitch but I've never known one of your raves to be wrong before.I'm fucking missing B.F. at Bookies because my friends are too lightweight to go,and I'm too light-weight to go alone-I don't even know where Bookies is.Shit. I know it was a great show.Oh well.
I missed the "peoples band" (Gang Of Four here too-8.50! those capatalist bloodsuckers-fuck em'Keep me informed on where to get the hot new indie U.S. releases.Schoolkids gets it half a year later if ever.What the hell is "Muscle-head music"?(Discords term)Seems to be real slow right now for Mich,gigs eh? I wonder why I didn't even hear of the Black Flag show till ye sterday.Not one poster or anything in Ann Arbor-somebody's not doing their job.
Later
A.D.
Ann Arbor,Mi
PS. Know anybody who needs a Stimulators 45?
If you're content to take our fluctuating word as gospel you'll run into problems-

DS&TV,
Gosh you guys make me sick!I've been spending all my paychecks on discs for months and now I get #14 and see what little I got(In alot of cases what we got aint exactly large,ED.)Guess I'll have to spend my next check catching up w/ ya'll.I consider your "venimous cut down of the rotten apple a public service for all T&G readers.Guess you have to see the disco turned p-unk slime for yourself to realize what a shithole that city is.Even though I've only lived near NYC for about 1 year,I can say with confidence that NY people are the ugliest dumbest,most selfish,inconsiderate, ignorant and racist scum on earth-(just typing that sentence was great! ED.)Didn't see the O Jerks in NY cuz I got depressed watching those trendy fartistes that go to those clubs.Only time I'll go is if there is a group that won't be playing anywhere else w/in 100 or 50 miles.However I did catch the Jerks in NJ twice.Show was great but barely lasted ½ hour with much of that devoted to Hetson repair-ing guitar strings.To think I only got a few bruises out of both shows.Saw Black Flag in DOver NJ-nearly broke my neck trying to leap over the riff-raff from a table close to the dance floor-landed on my head and sleepwalked for the rest of the show.It was great-the heaviest slamming I;ve ever seen.Even chicks were getting bashed down by bl-indsiders at 60 miles an hour.Dez and Charles got slammed pretty good but managed to survive.Also saw Stiff Li. Fingers since the show only cost 3 buc ks.Those Belfast boys can suck lepre-chaun dicks for all I care.Hardly did any of the early stuff,which I figur-ed would be worth going to see.Seem to be on a bunny Wailer kick these days who cares?Guitar hero Henry Cluney said that the band was ashamed of their 1st lp now that they've grown up and learned somuch about music."Sounded like a bu-nch of bloody amateurs back then" he stated.Bunch of old farts already-god-damn,fuckin' wankin' shithead puppets! How I hate those bastards(catch my dri ft)?
John Shine
Hackensack,NJ
Sorry to cut your letter so short guy-

thanx for taking the time ....
We buy records hit and miss-the real independents often times don't get picked up by the major distributors so it's take a chance(this was in resp onse to a question later in this let-ter about the records review ed in T&G......TV

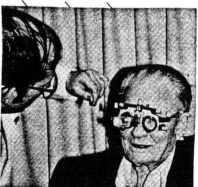

NOISE-Artist R.Moores journey into
the world of rock journalism gets
better w/ each issue-well no I take
that back...I liked #3 better than
#4 so it's pictured above-bitchin'
photo of greg huh?Good picture of
ol' Stevie"Slim" Soto on the last page-
food out there in L.A. must be pretty
tasty!! Sorry Bob baby got carried
off good job bob and next time you
steal a T&G picture don't apologize-
we've stolen enough to give anyone
plageristic fits!!!5 dollars for 10
issues-3588 Southbrook Dr.
Xenia, Ohio 45385

s u b p o p

SUBPOP-Bruce wins the award for smallest mag
in the country-even old Furry couch has'nt
released anything this small(has he?)There's
more here than in most large rags-everything
is divided up into regions of the country-and
even though he didn't review us I mean there
must be a good excuse n'his little thing is
so handy and informative how can I cut this
gent down-the best part of his latest
issue was a rundown of all these cool
films you can order from S.F. I mean
that's what it's all about isn't it?
Reaching out with something new to offer-
America's impoverished underground...
However some of his reviews I find lu-
dicrous(Comparing ALL NIGHT MOVIES to
B.FLAG?!?! Those pinheads hate the band-
but maybe he was simply at a loss for
words...Address all correspondence to
Bruce and mark it personal or something
because the dink that edits OP reads his
mail and then writes these excursions in-
on(And I lost his letter honestly or I
would've reprinted it-despite what the dru-
—mmer in IDLE HANDS thinks we do not throw out
our hate mail frankly we dun git any-to
speak ofSUB POP gets the hearty thumbs up-
next issue will be in cassette form...
LOST MUSIC NETWORK   BOX 2391 ·OLYMPIA
WASH(Is that where they filmed HERE CO-
MES THE BRIDES?) 98507

SMEGMA JOURNAL-COVERAGE OF the best stuff-
one of the editors is pretty open minded-
you know the carrot topped stud-the other
guy is strictly a rip-rocker and everything
else is art-and so it goes with others filling in occassionaly -only OHIO mag that
makes one split a gut-read it while you're
taking a choice herman and the old feces'll
just come a flying out so hard you'll splash
your ass with pee water...cool graphics of
enemic,starving and ugly children(they're
obsessed with black ones)A 5 star rating
send money to-BOX 421   MAUMEE OHIO 43537

DISCORDS

DISCORDS-Technically not a fanzine at
all this is more of a nationwide update-
that does what OP magazine wishes it could
in twice the space...Editor Howard Wuelfing
does a fab job on layout and copy-there's
reports on most major cities in the midwest
and east ...Besides you get great results
from their classifieds...now a supplement
to NY rocker(I'll reserve comment on that)
Strongly do I urge you to write and send
him money,,, 5018-8th road south
Arlington,Va. 22204

TRASHLAND ADVENTURES-Issue #2 just out
and it's got alot of interesting MICH
junk-good B.Flag review,questionable
East Lansing hardcore scene article
and a funny as shit Muffler of the
month page-..the last few pages is dedicated to stuff I hate but basically
this is a groovon papeles... 75¢ no
address listed....

LOUD FAST NEWS-One sided xerox from
NYC that's ok...only about 5 pages
long...good picture of Jello on the
cover and a BAUHAUS interview-
Jewel-215 park Row Suite #3   NYC
10038

HEY DADDYO-A clevland mag that features fiction-pretty good graphics and
a few musical notes-(reviews of The
Pretendrs and P.Gabrial and that's it?)
4939 Brooksdale Rd.Mentor Oh 44060

DAMAGE-THis is agreat magazine that simply
doesn't come out often enough-but they printed our MICH. report that Chris D. had asked
us to do for SLASH before they wimped out so
(don't you hate wimpy name droppers?) we can't
bitch...new one features' lots of great stuff
so get it...it may be six months before another
one comes out...

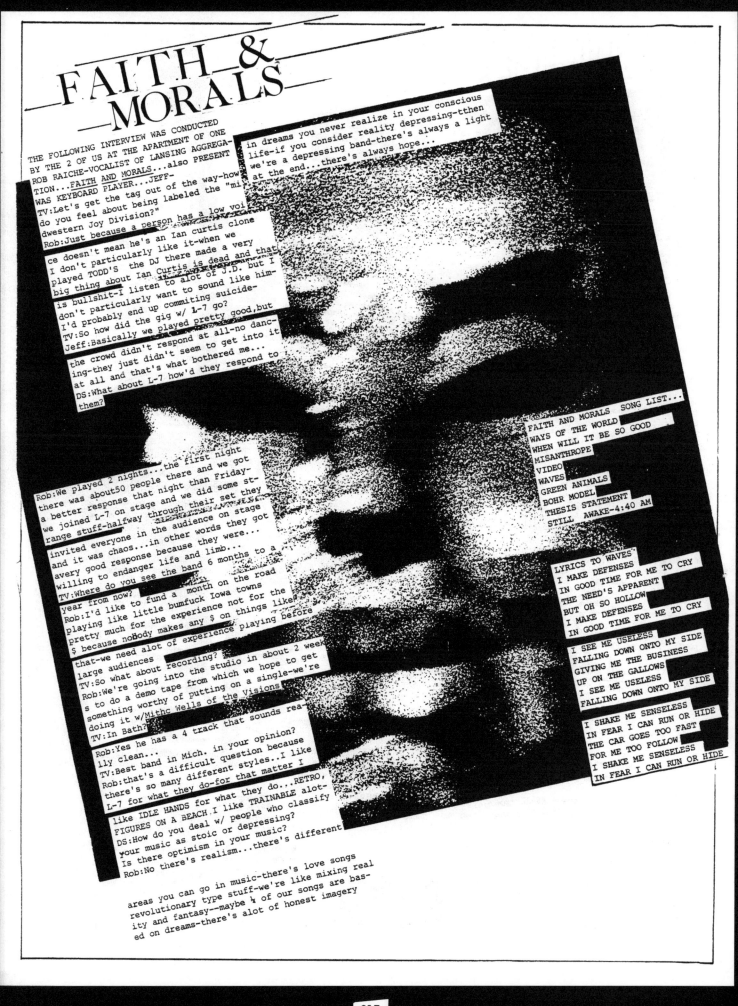

FAITH & MORALS

THE FOLLOWING INTERVIEW WAS CONDUCTED
BY THE 2 OF US AT THE APARTMENT OF ONE
ROB RAICHE-VOCALIST OF LANSING AGGREGA-
TION...FAITH AND MORALS...also PRESENT
WAS KEYBOARD PLAYER...JEFF-
TV:Let's get the tag out of the way-how
do you feel about being labeled the "mi
dwestern Joy Division?"
Rob:Just because a person has a low voi

ce doesn't mean he's an Ian curtis clone
I don't particularly like it-when we
played TODD'S the DJ there made a very
big thing about Ian Curtis is dead and that
is bullshit-I listen to alot of J.D. but I
don't particularly want to sound like him-
I'd probably end up commiting suicide-
TV:So how did the gig w/ L-7 go?
Jeff:Basically we played pretty good,but

the crowd didn't respond at all-no danc-
ing-they just didn't seem to get into it
at all and that's what bothered me...
DS:What about L-7 how'd they respond to
them?

in dreams you never realize in your conscious
life-if you consider reality depressing-tthen
we're a depressing band-there's always a light
at the end...there's always hope...

Rob:We played 2 nights...the first night
there was about50 people there and we got
a better response that night than Friday-
we joined L-7 on stage and we did some strange stuff-halfway through their set they
invited everyone in the audience on stage
and it was chaos...in other words they were...
avery good response because they were...
willing to endanger life and limb...
TV:Where do you see the band 6 months to a
year from now?
Rob:I'd like to fund a month on the road
playing like little bumfuck Iowa towns
pretty much for the experience not for the
$ because nobody makes any $ on things like
that-we need alot of experience playing before
large audiences
TV:So what about recording?
Rob:We're going into the studio in about 2 week
s to do a demo tape from which we hope to get
something worthy of putting on a single-we're
doing it w/Mithc Wells of the Visions
TV:In Bath?

Rob:Yes he has a 4 track that sounds rea-
lly clean...
TV:Best band in Mich. in your opinion?
Rob:that's a difficult question because
there's so many different styles..I like
L-7 for what they do-for that matter I
like IDLE HANDS for what they do...RETRO,
FIGURES ON A BEACH.I like TRAINABLE alot-
DS:How do you deal w/ people who classify
your music as stoic or depressing?
Is there optimism in your music?
Rob:No there's realism...there's different

areas you can go in music-there's love songs
revolutionary type stuff-we're like mixing real
ity and fantasy--maybe ¼ of our songs are based on dreams-there's alot of honest imagery

FAITH AND MORALS SONG LIST...
WAYS OF THE WORLD
WHEN WILL IT BE SO GOOD
MISANTHROPE
VIDEO
WAVES
GREEN ANIMALS
BOHR MODEL
THESIS STATEMENT
STILL AWAKE-4:40 AM

LYRICS TO WAVES
I MAKE DEFENSES
IN GOOD TIME FOR ME TO CRY
THE NEED'S APPARENT
BUT OH SO HOLLOW
I MAKE DEFENSES
IN GOOD TIME FOR ME TO CRY

I SEE ME USELESS
FALLING DOWN ONTO MY SIDE
GIVING ME THE BUSINESS
UP ON THE GALLOWS
I SEE ME USELESS
FALLING DOWN ONTO MY SIDE

I SHAKE ME SENSELESS
IN FEAR I CAN RUN OR HIDE
THE CAR GOES TOO FAST
FOR ME TOO FOLLOW
I SHAKE ME SENSELESS
IN FEAR I CAN RUN OR HIDE

UNSOLICITED

JEFF of MIDDLE CLASS

BLOOD SAUSAGE

MIDDLE CLASS/MDC(STAINS)/WARZONE/
FUCKUPS The Mabuhay in SF 7/15

The Fuckups have real neat sticker
s(you have to glue them yourself,
though). They fully live up to th
eir name and as a result can't get
many gigs, which doesn't seem to m
atter. They are real young and th
eir music is all Sex Pistols ripof
fs. They have extremely clichéd l
yrics and bland steretyped music t
o back them up. The kids love 'em
--something they can identify with
I suppose, a real cult band. The
lead singer is a long haired 16 ye
ar old fag(literally) who thinks h
e's Iggy and leaves the microphone
at the mercy of the audience half
the time, but he does have a lot o
f energy. They are terrible--lyri
cs include 'I just wanna die', etc
Exactly what punk should have neve
r become. Death to originality.
Warzone is great. True, they need
more practice(they aren't very tig
ht musically) but Jeff's Discharge
like vocals(and lyrics to match) a
nd the rest of the band's fast mus
ic more than makes up for any lack
of practice. The whole concept of
the band lies in thier lyrics, and
Jeff's madman energy on stage. So
ngs slagging nazi-punks, multinati
onal corporations, and their hit s
ong against the Moral Majority inc
lude some of the best lyrics writt
en I have ever heard. There is a
rumored tape they were going to pu
t on vinyl, but I think it may be
a while before these guys cut plas
tic.
The MDC/Stains(Stains from Texas--
MDC stands for 'million dead cops)
played a good powerful set includi
ng the all-time faves 'John Wayne
was a nazi'(but not anymore) and
'Born to Die'. Dave's UK Subian v
ocals and animated powerful stage
presence combined with Al's well e
xecuted drumming(where does the po
wer come from in that skeleton-lik
e body?) and Ron's great guitar pl
aying put this band up there with
the best of 'em. Frank is very co

mpetent as the MDC/Stains new bass
player, glad to see him in the gro
up. He's a great guy to boot, as
are all the MDC/Stains. Good luck
on your gigs with Black Flag. It
seems the MDC/Stains have a proble
m with the audience getting mindle
ssly violent at their shows, which

incites the band(particularly Dave)
to slag off the assholes and also
play with unmatched fury. Oh well
who said punks were intelligent?
Middle Class sound just like the n
ew EP, no more thrash. No more, n
o less. They have a little synthe
sizer they play with on the side o
f the stage that the lead singer p
lays with before every song. They
are real tight and do what they do
well. All the new wave girls get
up and dance, and everyone else si
ts down and watches--which sums up
Middle Class. I'll never pay to s
ee these guys.--Bonh@m

LYRICS FOR THE MEATMENS"
"ORGY OF ONE."

WHIPPIN' MY WOOD TO THE GIRLIE MAGS..
PROVIN TO MYSELF I'M NOT A FAG..
CUDDLIN' PUD IN THE TWIGHLIGHT LIGHT..
MY SWOLLEN JOYSTICKS' A SILENT FRIGHT..

STOPPED LOOKIN' FOR DREAM DATE FEMMES..
THE PULSATING POOZLE..
THE CREM' DE LA CREM'..
THE SINK AT HOME "LL DRINK IT DOWN..
A LOAD OF JISM'LL ERASE THAT FROWN..
(chorus)
LAYIN PIPE IS LOTS OF FUN...
BUT IT CAN'T BEAT MY ORGY OF ONE...

I CAN'T LEAVE THAT TOOL ALONE...
I'LL TORTURE IT TILL IT..
TURNS TO STONE...
WORK MY HAM TILL IT WINGS IT'S WAD..
A LOAD OF THAT CRAZY GLUE FROM MY BOD..

I LAY IN AWE AT THE SIZE OF MY TOOL...
MY BONER I KNOW WOULD MAKE THE BABES DROOL.
BUT WITH MY HAND I WANNA FUCK...
AN ORGY OF ONE WHO NEEDS LUCK?

LAYIN' PIPE IS LOTS OF FUN...
BUT IT CAN'T BEAT MY ORGY OF ONE...

CLUB REEVUE:
BOOKIES, DETROIT ROCK CITY

This fart house is on the first page of my"asshole management" hand book...
in the first place this old bitch runs around just looking for people to
toss out,even if it means going into the mens room stalls(no lie,she did)!
no mercy, because shes got Bruno and onionbreath to back her up...
Who died and made you queen? you can reef on my bureeto delux you slimy
whore bag!!!then she makes sure that every bouncer knows your face so he
can break your knees if you try to get in again...Even if you're 80 years
old and dont have your i.d., you can forget about getting into this place
and that giant Indian bouncer makes it perfectly clear that he dosnt like
you by tossing you at parked cars or getting you in a head lock for the rest
of your natural life...and then there are all the artsy faggos who tippy-toe
around and tell eachother how thier green hair and pink shoes are so fab,
and how they cant wait to get homo all over eachother...
GOD THIS PLACE REEKS TO HIGH HELL AND BACK AGAIN!!!
why dont you do us all a favor... BLOW DETROIT UP!!!

SADO-NATION--"I'm Trouble"/"Gimme
You"/"On Whom They Beat"/"Mom and
Pop Democracy" Trap Records

Some of that punky/pop we don't listen to much anymore. I guess I've
been brainwashed from listening to
"Warzone" too many times, corrupting
my once broadminded taste(who you
trying to kid?--ED). Clearcut Wipers
Ramones influence, with heavy emphasis on the former, which works to
their advantage, if you ask me. A
guy sings on two, and a girl sings
the other two. He lacks sincerity
while she maintains a sense of conviction. I'm sure I'll be chastized
for liking this, by what few musclehead friends I have left, but fuck,
I'll live dangerously.--DS
send $2.00 to Trap Records, PO Box
42465, Portland, OR, 97242

THE ALLEY CATS--"Night Along The
Blvd"/"Too Much Junk" Time Coast
Records

A preview of what we can expect
from their "Nightmare City" album.
Took me awhile to warm up to this
one, though. Great opening riff,
one of those gonad crunching blasts
like on "Too Drunk To Fuck". Hear
it once, and you got a jones for it
at least once a day. Randy's guitar break toward the end kinda
spoils it unfortunately. Not exactly the crispest idea he's ever
had and a far cry from his vinyl
melting frenetics on the Dangerhouse
single. But, what the heck, I can
live with it. "Too Much Junk" is
not too much different from the Yes
LA version and features the mammar-
ian Dianne on vocals. What more
could you ask for? A lot, I know,
but I can't give you everything,
now can I?--DS
send $2.00 to Time Coast Records,
8901 Sunset Blvd., LA, CA 90069

THE WALL--"Remembrance"/"Hsi Nao"/
"Hooligan Nights" Polydor

Well, they blew it! Got their big
chance to put out a single on a
major label, and they come out with
just their dicks in their hands.--DS

WASTED YOUTH--"Rebecca's Room"/
"'Things never seem the same as
they did even before they've happened' she added as an afterthought"
Bridge House Records

Martin Hannet sullies his hands and
soils his reputation with some mephi-
tically schlocky techno poop. It's
the same sort of superficial bilge
you'd expect from that faggot Steve
Strange. They thought they'd pull
the wool over our eyes with some
decidedly highbrow photography and
an equally absurd title on side two.
Suppose to make you think this is
some of that superfine serious music that NME is always talking
about. All it is, is some jerk
frigging on the dials of the mixing board, telling himself: 'wow,
what a statement!' At least they
got the name right, little boys
wasting our time.--DS

THE ERECTOR SET--"Inside Out"/"No
Room For Comfort" Erectunes

Gimme my wrap shades and my porkpie. I'm a wankin'. . . uh I mean
I'm a skankin' fool, yessire. It's
finally come to the Midwest and
sure as shootin', Cincinnati has
gone on a ska jag. Sorry, better
never than late, as the saying
goes. These guys have chosen to
emulate the Beat, how dumb, c'mon
fellas, how far do you expect to
get messing around with a fad that
was hot for about six months then
transported itself straight to the
graveyard where all revivalist trends
eventually come to rest. . . the
farthest recesses of our memory,
where we have neither the energy
nor the desire to recall them.
No offense, I trust, you know your
trade, maybe a year ago you could
have held my interest, but now. .
. never.--DS

THE PISTONS--"Investigation"/"Circus" Twin Tone Records

Ever wonder how come you never hear
shit about Minneapolis? One listen
to the Pistons and you'll know why.
Not good.--DS

CHRONIC GENERATION--Puppets Of War
EP Gargoyle Records

One look at the cover and you got
to laugh. Four young toughs ready
to storm the Bastille, but don't
stop cuz the real joke is the music
on this record. Crutches couldn't
help this band, their shit's that
lame. Oh yea, they may look punk,
but they couldn't break a grape.
Try to imagine four deaf guys goin'
thru some UK Decay covers. With
the British press quick to attack
our own punk bands, you have to wonder how some of these bands ever
missed the mesage. Sure put down
Black Flag and The Germs, but what
about your own proliferation of
'so-called' punk bands. . . all of
which would find competing with the
likes of S.O.A. or Minor Threat a
most humilating experience. Like
the old saying goes--if you don't
have anything to say, don't say it.
A must to avoid.--DS

WIPERS--"Better Off Dead"/"Up In
Flames"/"Does It Hurt" Trap Records

One of the greatest non-punk bands
ever. Sure, it's a sorry ass case
of hyperbole, but so what, it's
true this time, honest. Greg Sage
has got to be one of finest ax men
to break a string. We gave their
album the big rave up, and this is
their debut single that got the
whole thing going in the first
place. I don't want to hear no
heavy metal bullshit, either, the
Wipers are a fuckin' great band,
regardless of your inept ability
to label them. If you can put
your petty prejudices aside for a
moment, you'll realize that ol DS
ain't givin' you a bum steer. This
is a record with meat, not rancid
dung to be discarded after a couple
of bites. Buy it.--DS
send $2.00 to Trap Records, PO Box
42465, Portland, OR 97242

319

SIMPLY SAUCER--"She's A Dog"/"I Can Change My Mind Pig Records

Holy smokes! Just checked the date on the label(1978), no wonder I don't like it. Not really though, cuz this could have been 1968 for all I care. Side one is the Music Explosion plus some beefed-up recording gimmicks(the result of ten years of technology), biiig deeeal. Side two is worse with some sadsack Kinks posturing. Having just read something on The Pig Paper(they're connected somehow), I can see why some reguritated '60's slop would get the thumbs-up from this cleverly reflective Ontarian rag, they don't hold much regard for what's happening now and would much rather reminisce about the good ol days. They can have 'em.--DS

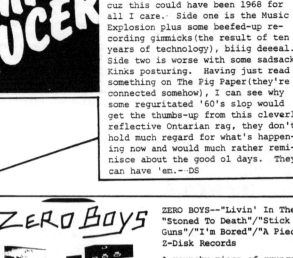

ZERO BOYS--"Livin' In The 80's"/"Stoned To Death"/"Stick To Your Guns"/"I'm Bored"/"A Piece Of Me" Z-Disk Records

A raunchy piece of grunge punk from Indianapolis of all places. A very crude authenticity screams out of the grooves with the force of a jackboot up the bum. Forget the Gizmos, here's the Zero Boys(I can be just as cliché as the next guy). For info write Zero Boys, 4022 N. Central, Indpls., IN 46205.--DS

NAKED SKINNIES--"All My Life"/"This Is The Beautiful Night" Naked House Records

Sonny Stitt(don't correct me if I'm wrong) once said 'mellow jazz' is the same thing as 'shitty jazz'. The Naked Skinnies can be written off in much the same way. "Mellow" is simply not a word to be found in my lexicon. This band is mellow, hence, they suck.--DS

BUDDY SHARPE and THE SHAKERS--"Jump Into The River"/"Dry Your Eyes" Bishop Records

Originally reviewed in the legendary INVASION fanzine, this shouldn't be confused with the other Buddy Sharpe, cuz this   one record easily rips the latter to shards. A rockabilly classic of the first order. They've been around since '57 and I've got no idea when this was recorded, but it sure as hell beats the fuck outa having to put up with modern day copy bands. The Stray Cats wish they sounded this good. This is the real thing. Thanx Scott.--DS

the PANTHER BURNS--"She's The One To Blame"/"Dateless Night"/"Drop Your Mask"/"Train Kept Ta Rollin'" Frenzy Records

So crudely produced and yet as vital as any rockabilly record I've ever heard. Proof to the old axiom that you can sound shitty and still knock 'em dead like all get out. Not just for rockabilly nuts.--DS

BILLY SYNTH and THE JANITORS--"Rock 'n' Roll Casualty" EP

On the surface it's nothing more than some pedestrian-type thud, but you get to thinking that this rock 'n' roll casualty has got something to say with this archaic schlock. Maybe not. Maybe he's just a hack with the synthesizer, and I'm wasting my time attempting to see anything in his music. An obscure item that somehow bridges the new music with something out of the past, I don't know exactly when. He and Mark Hoback(of No Joe fame) were obviously cut from the same piece of cheese. They both occupy a kind of limbo that is neither new nor old. Not for everybody.--DS

ERIC RANDOM-"23 SKIDOO"/"SUBLIMINAL"
Les Disques Du Crepuscule
Call me an old fart,an ex fan of Guru
Guru,or a schizophrenic hypocrite但but
Eric Random has just released 2 incredible singles-are we not ignoramous puck
rockers or am I talking to myself?Ser-
iously if there's any one else out there
who goes for this speak to me or forever
hold your hoodus-this music transcends
labels and categories and if I hear any
Cab Voltaire references I'll spit and
violate something or somebody,,,while
I'm listening to this record of course...

GODS TOYS-"EVERYBODY'S GOT A MOTHER"/PACKAGE
TOURS TO HEAVEN " Badge Records
The ultimate skunk piss,dung bag,neo psych-
adelia filled fuck disc the ils,I mean ILLS
I mean British Isles have ever had the gaul
to send this way...Don't make the same mistake that I did...

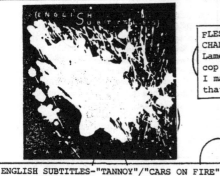

ENGLISH SUBTITLES-"TANNOY"/"CARS ON FIRE" Glass Records
Absolutely out depresses the rest...One band
member went to the subway during morning rush
hour and had a "friend" drive a 6 inch nail
through his hand into a block of wood-the sleeve was screened from a sheet of plastic that
caught his blood...let's face it even DS's dad
couldn't council these guys out of their desperate state...this is single #2 for this band-
the first being the "Time Tunnel"(all time TV
favorite) classic on Small Wonder...Not a trace
of optimism on this one-lots of imagery in "C
ars On Fire" but not much relevance to what is
obviously weighing so heavily on their collective minds...an outlet?Just another single?A
little of both...

THE TAN-"HOW COOL ARE YOU?"/WHO INVENTED SUN-
DAYS?"/"360"/"STOP SIGN"
It's funny ,when you do a mag some combos that
have never seen your rag think "Oh I'll send
them our record and they'll give it the hearty
""Rave up"Lots of publications further this
little cutesy underground "wer'e all in this

together so let's kiss each others ass
philosophy" that does nothing but lead
those incapable of any independant decision making down one dead road after anoth-

THE DANSE SOCIETY-"CLOCK"/ "CONTINENT"
Society Records
No period derivation here-one side rides
the cosmopolitan fringe,and the flip is
equally talent laden but quite opposite
in approach-both work incredibly well-
there's an air of mystery about this band that lingers after repeated playings-
That's about all I can say I'ts that great...

SLIVERS-"RESTRAINT FOR STYLE EP" NEW
ALLIANCE RECORDS
We thought since it was recorded in
Hermosa Beach and it was engineered
by SPOT it would be good,but Jack we
was wrong!

FLESHTONES-"ALL AROUND THE WORLD"/THE WORLD HAS
CHANGED" IRS(A&M)
Lame glitter band sound on this old remake-they
cop a million sounds none of which work-besides
I make it a point to never listen to any records
that have harmonica on them...

ZOUNDZ-"DEMYSTIFICATION"/"ZOUNDZ" Rough
Trade
It's easier to write a bad review than it
is a good one but by the same token there's
alot more lameness than goodness in the
music kingdom...and so it goes...

er...What I'm getting at is there's no way
I'm going to even play the "You were nice
enough to send us your record,press kit,a nd
letter,so we'll give you a pleasant,bland and
copiously thorough little pump up" game with
something like this....I've got more respect
for my readers than that...

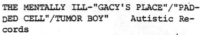

THE MENTALLY ILL-"GACY'S PLACE"/"PAD-
DED CELL"/TUMOR BOY" Autistic Records
2 year old Chicago release so why had-
'nt I heard of this before-probably because anything remotely unorthodox,and
non european gets squelched in the snot
filled windy shitty-the lamest big city
scene imaginable-but this is one great
disc-someone told me it's one of of Jello's faves and I can see why-the themes
are depraved and the band sound as if
they relish the thought of living to
their name...recorded sloppily with fu-
zzsaw guitar and haphazard vocals..find
it!!!

STAINS-"JOHN WAYNE WAS A NAZI"/"BORN
TO DIE"/Radical Records
What a hot one!Great everything-lyrics,
vocals,sloppy recording-that makes 2
whole bands in a state the size of my
dick we can get excited about...THE
HaTES and THE STAINS...the Bside has
a chorus that sticks-"NO WARS,NO KKK,
NO FASCIST USA" sung over a cool drum
beat-pec brained music that doesn't
get much better (especially out there
in the land of hats,spurs and yuchh!
armadillos,god I hate those things)
Comparisons to the now long since defunct
L.A. SKULLS are inevitable which would
undoubtedly hurt nobodys feelings-br-
idging the gap between greatness...

BLACK FLAG-"SIX PACK" SST Records
People are saying they don't like this
as much as "Jealous Again" but I say
bullshit this is the best thing they'
ve done in a long time..."I've Heard
It Before" and "American Waste" are
also on this and before you have a
chance to pick up on this there just
might be another single out according
to informed?sources...this one will
have Henry on vocals and will have
"Rise Above" and "Depression"...I'm
not sleeping too well waiting for that one....supposedly the band is going
to be hitting the midwest this fall
so it looks like we're in luck...

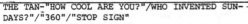

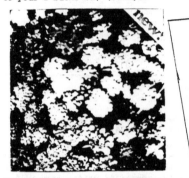

HUMAN HANDS--"Trains vs. Planes"/
"Blue Eel" IRS

Nothing here as brilliant as the "I
Got Mad" cut on the Darker Skratcher
LP. Actually this is terrible--sounds
not unlike a band from New York with
a bleach blonde on vocals--a very
new wave gravitation--Hue and Cry--
to your 2 bucks say goodbye.

SECTION 25--can't read the shit on
the sleeve Benelux Records

All the printing is in some foreign
language, gee it looks like French,
I hope it isn't cuz French=locust
shit-ok it sez made in Belgium that's
better, my old car was made there--
why was this damn record so expensive?--it sounds like the other one.
And they recorded the drums on one
side and forgot the other instuments.
These foreigners must be trying to
rip us off. I bet the European
copies are printed in real English
and there's probably instruments on
the B-side--besides Eric had this
guy named Pierre staying at his
house and he was from France and he
was typically wimpy, faggy, dorky--
he had two-tone topsiders on and
he tried to cut me down and French
people should go die--I hate them
more than Arabs, Iranians, or even
Dutch people!

45's reviewed by TESCO VEE

JC's MAINMEN-"CASUAL TROUSERS"/"EAR BENDING"
Fresh Records
The neither here nor there FRESH label
caught my eye on this one-this band features Arturo Bassick of the old LURKERS
and Eddie Case on drums among others-
front side is miserable pop-awful backup
vocals-the pits-the b side is as good as
the a side is bad...pounding drums &
Bar-room multi vocals...they got it half
right...

YOU'VE GOT FOETUS ON YOUR BREATH-"Wash It
All Off"   Self Immolation Records
A side is zany,and frivolous with an inane
guitar run and phrasing like
supercalifragilisticsadomasochistic...wot
fun we be havin' now Cleotis-a real laugh
riot...let's try the rubber vomit or the
doggie droppings or the fly-pin in dads
hotdog that should even top this for gags n'
thrills,,,uh oh suddenly we have the flip
to contend with this industrial high frequency annoyance-as different as night and
almost night-I cunt finger it out!!Twots
that?Tits alright we'll get the listener
all lightened up with a decidedly non-th-
reatenong tune-then shoot them off into the
world of bolex dementia...the plan is intact-

THE TEE VEES-"Doctor Headlove"/War Machine"
Good Vibrations Records
Everyone laughed at me when I bought this
bargain bin one off-I laughed along when
I played the A side-some off beat Jamaican
interpretation...But 'War Machine" is an
interesting piece sung in nasal tone with
effect...heavy theme-light pronunciation-
think I'll keep it...

SOUL-"TRIBES"/"LOVE" Cherry Red
A cross between alot of lightweight British bands- an unoriginal chorus on "Tribes" that talks about "the pictures on
my wall'and so on...heavy on rythym and
ideas-but sporting a rather bland pres-
entation-it just doesn't sound as new as
it could have...

SOFT CELL-TAINTED LOVE"/"WHERE DID OUR LOVE
GO" SBL
Their stll cloning the same old sound-
Depache Mode,Silent Types the list goes
on forever,,,my patience does not...

THE FALLOUT CLUB--"Dream Soldiers"/
"Pedestrian Walking" Happy Birthday
Records

Trevor is moving more toward high
ground on this, his second single.
Gone is the hypnosis of his earlier
effort--much as I like this record
I see the added electronics as an
act of confinement. . . his obvious
endowment of talent shouldn't be so
reliant on the forays of others. . .

VISITORS-"COMPATIBILITY"/"POETS END"
Rational Records
Taken at face value this single can be said
to blend in with many other recent releases-
But it posseses a dichotomy absent in most
Scottish bands particularly those on the
postcard label.It's that moody and mediatory creation that few bands can lay claim
to-that definition that makes or breaks a
single of this sort,,,With hundreds vying
for a place in the hallowed halls of the
genre of quiet intellectualism-VISITORS
are quite simply the most sagacious entry
in this months sweepstakes...A secular
classic...

FLUX OF PINK INDIANS--"Neu Smell"/
"Tube Disaster"/"Poem"/"Sick Butch-
ers"/"Background Of Malfunction"
Crass Records

Typically Crass in its condemnation
of those of us who still have this
somehow sick attraction for the
taste of meat. Let's attack not
only our political system but the
way we live as well. Maybe they
have a point however I see these
guys taking a rather self righteous
stance to the whole thing. As
though they've been right all along
and now they're gonna do a little
preaching. If you're at all interested, the music on this disc is
better than most Crass records.
Oh, it doesn't wander too far from
the original format, but this has
more drive and punch than most.
It's good, but I'm always wary of
those who take themselves a bit
too seriously. What's next. . .
vegetarians rule or something like
that?--DS

BUSH TETRAS--"Boom"/"Das Ah Riot"
Fetish Records

Big step forward. These girls have
graduated to a much fuller, denser
sound. More than likely, the result of having secured the backing
of some benevolent soul so as to
release a more professional product
(whatever that means). Shows all
the signs of that attempt to collar
a wider market. Pull some tricks
in the studio, make it sound a little more like everything else, and
you'll have the masses eating out
of your hand. Right?, well maybe.
They want to make it just like any
true blooded American, and now they
have gotten their chance, something
which may have eluded them had they
remained with 99. This record is
still distinctively BT's, and while
this was not intially intended to
be knock on the band, I prefer the
starchy uniqueness of the "Too Many
Creeps" disc. That was challenging
and fresh, and this is . . . well,
not so fresh.--DS

Some good
sheet, no?

SKI PATROL--"Cut"/"Faith In Transition Malicious Damage Records

Oh no, not another singer sounding
like he's on the brink of suicide.
Grab the old Gillette double edge
and get it over with, the sooner
the better. Generating a dreary
mood of desperation, so we'll feel
sorry for them, I guess. Should I
be moved by some poor pathetic soul
tortured by his neurosis? No thanx,
keep that shit away from me. There's
enough strife in the world without
having to subject ourselves to the
phony pain on some record. Music
for the mentally weak.--DS

DA--"Dark Rooms"/"White Castles"
Autumn Records

Chicago is funny in that they have
their ears focused intently on what
the hell is happening in Britain
while ignoring our own shores. DA
is a classic example in that even
before one side is over, you're
muttering to yourself; now they
sound like something I've heard
before, if I could only place it.
Trouble is, you do finally figure
it out. . . only to realize that
this town is full of technicians,
who while they may be very competent, don't have an original idea
among them. I'm almost embarrassed
to say who they sound like, the
resemblence is so clearcut. Alright
I'll spill the beans, the band I'm
refering to did a song called "Happy House", which comes closes to
what DA sounds like. A little like
any of the unsteadily wailing cuts
off of "The Scream", if you happen
to need more of a hint. DA sounds
fine, recorded very well, very clean,
but I just don't have an appetite
for this kind blatant emulation.--DS

ZYKLON--"Wir Sind"/"Gary, In"/"Part-
Time" Grim Records

Having little or no respect for GR,
this reocrd came as a surprise. Out
of the bible belt comes some irrever-
ently industrial noise, that will
quickly be labeled 'art damage' by
the majority of our readers. You
guys don't happen to paint in your
spare time, do ya? No affiliation
with Kendall, I hope. Anyway, these
guys and All Night Movies would have
been just jake together. Three guys
who were probably social outcasts in
school take their neuroses and put
it to music, just kidding fellas,
I'm no better judge of character
than the next Freudian hack. However your decision to record was a
bit premature, unless perhaps, this
is all you plan to do. The sound,
while original, lacks depth as
though it were standing still. Too
thin and one dimensional, "Gary, In"
works best simply because more instruments were used. To generate
any kind of atmosphere, you need to
operate on more than one plain.
Maybe I'm way out in left field on
this one, maybe your intention from
the start was the static approach,
hell what do I know.--DS

PLAY DEAD--"Poison Takes A Hold"/
"Introduction" Fresh Records

What a dud! Factoryesque vocals
superimposed on top of some delib-
erately plodding heavy metal punk,
obviously attempting to drive home
some profound message with their
oblique lyrics and a sluggishly
indifferent beat. Who cares, after
an infectual intro, they lost me.
Once, it's kinda interesting, second time around, well, let's just
say the surprise is gone. Fresh
flop number . . . uh, let me think
. . . shit I lost count.--DS

some chart, eh? - FF

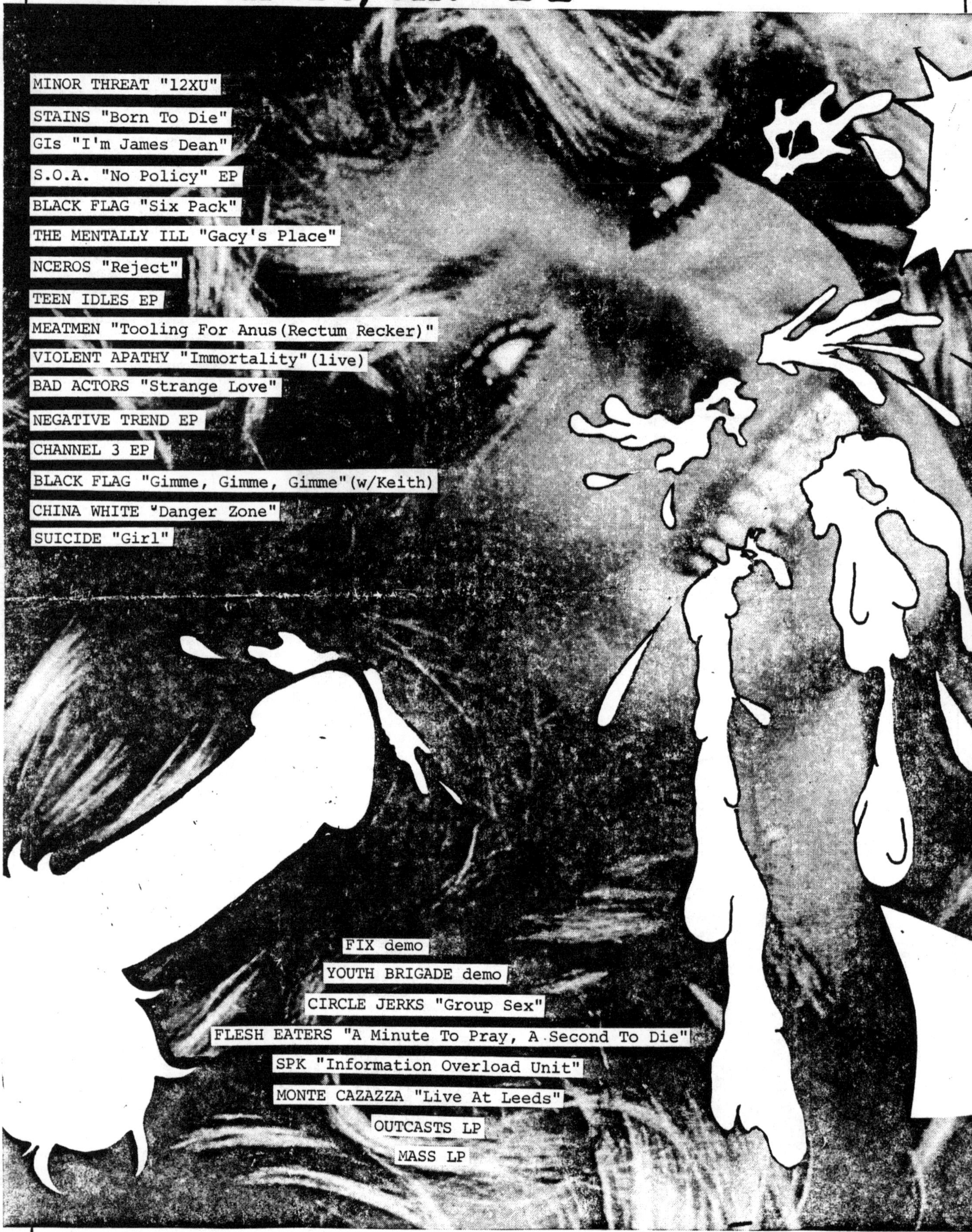
MINOR THREAT "12XU"
STAINS "Born To Die"
GIs "I'm James Dean"
S.O.A. "No Policy" EP
BLACK FLAG "Six Pack"
THE MENTALLY ILL "Gacy's Place"
NCEROS "Reject"
TEEN IDLES EP
MEATMEN "Tooling For Anus(Rectum Recker)"
VIOLENT APATHY "Immortality"(live)
BAD ACTORS "Strange Love"
NEGATIVE TREND EP
CHANNEL 3 EP
BLACK FLAG "Gimme, Gimme, Gimme"(w/Keith)
CHINA WHITE "Danger Zone"
SUICIDE "Girl"
FIX demo
YOUTH BRIGADE demo
CIRCLE JERKS "Group Sex"
FLESH EATERS "A Minute To Pray, A Second To Die"
SPK "Information Overload Unit"
MONTE CAZAZZA "Live At Leeds"
OUTCASTS LP
MASS LP

CHINA WHITE

DANGER ZONE

CHANNEL 3 EP   POSH BOY RECORDS
CHINA WHITE   "DANGER ZONE EP" FRONTIER
RECORDS

It's been a while since anything this
threatening came out of L.A. to back
up advanced hype...both of these releases are a welcome hard hitting pair-
that pick up where some of last years
releases left off...Where did CHANNEL 3
come from they are really exciting-eas-
ily the most aggressive thing posh Boy
has ever put out...and no wimpy vocals
like the ones that ruined the TSOL EP
Barry had to eat some crow and admit
that CHINA WHITE had come up with some
greatness because he was pretty down
on them because of a lame video tape-
but he bought it you know now he carries
it into the bathroom along with his
bottle of Rose Milk Lotion,his GENT
(Home Of The D-Cup Magazine)and his
assortment of french ticklers so when
he flogs his rib-eye he can groove on
some choice toonage...All in all the
greatest western stuff in along time!

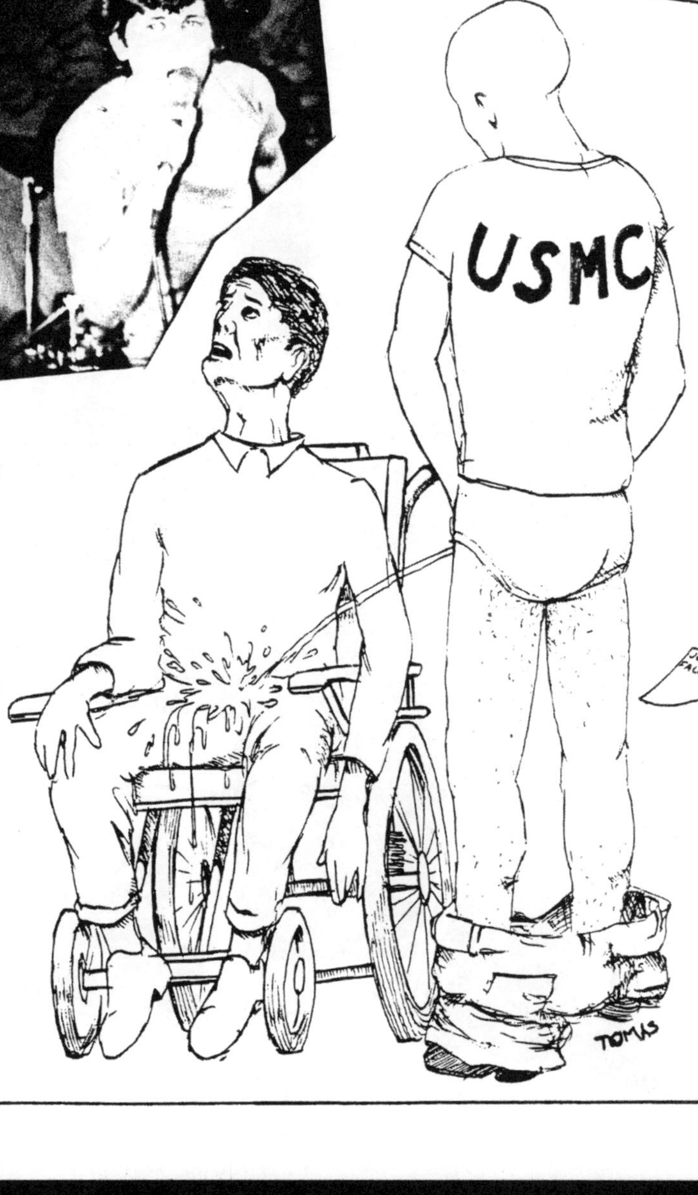

BIG BOYS AND THE DICKS -Recorded Live At
Rauls Club-Rat Race Records

Wholly pitoot Austin has one good band we
talk about elsewhere in this issue but watch out for both of these godawful turd-
balls-THE DICKS have a Divine type on vo-
cals-almost as good as SKUDDUR from Omaha-
They probably heard about this new music
thing down at the snakeskin cowboy boot
factory or something and thought "Hey
lets break into the hot Texas scene with
a fat guy in a nurses outfit-fans of DMZ
or LA PESTE will eat this record up-any
one with any taste will shit it out...
So on to the BIG BOYS....NO FUCK THE BIG
BOYS THIS IS SHIT AND I'M SHIT FOR BUYING
IT!!!

Keith in Joisey-THANX John...

Editors of Touch & Go,

    Some friends of mine and myself were
at the latest Fix show and about 10
minutes into the gig we see these 3 big
guys standing by the front of the stage
grabbing people and shoving them back
when they got too close to the stage.
People were just dancing nobody was
being threatening to the people on stage,
just enjoying themselves, that is, until
these big bouncer types started butting
in. Of course we started asking ourselves
who are these guys and started shoving
them back. At this point Steve (vocalist
for the Fix) leaned over to them and was
heard to say "Hey, leave those guys alone."
Right after that they started pretending
to dance right along with us like "Oh, were
just here to have fun". We found out after
the show that these 3 obeying brutes were a
mixture of roadies and roomates of the Fix.
I don't know if any of those guys in the
Fix had anything to do with it but it sure
looked like th'y did, that's an undeniable
fact, just ask anybody who was up front
dancing. If I want to be disciplined
at a show I'll go see a Led Zepplin concert,
or is that who the Fix think they are?

*I agree but only to a point-Im sure the
band put nobody up to that-And besides
we had some targets so we didn't beat
each other you dig?*

JERRY FALLWELL

USMC

TOM'S

THE BEST OF ALL WORLDS...

523 E. LIBERTY
ANN ARBOR, MI
48104
(313) 994-5103

'T and G

NUMBER 15 $1.00

16

Was Nothing Sacred a real DC super
group? Hell, I don't remember... Nice
Chris Bald cover artwork nonetheless,
and the first appearance of many of the
Bazooka Morris comics. What a stellar
lineup of interviewees here: Bad
Religion, Misfits, Negative Approach,
Red C; virtually all US coverage now.
No need to worship from afar; there
was enough aggro in our own backyards
to keep us fat and happy... Okay,
Steve Soto was fat, but we were happy.
Imagine this: On another junket to DC,
we went to a basement party somewhere
in Maryland and the lineup was—drum
roll—Minor Threat/Artificial Peace/
Youth Brigade/Red C/Iron Cross/
Deadline, and Nothing Sacred... Okay,
they were a band! Christ, I really
should have been paying attention...
How'd you like to have a time machine
and go back for that little hardcore
hootenanny? If video cameras hadn't
been the size of Buicks back then, I
coulda shot that shindig for posterity.
I still have the husk of a memory of it,
and will carry it to my grave.

TOUCH & GO

CROSSED HANDS CLOSED EYES

NOTHING IS SACRED

no.16 $1

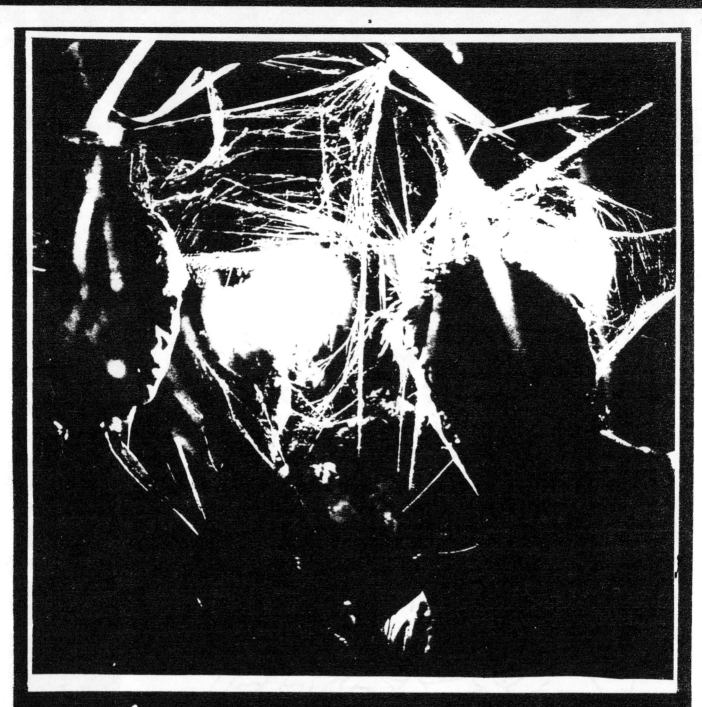

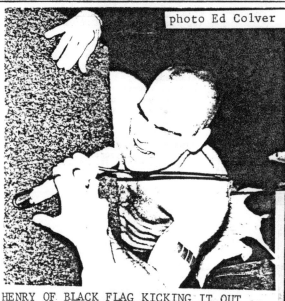

photo Ed Colver

WHAT TYPE OF MAN READS TOUCH AND GO?WHY A MAN WHO WEARS UNDER- WEAR ON HIS HEAD OF COURSE!!!BUT EVEN IF YOU AREN'T INTO SUCH ANTICS YOU CAN ENJOY T&G BY SENDING US YOUR MONEY YOU DIG???

#16

ALL CONTENTS TV UNLESS
OTHERWISE NOTED.......

ABBA MADE 64 MILLION
DOLLARS LAST YEAR...

HENRY OF BLACK FLAG KICKING IT OUT
THEIR NEW ALBUM SHOULD BE OUT SOON...

TOUCH and GO

BOX 26203 LANSING,MI 48909

SPECIAL THANX TO IAN MACKAYE,MORTICIA,
SHREDDER,JEFF NELSON,CHRIS BALD(for the
bitchin cover)SAB,VIVIEN,BAD RELIGION,
WASTED YOUTH)BERTO,MIKE WATT,D.BOON,
HENRY GARFIELD,ABBIE,BRIAN POLLACK,NE-
CROS,GEORGE,LORI

RARE PHOTO OF
NOTHING SACRED
BY MORTICIA

(this issue
dedicated to
the hatred of
French people,
armadillos,
Detroit fags,
pretty girls,
and drugs...

NECROS

VIOLENT APATHY
NEGATIVE APPROACH
BORED YOUTH
SUBURBAN ANGER

AT NUNZIO'S
SAT.,NOV.21
$4

all on TOUCH & GO RECORDS POB 26203 LANSING,MI.48909

SUPPORT MIDWEST HARDCORE   NECROS 9 SONG ep OUT NOW   PROCESS OF ELIMINATION ep OUT LATE NOV.   N.A. ep soon

LAFF IT UP!!!

S'AM

LYRICS

ROCK AND ROLL BULLSHIT by GI'S
Now I've got it I'm insane
Van Halen gives me a pain
And Supertramp gives me a cramp
And I don't want to go to camp
  And I don't wanna listen to it
  You don't wanna dance to it
  We don't wanna hear it
  Rock and Roll bullshit
I used to listen to the Clash
Now they suck like all the trash
The Ramones used to be a hit
Now they're just a pile of shit

MARK   SAB   DANTE

FREEDOM by IRON CROSS
It's such a bitch man
when you're on the streets
It's even worse
When they start to constrict
Feel so bad when you have no choice
Too bad you have no voice
  Young dog hasn't got a home
  Fuck you I don't want a bone
  Man all I want's my fucking freedom
Find yourself searching but all
Their doors are locked
Try and find the right road
But all the ways are blocked
      Sab 81

IN MY EYES by MINOR THREAT
You tell me you like the taste
You just need an excuse
You tell me it calms your nerves
You just think it looks cool
You tell me you want to be different
You just change for the same
You tell me it's only natural
You just need the proof
     (DID YOU FUCKING GET IT?)
It's in my eyes,in my eyes
And it doesn't look that way to me
In my eyes
You tell me that nothing matters
You're just fuckin' scared
You tell me that I'm better
You just hate yourself
You tell me that you like her
You just wish you did
You tell me that I make no difference
At least I'm fucking trying
    (WHAT THE FUCK HAVE YOU DONE?)
It's in my eyes,in my eyes
And it doesn't look that way to me
In my eyes
     Thanks alot,"Friends"
(MacKaye,Preslar,Baker,Nelson)

OUT OF STEP by MINOR THREAT
Don't smoke
Don't drink
Don't fuck
At least I can fuckin' think
Can't keep up(3 times)
Out of step with the world(MacKaye/
               Preslar)

PRESSURE'S ON by RED C
Laws on my back
Pressure's always on
Never able to do things on my own
The way we dress
Disturbs them all
They push us against the wall
They tell me my rights
Just because I fight
Can't understand at all
(chorus)
They keep their eyes on us
Ready for a bust,can't understand at all
(chorus)
The way we dress

GUILT OF BEING WHITE by MINOR THREAT
I'm sorry
For something I didn't do
Lynched somebody
But I don't know who
You blame me for slavery
Yet it was a hundred years before I was born

Guilty of being white

I'm a convict
Of a racist crime
I've only served
19 years of my time

Guilty of being white

SKINHEAD GLORY by IRON CROSS+
You always come and put us down
Say we're vicious
Or just following fashion
But you don't know the feeling
When we put the boot in
Skinhead glory
Skinhead youth
We know why we scare you
It's because we know the truth
Skinhead glory
Skinhead youth
Kids with shaven heads
Kids with heavy boots
Kids that won't listen to you
Kids that see the truth
Skinheads going crazy
Skinheads going wild
Skinheads going out tonight
and running to the fights
Tomorrows youth is really mad
coz we see no life
      by Sab Decay

NEW YORK ROTS

N.Y. is a place thats worth just about as much as the scum under your toe nail. The Undead with Bobby Steele are pretty great tho. They even wrote a whole song dedicated to our fair city. They are supposedly going to put out an e.p. in Oct. Well at least thats one thing to look forward to. The Misfits should be around soon and with them hopefully The Necros will open up. I've yet to see a N.Y. band with half as much energy as The Necros. When they played at club 57 with the Circle Jerks and the Stimulators The Necros, even tho they claimed it was one of their worst gigs ever, made the Stimulators look like watered-down pieces of shit.
Even Worse know they suck but thats a bit of an understatement. I think of Even Worse when I catch a whiff of one of Al's evil farts. The Bad Brains play around a lot. That makes up partly for N.Y.'s output of faggot maggot bands cause they are definitely not as fuck. Kraut are yet another N.Y. attempt at being boring and unoriginal. They succeed. They also have this strange obsession with cabbage. Kraut live are about as energetic as bowel movements. The False Prophets have a 3-song e.p. out called "Blind Obedience" thats really good. Unfortunately their bass player's jaw was busted by some considerate soul outside A-7 so they haven't played lately. Reagan Youth I liked. I saw them with the Undead and Kraut. They didn't quite have their shit together that night but I'd see them again. Oh yeah X played at the Ritz-(how utterly shiek) For a staggering $8.50. I didn't go and at that price I really couldn't care less. Thats about it.
      A. Mahler

THANX Abbie!

LETTERS

To Readers of T&G;
The August 13 FIX show at Ricks Cafe seemed to draw alot of fire on the FIX in regard to the "goon squad"- two "brawny assholes" in particular. First of all to blame The FIX for the stupid actions of these people is ridiculous.We neither need nor want protection from our fans.I have much respect for our fans.It says alot for people who support a scene in such a culturally backwards conservative area like the midwest.No we did not set these people up for our protection.Yes they did take it upon themselves to protect the band.They are aquaintences of the band who have no understanding of the scene.That is their problem.They now know they are not welcome.Nuff said-Thanx for coming to the show.FUCK EVERYBODY ELSE...

STEVE FIX

P.S.TV and DS actually seemed to take care of those apes pretty well...

Okay I admit that I think you guys are ignorant hillbillies,But look,Hey,I don't blame you for it.All the brides we ordered came from Mich.(who else would have come?)And they were good too until they all died.We offered to freeze em' up and send them to the Mormons(waste not want not we always say)But at the time they were getting in big trouble for having too many of them(huh?ED.)Finally we put them up for auction and got a very decent price from a political organization called the True Sons Of Liberty.I dunno what they did with them(target practice?) And I don't care.Hey Ho.Ya'll must come visit sometime.Your Pal   J

And all this time I figured it was the cultural dissemination of those gol' durned brides that was accounting for the diversity of tastes in your OP mag-(you know classical,reggae,rock,puck, folk,hat dancing music,gamelan,jazz etc.) Now I'll just have to lay awake some more thinking...pondering just why...(it aint easy sleeping in early Sept. anyway cuz you know that's when they spread the manure...and I might as well tell you there are people in my town that fuck livestock-and this kid that stole my bike has obvious mental deficencies so I asked one local just what his problem was and the guy told me he was at a party where this theifs older brother made him blow him in front of everyone so that explains it sort of doesn't it John baby? Ask my friends I never lie so I can't lie and tell you I liked your bands demo a whole lot...a tad mite,tidbit maybe...Actually I havn't heard anything so unique since I sold my Capsicum Red LPs and if that makes sense I'll respect you forever...TV

Dear Tesco-Sorry about the picture of T&G in here,somehow part of it got erased.We got a good laugh saying you lost your "touch" but that ain't true, last ish was great!When you gonna interview the NECROS for us huh?Oh well keep in touch, AL(FLIPSIDE)
Das cool mon gee whiz even having our mag in your mug I mean mug in your mag is like putting me into another dimension you know like FLIPSIDE is the icon,mentor,big brother(sorry Hud)of every rag east or west of etc.Thanx to you....

THANKS TO SHREDDER FOR the following choice LA column...

EVERYBODY KNOWS THOSE LETTERS STAND FOR LOBOTOMIZED ASSHOLES
IT'S A HUNDRED MILLION FUCKING DEGREES OUTSIDE.FEAR IS AT WORK ON AN ALBUM PRODUCED BY REO SPEEDWAGON'S PRODUCER GARY LUBOW,A FRIEND OF DERF'S SINCE HIGH SCHOOL.BLACK FLAG RETURNS WITH HENRY AT THE VOCAL NOISE PLAYING DAYTIME SHOWS AT THE CUCKOO'S NEST(FUCK YOU JERRY ROACH) THE CIRCLE JERKS RETURN AND PLAY THE WHISKEY.AUDIENCE TEARS THE PLACE UP AND ONCE AGAIN IT'S THE END OF HARDCORE AT THE WHISKEY.WASTED YOUTH AND OZIEHARES TAKE OVER THE CITY,SEVENTEENTH GENERATION OF PUNK.ADOLESCENTS DEMOLISH,RICK REFORMS FIRST BAND),TONY IS LEFT IN THE COLD OF ANAHEIM(SIC)DE DE(NOT DO DO)IS BACK AND REFORMING U.X.A.AND THE CARTUNES.CHINA WHITE RELEASES THEIR SIX SONG ALBUM,IS THAT PUNK ROCK?NINE MINUTE SONGS?T.S.O.L. GOES HORROR METAL,TO JOIN THE RANKS OF THE EVER POPULAR 45 GRAVE,BONEHEADS(IF THEY DON'T COVER THE MUNSTERS THEME THEY SHOULD)AND THE NOW NON-EXISTENT CASTRATION SQUAD.GERMS EP AND GUN CLUB LP OUT ON SLASH,GET EM YOU RETARDED FROG.RODNEY BINGENHEIMMER'S SHOW IS CUT IN HALF,THE GUY CELEBRATED HIS FIFTH ANNIVERSARY,BABY POWDER AND VASELINE AND ALL,PSYCHEDELICVELVETUNDERGROUNDETC.BANDS APHOCOCULTURE AND KOMMUNITY FK BECOME THE DARLINGS OF HOLLYWOOD.TOMATA DU PLENTY AND K.K. COME BACK TO LIFE IN THE WORST PRESENTATION TO COME ALONG IN YEARS.AS FOR LOCAL PRINT FLIPSIDE,PARANOIA,NIGHT VOICES CONTAGION,RAG IN CHAINS(A SLOWLY DYING MYTH)POSEUR,ETC.CLUBS ABOUND THIS SUMMER,THOUGH NONE AS HARDCORE AS LAST SUMMERS' FLEETWOOD.CATHY DE GRANDE,PUTTING ON SHOWS OF L.A.'s OUTER REACHES,INCLUDING THE BENEFIT FOR DERF SCRATCHE'S FACE.THE POOR FUCKER GOT THE SHIT KICKED OUT OF HIM AT THE STARDUST SHOW.THEY ALSO HAVE BLUE MONDAY FEATURING TOP JIMMY,AND A GOODBYE PARTY FOR PROMOTER BUNKY.THE VEX AND BARDS APPOLLO KEEP OPENING AND CLOSING IN THE GRAND OLE STARWOOD FASHION.IF ANY OF YOU SAW THE DECLINE AND PARTICULARLY HATED THOSE SCENES WITH EUGENE YOU TOO WILL BE HAPPY TO KNOW THAT A FEW MONTHS AGO AT THE VEX AN ENTIRE CROWD OF CIRCLE JERKS FANS BEGAN TO MOCK HIS LINES AND SMACK HIS FACE.'MEMBER WHEN EV'ERYBODY WAS SCREAMIN' BOUT THOSE "TOO ROWDY" BEACH SUBURBANITES?WELL IT SEEMS THAT YESTERDAYS NEWFOLKS ARE TODAYS INCROWD,AND THE VALLEY HAS TAKEN OVER AS THE SCAPE GOAT FOR CRITISM OF VIOLENCE.GOLLY THIS WHOLE TOWN. IS BEING TAKEN OVER,WHO'S NEXT?"MAYBE THERE'LL BE A HARDCORE BURBANK OR GLENDALE SCENE," SAYS JEFFREY LEA OF GUN CLUB.I'M SURE THE PEOPLE FROM WHERE YOU ARE HAVE TOLD YOU THAT X HAS PLAYED THE GREEK THEATRE,A HUGE STADIUM.NOW LOOK PUSSYHEADS,JUST 'COS X DOESN'T HAVE A SKINHEAD ONLY AUDIENCE-AND THEIR SOUND IS MORE DIVERSE THAN THREE CHORD-BEAT UP YOR GRANNY-SLAMBAMBOOM MUSIC X IS STILL ONE OF THE HARDEST CORE(WHAT A DUMB PHRASE)BANDS IN TOWN. THEY'VE BARELY EVEN MADE ENOUGH BUCKS TO MOVE OUT OF THEIR ONE ROOM FLAT.ON THE LIGHTER SIDE OF THINGS THE MEDIA IS STARTING YO TAKE A MORE INTELLIGENT VIEW OF L.A. HARDCORE.NO MORE LINES LIKE:PUNK ROCK VIOLENCE,FUN AND GAMES OR

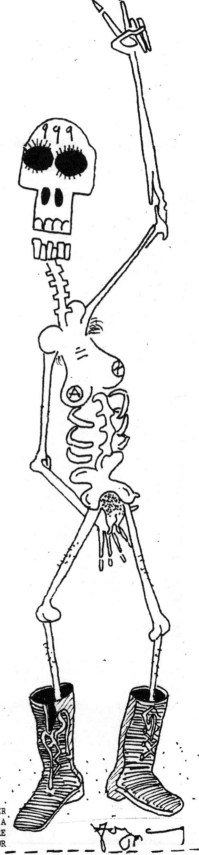

LIVE SHIT →

THE FIX/THE MEATMEN live at the Coronation Tavern Windsor, Ont.

You had to be there to believe it. Taking my word for it just won't do. There I was, standing in this scummy little dive, waiting for the Meatmen to make their first public appearance. What might have been nothing more than a pipe dream a month ago is no joke now . . these guys are for real. Cut their teeth on some Canadian slime before takin'

Sexist? you tell me. Offensive, of course, check out one of their lyric sheets for some more tasty gems. They're the only band on the local scene that takes such an uncompromisingly irreverent stand on absolutely everything. Nothing is held so sacred that it could avoid the wrath of the Meatmen stomp. As a closing thought, the Fix were great, they're always great.--DS

Momma!

PATHETIX/JERRYS KIDS/NEGATIVE APPROACH/NECROS/
MEATMEN/YOUTH PATROL/VIOLENT APATHY---Endless
Summer Skateboard Park   Oct.3

Kinda late in the year up in these here parts to throw an outdoor gig...but the weather held out...this was the coolest thing Detroit has ever had...finally a place where kids could go to hear some bands they'd heard about but never had an oppurtunity to see because of the fucked up bars who never throw any under 18 nites because then they wouldn't sell any fuckin' booze-you can take every lame bar with it's ultra gay employees in the whole motor city and chuck em' in the river...because this gig proved we don't need those assholes...the crowd was damn good-probably 3 or 400 came and went before the night was over(hey for here thats alot)I got a little depressed when the PATHETIX came out because they epitomize what a Detroit band would inevitablbly do to loudfast music...turn it into a pile of putrid pose...let's jump up and kick out like Weller or Townsend...let's strut way out into the (rapidly retreating)crowd-two guitar players playing the same chords-ya right...fuck off you wimps-besides you painted your little logo over the cool 3D Dukowski NO VALUES on the back of Bookies so when BLACK FLAG comes back in November they told me their gonna find you and kick your fuckin' butts...JERRYS KIDS were bad-real bad but this was probably their first gig so I'll give them the benefit of the doubt...
OK on to NEGATIVE APPROACH-words are gointo fail me here this band blows me away no two ways about...they could occupy any stage anywhere and hold their own...the singer has a fuckin powerful voice-like Ron on the Decline but with much more power and intensity...the crowd launched into a bruising bash they'd been waiting to do but the first two bands hadn't given them anything to headbang about...all I can say is go see em' they'll impress...‗‗‗‗‗‗‗‗...twas a shame VA couldn't finish their set because what they did sounded great...at least we got to hear IMMORTALITY" and La Bamba" but they had just driven 150 miles-there was an off duty cop that broke it up(as well as when three carloads of grits showed up with sticks)All in all it was fun as shit-a breath of life for everybody...

on the world. And that's just what will happen when people get wind(you know, the kind you break) of what these sickoes are all about. Oh, they're hardcore alright, don't fret about that, but it goes a lot deeper than your basic three chord slam in a spray of sweat and blood. Other bands play music. . . the Meatmen perform a twisted brand of carnage on stage that is, quite simply, beyond comparison. If the crowd isn't jeering and berating the band by the time their halfway thru their first song, then they've fucked up, the band, that is. With a shamelessly blunt Tesco Vee on vocals, the Meatmen expose our most fundamental inhibitions, grab them by the foreskin, and grind them back into the blushed countenance of our embarrassment. This is the stuff other bands wouldn't touch with even Mr. Watson's pole. . . it's too close to home. Go the political route, why not?, that's safe, and besides, everybody's doing it, but start singing about the dilemma or joy(as the case may be) of bashing the bishop three or four times a week and you've transcended the crap that's spewed at us from all the rest. Comes out of nowhere and hits you where you live. Sink your teeth into these choice lines from "I'm Glad I'm Not A Girl"---
'they look for love/we look for meat/ they think that's bad/we think that's neat . . . not being able to choose your fuck/ cuz some schmuck might beat you up/no fun like that in this world/just because you are a girl'.

HAVIN' SUM FUN...

NEGA APPRO

334

GERMS | WHAT WE DO IS SECRET

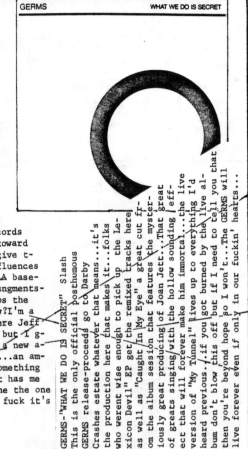

ANTI PASTI-"THE LAST CALL" Rondolet Records
With all the English"new punk" flooding the
bins these days one must be more tactful with his/her bucks cuz there's a burn mastered
every day...CHRON-GEN,4 SKINS,VICE SQUAD,EX-
PLOITED,INFRA RIOT,ANTI PASTI=shit,absolute
fucking putrid,boring shit...who the fuck a-
re they kidding??? Listen to any old SHAM 69,
UPSTARTS,or UK SUBS cut and then listen to
this new limey grunt...pretty funny innit?
OK so you're an avowed punk rocker and you'll
defend it to the death-you are a bastion for
the "hardcore"..you stand alone and wish this
"new punk" was listenable-you may even have
yourself convinced that it's hot..it's new
so it must be great=besides you just shelled
out 9.99 for this new ANTI PASTI album and
it would be a cardinal sin to admit you bought
a dog right?Wake up...get your heads outa your
arses long enough to see what this shit is-c-
leverly packaged redundancy-it's time to close
off some avenues and realize there's more relevant bands in our backyard no matter where we
are,that desperately need support...

THE GUN CLUB-"FIRE OF LOVE" Ruby Records
Although admitedly not predisposed toward
this type of music I can't help but give t-
his a hearty thumbs up.The bands influences
unequivocally point away from it's LA base-
there's a cajun,C&W feel to the arrangments-
whilst maintaining a drive that keeps the
whole thing entertaining.Old r&r?New?I'm a
bit befuddled as to just exactly where Jeff
Lea and companies' inspiration lies but I g-
ive them an A+ for approaching from a new a-
ngle and trying something different...an amalgm of styles,or the creation of something
totally new?Whatever-GUN CLUBS debut has me
asking myself why I'm so enamored one the one
hand...but on the other who gives a fuck it's
a great album...

GERMS-"WHAT WE DO IS SECRET" Slash
This is the only official posthumous
GERMS release-proceeds go to Darby
Crashes estate whatever that means...it's
the production here that makes it...folks
who werent wise enough to pick up the Lexicon Devil" EP get the remixed tracks here
as well as "Caught in My Eye" a great cut from the album session that features the myster-
iously great producing of Joan Jett..That great
of greats singing with the hollow sounding effect that will forever make him immortal...the live
version of "My Tunnel" lives up to everything I'd
heard previous..if you got burned by the live album don't blow this off but if I need to tell you that
then you're beyond hope so I won't...The GERMS will
live forever even if only in our fuckin' hearts...

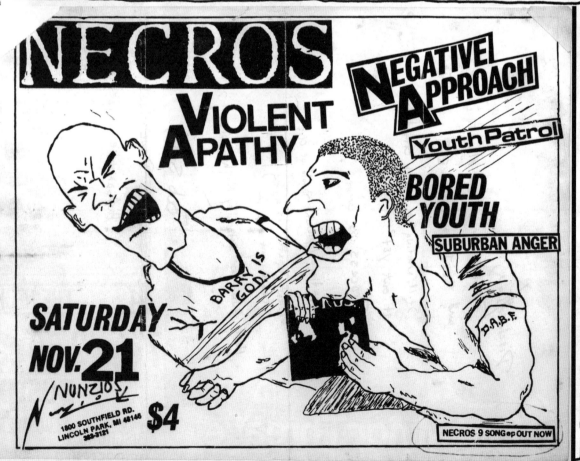

NECROS
VIOLENT APATHY
NEGATIVE APPROACH
Youth Patrol
BORED YOUTH
SUBURBAN ANGER

SATURDAY NOV.21
NUNZIO'S
1800 SOUTHFIELD RD.
LINCOLN PARK, MI 48146
382-3121
$4

NECROS 9 SONG ep OUT NOW

Subscriptions
$5
for 3
Issues
post paid...

from↓

touch and go
BOX 26203 LANSING,MI 48909

335

OUT SOON: D.C. 12" SAMPLER 30 SONGS BY: TEEN IDLES, UNTOUCHABLES, S.O.A., G.I.s, ARTIFICIAL PEACE, RED C, YØUTH BRIGADE, DEADLINE, MINOR THREAT, BEAVER, VOID, LAW & ORDER, IRON CROSS...

DISCHORD

Out Nov.-2nd Minor Threat e.p. Possible e.p. by Yøuth Brigade.

THE TEEN IDLES

1 8 SONGS minor disturbance E.P.

S.O.A

2 10 SONGS NO POLICY E.P.

MINOR THREAT

3 8 SONGS

GOVERNMENT ISSUE Legless Bull E.P.

10 SONGS

4 1/2 9 songs THE NECROS

7" e.p.s $2.50 each postpaid

SWINGIN' SINGLES BY DS...

SOLGER--"I Hate It"/"Raping Dead Nuns"
"Aman"/"American Youth"/"Dead Soldier"

I'll say quite emphatically that this record is one of those quintessential punk classics(whatever that's suppose to mean--ED). As great as it is poorly recorded, these brutes from Seattle have redefined the meaning of hardcore. Underneath an incredibly crummy production comes this rumbling commotion of guitars and drums. Nowhere near distinct, it's more like one long ominous fuzzy drone with some angst-torn tough shouting the lyrics. One can only speculate on what kind of havoc would have been wrought had they the money to do it right. Maybe they did. Greatness never sounded so bad. If you're gonna own one record, it's gotta be this one. --DS

THE MISFITS--"London Dungeon"/"Horror Hotel"/"Ghouls Night Out" Plan 9

Good, but far from my favorite Misfits' disc. They've slowed things down too much for my taste. Although on the A-side, there's no denying the fact that that Danzig guy can sing, he's nothing short of great. Don't let this review dissuade from seeing the band live. They are quite simply the best band I have ever seen(check out TV's live page elsewhere in this rag).--DS

THE TOOLS--EP#3
Subterranean Records

"Jeepers Whitey, why'd you go and do a creepy thing like that?" "Aw come off it, Beave, that ain't half as bad as this new Tools record." "Well, I don't know, let's go ask Wally, Hey Wally! have you listened to my Tools single yet?" "I'll say, I played it for Eddie Haskel and he went ape on me before the first song was over, and get this, they got a girl singing on it." "Kripes Wally, if I were a girl, I'd rather be dead." "Me too".--DS

MEAT PUPPETS--"In A Car"/"Big House"
"Dolphin Field"/"Out In The Gardner"
"Foreign Lawns" World Imitation Records

Definitely the big surprise of the issue. Come out of Phoenix with no particular look to speak of and start blowing people's shit away. Wildly hardcore and eclectic all on the same record. But that's not the whole story. They throw in a couple of curve balls along with their break-neck excursions of slothful pandemonium. "Big House" and "Out In The Gardner" not only have going: duh, what kind of shit is this?, but they also act as catapults for the fast stuff--cool things out for a sec, then POW! we get whupped upside the hade. Brain damage was never this much fun.--DS

BLITZ--"All Out Attack" EP
No Future Records

Best Oi band I've heard yet. About the hottest metallic assault you're gonna hear. A lot more crunch than the stuff from Discharge. I don't know about the 4 Skins, but these guys could whip the Gray Panthers into a frenzy. Great snarling vocalistwho must've been weened on Skrewdriver. They say punks' not dead.. . the proof's right here.--DS

4 SKINS--"One Law For Them"/"Brave New World" Clockwork Fun Records

A lot of adverse hype on these guys and they're already legends in their own time. Unfortunately the music doesn't come near my expections. Not exactly the kind of stuff I'd consider riot material. Granted, I'm overstating the issue, but they give us nothing 'cept for an accurate interpretation of early Ruts, big deal, file this one along with The Exploited, if you catch my drift.--DS

IRON CROSS (thats SAB with the braces)

PHOTO BY SUZIE J.

IRON CROSS is a band from Wash.DC-their vocalist Sab agreed to do an interview...
TV:You saw THE UNDEAD?
Sab:THE UNDEAD WERE BORING...I don't like the fast shit anyhow I'm bored of it-BLACK FLAGS great THE CIRCLE JERKS are boring in concert-but like MODERN WARFARE you can have that stuff...that's why I like the English shit...
TV:Is that what you're trying to do with your band?
Sab:Well like a cross cuz some of the LA shit is good and I like English stuff but we're not English so we can't sing about getting beat over the heads by Pakistanians,but the style is great-I like songs where you can sing along and get up on stage and shit...
TV:Do you have problems with the OI tag?
Sab:that sort of solved itself now,like everyone thought Ian and I hated each other...like we were criticizing each other supposedly without ever meeting each other face to face and by the time what we supposedly said got through it was total bullshit...some people give us shit about it but it's more in fun.
TV:Do you have problems in GEorgetown?
Sab:Occasionally-I got chased by Marines once that scared the shit outa me-you can't fight a marine-like with a grit or a redneck you've got a chance but Marines are trained to kill
TV:So what's going to happen to scene in DC...
Sab:It's either going to get really big or it's going to die out
Like now there's nothing going on
TV:No shows at the 9;30?
Sab:She's not going to hire bands cuz it's all kids and most of us don't drink so we don't give the bar any business...that's going to be a problem cuz our drummer is 14 and our guitarist is 13...I'm 18 and Wendels 15...I feel old...
TV:Don't feel too old...
Sab:I like to go back to Baltimore once in awhile...you see more real people-I saw this guy on the bus who had lumps all over hi face like leprosy...Baltimore is great if you like to watch cripples-

TV:What do you think of all these NF people getting thrown in jail?People in the media are calling them new nazi's and shit...
Sab:Msot of them don't give a shit about politics...sure there are Næi s to a certain extent I'm a Nazi everyone is

Alec:Everybodys racist not nazi necessarily...
Sab:Blacks are the biggest racists

TV:So...what do you think about DISCARGE?
Sab:Boring...all they do is sing about war...
DS:Same with CRASS?
Sab:Definately their just hippies...it's not love and peace time it's throwing bricks time I mean how can they fuckin' preach when the world is falling around our shoulders???

A TAPE REVIEW....

SUICIDE-"½ ALIVE" Cassette REACHOUT International Records...
New Yorks most original band right?This tape is a combination old live performances and home tapes...SUICIDE was playing this type of music since before DEPACHE MODE and the like even gave being in a band a second thought(which was probably last week)The only band capable of playing electronics w/ real feeling...the quivering Alan Vega will for years be the one looked to as the mentor of modern electro music at least by those with half an awareness of what he and Martin Rev have accomplished in the last 10 years-They transcend labels and totally ride without trends...shit they set them...If you haven't heard SUICIDE by now it might be too late...All I can say is I'll stake it all on the inventivness and brilliance of the material on th-

⩔

HE WAY WE SEE it- YOU ARE JUST LIKE YOUR PARENTS. DULL.

LP'2

cabaret
voltaire
red mecca

CABARET VOLTAIRE-"RED MECCA" Rough Trade
Easily their worst effort...from what I'd
read in the English Press I was expecting
some sort of all encompassing effort from one of my all time faves.I think Andy
Gill even went so far as to call this the
most important album in ten years or some
such shit...maybe I'm missing some obvious
overstatement,but this lacks the vitality
of even their live releases...they've shucked their monolithically rythmic approach
and seem to have found a friend in their
synthesizers' horn stop...a noise that takes from their overall sound in that it
gets grossly overused...they aren't quite
at the "going through the motions"phase but
this LP has me a bit worried...each of the
other three LPs have jumped forward as if
propelled by some mysterious divine inspiration...maybe it's just this boy but suddenly they aint sounding so new...but I
should clarify...even though this may not
be the bands most inspired effort,it still
ranks as one of the LP's of the year-they
just plain occupy that place in the peerless
pantheon of all time greatness....

CHUNKS

CHUNKS-NEW ALLIANCE RECORDS
Holy poop I'm not much on samplers but wait
a minute this one just changed my mind....
side one has no equal-all the greats are
here...starting off with one of L.A.'s coolest the DESCENDENTS..."Global Probing"is a
fast song that keeps getting faster...watch
for a new EP out as you read...CHEIFS are n-
ext with a new singer and another great song
"The Lonelys' is much more intense than the

stuff of their EP(BUT that stuff is classic
also)MINUTEMEN are next with "Clocks" another
venture into destruction of the time signature
as we know it...and it's over before you know
it...BLACK FLAG's "Machine" is next with Dez
on vocals...a little more bass would've been
in order on the mix-I've got a live tape where
they do dat one and I poop my briefs every ti-
me(aren't you jealous?)What can be said about
the STAINS cept' they're probably the coolest
(meanest?I hear the singer is merciless against
stage divers)new?band I've heard out there-
(well shit you know how carried away I get)
"Sick And Crazy" sez it all-nothing else my limp
commentary can do...

Uh oh now I've gotta review side two...
hmmm PEER GROUP let me see...sound a bit
like members of that free music society-
I'm told by Mr.Boon that VOXPOP is another
incarnation of 45 GRAVE,and "You're my Favorite is a good song...KEN(great name) does a
song called "Purposeless Attitudes"(lousy
approach ken baby-)I'll reiterate once
again SLIVERS blow the spud and their cut here
"Sport is no exception...

Posh
Boy

"THE FUTURE LOOKS BRIGHT" Compilation Lp POSH BOY
Gee whiz Posh Boy I get one of the super rare lp
versions of the popular cassette compilation how
do I rate...must be my bulging herculeean pecs...
I don't know if SHATTERED FAITH is "IN" right now
in LA or if the punks from here or there love them
or hate them they are easily one of my faves on this
record but then again we're dealing with some pretty
heavy competition..."Trilogy" is one of those tunes
that your brain won't let go of...it rings in my head
while I'm eating,drinking,spewing,sleepin all da time-
and they have an album cummin'/out soon...I HATE TSOL-
SOCIAL DISTORTION leave me pretty cold-I know my be-
leaured opinion don mean bloody poop but they sound pretty fuckin' nondescript....CHANNEL 3 are of course great-
you know what I think about them from last time...Oh
shit look at side 2 OK so SHATTERED FAITH is the best on
side one but this other stuff jeezus chris it jus friggin
kicks me in the dick...like the MINUTEMEN what a novel
fucking bunch of impossible to pin down,define,write off,
write about...It can't be done...it's like if you had the
chance to fuck Raquel Welch you'd be so nervous,uptight and
flipped out you'd never be able to get a boner and you'd
look like an idiot...so when I try to write about the MINU-
TEMEN the same thing happens...I get shakey,I look like an
idiot...and you're right I can't get a boner...they also
have an album coming out...THE DESCENDENTS-the folks at New
Alliance said it best..."Heavy and mean fish punk".......
I Like Food" is loved by all of course coz it's the old humorous relief English Lit teachers tell us about/..SACHARINE
TRUST sound different every time I hear them...here they display a more straight forward if off balance approach that is
admitedly great...still going to wait for the LP...(OH YA IN
CASE YOU MISCONSTRUED THE MINUTEMEN FUCKIN ROOL -I gET CAR_
RIED AWAY WHEN THEY ARE ON MY TURNTABLE)BLACK FLAG do "Six
Pack" here again for all of you out of' out of it's that did-
n't get —>

SACCHARINE TRUSTS "A Christmas Cry" makes me
curious as hell as to what their album is going to sound like...I'll reserve comment on them
until I hear that..."ARTLESS ENTANGLEMENTS"...
alright Spot...ya right "distortion is life"...
"Dildoes Bondage and Toys" is more fun than rubber cods stuck up NIG-HEIST is a real bald headed
the singer for NIG-HEIST is a real bald headed
stud...but he's found time in between his boner
messages to cut a new single which the world eag
erly awaits...Hey listen this NEW ALLIANCE label
is putting out alot of good stuff...definately
one to watch and support...

the EP...last but definately not least are the STAINS-
definately this one frenetic guitar stuff-so-those-of-us
wins my award for best-everything-
the most intense band for best-cut on the
the land...great frenetic guitar stuff won't suffer deck
whole album-great out more good them live won't suffer deck
Get this tape you'll play it till your play Robbie
not fortunate enough to see i'll play it some more...fanx
let's hope they put out them I play it some more...fanx
feeds on it then you'll play it some more...
baby....

LA'S WASTED YOUTH

ARTIST'S RENDERING OF D.C.s SKINHEAD STRIKE FORCE PREPARING FOR T.S.O.L. WHEN THEY DARE TO SHOW THEIR FUCKING FACES IN THE NATIONS CAPITOL ON NOV.11

LA'S WASTED YOUTH-"REAGAN'S IN" I.C.I. RECORDS Choice cover depicting Ronny with the WASTED YOUTH logo carved into his little forehead...fuckin' great new Hollywood sound from a band I'd been hearing alot about...some of it is lightning fast and others like my fave cut "Problem Child" has that great mid-tempo chug with a great bass ni High Beefrag"/"Fuck Authority" and line...lotsa more cool songs like "U-more...it's a pretty short LP but who gives a monkeys it's the quality of the burp gun boogie these guys shove in our faces that counts... If you all come to your neighborhood record shop sit on your asses and wait for this to then forget it...order it now direct-Don't bitch cuz you can't find it any-the band answers all correspondence... where here's the address...

to receive a copy of this album
Please send $5.95 to:
I.C.I.
P.O. Box 321
1765 N. Highland Avenue
Hollywood California
90028

EXPLOITED-"PUNK'S NOT DEAD" SECRET RECORDS OK so I'm not into winning friends and influencing all these undiscerning fans but this band is the shittiest.People seem to be in love with their look,their self righteous LP title and "rad" song titles.To call it three chord dull would be a compliment."I Hate Cop Cars" what the fuck is that?"I'm A Mucky Pup" aw that's too bad.4 English blowhards jumping a bandwagon that has four flat tires.I never had to buy this to review it because people keep subjecting me to it when I go to their houses.Spare me...

I.Q.32
MIDWEST MIDWEST TIME TO GO
I'D STAY BUT IT'S SO FUCKING SLOW
STUPID PEOPLE'S ALL I KNOW

I.Q.32 IQ.32!! —— CHORUS

STUPID CORN ALL IN ROWS
SIT AROUND AND WATCH IT GROW
YOU'VE GOT NOTHING LEFT TO SHOW

I.Q.32 I.Q72 IQ32
MIDWEST FUCK YOU!!

PEER PRESSURE
MY EVERY MOVE IS JUDGED BY THE COURT OF MY PEERS
WHEN THE SENTENCE COMES IT CONFIRMS THE WORST OF MY FEARS
THEY KNOW I'M DIFFERENT I'M NOT LIKE THEM
THEY WONT ACCEPT ME FOR THE WAY I AM
PEER PRESSURE PEER PRESSURE
MESS UP MY HEAD
PEER PRESSURE PEER PRESSURE
WANNA BE DEAD
PEER PRESSURE PEER PRESSURE
WON'T LET ME BE
PEER PRESSURE PEER PRESSURE
WONT LET ME BE ME
IT'S A NEW YOUTH MOVEMENT, A TEENAGE CONSPIRACY
A GROUP WHOS PURPOSE IS TO MAKE THE SAME OF YOU & ME
NEVER STOP IT MOVES FAR TOO FAST
HATE IT FOREVER BUT IT'LL ALWAYS LAST
—CHORUS—
YOUR SCHOOLS A SOCIAL CLUB FOR THE SELF ANOINTED ELITE
A PLACE WHOS ONLY FATE HAS GOT TO BE DEFEAT
NEVER STOPS IT MOVES FAR TOO FAST
HATE IT FOREVER BUT IT'LL ALWAYS LAST

RACE RIOT
EVERYBODYS FIGHTING FOR THE COLOR OF THEIR SKIN
EVERYONES FIGHTING JUST TO SAVE THEIR SKIN
THEY'RE FIGHTING IN THE STREETS THEIR FIGHTING IN THE HALLS
THEY'LL RIOT TILL THEY KILL & IT'LL NEVER HALT
RACE RIOT!! THIS AINT 1980
RACE RIOT!! RIOT OF SOCIETY
THEY RIOT IN THE STREETS & THEY RIOT IN THE HALLS
THEY'LL RIOT TILL THEY FALL & IT'LL NEVER HALT
SCHOOLS NOT A PLACE FOR EDUCATION ANYMORE
IT'S SIMPLY JUST A BATTLE GROUND THIS CAN'T GO ON NO MORE
RACE RIOT!! BLACK MAN FIGHTING AGAINST WHITE
RACE RIOT!! FIGHT TILL YOU CAN'T FIGHT ANYMORE
THEY'LL NEVER SIT DOWN & TALK ABOUT THEIR PROBLEMS
JUST WANNA FIGHT & CREATE MORE OF THEM
WHITES CALL 'EM NAMES DIRECTLY TO THEIR FACES
THEY SAY "HEY NIGGER GO BACK TO YOUR OWN PLACES"
— CHORUS #1 —

TOUCH & GO #3 DISCHORD 4½
ADDITIONAL COPIES $2.50 p&p ind. CHECKS
PAYABLE TO COREY RUSK OR BARRY HENSSLER

YOUTH CAMP
KILL THAT NIGGER, KILL THAT JEW
I'M MORE AMERICAN THAN YOU
WHITE RULE LIKE SOUTH AFRICA
THINK IT CAN WORK FOR AMERICA
YOUTH CAMP FOR THE K.K.K.
IT'S THE AMERICAN WAY
YOUTH CAMP FOR THE NATIONAL FRONT
WHEN WHITE RULE IS WHAT I WANT
KILL THAT PAKI, KILL THAT QUEER
WHITE STRAIGHT RULE IT'S ALL QUITE CLEAR
GENOCIDES HEALTHY DONT YOU SEE?
ESPECIALLY WHEN IT AFFECTS YOU AND ME

NECROS INFO:
P.O. BOX 421
MAUMEE, OHIO 43537

THANKS- T.V.D.S., IAN, HENRY, BRIAN H., ANDY,
MATT, MARC, LARISSA, BRAD, SEAN, ROGER, KIM
CAROLE, ALLISON, ABBIE & AL, GREG BOKOR, TYSON
FRANK C., VIOLENT APATHY, NEG. APPROACH,
YOUTH PATROL, D.C. PUNKS, DETROIT SKATE
PUNKS, GEORGE & LORI,

WARGAME
BURNED & CHARRED BODIES LOOKING UP AT ME
I'VE GOT GUNS TO THE HEADS OF PEOPLE IN CATAGORY 3!
WASTED BODIES PILED IN A MESS
HORRIBLE STENCH MAKES ME UPSET
CATAGORY 3 NO LOOKING BACK
CLOSED YOUR EYES ON NUCLEAR ATTACK
DEVISTATION THATS SO IMMENSE
A REALITY THATS TOO INTESE
THE NAKED TRUTH UPON THE SCREEN
A DOCUDRAMA SO OBSCENE

PUBLIC HIGH SCHOOL!! HOME OF THE FOOLS
PUBLIC HIGH SCHOOL!! IT'S SO UNCOOL
1000's OF KIDS & THEIR ALL THE SAME
MIGHT AS WELL HAVE THE SAME LAST NAMES
LITTLE WORRIES FOR SUCH LITTLE MINDS
FOR SURE MAN THEY'RE NOT MY KIND
— CHORUS —

I HATE MY SCHOOL
I HATE MY SCHOOL
MY TEACHERS ARE INSANE
THE KIDS ARE ALL FOOLS
& MY WORKS DOWN THE DRAIN
WHY DONT YOU ALL LEAVE ME ALONE?
ALL I WANNA DO IS GO HOME
FEEDING MY BRAIN
I FEEL LIKE I'VE BEEN HIT
CAN'T TAKE THE STRAIN
SO MAYBE I'LL QUIT

PAST COMES BACK TO HAUNT ME
A FASHION QUEEN NOT IN MY DREAMS
COMES BACK TO INVADE THIS STUCK-UP SCENE
WE HATED YOU BEFORE YOU LEFT
SO DONT COME BACK & THINK WE'RE FREINDS
DOCTORS DAUGHTER AMY GOOD
I THOUGHT THIS TIME YOU UNDERSTOOD
NEVER WANTED TO SEE YOU AGAIN
WE WERE NEVER EVER FREINDS
HAUNTED HAUNTED BY THE PAST
TO SEE YOU DIE WOULD BE A BLAST
HAUNTED HAUNTED BY THE PAST
HOPED THIS TIME WOULD BE THE LAST
A YEAR FROM NOW TUESDAY AFTERNOON
YOU'RE COUNTING DAYS YOU THINK IT'S SOON
YOU'LL HAVE BRIAN YOU'RE SURE OF IT
IT'S WRITTEN DOWN ON A SCHEDULED LIST

REJECT
I WOULD RATHER BE AT HOME
IN MY ROOM & ALL ALONE
IT'S TIMES LIKE THIS I FEEL SO BAD
WHY AM I ALWAYS SAD?
REJECT REJECT
I AM NO DEFECT
REJECT REJECT
IGNORE THE EFFECT
LOST COMPASSION IS THAT SO?
BUT I STOPPED CARING SO LONG AGO
IT'S NOT YOUR FAULT SO DONT LOSE FACE
MUST BE BAD TO FALL FROM GRACE
—CHORUS—
WHEN I'M HERE & ALL ALONE
DON'T THINK THAT I'LL ANSWER THE PHONE
NOT AFRAID OF THE BARBS YOU'D SEND
JUST MY REACTIONS TOWARD AN EX-FREIND

PUBLIC HIGH SCHOOL
HANGIN' OUT ON A FRIDAY NIGHT
THERE'S NOTHING TO DO & THERES NO ONE I LIKE
KIDS MY AGE HAVING TIMES OF THEIR LIVES
STEADY COUPLES FUCKING MAN & WIFE
HIGH SCHOOL LIFE IT IS SO LAME
WITH ENTERTAINMENT LIKE A FOOTBALL GAME
STUCK HERE UNTILL THEY GET OLD
HIGH SCHOOL SPIRIT TO THE PURPLE & GOLD
I GUESS THAT NOW I'VE NONE TO FEAR
NOW THAT GRADUATIONS HERE
GUESS IT'S O.S.U. FOR ME
& MY STUPID MAUMEE SOCIETY

CHUGGA CHUGGA CHUGGA

DEMO TAPE OF FOREVER...BEAVER!!!! THAT'S RIGHT AND DON'T LAUGH...SOME OF THE WILDEST MUSIC YOU'LL EVER HEAR..SOME STUDIO AND SOME LIVE-ALL I CAN SAY IS SOMEHOW HEAR IT...SEND ME A TAPE...SHIT I'LL DUB IT FOR YOU...

BAD RELIGION

TV:Is all the violence blown out of proportion?
Brett:It's not a real problem but it;s true
Greg:Yea it's real violence but the media
hypes it alot. that happen are usually some-
JayB:the fights like somebody says some-
punks vs. punks once in awhile
thing to a guy so they fight,once in 6 guys
there's a real good one though like warfare=
that's fun,the people that get stabbed
vs.10 or even better,full gang
usually deserved it,then the media blows
it all out of proportion.That's usually
when the shit hits the fan in L.A.the
cops go nuts and beat up everybody on the

scene.it gets pretty hairy with the
bad.they mace the sheriffs in L.A. are really
cuz their hangin' around. are the cops
TV:Does Bretts mom still get mad cuz you
guys drink all the milk? we have to d-
Group:That's gregs mom and now cuz she found out
rink the kool-aid from the Flipside article
about it

interest in people,if he does he wouldn't always ask people for money.The guys a million=

aire and he denys it.
TV:How's the response been from the religious
community?
Jay B:One time brett spray painted bad religion
on a wall and next day it was crossed out and
somebody wrote victory in christ so we crossed it out and put victory in ignorance.
TV:Who's the biggest asshole in LA?
Group:all the fucking posuer little faggots
that think their the meanest thing since Sid.
They're the assholes of LA

BAD RELIGION were interviewed by TV some-
time in Oct.
TV:How many grovelling little nubiles do
you get to suck your wangs after every g-
ig?
Greg:At least one every gig.
Brett:one...
JayB:Not too many,i'm usually way too drunk!!
TV:What's been your best show so far?
Group:We played with the DEAD KENNEDYS in San
Diego.That was a good one.There's a show coming
up called SLAM 81 with FEAR,TSOL,us (BAD RELIG-
ION,CHINA WHITE and about 10 other bands,that
one will be way hot!!
TV:What are you when you aren't BAD RELIGION?
JayB:A piece of air
Brett:Horny
Greg:A sex maniac who likes new wave chicks
with big tits and who MASTURBATE!!!
TV:What did your folks say when they first
heard your record?
Brett:"Turn it down"!
Greg:ga-ga..
JayB:Oh your in a band??How nice."
TV:What LA bands are your favorites...
Greg:I don't have any favorite LA bands...UK
SUBS!!!
Brett:THE ADOLESCENTS,but they broke up,the
RAMONES...
Jay B:WASTED YOUTH TSOL,you know the typical
LA band scene...
TV:If you saw Jerry Falwell walking down the
street what would you do?
Brett:I would tear off his eyelids so he would
have to see the real world around him,then I
would cut his toungue out so he couldn't tell
any more lies.
Greg:I'd box him for the belt!!
Jay B:i'd go right up to his face,call him a
liar and a sinner,then I'd blow his fuckin'
brains out.I hate that guy,all he wants is
money,money,i really don't think he has a true

TV:Any plans to tour outside of ca?
Group:wer'e going to try to tour if we get
enough money after we release our album
(next summer)
TV:What type of kids do you attract?
Brett:mostly hairlips and lutherans.
Greg:Not enough new wave chicks with big
tits.
Jay B:roaches,fleas and ticks.the average
in the clubs around here.oh ya crabs and
lice 'too.
TV:Opinion of San Fransisco?
Greg:i don't really like all the people
but the city is cool,if it didn't always
smell like cum.
Brett:It's a cool town and it's cold with
lots of hills and trollys you can ride on
for a quarter.
Jay B:I'ts weird up there.i mean people
are freaked out on drugs or something.I
love the city structural wise it's bitchen
and the nude ladies you can see for a q-
uarter that's OK.
TV:What do you want to be doing in a year?
Brett:I don't know.
Greg:living and breathing.
Jay B:nothing but a little of everything..
maybe a sail around the world in an 8
foot rowboat or something

TV:Where do you guys stand on drugs,booze etc.
Brett:anywhere I can
Greg:I don't touch the stuff.
Jay B:anything that's bad for you is good for
you,if you take enough to make you pass out!!

WRITE TO BAD RELIGION..ORDER THEIR HOT 6
SONG EP..WIN A DATE WITH THEM IN OUR CH-
RISTMAS WIN A DATE CONTEST(NEW WAVE GIRLS
WITH BIG TITS ONLY) WRITE......
BAD RELIGION 233713 VENTURA BLVD
WOODLAND HILLS CA. 91364

MISFITS

GLENN DANZIG - VOCALS
JERRY ONLY - BASS
DOYLE - GUITAR
GOOGY - DRUMS

THE MISFITS were interviewed by Brian
Hyland at Bookies in Detroit 9-81
Bd:So is this an official tour or what?
Glenn:Well we're heading back to New Y-
ork now and then we're goin' to San F-
ransisco and L.A. Then we come and do the
whole fuckin' thing over again.
BH:Are you playn' here again?
Glenn:Ya middle of October.
BH:Do you do any of the old stuff any more?
That stuff at sound check I'd never heard
before.
Jerry:You shoulda been there last night
(Chicago)
Glenn:That stuffs off our new album.
BH:When's it coming out?
Glenn:About two weeks.The problem with us
is that we had an album done but no one kn-
ows how to record us and we never like the
album.
BH:Did you re-issue "Night Of THe Livin Dead?"
Glenn:No way.
Googy:Go to Bleeker Bobs(NYC)they have the last
few copies.
Glenn:It was a Halloween free thing we did.
BH:That "Who Killed Marilyn" single;who play-
ed on that?Is it the Misfits or just you?
Glenn:Just me.
BH:Who played on it?
Glenn:I did everything on it.
Googy:I think it sucks myself(guffaw)
Glenn:Oh come on your better than Tom Snyder!
BH:Is PLAN 9 your own label?
Glenn:No there are other bands on it.Our old
guitarist has a record comin' out on it.
Googy:THE UNDEAD.
Glenn:There was another band on it along time
ago,THE VICTIMS.It really sucked though.
BH:Is that from PLAN 9 FROM OUTER SPACE?"
Glenn:YA
Googy:There is a new fiend club did you know
that?It's 3112 Grand Central Station,NY NY
10016.If you want you can use the zip plus 4
code but it's not in effect for two more years.
Glenn:The old Fiend Club was run by a bunch of
jerks,we run this one.
Googy:Jerry and I get the mail.I read it on the
bus,so don't send any letter bombs or I'll blow
up.
Glenn:We're gonna make a MISFITS catalogue.Ya
know MISFITS beach towels.
Googy:All sorts of shit,lunch boxes,and if we
really get into it,socks and stuff.
Glenn:Hey if you guys ever come across any dead

animals on the road or something cut
the fuckin' heads off and send em' to
us.
BH:I've got a cat head if you want it.
Glenn:Definately!
Googy:Ya like a dear head or horses head
BH:What was the Monster Movie Club like?
Glenn:It was cool-we just went there and hung
out.
BH:Can you get lyrics from the Fiend Club?
Glenn:Our new album will have a lyric sheet.
BH:On "Bullet" was that Bobby Steele or not,
(Frances Coma)

Glenn:No it was somebody else.
Barry:I told ya so ya dick!
Googy:Why dont you guys come to a party at our
hotel room?Bring all the nice girls you can find-
BH:There probably won't be any choice ones,may-
be a bunch of stew fed Canadian ones.
Googy:Great bring the Canadians!
Glenn:Enough about fuckin horniness Arthur!
BH:When did the new line up start?
Googy:Since the band got great Me and Doyle.
Glenn:That's Jerrys brother Doyle,he's always
been with the band but kinda you know.
Googy:He was always gonna be in the band it was
just a matter of time.
BH:Is Mr.Jim in another band or anything?
Glenn:He works at Crazy Eddies..
BH:Where are you going to play in D.C.? 9;30?
Glenn:Ya..
Googy;Chicago was greatThe people wouldn't
leave.They just kept comin' down goin' play"
We said"Look we ain't got no guitars left,no
strings,they just wouldn't leave.
Glenn:We played every song we knew all but two-
BH:Is "3 Hits From Hell" gonna be on the LP?
Glenn:Two of em are.Not "London Dungeon"
BH:How many songs are on the album?
Glenn.Guess
BH:Duhhh
Glenn:13
Googy:It wasn't planned though.
Glenn:Bullshit it wasn't planned!
BH:What's the album called?
Glenn:"The MISFITS WALK AMONG US"
"Night Of The Living Dead" you can't get any more!
Jerry:You can't get the 12'' either...
BH:There's tons of those at record stores in To-
ledo.
Googy:They go for 15 bucks in NY.
Andy:They're in this one store where they have
like a Barry Manilow record and then yours ri-
ght behind it.
Glenn:It'll just eat right through his record!
Googy:I don't believe that shit...
BH:What's the skull from?A movie or something?

Glenn:Ya what is it,"Crimson Ghost"(to Jerry)
Jerry:Yep
Glenn:It's an old serial but it's just a cool skull.
Googy:Hey you guys got any reffers?
BH:No we don;t smoke it!
Glenn:GOOD!
Googy:Oh ya,I remember outside of Club 57!I lit
up a joint and they just started saying "aw re-
efer sucks," and all this shit.About 90 people
from Washington...
Glenn:Good,they should have killed you...
Googy:That;s why I got my hair cut.I said ei-
ther join em' or fuck it!
BLACK FLAG was a nutty concert!
Glenn:I don't even care about BLACK FLAG.
BH:You don't like them at all?
Glenn:NO.I just said I don't care about them.
I like them.
BH:Do you guys listen to any hardcore L.A. stuff?
Googy:I sold all my records and stereo.
BH:So did I.
Glenn:I only buy records once in awhile.These guys
(Jerry and Doyle) got a few records.
Jerry:The've got scratches and beer all over em!
Andy;Do you guys have any direct influences or...
Glenn:US!
Googy:Everybody else is a wimp,right?Nobody else
rates!
BH:Why did Bobby Steele quit?
Googy:Bobby Steele got exterminated!
Jerry:Bounced.
BH:We talked to him in New York and he said he
quit
Jerry:It doesn't make any difference whether or
not he quit-he's just out...
BH:Well why did he quit?(get booted?)
Glenn:Cuz he couldn't play fast enough.Basically
that's it.I'm not gonna pull no punches.
Googy:He didn't get along with anyone either.
Glenn:His influence is Jimi Hendrix and I hate
Jimi Hendrix..
Jerry:He would always try to throw leads into songs
and then he couldn't play fast and he'd try to do-

uble up like upstrokes -like Chet Atkins.W'ed say
"No that's cheatingwe're not going to let you play
like that..Your out buddy...
Glenn:And when we recorded "London Dungeon" and ev
erything he didn't show up for a couple of things
and said let Doyle play for me,and we said,well
fuck it,why don't we just use Doyle cause he's play
ing with us at rehearsal all the time so fuck it..
we kicked him out...
Googy:It was impossible to get Bobby to go to re-
hearsals.He'd go once in a blue moon! Me,I'm out
there 5 times a week prompt for practice these guys
know!
BH:Did you really record "Horror Business" in a haunted house?
Glenn:What,you heard we didn't?
BH:No I was just wondering...
Googy:that's my fathers castle.It's been in the
family for years.
Glenn:Bullshit.

Glenn:They tore it down though.It was in New
Jersey on this old long highway.It's desolate
and there are all these old military training
stables and shit with big mansions,you walk in
the back and there are these bottomless pits
filled with water.You fall in em and you fuckin
die...we took a mobile unit and did it...
Matt:Did it have the reputation for being haunt
ed?
Glenn:Ya it had a reputation.I remember when I
was a kid we'd go driving down there bombed out
of our brains!It's by the cliffs.Why you guys don't
have any haunted houses down here?People get wasted in those houses...
Googy:Don't forget,all the nice girls,there's a f-
uckin party...
Glenn:You shuld see the girls he fucks,most of them

Googy:It's physical you know what I mean?You fuck
and shoot your load,then on to the next town.
Glenn:One of these times yer gonna fuck one of those
ugly chicks and you'll pull out and nothing will come
out with ya,it'll fall off inside!
Googy:I always have the best girls in the world.
These guys are jealous.
Glenn:Oh fuck you.He said he's a combination of
Errol Flynn,and Fred Astaire and he's out on the
dance floor fucking around,aw shit!
Jerry:Errol Flynn!
Glenn:Really...we were laughin for about a half
hour...
Jerry:Ya he keeps us jolly.

NEGATIVE APPROACH

NEGATIVE APPROACH were interviewed outside of the Coronation Tavern in Windsor by TV,DS,Corey and Todd...
TV:Where'd you get your inspiration in Detroit to play the kinda stufff you play anyway?
John;Inspiration?In Detroit?..fuck..
Corey:You must have got it somehere cuz there's no other bands like you around here...

Rob:NECROS
TV:Oh ya tell me what your names are otherwise I'll have a helluva time t-ranscribing this thing...
Rob;guitar,18
John:vocals,18
Lance:drums,18
Pete:bass,17
TV:Have you played out at all?
John:Our first gig was in Todds base-ment...this gig coming up will be our second(BOOKIES gig w/Negative Approach/Meatmen,Necros on Sept.30th,ED)
TV:Song titles?
John:"Sick Of Talk"..."Fashionable Idio-ts"
Rob:"Pressure"
TV:So that Bookies thing is all set for you guys?
John:I guess....
Todd:We can get anyone we want to play..
TV:What about this Meatmen thing?

Corey:Gawd I saw em' tonight you would-n't a believed it man they got this re-ally tall gay guy on voacals(laughter,ha ha hee,hee ALL)He was talking about like Tooing For Anus" in Detroit he warted my ass I almost beat him up what a queer...
(some people got no respect,ED)
Todd:They did this thing in one song whe-re the guitar player sticks his guitar up the singers ass...
All:What a bunch of queers...(Laughter)
JOHN:We don't think theres any other bands like us in Detroit like here everyone looks up to the Romantics as heros you know....
Corey:How are you different from YOUTH PA-TROL?

Rob:Our songs are alot longer...
Pete:Theres not as much power really to Youth Patrol...
John:Youth Patrol's just kinda there but were more raw...
Rob:The singers more controlled...
TV:So I take it you don't like that band?
Pete:Their the worst ...I hate em' (laffs)
John:No wer'e all good friends and shit..
All:He's their guitar player...
TV:Yor in both bands??
Corey:Ya and he hates youth Patrol HA HA...

TV:No wonder you were making all those caustic comments...
What magazines do you read?
All:Creem,Action Now,Hit Parader,Circus

(somewhat sarcastic young whippersnappers aren't they now?
Corey;Teen Beat,Sixteen...
TV:What about Iron Horse?

Pete:My brothers got a band called Iron H-orse..(yuks)
Rob:The Joys Of Anal Sex,Blueboy
TV:You realize you guys are outnumbered play-ing good music like this in Detroit don't you?
John:There's no other bands like us around he-re...
Todd:What's your stand on drugs and stuff
John:None of us use drugs...I drink a beer once in awhile...our drummers a mixed drink man...
TV:Todd how often do you beat off??

Todd:Twice....both times on wednesday...
Corey:God I get more than that in in a day.
Corey:(loud)BELCH...
John:The only cool kids in Detroit are skate-boarders like Youth Patrol...except for Pete..

TV:Do you get shit when you go to the skatepark?
Rob:Fuck no their all about this big..there's quite a few arguments and fights and shit
Todd:They spraypainted in the pool..

Corey:Ya "Punk sucks my dick"
John:They skate after hours and the boss has given us permission to beat them up...
Corey:No Shit?we gotta come skatin' with you

after hours that'd be fun to beat up a bunch of kids sneaking in...
Here comes some cops
Cop:How come you fellows aren't in the bar?
Corey:Wer'e interviewing a band...

Cop:Interviewing a band in the parking lot? Wheres the beer..
ALL:No beer...
Cop:Go back in the bar...(needless to say this about wrapped up the interview)

PARTY N' HEARTY IN D.C.!

ERIC AND PETE OF RED C

the classic cover of "12XU"...all I can say is R.I.P.ARTIFICIAL PEACE(formerly ASSAULT AND BATTERY)were up next and I hope I havent beat off too much already because this band was no letdown...only here can there be a band this great you've never heard of...hard and fast and all those other overused adjectives ...all songs great with titles like "No Escape No Excuse"/ "Enemy Minds"/and "Danger UXB"...definately an up and coming band...YOUTH BRIGADE are another band that at the time of this writing are break-

ARTIFICIAL PEACE

MINOR THREAT/ARTIFICIAL PEACE/YOUTH BRIGADE/ RED C/IRON CROSS/DEADLINE/NOTHING SACRED-- (at a bash somewhere outside outside of Washington) To say the location of this gig was a sad commentary on the state of D.C. clubs would be an understatement.Most promoters prefer the "safe" inocuous bands like the SLIKEE BOYS-there's a guaranteed almighty dollar-ya would hate to risk booking any of these young vital sounding bands...let's face it youth clubs don't exist in this country except in fantasy-and with the majority of D.C. punks shunning alcohol(in mass quantities anyway like the old farts,college students and wavers-theres growing numbers that don't drink at all)it forces the punks to go underground (ha ha so what if the party was in some girls basement)MINOR THREATS last gig...tsk tsk... the good die young...but the guitarist is off to college...let me just say that Lyle could do fuckin incredible things on that axe-a fact easy to overlook when you're hit with the overall power of this band...no mikes on the drum set but Jeff seems oblivious pounding away-a mohawked madman...Brian now plays bass with the GI's...an addition that shouldn't hurt their sound on bit...and we can't forget ol'Ian-screaming at a wall so to speak with an inferior pa but doing a more than adequate job of stirring the crowd up-if you thought you'd heard it all on their first EP you'll herm in your briefs when you hear the new stuff slated for release as a four song EP...I got punched in the nuts good but managed to stagger out for

ing up...you may be asking"what's with these bands...all splitting?"Search me except they just aint jivin' you know like those musical differences like what a shame...their in the studio recording a new demo for release(as D-ischord #5?)They've got some great new songs like "Barbed Wire" that will hopefully see the light of day along with their old faves like "I Object" and "Waste Of Time"...

their set was great...the crowd kept yelling for SixOclock News" I guess an old favorite...IRON CROSS had to cancell I guess because bassist Wendel(Formerly of S.O.A)couldn't make it but they do have a demo tape out...too my knowledge Americas only OI band...granted they're going to have to bend a bit ideologically ... but see interview w/vocalist Sab elsewhere in this issue...DEADLINE were next...their first gig...their singer

minorthreat

had a TSOL tshirt on-well nobodys perfect he seemed sort of nervous but I think w/ time they may be able to hone their sound into something great...they had misfortune of going on last when people were all just hanging out...oh wait...no there was one more band...it was...was it? Yes I actually think it was...NOTHING SACRED... jeez it was all like a swirling trip into another dimension...the highlight of their set was definately the classic "Abbie Mahler Is Going To Hell".... Bill Rollins,Mr.E,and a maniacal bass player make them a monster band that must be reckoned with...they only will perform in complete darkness...strange but true...

YOUTH brigade

Keep your fingers crossed...RED C are a band I'd heard alot about but never seen- And yes this too was their last gig...but don't get the wrong idea...out of all these

ashes theres bound to be some hot new bands (sorry that was bad)Hey why is the guitar player and the bassist bitching at each other?Their set ranged from loud raucous stuff to some guitar noodling by the drummer that was downright dull...but overall

344

I PLAY DRUMS FOR A WORKING CLASS BAND. I POSSESS EXPENSIVE ORNAMENTS

new alliance records
p. o. box 21
san pedro, CA   90733

BRAND NEW "GEORGE-TYPE" SHIT FROM L. A.:
FIVE SONG EP FROM THE DESCENDENTS, HEAVY AND MEAN FISH PUNK.
THREE SONG EP FROM THE MINUTEMEN, SOLID AND BENT FREAK OUT.
SALVATION ARMY DEBUT SINGLE, CHEMICAL POPTONES.
EACH RECORD $2.50 POST PAID. DIRECT AND REAL THRASH FROM
THE PLACE EVERYONE THINKS THEY KNOW ABOUT. HEAR IT. FEEL IT.
THEN GO OUT AND DO YOUR JAM. THAT'S WHAT IT'S ALL ABOUT. OK?

THE JOHNNYS/REVILLOS   BOOKIES CLUB

With a name like theirs there is no way THE JOHNNYS could be any good right?You got it =a three piece that played an incredibly long set that had us going in and out the door for the best part of 90 minutes.yet another fuckband from Ann Arbor that played a hodgepodge of modreggaedungbagrockandroll that noone danced to and not many seemed interested in bringing them back for any encores(thank god)Eugene was sick or something so FAYE had to carry the vocals single handedly and she did it with all the grace of a pregnant housewife-what a bitch!.She acted like we were all so out of it(well considering it was Detroit I guess she wasn't too far off)but I've had all the snot treatment from British(I know Scottish they should all die anyway)rock bands I need for a year...proficient but rather uninspired...seeing THE REVILLOS without Eugene is like seeing a porno film without a cum facial...TV

THE SHAKIN' PYRAMIDS/THE SWINGIN' MADISONS 9:30 Club Washington DC

A total waste of time. The Pyramids play about the most pedestrian rockabilly I've heard and I'm no rake-do aficionado, but these guys bored me rigid. The Madisons weren't much better with their cheesy cornball nite club act. Composed of three thirds Mumps, I liked them better before they made the swop for the penguin suits.--DS

SLICKEE BOYS/THE WANKTONES
Desperados in Washington DC

Got there late and missed the Wanktones which I guess was a blessing judging from all the bad mouthing they got after their show. I am no Slickee Boys fan by any stretch of the imagination, but here I am at one of their gigs. Entertaining would be the best way to describe their sound. Good time new music for all those Georgetown preppies flirting with the idea of getting into nu wave. Harmless fun where nobody gets hurt, nice huh? Well, it'll wear badly on me cuz the stuff is a little too saccharine for my musclehead diet. Trainable would see these guys and want to be just like 'em. The look similar 'cept that the SBs don't fuck off when they're on stage. They can be fun if you can tolerate the flood of squirmy college jerks who flock to see bands like these guys. I've seen them once, that's enough. --DS

This is not funny!
THE MEATMEN live!

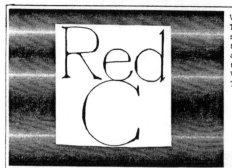

Red C

V:Why did RED C break up?
T:well basically because Tom was leaving for school in Georgia and all of us but Tom were tired of .Now Pete plays for Assault and B-attery.Eric may produce bands and I'm going to wait till something I like comes along.
V:Is your underwear always up your butt?
T:It's not and I've got beautiful eyes.

The following interview with Tony Young was conducted by Vivien..Sept.24
V:Was RED C the first band you were in?
T:No I was in a band with Chuck Biscuits, Keith Morris,and Angus Young.
V:Good answer.Who thought of starting RED C?
T:Officially Eric(vocals)He came up to me and asked me did I wanna play bass in his band. Ian(of Minor Threat)told him I could play bass. Back then everyone was asking me to be in their band.Even the Virginia Necros.
V:When and where was the first time you played?
T:Maybe in February.It was in Columbia,Ma.Leo was playing guitar and after that show we decided to get rid of her,although she's got potential
V:What's it like being the only girl in the band?
T:I put up with alot of criticism.
V:Who gets blamed for most of the arguments, in the band?
T:Meand then Tom.I get blamed because I won't settle for anything less than what I want sometimesTom gets blamed because he fucks off, is sarcastic and generally a nut.
V:So what about the music?
T:I wrote most of the music and Eric wrote most of the lyrics.Pete writes some songs too-he wrote music to "Boredom"/Scam Out"/"Assassin" and "Social Minority"
V:That was almost the name of your band right?
T:Yes now I'll tell you why we're called RED C so the whole world will understand.At first I liked the name Social Minority but nobody else did.So one day I got in a fight with my mom-will my mom ever read this?She's very religious you know.She pissed me off,I forgot about what so I said to her"Don't cross me woman because I'll swallow you up like the Red Sea."Whenever I'm angry I write songs.I thout it sounded like a good name for the band.RED C means power to overcome.
V:Why the letter C instead of the word?
T:Because we all thought it would be too religious as a word and people would misinterperate .But so what the fuck they do anyway
V:What about influences?
T:I was influenced by the Bad Brains old stuff-and Teen Idles.
V:Were you really?

T:Yea I loved Ian he had a neat style sort of..I can't explain it.I was heavily influenced by the U.K. Subs,Ruts and recently Chuck of Black Flag who's fuckin' great.He's one of the best.
V:H'es really a great bass player...
T:Yea and also heavy metal bands,I like AC/DC they have a steady driving bass line. Motorhead and Girlschool which is the best all girl band around...
VOk what about your demos?
T:We went to the studio once..It didn't come out that well at all.That was the first thing the band agreed upon.I was blamed for that too.Then we did a basement tape in Tom's basement.Eric set that up well.It came out really good.
Vi:I'm surprised because Eric told me he doesn't know anything about sound.
T:He doesn't.He's also very stingy with our tapes even the good ones.
V:With set lists too -he offered me money for the one I've used
T:At Wilson Center someone tried to take our set list and Eric stomped on his fingers with boots.

VIOLENT APATHY were interviewed in Detroit on Sept.12 by TV and DS...present were Kenny(vocals)Elliot(drums)and Dick(guitar)Jim (bass)was absent...
TV:Hey where'd you find those wint-o-greens-those are mine...
Eliott:Go like this and chew em' and they spark and look really cool...
TV:So where'd you get the name VIOLENT ENEMA-uh I mean VIOLENT APATHY
E:From Jims term paper
DS:What'd he get on it?
E:He flunked it...
Dick:Ya it described the attitude of prisoners on death row...
TV:So I hear you guys are going to have an ebony male dance review to go along with your show...
Kenny:Ya I wanna try it out   (lossa yuks)
E:Kenny and I'll be out there showing them up...
DS:Ya you guys'll be the siamese twins..
VA:That's right...
TV:Where were you joined?
E:At the penis!
D:EVERYONE ALWAYS ASKS IF their brothers..
TV:Who these guys?
Kenny:Yes we connect at will...
TV:You guys like tacos alot?
Kenny:Ya beefy tostados cuz you get the free pen...
Dick:I got diareah one nite from eating at Mi Ranchito...
DS:Ya I got diareah one night at Pizza Bobs in Ann Arbor...
Eliot:Ya did you ever get one of those banana-hot fudge shakes?They're great..
DS:I just got a vegetarian sandwich and their m-uta been boogars in it or something...cuz I'm walking home and got hershey squirts real bad
TV:Burning ring of fire?
DS:The burning ring isn't so embarrassing but when you got this big brown stain on your ass...
Kenny:Dribbling down your leg...
TV:Are you ever going to play Ann Arbor?
VA :Where?
DS:What's it like living in Kalamazoo?
Dick;Lotsa new wavers...
Kenny;there's new wave bands like Young Rossum and the T-Snakes...
Kenny:You guys aughta go to Harvest Table all the pancakes you can eat for a buck nineteen... All the farmers go there to load up...
TV:Where were you when the tornado hit...
Kenny:I was at work watching the funnel tear shit up...
Dick:The only people who like us are our friends..

(OK so some of these statements are out of context cuz transcribing is boring)

VIOLENT APATHY INTERVIEW

Bookings call (616) 388-5343

GOVERNMENT ISSUE
Legless Bull
E.P.

AGENT ORANGE-"EVERYTHING TURNS GRAY"/"P-
IPELINE"   Posh Boy Records
Can't decide if or how much I like the
A side of this one....not quite as torrid
as "Bloodstains" but it has a catchy guitar riff...whatever intensity is lacking
in the vocals is more than made up for by
the guitarist...and let me tell ya' their
rendition of "PIPELINE" is the best ever
recorded (Original included)it alone is
worth the money...great double beat snappin drum....

GI's"LEGLESS BULL EP"   Dischord Records
The only band that can be
GI'S "LEGLESS BULL EP" Dischord Records
These guys have you yelling curse words,
laughing and punching the walls during the
duration of their 9 song EP-"Religious Ripoff" is the best poke at the moral maj yet-
and check out the oozing sarcasm on "R&R B-
ULLSHIT" like "Wow man kick ass rock and
roll,I need a bong man I need some drugs-
this rock and roll bullshit is good".It m-
ight be funny for some of you but for others
unfortunately your'e only laughing at yourselves for being dorfy and out of it enough
to think drugs are cool...but jeez no one
who reads T&G would do that now would they?
"Fashionite" sez it all...."Anarchy is Dead"
sez it all...you've really gotta see them live to appreciate vocalist John Stab's hatred
for thethings he hates(redundant but effective)
but for now buy this choice EP...yet another
hot one on Dischords...

RADIO FREE
EUROPE

IT LIKES /A COUPLE
YOU / SCREAMS

RADIO FREE EUROPE-"IT LIKES YOU"/"A
COUPLE SCREAMS Mig Records
Strange band considering their point
of origin...Austin,Texas,really shooting for the SF crowd...members of this
band probably feel very neglected and
unapreciated...Don't get me wrong this
is an excellent record it just has me
perplexed as to where when,and why they
got inspiration in the land of armadillos
to create music such as this...I'd love
to kill an armadillo someday...

NEW ORDER-"EVERYTHING's GONE GREEN"/"PRO-
CESSION"   Factory
Charging synth that takes an alternating
front and back seat to guit-bass--the back
and forth works to a tee...alot more overt
than their first effort-they seem to be in
a more"let's hammer the point" mood like
they've recovered from any traumas they may
have been experiencing previously...OK like
shake the JOY DIVISION monkey whose claws
were dug deep in the back until...you got it
...this single....of course this is purely
conjecture on my part..and all of you who
can mentally negate my analysis on the grou-
nds that we cover loud fast music in T&G can
stick your narrow minded fascist(that's right
Bruce and John)attitudes up someplace brown
dark and stinky...oh ya this is one of this
month's best singles...

BAD RELIGION

BAD RELIGION--"Bad Religion"/"Politics"
"Sensory Overload"/"Slaves"/"Drastic
Actions"/"World War III" Epitaph Re-
cords

Unlike many LA based bands where all
it takes is one listen and you're already dripping slobber on the floor,
Bad Religion takes time before winning
over their legion of fans, which must
be many cuz this is a great record.
When you first hear it, you say same
old LA-styled punk, good, but nothing
to get excited about. Now that's
where you're wrong. This is perhaps
the best debut record since "Nervous
Breakdown". I can't quite put my finger on it . . . something like Black
Flag meets Neg Trend. Sure it's an
oversimplication, but like, hey man,
it's good and I like it.--DS

KRAUT--"Kill For Cash"/"True Colour"
"Just Cabbage" Cabbage Records

I don't know where to start with
this one, there's so many things
wrong with it. Shitty, affected
vocals . . . punk with no conviction, and some of the worst drumming I've heard in along time, the
guy who recorded it should get some
of the blame. He got the guitar
right and bothced the rest. And
what the hell is "Just Cabbage"
supposed to mean?! Too stupid for
comment.--DS

BLACK MARKET BABY-"POTENTIAL SUICIDE"
YOUTH CRIMES Limp RECORDS
Just where to classify this band..fr-
ankly I can't pass judgement in good
faith because all I've heard is this
single and "Crimes Of Passion" but I
might as well talk about this single-
"Youth Crimes" is a fuckin great song -
good production...don't like the A side as much...Fans of this DC band are
loyalists who swear by BMB and go to
all their shows...Good single

BLACK MARKET
BABY

LIMP
035

SOCIAL DISTORTION-"PLAYPEN"/"MAINL-
INER   Posh Boy Records
Mainliner" is the better song of the
cuts included here as well as the F-
uture Looks bright" comp.not harsh
at all like I figured they would be-
but a winner to boot...

THROBBING GRISTLE

PROCESS OF
ELIMINATION

Out
eNOV.
20th!!!

THROBBING GRISTLE-"WE HATE YOU LITTLE GIRLS"
"FIVE KNUCKLE SHUFFLE" ADOLESCENT Records
IF you missed the Sordide Sentimental release of this one then like me you were over-
joyed when this hit the racks...how the SF
based Adolescent got the rights to reissue
is beyond me...who cares I've got...it's sick
it's twisted...it's out...your turn...

T&G SAMPLER-featuring NEGATIVE APPROACH/NECROS/FIX/
YOUTH PATROL/VIOLENT APATHY/TOXIC REASONS/McDONALDS/
MEATMEN...8 SONG 7" EP ON TOUCH AND GO RECORDS!!!

7"

BILLY IDOL-"MONY MONY"/"BABY TALK" Chrysalis
Here we go the swift(?) rise to fame for Mr. Peroxide...but who picked this be-boppin classic done previously by one Tommy James from just down the pike in Niles...and no bitchin' picture sleeve for the chicklets to sieze prior to their excursions into another dimension via their first two well lubed fingers?

THE BIRTHDAY PARTY-"RELEASE THE BATS"/"BLAST OFF" 4·AD
Now is the time to dispense with all restraint, discretion and categories heretofore set down by you me them....to take into account everything and nothing that has transpired thus far-the epitome of powerful backbeat nixed with not a soft edge....opugnant as anything to come out of anywhere this season...from Presley to Pop Group and beyond man this is not the personification of safety and well being...anyone with half a wit left will jump on this now...

Il y a VOLKSWAGENS-"KILL MYSELF"/"AMERICAN DREAM" Mechanical Reproductions Records
Interesting enough I guess-warbling voltage over the traditional sharp sounding guitar-skip the baby cymbal sound.. that's already been done.Actually it's quite repetitive in a dull sense...For FIRE ENGINES fans only...

SKIDS-"FIELDS"/"BRAVE MAN" Virgin
My patience with Dick Jobson is wearing thin...no Stuart Adamson on guitar...and that adds up to a thin mix and more of the same sentiments regarding human struggle-but his lyrics are starting to read like the old testament-and with only 2 of them left I wonder how much longer the'll hold out before calling it Richard Jobson and Skids and then a dull solo career etc.Tis a pitty folks cuz I don't care what u say their other records are great...

JO CALLIS-"WOAH YEAH"/"SINISTRALE" "DODO BOYS" Pop Aural
OK Joe so I gave you one more piece o' my income...one last chance to bless me with some brilliant,manic riffs from your halcyon days with the REZILLOS...can't you see just how mundane your efforts now are??Pop music just don't cut it Jo baby...I could see a minor lapse of excitment but it's been 3 years...time to write this kilted klutz off...

GLENN DANZIG-"WHO KILLED MARILYN?"/"SPOOK CITY USA" PLAN 9
COOL AS SHIT... A solo single from the MISFITS lead vocalist...the bitchinist band east of the ol Mis'...guess both of these are ol 'Fits tunes and I gaurantee you'll play this mammy til the needle is riding the rubber...the themes aren't quite as heavy as his bands but this is such a hot couple tunes-and besides he's the only singer in the world that'll help you up on stage so you can dive back into the crowd...Limited I'm sure like all Plan9 releases so don't wait and accept your fate...

BLACK FLAG-"LOUIE LOUIE"/"DAMAGED I" Posh Boy Records
The final installment with Dezo the human dynamo on vocals...what a killer this record is...great production...I'm glad they decided to put this out just before their hot LP hits the streets...get your arses out to the midwest you rock and roll studs...

MINUTEMEN-"JOY"/"BLACK SHEEP"/"MORE JOY" New Alliance Records
MINUTEMEN-"JOY"/"BLACK SHEEP"/"MORE JOY" New Alliance Records
3 more greats from these speed merchants....this isn't quite as strong sounding as their first EP,nor is it as long(Three tracks totaling under three minutes)almost funk this time...this is short,great,brief,to the point,.expect the unexpected from these guys...

B PEOPLE-"YOU AT EIGHT"/"WEATHER TO WORRY" M.P.C.D." IRS
Full of holes...the sax is not necessary and adds to the mish mash hodge podge banality of this disc...That's the main problem with these buildups...by the time you get around to product...nobody gives a rip-the B side fares better as it's more direct-not nearly as nebbed out...the sax comes in short bursts that fits into the general scheme more effectively...Pat Delaney of the legendary DEADBEATS is here and M.P.C.D. could have been one of their outakes..Hey that makes two against one doesn't it?

MODERN ENGLISH-"SMILES AND LAUGHTER"/ "MESH AND LACE" 4·AD
This single picks up where the "Gathering Dust" 45 left off-somehow the LP however interesting lacked the conjunctive link between thought and deed... The same fierce guitar that comes out of nowhere on the GD single appears on both sides...the B side has a series of effective dynamics that keeps the energy from falling out...and a pensive break that does nothing but add to an already lasting effort...

SHATTERED FAITH-"I LOVE AMERICA" REAGAN COUNTRY" Posh Boy Records
Gotta tell you I'm real impressed with,like this band immensly...Jus check out all the good shit POSH BOY is putting out lately...this band doesn't sound that different from some other bands really but they have that fatal charm...lyrics+sound+image+a valid attempt to hate Reagan-they can't lose...strongly recommended...

O RDER FROM...
POSH BOY RECORDS
P.O. BOX 38861
LOS ANGELES,CA. 90038

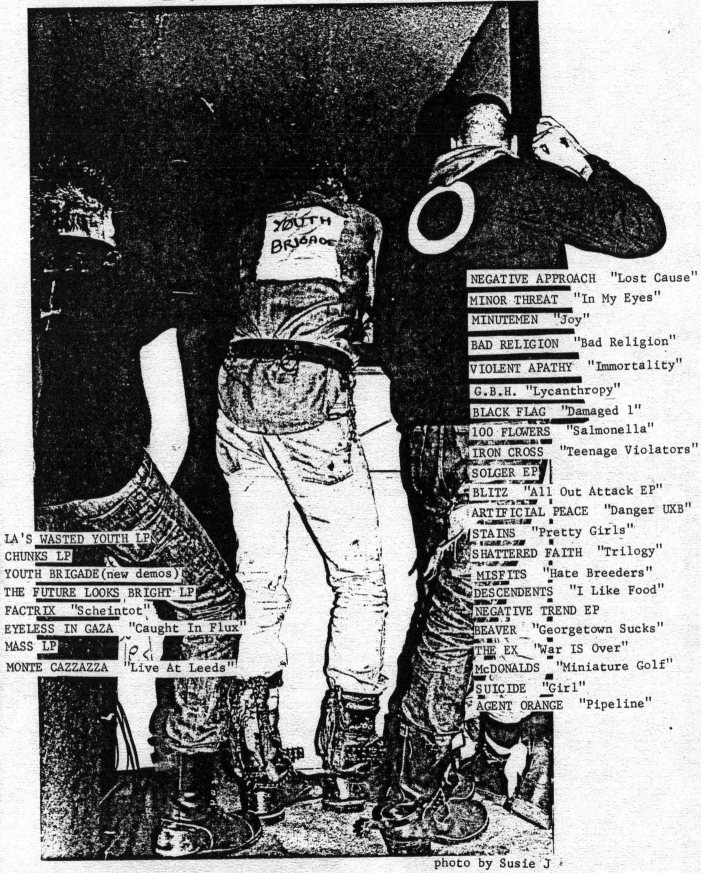

NEGATIVE APPROACH "Lost Cause"
MINOR THREAT "In My Eyes"
MINUTEMEN "Joy"
BAD RELIGION "Bad Religion"
VIOLENT APATHY "Immortality"
G.B.H. "Lycanthropy"
BLACK FLAG "Damaged 1"
100 FLOWERS "Salmonella"
IRON CROSS "Teenage Violators"
SOLGER EP
BLITZ "All Out Attack EP"
ARTIFICIAL PEACE "Danger UXB"
STAINS "Pretty Girls"
SHATTERED FAITH "Trilogy"
MISFITS "Hate Breeders"
DESCENDENTS "I Like Food"
NEGATIVE TREND EP
BEAVER "Georgetown Sucks"
THE EX "War IS Over"
McDONALDS "Miniature Golf"
SUICIDE "Girl"
AGENT ORANGE "Pipeline"

LA'S WASTED YOUTH LP
CHUNKS LP
YOUTH BRIGADE(new demos)
THE FUTURE LOOKS BRIGHT LP
FACTRIX "Scheintot"
EYELESS IN GAZA "Caught In Flux"
MASS LP
MONTE CAZZAZZA "Live At Leeds"

photo by Susie J

...my God after that long kiss I near lost my breath yes he said I was
a record on the turntable yes so we are records all yes that was one
true thing he said in his life and SCHOOLKIDS is open for you today
yes that was why I liked him because I saw he understood or felt what
music a woman wanted to hear and I knew I could always get round him
and I gave him all the pleasure I could leading him on till he asked
me to put the NECROS on and I wouldnt answer first only looked out over
the sea and the sky I was thinking of so many things he didnt know of
MINOR THREAT and DISCHORD RECORDS and the MISFITS and MICHAEL LANG and
old TESCO VEE and the boys playing all guitars and I say stoop and wash
up after they called it in ANN ARBOR and the poor devils half worked
to death and the girls laughing in their sweaters and the Detroiters
and the Kalamazooians and the devil knows who else from all the ends of
Michigan and the U.S. all clucking outside SCHOOLKIDS at 523 E. LIBERTY
and the poor other stores slipping half asleep and the vague fellows
and the help asleep in the shade on the steps and the big wheels of
the cars searching for to park nearby thousands yes and those handsome
clucks in t-shirts asking you if you need help in their shop and GEORGE
with the window through to his office and we missed the first shipment
and the workers going about serene at night dimming the lights and O
that awful deepdown torrent O and the sea the sea crimson sometimes like
fire and the glorious sunsets and the imports and the singles yes all
the queer little records and yes I shall wear red yes and how he kissed
me under the bin and I thought as well him as another and then I asked
him with my eyes to ask again yes and then he asked me would I say yes
to say yes and first I put my arms around him and drew him down to me
so he could feel my breasts all perfumed and his heart was going like
mad and yes I will go to SCHOOLKIDS RECORDS I will Yes.

I'm flying solo after DS's move to the nation's capital, and T & G would be my baby for the final six issues. Sexy Doyle cover shot when he was just a pup, taken at Bookies in Detroit by, I believe, my blushing bride Gerta Gompers. We loved the Misfits and they loved us back, many times gracing us with their poorly tuned, cheapo marine plywood guitars in glorious live shows. This issue features my recollections about our stint as slam dancers for the infamous Fear appearance on Saturday Night Live in NY. I was hanging in Ian's basement and he got a call from a dude at SNL named Mr. Mike, who said Belushi wanted slam dancers. So we drove up the 95 for our own little reward. It was quite a stellar lineup of Midwest/DC/NY HC kids in NBC's green room, cutting Mohawks into each other, sticking hundreds of 45s in the acoustic-tile ceiling of the room, and just generally fuckin' shit up. I walked by the dressing room where Belushi and Lee Ving were getting high and I almost walked in—but didn't. What a pussy (they woulda heaved my pencil-necked ass out anywho). Anyway, as you've probably seen, all hell breaks loose during Fear's first tune. I was mortified at all the pandering to the hardcore stereotype...what with mic cords ripped out, people who had never stage dived in their lives leaping from the stage like spawning salmon, guys bumping headlong into the band. I promptly left and went and hid in the green room. We had knocked a $60,000 camera over at rehearsal and the whole thing almost didn't happen, but Belushi had power and he was friends with Lee... At the end, on the tape, just before they pulled the plug, you can hear John Brannon bellow, "Negative Approach is gonna fuck you up!" I still have it indelibly etched in Beta hi-fi. Yes in the pre-five-second-delay days, all of America heard it... How cool is that???

TOUCH & GO

no. 17

$1

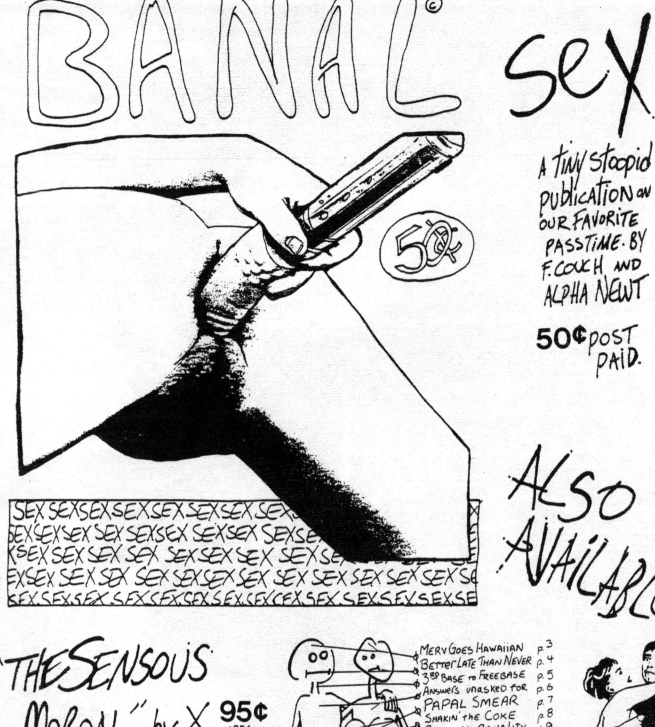

BANAL © SEX.

A tiny stoopid publication on our favorite passtime. by F. Couch and ALPHA NEWT

50¢

50¢ POST PAID.

ALSO AVAILABLE:

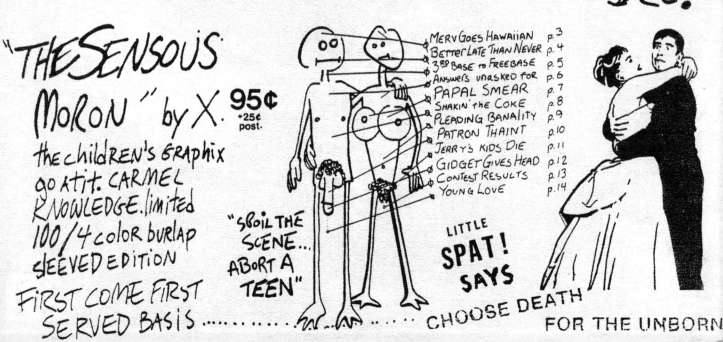

"THE SENSOUS MORON" by X. 95¢ +25¢ post.

the children's graphix go at it. CARMEL KNOWLEDGE. limited 100/4 color burlap sleeved edition

FIRST COME FIRST SERVED BASIS ....

MERV GOES HAWAIIAN p.3
BETTER LATE THAN NEVER p.4
3RD BASE TO FREEBASE p.5
Answers unasked for p.6
PAPAL SMEAR p.7
SHAKIN' the COKE p.8
PLEADING BANALITY p.9
PATRON THAINT p.10
JERRY'S KIDS DIE p.11
GIDGET GIVES HEAD p.12
CONTEST RESULTS p.13
YOUNG LOVE p.14

"SPOIL THE SCENE... ABORT A TEEN"

LITTLE SPAT! SAYS

CHOOSE DEATH

FOR THE UNBORN

354

#17

Graphic depicts improper skinhead haircutting technique...a swift but gentle motion with the razor will avoid skull damage as in the above...remember...going skin.... means safety first....(a pearl of wisdom from your editor)

HOMOSEXUAL*: A MALE WHO HAS SEX WITH MEN OR BOYS.
LESBIAN**: A FEMALE WHO HAS SEX WITH WOMEN OR GIRLS.

THIS ISSUE IS DEDICATED TO THE FILMS OF ZWARTJES CUZ HE'S DUTCH AND HE'S A REAL WEIRDO JUST LIKE ME YOU SEE?? (top that TKA you horny heathen...)

AND WOMEN STARTED MAKING LOVE TO OTHER WOMEN. THEY TURNED INTO HOMOSEXUALS* AND LESBIANS**: THEN IT GOT WORSE THAN THAT.

MEN AND WOMEN EVEN BEGAN MAKING LOVE TO ANIMALS AND STILL ARE . . . THIS IS ANOTHER WAY V.D. CAN SPREAD.

A WORD FROM YOUR FAVORITE EDITOR...

Well gang here it is the Christmas,Two year anniversary,year end issue all rolled into one...the last month saw 1)The total destruction of NUNZIOS in Detroit...(plumbing,furniture,the new wave painting the work)by the giant crowd at a recent gig...2)The move by your editor and his lovely assistant Gildee into a spacious home in Lansing(where gee I even have my own office) 3)The departure by THE FIX on another journey westward 4)The release of tons of new records so this issue will feature some of those new releases and some stuff I had to assimilate before reviewing you know....As some of you already know my co-editor has moved to DC so it's basically mah baby....with much thanx to those who helped me out this time namely...JEFF NELSON for the cover art for the "PROCESS OF ELIMINATION" EP that got "lost in the mail"....it was cool as shit and I am indeed in mourning-also ABBIE MAHLER,AL PIKE,MA PIKE,BRIAN POLLACK,J.CRAWFORD,FURRY COUCH,SHREDDER,THE MINUTEMEN,JODY FOSTERS ARMY,COREY RUSK,JOE McCREARY,AUTUMN RECORDS, ,GEORGE,LORI, and everyone else I dun forgot...The Midwest scene is alive and growing but already starting to fragment into petty little arguing factions that if left unchecked will destroy what little scene there is in no time...it's band together(no pun intended) or die alone & it's time people realize that...Nobody's big enough to stand alone...we're all dependant on each other whether we want to be or not..sure trashing a club is fun...but the end(no more gigs in this case it didn't matter because the club was closing anyway)hardly justifies the means...perhaps that's why the "Process" release party is being held in the heart of Motor City Murder district...which in actuality is fine cuz the wimps will be too scared to come anyway....so keep something shoved up your dicks and enjoy this hot new issue...it's the least you can do after all the time,money effort,mileage,sweat etc.i got on the line... AND SEND IN YOUR READERS POLLS... I SWEAR I WON'T TAMPER WITH THE RESULTS.... (your friend with the savory scrotum..

rare photo of NY Rocker Editor Andy Schwartz [a real stud by big apple standards]

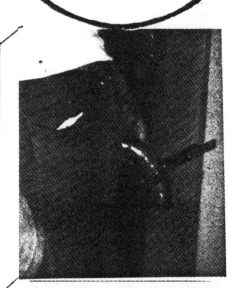

order <u>BANAL SEX</u> from 679 Arbor Lane W. Warminster,Pa. 18974

This is not funny!
<u>THE MEATMEN</u> live!

TOUCH and GO

BOX 26203 LANSING,MI 48909

from our readers

Tesco,
Thanx a million for sending me the new T&G and NECROS EP(fucking great record)I really appreciate it..We(7 SECONDS) are making a bunch of new tapes so you'll be the first to get one... What's going on in Mich?Any shows?We've had a few gigs in Skeeno.A great show happened in the basement of an art studio,it was great for sure,loads of fun,tons of new punks have been showing up,most of them skinheads.All the skins are skateboarders and they KILL... Super radical.Just like all of us die hard" hardcore punks.We had another gig last week that was cool,not too many people showed up(about 60)hardly any promotion out because we had only 2 days to put posters out. It was D.O.A. that ripped up the night,by doing a great set.They brought REALLY RED up(from Texas) They were OK but the PA kept going out so what can I say?Also the WRECKS played,they ate tons of shit(huh?ED.) that night(why?I don't even know why?)Also a band from "Carson City"(a town about 30 miles from Skeeno)played,they were called the yobs,they did alot of old punk classics(circa 77)but they were still cool.Well thanx again for sending all that cool shit,it's great to make friends out of state. Well anyway Skeeno's super fucking radical,but we're in it for fun,not blood,like the jerks that live in LA.Thanx   Steve Youth
RACISM SUCKS!!!DOPE SUCKS!!!BOOZE SUCKS!!!T.S.O.L. SUCKS!!!MEATMEN RULE!!!TOUCH AND GO RULES!!!SKEENO H.C. RULES!!!DC H.C. RULES!!!
Geez Steve could'nt a said it better myself...wish i could be out there in Skeeno to partake of the onslaught-but pen pals it'll be till I get the overriding urge to check out the real western sound for meeself...(till he gets the money and off his bleedin' arse is more like it,ED)

Thanx for the cool letter...your town indeed sounds cool as shit...

Dear Mr. Touch and Go,
    I'm not quite sure what issue I want, but could you please send me a copy of the issue with the highly caustic PHANTOM LIMB flexidisc review in it? I enjoy the bad reviews as well as the good, perhaps for the same reason I can listen to music from very diverse schools of thought. I used to have a "punk" band together called the La-Z-boys here in Columbus, but perhaps your reviewer would not have liked that either because on occasion we played more than 2 chords or one time signature within a given tune. Honestly, keep an open mind on music, or I'm afraid you'll see your self-proclaimed culture go the way of many others that maintained rigid and narrow parameters.
    Thanx, Kurt Tuckerman (guitar)
                    Columbus, Ohio

You are probably one of those people who stands at the back of the bar and screams 77' when in actuallity you wish PHANTOM LIMB Sounded that current...you see what you want to see...you are middle aged youth...it's easy to write us off as hardcore mag right Kurt...that's cool don't bother to look through anything unless it's about you...drink a cup full of my sperm and see the light-ED.....

TOUCH AND GO-
I live in Tokyo Japan and one of Tokyo's new wave fanzine's editor.I knew your name from FLIPSIDE.Why I interesting your fanzine.So I want know Michigan scene cause Michigan's scene is unknown in Japan but I know.Unknown scene where have good sound.Right? ha haWell if you interesting my letter I hope connect with you & exchange information.If you think so too hope to hear from you soon...
    Love Masako Sakurai TOKYO

TV-Thanx for #16.It's a great mag. But why do you hate TSOL?Do you hate the EP or just the LP?Or do you hate face paint?They sound great. (actually I just saw them last Sunday & they were really lame and bored and mechanical,but then the crowd was small and dull,I couldn't blame em! Interesting there's so much puritanism about alcohol and drugs out there. In SF kids get fucked up to go to shows,women sprawled out on the dance floor clutching hopefully at passing boots,fighters falling over with every other swing."Neutralized" as Chuck says.
            Murray Bowles
            San Fransisco
PS.Geez if you hate TSOL what must you be thinking of the ne ADOLESCENTS EP?The antichrist.The angel of death. (but Casey looks great in a cassock)

HEY TOUCH AND GO.
Can I 'ave a copy of 'yer mag? Sure I can.Here's $.
P.S. You wanna story on PUBLIC NUISANCE,Green Bays' only(BUT GREAT) H.C. band? Sure ya do.Send for it today(before midnight tonight.
        NOrbie Ugly
        Green Bay,Wis.

hello touch and gos
well i got your mag and i surely do appreciate it...seldom do I get to see a mag that i read from cover to cover as they say...that is there is little to choose from here..there is short news(good subway reading...non lp b side(which everyone I know hates)(add me to da list,ED)and sometimes mouth of the rat but seldom..you see, i get lot's of info from you guys..the scene here is somewhat lacking due to nys going backwards attitude clubwise..i mean we take bets on how long each new club is going to last...what I find humorous in your mag is the HATE directed towards ny..particularly the lad in the letters section that mentioned how blah blah the scene was here-poor guy..see there is quite an underground here but it keeps basically to itself...there are several clubs,A-7, 171-A,2x4,THE WAREHOUSE,BC(before closing)to name a few...these places are purposely kept quiet...keep the jerks out,keep away the pirates and students etc...but fuck the best scenes are the private parties where several bands get together and play for free-load bands here do,not do well enough money wise to be able to play in the big clubs...we never go out to clubs any more...so i'm sending you some issues of the hippie mag that we just finished and I know that it's slick in fact we were going to call it SLICK AS ADDICT GUESS i'm just getting old..in fact i can tell by the way my friends say "i like your new mag"instead of "I don't get your mag like they used to in the gold old days of 78 when we were ten times more violent...this issue even has a poem in it only because the guy uses the word "death ray"...keep up the good work and don't get old...the death of all punks.. most people i know can't handle much of the music around here so we stay underground but believe me b.flag and angry samoans(my faves) get quite a following around here but noone ever talks about it...i mean when you been there for going on thirteen years you start to say " who the fuck cares right?"I dress like I feel like dressing and i don't care..ricko
            i heard it before

Tesco-So yeah if I was part of the crew cut crew-I'd be bent outa shape...Geez FEAR looked lame,and so did the crowd(reference to Saturday Night Live,ED)And what is that stupid crouch that they all assumed while running across the stage?Talk about posing.Geez David Bowie wore a dress/Klause Nomi Always wears a dress,does that make them ultra cool too?If you ever see a video tape of that show yer gonna agree it was a lame game...it was interesting that they cut them off short...I'm writing you as a helluva storm whips up. Geez all the neighbors trash is being blown far away.I raed an interview with FEAR and they were mundane and insulting-not offensive and insulting.Not a speck of good humor either,oh well...
                    T.Stool
Hey gang is it my responsibility to respond to this type of mentality? Thought so....

PRIME TIME JOKE

Headliners

'Fear' riot leaves Saturday Night glad to be alive

DOZENS of punk rockers wrecked the set of *Saturday Night Live,* shouting obscenities over the air as they smashed furniture, equipment and props.

"It was a riot, mindless, out-of-control destruction of property," one Saturday Night Live insider told our man Alan Markfield.

"We had to switch away from the live show and go to a tape.

"The studio audience wasn't aware of the extent of the fracas. But the audience at home did hear some of the swear-words go out over the air, and all hell is breaking loose now from the affiliates."

The punkers — nearly 50 of them — were guests of the rock group Fear.

Things started going out of control during the dress rehearsal, insiders say, when Fear fans jumped up and started slam-bang dancing — a new punk craze that involves dancing, biting and kicking.

"But they just got carried away," said one stunned observer.

"Even the audience wasn't aware of just how bad it was . . . It became a total, out-of-control free-for-all."

Producer Dick Ebersol tried to usher the groupies into the Green Room, hoping to calm them down. Instead, they wrecked it.

"They destroyed the Green Room while waiting to go on," said one crew member who was there. "They destroyed a mini-cam camera, they destroyed two viewers and wrecked the viewing rooms."

That added up to $90,000 in damage. Additional vandalism brought the total to an estimated $200,000.

Ebersol and the show's chief of staff, Michael O'Donohue, will meet with NBC president Grant Tinker tomorrow to discuss the incident.

"I've been in this business for years and I've never seen anything like this," one NBC technician told The Post. "This was a life-threatening situation. They went crazy. It's amazing that no one was killed."

One slam dancer knocked over the support box for a handheld camera . . . resulting in a quick rewiring job that cost about $42 in engineer overtime, according to Ebersol . . .

And surprise cameo guest John Belushi, who at one point planned to join the skinheads for a little slam dancing, watched them in action and decided against it . . .

ED COLVER

TOTAL SHIT

TRUTH

HA! HA! R

As usual I had just the right thing written out in response to all of this(in this instance on the back of a bag at work)but here I am again ...but then I guess my head is cleared sufficiently for a better pubic reaction....the above article is a ludicrous example of creeping conservatism,or rampaging fascist journalism is more like it...what we've got here is scare tactics for middle America...what the public wants to here-I speak from experience as I was one of about 40 in attendance for Madison Avenues version of what the music is all about...I suppose we all shoulda told em' to reef on the bloated loaf,but hey who would pass up a chance to make a mockery of national TV?They herded us into the "green room" whatever the fuck that means(the walls were white)There was some guys from West Point sitting on the sofa (I swear I'm not making this up.)and they took it all in with little impish,brainwashed grins on their faces...well after awhile they got up and left saying something about being around us was contrary to everything they stood for(I aint gonna touch this one at all,ED)So they give us Cokes and everyone spills them on the carpet...the producers started shitting when people started throwing old records around and sticking them in the acoustic tile ceiling(very punk dun u dink?)Lee was cool and John Belushi was there and so was Brooke Sheilds that dumb cunt and we all went out and did a dress rehearsal and all the ultra-hip-over-thirty-sophisticated-boring NY audience made comments and Lee cut them down with fag jokes and the producers told

him he couldn't say that....FEAR's dressing room stunk like they were smoking heavy muggles in there(yukky poo)and one by one the NY assholes started trickling in...there are cool people in NY city like(Abbie, Big Al and his mom,Glenn,Googy(who got a green weenie from fuckin gangrenous gurls) Doyle,and Jerry,R.Kern and a few others...) but mostly they are just fuckheads that should eat my dung and go die downwind... and the bands?Don't make me laugh...KRAUT? CRO-MAGS?(Suck me Harley and who was that ultra chic baldy with you?) Bunch of drunk assholes copping onto whatever stops at the dock....OK enough already...the lamest

town in America...so here it is time to go on TV so suburbia can say"Ohmagosh willya look at that....and so the people in LA can say we did it first and so all of us cool midwesternandDC people could go ape(OK so everyone over reacted a bit that's to be expected...

but 200,000 dollars in damages??? That aint even funny...especially when the 90,000 camera was repaired for 42 bucks as was reported later...of course it looked staged...it was staged jeesus it was a lame idea but we had fun doing it ,,,but then people started swearing and someone smashed a pumpkin(very punky again coole) so they switched off-oh weeII life goes in...I guess the old rent a pig said it best after he escorted us out of the building"It'll give em something to talk about..."

SUZI, I KNOW HOW SICK YOU FEEL WITH THAT FEVER, AND ACHES. THOSE PAINFUL BLISTERS WILL SOON BREAK AND TURN INTO ULCERS AND THEY WILL DRY UP IN A FEW WEEKS.

BUT THE DISEASE WILL REMAIN ACTIVE IN YOUR BODY AS LONG AS YOU LIVE.

WHY DID GOD DO THIS TO ME?

MORE THAN LIKELY THE BLISTERS WILL COME BACK . . . ALL IT TAKES IS AN EMOTIONAL UPSET OR PHYSICAL STRESS.

DON'T BLAME GOD, SUZI. GOD TRIED EVERY WAY UNDER THE SUN TO KEEP YOU FROM GETTING THIS TERRIBLE DISEASE.

SUZI, JESUS SAID THE DEVIL IS A MURDERER AND A LIAR.* HE IS THE ENEMY OF ALL RIGHTEOUSNESS.** THE DEVIL HAS A TREMENDOUS POWER STRUCTURE† OF DEMONS TO DESTROY PEOPLE.

I BELIEVE DEMONIC ACTIVITY IS THE BASIS OF HOMOSEXUALITY TO DESTROY THAT INDIVIDUAL.

The new adventures of runaway fetus.

They'll never take me alive!

what th' fuh?

pop!

Hurry Doctor! If the Bishop finds out he'll ruin everything!

Geez, how was I supposed to know mom and dad would rather have a K-Car?

Come here you!

©1981 CRAWFORD

J.F.A.

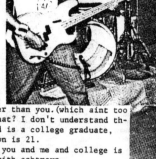

JODY FOSTER'S ARMY are a band from Arizona and they were interviewed sometime in november....they are..
Vocals-Brian(Stupor)Brannon-BB
Bass-Michael Cornelius-MC
Guitar-Don Pendleton-DP
Drums-Bam Bam-Bam

TV:What's it like living in Arizona?
Bam:it sucks
Don:it's like living in your oven with cowboys.
Brian:I like it.
Bam:it figures!
MC:Every time it gets really hot here I think "Someday I will leave"- it's boring.But there are a few good things that hold me here...
TV:So Rodney is spinning your record?
Bam:No he's playing it.
MC:Ya it was in his top 20 in FLIPSIDE magazine(huh what's that?ED)
TV:Is there any scene at all where you live?What other bands do you play with?
BB:Does Dolly Parton have tits?
MC:It was kinda lame except for a few shows.Now it's getting better because of Tony Victor's shows at Mad Gardens. All other places suck here...
DP:This is our scene-the skaters(Hardcore stuff)Besides that there's a few freaks left over from '77 and three Blitz people.It's mostly college talking heads preppie bullshit topsider people and kickers.
BB:There's the skaters and that's all that matters...
Bam:Well there isn't really a"scene" it's just a bunch of gooks who need somewhere to hang out cuz the hippies all beat them up anyway.
Dp,MC,BB:WHAT???
MC:We play with the MEAT PUPPETS,they are the best..and the FEEDERZ,they are the worst.We open for most all of the out of town hardcore bandss like TSOL BLACK FLAG etc...we play parties
TV:Do you get your rockets sucked after every gig?
MC:Don gets it before the show.I get it during.Bam thinks sex is too arty and Brian just slaps his monkey all the time.
DP:Brian's even uglier than all the girls out here.Most of them are violently ugly BB:Let me tell you about my vision!!!
DP:oh no!no!. not the vision!
Bam:No way It's not going to happen!Impossible,Brian you're such a geek,,,you're ugly too!
BB:I am not!Well here it goes,see I'm going to be just standing there at a gig and a way burly chick with a dress on is going to come up to me,put her hands on my feet and stand on her hands.Her dress falls down and she wraps her legs around my head and well...you can guess the rest...
MC:Stinky poon!
TV:What's your opinion of other scenes...
DP:I like Orange County cuz I'm from Aitch Bee ...England is stuck up...the Clash sucks...I like the JAM,what is the midwest? I hate all the Rockers from NY(AKA Johnny Thunders clones) and the wimp rock bullshit.
BB:This must be one of those trick questions.MC:I think there are little pockets of good stuff all over.LA seems like it's slowing down.I could never relate to the English stuff.
BAM:If you don't skateboard you suck and can't even have a scene.
TV:How old are you guys?
BAM:15,but that doesn't mean I can't talk to girls.....BB:Old enough to know but young enough to still be able to get away wi-

thit.....DP:Younger than you.(which aint too difficult,ED)BB:What? I don't understand that...MC:I is 22 and is a college graduate, Brian is 15 and Don is 21.
DP:That;s 105 for you and me and college is just high school with ashtrays...
TV:So Tucson has a lame crowd?
BB:I refuse to answer that question.
MC:Yeah very,the girls from phx could outslam all those wimp guys there.Tucson has tons of hairy dirty hippy bums with ugly dogs and girls.That's not what you thought when we played there.(BB said that)
DP:We played Tucson?Oh yeah...free pitchers of brew.The crowd wasn't hardcore,just poor and ugly.There was a pregnant retarded lady wh gave herself a ceaserian section in the hotel room next to us.We stole her t-owels.
BB:We still have the keys to her room.
TV:Any write ups or interviews with any other mags?
MC:Is that an offer?

DP:I got to be on Rodney's radio show.there was that FLIPSIDE thing. Locally not much,out here you have to have les Pauls and Marshalls and be a cover band.We get little mention when we trash entire bars.
MC:One club owner even called the cops on us after he threw us out.We have kind of a reputation now...
TV:What has the response been to your radical name and lyrics???
DP:What radical name and lyrics?
MC:Deny everything!
BB:Jody who?
BAM:Who can understand what Brian sings.
TV:YOU aren't worried about the FBI and the rest cracking down on Reagan haters?
BB:Aren't they afraid of BAM BAM?
DP:They can't crack down on everybody...
MC:Just us...
TV:What the hell does the song "Do The Hannigan mean?
MC:The song is a twenty second explanation of the actions of two Hannigan Brothers and their dad.They own a ranch in Douglas,AZ.They found some wetback mexicans on their land and tortured them.Tied em to trees and beat em for a few days.they didn't go to jail for it.Then one of the brothers gets caught with 500 pounds of pot in the back of this pickup.He claimed he was taking it to the dump.Yeah sure.He didn't go to jail for it.He is arich white man in a poor mexican town. Justice lives in america...
TV:Is Placebo Records your own label? No it's Tony Victers,the guy who puts on the shows at Mad Gardens...
TV:What would you do if Jodie Foster walked up to you witha mouth full of cosmic candy and offered to nurse your trouser snakes?
BB:I'd ask her how she was at handstands.
MC Too much candy is bad for your teeth
DP:Not with a mouthfull of that stuff.. Besides i gotta 45 and she only goes for guys with glasses and 22's...
TV:Geez wheres your spirit of adventure guys i got a boner just thinkin about it....so what inspired you to call yourselves J.F.A?

DP:I came up with the concept..MC:And we all agreed it was our destiny...we changed our name to JFA when we realized it was more than a song;it was a whole movement.All the skinhead skateboarders are JFA not just the band...
TV:What do you hate more than anything in the world?
MC:Reagan,I hate our president Ronald Reagan more than anything else in the world

Jodie Foster's Army

He shot Reagan, he shot the Pig, didn't he?
He shot the secretary in the head, didn't he?
Between the eyes, in the chest, .22's are the best.
For your dear,for your honey, kill the prez, leave the rest.
We're Jodie Foster's Army, Jodie Foster's Army!
In your room, plot the crime, Mom and Dad's house.
People Mag, Jodie dear, for you I'll kill that louse.
Shoot the prez, shoot a cop, the secretary too.
We're Jodie Foster's Army, we've got guns, how 'bout you!
We're Jodie Foster's Army, Jodie Foster's Army!
Kill!

DP:Girls with red hair,they all have yellow teeth and clear eyebrows and freckles...Girls with control top underwear.I like the kind with small sides.
BB:Chicks who don't perform my vision.
BAM:Brian
TV:What is your favorite food,band etc?
ALL:Santa Cruz,skateboards,indys,cokes and snickers.The MEAT PUPPETS are the best.Japanese girls with tiny hands and high heels.Empty swimming pools...the GERMS,BLACK FLAG,TSOL,CIRCLE JERKS etc. .22s loaded with jelly beans...
TV:Do you like your dads?
DP:Yeah
BB:Yeah
BAM:My real dad is OK,my stepdad sucks shit,but he was nice today because he bought me a drum pedal.

continu-ed→

J.xF.xA.x

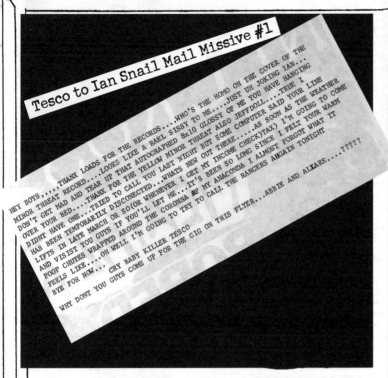

Tesco to Ian Snail Mail Missive #1

HEY BOYS,,,,THANK LOADS FOR THE RECORDS...WHO'S THE HOMO ON THE COVER OF THE MINOR THREAT RECORD...LOOKS LIKE A RAEL SISSY TO ME....JUST UH JOKING IAN... DON'T GET MAD AND TEAR UP THAT AUTOGRAPHED 8x10 GLOSSY OF ME YOU HAVE HANGING OVER YOUR BED....THANX FOR THE YELLOW MINOR THREAT ALSO JEFFDOLL...TRUE I DIDNT HAVE ONE...TRIED TO CALL YOU LAST NIGHT BUT SOME COMPUTER SAID YOUR LINE HAS BEEN TEMPORARILY DISCONECTED...WHATS NEW OUT THERE.....AS SOON AS THE WEATHER LIFTS IN LATE MARCH OR SO(OR WHENEVER I GET MY INCOME CHECK)TAX) I'M GOING TO COME AND VISIST YOU GUYS IF YOU'LL LET ME ...IT'S BEEN SO LONG SINCE I FELT YOUR WARM POOP CHUTES WRAPPED AROUND THE CORONNA OF MY ANACONDA I ALMOST FORGOT WHAT IT FEELS LIKE....OH WELL I'M GOING TO TRY TO CALL THE RANGERS AHGAIN TONIGHT BYE FOR NOW... CRY BABY KILLER TESCO WHY DONT YOU GUYS COME UP FOR THE GIG ON THIS FLYER...ABBIE AND ALLARE....?????

HAY GANG DID YOU KNOW SPERM DIES AT 110 DEGREES FARENHEIT???NOW YOU CAN TELL YOUR MAIN SQUEEZE SHE CAN THROW AWAY ALL THOSE PILLS,FUNNY LOOK-ING RUBBER HATS AND CREMES...BECAUSE HYLANDCO. INC. PRESENTS THE BRIAN BRAND®"JUEVOS STEAMER" THAT WILL UNCONDITIONALLY KILL ALL THOSE UNWAN-TED TADPOLES (and all your worries)IN JUST 5 S-HORT MINUTES...NO MORE"I'M PREGNANT IT'S YOUR FAULT AND YOU GOTTA PAY HALF"or"IT'S SAFE GO AHEAD BIG FELLA"   SEND$19.95 TO 614 S. PUTMAN #2 WILLIAMSTON MICH...ORDER NOW.....

MC:My dad works for Reagan He is very Republican...
TV:How come your record is so great?
DP:Cuz I'm from Huntington Beach...
BB:Cuz I sing on it...
MC:Because we're skateboarders.
BAM:Because it's us!
TV:Views on racism and sexism and the moral majority and and...
MC:The moral majority are the new NAZI's and the new right are the fascists of our day.Sexism and racism are based on narrow mindedness,stupidity and mans t-endency to destroy what he doesnt und-erstand.
DP:Alot of people are dicks..the moral majority and anybody that tells you how to live are dicks.Abolish government! If you are a dick you make yourself one. Sex,race it doesn't matter.You do it to yourself and deserve to be thrashed.
BAM:The moral majority just sucks.sexism is doing ok I guess...Racism is well you know haow it is...

BB:Of the three sexism has my vote for president...
TV:Who gets most of the girls?
BAM:I DO
BB:I DO
BAM:Fuck u Brian you're too ugly!
MC:You guys call anything with a wet hole a girl...How sick!
DP:Lorne Greene...
HAY GANG WRITE TO JFA AND ORDER THEIR COOL RECORD FROM MIKE COR-NELIUS 1347 W. 10 PL   Tempe Arizona   85281

Do the Hannigan
Get a mexican
Get a whip
Get stupid
Get pissed
Get your brother
Get your dad
Get abusive
Get mad
Get in jail
Get out
Get some dope
Get caught
Get a mexican
Get a whip
Get stupid
Get pissed

JODY FOSTER'S ARMY-"BLATENT LOCALISM" EP
I betcha when these guys whip out their flacid cranks to make some dew they look like boards with trucks...well ok they live and die by swimming pools with no water in them...their record?Oh ya it's of course boss-o-matic with hairaising tun-eage like "Cokes And Snickers"("is all I eat...health sucks,health sucks")Young brash and twisted...everything you used to be before your punkiness jaded out n' you got old and we forgot about you... ME? I've been reborn...

SHREDDER SPOUTIN'

GOO GOO DA DA
I'm sick..Yes I mean Robitussin-by-the-bed and Twilight-Zone-on-the-tube-sick. As for this city,she and I are pretty much in the same condition.There has n-ot been a hardcore gig in a loong time and there is only one in sight/WASTED Y-OUTH,CIRCLE JERKS,999 at the Florentine, in 3 days,everyone knows the local bald-ies and black hatters are gonna fight... again.But alas...there has been some gr-eat plastic worming it's way into the l-ocal disc shops.AGENT ORANGE have a sin-gle("Pipeline'/"Everything Turns Grey') and an EP (Living In Darkness)out on P-osh Fag records-what an amazing band.. the infamous Posh has also released the second ROTR disc which is another gem... including,,,everybody.45 GRAVE is simply going up,up,up with a "Black Cross'/"Wax single in the stores....in the softie d-ept is TWISTED ROOTS who've just releas-ed a single.What do they sound like?They sound like people who have never heard t-he GERMS,SCREAMERS,SEX SICK OZIEHARES etc. The trouble is...they are all ex-members of those bands.A new ADOLESCENTS single is out,post mortem.Also out on the Front-ier catalogue is Choir Invisible,ex FLY-BOYS go scaredom.NERVOUS GENDER(who are the only band deserving to open for Bob Dylan if he hits LA)are soon to release their long awaited "Music From Hell"LP.

Also under Lucifer's influence is the c-ompilation EP "Hell Comes To Your Home" including 45 GRAVE,RED CROSS and more,o-ut on Bemisbrain Recs.Halloween saw the CRAMPS show...a slated event,an actual flop,the ECHO AND THE BUNNYMEN show(I l-ove them,however I'm not thrilled by R-eceda audiences,and the same old Oki D-ogging.That's what L.A. punks do when t-here are no shows.They eat teriyaki hot dogs and kiss each others' asses.Thrills.
    As for extra terestial happenings hap-penings the greatest Rock and Roll band was on Saturday Night Live and you know I don't mean those 5 lesbian sell outs.
        Jesus died for your mother's sins
                SHREDDER

Get the comic strip that bites the... hand that feeds it!! Baboon Dooley ROCK Critic!! write: J CRAWFORD 7 So. Pt. Trr. Kinnelon NJ 07405

SNAP! SNAP!   snap!

"the best of its kind!!" -OP MAGAZINE

THE EFFIGIES-"HAUNTED TOWN" EP Autumn
Records
Holy shit what can I say except when
this rips through my apartment the p-
aint peels and the cats run for cover-
THE EFFIGIES prove to be light years
above their fellow Chicago competion
with this their debut effort...Whoev-
er made the Angelic Upstarts comparison was way off base...fast and heavy
duty and the English wish they had b-
ands this good(with some exceptions
come on you know)Some people are bitching that they've mixed down the aggro
in John's voice but I've got no problems in regard to that(but it does lack
some of the gutpunch exhibited on the
BUSTED AT OZ LP....this was one of those bands_I WAS SICK OF HEARING ABOUT
HOW GREAT THEY WERE I WANTED PROOF...
and now that it peruses my turntable
on a daily basis I can expound on it's
virtues as the unrelenting strains of
"Below The Drop" start each new day w-
ith the thought that all in Chi-town
is not lost....Order from AUTUMN RE-
CORDS 2427 N.Janssen   Chicago,Ill.
69614

TAV FALCO'S PANTHER BURNS-"TRAIN KEPT
A ROLLIN'/"RED HEADED WOMAN Frenzi
Real authentic loose tube rockabilly-
this second effort features Alex Chilton ...with all the fluff coming
out in this genre it's nice to hear
something with immediacy...crude production which is their trademark t-
hankfully so...

DESCENDENTS-"FAT" E.P. New Alliance
Records
I betcha these zanesters have that
rare disease where they need to order pizzas under false names at least
once a night or else give themselves
fresh fruit enemas and cut tropical
farts in front of old people eating
at the 5and10 or else they fish for
a living cuz deep inside the latent
need to make great music drives them
on into the outer reaches of culinary
rock cuz you see what they do no one
does better like make me happy cuz
they play good music you see and "My
Dad Sucks" is the name of one of there songs and they will succeed in
turning dining back into eating I am
sure the end...

DISCHARGE-"NEVER AGAIN"/"DEATH DEALERS"
"TWO MONSTROUS NUCLEAR STOCKPILES"
Clay Records
Someone at Clay called up the band and
said"Time for a new one and hurry up"-
well it seems that way...hardly any s-
emblance of progression...not that DIS-
CHARGE is into that,but the brilliantly
presented 12"is a fleeting memory in t-
erms of this piece of dogma...check out
this line "Choking lust crazy with thirst drinking from poisioned pools and st-
reams"..I mean a bigger fan of this band than myself does not exist,but their
narrow scope has them so bound up with
sociological ranting they seem now to b-
e running in circles..it would seem they
rode hot rails straight into the arms of
Armageddon...and now they must limp back
home...

VIRNA LINDT-"YOUNG AND HIP"/THE DOSSIER ON
VIRNA LINDT" Act Records
Fans of LORI AND THE CHAMELEONS will go
for this mammy with it's bitchin cosmo
dance twinkle...as much a product of the
cloistered young Scandinavian ultra cools
as anything this season...if those grand
Parisien palaces with the multi rooms still exist this is being spun right this
minute...will ya look at that face??

FLIPPER-"SEXBOMB"/BRAINWASH" Subterranean
If this was any other band people would
be saying "Hey this sucks" but since it's
FLIPPER everyone is beating meat over it
but"Hey this sucks"...

PIG BAG-"SUNNY DAY"/"ELEPHANTS WISH
TO BECOME NIMBLE   Y Records
About the only English funk capable
of setting me on my ear...sure some
of it is good...like a McDonalds b-
urger is good...but more than once
in a great while no...(tis my analogy)P.Bag bags the in vain attempts
at border soul and plays a straight
and clean funk that is good for white
people....

SUBVERTS-"INDEPENDENT STUDY" EP
Clandestine Records
I dont know why exactly but I can't
review this record.And since I do
it alone here I can't say"Here Clem
you take this one"or"Hud if you like
it so much etc....cuz boo hoo I don't
(sob)like this at all garsh(sniffle)
Brian I don't(gurgle)think you can
sing at all and when I break wind it
sounds more(sigh)melodic and ,and,
I feel better now...the records over
and so is this review...

MAD SOCIETY EP-Hit And Run Records
....short primitive songs with Stevie
singing who is a youngster...the image and name are better than the sound
but who cares it's still something d-
ifferent....Steve was also in this g-
reat video a while back with the WEI-
RDOS that you gotta see...running around in a coonskin cap smashing statues-
order from....HIT AND RUN RECORDS PO
BOX 480497 Los Angeles,Ca 90048

DEAD KENNEDYS-"NAZI PUNKS FUCK OFF"/Mo-
ral Majority" Subterranean Records
Finally the voice of someone on a pedestal is heard...thanx Jello...

Safety Instructions

Schoolkids' Records and Tapes

523 E. Liberty
Ann Arbor, MI 48104
(313) 994-8031

LIFE VESTS

SEAT BELT RELEASE

EMERGENCY LANDING POSITION

OXYGEN MASK

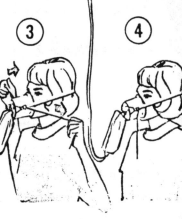

362

THE FARTZ-"BECAUSE THIS FUCKIN WORLD STINKS EP" Fartz Records

Blasting from the bunghole of Wash. state are this bunch of methane monsters whose 9 songer has gotta be one of the years best...bang bang and the KLAN(KKK THAT IS) is dead...or so they wish cuz inside comes all sortsa propaganda about them holding rallies on Lillian Carters land...I had to beg borrow and steal to get this godamn thing cuz the band must think their too cool or something to send me one even after I sent them a mag(not really but this'll piss em off so they'll write the FARTZ will look like...my loaf is I'm dieing to see what hate mail from turgid jus thinking about it...crude, sloppy,pounding,heavy duty,hit your granpa with a baseball bat when he's not looking type of music you gotta have if you ever want too find happiness....

45 GRAVE-"BLACK CROSS"/"WAX" Goldar Records

....makes it tough for an all American spooked out combo to live up.... "Wax" is sludge plain and simply.... as unoriginal as the day it was first conceived...at least the other side moves but hardly any qualification for any rave reviews...I expected something earsplittingly weird and got some decidedly heavily hyped squat from the west coast...life is never what it seems to be.....

CRISIS-"ALIENATION"/"BRUCKWOOD HOSPITAL" Ardkor Records

A posthumous release from some late 78 Peel sessions...not unlike old MENACE or DRONES-mysterious delay in the release of this as if awaiting the cult following somehow the media would like us to believe still worships the dead corpse of this band(who brokeup in June of 80...one of the members is in THEATRE OF HATE now if you are interested-I guess the bottom line is this is for CRISIS' total fan if that still exists-"White Youth" was still their high point.......

HATES-EP

This is the third EP from Houston's HATES....a band that can play virtually nowhere in that city of immigrants(from where I live over 100,000)All the clubs say something wimpy about not wanting the crowd they attract or some such shit...I don't like this as well as the other two records....not quite the drive...but a good record nonethe less...Write 4200 W 34th Box 132 Houston,Texas 77092

MIDWEST UPDATE

YOUTH PATROL/SUBURBAN ANGER/BORED YOUTH
MEATMEN/NEGATIVE APPROACH/VIOLENT APATHY
NECROS (the last night at NUNZIOS-Detroit
Well it finally happened the final Nunzios show...big deal...there have been at l-
east 4 last night at Nunzios over the last
couple of months,but this time it was really the last night...the shows up till n-
ow have been really lame with bands like
the CULT HEROES playing...this one was different...never before has there been this
many bands at Nunzios....especially this
many good bands...and the cover was only
4 bucks...also a very important aspect of
this show was anyone with an ID even if it
was obviously fake was let in....that's a
big step in the right direction for this
area....YOUTH PATROL started out and played
their best set ever....SPIKE put more energy
into his singing than ever before and the m-
usic was pretty tight....YP has gone through
more line up changes than Tesco has vibrating butt plugs....but this lineup looks as
if it might be stable....this gig they projected a more confident and energetic image
SUBURBAN ANGER were next..thhey formed just
3 months ago and none of them had ever played an instrument....they just wanted to start a band and it shows...they aren't very
tight or in tune but this isn't to say they
are bad...they improve with every show and
practice alot and Lozon is sort of a local
cult figure...tonight however was not one
of their better nights...musically they w-
ere as usual but the energy just didn't s-
eem to be there...there wasn't as much crowd participation or dancing as their last
show...BORED YOUTH took the stage and they
were the hottest band of the night...they'
ve been playing on shit bills like opening
for the SEATBELTS...and they don't deserve
to have to play with the shitty old farts
of Detroit...they're young and fast but t-
hey are also very musical...they've managed to be fast and energetic but their songs
arent boring and all the same like so many
new fast bands these days...also they have
a new singer now...they used to be a three
piece and the guitarist would do most of
the singing but they realized the need for
a vocalist whose not tied down to an instr-'
ument....but the guitarist still sings on a
couple songs....Rob can sing he doesn't just
scream....NEGATIVE APPROACH is Detroits hottest band..their music is more original
than some other Detroit bands and John
the vocalist is incredible...I've never
seen anyone so into his singing...the w-
hole time h'es on stage he's a madman-
a screaming banshee....simultaneously
stern and lucid and a man not playing with
a full deck as far as his feelings for the
rest of society...his face turns red and
his eyes bulge out as if the inner rage
will surely send blood streaming through
the sockets at any moment...tonight John
was sick and their were a few fuckups but
I've never seen them do a bad set...there
were plenty of kids dancing and helping
with the vocals...after watching FEAR on
a video of Saturday Night Live(in person
was a helluva lot more fun)VIOLENT APATHY
took the stage....tonight was one of their
better nights and they played all of the
audiences faves like the "Hoo Hoo" song...
their sound was garbled but that was the
fault o f the PA...Kenny's performance was
one of his best...it rivalled his Don Nei-
ls presence....he was spitting out his
lyrics with his best maniac"just released
from the mental ward quality"..the last
band to play was the NECROS...I don't remember what song they started or stopped
with but the energy level was unusually
high.....they managed to be wild and still
keep it together...the club was packed
and half the audience was underage kids
who were mostly all dancing...about half

Continued

NEGATIVE APPROACH

BORED YOUTH

NECROS

Hi,
I just finished reading the interview with Ian Mackaye and got so h-
ostile I thought I'd better write
before I smashed something.Who the
hell does he think he is?With his
we were diving before Black Flag b-
ullshit.Who gives a fuck?It's like
the Tubes singing "I was a punk before you were a punk.I mean really
do you think the recognition has to
be somewhere?I thought anti vanity
was the key ingredient,and as for h-
is anti-pot and anti drink thoughts-
ok great,it's sensible and all that-
everyone knows that.But how far does
hi belief take him?Is he willing to
only associate(business and otherwise)
with people of said beliefs or only
verbally obuse them in publications
and at public functions?I'll bet the
people that press hi records and d-
istribute the shit he says and allow
him to play his music places don't
share similar thinking.So it seems to
me that his philosophy is in action
only when it suits his needs--one more
thing to bitch about.I mean really if
you're going to hold some thing to be
gospel then it means that your whole
life should reflect those thoughts
right?He says that he hit some kid in
the face for blowing pot smoke in his
face--wow--I could get a gun and blow
him off the world,does that make me
the best?The only thing he taught that kid was that he'd better have better
means to protect himself.More violence-
it's really sick.Then he talks about
people who only associate with certain
people ending up thinking like them-
oh god I couldn't believe I read that.
And he's not suscepable to that huh?
There's 230 million people in these g-
reat states and he chums with maybe
200 hundred(huh?ED) and he thinks he's
not being one of a crowd?The depth of
his thinking is as shallow as Johhnyy
Rottens skin.The man has no sense.But
despite the fact I'm willing to like
his music and enjoy the fact that at
least he makes a statement,however m-
isguided it may be.I wonder if that's

allright with him,I mean i consort
with known drinkers,smokers and p-
eople that actually enjoy sex.While
that doesn't make me better I think
it makes me more honest.
                    PAT
                    GRAND RAPIDS

THE FOLLOWING RESPONSE IS FROM ONE WHO SAW
COPY OF PRECEDING LETTER PRIOR TO PUBLISHING
DATE...

Pat,
I just finished reading the letter
you wrote concerning the interview
with Ian MacKaye and got sooo hostile I thought I'd better write before I smashed something.Who the H-
ELL do you think you are???Your letter is so pathetically full of pre-
varications and total misconceptions
it's a joke.You've never heard of p-
eer pressure before huh?Let me expl-
ain.You see many young adolescents
are very much influenced by their friends,and such and they want to be a-
ccepted by them,you know "fit in."Unfortunately this mostly deals with drugs
alcohol and sex and some of them don't
even enjoy what they're doing but they
think it's the cool thing to do ya dig?
What Ian is offering,,yes go look it up
in your dict-
ionary...no it doesn't mean demanding
that one believe in something or ridiculing others if they don't happen to b-
elieve the way you do)is an alternative
...to simply let kids know they do have

a choice and a sensible one at that.You
seem so ANGERED and INTIMIDATED by a p-
erson who thinks for himself and disre-
gards drugs and alcohol etc.And yes Pat
some of Ian's friends and business associates do use drugs and alcohol and he
doesn't condemn or think any less of them
so try not jumping to your jaded over
the hill and jaded conclusions....Did you
decide to fabricate his statements so it
would fit into your own train of thought?
In no way did I even get a slight implic-
ation of the "I was a punk before u were"
syndrome.Ian simply answered the interv-
iewer's question"Compare the DC scene now
with a year ago" and Ian proceeded to explain which bands were happening...what
they sounded like and how the scene developed and how it's not just an LA imitation which is of course what is going to
many peoples presumption...But you made
it clear you don't give a fuck about any
of that.OK if some people enjoy drugs and
alcohol and they feel it's benefiting them
in leading a better life then fine-I can't
condemn them,after all it's their choice,
but I do not believe in the use of drugs
alcohol or pot and I command the severest
respect in that area,so if someone ever in-
tentionally blew pot smoke in my face,my 1st
impulse would be to ram a blunt instrument
down that assholes throat so fast has atrophy-
ing brain would spin.You call it unecessary
violence...in your eyes perhaps... but are
you so passive that if someone antagonist-
ically defied your creed and inflicted elements onto you that you beleived were harmful to you own well being(and purely for
his or her own folly) would you stand by and
take it?Oh and aren't we so priveledged...
you're "willing"to like Ian's music...EITHER
YOU LIKE IT OR YOU DON'T,even though the statements made are so "misguided in your eyes-
It's apparent you totally misconstrued the
whole interview and WANTED something to bitch
about...Sorry Pat you directed your binge of
defamation at the wrong person.Ian is one individual I happen to respect a great deal and
it pissed me off good to read a letter containing such injust calumny by a misguided woman
such as yourself..I'm sure Ian cares who you
associate with as much as you care who he associates with and NO IT DOESN'T MAKE YOU MORE
HONEST THAN IAN to admit you consort with drinkers,smokers and people who enjoy sex...bec-
ause he never said otherwise...Let me see if
I can sum this up for you in a manner you w-
ill understand because it seems your thinking
runs about as deep as a stagnant puddle...plus
you have a habit of putting words in peoples
mouths..Ian does not drink or take drugs.He d-
oes not like the way they effect his mind and
the obvious effects on others.Everyone knows
that's sensible right?He does not choose his
friends and associates on the basis of whether
or not they use intoxicants...that is a ludicrous presumption on your part...oh and please
do reply Pat,I'm interested how and in what
manner you'll misconstrue my letter...
                    ABBIE MAHLER
                    NY NY

Dear Touch and Go:
I recently moved back here,to
Jackson from Los Angeles.Circ-
umstances in Hollywood forced
me to leave.Anyway your magazine was recommended to me by a
friend there as a possible contact,since I have not lived here since 1972.I would like to f-
ind out where I can get a copy of
the magazine or how much it costs
and if I can order it by mail.I a-
lso need to find out where gigs
are.I had very many friends there-
i have none here(except for my family)Another thing I am interested
in is forming a band.I had a band
in hollywood.I was the singer.My
boyfriend was the bass player,and
my best friend was the guitar pla-

yer.They ran off together.End of
band.End of Hollywood.End of my
life.Here I am.Help me.Where is
everyone?
                    Shirley Lewis
                    Jackson,Mich.

DEAR FRIENDS,
I'm a journalist very interested in
new american rock.I work for many magazines and newspapers,and I direct also the new wave section of a rock magazine called "Il Murchio Selveggio"
(45,000 copies printed)I read something
about your bands FIX and NECROS and I
decided to write you to know if it's
possible to receive their records along
with some information.If I'll write som-
ething(as I think I'm preparing an article about not-californian american punk)I'll send you the magazine.I hope you
can help me sending me the two records
and informations.Thanx alot for all,hope
to hear from you soon.
                    Frederico Guglielmi
                    Via Ugo De Carolis 53
                    00136 Rome Italy
note....bands and fanzines should contact
this cat unless a writeup times 45,000 doesn't turn you turgid like it did me,ED.

hey!
got any good
Blindie jokes?
wanna run my
comic strip??
write: JCRAWFORD
75o.Pt.Trr.
Kinnelon N.J.
07405
"refuze to be ignored!"

HEAPS MORE SHIT:
"JOY" EP FROM THE MINUTEMEN -
3 SHORT, SHARP, & TANGLED SPAS
ATTACKS FROM L. A.'S STUPIDIST
LOOKING BAND.

"FAT" EP FROM THE DESCENDENTS
5 WOOPERS THAT WRENCH THE
FISH STENCH OFF OF BILLY'S
BOOTS. IAN HAS SOLD 50 TO
FANS IN THE D. C. AREA SO
BUY ONE AND FEEL COOL.
(SORRY IAN)

SALVATION ARMY -
THIS SINGLE IS POP MUSIC
WITH OBVIOUS DRUG WORDS
AND/OR IDEAS. YOU WILL BE
EMBARASSED BY LIKING IT.

ALL THREE OF THE ABOVE
AVAILABLE FOR $2.50 EACH
(POST PAID).

SEND FOR OUR MAG,
"THE PROLE" (EDITED
BY D. BOON). 75¢

COMING OUT SOON:
"LAND SPEED RECORD"
BY HUSKER DU
LIVE ALBUM RECORDED ON THE
LAST STOP OF THEIR "CHILDRENS
CRUSADE" TOUR.

"FEEBLE EFFORTS"
9 SONG COMPILATION 7" (33 1/3)
OF SOLO CLOSET CASES PLUS A
COUPLE OF CLOSET TEAMS.

NEW ALLIANCE RECORDS
P. O. BOX 21
SAN PEDRO, CA   90733

WRITE FOR INFO ON PRODUCT
BY ARTIST RAYMOND PETTIBON OF
ALBUM COVER & COMIC BOOK FAME
(BLACK FLAG, MINUTEMEN, &
 "CHUNKS", "CRACKS...")

GEORGE DID THIS DRAWING

LIVE CRUD

TOTENTANZ/MX 80 SOUND at BUNCHES
Alright another place where something original might happen...the
first bands' name means "dance of
death" or something like that-th-
ree guys sitting in total darkness playing synthesizers and treated guitar etc...to say they were
long winded would be a compliment
(this is the 3rd time I've seen
them so save your hasty judgemeant
commentary for something else)Oh
lot's of people probably liked t-
hem if only because they played at
a volume conducive to smoking,dri-
inking little watermelon drinks in
skinny glasses and neo cosmopolitan
chit chat...a mixture of dull and
uninspired electronics played in
the style of mid seventies monolit-
hic,eastern european hippie drone-
probably put their target audience
(people enjoying some form of euphoria)to sleep and us well we went
out near the end of their set to
steal some Haagen Daaz and get the
bad taste from our mouths...All the
way from San Fransisco comes MX 80
SOUND...I guess I have to admit they have alot of interesting ideas-
something was lacking in their weak
presence(don't you think bands on
RALPH are better heard than seen)I
guess I expected 4 guys to walk out
looking like armageddon personified
or something but right that's my
hangup...some of their tunes were v-

ery unique rythmically but came of
exceedingly flat vocally...a couple
of their songs sounded like R&R c-
irca George Thorogood or something-
quasi boogie that had the crowd unfortunately turned on...perhaps it'll
never be time for the crowd here to
truly think for themselves...a dose
of something fleetingly new before the
youth their convinced is fleeting fast
fades into the image of mom and dad...
the embodiment of midwestern morays...
more chatting...more smoking...and
more watermelon drinks...■

THE MISFITS/NECROS Ukranian Hall NYC
Another trip to the big apple this t-
ime on Halloween to catch the ultimate
band from the big shitty that is NY...
it was pretty funny cuz this old codger
who was in charge(I mean old like 80.)
had no idea what was in store for his g-
rand old palace of pomp from yesteryear-
I guess he kept asking guys in the MIS-
FITS "What type of music will this be?"
And their rather humorous reply was something like"You know man just rock&roll
it won't be very loud,don't worry...yuk
yuk...no doubt the first and last gig at
the Ukranian Hall...New York is weird I
can't deal with it at all...the hardcore
bands from there that I have heard suck
shit(KRAUT,FALSE PROPHETS,UNDEAD)and most
of the ones I havn't like REAGAN YOUTH,
and the CRO-MAGS probably a-
int much better(go fuck yourself Harley-
you little twerp)Of course the fuckin'
MISFITS are only like the most incredible
band consistently putting out records for
the last three years so when they came to
Detroit last month I was sure there was no

way they could live up to the freakin'gre-
tness of their image,records etc...Wrong
again they fuckin' knocked us silly with
all their great new songs like "Hate Breeders" "Skulls" and "Devil's Whorehouse"
With the current scampering by bands to
be the spookiest all the MISFITS need do
is sit back and laugh at the rest...TSOL
are a fuckin'joke...I can't believe people
can even listen to that shit cuz it don't
cut it not even...right Bonham walking around Chicago with them with theirwhite f-
aces was cool...their so much cooler than
Black Flag...what the fuck does that mean?
 Anyway back to this old decrepit hall in
NY...a pretty good turnout...the NECROS ran
through a typically great set except I got
cracked in the jaw and then broke a bone in
my hand when I punched back...fortunately
I hit him in the eye so he could'nt see w-
here I ran off too(hey I can't be expected
to be good at sex,writing,beatin' off,being
nice to small children,and be a good fighter
too can I?)Lots better than their debut at
Club 57 last summer that's for sure...The
MISFITS came out even wilder than they had
in Motor Town...maybe the old home town a-
dage holds true...it was cool cuz they showed old science fiction clips on a big s-
creen before they came out...old Googy was
on a drum riser and he almost got brained
when Jerry Only winged his bass at this big
plaque on the wall
     ...All I can say is I'd be n-
ard pressed to think of a more exiting
band live anywhere...they did a great new
song called "Mommy Can I Go Out And Kill
Tonight" plus all the old faves...the
show of shows...seeing this band on
Halloween....I popped a boner...

CARRY ON OI-Secret Records

OK so I went a bit off the deep end in regard to the Britshit last month so what if I like this new OI compilation alot it aint the first time I've gone ape with vehemant hatred only to sheepishly admit there is something valid in what I was railing against right???Holy poop the INFA RIOT cut here is good and so are the PARTISANS whose single on the OI label didn't turn me around...the LP starts off with an exceedingly stupid poem that leads into a bore of a ska tune by JJ ALL STARS that proves once and for all that medium should be buried...but the highlights have to be THE EJECTED who look like total motorhead cum studs and spikes types...but "East End Kids" and "Youth" by BLITZ are in my slightly tainted opinion the best two cuts on this mammy...all I can say is I'm much more heartened by this than anything else this mode of the isles has pumped out of late....but I still hate THE EXPLOITED, ANTI PASTI,VICE SQUAD and the other droppings...the DC kids tried to beat me up in NY cuz I hate THE EXPLOITED so when people say do you really hate em' i say...do my farts smell like meatloaf?

MATT JOHNSON-"BURNING BLUE SOUL" 4·AD

This LP is a very pleasant change of pace for the 4·AD label(although the first 30 seconds sound like a Lewis& Gilbert LP)It presents Matt in his first solo outing away from THE THE and THE GADGETS.Through a combination of serious percussion and synth hooks, quiet and very well placed guitar parts,and Johnson's breathy voice,a picture is delineated that has the inate ability to make the listener sit down and listen...(and deal with what a great fucking album this is.)The record fits together very well,to give one a very satisfying,if somewhat confusing view of the artist and his work.The lyrics alone will keep you wondering if Mr. Johnson is possessed by a rare genius...or simple possessed(Jerry Falwell should exorcise)Given the aforementioned commentary you should rush down to your nearest hit shop and grab "Burning Blue Soul"....after hearing this one you'll be craving it in the night.TJ

CHRIS AND COSEY-"HEARTBEAT" Rough Trade Records

Well since THROBBING GRISTLE is no longer together(why?) I assume these two either banded together as one half of the tiff that broke up the band or everything is amicable and they just had the ideas and the will to cut this-Cosey has been doing alot of girlie mags lately portrayed as some British wench in heat(see this months chart)The LP itself is magnificent...the same sort of twisto bouncing harmful synth such as was heard on the "20 Jazz Funk Greats"LP (the Discipline 12" was getting to be a bit much didn't you think?)It's great when you get all upset and depressed that a band bites the stiffy...but then isn't it grand when something really choice rises out of the ashes that more than makes the witto sadness go away...goo goo gaa gaa.....

GARRY BUSHELL PRESENTS FOR YOUR PENULTIMATE STIMULATION,RELAXATION AND EXULTATION — OI 3!

CARRY ON Oi!!

DISTURBING DOMESTIC PEACE

RODNEY ON THE ROCK VOLUME 2 Posh boy Records

Just in time for Christmas giving is installment #2 from what Rod plays on his show....TARGET 13 who apparently totally prostituted themselves by singing a song that gaurantees airplay-pretty foul stuff spiritually and physically...."1945" is the best song I 've heard yet from SOCIAL DISTORTION.. catchy as is the SHATTERED FAITH cut which follows...they will be releasing an LP soon I guess...BLACK FLAG does "Rise Above" that sports great vocals but a very poor mix...what can I say about the MINUTEMEN except this makes 109 different records I have with them on it which is fine with me....RED CROSS do a ho hum cut....CHANNEL 3 do "You Lie" which makes me drool ovre the prospect of their forthcoming album.... alright AGENT ORANGE another wigged out cover "Mr.Moto" with...you got it that great double beat snappin drm just like "Pipeline"...fucking choice...Venus does "Boys" which is great but the rest of side two is strictly sloth dropping.... save for the great re-recording of "Room To Rock" by LEVI...all in all it's a compilation well worth the funds so go out and be a consumer...besides you aint gonna get FLIPSIDE #28 any other way...

RIUICHI SAKAMOTO-"LEFT HANDED DREAM"

I'm not quite sure if this is available in this country but I believe this ex member of YELLOW MAGIC ORCHESTRA has at least one in the import bin over here....some of it sounds real rootsy which I guess for Japan means traditional...you know like in a Egg Roll take out place...but some of it is real interesting....on a par with John Foxx-a bit too repetitious at times but nonetheless an interesting LP...thanx to Masako Sakurai of VOICE CHIPS fanzine for sending me this......

THE EX-"DISTURBING DOMESTIC PEACE" Verrecords

Earlier material than their dynamite "Weapons For El Salvador" and the single shows a marked progression from what the band was attempting here... of course there's no way I'm going to try to negate whats going on here.... about as crudely simplistic as they come...rythym,structure and lyrical content seem to be the primary considerations,..melodic progressions and all semblance of trend is missing...from Belguim or Holland....very worthwhile.

DOLL BY DOLL-MCA Records

You know I'm making history...how many other fanzines or full fledged mags for that matter have given two shits in regard to any of the 3 D by D LPs?Well you know I've always stood by the genius of Jackie Leven as my friends heaped on the abuse all the while incredulous that I could listen to such a band...but onward I'll tread into the ranks of unpopularity...it's polished,it's clean,I like it.....But how much longer will labels stand by while the band continues not selling records in mass quantities?Not much longer I'm afraid...

LP's

WIPERS-"YOUTH OF AMERICA" Park Avenue Records

The WIPERS owe no debt of allegiance to anyone...their creation is externalized from the realms of categorically laid out(musical labels...) This second LP rose seemingly out of the ashes of silence...where the fuck is the press coverage,fanzine plaudits,or even chit chat at cocktail parties concerning this????Or am I simply losing any semblance of where my "hardcorepunkborderlineartsybraindamage" image fits in with the schemes and heirarchies of music in 1982?All I know is the bottom line is this is an incredibly hot fucking album and I'd be hardpressed to find a better guitarist in America today than Greg Sage...we said it before...ol' DS got nipple boners over their last LP-as did I....I'll never forget the time I played it for TJ one night when we were tooling for clam downtown...he simply went beserk and the passenger seat of my car was never the same...and from Portland Oregon no less...well I should n't say that what difference does that make?What is important is that if you aren't so fuckin hung up with whats hard enough to fit your punk image and what you can't write off as a r&r LP... what I'm trying to sputter is think for yourself...don't listen to me...don't listen to anybody...the WIPERS fit nowhere...they've created their own style totally..there are guitar sounds on this that are totally new and refreshing... totally,totally,totally hot....well I like it anyway....

ORDER FROM....PARK AVENUE RECORDS P.O. BOX 14947,PORTLAND OREGON 97214

THE BLASTERS-Slash Records

On the one hand this is as gussied up as a farm boy headed out on Saturday night if you catch my drift...slick production and the whole shebang..but somehow the whole thing doesn't come off...well no better than any Robert Gordon album...or Catfish Hodge for that matter...the singers good i guess-he does emote a lot more than most of these types...but it's just old R&R isn't it?Best songs are "I'm Shakin" and the C&W sound on "Never No More Blues" But I guess I'll shut up because if had to listen to a steady diet of this I'd throw up....

U2-"OCTOBER" Island Records

Some asshole like Lester Bangs would no doubt call this"the accepible face of new wave" or some such rot but I've never had any qualms about what is cool regardless of it's mellow nature.DS...let's talk about what he said about their first album...whoops he said the same thing...they have alot of great ideas...soothing harmonies and I'm sure they feel as noble as they look on the cover...but there is something about their clinical and smug appro-that really bothers....subliminal hooks maybe are in effect but as many times as I listen to this I can't keep one piece of phrasing in my mind for more than a few seconds...bland music for a bland culture....

FACTRIX-"SCHEINTOT" Adolescent Records

With age comes wisdom(alright no comments from the peanut gallery)and I now have the maturity to let some of these twelve inch platters age gracefully on my turntable before I give them my divine seal of approval or a hearty hands down...What I'm trying to say is I'm still up in arms over what where,when and etc.regarding this FACTRIX LP...certain things can be stated in earnest,,,it is an album of incredible songs bestrewn with smatterings of psychosis...if you are languishing in your semi comatose suburban state then you're fair game for the twisted lapdog of subconscious sickness that writhes in it's maggot infested state on your living room floor in the form of songs like"Phantom Pain" "Ballad Of the Grim Rider" and "Center Of The Doll"....
A one of a kind exercise in something bigger than all of us.....

EYELESS IN GAZA-"CAUGHT IN FLUX" Cherry Red Records

The second effort from this duo is even more astonishing than their first in regard to consistency and natural progression.A beautiful package with a FREE(yes this one's actually free)12" that is essential to the product as a whole...entitled "The Eyes Of Beautiful Losers" it is a slow,enchanting and melodic introduction to the long player...always moving foward...slowly moving up the pace,preperation for the sheer dynamics of the album-The title cut of the EP could have been recorded in a monestary,and as the disc plays you begin to see why.The LP starts of with the ever familiar(to those cool enough to be attracted to this band,ED) E in G. sound,swirling and hidden in many shades of tempo and style...through 12 cuts a satisfying effort albeit one filled with lyrics

as disturbing as their "Photographs As Memories" LP of earlier this year... The disc shudders to a close leaving no room for the questioning soul,lost in the intricate weave of word and melody-These guys break new ground without being the least bit pretentious...In a league if you will with the BIRTHDAY PARTY,JOSEPH K, and MAtT JOHNSON..... A brave and adventurous work that is among this years' best...TJ

ROTTEN 🍎 APPLECORE

N.Y. is still plodding along. We've had some pretty choice visitors in our area lately. The Misfits and The Necros played a gig at The Ukranian National Home the night before Halloween. Two bitchen bands, one great show. The Necros were great. They ripped through their set with undying intensity and Barry's vocals were strong and clear. The band is definitely a "MUST SEE". The Misfits are a classic. Glenn's killer voice booms. One of the best bands around for sure. S.S. Decontrol recently played a gig at A-7 with Kraut and Reagan Youth. First off- A-7 is about the size of your linen closet with a hundred human sweat wads smashed together, all wheezing from asphyxiation. Secondly, the sound pretty much sucks. To make things worse Kraut (AKA The Cabbage Kids) came on first and played a pathetically lethargic set of dragged out cabbage music which brought on a massive yawning fit. S.S. Decontrol air from Boston and judging by this band, their scene must or at least should be hot. They played a good, aggressive, powerful set of about 20 songs with a cool cover of Discharge's "Decontrol" for the grand finale. Friday the 13th I had a blast. Know why? Cause I wasn't in N.Y. I was in Washington D.C. and needless to say they have the absolute best scene on the east coast. Youth Brigade started off a five band gig held in a school cafeteria, I believe it was, and played what might have been their last gig. Artificial Peace, Deadline, The Faith and Iron Cross followed. All these bands were great. The D.C. tradition- its hard to say one was better than another so I'll just say my favorites were Iron Cross and The Faith. Reluctantly getting back to N.Y., Heart Attack put out a 3 song e.p. entitled "God is Dead" Its considerably more tighter and energetic than the usual N.Y. slug speed shlock- Originality is lacking but remember- this IS N.Y., nevertheless its a good single. The only N.Y. band that matters, The Bad Brains, are going to release a cassette-album soon and Bleeker Bob has dogbreath due to the fact he tantilizes his Doberman's asshole with his wet, pointy tongue then sucks on it's stubtail. Y'all saw him in D.O.A. Meatmen Rule.

A. Mahler

MCCREERY 81

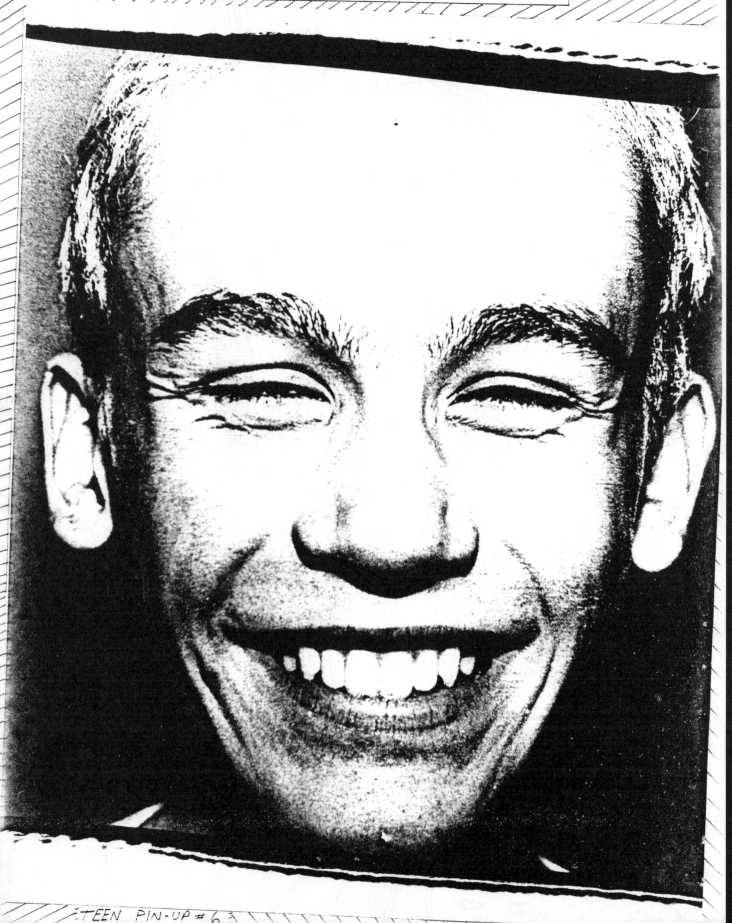

TEEN PIN-UP #6

MIDWEST CONTINUED

way through their set Brian their guitarist
suggested that the kids rid the club of
the pretentious new wave painting forever...you know the one I mean...the big
one that was obviously painted by a queer
hanging on th e left wall.....the painting
was then ripped to shreds in the ensuing
riot and the tables and chairs were soon
without their legs...I think this made N-
unzio realize that this really was the last
night at his club...

                    Ted Rollins

Thanks for the review Ted whoever u are-
MEATMEN portion of review removed-posit-
ive as it was so folks won't accuse me of
Catholic Discipline syndrome...see how easy
it is to get your writing in T&G folks?Sim-
ply submit it....And in my professionally
biased opinion BORED YOUTH fuckin kick dick-
with their driving bass...I hate the
name because "bored" takes me back to
hot summer nights in Ann Arbor listening to DESTROY ALL MONSTERS and there
is a million bands with "Youth" in t-
heir name...but who gives a fuckkk-f-
inally the midwest is coming up with bands
like this young one...to rival bands any
where....and I fuckin' mean it...one listen to NEGATIVE APPROACH will convince...
so they will be on TOUCH and GO records
hopefully if John doesn't start hating me
or something(that fucker is intense to say
the least)let's not neglect the other guys
either jeez Rob Pete and the legendary Za-
heir all provide some of the wildest music
going by their own right....call my comments
self indulgent biased garbage but the Midwest
behind bands like NECROS,EFFIGIES,FIX and
the aforementioned combos are to be reckoned with...all you locals that hate my guts
believe me the feeling is more than mutual-
cuz you are all safe and lame and don't even
deserve my criticism .....,"Tesco's an asshole
....the only bands he covers are hardcore"
that's my town's feelings in a nutshell...my
opening column may appear critical to some-
but my criticisms are intended to be constructive in regard to the local bands that matter....cuz together we have the inate ability to fuck up alot of people....mentally
and physically if they wish....granted some
of those involved will begin to lose touch-
like one guy who used to be cool as shit but
is now a prick to everybody for no apparent
reason....we've <u>got</u> to stick together if
it's going to work and it fucking will cuz
there are people involved who are fucking
<u>DOERS</u> like Corey Rusk whose investature of
time in regard to the midwestern scene is
mind boggling...sometimes abrasive,but always effective...whether you like him or
not he <u>gets a job done</u>.....his contribution
to a once struggling TOUCH AND GO RECORDS
won't soon be forgotten....thanx bud.....
and before I hop off my soapbox I'd like
to put in another commendation for Detroit's
L-7.....Larrisa,frank,Corey and all you
guys deserve alot of credit for putting
out the most intellectually entertaing m-
usic(can I get away with that Larrissa)and
also David Rice whose received a few hard
knocks from the bonehead community but
has shown his true colors by rising above
and involving himself in helping out bands
regardless of ideological persuasion...thanx
Dave(by hard knocks I mean...like remember
Ian's boot?) So qualification was in order in
regard to my opening column and I got carried
away...so what else is new???Take care...for
all that have supported the mag and the record
label...thanx a pooplead..... TESCO(the editor-
the dick....theperson)

ALSO THANKS TO T.J. AUTUMN RECORDS.AND EVERYONE ELSE I FORGOT..

<u>CASSETTE COMMENTS</u>
7-SECONDS has a really great cassette
out that you've gotta hear...fast as
shit...one hot one after another...th-
ey are a three piece from Reno(home of
a great youth scene)where load of good
bands are starting to happen...they are
a three piece and the sound is raw and
powerful...it says "bootleg quality"on
the package but it's alot better than
that depending on your definition of b-
ootleg...get it...order from 2302 Patton
Drive...Reno Nevada 89512 oh ya its
called "3 CHORD POLITICS"....and they
call it Skeeno hardcore but it has yet
to be explained to me what the hell Skeeno means...I got a new FRICTION live
tape in the mail the other day...they've
lost their original guitarist Tsunematsu
Masatoshi who has gone on to pursue it sol-
and by the way his new material I also
have on tape and it's a definate winner
but I don't know if this is a record,EP
tape or what so I'll review it for sure
nest ish...two more tapes from REACHOUT
in NY have been released...early Dolls
sessions and the tape is called "LIPSTICK
KILLERS"and also a live tape by SHOX LUM-
ANIA...can't wait till they release the
BAD BRAINS tape...also they will be releasing a GERMS live tape(this is off the subject in regard to tapes but the MISFITS LP
will be coming out on SLASH Records)it's
weird when I get tapes like this SOUL PAT-
ROL band from Louisiana because I don't
like it at all but feel it's my duty to
review it but then I realize it's hopeless...there will be a compilation tape
featuring Hardcore bands put out by the
gent who edits NOISE mag/and Kevin Seconds
and the gang from RENO...so far bands like
Social Distortion,Wasted Youth,Necros,7-S-
ECONDS,FIX,MEATMEN are scheduled to appear-
more on this later...any bands interested
should contact the Reno address above or
R.Moore 3588 Southbrook...Xenia,Ohio 45385
  Oh ya the FRICTION tape...what can I say?
  It's simply a cardinal sin they aren't the
  biggest band in the world...puts most Western esoterica too shame...write FRICTION
  (c/o WATCH OUT) c/o Mr.Mitsuhashi 2-37-12,
  UMESATO,SUGINAMI-KU TOKYO JAPAN

THE MISFITS-"HALLOWEEN"/"HALLOWEEN 2"
Plan 9 Records
All it takes is one night with this
bunch live and you are an instant fan-
unless they don't fit your little image but then who cares about you anyway-
there's this bunch of weird kids in Ohio that have MISFITS on everything they
own..their clothes,their mothers lasagna,
their dad's car...even their dicks...li-
ving proof that this band is on the verge
of world domination...bitchin' band..ano-
ther great single...can't stop em' now,,,

BART AND JAN-"DE DAG DAT DE DERDE WER-
ELDOORLOG OOK AAN ONS LAND NIET ONOP-
GEMERKT VOORBIJ GING"Torso Records
Don't ask me...ok so it's German and
very sstrange to be sure the b-side
is called Messerschmitt Parade" and
it features some guy ranting,orchest-
ral screeching,machine guns,strange
electronic dementia,sounds of doom,
sounds of the end as it approaches-
bout' time these people realized they
will be the super powers dumping ground-

still MORE 45's

RUDIMENTARY PENI EP-
12 songs from an English band that
has put out a record that is never
typical and always wild and exciting-
quasi Crass sentiments regarding n-
ukes and sexism but loads more exciting than anything they've been putting out lately....i heard there were
only 300 of these made but it is going to be released on CRASS records
I guess which will undoubtedly get
this heartwarming effort into each of
your living rooms soon...as good as it
gets/////

SPECIAL DUTIES-"VIOLENT SOCIETY"
Sarcophagi Records
someone walked up to me on the street the other day and said"Hey TV
how bout' rating the 5 nastiest,w-
ildest,most grating,intense vocalists in the world...you know big g-
uy the singers that make it sound
like it's all over"....so I said to
this guy(besides "Do I know you?")
"OK there's Cal DISCHARGE,Carl of
BLITZ,John of NEGATIVE APPROACH,
Steve FIX and this guy in this new
OI band SPECIAL DUTIES...Steve Green-
ok so I coulda said that a mite more
succinctly...OI music at it's best
here...not no speed merchants...but
as tough and authentic as they come-
one of this months hottest...

373

images of just such patriotic mishmash, as when a party opens on a caviar American flag

Joan Crawford: "What do you want to hear?" Sterling Hayden: "Lie to me—tell me all these years you've waited."—Johnny Guitar (1954)

"I'm not one of those 'eye' for an eye' men. No, I always take two eyes."—Luther Adler to John Wayne in Wake of the Red Witch

Barmaid: "What about you, Jonny, what kind of trouble are you looking for?" *Brando: "Whaddaya got?"* — The Wild One

LOCAL NEWS FROM PHILADULLPHIA

phila news....lotsa new zines, most are copies of all wave seen already. THE BOBmag will feature a flexi in thier feb82 issue($1) w/2local bands. TERMINAL! ,philas only new music monthly now features comix regularly, among the funnies seen exclusively there are;ZIPPY,BABOON DOOLY,as well as local talents,soon more are planned........ One club features full time music, and a batch of bands are getting at—tention! Sadistic exploits,Nomilk, Mother May!, Headcheese,and BUNNYDRUMS who've been signed to CBSfor world wide dist..

JAH WOBBLE
JAKI LIEBEZEIT
HOLGER CZUKAY

(Island)

Never thought I'd see the day when punks would be dancing to Can, much less playing with them. That's right, Jah Wobble, PiL kickout and tari driv—er, working with two of the originat—ors of Duetschen rock.

Heady mix, too. Czukay dubs Wobble and drummer Leibezeit into one differ—ent mix of Continental/Jamaican. Dark, gloomy, it doesn't really hit you un—til you listen to the last track "Twi—light World" and then realize that the dedication to Ian Curtis is the only fit one on vinyl.
—S. Dunhill

NEW CATCHES
from CONSTANT CAUSE

new stock;NO mag(w/ great flexis by Geza&,andWildKingdom).FAMOUS POTA—TOEMAGis the silliest and goofiest yet, #6 has s,clay wilson, and every issue is a load of vyuks,the mag for modern morons.Along with that we got PONTIAC TEMPURACOMIX, a swell book that features CAROL LAYS"reach out and touch somone"(with venus of milo)

.......URBAN ANIMALS is a comixpub by fred t, seen monthly in FLIPSIDE, that are angry, angst and animated in a sorts steadman like way.\$1,50 cover price.

CONSTANT CAUSE IS THE ONLY MAIL ORDER DISTRIBUTOR OF INDEPENDENT AND SELF—FINANCED PUB.S, MAG., ZINES, AND PRODUCTS.....MAIN CATALOG—50 CENTS........TO:

CONSTANT CAUSE /679ARBOR LN. WARN WARM. PA 18974

SOCIAL CLIMBERS
(hoboken/gultcher rex)
Remember the new found joy yer ears gave ya when you heard T.Heads 77, well re—live it , now with the L.P. of the year.simply titled "Social Climbers", the swell variety and power of the ROCK music included is sure to turn as many heads as the heads. A banquett of tunes both nasty and funny, melodic and malic—ous. Unlike any other group but similar to many popular sounds. Exceptional uses of vioce,rythmn units,and keys. DONOT PASS IT UP , bub.

ZEV
(lust unlust)
...Zev , has had a few shows from his 81 tour released on a (disco)12 inch e.p. ; Sounding like a junk yard revolution, zev thrashes about pounding metal and bells causing enough niose to give all but the most manic a headache. "the salts of heavy metals" is brilliant.

OH! IT'S ANOTHER GOOFY PAGE BY FURRY COUCH

SEXISM SUCKs
[but it sure makes my spud go turgid]

RUDIMENTARY PENI EP

THE MISFITS-"DEVILS WHOREHOUSE"

THE EFFIGIES-"GUNS OR BALLOTS"

MINOR THREAT-"IN MY EYES"

GBH EP

ALL PAGANS

SOLGER EP

NEGATIVE TREND EP

ALL CRIME

BLITZ-"YOUTH"

SUICIDE-"GIRL"

OUTCASTS-"BEATING AND SCREAMING PART TWO"

YOUTH BRIGADE-"BARBED WIRE"

BORED YOUTH-"OUTCAST"(live)

DEUTSCH AMERIKANISCHE FREUNDSCHAFT-"GOLD UND LIEBE"

WIPERS-"YOUTH OF AMERICA"

MINUTEMEN-"THE PUNCH LINE"

CHRIS AND COSEY"HEARTBEAT"

BLACK FLAG-"DAMAGED"

7-SECONDS-"3 CHORD POLITICS"(cassette)

LA's WASTED YOUTH-"REAGAN'S IN"

SUICIDE-"½ ALIVE" Cassette

THE FUTURE LOOKS BRIGHT LP

VOID DEMO TAPE

FRICTION-"LIVE CASSETTE"

PANTHER BURNS LP

COSEY FANNY TUTTI OF THROBBING GRISTLE

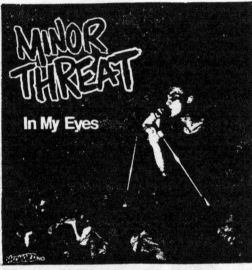

Action shot taken by Gerta of Oil, the axeman for Chicago's Effigies, who sadly wants no part of their current comeback... taken at Bookies, where else? At this point, I'm still toiling out of a rented house in Lansing working part-time shit jobs, having been laid off as a teacher... stealing baguettes from a bakery where I slaved to survive, realizing how much fuckin' work it was to continue this noble endeavor solo while also running Touch and Go Records, though by now, Corey was my partner. My body was still in Michigan, which was sportin' like 16% unemployment, and my brain was already East Coast. Hadda talk Gerta into marryin' my ass so we could hitch up the covered wagon and pull up stakes on what I described at the time as a "grey bogus dump." The "Good Shit" page featured none other than one of yours truly's intestinal sculptures... You know yer a real man when that fecal king snake dead-ends in the hole and comes all the way outta the water like a poopy gator sunning itself on a riverbank... Top that, fuckwads!

number 18

TOUCH + GO

$1.25

IT'S OUT

32-song D.C. sampler-

$5.00 POSTPAID
('6.00 OVERSEAS)

SEND ORDERS TO:
DISCHORD,
3819 Beecher St. NW, Wash., D.C., 20007

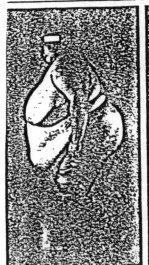

Woman patient before intestinal bypass surgery, and after.

KIDS IN FINLAND WHERE GREAT THINGS ARE HAPPENING

FURRY MOUTHS OFF

HOWS THIS; one general gets nabbed and a whole Mediagoes ape. The red brigade should grill Dosiers balls and mailthem to reagon in a big mac box. REALLY. do you know that this may be the 1-st year of life as we now know it. If the facists dont get us the Enviroment will. When all nine important planets line up this december What will be the effect? well noone knows. it never happened before, THIS is our equivilant to the HirosimaBomb.Some scientists think we will all die or a lot of us anyway,,,some think itll be a normal day but There is predicted a Violent turning piont for Xmass day 1982. Then if we dont get offed(oroptimisticly thinking changed) we must come back to all this.Ronnie will host his version of Howdy Doody goes to Washington, Haig will watch t.v. and fuck his little brains out(he looks like a "swinger"). Soon they will begin work on the scariest piece in this puzzle. From deep down in the bowels of TRI-Lateral thinking sprouts the most Orville like idea yet.Dig; there is a plan or it is planned to Construct Huge steel(ornatalic) PYRMIDS,to store atomic waste for the next Io,ooo years or so?.... Yowl and these things are gonna dwarf those Eygptian ones you bet. Every state and Township will probably have them since the underlying Idea of these things is certainly NOT storage of dangerous materials (pyrimds, in populated areas,unsealed?0) but to permiate the skyline With huge impressive Calligraphy ornate pyrmids shining ,reflecting the progressively Dimmer solar rays.The planned time for erectin these collosal incubator s just Happens to co incide with a projected ; "Suspension of Believes" and both natural and man made depressions. Heres the scenario;: Suburbia is unemployed,intercity unemployable or bordering on it(a post jubille -ituation) millions live on govt.food (probably proved to dontain up to 5 of 6 hunred times the save levels of Sugar/charbos/and chloresteral as well as XXXXXX unidentified chemical componts), getting pretty hairy, not much left for a guy to do outta work(feel like a schmuck) nothin to do but, watch t.v. nothin left to wonder at but these big things......................... And what makes this believable...Why there is planned a elite group to rule theseterrible tryangles ,who pick thier own successors. and its already termed the"Nuculear preist hood". YIKES. is rude but true. eek like now its too wierd to sound feasable but at first signs of activity go ape,trash the land and stomp the WHITEHOUSE ! now forwarned is....

Sorryn all that for taking so long but it's quite the burden doing the whole thing...so anyway 4 pressers wouldn't touch our latest release the MEATMEN'S "BLOOD SAUSAGE EP" BECAUSE THEY said it was too vulgar or something...anyway we now(keep your fingers crossed)are teamed up with ALCO Research in LA..thanx to all who wrote the choice hate mail to Nashville--- Touch and Go now has it's own 8 track studio in Ohio where the bands can record at no expense....we have also started a subsidiary label called SPECIAL FORCES-- the first rel ase will be the EP by L-7...we look at this as a branching out of sorts to present new types of music...with a solid new line up NEGATIVE APPROACH will finally be recording the first week in April... no release date as yet on the BORED YOUTH EP but it should be out sometime in April as well...second pressing of the NECROS EP lasts only a few days...PROCESS OF ELIMINATION EP will also be in it's second pressing very soon...FIX "JAN'S ROOMS EP" is selling very well on the coasts....thanx to all who have bought our records and supported our label...also thanx to Systematic,Rough Trade and Skydisc,Tim Yohannon,Tim Sommer,Lori and all other Dj's for the airplay...special thanx to George...

COVER-OIL of THE EFFIGIES...photo-GILDEE

THIS MAG WAS WRITTEN BY TESCO VEE

thanx to PUSHEAD LAMORT,Corey Rusk, Dischord Haus,J.Crawford,WX,Gildee, and everyone else...like Furry Couch AND especially Brian Pollack!!

steve Youth pondering metaphysics, female masturbatory techniques and why Freud was wrong!!!

ISSUE 18

MORE SLOP

DEAR TESCO &CO.,

At twenty three I'm probably older than most of your readers,(so what? ED)yet I listen to and enjoy some of the hardcore groups glutting the marketplace(Black Flag,MEAT PUPPETS, MINUTEMEN and MINOR THREAT are my current favorites)Been reading whatever issues of your rag filter out to the east for about 3 years-it certainly is one of the more uh,committed punk fanzines around.I would like to make some comments re:stuff in recent issues,though...What is this shit of headlining a page "Sexism Sucks" yet printing a blatantly pornographic(and not particularly flattering-you sure know how to destroy a guys fantasies)shot of Cosey T. Gristle on the same page?George Orwell had a word for it:"doublethink".. Perpetuating this "do as I say,not what

I do "crap attitude makes me less and less certain 1984 is gonna be just amother year.What's next a pic of a burning cross with the headline "Equality For all?"I also wonder what your female readers think of such demeaning displays.If you're gonna run porn the least you can do is give the women something to wank over too... I'm not very proud that DC has become the East Coast HQ for Central Casting (Punk Division)FEAR must've had a change of heart (or wallet) since telling record execs to go die in THE DECLINE...though I am proud that Ian Mac-Kaye and Henry Garfield are locals who made good-what they do in the future should be interesting.
One more observation;aм ÷I the only one who feels that blind pessism has become just as much of a fashion today as blind optisim was in the 60's-and ultimately just as reactionary?Come on-come on-communiacate."(ATV)

Keep em' flying
MIKE HEATH
WASH DC

People who write letters and don't give return addresses don't get much respect from me not that this guy's close....any self respecting editor would do all those mediatory antics to assuage rest assure and appeal to dear Mike to let that smug feeling set right in there in the midst of all his stereotypically humanitarian gaff that I'm supposed to take to heart....I hear having your heat shut off is now fashionable more and more people in my neighborhood are doing it...they are all happy too don't get me wrong....being cold is no reason to get pessemistic and trendy....so what if unemployment is 16%?Be happy-why did my neighbor shoot himself in front of the Social security office?Because he realized he was jumping the bandwagon of despair...sort of liken it to rubix cubes or video games.... It's great to be alive in 82' aint it Mike doll?so what if we're getting sludge rammed up our noses at every turn...let's be anti sexist,anti nuke,anti democrat,anti poor,anti black...pro Reagan,pro big business,pro Sun Belt,and be truly happy like the brainwashed of the nations capital would have us....OK?ED

SUBSCRIBE
$5.50
FØR 3
post paid

CRUCIFUCKS/CULT HEROES at Bunches 3/11/82
So unabashedly shameless the Crucifucks give me heat rash...uncategorizable in their approach to premeditated irreverence ...ready to shake the lame East Lansing crowd out of their perrenial stilted stupor and they go down hard to make an otherwise disastrous evening great...Unfaltering energy,great rythyms...singer Doc is as obnoxious as they come...spitting out the verbiage with all the tact of a manic depre-

for the faggot dough boy that the club owners use as an advisor let me just say that we all know how two faced you are... and you probably revelled in the destruction ddeep inside so you wouldnt have todeal with anything other than lame crud like the I-TENSE to keep your over thirty nazi gay crowd happy...you'll be dead soon we all must pray fuckface...

BORED YOUTH/MEATMEN/GUN CLUB
Statehouse-Ann Arbor 3/5/82
A big old wharehouse is where some people be trying to start an alternative to the bar scene in this town...BORED YOUTH comes out and plays hot tunes but about halfway? thru their set the fire marshall and the cops waltz in and shut the place down....seems they came in earlier to warn them they would do just that if they tried to have a gig and by joe they came back and done it....the bands got paid...the cops were all real old like they were called away from retirement and given riot gear...they shined their flashlight on people outside and laughed... THE END

CONTINUED SIDEWAYS

ssive evangelist on LSD(sounz like something David Pimplebutt I mean Winkelstern would say) I'm not even going to tell you how bad the other band is...you know that already....and for the asshole friends of their neat fans that kicked holes in the walls and for the two little new wave pixie dick sucking hog slitted cunts that wrecked the bathroom all I've got to say is thanx to u little worthless excuses for humans the EFFIGIES/MEATMEN gig got cancelled...I wouldnt even grace your integrated faces with a load of my penis snot..all you deserve is a good ass fucking till you bleed to death...as

Ernie
Haygood

Hey Tesco,
There's this guy at our school named Ernie.He beats his hoodus before and after school.He also eats his juicy jism.When we ask him about it he answers with "God Rick,it's your own stuff" He also admires girls armpits and necks-He fantasizes about having sex with 60 year old librarians and study hall teachers.When his mattress gets too juicy he pops it over and keeps on whacking, he also thinks he looks like Fabian and sticks his fingers up his butt...
Rick-Dayton
Thanx for the profile Rick...we should start a typical T&G readers profile thing like DEWARS scotch so everyone will know your basic reader aint just the guy or gal next door...but rather a sick,twisted,brainbent youth of the 80's....ED.

JIT ON ME

CUNT QUEEROS

MICK JONES EAT YOUR FART OUT

MY fingers stock Hiawatha

CLOSED MIND... OPEN Dirt Chute

LETS GET PHYSICAL

"CHUCKLES THE CLOWN"
(Preamble)
I snicker and chortle as I flip through the news
And come across an ad of mine
It sez "Chuckles the Clown is sure to amuse"
Small kids when they have partee time

Oh yes I'm a bundle of laughs as the kids well know
And the parents seem to quite like me
From house to house I chuckle as i go
Making a mint so very nicely

Ring,ring,ring,goes the front door bell
And is answered by a gent quite soon
"Chuckles is here with a bag as well"
He yells into the adjoining room

Crowded by kids I step into the hall
And am asked "What's in the bag that goes "Clink?"
"Why,devices for fun and having a ball"
"Everything but the kitchen sink"

I stand on my head and make a face
The parents smile and kids scream for more
I eye the well stocked liquor case
And wave to the parents at the door

We'll be across the street having our tea"
"Unless there is anything for you we can get"
"We'll be going now so have some fun"
"Aren't they darling dear little pets"

Indeed they are a frolicsome troupe
All boisterous and blowing out candles
2 grams of Seconal in the punch
Should make them easier to handle

(one lad queries)
"Where are you going with my Boy Scout shovel?"
"The one I just got today"
"WHY WE'RE GOING TO THE BASEMENT TO PLAY A GAME"
"OF COURSE,IF YOU SAY IT'S OK"

I polish off the last of the Cutty Sark
And head for the Seagrams Seven
I'm teaching the kids to play"Lights out in the Dark"
My god this is a clown's kind of heavan

The basement is quiet ,soundproofed with panels
Just the way Chuckles likes
I stand by the switch and say "Ready KIDS?"
And off goes the overhead light

Giggles and the sound of little feet
Patter throughout the room
My infra red glasses are a bit of a cheat
But my shovel won't stray in the gloom

"THIS MUST BE A GIRL,"delighted I snort.
"HERE PLAY WITH THIS TOY RUBBER SNAKE"
"FEEL HOW LONG AND LIFELIKE IT IS"
"AS IT SPITS SOME VENOM IN YOUR FACE..."

Johnny is over here,"cries one little boy
"He's laying in a puddle of punch"
"He musta spilled a glass of that sticky stuff"
"Gee whiz,there sure is a bunch"

"COME ON KIDS,"I call out loud
"THIS ISN'T A GARDEN CLUB LUNCHEON"
"MAKE A NOISE OVER THERE AND BETRAY YOURSELF"
TO ME AND MY IRON TRUNCHEON"

"My joint is straining to get out once again
As I spy a dazed little girl
I'm attending to a call of nature kids"
"BUT I'LL BE RIGHT BACK TO GIVE YOU A WHIRL"

EXPENDING MYSELF,I clump the lass
But not a clump is needed more
Cuz as I raise my arm for a second shot
Her brain slips out on the floor

One child catches on and slips on the gore
As he hurries across the room
Chuckles laughs as he opens the door
He won't get too far too soon

RZZZZ goes the saw as Chuckles gives it some gas
And lopes at the frightened child's heels
the boy trips and falls in the backyard grass
And gives the McCULLOUGH a meal

Horrified parents stare at the scene
And the clown holds aloft some hunks
"HIND QUARTER FLANK OR ENTRAIL STEAK"
He says,"YOU'LL LOVE MY CHILDREN CHUNKS"

Around the basement the parents survey
THEIR whelps with clefts in their beans
The clown was thoughtful and left the recorder play
The sounds of the childrens' screams.
                                R.Ramsey

CHUCKLES THE CLOWN

GOES TO THE FANZENE CONVENTION

©1982 TESCOVEE/JCRAWPORD

Singles Up The Butt

DANCE CHAPTER-"CHAPTER TWO" 4·AD Records
Nothing that's going to reach out and grab you or anything,,,,nor is this going to win a horde of new converts but those predisposed to this brand of mild manner-ed obscurity will see this as I do as a well executed follow up to last years de-but single...One of those bands that cho-ose to hide in the shadows of their chos-en profession letting little glimmers of their contemporarily stark little frames of mind out via the patter of acoustical sound progressions and vague banterings a-bout this or that...Solitude,sex,and moth-er....ahh such an arduous veil of tears...

4-SKINS "YESTERDAYS HEROES"/"JUSTICE" "GET OUT OF MY LIFE" Secret Records
Tell me why this band gets any hype-this fucking blows my dogs dick....an archaic R&R progression with equa-lly old fashioned studio production-dumpy keyboards.... "Justice"is ok...but on the last cut we can really hear how lousy the singer really is-cuz there aint no backups...like l-eaving yourself in a snowbank with no clthes on...stupid bullshit give me a break..(Good cover however) Overweight in body mind and spirit...

THE STUNT KITES-12" ep Pax Records
Quite the different approach from their awsome debut on the Neutron Sampler...more like ev-ery other inner reaches of the cerebrum English band with a s-ynthesizer and a monotoned sing-er..nothing to really set it ap-art,apart from it's obscure avai-lability...pretty overlookable...

OUR FAVORITE BAND-EP Praxis records
Some gutsy hick uppy,basement tape type rockabilly that will endear f-ans of authenticity and alienate t-hose of the commercial persuasion-"When Am I Gonna Win?" is awful but the first cut "Pink Cadillac is cool-like Panther Burns(can I get away w/ that?)"Praeceps Lascivus" is some s-ordid cajun ode to either history or someones vivid imagination...The ca-dillac on the cover belongs to..is it Sleepy LaBouef?Remember him TJ? "What's Inside Of me" is strangely satisfying but don't ask me why?not for everybody,but I think overall it's pretty cool and so does Marlene-so there...PRAXIS RECORDS 152 KEN-NER AVE. NASHVILLE TENN..37205

VARUKERS EP-Tempest Records
Hardly original but hardly unexi ting...spiky,studdy stuff from t-he Isles which is quietly sudivi-ding all these new sounds for us into OI,crash and spurn and cast-igate,and the redundant bilge we all try to avoid,,,,this falls i-nto category two...well worth yo-ur cash...lots of energy...support this....TEMPEST RECORDS LTD. 170-172 CORPORATION STREET BIRMINGHAM ENGLAND....

RAZOR PENGUINS-Moment Records
Neat sleeve..let's see 1....2 3 colors...musta set somebody back a few...lossa treatments on everything...on the "Indif-ference" cut anyway....sounz t-o me real English and unorigi-nal..."Paris" is better but s-till not breaking new ground.. it will forever remain a myst-ery to me how people can call this new music,a step forward, a progression,when it's about as new and exciting as a Big Mac...or should I say 3 year old tea and cakes?

DISORDER-"DISTORTION TO DEAFNESS" Disorder Records
How come you aint loving DISORDER like you should,I tink dey be sou-nding quite on the goont side here-strongness installment #2...so why stop now put out lots and give me some real heat...lay it on so I can hotbox all this steamy shit,and so tell me why your counterparts don't sound half this good...
18 WOODBURGH ROAD EASTON BRISTOL ENGLAND

CRUCIFIX-EP Universal Records
I'm not sure what regional locale, or incrowds we are dealing with here but the bottom line is what's on the bleedin disc and it pleases my ear to no end...singer's got it down,heavy P-ACK type guitar...makes you feel like going out and bludgeoning some old l-ady to death,or call your sister up n' telling here what a lame fuck she is.. this one cut is slow and mean called "Brazen Hell"....sets itself apart an-d is my fave ....6 bux? from UNIVERSAL RECORDS 2309 TELEGRAPH AVENUE BERK-ELY,CA. 94705

MOZABITES-"SOUL TO SAVE"/"A-NANTA SNAKE DANCE" Rock Ste-ady Records
You mean I like it and it has sitar on it?You bet...this is like getting massaged by abo-ut 100 Indonesian 12 year old girls in an opium den covered in bavarian cream eating seed-less grapes,wearing a turbin with a big ruby in it,whilst I get a pedicure and a BJ all at the same time....

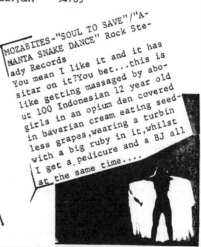

MINOR THREAT "IN MY EYES" EP
There was something about this band that made them the most exciting live assemblage I've ever seen...it was the sum of four parts,the total package that oozed sincerity....rigid and forceful as shit(im trying to put this succinctly w/o going overboard but it's tough)4 new songs from MINOR THREAT recorded shortly before their split are featured here on red wax- including the ultimate version of DC anthem "Stepping Stone"....(the SOA party version is a buster too)purchase and enjoy...

HEART ATTACK-"GOD IS DEAD" EP
DAMAGED Goods Records
Hey dis is a beater...pretty fast and thudlike,like maybe there's hope for NY after all..but it's much better to listen from the safety of my midwestern confines than to brave the inner world of leather studs,and buggery that is the big A.GBH with makeup- Admitedly a helluva lot more promising than the other stuff I've heard ...singles are out soon by EVEN WORSE and the UNDEAD....and don't forget(we're stepping up here)the MISFITS LP(if they get it out by 83.......)For the HA single write Damaged goods c/o Lyle Hysen 8 Wyngate Place Great Neck NY 11021

THE INSANE-"POLITICS"/"DEAD AND GONE" "LAST DAY" Riot Record
An angry blast of distorted speed from a shot in the dark purchase on a new label.to me....as debuts go it rivals the best....three boys that'll beat their way into the cockles of your savage punky way of life...if you buy two singles from Britian this month make it the BLITZ single and this...and one of em wears a tie to boot-can you deal with it?

GET SMART-"WORDS MOVE" EP
Syntax Records
This bands' condensed brand of simplistic beating continues to be exciting and imaginative...nothing worse than a band content to ape Gang Of Four or some other rythmic puke from jolly old nowhere...not the case with this Kansas based three piece...they be doing their own ding you dig blood?

Heavy on bass and drums with snappy syncopation and original songwriting. This thankfully aint pop music but other lame rags'll try to convince you it is no doubt...order from PO BOX 493 LAWRENCE,KANSAS 66044

UK SUBS-"COUNTDOWN"/"PLAN OF ACTION"
Nems Records
The Subs return to a semblance of reality,following up their last 7" debacle with a couple heavy handed tunes that got more meat than I ever thought dey would.....gone are the garrish scarves,fluffy pants and day glo colors...it's as if this time they set out to become what they've always been...one of Englands longest running bands in the old gaurd tradition..this is a good opportunity to get back into what the band is doing....

SHELL SHOCK EP
Vinyl Solution Records
Good stuff....midrange drive,high on spirit....a little low on originality....live I'm sure they lose the clean edge and drive home a much rawer sound,no?Lots better than shit like the RED ROCKERS....order from SHELL SHOCK co VINYL SOLUTION RECORDS 4304 JAMES DR NEW ORLEANS LA 70003 only 2 dollars

COME1-Come Organization Records
As is by now apparent this is the time and space in which I discover the undeniably twisted world of COME ORGANIZATION....this is installment #1.....a little innocent looking platter filled to the brim with the daily depravity I need to function in this culture....so prove to me you aren't crazy...

TOXIC REASONS-"GHOST TOWN" EP
Risky Records
Uninspired and lackluster stuff from the Toxics...their debt to DOA has them sounding surprising bland and the wimp who produced this is in bad shape-there's none of the drive they possess live and the A side is an awful reggae type of tune that I can't even think about much less write about...(whoops I just noticed it was produced by East Bay Ray,sorry Mr.Kennedy)Big Mr. Pittman'll probably draw and quarter me for this review, nothing personal Ed baby...but this record blows...

THICK PIGEON-"SUBWAY"/"SUDAN"
las disques du crepuscule
Pointless electronic noodlin?An artistic endeavor of eternal duration?Probably neither...more like me in a record store with money to burn(believe me a rare occasion) so i springs for another record on this rather,sometimes,occasionally interesting label...a girl whimpers about smething or other.as if she's some shy coquette who while maintaining her demure impish,ballerina shoed image 99% of the time,would probably have one highball and reef on the bloated loaf till it spat angry jism all over her rosy red unblemished cheeks...let's see the B side....better...more off the deep end...I like records with that heartbeat rythym....check your astrological week in review before buying this one...

G.B.H.-"NO SURVIVORS"/"SELF DESTRUCT" "BIG WOMEN" Clay Records
Outing #2 from a band that gets a pretty luke warm response from the people I know,but to me dey is doing no wrong...especially with the zany tune "Big Women"..proving bands from over there got a sense of humor- "big women love the size...big women flabby thighs...big women fill my eyes"...the hearty thumbs yup here-

LIVE AND IN POISON

BORIS SAVAGE AND THE PRIMATES/EFFIGIES
BOOKIES Detroit
Sure Shot Productions is now booking this hole...so the EFFIGIES manager Jon Bonham calls the club to get one of the good young bands(you know like the groovy ones we put on T&G yuk yuk) so this dorf name of Cameron something or other sez "Those bands aren't happening,I'll get you a good band"..so who does he book?Some nonentity piece of schlock,whose members undoubtedly had to either reef on his monorail of flesh,or give him enough cocaine to satisfy his lamefuck promoter new found ego trip....THE EFFIGIES are the fucking meanest sounding band...all their songs get to the marrow of the matter...not with speed but rather with just plain power...they take the whole thing seriously....no banter with the crowd...nary a word betixt themselves....just a subtle nod and then a continuance of the mean thud they lay down the entire set...they are truly a credit to the Midwest(hows come there aint more cool bands following suit in Chicago?)A new single will be out as you read this "Body Bag'/ "Security" on their own label RUTHLESS RECORDS...

GOVERNMENT ISSUE/NECROS/MISFITS 9:30
Club Wash DC
After 8 hours in the camper from NY (it;s a 4 hour drive)we roll into the nations capital...GI have a new lineup with Brian Baker(former bassist from MINOR THREAT)on guitar and Tom of BEAVER on bass,and these new additions make them totally great....vocalist John Stabb had the zanyest suit ...what a wardrobe but dont get that wrong their music is dead serious....they even did a rousing rendition of "I'm A GI" cuz you see they fucked up by not putting it on their record....me and Stabb agree on next to nothing but I think we both agree that these new boys make the GI totally supoib(that's whats nice about doing a mag you always get the last word (the MISFITS rool John,ED)The dancers lose some intensity when the NECROS come out cept for the Midwest kids who drove out and a small band of loyalists from DC who seemed to remember something about the band being partly on Dischord but for the MISFITS it was like all of the farmers hit the dance floor...dried pig dung breaking loose from vibram soles as the men in black raged through their first set....the first tune was a new one called "Demonomania" which is fast as shit and they did all their favorites too like "Vampira"/"Devils Whorehouse" and another new one called "We Bite"... some of the DC crowd seemed to have trouble with the bands image or something but part of that's gotta be one has a tendancy to freak when seeing this band for the first time...light years more powerful than most anything around you know like these studs jsut won't quit...and if you have any doubts just listen to the lp and shit your diapers- (hey Ian And Sab hope you guys had fun doin the crab walk beating the shit outa poor old me cuz my achin' bones still aint recovered...I'm telling you those bald guys are big meanies...it just aint fair,,,sob)

NEGATIVE APPROACH/NECROS/THE DAMNED
Clutch Cargos   Detroit
Vince and Jade Productions finally leaves BOOKIES and opens this posh mega-hall in an old hotel downtown. He's always wanted a club "Like the ones in NY and by god he's got it-complete withe video room(cushy carpet and statues) and 700 people show up at 7 bux a head-suddenly all the faces reappear we haven't seen since the halcyon? days at 870....fashion sluts abound as we snip at the chickys "punk out " or "Neat Dress" or some other typically rude male commentsos we can see the flare of anger only as a passing thought as they realize their studly do right date who'd just been poured into his pantaloons aint exactly a scrapper...the place is crawling with 35 dolllar a night security gaurds...all nervous that they may get punched or something,all carrying little flashlights like they aint sure if dis is Cobo o Masonic cuz sheeit man ah could be home in mah crib reefin' on some muggles not lookin at all deez jive ass mo fuckers".. all the fat guys in leather jackets are slugging beer out of paper cups and negative Approach comes out and plays a great set with the hot new lineup(I'm totally into it Jon mama)One chaotic binge into the outer reaches of savagery(good line huh?) (how about this)an atomic assault of new generation punk rock(sound like CREEM yet?)NECROS get hotter with every outing (and faster)the burden of this daily speed increase seems to ultimately land on Todd who somehow manages to keep up...body and soul caught up in a blur of sticks and sweat(this is music journalism at its finest folks)The Damned had actually called the club and said "no slamdancing" or some thing to that effect...anyone who listens to and supports this band should fuckin be taken out on the back 40 AND SHOT...old tunes,old jokes,old clothes,old egos...man these dicks did the same slush they did shitilly 3 years ago"Go home and listen to your Rolling Stones albums"Ya...neat joke

Captain...real relevant to the crowd... they come over and get fucking 4000 bucks a show and have the fuckin balls to slag the crowd while the warmup bands play a million times better and get nothing and 50 dollars respectively....neat club...neat crowd....so then they do an MC 5 song and everyone goes ape...i swear to god my mind flashed back to URIAH HEEP and Deep PUrple concerts I went to 10 years ago...thats how outa touch and fucked these guys are...its like some 40 year old rock star said in an interview on that stupid M TV show....as long as people keep coming to see us and buying our records we'll keep doing it..." A senseleess waste of time for all involved

YOUNG BROTH/ZYKLON at Bunches Lansing
YOUNG BROTH is Tom Scum from the never legendary THWARTED and some girl who just sits in a chair looking embarrassed and sings along once in awhile...looks a bit like a sheepish third grader reciting the books of the old testament in front of her bible school...all tapesfarts for farts sake...go eat your moldy Cheerios...hardly anyone came out to see ZYKLONS last gig...great stuff they did..real original...loud rythmic electronics and not redundant...they even did "Brand New Key"(wheres Melanie?) and you're dorfy for missing this and the band will collect its plaudits after the split like all good artists...

(HOUSTON TEXAS   1981 & BACK)
After a HATES practice on Jan.9,1982 I went down to the PARASITE CLUB on Main St. to ask for an opening and they said they would not hire us because we were hardcore.In the past year the Discos,"LIMIT" at 290 NW freeway, Rocksy's at Westheimer,STRUTS at Airline and ALLEY'S on Harwin reopened as rock clubs.Some of them feature New Wave Mondays but they just have the same rock bands from other nights.RHINESTONE WRANGLER at S.Main and CARDIS at Fountain and newly reopened ROCK SALOON at Westheimer have rock bands and are being mentioned in this article because groups like The RAMONES and IGGY seem to have enough influence to be booked into these clubs...DOME SHADOWS went out of business and reopened as the BANANA BOAT featuring Reggae...Country Western club GOOD OLD BOYS closed and reopened as Caribana Reggae and it features new wave on Mondays.. CARIBANA REGGAE and OMNI gameroom at this time stand the best chance of featuring Punk and New Wave locally.In December 81 c7w club Whiskey River at Gessner and

Continued→

BLITZ-"NEVER SURRENDER"/"RAZORS
IN THE NIGHT" No Future
What can I say?By far Englands
best bludgeon band...so i was
walkin thru the mall with my
ghetto blaster blaring this 45
and I walked by this old man and
beefed....he didn't hear it but he
sure as shit smelled it and I sez
to myself..."Fuckin' BLITZ is
boss" as I swaggered offin a mellow trail of stenchwind...

KAAOS-"Kytat on Natseja EP"
CADGERS-"Riistetyt" EP
A unique EP that features two
bands on the same disc..KAAOS
is too good for words...things
in Finland must be going mad
with bands this good playing
around...on a par with DC or
Midwest or La....the voice of
dissent cept I can't make heads or tails ah what they're
saying...CADGERS' singer aint
quite as awe inspiring but they play a good breed themselves...from the sleeve they look
like the sleeziest bunch of sw-
eeties...and when I think of
the place where they live I
think of steam rising off of
a tranquil bay...i'm glad it
aint as dull as all that...
must be heard...

YOUTH BRIGADE-"POSSIBLE EP"
Dischord Records
If you're reading this mag
odds are you already own this so my analysis won't be of
any consequence but here it is
anyway...the band released this
just before they self destructed
and of course it's hot poop from
the nations capital,and tis a s-
hame they ain't still around...
the sleeve looks like it was re-
produced on a xerox machine at
Safeways but it's the rockin'
punkarama contained on the disc
that counts...one of this seas-
ons beasts...my fave?"Barbed W-
ire"....

LEVI DEXTER AND THE RIPCHORDS-"I
GET SO EXCITED"/"OTHER SIDE OF M-
IDNIGHT" Fresh Records
I don't care what you say...oh
scooby doo(I'm covering my ears
and singing like when you wanted
to get the last word when arguing
with sis)as far as rockabilly re-
vivalists come Levi has always be-
en the best and most authentic
sounding and now that all the assholes have shot their wad on the
latest resurfacing it's Levi who
sez F.T.W. and puts out a couple
great singles...wot a teen idol
he woulda been back then...but i'm
aferd he'll be marooned to a life
of obscurity unless he either goes the route of Mr. Idol or becomes born again and does r-a-billy
crusades or something...

TERVEET KADET EP Ikbals Records
Another great Finnish band...total
distortion...vocalist sounds like
a raving beast,but they didn't turn him up loud enough...4 songs on
the A side with a blank B side...
the crude mix puts this in a class
with such greats as the SOLGER EP
and the "Night Of the Living Dead"
45...I only wish this were more r-
eadily available so the world could get their paws on a copy a dis.

MAN TIT-"MAN TIT"/"PUSSY PUSSY"/
"REMEMBER ME" Dunlap Records
Is this not the choicest name e-
ver thought up?each sleeve is hand screened...what does it sound
like?I'm not telling...

THE OFFENDERS-"LOST CAUSES"/"ROCKIN
THE TOWN Suffering Sounds Records
A side is straight up and an inspired one...not unlike Toxic Reasons
cept Mick Buck aint as big and mean
as Ed...B side blows...

SVATSOX-"EMPTY CORNERS"/"VOTE"
"REVENGE"/"PROBOT" Wand Records
Another promising band from
                 Holland along wi-
the THE EX...heavy on the denou-
ncing trip...he kills his unfaithful wife as she embraces him-
but the best sentiments hit the
spirit of the Olympiad every country tries to encourage..."We m-
ake you win...an injection...we
programme you...to have our system win...robots beat the record
happy sporting people...in the b-
est system...(from the song Probot)also included is an anti nuke song...they do it well...the-
se bands all seem to sport a neat
brand of out of tune cacophony t-
hat really grows on ya...

LAMA-"NIMETON"/"AINOO LAJISSAAN"/"JEESUKET"
Johanna Records
Pretty fuckin choice again he ah mates from Scandinavia agin...good poop whose mat-
uration is instant...we aint ape in' the
west they are sounding like...wonder what
LAMA means...you probable saying 'Why is
he reviewing all these records we'll never hear"... and I say I can't help it if
I'm so fuckin wordly I mean worldly"(that
too)

13th CHIME-"CURSED"/"DUG UP"
This fucking blows me off...ser-
iously great as reading the Book
of the dead whilst digging for an-
tique jewlery in an eroding grave-
yard(that about doesn't sum it up
huh?)Something you'll buy and say
"where was he coming from?"

RED ALERT-"IN BRITIAN"/"SCREAMING AT
THE NATION"/"MURDER MISSLE" No Future
Records
Typical new stuff..a side is the Rejects-
the others are better....what's this shit
No Future/Cherry Red music...a great indie on it's way out...the minute these so
called independants stick their hands in
the pie it's only a matter of timebefore
things get watered down...

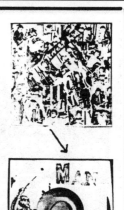

12"

HOISTING THE BLACK FLAG Compilation featuring LEMON KITTENS/MENTAL AARDVARKS/NURSE WITH WOUND/TRUTH CLUB/WHITEHOUSE/DAVID CROSS/PAUL MILTON/JOSEPH DUARTE first band is too annoying and unmoving-don't threaten at all with their silliness....TRUTH CLUB.....nondescript chamber music...supposed to be nerve wracking I suppose...NURSE WITH WOUND wake up side one a bit with bone cracking dissonance-voice tapes...they play around...part of COME ORGANIZATION....I never got around to listening to side two..

FLEX YOUR HEAD-Dischord Compilate
What can I say about this...the best sampler ever would be selling it short...alot of unreleased material by DC's finest bands...classics all of them...this label has proven itself time and time again...but they've outdone themselves this time...standouts include RED C's version of their best tune "Pressure's ON" which is sure to make you shit...MINOR THREAT's "1 2 X Ū" and the list goes on and on.... nothing short of the best...32 songs for 5 bucks?You'd be a fool to not own this mammy....order from Dischord-(see ad)

WHO CARES

Right,Who Cares?

HELL COMES TO YOUR HOUSE Compilation
Bemisbrain Records
45 GRAVE are pretty choice sounding here-I've renewed faith in their approach no thanx to their debut 45 which was pretty mundane...they sound more like they mean it here...three cuts that whip something around spookily/..CHRISTIAN DEATH....what would my Christian Reformed,Dutch,conservative parents think if they knew I was listening to a band that was called this and what if I went so far as to say their cut was probably one of the more exciting cuts on this mammy?He'd probably like that about as much as when he got death threats from the FBI and the R&R Bankrobbers father in law...(faithful T&G readers will know what I'm talking about...anyway CD are hot and they have a new 12" coming out on this very label...100 FLOWERS continue to pump out their unique brand of garage grunge-a little low on overall energy but never a dull one with them...RHINO 39...thus comes the problem if this is supposed to be some sort of cohesive package cuz this wimpy cut sounds as if it shoulda been on the ROTR 2 album or something not something like side one of this thing that up till this point made me chew on my dogs tail...SOCIAL DISTORTIONS records keep getting better...."Lude Boy" is great,with a hot guitar solo....a dying interlude to be sure but effective here.. LEGAL WEAPON ...Pat Bag right?Good singer-RED CROSS do a New York Dolls cover... Hmmmm....MODERN WARFARE have changed a bit and put out a couple chargers...both of their earlier singles are well worth having and you can order them here...good poop Stevie...SECRET HATE....im plum out of good analysis...the clock on the wall sez 4am so I'll leave you with this...if you don't go out and get this super compilation then,then....I'll come over to your house dressed like some of the wimpy people on the back cover and look in your bedroom window with a flashlight on my face and a load in my slacks...and thats a promise....send about 6 bux? to BEMISBRAIN RECORDS 200 TERMINO AVENUE LONG BEACH CA 90803

ENGLISH SUBTITLES-"ORIGINAL DIALOGUE"
Glass Records
One side live and one studio...about the only sad band that still does it for me....a melodramatic binge of of human emotion and all that biz..all three of their records display that sense of being where nobody should be-I dunno anybody who hammers their hand to a board is OK by me...both sides differ dramatically but are both a firm reminder ive still got a taste for this doom from the Isles...

A COUNTRY FIT FOR HEROES-No Future Records....11 punk and skin bands that sent their tapes to this label...some mediocre but mostly raw and inspired.. this prolific label keeps spitting out greatness at a breakneck pace...hope they don'T burn out because if it was' nt for this label England wouldn't be doing diddly....my fave cut is HOSTILE YOUTH's "Fight Back"....No future... 3 Adelaide House 21 Wells Road Malvern Worcestershire England

MINIMAL MAN-"THE SHROUD OF" Subterranean Records
What the hell makes these guys tick-? If this isn't the LP of the year from the left bank then I didn't just bash my bishop listening to these people n say to myself"Minimal Man should be massive...but then so should FACTRIX and that aint happening either..the

old bottom line rears it's handsome head again...this is one of a kind greatness that no one should be without...unless that is you aint up to dealing with it...it isnt pretty... write....912 Bancroft Way Berkeley Ca 94710

PUBLIC SERVICE

PUBLIC SERVICE-featuring RED CROSS/BAD RELIGION/R F 7/DISABILITY/CIRCLE ONE
Smoke seven Records
Great sampler(the months of the sampler have arrived)featuring some of LA's finest...the only shit is Disability..all else kicks dink..the Bad Religion is produced songs that appear on their 7" but are tons better here...Circle One kick my ass...this is a little too unheralded don't you think you should've bought this along time ago?It aint too' late...write Smoke 7 Productions 7230 DeSoto Ave Suite 104 Canoga Park Ca. 91303

BORED YOUTH were interviewed by TV here's how it went...
How long have you guys been together?)thought I'd ask something different and unusual for the first question)
Fred:(drums)We've been together as BY since August but we've been playing music for about a year
John:If you could call it music...
Fred:Ya a year ago none of us could play our instruments....so we just did whatever we could but then in about August we got serious about what we wanted to do...

TV:Opinion of Detroit?
Rob:I think we have some of the best bands in the country actually...i wish SUBURBAN ANGER and YOUTH PATROL hadn't broken up though...
Fred:It's great here...great bands..what do you think Robert
Robrt:I've never been anywhere else
John:What do you think of bands around here?
Robert:Great...'

BORED YOUTH

John:He thinks there great...he's very soft spoken...
TV:How did the 4 track come about
Fred:David Rice(L-7) was nice enough to do it...it came off really bad..we rushed it and made alot of mistakes
HOHN:If anybody wants to get an impression of the band off of that...they shouldnt and it'S really bad...
Rob:I can't believe we did it..I've never listened to it the whole way through...

Rob:(vocals)They played in a friends basement then I'd go down and sing and play "My Generation" and we made up all these songs we laugh at now... They played around then in November I started singing with them was at Nunzios on Halloween with FIGURES ON A BEACH
Robert:(bass)When Rob became a man...

Fred:We want to go to NY and DC this summer..
John:Our African tour...hit the Ivory Coast and Swaziland...
Fred:Hopefully we'll be able to get back into the Detroit scene with Coldcock and the Monsters
John:Play Cobo hall with the Rockets...

TV:Influences and inspiring force???
All:Sham,Rejects,Upstarts, Eater
Rob:They were into different bands than I was so for the music you'd have to say SHAM 69
Fred:Until Rob came along our influences were British...
Rob:Then I introduced them to groovy bands like THE MISFITS,and DC bands.. the music is more of an indirect influence...id hear it and it would give me an idea but I can't say I credit anyone but ourselves and a lack of things to do,,,

TV:What do your parents think?
Fred:My parents really like it...
John:Well I don't think my mom really cares Fred:Yes she does..John:As long as my grades don't falter and we don't get killed going to jobs
Fred:It's a rough world out there...if we go to Detroit we can't talk to strangers....cuz they're mean...
John.....very bad people...
Rob:My parents never really got involved with anything I ever did...
Fred:My mom wanted to come see us but I wouldn't let her
Robert:My mom is happy with me as long as I stay in school

TV:What were the earliest gigs LIke?
Fred:Let Robert talk...
Robert:I'm playing with my bass...
John;They were fun...
Fred:They were stupid...we played with bands like DESTROY ALL MONsters....
TV:Crowd reactions?
Fred:Somw of the people liked us...
John:(yells)they were just jealous that's all...
Fred:That was John...he was kidding..
Rob:If this scene hadn't started happening we probably would still be playing with the SEAT BELTS and shit
John:and living a horrendous nightmare

Fred:My mom's proud of our music...
Future plans:???
John:I think they should have these neato cars that run on air...
Fred...moving sidewalks
All;More money should be spent on the space program
Rob;Ya the most important thing is beating the soviets..any communist expansion
Jon:I plan on dieing later in life...
Rob:in space would be very detrimental to freedom and democracy
John:Hey the little Rascals are on...

songs
"TO LABEL IS TO LIMIT"
"OUTCAST"
"THEY DON'T HAVE THE RIGHT"
"SHOCK VALUE" (rip)
contact the band
c/o Rob Michaels
5357 Tequesta
West Bloomfield mi
48033
EP out April....
on Touch and Go

ZYKLON INTERVIEW

→ Houston Continued

SW Freeway opened as a new wave club but it's too soon to say if it'll be any good because so far it has booked only pop acts. WILD DOG MAGAZINE be print it's last issue because it feels it doesn't have much punk rock in Houston to report.

CHRISTIAN ARNHEITER

NECROS/FLIPPER at Second Chance Ann Arbor 3/15/82

The kids vs. the jaded adults?The happenning vs. the "we've seen it all now we're setting trends(plod....plod...stumble...plod)not following them...sure I'm biased as hell-and by no means blind to the obvious...if the singer in Flippers little quotes hold true and if they are the future of music I'll gobble fecate on rye bread before plugging myself once and for all...get these choice gems of wisdom- "No more punk rock" or "Skinheads are for little kids"..ya and dyeing your hair blond is the adult thing to do...one dimensional piss with limitless noodling added up to one pitifully apparent hype...add to the list"I've had enough of you assholes stage diving as he jams his crutch into a kids rib cage...Rich said it best- "Basically those guys can blow me".....

BANDS, mags, asswipes- send promos for honest appraisal- NO ASS kissing w/T + G... send em' now butthead....

THE FIX are currently without a permANENT drummer following the departure of Jeff following their most recent west coast tour...if you are a skin man (or women)with the right attitude contact Steve at 517-371-4841 or Craig at 517-332-7755...touring,videos,and recording is imminent as soon as a replacement is found...anyone willing to relocate is more than welcome... write... 2204 Stirling Lansing MI. 48910

The following interview was conducted with Steve Zuidema of ZYKLON following their Feb. 4 gig at Bunches in Lansing...it was the bands final performance...

SZ......we've only been playing actively since May,but we've been together on and off for about 2½ years...me Brian and tom....I was going to school at Western and Brian bought a Korg synthesizer and i just used to show up on weekends and we'd mess around with tapes and gradually it evolved....I moved back from Ann Arbor and used my student loan to buy a synthesiser and Tom had bought this fucked up used Roland... the first thing we did was put out the single...in fact two of the songs were recorded on something that looked like that(points to my shitty tape deck,ED)and the other one was recorded live and we figured ZYKLON always existed on a day to day basis and we just wanted something we could put out right away that we would like e and it didn't really matter what anyone else thought....we knew that with what little money we had anything we did was going to sound sorta cheap.. plus I think this is the kind of record that should come from Grand Rapids...

TV:What's this about people tearing down your flyers?

SZ:ZYKLON B was the gas used at AUSCHWITZ to exterminate the Jews.. it was developed as a disinfectant and they found it had this additional application...there's also the TG song(Throbbing Gristle,ED)and that's a whole nother thing...

TV:An influence?

SZ:Well to some extent there have been alot of influences...we're pretty eclectic band in that regard...we tend to think of most of our influences as environmental...the kind of sounds we make are a kind of camouflage for our personalities...and bands like Cabaret Voltaire and TG...they sound closer to alot of the things we do... but I think it's just a matter of

parallel evolution...you have a synthesizer and you can get nice sounds out of them or you can get other sounds... but I never thought the name would offend so many people but Jews tore down our posters in Lansing and Ann Arbor and I think thats pretty bad..with Reagan and everything you have this fear of Fascism and it seems really similar to the Mcartyism of the 50's where you have this college student liberal thing and these people are just really shallow...and just can't investigate anything...this emotionalism ...they can't think and examine something you've just got to react...ZYKLON ARE NAZIS" you know...this is the 9th gig we have played....our first was last march with THE INFECTIONS ever heard of em? TV:No...

SZ:They r Grand rapids' punk band... it was in a big polish hall on the west side filled with 3 or 400 drunk obnoxious people .....probably the most negative response ever in GR...they yelled "fuck you" and threw ice....Grand Rapids people are just so lame....as far as other influences I should probably mention drugs- there's nothing else to do in GR apart from this and all of us were pretty severe PCP and acid casualties the last year of high school..and I just really went over the deep end...the whole inspiration for ZYKLON as a matter offact came from the summer of 79...I was convinced my life was worthless and I was going to die...and we'd ride around in our cars and smoke enormous amounts of pot and plus I have these health problems... there was this one day when a friend of mines car ran out of gas on the freeway and it somehow happened this gas can exploded in my face and I inhaled all these vapors on top of this horrible combination of chemicals I was doing... and for quite a while I couldn't talk and everything was stripped down to this animal type of thing where I could only think in pictures....and this is the big reveleation in my life... that's one of the themes of ZYKLON is a form of escapism...

Interview Abbreviated due to length... Contact Zyklon at

Grim Records Box 9539 Wyoming,MI 49509

Single + Cassette Available

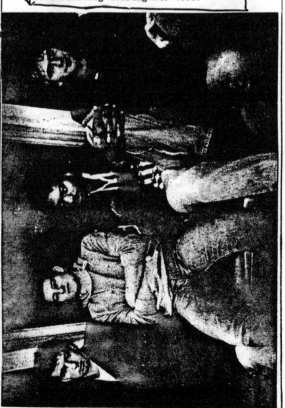

THE KOMPETITION

FANZINE UPDATE-Here's some of the latest zines I've gotten...don't get teeed off if yours got lost in the piles of debris I call home... here I go passing judgement...

FIRST OFFENSE-Everything reviewed from DEF LEPPARD to LOVERBOY and DISCHARGE and inside stuff regard the scene in the Cape Cod area... write CLIFF HANGER PO BOX336 WEST YARMATH MA 02673 25¢ & post..

TIPS AND TOURS - New issue out soon of NJ's "oldest punkzine" write 1453 PAWNEE RD NORTH BRUNSWICK NJ 08902 1 buck & postage

FUKT-Indeed a pleasure to see a mag of such high quality dementia exists-get this line from one of the stories- "I shot off my sperm cannon into her gravy pit is this not enough to make you all want it bad?write c/oGARBAGE 146 S Water ST APT #2 Kent Ohio 44240

BOREDOM-#10-Lots of greatness from Tommy and Co.Literature for the high-brow masses and record reviews..highly recommended Write Garbage INC.(same as FUCT)

SICK TEEN-Incredible how good this one is....put out by Norbie in Wisc. it features some jerks on the cover but thats where the lame ends...total HC great inside..insights from tomorrows youth,N.UGLY lays it down with Satan in tow...he got the spirit...***** write to NORB at 708 St. JOSEPH st. GREEN BAY,WISC. 54301

NUKE THE DISCO-It's all written in Italian so I can't give you much info except he reviews all US indie from Dischord to the Fartz to the Germs, Wasted Youth and the Necros...come on support it even if you can't read it-900 lire...from CASALI MASSIMO-VIA della Transfigurazione,6 00151 Roma Italy-----OUTCRY-- Finally another one-well I guess it came out sooner than I got...so it's great again-good pictures and writing..Wasted Youth interview...   ...OUTCRY 1001 FREEMONT PO BOX 1194 So.Pasedena,ca91030 75¢ plus postage

HYMNAL-Great chaotic layout here with the best in Texas meathead boogie ala Recipients,Really Red,Stains and coverage of other areas too..good pictures and copy quality***** $1.50 from B.Cotman 5307 Green Springs Houston Texas 77066

RIPPER-New ish is groovy with lots of features and incisive writing-Tim knows his punk rock dung,and he presents it with a serious tone and good editorials....order this one you creeps...Ripper 1494 Teresita Dr.San Jose,Ca 95129

ANTAGONIST-Sparse but effective layout-another Ohio mag with the right idea-but oh no a GG allin interview..that guy is to punk what Mark Fydrich is to baseball....cept GG never had his day...146 S.Water St. Kent Ohio APT 2 44240

FLIPSIDE-So all the rumours were untrue-the new Flipside finally comes out.typically great as usual $1 plus from po BOX 363 Whittier Ca90608

FLESH AND BONES-Ho boy a mag from NY that is actually good-fantastic photos of certain local luminaries as well as an interview with the defunkt Beastie Boys,the Nihili stics and Reagan Youth-

really good mag-*****write Jeff 351 Beechwood Avenue,Middlesex NJ08846

WHITE NOISE-HC publication from Madison with good coverage and reviews... 12 N.Franklin st Apt 1 Madison wisc 53703

MEDIA MASSACRE-Latest one is #4 with a bitchen pic of kevin seconds on the cover....a must as faraswho is importnt in america today....Jane~wotta fox 2302 Patton dr Reno Nevada 89512

BURP-What can I say about burp...the zanyest most fun filled tabloid-anywhere in the free world....Berl and Clive are into skateboards,autofellatio (blowing yourself)and their fave mag is PHENIS written by Mr Chicken Butt himself....write BURP at box 421 maumee Ohio 43537

THE OFFENSE-get some of these quotes from Book 13...all these (west coast) bands are finally learning how to play a little bit,especially the drummers-now you tell me can I take this guy seriously?Or regarding THE EFFIGIES... "stink,then smash metal,biker music" or "Everyone knows how much I like ORANG E JUICE and how I feel about love" but he does have those who swear by his magazine and the rest of us who swear about it...as narrow minded as they come regarding music by young people...write 1585 N. HIGH st. Columbus,Ohio 43201

PUNK LUST-5021 43rd ave So. Seattle Wa. 98118 mobing raht along..hmm

NEGATIVE ARMY-Hey man dis ones got it all...tradition of crudeness and good articles like a FEAR interview and good pix by Glen Friedman...get it clowns...PO BOX 1062 Santa Monica Ca 90406

SHORT NEWZ-LOTSO news on a one page double sided piece of papre about NY and other zines and stuff.a noble effortt...po box 1028 nyc 10028

SUBURBAN RELAPSE-Another mag from Cuba I mean Florida...good Bad Brains pics...50¢ plus from PO box 610906 N.Miami FL 33161 ps I agree with your SOA why did he leave philosophy Barry)

SUB POP-Number 6 is like 8½x11 from the man Brucey who loves little. Good editorializing...the man who keeps an open mind about all music like everyone should try to do... anyone who doesn't have the SUB POP cassette is missing out on some great stuff....in #6 he runs down the country(in his underwear? no just kidding ...by region and you should write to him c/o Lost Music Network Box 2391 Olympia Wash. 98507

ALLIGATOR ALLEY-Pictures of alligators on boobs on the cover with ⊙ thru them...as good as a college paper could ever be,,,send a buck to 1112 NE 4th St Ft Lauderdale FL 33301

SMEGMA JOURNAL-Some girl sent editor bra in appreciation the other day... that about sums it up...people get mad at them alot so they take hermans in Bell jars and mail em back so if you send em hate mail forget to put your return address-doesn't come out often enough..could BURP take over???People are scared of the editors of SMEGMS JOURNAL BOX 421 Maumee,Ohio 43537 send $1

POll RESULTS

Well heren' be the results of the 1981 readers poll...I promise I ain't tampered with the data...as far as the zany answers of course they were all different so if a Z appears before a list it was my own judgement of funnyness...other wise the answers went by number of votes cast.....here goes

PERSON MOST LIKELY TO GET MURDERED-
1)Ronald Reagan
2)John Lennon

LAMEST MOM
1)Mine
2)Yours

Z LAMEST DAD
1)Dick Van Patten
2)Mr Rodgers
3)Greg Bokors dad

Z WORST TIME TO HAVE DIAREAH
1)While modeling bikini briefs
2)In Bed
3)When taking a breathilizer test
4)While watching "On Golden Pond"

Z BEST TIME TO HAVE " "
1)In the outdoor pool at MSU
2)In the bathroom at the Crooked Beat
3)7:56

BEST ALBUM
1)BLACK FLAG "DAMAGED"

BEST SINGLE
1)MINOR THREAT EP
2)NECROS EP

SHITTIEST MOST OVERRATED NEW BAND
1)MEATMEN
2)MCDONALDS
3)TSOL
4)KRAUT
5)FLIPPER

HOTTEST NE BAND
1)MEATMEN
2)NEGATIVE APPROACH
3)BORED YOUTH
4)THE FAITH
5)VOID

Z FAVE PIZZA TOPPING
1)URINE ICE CUBES
2)RABBIT ANUS
3)HERMANS

Z BEST HOBBY
Shoplifting at Goodwill and getting caught
2)Collecting splew samples

WHO IS THIS MAN?

TAPES

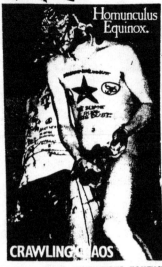

CRAWLING CHAOS

CRAWLING CHAOS-HOMONCULUS EQUINOX"
Foetus Products Tape
Words don't fail me now because what we
have here is one of 81's top releases-
a whole bunch better than their LP..this
tape springs from many backdrops...cover-
ing each base with an air of belligerant
(well subtle you know)authenticity..even
their cover of "A Taste Of Honey" with t-
he genuine sentiments like "Because we
felt like it"...fans of their debut 45
"Sex Machine" will groove on "Mummy's T-
ummy" which features the same supremely
disturbing garbled voice effect that makes the epidermis crawl in even the most
staid frames of mind..."One More Peso" is
the best spaghetti western theme ever written and all one has to do is close ones
eyes to see Charles Bronson dusting off
into a fake Mexican backdrop....if you see
this tape fucking buy it...limited edition
and all that so get it now

BAD BRAINS-Reachout International Cassettes
Are they the greatest band in the world or
what?As fast brash and loud as they come-
some old material and some new (I think)
and some dull reggae but all in all some
of the fastest gutpunching stuff being p-
umped out anywhere in the world...a vastly
underrated band to say the least...easily
the most profficient speed merchants in
America today.....GET IT....GET IT...GET IT
write 611 BROADWAY SUITE 214 NYC NY 10012

SEND BUCKS TO THE WRECKS
FOR THEIR TAPE OF CUNT FARTS
AND NEATO TUNES...
PO BOX 20391 RENO NEVADA
89515

DELINQUENTS-Demo.....Ohio's DELINQUENTS
have a choice tape out that blows away
their other effort...they sound totally
balls off da wall hot....not unlike 7
SECONDS from Reno....good ideas...good
changes.....another up and coming Ohio
band that is doing something original..
and you are right Rick Baby-you are better than CHINA WHITE...write 3013 Village Green Dayton Ohio 45432
songs include "Cowboys Are Fags"/"Crime
Wave"/Bible School"/ "Atlanta Murders"
"Timebomb"

L-7's
LARISSA TALKS TO TV

THE FOLLOWING INTERVIEW WAS CONDUCTED
BY TV WITH LARISSA OF L-7 WHO HAVE AN
EP COMING OUT SOON ON TOUCH AND GO'S
NEW LABEL SPECIAL FORCES RECORDS....
TV:So where are you coming from in
terms of L-7....philosophy etc..
L:IT's like when we write new material
everyone in the band writes what they
want to...it's never been a situation
where like someone comes to practice
and sez here's a song and here's how
you play it...everyone's involved..
TV:What happened to the old members?
L:They got fed up with my attitude a-
bout hardcore...
TV:Like....

L:They didn't want me liking any type
of punk music,so at first Mike wanted
me to quit and the band didn't so he
quit and then later Chuck quit...
TV:Mike's the guy who joined figures
on a Beach right?What do you think of
them?
L:I think they're horrible and predictable and not anything different...
TV:What do you think of Detroit now?
L:It's shitty but I wouldnt leave..
like why go somewhere else where there's a ready a scene you had nothing
to do with it..here you can work hard
and try to make it better
TV:So tell the world about your new
plush penthouse suite....
L:Ya I live above Clutch Cargos
TV:Which is for the rest of people
who don't know....
L:It's pretty much new wave..it's
really big....it pretty much sucks
cuz it's all new wave..but they're
getting stuff like the UK SUBS...
TV:So what lies ahead for the band
L:We're going to releases our record-
were hoping to go on tour with Killing
Joke in May...like an east coast and
Midwest thing...Youth their bass player wants to produce our second single-
TV:Do you worry living down in the sl-
ums?
L:No I love it but cops down there hassle
me and John(NA) all the time...they yell
"new wave"...like your boots..stuff like
that...write L-7 at
20107 MADA AVE
Southfield,MI
48075

ONE BAD APPLE

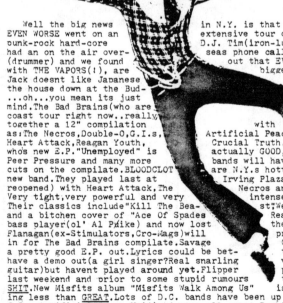

Well the big news
EVEN WORSE went on an
punk-rock hard-core
had an on the air over-
(drummer) and we found
with THE VAPORS(!), are
Jack doesnt like Japanese
the house down at the Bud-
...oh...you mean its just
mind.The Bad Brains(who are
coast tour right now..really
together a 12" compilation
as:The Necros,Double-O,G.I.s,
Heart Attack,Reagan Youth,
who's new E.P."Unemployed" is
Peer Pressure and many more
cuts on the compilate.BLOODCLOT
new band.They played last at
reopened) with Heart Attack,The
Very tight,very powerful and very
Their classics include"Kill The Bea-
and a bitchen cover of "Ace Of Spades
bass player(ol' Al Pike) and now lost
Flanagan(ex-Stimulators,Cro-Mags)will
in for The Bad Brains compilate.Savage
a pretty good E.P. out.Lyrics could bet-
have a demo out(a girl singer?Real snarling
guitar)but havent played around yet.Flipper
last weekend and prior to some stupid rumours
SHIT.New Misfits album "Misfits Walk Among Us"
ing less than GREAT.Lots of D.C. bands have been up to N.Y. (Double-O,
G.I.s,Artificial Peace,Void)and were all great.Double-O to release an
E.P. on Bad Brain Records in which only 300 will be printed up.Misguided
will be on cassette-compilate "Charred Remains"and you should all know
by now The Bad Brains cassette-album is out on R.O.I.R.and is one of
the best releases of the year.   A.M.

in N.Y. is that famed local band
extensive tour of Japan.Yes,N.Y.
D.J. Tim(iron-lungs)Sommer even
seas phone call from Jack Rabid
out that EVEN WORSE played
bigger than KISS and
food.They brought
okan and...huh?
a joke.Never-
on a west
are putting
such bands
Scream,
Kraut...
also
are N.Y.s hottest
Irving Plaza (recen-   tly
Necros and The Bad Brains.
intense stage presence.
st"We Wont Go To War"
Reagan Youth found a
their drummer.Harley
probably be filling
Circle(Bronx) have
ter.Killer Instinct
vocals and fast
played The Mudd Rub
they were HOT AS
is out and its noth-

with
Artificial Peace
Crucial Truth,
actually GOOD,
bands will have

good shit

ROZZLYN RANGERS DEMO

NEGATIVE APPROACH-"READY TO FIGHT"

SEVEN SECONDS-"HEAVY METAL JOCKS"

KAAOS EP

McDONALDS-"GREG'S ROOM"

IRON CROSS-"TEENAGE VIOLATORS"

THE INSANE EP

EFFIGIES EP

GI-"TEENAGER IN A BOX"

FEAR-"BEEF BOLOGNA"

THE FAITH DEMO

THE WRECKS"I LOVE TO SHOPLIFT"

NEGATIVE TREND EP

BORED YOUTH-"SHOCK VALUE"

YOUTH BRIGADE EP

BLITZ-"NEVER SURRENDER"

ANAL SERVANTS-"REST ROOM RAPE"

SUICIDE-"GIRL"

FLEX YOUR HEAD LP

THE MISFITS-"WALK AMONG US"

MINIMAL MAN-"THE SHROUD OF"

CHRISTIAN DEATH-"ONLY THEATRE
OF PAIN"

ARTIFICIAL PEACE DEMO

WIPERS-"YOUTH OF AMERICA"

DELINQUENTS-DEMO

FACTRIX LP

HELL COMES TO YOUR HOUSE LP

PETER BECKER-"BY TRAIN TO
THE COAST"

BAD BRAINS ROIR TAPE

FRICTION LP

March 12, Clutch Cargo, Detroit
U.K. SUBS and THE ANTI-NOWHERE LEAGUE

There was hardly anyone when we got here
at about 10:30. Half, us kids and the other
half, a mixture of nu-wavos and stud-bandana
harder than hardcores. All of us were up front
having a zany time before the ANTI-NOWHERE
LEAGUE came on, so we were all loosened up and
shit. They came on in full geer, Winsor showing
off his tattoed arm and Animal with his studded
penis guard or whatever it was. They played
about 15 songs that were all great and everybody was diving, like it used to be at the
shows. They played So what at the end and the
stage was full of kids diving and banging into
the band.There were wimpy girls thrown up on
stage with their shirts half ripped off, it was
great, fun band. twenty minutes later and a
quart of coke the SUBS were on. We were all
worried that they would play all their new
stuff off Diminished responsiblity or something
but when they started off with C.I.D you knew
it was going to be a great show. They were so
tight, they played practically all the stuff
off the first album and everything else was great
too. Charlie Harper is a fucking great singer
skanking around the stage and grabbing peoples
heads and screaming in their ears and shit, the
guitarists were great, doing jumps off the
drumriser and the stage every 10 seconds. When
they left everyone started yelling SUBS until
they came back to do STRANGLEHOLD and 4 other
great ones. When they came back for the 3rd
time , their drummer who I guess had the flu
wouldn't comeout so everyone threw Todd Swalla
of the NECROS up there and they did waiting
for my man.Todd did a better job than their
drummer I thought and so did the band it seemed.
This was one of the best shows I've ever seen
and I hope they stop in detroit on their way
back. If you get a chance to see this band,
don't pass it up for anything.
Greg Bokor

Yes, this is the cover shot selected to represent <u>T & G, the Book</u>. Why? It sums up what we were about... John Brannon from Negative Approach glowering at the shooter between songs at the Freezer Theatre (bonus Don Van Vliet graffiti on the wall behind him). For me, punk rock was all about the front man, and nobody embodied the Midwest musclehead manifesto like Brannon. Screaming so hard you swore his zits were gonna pop in your face, the guy was born to be a belter. The biggest crime in music today is that his current band, Easy Action, isn't a household name. He still has the bellicose bellow of a man half his age, and all the Marlboro Reds and cheap whiskey have only further turned his pipes into parlors of tortured, tonsorial perfection. This issue also features Dirk Gunga's (Rich Ramsey's) column, which was one of the funniest we ran. Crucifucks, 7 Seconds, Battalion of Saints, NA, all present—the interviews were coming fast and furious, most conducted via the Pony Express, or snail mail, as we call it today. Flyer for the infamous Minor Threat show we put on at the Lansing Civic Players Hall. What a nite... This is one of the best fucking issues of <u>T & G</u>... Yes, I said it, so suck me.

TOUCH AND GO

no. 19

RUTHLESS RECORDS
PRESENTS:

THE EFFIGIES
BODYBAG /
SECURITY

new single out now !

T.of infamous K+T.INC.
caught with egg on
her face...or is it...
oh...well...No they're
such nice girls...

All these people who've got nothing
better to do than make commentaries
on other cities' scenes should shut
their yaps and concentrate on doing
something positive instead of always
passing judgment....9 times out of
ten they don't know what the fuck t-
hey are talking about...all the areas
that have viable scenes deserve your
support...for one people who say LA
sux...I know nothing first hand about
their scene,but I do know one thing..
they've been doing it for a long time and like it or not all of americas
youth scenes owe a debt of allegiance
to that city...and know that we in the
midwest have something to cheer about
and have for quite some time..it's no
time to get all power trippy and say
anything about anyone else...DC,Boston,
Reno all are getting greatness togeth-
er-assimilate,appreciate,and keep your m-
ouths shut....this is one soap box I
won't twist my angle coming off of...

BUTTS

SOMe People Got No SCRUPLes YA KNOW?

SUBS.
$5.50 for
3 issues
postpaid

We at T&G salute the people
of the great state of New
Jersey...for every letter we
get from somewhere else we
get three from NJ...CHOICE!!!
Who would've thought that Craig of the late great FIX would abandon all his principles and sink to playing in a
rock abilly band....he touched greatness....and let it slip
through his fingers.....On fast
music....GANG GREEN is a sirlo-
in tip....HUSKER DU are strictly
cube steaks.....Who was that rich boy cum rasta man kissing the
BAD BRAINS behinds when they stayed at the FIX haus?Who is Jah
anyways?Must be one of their
roadies....TSOL gets $500 bux-
NEGATIVE APPROACH GETS 15...in
Canadian money no less...swell
guys Vince and Chatto....fucki-
ng capatalist cunts out to make
their own asses cushy.....if y-
ou live in Ypsililanti I feel s-
orry for you....Pushead Lamort,
J.Crawford,Vince Ransid...three
of the best with a pen....support
these animals....soon art femmes
will be nursing the oil base out-
of yer pastry bags....wher did
the singer in ZERO DFX get that
hair???I fuckin hate sluts.....
no fanzine thing this time/too
friggin lazy....but heres my faves...of course FLIPSIDE always
rools..always will...Al's blood
viper is the envy of all zine ch-
airman..the new RIPPER kix some
serious ass!!!.Hats of to Toonooka...
Sick TEEN,SMASHED HITS,Cralys I
mean Carly's mag...whatta serious
teen Babe De Sade...floggable buns
guys...check her out...new WE GOT
POWER is choice..the list is endless....lotsa good zines comin in-
new ALLIED lineup...interview next ishuee...CRIME broke up after
8 years...shit,they were cool and
the rest of you can pack your m-
others spiral of anal flesh...
BLIGHT is the music of the year
2000....

ya thanx to Aaron for the cool
illoQ:Why does a baby have a s-
oft spot in the top of it's head?
A:So the doctor can carry 10 of
em at one time....sorry....thanx
for your support....love and a-
nal sex....,Tesco....PS...song
title of the month is VENOM's
"1000 DAYS IN SODOM."..wish I'd
thought of that...oh ya and thanx to all the cool bands who
took the time to send me demo
tapes like SIN 34,WHIPPING BOY
REBEL TRUTH,YOUTH KORPS and as
always all that slip my aging
cerebellumI'll leave you with
some classy quotes...."My con
dolences on the death of the
late T&G,"Frank Blank-Ann Arbor-
"Your lyrics are too fucking
gnarly but I still crave"Glen
E Friedman,Los Angeles"My guidance counselor used to be a
NUN.Carly Sommerstein....I'll
quit babbling...enjoy the issue.

I fuckin said that....

who dat?

TESCO SAYS:
TOUCH REALITY
OR GO TO HELL!

MEAT MEN
Q100
OUT IN August!!
6 songs
"Crippled Children Suck" EP

EDITOR-TESCO VEE
SENIOR VICE PRESIDENT IN CHARGE OF
ART PRODUCTION-PUSHEAD LAMORT
BAZOOKA MORRIS COMIX BY-LAFF YERSELF
INTO A MUGGLES STUPOR COMIX
ROD RAPE- BY THE MAN FROM THE EAST
J.CRAWFORD....THANX TO ALL WHO HELP-
ED OUT THIS MONTH AND SENT ME COOL
SHIT....

QUOTE OF THE MONTH....
Jack of TSOL to Ian MacKAYE in
DC...."Ya like skinheads are going
to beat up the band that invented
the skinhead"...

This
issue
costs
$1.25
Forgot to
put it on
the cover...

DIRK GUNGA

my dick is much like a cobra...it slowly uncoils,raises its head,and spits venimous jism...this hooker I had once in the Philappines helped me fulfill one of my own very personal fantasies:to have dirty brown enema water deluged in my face: included...feces with roots...sometimes when I walk into a porn shop it seems like,well,you know,like coming home...it seems the same people who are wearing mohawks now were the same ones wearing skinny ties 3 years ago.....Barry says he has created a bicep on his dick by stringing a weight on it and flexing his powerful groin muscles....any rad feminist who sez the Meatmen are sexist can simply blow me....if you are ever in Lansing and want to talk to a local skin you have to go to the Greenbriar Convalescent Home or the Divine Light mission for Krishna consciousness,,,my dad says he would forego sex with Mamie Van Doren or a sumptuous meal just to be able to take a good dump...remember the commercial with the little kid handing a Coke to a thirsty Mean Joe Green?Well as a kid I can remember handing a black man a drink of water as he slammed my mother's passive midsection with his ebony power kong...i think he was my dad's caddy...your typical East Lansing new wave slut will almost assuredly sport a

bleached mop,a cavernous blood raw love tunnel and a myriad of prescription drugs to keep them in a perrenial drug-n'-dance stupor...yea we know hardcore sucks..look in the mirror sleazbags...if you happen to be gay and can't accomodate your buck stud's hoodus you're probably not eating enough fried or greasy foods,.A Hostess fruit pie or some French Fries should make parking no problem for him.After a particularly hard day at work when I'm floggin' it to relieve tensions...the hood of my gladiator turns into an angry face spitting pearly splooge in all directions...sometimes I wish I had a butter knife to assist in the lopping off of a particularly stubborn stool that can't decide if it wants to stay or exit my sphincter gates.Last seen...Jah cruising the quarter booths at Cinema X... Guys:Ever blown your wad so enthusiastically that your hot seed came flying out in arcing

X's?Sometimes if I lay still in bed for a while,and then shine a flashlight into a mirror pointed at my anus,I can catch a glimpse of a surprised worm squiggle back into the darker regions of my coal chute.. A certain young man known to us only as Gregg Bokor was seen being called "beautiful" by new wave crowd outside of crowded club in a seamier side of Detroit... Ever dug your itchy ring so hard you had to pull your undies back out?It'll no doubt look like you tie died your briefs in dung...the only balanced thing about my diet is roughly the same amount of slime that enters the body also leaves...the other day I stopped by the folks house unexpectedly and caught a glimpse of my dad clad in a ballerina costume scampering playfully after my mother who bore an authentic in every detail Houston Oilers footbal uniform....speaking of said sexpot earlier...what ever happened to Mamie Van Doren?What about Lani Cazan? We'll catch ya next month scum rot......

OI!-THE COLUMN
By Dave Lozon

First off,I'd like to straighten out a few things about OI.Many people seem too think that people who like and support OI are hell bent on violence and facism.This is a load of shit.In England many different types of people support OI such as blacks,straights, skinheads,west indians,pakis,and herberts. So even if your totally into hardcore punk, buy one of the records mentioned below and give it a chance.INFA-RIOT has a new single out on SECRET RECORDS.It's called "THE WINNER" and is amazingly better than the fantastic "KIDS OF THE 80's single.The reformed 4 SKINS(without Gary Hodges)have an album out on SECRET RECORDS titled "THE GOOD, THE BAD,AND THE 4 SKINS".It features a live side and a studio side.The studio side is okay but the live side is horrible.The new singer just does'nt posses the power and presence that the immortal Gary Hodges had.THE INSANE(a punk band)have just relesed a three song e.p. on NO FUTURE RECORDS.The record is alright,but it comes with a great fanzine from England titled "RISING FREE". This summer NO FUTURE will be releasing a BLITZ album and a PETER AND THE TEST TUBE BABIES album.NO FUTURE will also be issuing new singles from BLITZ,THE PARTISANS,THE VIOLATORS,ATTAK,and RED ALERT.The last OI! album titled OI!-"A WAY OF LIFE" should be out by the time you read this and will feature THE VIOLATORS,DEAD GENERATION, ATTAK,ANGELA RIPPON'S BUM,SKIN DISEASE, ATTILA THE STOCKBROKER,THE BUSINESS,and many others.It will also feature two American bands who are so shitty I'm not even going to mention their names. The long awaited LAST RESORT L.P. has just been released.It's titled "SKINHEAD ANTHEMS" and it's the best record I've ever bought.Well,thats about it except that if you'd like more informatin on OI! theres a fanzine to help you.Write too

REAL THREAT
818 CADULEX
GROSSE POINTE,MICHIGAN
48230

So until next issue SO LONG DROOGS!

NECROS
VIOLENT APATHY
BORED YOUTH
Negative Approach
MEATMEN
Youth Patrol
mcdonald's
SUBURBAN ANGER

TOUCH and GO
PROCESS OF ELIMINATION ep
RECORD RELEASE GIG

SAT. DEC 12
THE CROOKED BEAT
3958 cass detroit

SUPPORT MIDWEST HARDCORE

NEAT SCROTUM you got huh?

TESCO: WHAT WAS YOUR MOTIVATION FOR STARTING THE ELOQUENT AND SCINTILLATING L-SEVEN IN THE LICE INFESTED, RAT ENCRUSTED, HELL HOLE OF DEPRESSING DETROIT?

FRANK: I GOT KICKED OUT OF RETRO, THANK GOODNESS AND I WANTED TO PLAY IN A BAND WITH A HARDER BEAT AND A LESS WIMPY IMAGE. DAVE RICE WAS THE FIRST PERSON I THOUGHT OF AND WHEN I BUMPED INTO HIM BY CHANCE DOWNTOWN I FIGURED IT WOULD BE A GOOD IDEA NOT TO BLOW OFF HIS INVITATION TO JAM. WHEN I GOT THERE, I MET THIS CRAZY INSURANCE SALESMAN OF A DRUMMER AND THE PUNKIEST LOOKING GIRL I'D EVER SEEN. I FIGURED I WAS ON THE RIGHT TRACK, RIGHT AWAY.

DAVID: THERE WAS NOTHING ELSE TO DO EXCEPT DELIVER PENCILS TO RECEPTIONISTS AND PLAY IN THE BLIND, SO...

LARISSA: BECAUSE I WAS FED UP WITH ALL THE OTHER DETROIT BANDS, AT THAT TIME (NOV. 80) THERE WASN'T ANY HARDCORE BANDS EXCEPT THE NECROS, SO IT GAVE ME A REASON TO CONTINUE TRYING TO DO SOMETHING COMPLETELY ORIGINAL. DAVE ASKED ME TO SING FOR HIS BAND, HE WAS JUST PUTTING TOGETHER, SO WE WENT ON FROM THERE.

KORY: LIKE SO SCOTT AND I HAD A BETTER OFFER TO EXPRESS OURSELVES, SO WE JUMPED ON IT. ME AND DAVE HAD BEEN JAMMING ON THE SIDE ANYWAY AND IT SOUNDED GREAT. IT WAS JUST A LOGICAL CHOICE.

SCOTT: I GUESS I DON'T HAVE ALOT TO SAY ABOUT THIS, BUT WHEN THEY ASKED ME TO JOIN I FELT GREAT ABOUT CONTINUEING THIS FINE SOUND THAT THE ORIGINAL L-SEVEN STARTED BUT AS TIME WENT BY WE SEEMED TO FALL NATURALLY INTO THIS NEW SOUND THAT SEEMED... MORE APPROPRIATE FOR US. ITS FOR REAL!

TESCO: HEARD YOU GOT A LITTLE ROUGHED UP AT SOME RECENT GIGS...

FRANK: WE PLAYED IN A LUMBERJACK BAR IN LONDON ONTARIO AND THE FUN IDEA WAS DRINK AS MUCH BEER AS YOU CAN AND HASSLE THE BAND. WE REALLY DIDN'T GET AS MUCH PHYSICAL ABUSE AS THE SCRIBBLES. THOSE GUYS CAN'T GIG WITHOUT GETTING BEAT UP. WE WOUND UP GETTING RIPPED OFF FOR OUR PAY OVER EXCHANGE RATES AND BULLSHIT. AND THE THING IS, YOU DONT HAVE ANY WAY TO MAKE THEM PAY YOU DESPITE ALL THE BUREAUCRATIC PAPER SHUFFLING AND RETENTIVE ASSHOLE CRAPOLA WE WENT THROUGH. WHEN IT COMES DOWN TO REAL PHYSICAL DANGER AND THE BAND GETTING RIPPED OFF, THE AUTHORITIES ARE NO HELP. THEY JUST WANT YOU TO GO THROUGH THE PAPER MILL. IT JUST GIVES THEM A JOB.

DAVID: WELL, I GUESS WE'LL JUST HAVE TO GROW UP AND NOT DO ALL THOSE NASTY THINGS THAT PROVOKE BOUNCERS—LIKE LOOKING AT THEM AND PUTTING DIURETICS IN THIER BEER AND PUTTING IGNITION BOMBS IN THIER CARS AND EATING ALL THIER FOOD AND STARING AT THEM, ETC...

LARISSA: LONDON WAS A COMPLETE DISASTER, I GOT IN A FIGHT THE FIRST NIGHT, THIS GUY JUMPED ON STAGE AND GOT THE MIKE AND SAID WE SUCKED, HE JUMPED OFF THE STAGE AND SAID "ALL YOU SUCK AND I DONT WANT TO HEAR ANY BULLSHIT ESPECIALLY FROM YOU BALD GUYS." I WAS SO FURIOUS, I JUMPED ON THIS CANADIAN. THAT'S JUST THE BEGINNING IT WAS THE FIRST NIGHT AND IT WAS MY BIRTHDAY. IT SUCKED. THE SECOND NIGHT WASN'T SO BAD, BUT THE THIRD NIGHT, THEY WERE SUPPOSED TO PAY US AND WHEN THEY DIDN'T, WE GOT IN A HUGE FIGHT ALSO THAT LAST NIGHT ON STAGE THIS FUCKHEAD LIFTED MY SKIRT SO I HIT HIM WITH THE BASE OF THE MIKE STAND. I SWEAR I'LL NEVER PLAY CANADA AGAIN. RIGHT NOW WE'RE TAKING THEM TO COURT TO GET PAID. BUT WHO KNOWS IF WE'LL EVER GET THE MONEY. THE U.K. SUBS AND ANTI-NOWHERE LEAGUE PLAYED THERE BEFORE WE DID. WHO KNOWS HOW THAT WENT.

KORY: WHEN YOU GO INTO A BAR FOR A SOUND CHECK AND YOU SEE TEN ASSHOLES IN HOCKEY JERSEYS SLAMMING LABATS DOWN, YOU CAN PROBABLY GUESS THE OUTCOME. WHEN THE FIRST BAR ROOM BLAST STARTED I JUST DOVE ON SOMEONE'S BACK AND HELD ON. AFTER THAT I JUST WATCHED. IT SUCKED. WE STAYED FOR 3½ DAYS, BUT FUCKING CANADIAN ASSHOLES DRINK TO MUCH.

SCOTT: APART FROM A LITTLE VERBAL ABUSE, PERSONALLY I'VE ONLY RECIEVED A COUPLE ELECTRICAL SHOCKS ONSTAGE, BUT REALLY THE BOUNCERS THAT WE'VE ENCOUNTERED RECENTLY HAVE BEEN FUCKING UNBEARABLE, JUST ASK DOC DART.

TESCO: HOW DID YOU GO ABOUT THE ELABORATE PROCEDURE OF SELECTING THE CUTS FOR YOUR EP?

FRANK: "INSANITY" WAS GOING TO BE ON FOR SURE, AND THE OTHER ONES SEEMED TO AROUSE THE LEAST FRICTION WITHIN THE BAND. EVERY SONG HAS REASONS FOR AND AGAINST SO YOU WIND UP DECIDING ON THE BASIS OF SOMETHING MORE ARBITRARY THAN JUST A STRAIGHT-AHEAD DECISION HOW RECENTLY A SONG WAS WRITTEN HAS A LOT TO DO WITH IT.

DAVID: A DART BOARD.

LARISSA: THEY WERE THE BEST SONGS, AT THAT TIME, WE HAD JUST WROTE "SECRETS" AND WE DECIDED THAT WOULD BE ON THE 45.

KORY: THE SONGS TOTALLY FUCKING JAM. THEY'RE HEAVY METAL HITS.

SCOTT: WELL AT THE TIME WE PICKED THEM IT WAS PRETTY MUTUAL THAT THEY WERE THE BEST WE HAD.

TESCO: WHO IS THE MOST ESOTERIC, ENIGMATIC, UNIDENTIFIABLE MEMBER OF L-SEVEN AND WHY?

FRANK: I WOULD HAVE TO SAY CHUCK IS THE MOST ESOTERIC, ENIGMATIC, UNIDENTIFIABLE MEMBER —HE'S SO FAR OUT— HE HASN'T EVEN SHOWN UP FOR PRACTICE SINCE LAST MAY.

LARISSA: DAVID RICE, BECAUSE WHO KNOWS WHO HE IS ANYWAY. MOST OF THE TIME I THINK HE'S

GLEN BUXTON, BECAUSE HE IS THEE GREATEST GUITARIST. HE USUALLY NEVER CARRIES ANY I.D. WITH HIM, ANYWAY AT LEAST HE SHOWS UP FOR PRACTICE.

KORY: DAVE RICE IS OUT OF HIS MIND. ANYONE THAT PLAYS GUITAR PARTS LIKE THAT IS OUTSIDE. ON STAGE. HE'S IN ANOTHER WORLD, LAUGHING HIS HEAD OFF, GOING NUTS, DAVE'S GREAT.

SCOTT: I DIDN'T THINK I WAS TAKING A VOCABULARY TEST, BUT ANYWAY I'LL MAKE IT ALMOST UNANIMOUS, ITS GOT TO BE RICE. THAT GUY, I JUST DON'T KNOW MAAAANN.

DAVE: A. ME. B. BECAUSE. (P.S. YOU FORGOT GOD LIKE)

TESCO: WHY DID THOSE GUYS QUIT "FISH ON A BUN," I MEAN "FIGURES ON A BEACH?"

FRANK: MIKE THOUGHT IT WAS A WISE CAREER DECISION — LITERALLY. HE THOUGHT IT THROUGH FROM A STRICTLY BUSINESS POINT OF VIEW AND IT MADE SENSE. HIS BACKROUND IS HEAVY GROSSE POINTE — CHAMBER OF COMMERSE. HE STILL LIKED PLAYING IN L-SEVEN BUT DIDN'T THINK LARISSA WAS HEADED HIS WAY. HE'S NOT ENTIRELY SURE OF HIMSELF ARTISTICALLY, OR HE WASN'T THEN. HE SEEMS TO HAVE FOUND HIS ELEMENT. CHUCK JUST GOT LOST IN THE SHUFFLE. IT WAS KIND OF A RAW DEAL FOR HIM BUT IT WOULD NOT HAVE WORKED OUT OTHERWISE.

DAVID: WHY DOES THE SUN RISE? WHY DO THE SALMON SWIM UPSTREAM? WHY DO THE MASAAI CIRCUMCISE THIER WOMEN? WHAT IS THE SQUARE ROOT OF 38794446228?

LARISSA: AT FIRST IT WAS EITHER ME OR MIKE. MIKE STARTED JAMMING WITH FIGURES ON A BEACH, THEN HE QUIT L-SEVEN. THE FIGHTS WE WERE HAVING AT THAT POINT, RIGHT BEFORE WE BROKE UP WERE ABOUT ME AND MY TASTES FOR HARDCORE MUSIC. CHUCK CAME TO ONE PRACTICE AFTER THAT THEN NEVER SHOWED UP THANK THE DEVIL. WE SOUND SO MUCH BETTER WITHOUT THEM.

KORY: I FEEL THEY COULD EXPRESS THEMSELVES BETTER THAT WAY. I MEAN THEY'RE GOING FOR CHICKS, COCAINE AND BIG MONEY. LARISSA, IN MY OPINION BY BEING HERSELF I GUESS THEY FELT THEY COULD'NT ACHIEVE THIER MUSICAL GOAL, BUT I'VE SEEN THE BAND. WHAT CAN I SAY VINCE LIKES 'EM.

SCOTT: YOU MEAN FISH ON A BUN, YOU'LL HAVE TO ASK THEM. BUT DON'T BEND OVER TO PICK UP THAT STRAY QUARTER WHEN YOU DO. BUT AS YOUR EARS CAN TELL YOU ITS OBVIOUS.

TESCO: WHERE DO YOU PLACE L-SEVEN IN THE LABYRINTHIAN MAELSTROM OF THE SWINGING MOTOR CITY?

FRANK: SOMEWHERE BETWEEN THE RAILROAD CROSSING, CARMEN'S EAST, BOOKIE'S, NUNZIO'S, AND THE CITY DUMP OR ANY PLACE ELSE WHERE YOU FIND OUT THAT YOURE GOING TO PLAY FOR FREE AFTER YOUR DONE.

DAVID: RIGHT IN THE THROBBING SUCCULENT CENTER OF THIS DELIGHTFULLY DECADENT LABYRINTHIAN MAELSTROM.

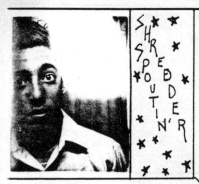

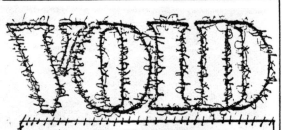

S*H*R*E*D*O*U*T*I*N'*R

MY MOTHER WAS A LADY,PAPA WAS A ROL-
LING STONE,HE'S NOT HEAVY-HE'S MY B-
ROTHER
Cruisin' 82:'tis wonderful,'tis mar-
velous-new trends like HAIRABILLY:Th-
ey play on big stand-up phallus/wee-
nie things,and smear on the Lucy Ti-
ger and look cute in scarfs and gor-
geous in pink frock and sing about a-
ll the controversies:taco stands,dri-
ve ins,ears,hair.PUNK ROCK:what this
one is all about I couldn't tell ya-
cept that they write alot of letters
to FLIPSIDE talking about each other
and their mommies and complain about
complainers.PREP:pink shirts and cu-
rly short hair,pizza at westwood,olde
english beer,GQ magazine inc.RELIGION:
masturbate kneeling in front of theat
hippie-on-a-stick until it hurts and
bleeds and tell their pops that it was
stigma.LA.POETS:drink too much sneaky
pete,write self consious blurbs about
fuckin their moms and have a tendancy
to be old and homosexual.NORMAL CHIL-
DREN:undecided fools who can't decide
whether they should pop a pimple or w-
ash it with dryandclear or vaseline it.
GIRLS AND WOMEN;mexicans with too much
make-up,frail white vulnerable and insecure lil misses with problems,and oh
those snots those keeny teeny bikini
fleas that make your weenie go...WEAT-
HER:a steady 85 degrees going up and
up.WHAT FANTASTIC NEETO COOL BEAT FR-
ANTIC PEOPLE DO IN LOS ANGELES FOR R-
ECREATION:eat at song hay inn chinese
food palace,watch all the in boobtoob
flicks such as sanford and son,JEFFER-
SONS GOOD TIMES,WALTONS,HAPPY DAYS T-
WILIGHT ZONE and THOSE GOD LIKE BOWERY
BOYS.READ ALL the in authors such as
kerouac and burroughs and ginsy and
walt disney.drink only jack daniels
and banana liquer,still only will smoke marlboros and will never stop believing in the glamour capital of the
world.PARENTS:do alot of speed and watch
alot of blue movies on their new video
machines,GRANPARENTS say things like'
nuttin' I like better'n chewn tabacky"
and "When i was your age" and TEENAGERS
are rebellious and bitchin' and radical
and say things like;"you was nevah my
age man..until they get old and finally
learn the correct way to stroke weenie,
and finally fall in love with one of the
beach boys or crystals and listen to buddy holly and paul robeson and judy gar-
land"Forget your troubles c'mon get happy,better chase all your cares away,shout
halleluah gmon get happy get ready for th
judgemant day" but you know what they say
('no what do they say...0")well this is
what they say"HARE TODAY GOON TOMORROW"
         have awonderful today and a
         pleasant tomorrow
                s-h-r-e-d-d-e

VENOM-"WELCOME TO HELL" Neat Records
I'm sitting here...diapers inundated
with liquid...where was VENOM 5 years
ago...all you kids who think Motorhead
takes you to the outer realms of distorted end of the world grunge metal-
feast your schoolboy tastes on this...
the epitome of raw,fast mean heavy metal....45 GRAVE talks it...you know all
the burnin up stuff...VENOM beats it into our heads with a strict evil sledge-
hammer approach that makes this one of
the years best albums...fuck labels...
this album kills,raids your little sisters unblemished hymen and leaves it a
bloody mess of   semen encrusted
veins....recorded like it should be-
puts the FEAR LP in a polished class
with ALPO NOVA and Huey Lewis...would
send AC/DC assholes running for their
grandmas sappy undergarments...
       ....VENOM FUCKIN RULES......

     THIS IS BOSTON NOT L.A.COMPILATE
featuring 7 Boston Area Bands Modern Method Records 268 Newbury St.Boston,MA 02116
There truly is an exploding scene in this
city formerly known for it's dimwitted por-
trayel of music as a sickly mop headed hip-
ster cum kid of the 80's...finally some real fuckin life....something that hits you
between the legs with a brass knuckled sucker punch,lots of it akin to the burgeon-
ing scenes in other areas of the country...
but I've got some serious problems with the
fucked title of this record...whether it is
supposed to be a stab at palmtree land or
simply a good natured explanation of the
cover photo..this comes off very self def-
eating and indulgent bite in the ass...seems
people are quick to say this or that about
LA,all the while ignoring some really great
west coast happenings simply on the basis
of petty jealosy or"now we have bands and
don't wanna worship anywhere but here."..
I won't belabor the point when this great
record deserves all the hype i can smother
on it...GANG GREEN....faster than shitskis
man...gotta check em out live so I can blast my shorts full-o-day old meat...above a-
verage to killer beat your ugly aunts face
in music...that gets this months 5star rating...all worthwhile stuff...get it you
cro magnon morons......

VOID

HERE'S AN INTERVIEW WITH VOID-

TV:Do you consider yourselves a DC band?
VOID:Yes but when it comes to shows we g-
et forgotten every now and then,no probl-
em.TV:How long have you been together?
VOID:A year and a half but it feels like
a week.TV:What are your fave bands,TV shows,girls with big tits,cars?
VOID:We like most hardcore bands.We love
MOTORHEAD..Chris likes funk,most heavy
metal also.Sean has cable TV so he's a
vegetable,and watches movies all the time.
Who cares about girls or cars.Motorcycles
are cool.
TV:Where do you think the DC scene is he-
aeding?VOID:DC will get real big,more violent and lose control,however it will take
awhile and it will be the most productive
and constructive?
TV:What do you hate more than anything in
the world?VOID:We hat Columbia(the people)
We hate fucking up at shows,breaking guit-

ar strings and drum sticks and especially
school.TV:Did you have fun being on Saturday Nite Live?VOID:It was great but I
got my nose smashed on Lee Ving's guitar
(Sean)Met John Belushi,trashed the dressing room.TV:What's been your best gig?
VOID:Wilson Center April 30..Bubba became a guitar hero..Autographs..Throwing
my sticks into the crowd.
TV:Who's the biggest fag in the world?
VOID:The new wave motherfuckers that
hang out at the 9:30 and DC Space,some
guy called Red Elf who called Ian gay-
TV:Any plans to put out a record?
VOID:Maybe but it will be a surprise.
TV:Any relation to LAW AND ORDER?
Sean:Mike Finnegan is my brother..they
were fun when we all practised at my

house-also when William put his foot
through a wall at a gig.
TV:Wha t mags do you read?(dun ya luv
theese loaded questions/?
VOID:Touch and GO(when it's free..)
Flipside,Columbia Flier,Wash.Post,
Newsweek...all fanzines....
HEAR VOID ON THE CHARRED REMAINS CAS-
SETTE on NOISE RECORDS OR WRITE THIS
COOL BUNCHA GORRILAS AT 5373 HESPERUS
DR. COLUMBIA MD. 21044

LARISSA: ON CASS AND WILLIS, OR ON THE WEL-FARE LINE, OR AT THE PAROLE OFFICE, AT THE CORNER STORE OR AT THE VIDEO ARCADE.

KORY: CASS BURGER KING OR RAY'S BOYS.

SCOTT: RIGHT NEAR AN EXIT BUT NOT QUITE OUT.

TESCO: IS IT TRUE, LARISSA YOU STYLE YOUR HAIR AFTER A MOP YOU ONCE HAD A CRUSH ON AS A YOUNGSTER?

FRANK: I SAY R, R., A, R.,.A.,G, R.,.A.,G., G.,.M..O....P...P...P...

DAVID: LISTEN BUDDY, MESS WITH OUR SINGER AGAIN AND WE'LL TAKE AWAY ALL YOUR DEGREES SO YOU CAN'T USE BIG ADJECT-IVES LIKE LABYRINTHIAN AND ESOTERIC ANYMORE, O.K.?

LARISSA: YES ITS TRUE, MY FIRST SEXUAL EXPERI-ENCES WERE IN THE BROOM CLOSET, ITS LUCKY I NEVER GOT CAUGHT.

KORY: ITS A WIG, TESCO. WHAT THE FUCK, YOU THINK THAT SHITS REAL? GET A GOOD LOOK AT THOSE BOOBS, TOO. WHO KNOWS IF THEY'RE REAL OR TISSUE.

SCOTT: WHAT DO YOU MEAN? SHE IS A MOP.

TESCO: WHAT MUSIC DO YOU ALL LISTEN TO BEHIND CLOSED DOORS?

FRANK: MORE PAPER PLEASE...YARDBIRDS, ROLLING STONES UP TO AFTERMATH, ROLLING STONES AFTER AFTERMATH, OLDIES, GREEK MUSIC, PSYCHEDELIC FURS, TALKING HEADS, MC5, PHAROAH SANDERS, JOHN COLTRANE, IGOR STRAVINSKI, BOB DYLAN, THE DOORS, THEATRE OF HATE, BIRTHDAY PARTY, TURKISH MUSIC, IGGY, ELVIS COSTELLO, EDDIE COCHRAN, FLOWERS OF ROMANCE, HONEY RADIO, JERRY LEE LEWIS, IKO-IKO, MACK THE KNIFE, BLUE MAGOOS, FAMILY, NEIL YOUNG, TONIGHTS THE NIGHT, L-SEVEN TAPES, MINOR THREAT, JIMI HENDRIX, OLD FLEETWOOD MAC, PROCESS OF ELIMINATION, JOY DIVISION.

DAVID: CHET ATKINS AND LES PAUL, SCREAMIN' JAY HAWKINS, JIMI, ANY BAND THAT WEARS TIGHT RED SUITS AND SKINNY TIES, SLIM WHITMAN AND ROGER WHITTAKER, THE MANDREL SIS-TERS (I'D LIKE TO BEND BARBARA OVER A COUCH AND DRIVE IT HOME), THE VEL-VET TALKS (APRIL 1980) ISSUE WITH PORN SUPERSTAR EDY WILLIAMS, WHERE SHE SCREAMS "AAAAAAAARRRGGGH! IM COMMMMM-III NNNG!!!"

LARISSA: CRIMINAL CLASS, ALICE COOPER, NEGATIVE APPROACH, T. REX, 4 SKINS WITH HODGES, MOTORHEAD-IRON FIST, ANTI-NOWHERE LEAGUE, L-SEVEN, UPSTARTS, DEEP PURPLE, BIRTHDAY PARTY, LAST RESORT, SLADE, ALL TOUCH AND GO EFFORTS, JOY DIVISION, VENOM, STATIC, MEAT PUPPETS, SWEET, MORE ALICE COOPER, RAINBOW, INFA-RIOT, THE STRIKE, RED ALERT, NECROS, BLITZ, S.O.A., RED CROSS, GERMS, LEATHER NUN, KILLING JOKE.

KORY: BLACK SABBATH-MASTERS OF REALITY, JIMI HENDRIX-CRASH LANDING + EXPERIENCE, MAHAVISHNU ORCHESTRA, MOTORHEAD, BEECHER BRO, TOP 40 DISCO, DON VAN VLIET (CAPTAIN BEEFHEART), INSTRUMENTAL ZAPPA, NEGATIVE APPROACH, MINOR THREAT (THE MUSIC), THE SHAGGS, BLACK FLAG, BLUES MAGOOS,

BLUE CHEER, STEVE GADD (EVERYTHING), FURS, PIGBAG, JOY DIVISION, I COULD GO ON FOREVER, I'M SO SERIOUS, WHAT A DRAG.

SCOTT: THE GODLIKE GENIUS OF SCOTT WALKER, HENDRIX, LED ZEPPELIN, ALL TOUCH AND GO, FLIPPER, MINUTEMEN, EVERYTHING ELSE IS SUBLIMINAL.

TESCO: WHAT HAPPENED TO THE ATTITUDES?

SCOTT: I GUESS, I DON'T KNOW BUT WE JUST DIDN'T HAVE A STABLE BASE FOR ANYTHING WE DID AFTER A WHILE. IT STARTED AS GENUINE TEENAGE AGRESSION. BUT FOUR PEOPLE PULLING IN FOUR TOTALLY DIFFERENT DIRECTIONS JUST DOESN'T CUT IT. ON WITH L-SEVEN.

KORY: WE TOOK IT TO THE LIMIT. SCOTT COULDN'T TAKE THE LEAD SINGER AND BASSIST. I WAS SICK OF SINGING AND I WANTED TO CON-CENTRATE ON PERCUSSION. MAINLY IT WAS TIME TO MOVE ON. IT WAS FUN WHILE IT LASTED.

FRANK: WE TOOK THE BEST AND LEFT THE REST.

DAVID: WE STOLE KORY AND SCOTT AWAY FROM THEM! AAAH-HAHAHAHAHA HAHA!!!

LARISSA: DID YOU KNOW SCOTT USED TO PLAY BASS IN THE JAM?

TESCO: HOW DO YOU KEEP THE PEDESTRIAN ROCK FANS OFF YOUR FLAXEN HAIRED DRUMMER?

LARISSA: I BEAT THEM WITH STICKS OR SHOOT THEM WITH RUBBER BULLETS WAIT TILL THE RECORD COMES OUT AND WE'LL HAVE TO CALL THE RIOT SQUAD.

DAVID: MACE AND DUM-DUM BULLETS AND A SPECIAL CHEMICAL THAT CONVERTS BLUE EYE SHADOW INTO HYDROCHLORIC ACID.

FRANK: WE SPRAY HIM WITH OFF!

SCOTT: I LET HIM WORRY ABOUT SUCH IMPORTANT THINGS. IF HE NEEDS MY HELP HE'LL ASK.

TESCO: IF YOUR DWELLINGS CAUGHT ON FIRE AND YOU ONLY HAD TIME TO GRAB ONE THING WHAT WOULD IT BE?

SCOTT: MY HAROLD FLYER (WITH FREE LINT)

KORY: MY DICK.

FRANK: MY RECORDS. (MY GIRLFRIEND? MY CAT?) MY RECORDS.

LARISSA: MY RARE TOUCH AND GO's.

DAVID: MY MONEY.

TESCO: HAVE YOU RECIEVED MUCH CRITICAL ACCLAIM?

KORY: ROCKER AND NOW TOUCH AND GO, THATS ALL I CAN THINK OF.

SCOTT: PUBLICALY OR PRIVATELY? I SURE KNOW! WHAT THE WORD CRITICAL MEANS, NO, THE KIDS AND SOME OTHER PEOPLE WHO MAKE AN EFFORT TO COME TO OUR SHOW SEEM TO ENJOY IT AND SOME MAY EVEN BE INSPIRED, BUT IT THIS WAY, I KNOW WHO LIKES US AND WHO DOESN'T.

FRANK: YEA, BUT NO CRITICAL MONEY. (BELIEVE ME, ITS CRITICAL).

LARISSA: ARE YOU KIDDING? N.Y. ROCKER'S THE ONLY MAGAZINE THAT'S PRINTED ANY THING KIND ABOUT US. THE OFFENCE REVIEWED OUR GIG WITH KILLING JOKE, AND THEY SAID WE WERE O.K. TOUCH + GO WITH THIS AND OUR FIRST GIG. WE'VE GOTTEN TONS OF CRITICISM IN TALK-TALK AND SMEGMA. BURP AND REAL THREAT WROTE NICE THINGS. STATE NEWS (LANSING) SAID WE WERE A ALL GIRL BAND.

DAVID: DOES THAT INCLUDE DIPPY WAVERS WITH WISPS OF BLUE IN THIER HAIR WHO SAY THINGS LIKE, "YOU GUYS ARE LIKE, KICKY!".

TESCO: WILL YOU BE RELEASING MORE PRODUCT IN THE NEAR FUTURE?

SCOTT: IF THE REACTION TO THE FIRST SINGLE IS FAVORABLE, CERTAINLY I HOPE SO. BUT ONE IMPORTANT FACTOR IS THAT ALMIGHTY BUCK. IT COSTS MONEY TO DO THINGS LIKE THAT.

KORY: I'D LOVE TO. RIGHT NOW I'M EXPERIMENTING WITH A COUPLE OF IMPROVE FREAKS. WE'RE DOING A VIDEO JUNE 4. IT'LL BE SHOWN ON PLYMOUTH CABLES. SOMETHING WILL BE OUT BY FALL I HOPE.

FRANK: OH YES, OUR RESEARCH AND DEVELOPEMENT PEOPLE ARE HARD AT WORK ON MORE PRODUCT DESIGNED TO MAKE YOUR LIFE MORE.

DAVID: YEAH, WE'VE ALL GOT SOLO ALBUMS COMING OUT IN AUGUST, JUST LIKE KISS. BARBARA MANDREL SINGS ON MINE AND HER SISTERS ARE THE RHYTHM SECTION.

TESCO: TOUR PLANS FOR SUMMER?

DAVID: COCKTAILS FOR BREAKFAST?

LARISSA: LANSING, DETROIT, LANSING, DETROIT AND MAY-BE LANSING.

SCOTT: THAT'LL BE TALKED ABOUT IN MY NEXT BOOK. — THE GODLIKE GENIUS OF KEN WAAGNER.

KORY: KEN WAAGNER IS CAPABLE OF DOING ANY-THING. WE'RE GONNA TRY TO GET ABOUT FIVE DATES ON THE EAST COAST.

FRANK: JELLYSTONE PARK, WITH THE WIFE AND KIDDIES.

SCOTT: WHATS THE NEXT QUESTION? WHAT DO YOU MEAN NO NUMBER 15?!?

KORY: TESCO, YOUR TOTALLY COOL.

FRANK: LOVE, TESCO.

LARISSA: THANK YOU, UNCLE TESCO.

This guy from Bomp Records calls me up the other day and says he would like to put a couple of T-ouch And Go bands on his new Ha-rdcore compilation.....so I says sure I'll ask the bands who th-ankfully said "No Way"...cuz you see folks 2 years ago it was the-se people at Bomp who wouldnt even buy TEEN IDLES singles or even think about carrying any independant stuff from the east-now all of a sudden HC is in and look who wants to cash in...ya thats what they are doing,,,fucking making asses outa the punks by sending out a contract that doe-sn't mean shit...ya look at it (our lawyer did and she said that in order to get your money u w-ould have to go Ca.,get a Calif-ornia attorney etc.)thankfully the DC punks and Chicago punks said fuck off too...BEWARE OF THOSE OUT TO RIP YOU OFF...DON'T TRUST ANYONE...FUCKING DO IT YOURSELF......................

ANOTHER LIVE REVIEW
ZERO DFX/NEGATIVE APPROACH/GI/
NECROS....Freezer Theatre
Hot show here...0 DFX hail from
Ohio and show lots of promise...
NEGATIVE APPROACH played the best
set I've ever seen them do...GI's
drove all the way fro DC to play
this show...fucking cool...new lineup cant miss....stabb is a great s-
inger and I did a great interview
with them and the godamn tapedeck
didnt work...NECROS guitarist Brian did a flip off the pa and everyone moved and bang his elbow
shattered so Andy filled in and
played a few tunes...it was choice-
oh ya and RIOT 1 played last...it
was the show of shows...the creme
on the cake or whatever that saying is....fucking hot stuff...

NECROS

TOUGH AND GO REKORDS POB 26203 Lansing MI 48909

HEALTH NUGGIES

BALLS OFF DA-WALL LIVE ACTION

CRUCIFUCKS-at Howland House
This place has some sort of reputation as some sort of decadent c-
oop where those in residence are p-
redisposed to some sort of alien s-
ex frothing but that was the last t-
hing on my mind this nite...#1 was to
deduce whether orange juice and vodka
& Carlsburg Elephant Beer would make
me spit up,and #2 was seeing the fastest rising of midwestern starlets CRUC-
IFUCKS...well all these bashos have themes and tonight was perversion night
so the walls were covered with pictures
of women with strap on cods and people
tied up and so on and all in attendence
probably felt so naughty being all this
distance from ma and dad in suburban D-
etroit a little drag for the boys and
a little artificial power kong for da
femmes and they get all the titillation
necessary to go behind those legendary
closed doors...where reality steps in-
and it's about as kinky as missionary
style and three pumps on their tired
out fish factories before dumping a m-
eager clotting of half inebriated tadpoles....real depravity...the longhaired
curiousity seekers wanna make me do one
thing no matter where I am...lay down on
me belly,and 'ave me mates force them to
eat from the bubbling mud spring of fecat-
e I call my asshole......but then the time
for hating those types was lost years ago-
AHHH CRUCIFUCKS....no scaryness,no sex-
pure hate it is...I'm inclined to smile
when I see them but it's only because I
like to see the mind of a tormented genius like Doc laid out over a great beat-
Plus I revel in seeing established cultural and social institutions ripped out
by the decaying roots...the drummer looks like the proverbial boy next door-
but lays down the most intricate textured,but fucking powerful drumming arou-
nd.one guy that really doesn't need m-
iking to sound meaty...Doc really got in
the crowds' face and shredded em with
choice bits of accurate putdown...all without a whimper in response(of course)
Of course there were a few morons who
tried to get wild and one moron got kicked in the aggots so hard he had to be
taken to the hospital.....just desserts-
Gee what can be said about that bass
player cept he's a wild unpredictable
sort of fellow who gets fuckin violent
while playing his bad green thang with
consistent riffs...and their madcap guitarist seems at all times ready to take
Mason by storm and rape and pillage at
the Shp Rite....really a band to watch-

THE MISFITS at the FREEZER THEATRE....
it ain't really a theatre at all-rath-
er a dank grotto in slumtown where the
kids run the show....no fuckwad promoter ready to throw ticket stubs away &
pimp the bands...the fact the MISFITS
made just as much here as they had the
night previous at mega hall CLUTCH CAR-
GOS is but another graphic example we
don't need businessmen running our scene...they can stick to the commercial
side of it all cuz sheeit they do it so
well...this review aint gonna be temper-
ed with one more iota of hostility cuz
this just happened to be the greatest
show Detroit has seen....got there too
late for BORED YOUTH...but folks said
they did a hot,short set of new tunes-
next was your basic NEGATIVE APPROACH-
who wailed as usual...driving the place
gonads and setting the tone for wot wos
to cum...NECROS raced through their set
with the same hotness always displayed-
I bet I've seen em 25 times so I'm dyeing for some new tunes although stuff
like "Your Version Of What I Think"and
"Reject" never get old....next comes
the guys everyone was waiting to see-
it's not like half of em werent there
the night before...but the lure of seeing this band in our homey confines
got us all back down to Murder City to
witness the spectacle again...Googy and
his trap set occupied the balcony so as
to free up some space...what can I say
cept they blew the place down with all
the greats and they even did the heart-
stopping "Devils Whorehouse" and their
classics like "Bullet"...after I clean-
ed the hermans outa my briefs I strolled
out of the club full knowing there werent nothing else transpired this eve anywhere on this glorious globe that coulda
matched what I had just witnessed....

DOC of the CRUCIFUCKS

Stopped in at Wax Trax the other
day in Chicago and never felt more
out of place...crawling with jerk
clerks with Jack Lord greasy do's-
there racks are overflowing with
sappy german synth avant garde drivel and two little racks of good
music...the EFFIGIES were right on
when they slagged these jackoffs
in the Flipside interview....

The Ultimate Dumping Ground!

A photo for No reason of Lisa De Leeuw - the fave-urite porn star of your editor

How come fat people got tiny dinks?

Cuz there aint enough skin to go around...

Cromax

NOW OUT ON Smoke Seven

battalion of saints

TV:Where,when,how,come,why,and what
inspired you to form BATTALION OF S-
AINTS?
Chris:I was into forming a band and
became indirectly associated with G-
eorge through a rumor that the band
he was in was breaking up up he was
looking to form another one.George
and I are the only two original members left.At that time we were the N-
UTRONS,with Ted our present drummer
and some hack guitar player.Then we
met Dennis who murdered the old bass
player which immediately racked up p-
oints with us.We got rid of the hack
changed our name and hence Battalion
of Saints were born.
TV:Is there any kind of scene in San
Diego or do you have to travel to m-
ost of your gigs?
BAT:There is a small(300)but dedicate-
d hardcore scene with Dead Or Alive,
the local promoters of hardcore shows,
about 8 good bands and a few fanzines.
We're really just an extention of the
LA scene.
Q:What would be the most exhilerating,
nirvanic thing that could happen toBAT?
BAT:A cross country tour,England and
spreading the gospel as far and wide
as we could reach.Dennis:Make enough
money off playin to be able to quit my
job.George:To be able to buy a new leather jacket.Ted:To get my car tuned
up and the album cover painted on the
door.Chris:Rx
TV:How many femmes are ready to fondle
your M-16's after you play out?
BAT:FUCKLOADS.
TV:Why a 12" single as opposed to a 7"?
BAT:Alot easier to see and they fly be-
tter.Better sound quality,and people
feel like they're getting more for their
money.Plus we wanted an eye catching p-
ackage.Originally we had six songs but
2 songs left with the hack and we kept
the original 12' plans.
TV:What did yer mom's say when they
heard the record?

Dennis:My mom won't listen to it,
she thinks it's devil music.George:
My mom liked it but she doesn't like my tatoos so she kicked me out..
Ted:She says she liked it but she sez
she likes alot of things.Chris:She likes the cover but she hasnt heard it
yet.TV:Where would yall like to be
when CA falls off into the ocean/?
BAT:Vacationing in the Falklands...
Dennis wants to be right on the edge.
George:Cruisin Chicago in a coup de
ville with my new leather jacket and
2 foxy HO's.Ted:Some place with a good
view.Chris:In New York on drugs.
TV:Any major writeups in mags yet?
BAT:No major write ups but some minor
ones in Flipside,Ripper,Sickteen,some
mag in NJ,we got an interview and review and Marc drew the cover for next
months issue of Noise from Ohio,Punk
Lust,Paranoia,Suburban Relapse,Public
Threat(Hi Dit.)We went down the list
of fanzines from Flipsides list and we
are expecting lots of good reviews from
all of them,and we have been getting
lot's of nice letters and good shit in
the mail.TV:Future plans?BAT:We are going to be featured on the Noise magazines Meathouse compilation.Some songs
on a vinyl comp put out by B.Y.O.(Better Youth Organization) The Stern Bros.
More indepenent vinyl and we are trying to set up the BATTALION OF SAINTS
WORLD CONQUEST TOUR.....

BELIEVE It or NOT..

LIVELIVELIVELIVELIVELIVELIVE
J.F.A./RIOT 1/ROUGH GLIDERS/
WALL OF WATER/TUNNEL CONCAVES
What a lineup.all the makings
for a rad,gnarly,boss nirvanic
show...JFA did all their greats-
"Ramp Scamp"/"Wheels On Fire"/
and Your Vans Smell"..but mid-
way through through their set w-
as when the trouble started...
all the skateboarders including
members of Riot 1 and Garfields
Maulers began their chanting-
WATER SKIIERS SUCK SISSYPRICK-
HANG GLIDERS FUCK OFF".....over
and over...the contigent of angry suburban razor cut skiiers c-
ircled the mob angrily picking
out the peripheral boarders and
pommeling them with clubs and
rubber cods...the hang gliders
circled overhead dropping steaming hermans on the crowd and by
the time WALL OF WATER came on
the skiiers had taken over...T-
odd Wudda Buldie leader of the
shredders was in the spacious b-
alcony firing pyrotechnics at the
crowd while he was on the reciev-
ng end of a choice reefing from one
of those little girls who take pictures at all the shows so they can
feel needed and wanted....lemme tell
ya it was pure chaos...Al was right
Detroit has subdivided into warring
sportsman whose caste system must
end before our scene is destroyed...
Watch out cuz with bands like the
Wind Surf Punks" and the HOBIE CATZ
coming to town it'll be a long hot
summer...

CHildren Of Lansing(or any other small
scene anywhere)Heed these words of wisdom,enjoy your scene while you have id-
entity.It won't last long.You can't be
a punk in LA anymore,you can't make a
statement out of being a punk here,all
you do is do what all your friends plus
a few hundred thousand other kids do.W-
hen it started here it was great but it
has gained such wide spread attention a-
nd acceptance that it just can't be the
same.Not to say there arent great bands
here(45 GRAVE,VOXPOP Christian Death,
The Mentors,Nervous Gender)and plenty of
real people but the whole attitude is
such a watered down version of what it
once was,I guess you can only be angry
for so long,but never mind our dilemma,
realize the energy you have and enjoy
it to it's full potential cuz in a year or two all the kids that give you shit at school are gonna be shavin their
heads and you will become alienated
and bored.sincerely.Raynard Dean
Editor/Publisher
gothic shock
ED's Note:This is typical of the mail
i receive from So.Ca.Whether it be a
word to the wise or sour grapes I don't
know...as of last issue I discontinued
the letter column as it's basic function had become a place for people to
argue with each other about stupid things..I will however in issue#20 give
space for those of you who would like
to comment to or respond pro or con
to Mr.Dean's comments...I guess it's
something people should think about-
or is it?

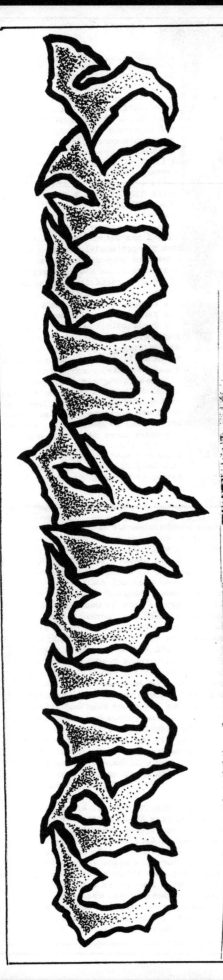

THE CRUCIFUCKS WERE INTERVIEWED ON MAY 5th IN LANSING...

TV:So your last couple of gigs have ended on a violent note I hear... tell me how much you like Flint....

Scott:It's OK...it's the bouncers

Doc:We didn't see much of the town just the disco...

Scott:It has a really strict dress code....(talking about the Micotam)

TV:How many of you got beat up?

Scott:4 or 5...

Doc:Scott got shoved around alot and my back is really starting to bother me

TV:You gonna sue em?

Doc:I'm gonna try...probably find out it's the mafia and you'll find me in a ditch somewhere..

TV:What about your gig in london,Ontario?

Doc:there were people who came to that bar just to cause trouble...ya long haired leather jacketed guys with

gloves with knuckles exposed...the guy that booked us in there,he got sucker punched twice before we even played...and it just got worse...it was chaos..people were throwing glasses...

Scott:It ended up we didn't get paid...

TV:Had any problems here in town because of your name?

Scott:We can't play...

Doc:Some people find our name offensive...

TV:I say bring back club DOO BEE...

Doc:That place was perfect almost...

TV:So what do the CRUCIFUCKS stand for ideologically,socially,politicallly, morally,sexually.....blah...blah...

Doc:I can't speak for the other guys.. we're all really different...we like to think that compared to most bands we've got a better idea of the different ways the government is fucking people over...and how religion plays a part in that...

TV:Hence the name.

Doc:We have to play around here as the SCRIBBLES....it's always been an asset of mine to offend people...basically .. I hate police...we've got a couple of songs about them...most of the songs

are directed to people like that who have little or no intelligence whatsoeverTV.that was great when we did we being the MEATMEN)FUCK THE COPS and you started screaming and the whole crowd went apeshit...

Doc:Ya the same thing happened in Flint- we started the song "Who Are Those Fools in Uniforms" and I just screamed KILL THE PIGS....there's alot of good sentiment out there it's just people are subdued cuz they are afraid of the consequences.

TV:Whats "Positive in A Negative Town" about:?

Doc:Ask Steve..

Scott:Bagels....Steve:It speaks for itself....Scott:Well he doesn't know...

TV:When you guys do "Go Bankrupt And Die" I always think lovingly about my boss

Doc:That's good that you thought about that...it can be applied to anything or anyone establishment...just look at all the man hours logged through out history and now it's all stockpiled in gold for the rich...and theres all these people with no jobs and no future... it's like in "Democracy Spawns Bad Taste" I say "put a gun in my back and i'll do what you say but if you let me get away you'll get yours...and I'm not a revenge seeking person..but if someone does something it comes back to haunt em'...

TV:So how did the incident with the EL cops come about...

Doc:There's this bar in Eest Lansing called the Americas Cup that's really preppy and all the assholes go down there and drink...it was right before our gig with L-7 and we were passing out flyers and as we went in there was a cop so I yelled "asshole"....the guy didn't hear me so Scott said a couple things..what did you say..

Scott:Shithaed...Fuckface(that outa do it,ED)Doc:A bouncer grabbed and put me out the door and then I elbowed him really hard and there were the cops..when they had me in the cell they were hassling me saying "We have some tinker toys for ya" and then I said I wanted a phone call so they made the phone ring in the outer room and they said go get the

phone go get the and they were laughing at me ...

TV:SO what else would you like the world to know about your band/?Doc:We've been accused by our parents.Joe has and I have that it's just a totally negative message

TV:Have your folks heard your music?

Scott:My mom has a tape of us and she gets up in the morning and listens to it...she played it for her fourth grade class..you can't understand the bad words so she played it for em...she's seen us twice...

Doc:People around town accuse us of being trouble makers but we don't actively try to cause trouble it finds us...people are intimidated by what we say,and we're saying things that are true....every thing we do is borne out of concern as to like why things are still this way-

Contact the Crucifucks c/o Touch + Go....

Gildee photo

TOUCH and GO REKORDS

OUT NOW...NECROS EP,FIX"JAN'S ROOMS EP"/MEATMEN"BLOOD SAUSAGE EP"/L-SEVEN EP....
THE EP FROM BORED YOUTH HAS BEEN CANCELLED....NEGATIVE APPROACH EP WILL BE OUT
IN JULY...PROCESS OF ELIMINATION SECOND PRESSING AVAILABLE NOW....FUTURE PROJ-
ECTS INCLUDE AN EP BY THE CRUCIFUCKS AND A CASSETTE RELEASE FROM BLIGHT...ALL
RECORDS ARE $2.50 POSTPAID...

KEVIN SECONDS-Guitar and vocals
STEVE YOUTH-Bass
Bix BIGLER-Drums

SEVEN SECONDS exemplifies the growing
number of solid youth bands worthy of
a helluva lot more exposure....thus
the following interview(i'm a noble
sort aint I?)
TV:How's the EP coming?How did you land
the Alternative Tentacles deal?

K:The Ep should be out this summer.It'll
be 9 songs.Jello is talking to Faulty P-
roducts about distribution.We got lucky.
I was talking to Biafra on the phone and
he said they could put the record out.We
originally gonna do something on Dischord
but the money wasn't there...
TV:How's the Skeeno scene these days?
S:Fucking great!Things up here look g-
ood gig wise.3 clubs have offered us t-
here places so things should start picking up,just like the old days.We had a
great show with DOA and TSOL on the 25th
of April.Once again alot of new kids showed up.The hall was super cool.Great s-
tage for diving,great floor for rucking,
I swear it was so fun.Tons of thrashing
and stage diving and not one fight.Any-
way MINOR THREAT are coming out in July
and that'll definately be killer!
K:Another thing about the scene here is
that it's factioned out into several g-
roups of people.Like you've got the 1st
generation of punk here who for the most
part have remained totally committed to
the local hardcore scene.That's where
the creative output starts.Bands,fanzines
people putting on shows,all come out of
this group of people.Then you've got the
2nd generation which lives off the reputation and work of the first,but come to
the shows and give support nonetheless.
Then of course the third and most recent
faction mostly consists of real young
high school kids like the skatepunks and
the Wooster high crew.They're the majority of our following and fucking totally
cool.The scene here is very touchy but
the dedication is unparalleled.
TV:Where and how recently did you play
out?S:We played in SF with the Dead
Kennedys,TSOL and the Bad Brains at the
Elite Club,probably one of our best shows,that's what everyone said anyway.We
got a great response for not playing SF

for awhile,we even made $240.00,that's
the most we've ever made.We had a great time.TV:Is the EP all new material
or stuff from the tapes?S:A few old,a
few newK:Ya the songs on the Ep will b-
e;"Skins,Brains,and Guts"/"No Authority
"Redneck Society"/"Baby Games"/"Racism
Sucks"/"we're Gonna Fight"/"This Is My
Life"/"I Hate Sports"/and."Anti Klan",
All the songs have been newly recorded
and are quite a bit faster than before.
We've also recorded a song "Fuck YOUR
America" for an album coming out on A-
lternative tentacles called "Not So Q-
uiet On The Western Front"which will f-
eature 47 bands from all over northern
California and Nevada.The Nevada bands
are us,SECTION 8,THE WRECKS,URBAN ASSA-
ULT and MIA who are from Vegas.TV:What's
the status of YOUTH CRISIS?S:Youth Crisis was a very brief project,we never
played out.I don't wanna brag but Y/C
was a fucking killer bandwe had alot of
great songs.It was a good idea but at
the time we were too busy working with
7 SECONDS.Maybe someday we'll play
again,but it's hard to tell.We're still
putting out something on Viscious Scam.
K:Plus Steve and I are putting our other efforts into UNITED TRUST(formerly
MORAL DISRUPT)our new band which is closer to the English Hardcore sound than
the stuff we do in 7 SECONDS.By the way
Steve and I play in more Skeeno fuck bands
than anyone.Wait'll you hear the Skeeno
HC Compilation tape!
TV:Any plans to tour the midwest or East?
K:We plan to tour probably in August.Our
goal of course is to hit DC and The Midwest above all! S:Ya Kev and I made a promise to ourselves that we would definately play out there this summer and we wi=
ll.K:So anybody out there who can get us
gigs call us at (702)322-8496.We'll trade
a gig in Skeeno for gigs in other cities.
TV:Why is your music so absolutely choice?
S:I don't know is it?
K:Cos' we don't do drugs! No,we just take
our music seriously,we firmly believe and
commited ourselves to the music as well
as the lifestyle.If you're a punk you h-
ave to be 100% a punk.If you're a hippie,
be 100% a hippie,but don't just fucking
stand in the way.People think all you

have to do is shave your head,lis-
ten to all the L.A. bands and beat
the shit out of your friends and
other punks and that's total fucking shit! We care about people,ab-
ove all,the kids who make the shows so fucking great!That's what is
so fucking great about the kids h-
ere in Skeeno.If it wasn't for them
we wouldn't play.We believe in youth
totally!100%!
TV:How is Ma Seconds these days?
S:She's fine,still tryin' to convince
me to stop shavin' my head.Oh ya she
says hi to THE FIX...K:Yeah her favorite bands are 7 Seconds,Black Flag,
The Fix,and D.O.A.She sipports what
we do entirely,except when we shave
our heads,she really believes in what
we do.TV:What happened to Dim?
K;He's playing in SECTION 8 now and
may move to L.A. this summer.He's one
of my best friends and is a great s-
inger and performer.S:When Dim was
in 7 Seconds we had alot of band prob-
lems.Things were just not working
out so we went trio and Dim formed
Section 8.He's one of the coolest
dudes around and alot of fun to be
with.He might roadie for us on the
tour......WRITE 7 SECONDS.....
2302 PATTON DRIVE   RENO NEVADA
89512

SKEENO HARDCORE KILLS!!

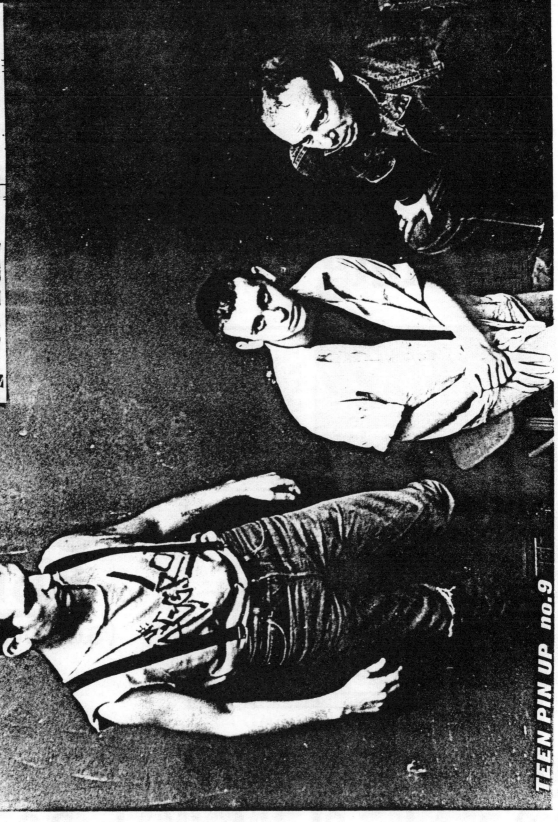

7 SECONDS

PHOTO: GARY BUHM

TEEN PIN UP no.9

NEGATIVE APPROACH ARE
O.P.-Drums
Graham-Bass
Rob-Guitar
John-Vocals

Graham:It's going to get larger...it's growing now.John:Summer's going to be good,
new bands are forming left and right...
TV:Do you agree with certain outsiders who
say it's only a matter of time before 'out-
staters start subdividing the Detroit/Mid

TV:Are you happy with the demo for
your EP?
O.P.We're pleased with the way it
came out.John:I can't wait till it
fucking gets pressed.Rob:Gosh I like it swell.Graham:Yes...
TV:How do you think the new lineup
differs from the old one?
Rob:We're having more fun at pract-
ices:John:The reason the old band s-
plit up was practicing wasn't fun at
all.It just got to a point where we
couldn't practice together.We were
fighting all the time.I just couldn-
't take Zuheir's complaining about
white slavery.Pete quit the band b-
ecause of that.Then we kicked Zuheir out.The new band is great.Every
one is into practicing and everyone
writes tunes;TV:Has having a red haired drummer improved your sex lives?
O.P.Duh I dunno.Graham:They can't get
enough.John:Yea it's great.People co-
nfuse him for that sex god Barry Hen-
ssler.Rob:We get all their leftovers-
O.P.Yea right...TV:Hey big John what's
it like living above Clutch Cargos?Do
you miss the clubhouse?
John:It's pretty cool.We don't have to
pay for shows.They're getting some cool shows there now.We still practice at
the clubhouse.It got to a point where
it was fucked living there.We didn't h-
ave heat or running water.The clubhouse
is still a cool place to hang out though-
TV:Why did YOUTH PATROL break up?Come on
give us the hot poop...
OP:I wasn't having fun.I'd rather play d-
rums than guitar...Graham:I realized that
it wasn't going anywhere.Our songs were'nt
very original...but it was fun playing with Bud.TV:Where is this scene headed?
Rob:Nowhere,it's staying right here,yuk yuk

Write NA...
PO Box 141
St. Clair Shores, Mich.
48080

west scene?John:All the bands know
each other.It's not a who's best si-
tuation.Detroit's cops are nothing l-
ike LA's.Cops here don't fuck with an-
ybody.New punks and skins come to every show.I think it;s great that our s-
cene is so strong now to let any outsiders divide us all up.
Graham:No ones going to let anyone fuck with anybody...
TV:What are your current fave bands?
John:4 SKINS with Hodges,MISFITS,SOA
and ALICE COOPER..Graham:BLACK FLAG,
MINOR THREAT,SOA and THE MISFITS...
O.P.:NECROS,MINOR THREAT,MISFITS and
THE ALLIED...Rob:SOA,NECROS,MEATMEN,
and SWEET...TV:What do you think has
been the hottest thing to happen of
late in Detroit?John:"Harold" and ev-
eryone is skating again...
O.P.Definately.It's the re-established
skate scene...Graham:The opening of the
FREEZER Theatre...Rob:They opened the
Mini Baja season at Endless Summer(Ska-
teboard Park,ED)TV:Any new tunes in the
works?Who writes em?
Graham:"Live Your Life" and "Your Always
Wrong"John:I write the lyrics and all of
us write the music.
TV:Who does the angry rabbit on your tape?
Who is Bud?Is he gay?
ALL:Graham does the "angry rabbit"
Graham:Bud is only the swing-iest sex god
I know besides Tesco.John:He drums for the
Allied...Rob:He's not gay,he's just miser-
able,not very gay...
TV:Why is D.A.B.F. being left off the EP?
John:D.A.B.F. is going to Finland for a
compilate record.FINLAND loves fast music
TV:Why do John's buns send the girls into
cold fits?Why is Rob into listening to
Gino Vannelli records while he beats off?
Graham:It's not his buns it's his wavy
hair...Rob:It's his penis length.John:F-
uck that Robs favorite mag is Phenis
O.P.:Let's face facts John sports some
nice buns...
(b)Rob:Because the MEATMEN ep wasn't out
yet...END

PIC PAGE!!

→NeGATiVe APPROACH and MIdwest KIds

SAMe TO YOU DOYLe!!!

McDONALDS RooooOL

Member of professional punk rock band

GLeNN backstage at the FReezer

Wotta fag!!

Greg Helping out oN "Riot Squad" as the Bad Brains play to shitty crowds in LANSING...

MINOR THREAT

TWO MIdwest dates Only

WED.
June 16
Civic Players Hall
Lansing
Corner of Hayford + East Michigan

All AGES

Don't Fuck up this hall AND WE CAN USE it again sometime!

with...
FROM SF...
Whipping Boy

Also Appearing...
meatmen
CRucifucks

$3
8PM

Fri. June 18
Freezer
Theatre
Detroit

with...
Whipping Boy
NEGATIVE Approach
MEATMEN

All AGES

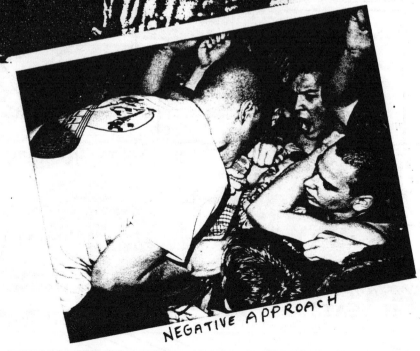

NEGATIVE APPROACH

414

So anyway we're driving all around the city,rush,rush dropping amps & drums & shit off and picking people up (four skins,cute huh?)three normal haired people and a woman so we could go see TSOL in time.Now I don't even like TSOL but punk shows especially under 21 minors welcome shows are few and far between.Besides this Minneapolis thrash band that we all love and you hate was supposed to be playing,So we finnally get there an hour late and haven't missed a thing because the under 21 show only TSOL are going to be playing cuz us minor threats by law gotta be out by 10:00PM.So they come on and this is a sight to see.Dey got long hair talking about how it's the next big trend in California and they're acting like prima donna rock stars and they gotta fucking keyboard.They start playing this awful AM pop muzak. We had heard that a pop band was going to be starting things off so we go back and ask the bouncers Who be dis band?" (oh I forgot to say HUSKER DU cancelled) and TSOL start playing "Superficial Love" and we now know it's them.They are really terrible,playinga fusion of heavy metal,pop and AM muzak so the crowd starts yelling "Go home fuckers" etc. So I'm like incredibly bored right and their faggot lead singer using his microphone as a whip hits me square in the nose(and this was one of those heavy deluxe rock star jobs too) with precision like he'd practised doing itafter 23 minutes of shit they leave the stage,they were bood off so as they leave everybody (trendies included)yay.

is screaming obscenities at em and giving em the old index finger so I yell "TSOL can suck my cock faggots."and their roadie who by the way is as tall as you and also mucho muscular with TSOL tatoos and spikey red hair he had copied from the Exploited leaps off the side of the stage screaming "Little shit" and knocks me into the ground and hits me on my head but he doesn't really hurt me and then he dissapears into nowhere and I pick myself up and everybody is patting me on the back and going "ya" and stuff,so we leave the club in a huff and then everybody else gets herded out.So the cops are waiting outside(we never got harrassed by the police before)and they start herding us down the street how we are going to burn TSOL records and how TSOL can lick a dogs asshole til it bleeds and thsi guy who is about 5 foot nothing gets beaten in the back with a billy club and the macho cops friends are all watching and he grabs my friends coke and sez "what is this shit" and my friend goes "It's coke honest taste it".and mister blue man goes "shit" and grabs the coke and throws it in the gutter and does the same for some 45 year old hardcore fan women (cool)who is clearly old enough to drink and goes "move along or we're gonna lock ya'll up and bust some heads.....(letter abbreviated due to length)   Jay Yuenger
Chicago Ill

The main reason I discontinued the letter section was basically because all it had turned into was a forum for senseless arguing and rantings about particulars...of all the mail I get about 97% is either overall critique,praise and so on.... some of it(not enough) resembles those genuinely angry about something I stated or the scene in general...it seems people are too complacent most of the time to say what they really think,,,or maybe they dont wanna hurt my feelings or hey meybe they really do like what we are doing... whatever...I'm sure people who don't get their nasties printed go off and say TV's a wimp because he wont print what I said....like Frank Blank of Ann Arbor who called me old and the midwest bands inane...but if I print that I've gotta print all the yes votes,so you see what a pain in the ass it is and fuck it...but here is one or two entertaining ditties I thought you might be interested in...

PROCESS OF ELIMINATION E.P. II? WELL NEVER TELL

FLESH EATERS
UNDERTAKERS
TUES APRIL 21 WHISKY

the FLESH EATERS
A MINUTE A SECOND
TO PRAY TO DIE
RUBY RECORDS

HEAVY METAL JOCKS

Make my life so fucked,you think you're so tough, Yeah,Hippie fuckoff,prove you're mean,get rough, (chorus)Freaks and Hippies,smoke your dope,Heavy Metal Jocks, Freaks and Hippies,smoke your dope,Heavy Metal Jocks, You call me Faggot,ask my girlfriend scum, Who would fuck you,man?,dirty longhaired bum, (chorus)
AC/DC freaks,all so fucking weak,never mean a thing,to fucked u, (chorus)

fuck lyrics!!
7-Seconds/lyrics!! choice!!

Red Spot continued

so cuz it's the cool thing to do-
their LP is unlistenable...gimme
"earthworm"any day...quit listening
to what your friends say and start
buying things like this RED SPOT c-
ompilation because you wanna start
listening to other forms of neurosis-
unless you need overt teen rant and
chant as a stedy diet but me I need
variety...SUBTERRANEAN RECORDS 912
BANCROFT WAY BERKELYED CA 94701

WILMA

LOST CAUSE-EP
Yes sir don't know what they
did to ingratiate themselves
to me in this way butthis record has it all...immediacy b-
ut still a nagging we don't c-
are attitude not to placate
but....then the chorus blasts
out....anyway the change in
"Born Dead" works...and so does
the rest of it...highly reccom
ended

**WILMA-"Alexander Haig"/"FAST
Fascist"/Pornography Lies"**
Subterranean
I've given up my search for y'
our basic shittiest record ever-
just what I wanted to hear is
three butch femmes singing some
gaff to a violin and synth backdrop...gives me more of a pain
in the ass than a prostiscopic
at the Mayo Clinic...(that's
when they stretch your colon out
straight with a long lighted t-
ube to check for polyps...doctors
say it will soon be standard procedure for males over thirty---
you heard it here at T&G first
guys....)PornographyLies?Ya on
my living room floor...I mean
what would life be like if there
were no magazines of well hung
black men sticking their stretch
monsters up some fat white girls
rectum?

**100 FLOWERS-"PRESENCE OF MIND"/
"DYslexia"/MOP DUB" Happy Squid**
Records
I miss the breaking a toilet over
your aunts head sound of the URI-
NALS but these guys are cool too
if somewhat more predictable...
but then again if this was done
by a band called the "Frolicking
Typewriters" I would probably s-
ing a different tune...the dub
thing is cool...Happy Squid...
Box 64184 LA CA 90064

REJECTORS-"THOUGHTS OF WAR EP"
FARTZ RECORCS....
Fuckin aye man more great stuff
from Seattle...9 songs that will
please fans of speed...not standard farepunk...top of the line
domestic shit from the land of
the FARTZ....we'll all be dead
soon...so grab a peep show at
the future here clods...write
1112 So.211th Pl Seattle Wash.
98148

**THE INSANE-"EL SALVADOR"/CHINESE
ROCKS"/"Chinese Rocks" No Future**
This is OK not ½ as exciting as
their first record...who cares
about El Salvador?I'd rather save the whales.....

HEADCLEANERS "DISINFECTION EP"
Malign Massacre Records
You are probably going to get
mad at me again like last issue
cuz people wrote in and ragged
on me for reviewing these international ditties hey but this t-
ime I have an address so....this
kicks hardcores ass...singer is
cut throated meanie...growling
Swedish meanies that have laid
out this grand piece of 7 song
mania....hey if you hadnt noticed heavy punks are sprouting
up all over the world...so quit
supporting dead assed English
shit and start writing letters-
MALIGN MASSACRE BOX 9004 UPPSALA
A9 SWEDEN(limited Ed. 500)

I wasn't expecting anything
as great as this...another
band with that meaty sou-
nd of alot of the early LA
bands...alot more punch
than some of the other records from this locale of
late...Im telling you everything on this Smoke 7 label
is cool as shit...if you're
a fan of the Skulls or the
early Controllers then bite
down hard on this one!

DALLAS/FT. worth

DALLAS/FORT WORTH UPDATE
Best band in D/FW is the HUGH BEA-
UMONT EXPERIENCE.Their sound used
to be very 77'ish in style and bite
but they've accelerated their speed
and Brad Stiles has really shown signs of shedding his Rottenish vocals...he can really belt it out now.
They have a four song EP that exemplifies their previous 77 state(of
which "Zyklon B" is one of my all t-
ime favorites)They also just released a 30 minute 18 song live casste
that was recorded at the Bowie Theatre in Ft.Worth.Now that was a wild
show.12 or so punks showed up to s-
upport the HBE while 50 jock redneck-
s showed up to see the second band
which was heavy metal.To make a long
story short we were lucky to get o-
uta there without getting our asses kicked.Write VVV Records 3906
Cedar Springs Dallas Texas for details and prices...the cassette is
super cheap,about $2 I'm sure...
BOMB SQUAD has released their 4
song EP.If your tastes are jaded
toward the fast,fast,faster DC/Mi-
dwest/Boston thrash you'll hate
this.But if you're into raw medium speed minimalist Texas punk-go
for it.The tunes are good and production is a little lacking but for
$1.50 postpaid you cant afford to not
take a chance...send all orders to
Johnny Chaos 2959 Latham Dr Dallas
tx 75229...other D/FW bands are stuck
in the garage still but it seems like
everyone is waiting for a scene to "H
appen"Don't they know they've gotta
build one?Anyway,MILITARY INTELLIGENCE
(ex MDA),MIA's,FALSE PROPHETS,WARMAMAS
AND ZERO FACTOR are out there someplace but remain doomed to the garage
and parties because the club situation
sucks...The Hot Klub,a neewavee venue
has a monopoly over all but there have
been some good shows set up at the B-
owie Movie Theatre in Ft.Worth.Some g-
ood Texas Fanxines to chexk out would
be XIPHOID PROCESS for Austin info---
write 401 W.32nd st.Austin TX 78705...
For Houston info write WILD DOG po
box 35253 S.Post Oak Station Houston
TX 77035...for D/FW info write
me at PO bOx 223 Boyd TX 76023
and watch for the upcoming AKA
fanzine...oh ya and for some
more general Texas info write
NEW MUSICAL EXCESS 3118 43rd ST
Lubbock TX 79413......

TOUCH and GO
BOX 26203   LANSING, MI 48909

SEND All Records, promos, Nude photos
to the above address for proper
consideration...

416

THE WRECKS

Hey here's yer chance to get to Know this all female assemblage, intimately. Write them and they'll bend your ear with lotsa bad mouthin'

Lynn Lust of Reno's The Wrecks Whatta Women!

TV:What's life loke when you're a WRECK?Jone:Life when you're a WRECK is filled with Excitement! We frequently go to live sex shows and do guest appearences.Often times the WRECKS are asked to go to old folks homes and teach the old coots how to handle their feces properly.Bessie:Hey what can I say except "wild and crazy!" Naw sometimes it sucks but usually it's pretty fun.Lynn:Let me tell you;it's hell:you got to get up at the crack of dawn and feed the chickens,milk the cows and cook breakfast for the whole family. Go to school.Urinate when you come home,go to work,come home again wash up and mop the furniture. Hell-N:A living breathing walking hell...sometimes I'd rather die... TV:What do you do at your infamous slumber parties:Hell-n:Sing gospel music.Jone:One time Bessie and I had a boxing match and charged admission,we made about $2.50.Bessie:We really do have slumber parties at my house.Like after gigs and stuff when it's too late for people to go home they sleep over here.Lynn:Well why don't you come to the next one and find outTV:Cuz I would probably pop a king snake and spray all your youthful supine forms with my mellow coconut oil...by the way who is the most voluptuous WRECK?Hell-n:Jone because of her sexy nose hairs.Bessie:Me of course because of my two slender 94 inch penises.Jone:I.B.W. oh she's not really a WRECK but she sure is sexy!She sorta counts as a Wreck cause she lived in the Wrecksmobile for months.Lynn:Hell-n's VW bug is by far the most voluptuous Wreck.With 2 crunched rear fenders and the front end smashed in how could one resist?(sounz like a gurl I used to date,ED.har,har)TV:When was the last time you had a good knockdown dragout orgasm/?Jone:That would be last summer when a large bird attacked me.Have you ever had sex with a bird?It's great,the ult-

imate orgasm!Lynn:While cleaning the toilet.Bessie:When I inserted an uninflated basketball up my rectum until it lodged there snugly and then simultaneously inflating the basketball and sliding a searing hot curling iron into my vaginal cavity.Hell-n:When you sent that picture of the guy jakin it off.mmmmyeh!TV:So what is Reno like?Jone:I'll have to say fecal material.Reno is like a piece of shit. It has all kinds of stuff in it and it's filthy and it stinks.Hell-n:It sux!! don't come here.Lynn:Boring,uncultured, no clubs w/lots of snobby jocks,varnets and cowboys.But the weathers great-- TV:How's been the response to your tape?Bessie:Good enough for a homo-zine'- new wave chronicle like Touch and Go to interview us I guess.Actually pretty good-I think it's cuz we put alot into it, Lynn:So far pretty good.We get a couple of letters a week for tapes.Jone:Pretty good,I'm surprised.We've been getting good reviews except those that say we're an art damage band.fuck yeah we sound like a combination of Rik L Rik and The Slits and David Bowie...I'm sure! Hell-n:Great-I even saw one in Recycled RecordsTV:Any plans to put out a record?Hell-n:Yes we would like to put out a double live album soon.Bessie:Not at the moment unless of course someone offers to do it for us and gives us 20, 000,oooJone:If you want to pay for it we'll do it,Yeah Wrecks on Touch and Go what do you say?TV:Corey wouldnt like that idea too much...anyways folks write to these teen babes in a fit of lust at PO BOX 20391 RENO NEVADA ... RF-7 'Weight Of the World LP Smoke 7 Records

You could have bought this space for 62¢....

Write for the Wrecks tape

Double O-were too busy skating to do an interview

golly they must like straight EDGE better!

NO Dis Ain't the Wrecks

Its Richard Bert + Tom of DC's hot new combo Double O!

THE LAST WAVE

ROCKGOD! Baboon Doooley · VISITS

BUTCHES CONTINENTAL CAFE!

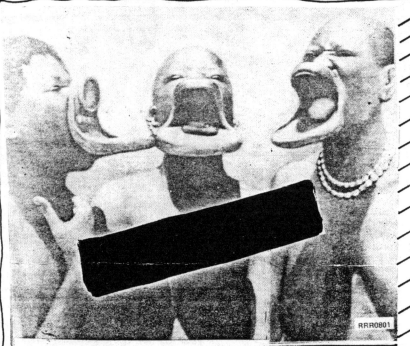

RRR0801

BLITZKRIEG-"LEST WE FORGET EP"

No Future Records...
Basically most British punk rock
records coming out these days can
blow me...it continues to be one
or 3 independant labels like this
that hold my interest...an extremely prolific label this....they haven't issued a dud yet...this one is
heavy duty...good staggered drum-
ing and thudlike bass...good content
too..gotta remind these kids once a-
while...so what if the bands own assessment sez it all "10 minutes of
pure noise..."

(the following came scrawled with the interview)
VOMIT VISIONS formed in Summer 1979.
Until then the German punkscene was
non existant.The GERMS were their h-
eroes then.Even after their split a-
long time ago,The GERMS are the only
group the VOMIT VISIONS want to be a-
ssociated with.In Rola Supersex the
VOMIT VISIONS have without any doubt
the best punk singer ever...and Eric
Hysteric's guitar playing is ear des-
troying...VOMIT VISIONS are the only
known band on the wrong side of the
Atlantic (Europe)who play without any
comprimise.Love them or hate them,but
don't forget:the name "VOMIT VISIONS"
is a promise-you will never be dissapointed.....here's an interview.....
TV:Where are your roots?eg;(institutions,
abused childhoods,victims of ground w-
ater contamination etc.)
VV:Listening to "Forming" on a Zody's
mono-stereo deluxe,after eating too
many frankfurters on an empty stomach.
TV:Do you consider yourselves to be a
garage band,a professional weird band
or a band whose cult following will b-
lossom after you are all dead?
VV:We are a straight professional band,
we are so good at it that we don't even
need to practice.We're only in it for
the money....
TV:How many government blacklists are
you on?VV:None we know of.However we're
amongst the nominations for this years
grammy.....TV:Where was the inspiration
garnered for your name?
VV:After Lydia Lunch puked in front of
us at a gig of Teenage Jesus And The
Jerks in Holland.Lydia Lunch alsohit
our drummer with a mug in his face.
TV:Opinion of England,usa,Turkey,Zim-
bawe etc...VV:England stinks-USA sucks
(Jello Biafra:You owe us $100 worth of
records)Turkey:we prefer chicken,ZImb-
awe-They're really behind us.Our last
tour there was to very little response.
TV:How will your new 45 differ from your
previous 2?VV:We have gone commercial
(in our own terms)in fact Rola Supersex
and Hans Wurst were against putting it
out because they thought it wasnt up
to Vomit Visions standards...

TV:Got any parting comments to your
American friends?VV:If you're at it
but our records now...before they
get as rare as "Six And Change'.....
contact the band c/o Eric Hysteric
40 Ellerslie Rd London W12 England...

45 Reviews

FUNERAL-"POLITICIANS ARE SICK"/
WAITING FOR THE BOMB BLAST"/"PL-
ASTIC GOD"   Peace Is Shit Records.....Soundz like something
that woulda fit on Upsetter or
something...great Controllers/
Skulls sound(what a lame cop out
TV...that's like saying...what
does she look like?A cross between Shirley and Mabel...really
tells the public nothing cept this is in the old gaurd style of
So.California grunge and I play
it constantly...every day..got a
12" out I havent heard...get this.

EFFIGIES-"SECURITY"/"BODY BAG"

Ruthless Records...
The boys show us again why they
are the best...both sides great-
"Security" is a really cool song
with a different style than most
of their stuff...shows off their
diversity...what can I say?They
are always outspoken and always
awe inspiring...write 319 S.Jef-
ferson Chicago Il 60606

Live
Shit

BLIGHT/CIRCLE JERKS at Clutch Cargos
The CJ's were totally on this night-
the only other times I'd seen them
was with Charlie of the PLUGZ filling
in last summer when Lucky had a broken
arm...well this little guy made alot
of difference(although when I pointed this out to Keith he reminded me
what a great guy Charlie is)Speaking
of cool guys Keith Morris is a mellow

jammer that refuses to be punk rock
star/....he's a fuckin nice guy-the
rest of em and their manager seem to
be more into lets scam on gurls and
all that and sit in our dressing r-
oom,but Keith seemed more into what
the Detroit kids were up to...their
set was great...some old tunes some
off the new LP...all right on the
mark....too bad while they were playing there were a couple Sammys
breaking into BLIGHT's van stealing
equipment...that's cool...Clutch
Cargos payed them 50 dollars...that
ught to about cover it right.?I
spit in your fucking eye Emir....

THE EX-"HISTORY IS WHAT'S HAPPENING
More Dirt Per Minute Records
A 20 song LP from one of Holland's
most prolific(and proficient)out-
fits...this is album 2 and one easily spots the progression...still
the same basic reliance on rythyms
but the delivery is less forced--
the content is right on...heavy on
politics in all regards from anti
police,sports,drugs,...whatever
society in conjunction with faceless vanity tries to instill in
us through the media and through
ourselves is laid waste here...for
$4.99 you get an LP,a poster,and
a booklet with the greatest pictures and lyrics...get off your
fucking asses.....

I smeared myself with paint and
walked downtown and people stared at me...I swallowed a chain
and winced as I passed it...the
distraught psychologist broke i-
nto four pieces when he hit the
ground...now I can't sleep well
at night...she can't stand the
thought of eating...he has to p-
urge himself after heavy eating-
he looks at it as psychological
cleansing...I wash my hands at
least 40 times a day...they just won't come clean...

DISCHARGE-"HEAR NOTHING SEE NOTHING
SAY NOTHING Clay Records
Minor change in the guitar mix-major
update of the sound...same relevant
words of wisdom....Cal is the best-
after that last limp wristed effort
I needed to hear what's here..namely
some of the most intense shit ever...
All of the analysis is for naught...
You must own this innocent looking
piece of black glycol......

RED CROSS-LP Smoke Seven Records
Some things in life are overt...
a cold gin enema,nude snow skiing,
and Andy doing a stage dive in yer
head....still other things in life
grab ya subtly...dear old mom sob-
bing uncontrollably cuz ya don't
go to church...being on a slow bum
cuz all yor frenz smoke dope,,,and
having a mudslide slowly seeping
outa yer bunghole cuz all you've
been eating is mexican all week...
then thirdly there are things that
inexplicably give ya an auditory
boner like this LP...sloppily done,
impish obnoxious,pubescent vocals,
and a boss package ...oh shit and
some of the shittiest(eg,THE BEST)
guitar solos ever...all together
you have an LP to hang yer beanie
on folks...cuz you maybe can sub-
sist on leather jacketed meanies
all yor life but I find diversions
in albums of this sort...it's like
Carly said just the other day...as
soon as you decide yer old there's
no coming back...this record is for
those who wanna feel like a weirdo
who likes to have young gurls tickle his/her genitalia with blue jay
tail feathers...cmon you know me-
I dont pull no punches..this is
fuckin great....

IN CAMERA-Peel 12" 4·AD Records
Brilliant,haunting,esoteric,awe
inspiring,Christlike dirge,the
coterie of the intelligencia...
pallid prognosis of futureless
souls wandering in the abyss of
futility...instancy without re-
pression...

BATTALION OF SAINTS-"FIGHTING BOYS
EP" Nutron Records
Hot 12".........it's great when
a band comes out with a record
before all the in-talk and hype
has everyone knowing ahead of
time if they are going to like
a band...this is killer stuff--
proving San Diego has something
to cheer about...hey anyone who
gets in a fight with Iggy is a
jammer in my book...clean production here works to the bands
advantage....big,mean sound....
one of the more impressive debuts in a long time....

RED SPOT COMPILATION-Subterran-
ean Records...
What can be said about this label
except they are SF in terms of the
bands who all wanna fuck their mom's-
ie.what you might also classify as
people who swing on ropes and paint
with their feets on big canvases dr-
aped about their tenemant slum dwellings,that cost more per month in
SF than a nice house rental anywhere
else(less exciting)The bands on this
are MINIMAL MAN(if you still havent
bought their album,listen you suck)
anyway,RESEARCH LIBRARY,MICON,FRIED
ABORTIONS,ANIMAL THINGS,WOUNDZ,ARSE-
NAL,and JED SPEARE & EAZY TEETH....
if I wanted to run down all this
stuff and analyse what it all means-
I'd be a drooling neurotic(like some
of the "people" on this record)or
I could make a fingers crossed little
statement and say hey if you like
Flipper u will luv this,because I'm
convince half the people who give
all the lip service to Flipper do

OHL-"HEIMATFRONT"Rock-)-Rama
Record reviewed by PCE
They're fast loud obnoxious and
among the best hardcore bands I've
heard in a long time.Some of their
songs are "dying is humane","Is it
allowed to ask questions"/"We're the
unprepared"/"Resistance"..the only
gripe I have concerning this album
is the hiss on it...this probably
stems from poor recording tape or
mastering equipment.Anyway if you
understand German and can decipher
the lyrics,you get a pretty good
idea of the shape Germany is in right
now,and how some Germans feel about
the world as a whole,but even if you
don't have a grasp of this wonderful
language,I still highly reccomend
this album so get out your Deutsch
Marks and buy it..PCE

VOX POP 12" Mystic Records
Gee whiz I dunno...these people
look like they sin alot...

YOU'RE NOT BLACK.....
YOU'RE NOT WHITE.....
YOU'RE BLIGHT,.....
ALL THE SAME
IT'S BEEN INGRAINED
IT'S ALL IN VAIN
SEXISM GREED
FASCISM FEED
IT DON'T MEAN SHIT
HERE'S A HOLE
HE DUG FOR YOU
WITH TWENTY TEAM MULES
SHOW FUCKING GRATITUDE
ALL THE WORLD'S A STAGE
SO DARE NOT ENRAGE
CUZ THE BUTTONS THERE
FOR STANDARD FARE
YOU WON'T BE RICH
YOU WON'T BE POOR
WHEN THEY SLAM THE DOOR
TONIGHT YOU'RE BLIGHT
YOU'RE BLIGHT

BLIGHT

HARDCORE FROM SLOWDEATH

BATTALION OF SAINTS

BATTALION OF SAINTS
4 SONG E.P
FIGHTING BOYS
  FOR GIG INFO CALL: M. RUDE
  (714) 239-5597

SEND $4.50 p.p. TO:
BATTALION OF SAINTS
NUTRONS RECORDS
2015 MEADE AVE.
SAN DIEGO, CALIF. 92116

Distributed by Skydisc, Bomp, and Rough Trade

This Could Happen To You!

424

LARISSA of L-7

Pushead and his art were a fixture at T & G in the later issues. Sadly, attempts to reach out to him for comment on this book went unheeded. This cover sports one of his best works, with inset of the man himself. High-gloss, heavy card stock, front and back cover to show off his pen-and-ink profundity here. More Pus inside—and Biafra's head on a wang and back-cover shot of Rollins as a longhair—yes, this ended my and Hank's friendship. He called me up and screamed at me, as he did Pushead, and a decade later in 1992, the Hate Police were doing a show at City Gardens in Trenton, New Jersey, with the Rollins Band, and my drummer forgot his cymbals... As we stood in the darkness of the club, I said to him, "Maybe we can get Rollins's drummer to let us use his?" From the darkness, an angry figure approached, clad in only black cutoff sweats and gripping the pool ball (that was his trusted friend back then), squeezing it as if he wanted to turn it to dust. I extended my hand and tried to break the 10-year freeze with "Hey Henry, how are ya?" He refused the hand and snorted, "You wanna borrow anything, you'll talk to me, and the answer is probably NO!" and he then stormed off into the darkness. That was the last time I saw him, but all lingering hostility aside, thanks to Hank for offering up some remembrances for the book.

TOUCH AND GO

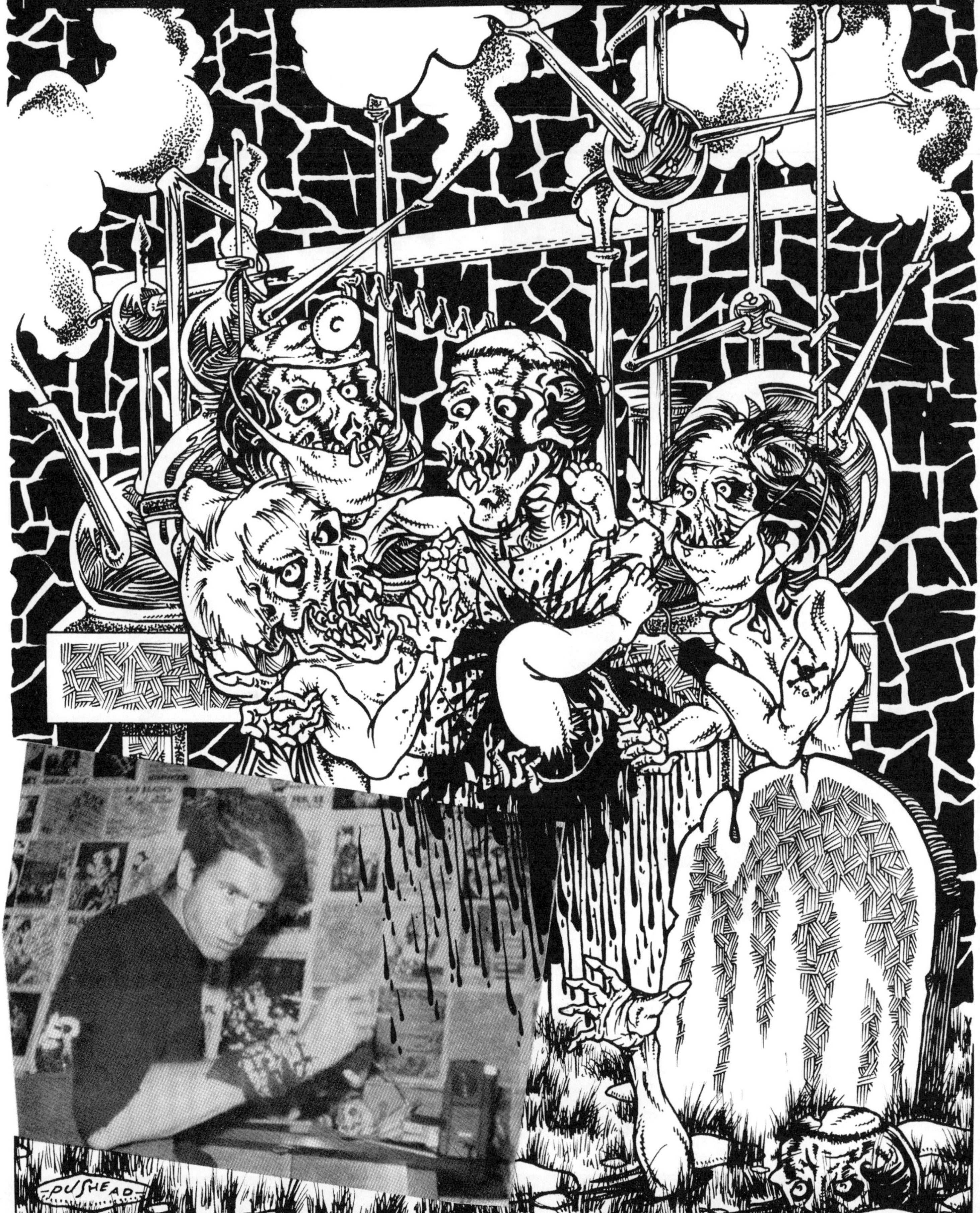

TOUCH and GO
THE ONLY RAG THAT MATTERS, OK!!

F-101

FISH

Well peoples I be back...after too many months away from yer hearts' warm cockles so with new locale and a new improved penis I have returned to instill some more insight and trashy verbiage on you the kings n' queens of studrock, the now-it-alls-the shameless of society...so why you may say did the big TV move 'is arse to the nations capital? No I didn't abandon the midwest because of music,no I wasn't ran out of town on a rail...you see I'm addicted to this stuff called food and to buy the stuff you know what?You've gotta work and stuff and when the cars arent being built Michigan slides so here i is..working-eating-screwing-shitting-and writing about music again and be-in ever so happy...of course all of my swell Detroit buddys I will miss you dearly-do drop me a post now and then...hopefully various of you will keep me up with gig reviews...please note the new ad-

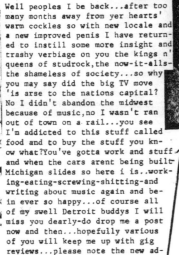

ress of TOUCH AND GO RECORDS... PART of the reason the magazine has been so inconsistent was due to the volume of mail and related T&G records work,plus everything else...with the label now in the hands of Corey everything will begin to pick up mag wise and I won't make yall wait a million years for mail to be answered..also all of your requests for records will' be whipped off to you so fast your hands will burn....many projects coming up...CRUCIFUCKS/BLIGHT/new MEATMEN/NECROS LP??Come on guys time for a biggun....anyways enjoy the issue and drop me a line... Any photographers/correspondents/ or other unsolicited materials are welcome...all are subject to editors strict scrutiny and can be returned...

Hey gang I'm Slim Jim from Hex I mean Stench mag and lemme say It's great to be fat,i mean obese...well p-ortly and reporting on this punk rock after 6 months on the scene...cuz living here in Holland I get all the hot poop on Tolchock and uh Tolchock and even uh Tolchock and carbohydrates I mean B-lack flag rools...an I aint no feeble bastard...wah you say?Ah sits on yor face...

my Little flesh bomb!

AL GREEN GETS NEXT TO YOU

What mixing, what fidelity, what romantic themes, what a coiffure What a suit!! What a jammer.....

TOUCH and GO

BØX 32313 WaSHINGTØN DC 20007

On a recent stopover in Detroit the band MDC reportedly called the Motor City skin contingent fascists and nazis............ hmmm...

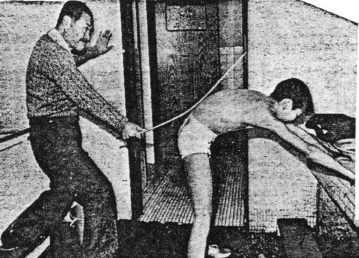

As rabid record collectors the staff at this rag would like to place here a list of wants...if you have any of these records and need the $$ and don't like the re-cord or would just like to make us happy-let us know............ (the $ is the price we are willing to pay)

ADOLESCENTS-"AMOEBA"(gold vinyl DJ) $20
                                    5
                              NGLER" $7
VOX POP(1st 45)
CRIME-"GANGSTER FUNK"(with limited sl-eeve featuring band in police uniforms)$25
WEIRDOS-(1st 45 w/color sleeve) $20
DICKIES-"EVE OF DESTRUCTION" $10
GENERATION X-"NO NO NO/45 with Wild Youth cover $15
PAGANS-"SIX AND CHANGE"(best offer)
   all must be with pic sleeve)

A parasite attacks gays

Boston (AP)—Two cases of a rare form of diarrhea caused by a parasite that usually afflicts ani-mals have been discovered in homosexual men, and doctors have named the new illness "gay bowel syndrome."

Dr. Pearl Ma, chief of microbiol-ogy at St. Vincent's Hospital in Greenwich Village, said two pa-tients suffering from the ailment were treated there in December.

The illness is caused by a pro-tozoa called Isospora belli that ordinarily attacks animals in tropi-cal climates. It is extremely rare in the United States.

Ma said that the syndrome is another in a series of unusual ailments plaguing homosexuals throughout the country. She is presenting her findings to the In-ternational Congress of Microbiol-ogy meeting here.

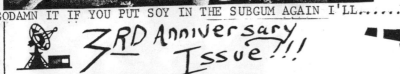

GODAMN IT IF YOU PUT SOY IN THE SUBGUM AGAIN I'LL......

3RD Anniversary Issue!!!

LIVE

DISPLACED/SOCIAL DISTORTION/YOUTH BRIGADE FATE UNKNOWN/GERBILS at the CLUBHOUSE in Detroit

The Displaced are easily Detroits' best new band...good mean sound and a killer vocalist,and they are real and young and will go far this old man predicts...SD were real tasty wave also(remember that gay expression DS)? No actually I thought considering the pa was poor they played a great set...they dress real punk rock and all of that...oh ya the Nigheist played and were quite the hit with all the penis and cunt jokes...muggers wig looks like it's authentic...Black Flag was supposed to play but didnt and I left before the other bands played...with Vince and Emir pulling out of Clutch cargos it being now called the City Club and the Freezer closing the scene needed something like this clubhouse to tide it over..there are two more potential clubs opening up so,,,but I think Larrisa and John both deserve a peck on the genitalia for doing this...the cops have been cool about it thus far also so.....................

ARTICLES OF FAITH/VIOLENT APATHY/CRUCIFUCKS at Knights Of Columbus Hall...Kalamazoo review by Craig....... This night had a rather inauspicious beginning,as there was a redneck wedding reception upstairs and drunken,tuxedoed revelers were hassling the bands as they came to set up.However the nuptial celebration ended before any bands took the stage and the evening proceeded without incident....the notorious Crucifucks stormed the stage with their customary assault of funky bass,slashing guitar and tribal drums-a sound like none other. A disturbing set-not necessarily provocative,just disturbing...I've never seen them quite outdo the sheer terror of the first time I saw them,but this came close, with Doc tumbling around the stage,writhing on the floor while singing "Hinkley Had A Vision"The intellectual level of alot of their lyricsmay be somewhat depressed but musically they trample all competitors.......VA was hampered by less than perfect sound,as were all the bands-Todd could plainly hear nothing but his own bass-but as always,a Violent Apathy set is the basis for a riotous good time. They had a cool stage presence that night with Kenny pacing the stage and Elliot the Love God pounding out the primal beat.They played all their greats,even throwing in La Bamba"& "Paranoid" which I havent heard them play in quite a while.V.A. are kind of the best partiers on any stage OK?....I had never heard AOF before:some people told me they were great,but my other fave Chicago band says they suck(not to step too deeply into that publicity war)so I didn't quite know what to expect.. Imagine then the carnage as these guys blasted their way into their own special niche in my top band list.The brutal power took hold and shook you,threw you against the wall: Vic's guitar kills like a machine gun, Joe's like a sharp steel blade.There was a bit of sloppiness,but I can forgive many slight technical errors in a band that pours forth this kind of energy.Don't get me wrong:they're no

slouches on their instruments and it is clear they practice alot."Poison In mY Sweat" "Everyday" and What We Want Is Free" were among the hottest songs in a well varied set that left me sufficiently slack jawed to make me buy their tape and even purchase my first concert T shirt in about a thousand years (fo 3 bux)best time I've had at a show in a while......CT

DOUBLE O/FAITH/IRON CROSS/EFFIGIES/ YOUTH BRIGADE/SOCIAL DISTORTION at the Wilson Center DC

Holy arab shit what a hall,what a night,what an oozing burrito in my pantaloons oozing beans in orgasmic delight at what befell my I balls... so out walks Thomas the legendary ex RED-C eccentric,off beat one of a kind stud(the only guy I know who wears his jockey shorts outside of his pants)and he proceeds to bless us with an earsplitting earth-shattering ode to Hendrix or acid guitar noodling call it what you will..got the night off to an interesting start...then comes DOUBLE O and wails as usual...any band with Bert on bass rages and the others aint slouches and the new guitar player is great and I love doubel O so there...then the FAITH one of two of these bands I had yet to see and they were all and more of the band featured on the new Dischord 12"...a serious pre frontal,with everything where it should be-cept when their singer disssspears into the sea of bodies...what a future a band like this has when the members are still in High school... serious bone....then comes Iron CROSS..the mislabeled,misunderstood metal machine monsters of sludge like steam roller vicious punk that I have loved on tape and have wished to see live and again the hearty thumbs up(getting bored of all the hype keep reading)the diminuative Dante flailing away on the skins while the gargantuan Sab fires off his dogma with looks of utter contempt...great set...then comes those lovable guys from Evanston Ill(that's Chi-town doofs) who never dissapoint...they have to be the tightest,meanest,most awe inspiring outfit going...seems like almost all bands peak,both musically

lyrically and as a live working unit, but the EFFIGIES never seem to hit such a plateau...their new tunes like "Smile" and the danceable ones prove diversity, a will to survive in a thankless,business,and most importantly real fuckin' talent...always outspoken and controversial...and never a dull moment...the only dissapointment was they didnt do "No Prisoners"....next came YOUTH BRIGADE..from LA..a band with the unenviable task of going on late and after the Effigies people were sweaty,bloody and tired...but alas stares of interest from the DC crowd(perhaps curious to see what this YB from way out there could do) turn to smiles,nods and motion...three brothers who get a great,noisy sound by all doing vocals and exuding a sense of sincerity about what they are doing... SD were'nt on this night,,,too drunk and I liked their Detroit show much more...by the way the Wilson Center has to be one of the greatest places to see a show around...the cops in DC are generally pretty cool and the night went without incident...

Editor-Tesco Vee
Art direcor and Advisor-Pushead Lamort
Contributors-John Stabb,Craig Taatjes Byron Colty,Joe McC-reery...Special thanx to J.Crawford...also thanx to Pete from the Allied for being totally cool and sending me all the new fledgling zines and all else....(†Dirk Gunga)
Staff photographers-Gerta,L. Clague,Morticia...

L.Clague © 82'

GI's/MINOR THREAT/VELVET MONKEYS at U. of Maryland...............
Definately a head scratcher bill with a starange mix of bands...came in as GI's were blistering thru their set and the pa was really clean...hadn't seen them since they debuted the new lineup at the Freezer and it has totally solidified since then..the new tunes like"Lost In Limbo" are much more complex undoubtedly due to the amazin' axe work of Tom Lyle...a great set and Stab's voice sounded cool as shit through the ranging catacombs of a large(unduly suited actually--too big) ballroom...then comes Minor Threat with their new line up" which sees Brian now joining Lyle on guitar and the addition of a new bass player...their set was...uh..unique to say the least-their set was somewhat marred by technical difficulties but when they were on it was"log in shorts" time but the crowd stood mute--and to the front man of this here group this spells dog dew so he turns around and says "you sing" on "Out of step" and it takes the crowd a bit of standing and staring at the back of Ians head before they jump into action and its hectic from then on...then comes the confrontation...someone steals the microphone...the sound man starts freaking out...someone hands Ian a mike from the drum kit in the interim...the sound man lunges at Ian and grabs the mike rather unseriptitiously and is followed off stage by a mob led by said front man firing right hooks and left jabs into said sound mans face.. mob faces off with the "security" force and the police...with FEAR written all over the latters eyeballs as the crowd sings "In My Eyes" into their faces...definately a moment when a video would have killed...oh well..gave those suckers a shit bricking they'll never forget...sorry missed the other ba-

Here it is...T&G's first in a continuing series of our version of Dewars Profiles or the NME's artist profile..this month's feature is on your editor TV...for you uninitiates- "Gay Tads In Bondage"/"Inside Seka"/"Annete Haven Anthology" Favorite Food and Drink..... YooHoo/Tab/Whitbread Ale/NY pizza/Guacamole Tostadas/Ham Steak and Cheese from Marios... so you can get intimate-you know groove on my karma--like cappucino with carol Lawrence or something...

Last books read-"Philosophy IN The Bedroom"-Marquis De Sade and "The Death Of Satan" by Antonin Artaud.......... Last Movies Seen..........

NEXT MONTH WHO KNOWS!
T+G MAG BOX 32313 WASH DC 20007
Write!!
☺
©L.Clague 82

© L. Clague
WILSON CENTER →
Shredder

CROSS-COUNTRY

P.O. Box 50416 Wash., D.C. 2000

order
records
from
Bru
a t
CO

(202) 393-3660

...so any-
way-she's
fellating this
bison..and this
little thing is
jamming penny
candy up her
land-mine
so I whip
out my...

DIRK GUNGA

THE RELTNEY PHENONMENON by Byron Coley

If you'll be so kind as to take your tool outta your trousers and submit it to a (visual)once over,you'll probably notice it's gotta cleft right at the very tip,The cleft is called a "diz",and those in possession of one should note that it has several functions.I've observed my personal diz emitting four distinct fluids over the years(piss,jiz, blood and pus-one for every season)and who knows?This list may grow and grow as the years roll by,so that wood chips,pebbles,hair,rubber and many other droppings will have been added to the trail of penile spoor leading to my tomb. The reason I mention this is that when I was a youngster roving around the wilds of North Jersey I knew that my diz had one function only-easing bladder tension.Subsequent discoveries of a Ewa Aulen pictorial in Playboy street fighting,and Caroline N.'s diseased crack(in that order)suggested that my innocent belief in the monist tendencies of my diz were fraudulent however and I eventually grew to see it as a virtual well of pluralism. So it is with another set of holes drilled into the human form-the ears.And where the diz can push out any number of somewhat disparate but elementally linked substances the ear can accept an equally wide berth of shit with the greatest of ease and what's more the ears themselves are crying out for dietal variations.About the best dietal variation around's local crap from the sixties.....The punk scene back then wasn't too different than the one that's around now,in that bands' basic motives were to unleash as much goddam pent up frustration in as noisy a way as they possibly could,and 'though the lyrics then were more about personal problems than the world's situation,—

Coley Continued -

there's alotta crap that sounds every bit as grungy,manic and wild as anything that's around(even if it is slower)Best part about this stuff's that a whole shitload of it's been re-released over the last coupla years on records that cost about 1% of what the original shit would run you(tons more expensive than even the Pagan's "Six And Change") and ya could buy it from a whole buncha places.To suggest that ya do so is bullshit,however as you'd still haveta drop hundreds to actually hab it.what I'm gonna do is make an offer.....if any of you jerks who think sixties stuff is shit wanna mail me a 60 minute cassette by December 20th I'll make you a tape of a buncha the best crap and if you don't like it you can just record right the fuck over it.I mean.stuff like "Spazz" by the Elastik Band is damn near as whipped as the Meatmens'"Tooling For A" (taken in the context of the time)and whoever produced that Solger ep got all their ideas from the guy who recorded "Green Fuz " by Randy Alvey.And hey when this guy from Unsettled Society yells, "I've got to live my life in the world of the Underground" it'ss not that different from anything the Fartz ever crowed.Christ this stuff is really great and ya outa hear before ya go round telling folks that only current noise really growls.It's virtually the same as admitting that you've never popped your rocks,so wise up. 847 19th St. Santa Monica Ca 90403

My dick no longer get's stiff...just heavy....Dick Bowser,guitarist for V-follent Apathy doesn't smoke marijuana but prefers long hits of his own private mixture,boogers,dingleberrys and dead bugs..I like girls who don't particularly take pains to change their drawers every week...Altough I am still working on perfecting this method,I am finding defecation during masturbation to be most gratifying...as long as orgasm is reached just prior to the log snap....In Boston there is straight edge,in NY bent edge,and in Lansing it's queer edge....at 65 Craig Fix will be a doddering,incoherent old man half insane from syphilis,his body ravaged by drugs..what about the guy from NJ who wanted to organize a punk Woodstock?My hooter starts off resembling a lazy grub,then begins to flop around like a lobster in a hot boiler and ends it's state bearing a close resemblance to an enraged royal cobra...has anybody seen the movie "Rear Deliveries"starring Barry Hansssler?All this Husker Du hype can be likened to Fords claim that the Edsal was the car of the future...whats worse than Whipping

Boy live?not much.....I rolled over and looked at the clock..3 AM..I had fallen asleep for a short while but felt refreshed now.The moonlight shone through the curtains and as I got out of bed and looked out over the night..the light illuminated the veined and permanently bloated and seething three toed sloth I call my crank...I cuffed it sharply once twice and watched it fill with blood in swift obeyance to it's master.I grabbed an Adult Cinema Review and continued the torture..Originally I penned a Meatmen song entitled"Blow Me God" but Tesco was fearful that his past would inspire the wrath of you know who-and a bolt of lightning would nail him in the peckwood at some gig....East Lansings "Dawn Patrol" are so proud of their drug addictions they want Attigraphix to immortalize their abuse on T-shirts...

SEE YA NEXT ISSUE !!!

Freedom For Paralyzed Dogs

- adjustable
- no training required
- fully maneuverable
- able to eliminate

FOR FREE INFORMATION WRITE OR CALL:

K-9 Carts

K-9 CART COMPANY
101 EAST KING STREET
MALVERN, PENNSYLVANIA 19355
(215) 644-6624

*PATENT PENDING

431

FAITH

THE FAITH were interviewd upstairs at the U of Maryland show by TV....all were present...Alec-Throat gurgles and bellowing-Chris-bass slappin and idol chatter..Iver-skin pounding and overt female solicitaion-and Mike-serious axe work and advanced malnutrition...(interview begins with conversation concerning gurl who had just whipped off her shirt on request and exibited a sad set of glad bags)CONVERSATION drifts in and out of lucidity and covers who writes songs and lyrics ...(to Iver)TV:So what do you play?Iver:Prémier drum set 5 toms 7 cymbals-TV:Sounds wealthyChris:I've basically got a Fender Precision bass with a piece of shit body and they sanded the sticker off so nobody will believe me,and I broke the other one..Mike:I have a Marlboro 37 Watts Of Hell amp..very rare...(band talks about lack of recent capital gains)TV:Ya but you played CBGB's garsh...Iver:That was Dec.26 1981;TV:Oh it must have been a thrill.. Chris:Ya because today I was looking at a Blondie book and I said hey "I was there". Mike:And there was a big gay man with loud clothes and leather pantz;Alec:And he burnah ass...TV:So do the former members of SOA demand celebrity status;Chris:Yes we have to perform sexual favors at practice and stuff...getting in the band was really difficult ...for Alec it was easy because he was in the Untouchables but me I wasn't in anything so i had to sleep with all of them..... TV:So what do you write about for instance "You're Xld"..Chris: People we don't like--people who drink.. Alec:But not just everybody...people who drink but dont wanna tell you they do... people like "ahh I hate everyone who drinks---and then sneak off...CHris:People who mess up the scene..TV:Do you get tired of the straight edge getting so much lip service?Alec:No because half the people don't know what they're talking about... Chris:No because straight edge is a really good thing...people can choose if they wanna be or not but then people give me shit because they arent and I am-- TV:Defending their vices...Chris:They make a big thing out of it fuck em.... (conversation drifts to NY)TV...best pizza in the world...Mike;New York is a dirty stinking shithole...Chris...Good

pizza and there's 5 people there I like...Tanya and Rebecca I love em' both...TV:ANy new songs these days-- Chris:"Subject To Change"/"Limitations' Eddie:What doess the logo mean? Chris: I thought of it the other day...the lines break up the cliques..uh..the cliqueivity....but then those lines all come back and point to the F...Alec:I never thought about it that deeply... Alec:The main reason we picked it was because it's a postive type of name.. you've got bands that call themselves the Nihlistics Mike:Christian Death.. Chris:Bad Religion....we hate the world so fuck off etcetera...Iver:Anorexic Surfboard(Boyd from Black Market B.enters)Boyd:You all know Tommy dont ya?Tommy and I are starting a disco band... Chris:Black Market Bootie...(conversation drifta from Lunar exploration to the Viletones to....)Chris:You see to be truly staright edge you must be gay.. Alec:That's what some people from NY though...came down here and didnt see a whole lot of girls and thought everyone was gay...(talk of Von L MO)fake like I'm wiping a bugur in Alec...Chris proceeds to hang an 8 inch loogee off his finger and drapes it on Bert's tape machine...ughh................fin........

shitty attempt at Faith logo

Flash! Issues of Cle Magazine 3A (the huge issue) are available for $2.50 from Cross Country distributors-Includes Pagans/Throbbing Gristle Art + lots more -get one before theyre gone-see address on the next page-

>>>>>>

FRICTION-"SKIN DEEP" CBS Records It really is a crime these records aren't better distributed as once again I proclaim the complete merit and global totality of Friction's greatness...less manic here than their first long player...this one is "basically concepted and performed by Reck the original founder of the group".. it stands to reason the bands that can diversify and explore new turf with each outing are the ones best capable of holding interest-a theory which obviously holds true here...as vicarious and as difficult to categorize as they come. Again heavy on rythym structúre and as free from modern day cliches as is humanly possible..no it doesnt sound like this or that..it sounds like fucking FRICTION...this is fucking CHOICE..................... write Friction c/o Watch Out Sasaya-so 2F 4-30-24 Koenji-kita Suginami-ku Tokyo Japan

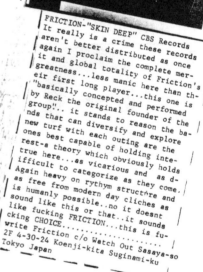

HEY GANG! No Glenn FRIDMAN PHOTOS! IM TOO "SCARED"to RUN THEM..I might get vibed on,or get too GNARLY,or RADICAL the way BY HUSKER DU + "shit! TSOL suck Teseu Joe

Write 3819 Beecher stNW Washington DC 20007

MY THREE SONS (1982)

432

MIDWEST HITS EAST...DETAILS BELOW

So the tour we had been planning for months finally happened during the middle part of august..we left in caravan with NECROS/NEGATIVE APPROACH and MEATMEN all stowed away in a camper,an elderly van and my red roadster...actually one of the most excruciating parts of the trip was smelling Rich(MM axe man)and all of his gourmet foods(herring,tofu,cheese,nuts,fruit-doesnt sound bad?Let it sit in the sun awhile)anyway we get to NJ at a million o'clock and catch a few zzzz's...next night to play the infamous MUDD Club in NY...the show is scheduled to be at 10 and the club wanst us to play at 8 and all the NY crowd is standing outside bitching about the cover...actually the pa is one of the best I've ever used and the show goes ok considering it's NY and fuck I hate that place...the goons and their circle indian jerkoff dances and so on... then it's off for a benefit show in DC at the Mill which is a historic place that rents for $25 bux a night...Double0 were great anyway...Terminal 406 in Baltimore is a pretty cool place not unlike the Freezer in Detroit but since there are about 7 punks in Balt. it was the DC kids who drove up that saved this one from being debacle #2... all in all a shitty night...then a 10 hour drive to Boston where we easily saw the best little date on our little mini tour...crowds of maniacs all piling on and going ape

shit and the Gallery East is a really cool place despite the echo due to the wall configuration...DYS were great as were GANG GREEN despite the fact they need a permanent singer as the guitar player can't do both... this show was really a hot one--made the tour...but then we hadda drive back to NY...kinda like forcing yourself to eat your own spit up going back...on the way the van breaks down numerous...times...and the A-7 annex is a lame place to play and the PA sounded like shit...more circle dancing from the bohemoth NY skinheads,which can be likened to neanderthal henchmen from some medeival age without a brain betwixt the 10 of em'...not really caring about the music-just flexing their limp dicks beating on the kids that were there to see the bands...singer for this band Agnostic Front cuts down DC and then apes every move out of his "How to be like Ian MacKaye" Digest complete with holding shortened mikestand...oh well...I've seen it before...it isnt going to say New Y... i know if you don't have anything good to say f and sing me... ...can't do something good to say it at shake...i don't say it age milk-years...p... said when this type of music got popular there it would spell the end of it...ya the end of it there-thank god it's got the brains,creativity and balls to stand out practically everywhere else in this big beautiful land.......

THE EFFIGIES

ALthough I have ranted and raved about THE EFFIGIES i never undertook the quitessential interview with the powerhouse quartete from Chicago so backstage of the Wilson Center where there present was the band,two sluts,made to look like french waitresses and myself and Ian Mackaye...and here is what they sed....
TV:Where'd ya get the bitchin SHAM shirt?
John(vocalist)The only good thing we did in Montreal was buy this shirt...
TV:Were Discharge up there?
Bonham:We played with em in Toronto...
Paul:They were a bunch of scumbags...
(long section of tape here is fucked up because of technical difficulties)
Bonham:and also we wont sign everybody and their brother to our labelJOHN:Ya we're trying to get a label organized and basically get a crossection of good intelligent bands that might not necessarily be thrash...we get alot of shit for sympathizing with bands that tend to be a bit more experimantal and don't adhere to the straight hardcore punk type of thing...cuz the thing is-theres alot of good hardcore bands but for every good one there's ten shitty ones right?Like some of these guys are like our friends and we tell them"sorry man-you're a good guy but your band stinks...TV:So whats the best band in Chicago besides...uh...6 FEET UNDER(much laughter)John:NAKED RAYGUN AND TRIAL BY FIRE...alot of these bands (here a long diatribe against band with Clashaspirations,you know who) alot of these bands you'll hear about from one tape but they're so fuckin' lazy...tv;Whens the new record coming out?Paul:you arent supposed to ask questions like that...John:Were trying to get the other bands going...
Ian:Is this your first stop or what?
Bonham:No we played Toronto and this guy named Jameel Emir who should be shot-noone should ever deal with him. :John:He was supposed to get us 5 gigs and we gg one...Bonham:We played Toronto with Discharge and Vice Squadmore people came to our gig alone than their gig with us...

(Much talk here about how everyone present didnt"care for the DK's on their recent tour and otherwise...much arguing with slut over whether band gets free cokes...TV:So whats ....(Ian bitching about how someone stole his effigies shirt...

makes mention of flipside interview ...John:Listen man I say this publically to the dc audience..the comments we made were stupid alright-alright we're pissed off in So.California its the low point of our tour-we lost three gigs in a row...so we get an interview with Flipside and we just start ragging on everyone we could find...Ian:and they called us prima donnas...Bonham:We've been called alot worse...slut barges in and announces "FREE COKES"(slight delay in interview)..much talk about how english bands comeover and smell and take home large quantities of US cash...Ian But I do like the UK Subs a fuckava lot..Bonham:Ya they were real good...John:They are one of the few bands that have come over here and not slagged anything off...
Ian:Like over there it's like"You're an american...fuck you...John:I've been there twice the same fuckin st-

ory-sept last time we went to the last resort and people were really cool-first time we went down Kings road and they were sayin all this shit...(much talk here about how no British label would put out their records n UK-a necessity if you wish to go over there at all...)John..thats like basically this whole thing is a piece of shit that nobody really cares about...look how much time and energy people have devoted to this thing and it's just never going to get off the groundIan:That's cuz it's not a movement its an individual thing..Slut: Does that make you unhappy though?You should be proud that..Ian.SHHHHH.... John:There comes a point where like I'm doing my job and I'm coming home and I'm doing gigs,and I'm not even making enoufmoney to live so what the fuck...if a band like the Plasmatics makes 10 million dollars a gig and I can't even be making my living...like this place is really rare(referance to the choiceness of the Wilson Center)Ian discusses his role in day to day Dischord) John:Ya but the question comes up"What are you going to do in 5 years or 10 yearsIan:Ya but I don't think in those termes...John:That's true for yourself but then if you look at it you say fuck man this shit is so great its timeless...peolple say its not a movement bullshit...Ian:As a fuckin group-all

the punks in America we havent accomplished shit except for showing people...but as individual scenes we've accomplished a fuckuva lot...John:as long as these dicks like Wendy are around it's just another kick in my ass these people gotta be brought down...the whole thing about uniforms and all that...uniforms define certain things...and nobody can teell me "I don't believe in uniforms"long hair or short" and that's bullshit..you make a statement and thats the way you fuckin are..and I know what I fuckin' wear and I know what it means...I know exactly what it means-there's a fuckin code-it's unwritten but its there...Ian:I totally believe in gangs personally-I mean not bull-shit gangs...but people who find they have something in common and by being together they are stronger than 1...but not Hollywood shit like lets go out and beat up people over 60...I like the idea of territory...I like the fact that like we're from washington and you're from Chicago and I think that's fuckin cool as shit-we're doing something here and you're doing something there and somehow it works together...John:That's theway it's gotta be..every band basically has it's domain..it's like a dog pissing on a tree..every band is that way....(much talk here about people who work to build a scene and those who bitch and moan about things etc)Oil:I've always said man you only get out of it what you put in

John:And all these people want it on a silver platter...theres two groups of people...movers and dreamers-in Chicago all you've got is dreamers...Ian:On the fuckin coatails:Oil:Oh you're in the Effigies oh wow....Ian:That's like when Lyle went out there to college he doesnt look real punk rock and ppeople were like "fuck you" till one day they found out he played in Minor THreat and it's kiss ass cityJohn:XKX John: the one thing that really pissed me off about Chicago was they could never get a decent fanzine going...to me...theres this dick mag called the Coolest Retard.. these two chicks who run this are group-ies...this went on for quite a while longer but my typewriters over.... overheating..bye folks

Write Ruthless Records
PO Box 1458
Evanston Ill 60204

MINOR THREAT

> chatting
> denouncing
> squablin'
> laughin'
> fartin'
> burpin'

TV:So what was your impression of the Midwest?Jeff:Great fireworks.Lyle:Great fireworks..it's got a good scene...Jeff: It's good...i mean I guess we wer'ent there on a night to see whats wrong with it...but everyone bitches alot about Clutch Cargos,and I did't see anything wrong with it...I mean that and the Freezer are both something we don't have in DC... Brian:Great bathroom...TV:Where?Brian:Freezer...TV:Someone was back there watching the girls pee...Lyle:That's what Brian did instead of playing "Scream At A Wall"...TV:So you're going to cut an LP? Jeff:Ya that's what we're going to California for...All:Laughs...TV:What's your favorite band besides Joy Division?TV: The Pop Group...(all chuckle agin)TV:So what's the hottest up and coming band in DC?Jeff:They are still on the way up so

ing wonderful(guffaws)the majority of em I saw were swooning over Steve from Whipping Boy...you see it everywhere..boston it wasnt too bad...TV:What was Boston like? Lyle:Strange:Ian:They are so extreme in each of their particular directions that they can't unify...it's like even in Detroit I get the feeling people don't know each other sometimes...in wash. peoplee seem to know each other.Jeff:Alot of them come from far away suburbs unlike DC... Detroit seemed pretty tight...Jeff:Boston seemed pretty tight..Ian:There's a crew in BostonJeff:But there is still division-

we saw here were great...at Lansing the sound was working against them but...I thought the Crucifucks were great..Lyle: They were...JEFF:The Meatmen were hairy: Ian:They were gnarly but I still crave (laughs)TV:These skateboarders need to learn to speak English..Jeff:No we need to learn to talk skateboarder...Ian:Negative Approach were fuckin awesome... Jeff:Fuck I crave...Lyle:HOT...they were definately gnarly...Brian: reat... Ian:The Sleestak brothers are pretty mean...Ian:The whole skinhead thing up here is...Jeff:I think they outa color their heads different colors so they can find their friends(chuxles) Lyle:Or put No on the side of your heads..TV:Draw your name on your heads... TV:What about the detroit motor city OI contigent?Ian:All I've gotta say is we went through the whole thing.last

Photos by Gildee

we can't tell...TV:So why did you get back together,is that a lame question? Ian:No that's something we want to clear up...the main reason we broke up is because Lyle went to college...the reason we came back is because Lyle came back from college...lots of people seemed to think"oh they're really popular and the're cashing in on it...the truth of the matter is just that Lyle was coming back and Jeff and I were frustrated...Jeff:In a big rut:Ian:Going nowhere with what we were doing...and we asked Brian apparently there was some problem between Brian and the GI's,I'll let Brian comment on that...Brian:No problem I said "I'm not playing with you anymore and that was that...TV:John Stabb didnt have a bird?Jeff:I think they were happy...I mean they were sad because it

was a good line up but they were sick of BrianALL:Yuk yuk....Ian:As far as I'm concerned since we got back together It's felt alot better.Lyle:Than it did before we've all got our heads together..Jeff: But it's still the same bickering..Lyle Well sure:Ian:We're still the same people as before...TV:So what effect has your music had on people?Jeff:I think it's blown their minds(laughs x 10)Ian:Like Straight Edge:people have taken it to e'xtreme...as far as I'm concerned all we did was put out an idea...if people wanna hear it as preaching if that's what they want:Staight Edge to me is someone who is

Al of Decontrol has taken Straight edge as a personal lifestyle...Ian:His straight edge philosophy is taken to an extreme as far as...Jeff:His lifestyle:Ian:So has mine-everyone of their songs is about the same thing pretty much-you'll see something about that in all their songs, that's Al and thats cool cuz al has created that scene pretty much single handedly...TV:What about NY?Brian:Neat place.. Jeff:Nice buildings...Ian:It's a shame they have so many clubs and...Brian.Wasted Youth should play there...TV:What do you guys think of Gerta?Ian:Top drawer Jeff: Great...Ian:I wanna be the doctor where she works...insert rectal thermometers Ian:Ask us a questions...all the bands

year and ist stupid,let each other be what they wanna be...its stupid to diversify but if thats whzt they wanna do fine...go see the Bad Brains next time Lozon you fag...TV:Should I print that? Brian:Ya...Jeff:So here we are still beting gnarly but craving...TV:All I have to say is since you've been here my toilet has been shit in more than ever before...Jeff:Cokes drunk and hermans dumped...TV:60 cokes you guys drank... Jeff:They were pepsis...Brian:Pepsi is rat poison...TV:You guys had better start eating right like Henry..tofu and the like..Jeff:AL-FUCKINALFALFA..LYle: Let's talk about the demographic considerationa of...Ian:The analytical ramifications of...

alert enough to benefit from what he or she is doing...Lyle:The drug and alcohol is only one side of it anyway,it's alot more than that there are other things that can sidetrack you.......Ian: That's what"dOn't fuck" means...alot of these people think that to be straight edge you can't drnk,smoke or have sex and that's silly...what the don't fuck line is that the whole getting laid and getting head thing..Lyle Living for sexIan:Following your penis around is fucking people up more than anything,and Detroit seems to have quite a few of the spread leg...slut things running around (mo laughs)TV:You'll makw a few pen pals on that one..Ian:I have nothing against them some of the Detroit girls are fuck-

Jeff + Brian getting gnarly but still craving on the roof of my garage !!!

TOUCH and GO RECORDS

NECROS T&G 1 4-SONG E.P. THE MIDWEST'S FIRST HARDCORE RELEASE. OUT OF PRINT.

THE FIX T&G 2 "VENGEANCE" B/W "IN THIS TOWN" IMPORTANT LANSING BAND'S FIRST RELEASE. OUT OF PRINT

NECROS T&G 3/DISCHORD 4 9-SONG E.P. A JOINT RELEASE IN CONJUNCTION WITH DISCHORD RECORDS OF WASHINGTON D.C. NINE INTENSE BLASTS OF TEENAGE FURY. FEATURES: "I.Q. 32", AND "RACE RIOT".

NEGATIVE APPROACH
NEW RELEASE

PROCESS OF ELIMINATION E.P. T&G 4 A 7" COMPILATION E.P. FEATURING 8 SONGS BY 8 BANDS. INCLUDES, NECROS, MEATMEN, NEGATIVE APPROACH, YOUTH PATROL, TOXIC REASONS, VIOLENT APATHY, McDONALDS AND THE FIX.

NEW RELEASE

THE FIX T&G 5 JAN'S ROOMS E.P. THE SECOND RELEASE OF THIS NOW DEFUNCT LANSING OUTFIT. WELL DOCUMENTED BY THIS FOUR SONG E.P.

MEATMEN T&G 6 BLUD SAUSAGE E.P. WHAT FEAR SET OUT TO DO THE MEATMEN ACCOMPLISH WITH THIS SEVEN SONG E.P. GUARENTEED TO OFFEND ANYONE AND EVERY- ONE. FEATURES THE NOW CLASSIC, "TOOL- ING FOR ANUS", AND "ONE DOWN THREE TO GO"

NEGATIVE APPROACH T&G 7 10 SONG E.P. SO INTENSE IT'S MIND BOGGLING. GNARLY DESPE- RATE VOCALS OVER SEARING GUITAR. FEATURES "NOTHING", "CAN'T TELL NO ONE", AND "FAIR WARNING".

MEATMEN T&G 8 CRIPPLED CHILDREN SUCK E.P. WHAT WAS ONCE A DREAM IS NOW A REALITY. AS THE MEATMEN ONCE AGAIN OUTDO THEMSELVES NO ONE THOUGHT IT COULD BE DONE BUT IT HAS. THIS E.P. MAKES THE BLUD SAUSAGE E.P. SEEM TIMID AND SUBTLE IN COMPARISON. FEATURES, "BLOW ME JAH", "I SIN FOR A LIVING" "ORGY OF ONE", AND "SPREAD SCAT BOOGIE II" AMONG OTHERS.

TOUCH AND GO RECORDS, THE MIDWEST'S FOREMOST HARDCORE LABEL PRESENTS THE LAUNCHING OF A SUBSIDIARY LABEL; SPECIAL FORCES. THIS LABEL IS DESIGNED TO RELEASE RECORDS BY BANDS WHOSE MUSIC IS JUST AS INTENSE BUT DOESN'T FIT INTO THE REALM OF HARDCORE. SPECIAL FORCES FIRST RELEASE IS BY DETROIT'S L-SEVEN. FUTURE PROJECTS INCLUDE A TWELVE INCH BY BLIGHT.

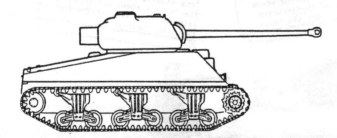

TOUCH and GO

SPECIAL FORCES
RECORDS

ALL RECORDS $2.50. P.P.($3.00 OVERSEAS)
TOUCH & GO RECORDS
P.O.BOX 716
MAUMEE, OHIO.
43537

No Punk Censorship!

ROCK GRTH! BABOON DOOOLEY!®

Our Story: "Now it is 1984/ And in the San Francisco Republic they are evening the score!/Baboon was visited by the People's Police/And they found a Misfits Album in his valise!" (Baboon was immediately arrested and taken to the People's Court Citizen Jello Biafra presiding.)

Listen you reactionary runt, don't you realize its people like you with your MISFITS albums and crummy east coast accents that are causing the war in EL Salvador?

Don't you know how many whales are killed because you—you dumbshit jocks want their skulls? Huh? Do you? Have you nothing to say?

?

M-Mr Biafra, c-could I have your autograph?

What? Are you accusing me of being a ROCK Star? TAKE him away!!

Good enuff for op?

Note: This is artistic

TAKE LSD And it looks just like Jello!

You heard him, get moving, reformist cockroach!

OH!

Baboon is taken to the deepest darkest dungeon beneath San Francisco CHX Republic Hall..

Ooooh! Ooooh!

...and there, safely locked in his cell, he is given the punishment he truly deserves!

NAZI PUNKS! NAZI PUNKS! NAZI PUNKS! Fuck off!!! (etc.)

Human rights violations.

24 hours a day.

IEEEE!!

437

ꝺꜧe ꝯꝹꝹꝺ

jus' think...in just a few moments all these voluptuous flesh pods'll be coddling my veined and bloated leather bag..ah..

7"

BANANA WAR
EFFIGIES-"SMILE"
OUTCASTS-"JUST ANOTHER TEENAGE REBEL"
LAMA EP'S
DIEKREUZEN CASSETTE
GOVERMENT ISSUE-"LOST IN LIMBO"
WIPERS(all)

ALL MINOR THREAT
CRUCIFUCKS-"DEMOCRACY SPAWNS BAD TASTE"
DOUBLE 0-"THE END"
BIG BOYS-"HOLLYWOOD SWINGERS"
IRON CROSS-"CRUCIFIED"
CHILD MOLESTERS-"13 IS MY LUCKY NUMBER"
NEGATIVE TREND EP
VOMIT VISIONS
WIKED CITY
SUICIDE-"GIRL"
DEADLINE TAPE
FLESHEATERS-"PONY DRESS"(new version)

12"

FAITH VOID LP
SCREAM LP TAPE
SS DECONTROL LP
DISPLACED(LIVE)
FRICTION "SKIN DEEP"
YOUTH BRIGADE-"SOUND AND FURY"
MENTORS 12"
FACTRIX/CAZZAZA LP

438

UNSOLICITED

EMERGENCY

BLOW ME YOU PRICKS

MERCY HOSPITAL

McCREERY

BLACK MARKET Baby at the 9:30

a single cadaver
Copyright 1982
Cindy Warren

In the phobic, grey room, the human stared out of the mirror. No reaction was visible to the detached horror of the corpse rotting in the corner. Look what's happening to my body.

The human retreated from the grey room strewn with shreds of mattress and flesh. Down the long, dark hall to the alley below. Two manques on the fire escape snickered.

The boulevard writhed with neon flashes. The human sauntered around the corner and pushed through the crowd to the nightclub.

Upstairs, it was too noisy to hear the video. A manque in lipstick mouthed silent words. Looks like a rockabilly band. Wonder who it is. A group of manques watched sullenly. A skinhead handed out flyers.

Downstairs, the definitive hardcore band was getting on stage.

"I met you at a dance party," a manque said.

The human confusedly recognized him from Duran Duran, not from a dance party. Restraining an urge to shred the manque's face with its teeth, the human grinned and mumbled amiably.

A guitar slashed through the companionable silence of the human. The singer was mobbed by manques screaming anthems into the microphone with him. Manques dove off the stage onto the roiling riot in front, the singer exhorting, "fuckin' kill yourselves," between each song.

The human pushed forward into the slam dancers, leaving the manque in an undisturbed oasis.

The human's glasses were knocked to the floor. The human fell to its hands and knees and grabbed them. A hand reached down from the chaotic turmoil above and helped the human back into the melee. The human smiled thankfully. A manque apologized for the glasses. Fingers and glasses unstepped on, the human laughed at warnings of the violence of slam dancing and slammed happily.

After a brief void, the next band commanded the stage. The human had purchased a piece of vinyl from this band and mouthed the words in a silent echo. Once in awhile it ducked behind a tall, immobile manque to rest. It shared the space with a manque who returned from slamming with a satisfied grin on her sweaty face. Another manque pogoed freneticily.

The disorder was stilled. The human pushed through to the bar and reluctantly paid for a cup of water. Its mind repeated a tape loop of hot, hot, hot... The human drenched its hand in the cool liquid and rubbed it across its face, neck, and shoulders. The remnant of the water it poured down its shirt.

The human put its glasses on. Jello Biafra impatiently paced the edge of the stage. An amp refused to function. In the interim, he offered us a chance to voice our intelligence. A manque shouted, "holiday in the Falklands!", and we cheered.

The Dead Kennedys silenced us. The human pogoed and slammed enthusiastically. On the side of the stage, a group of manques joked and laughed together. A manque about ten years old chorused, "I kill children. I love to see them die. I kill children. And make their mamas cry," an expression of angry euphoria on his face.

In the street, a manque selling vinyl screamed, "support the fuckin' city!" Few did.

A line from an old horror film echoed in the human's mind, "We've brought civilization to the planet."

439

LAMA-(third ep?)Johanna Records
Finlands best band prove it again...
uncredible vocals...sound like they
are all in unison minus OI trappings-
rather than cop on UK or US they've
got a good clean approach...the kind
of plucking Rickenbacker type bass
that cuts deep ...the production to
makes it a classic 45 for this seas-
ons top ten...(their lp is a must too)

BLITZ-"WARRIORS"/"YOUTH" No
Future....By John Stabb
Not your average Blitz material
(you are right it's dud material-TV)
More rock and roll oriented and not
very fast(oh well)Warriors even uses
an Adam type chorus but gets away with it.The flip "Youth " is also cool-
definate chant material.If you're used
to the first singles you will be sur-
prised(but probably for the better.)
BLITZ by your editor....
This 45 is about as useful as a limp
spud when Victoria's principle is
lowering in a squat to hone your
whalebone...got to give the sleeve
an A+ however...all the imagery of
a Henry Miller novel but the grooves
contain less than standard fare..the
long and short of it...this record
is a prick...

VENOM-"BLOODLUST"/"IN NOMINE SATANAS"
Neat Records...I made my feeling pretty
much known last ish...the best,most violent,satanic grungiest heavy metal band
ever...I'd love to lock JIM BAKKER and
his sleazy Miss Tammy in a room and force them to have sodomy while Venom blasted from all four corners of the room-
a hateful response from the bowels of
Englands outskirts...if I was into worshipping graven images I'd pray to
venom as I vomited blood on men of the
cloth...you betcha...

STRAPS-"BRIXTON"/"NO LIQUOR"
Donut...I hate people who give
their kids tang instead of real
OJ...I hate lesbians with cellu-
lite dimples on their thighs big
enough to park my dads snowblower
in...I hate the Fruit Loops magazine from Battle creek..I hate J-
ello Biafra...I hate the Damned-
but I love this bleedin record
with a passion..................

UNSAFE AT ANY SPEED-Modern Method
Records...Outakes from the LP...
nice sleeve...or picture bag if
you will...I'll say what all the
fanzines are saying about ever-
y sampler like "wow a million s-
ongs for a penny how can you go
wrong-and hey fuckheads if you
be over 7 fuck you....."'''''''''''''''

THE BUTTOCKS-"KILL THE PIGS"/"NEIN
NEIN NEIN"/"LAW AND ORDER"/"ARMY
LIFE" ....NOT QUITE as unique as
their first effort...besides they
looked cooler with two spikers and
two destitute looking longhairs but
this is still a jammer as are all
Buttocks tunes...they are no longer
together cuz I guess the singer got
jaded or something...anyways.......

NIHILISTICS-EP Visionary Records
I base my record buying-lots of
it on pure noise...from CRIME to
SPK if it's savage and sleazy odds are I'll buy...that's why I
say unequivically this is the best record to come out of the new
type NY bands...ya fuck you why?
Because they don't steal influences from Infa Riot or Black F-
lag and how much you wanna bet t-
hese guys don't hang out with all
the SF assholes in NY???

RED BUCKETS-"PALM SUNDAY"/XACTO
KNIFE" They'll call me a HC narrow minded punk if I dont love this...it's what GET SMART does a
helluva lot better...next?

IRON CROSS-SKINHEAD GLORY EP"
Dischord/Skinflint Records
Say what you will about Iron
Cross--the fact that all the
HUMAN RIGHTS PUNK ROCK PEOPLE
IN SAN FRANSISCO CAN SUCK COCK-
if they have it bad about this
band-they arent nazi's and this
record kicks my fuckin ass and
show me more commited members
of any band and I'll pound yor
mothers lard ass...electronic
distorted sludge with mean as
shit everything...yesir it'll
be controversy that fuels their fire into stardom......

The OUTLETS-"BEST FRIENDS"/"BRIGHT
LIGHTS" Modern Method
From whence they cometh-with an
eye on godollar or a lust for the
pop spotlight-hell i don't know-
not as bad as the bag might lead
you to believe....268 New bury
ST Boston 02116

ARTLESS EP-Knoblauch Records...PU this
is godawful-as underproduced and dull
as they come..not even leather jackets
and...chorus vocals help...shitty...
write..Busackerstr 14 41 Duisburg
W.Germany

BIG COUNTRY-"HARVEST HOME"/
"BALCONY" Phonogram
The cover imagry is a bit
nauseating--all the flair
for Jon Boy chic and giving
thanx for a cornacopia of b-
lessings..Stuart Adamson--
guitarist for the SKIDS in
their halcyon days is the r-
eason I bought this--and his
style is reminiscent of the
days in europa phase of the
band when as far as I was
concerned this could do no
wrong...hard to say where this
will fit in...I'll give it a B+ and
buy the next one................

MODERN ENGLISH-"I MELT WITH
YOU"/"THE PRIZE"4-AD Records
It's obvious the band wants
to shake the 4-AD stigma and
create something upbeat--as
there is apparently a sort
of backlash against the sort
of records these dank labels
have put forth for the last
few years...dangerously close to innocuous pop from s-
ome of the faculty of the school of the obscure...nothing
as awe inspiring as "Mesh &
Lace".....................

THE MOB-"UPSET THE SYSTEM" EP
Mob Style Records...
The only NY bands I seem to
enjoy employ the sledghammer
technique--rudimentary approaches to the obvious--don't
really care what they have to
say--they've got the right idea...write 246-14 54th Avenue
Douglastown NY 11362 ($3)

SLIME-45--The cops want to confiscate
all the SLIME records in existance--
they feel the contents to be subversive and so on...this is ok for the
collectable side but the LP's are
much better...

EINSTURZ ENDE NEU BAUTEN EP-ZICK
ZACK Records...Ok admitedly I'm
hopelessly out of touch with this
prolific label--could it be I was
wrong in safely assuming these all
were dung?Besides this stuff is
all the rage with the oil-base-
quiff post-everything crowd so
how can I be liking this...any-
way I do,as as the percussive
elements re-create some sort of
ritual or mystic revelatory experience that is beyond this boy--all I know is when music is reduced to it's basic elements it catches hold---classic
example (double pack 45)

ANDREAS DORAU & die MARINAS
"FRED VOM JUPITER"WR9
Top ten fare from West Germany featuring 5 13 year o-
lds over a boingy synth--
catchy as my dick is long-
young liepshens crooning
their way into your twis-
ted slacks with socially
unimortant ditty about a
guy named Fred...Presley
would have loved this in
his waneing years........

SAVAGE CIRCLE-EP Savage Circle Records...It's all differentiating between content,intent,latent subconsious desire to be hated and all t-
hose vibes these guys set off....
sometimes insipid banality deservedly falls in everybodys laps glee-
gleefully for Andy Schwarz and his
crew of jaded phonies--discrediting
and conversly hyping the Phosphenes-
the Feelies-and that is so positively
unregressive isn't it you fucking
jerks are so blind---all well and
good in NY...a little of everything-
And Larry C. poofs about daintily
oozing about at shows hoping no
$7 A weighs in at 280 and will st-
omp on the lower east side of his
face........$2.50 from 2329 Vance
St Bronx NY 10469   C+

440

Smoke Seven
PRESENTS

Last Rites for Genocide and M I A   SMK 7-104

Smoke Sevens newest release combines the steaming hardcore of N.Y.'s Genocide with the blazing tight sound of Las Vegas' M I A – 19 songs that will kick your ass!

RED CROSS   SMK 7-103
BORN INNOCENT

Acclaimed as the best album of the year Born Innocent features the Mc-Donnalds at their worst (best) Don't miss out on this classic

R F 7   SMK 7-102
Weight of the World

R F 7 has received world wide recognition for this brilliant debut L.P. Hard strong songs with excellent lyrics R F 7 has a message they want to pound into you

PUBLIC SERVICE   SMK 7-101

New music compilation with Circle One, Red Cross, Bad Religion, R F 7 and Disability This L.P. features the first recordings from Circle One L.A.'s most controverisial band Plus great songs from Bad Religion, Red Cross and more

---

NEXT FROM SMOKE SEVEN...

"SUDDEN DEATH" L.A. comp. with Naughty Women, Sin 34, Youth Gone Mad, Red Cross, Moral Decay, Demented & more.$ 5.00
"FALL IN"- A 12" E.P. from R F 7, includes "Fuck Money", "6 6 6 Head".$ 4.50
The 2nd L.P. from the unpredictable Red Cross
...All 3 due out by Nov. 1st.

For Mail Order Send $5.00 for each to:
Smoke Seven
7230 De Soto Ave #104
Canoga Park, CA. 91303

*overseas residents add $2.00
*allow a couple of weeks for delivery

441

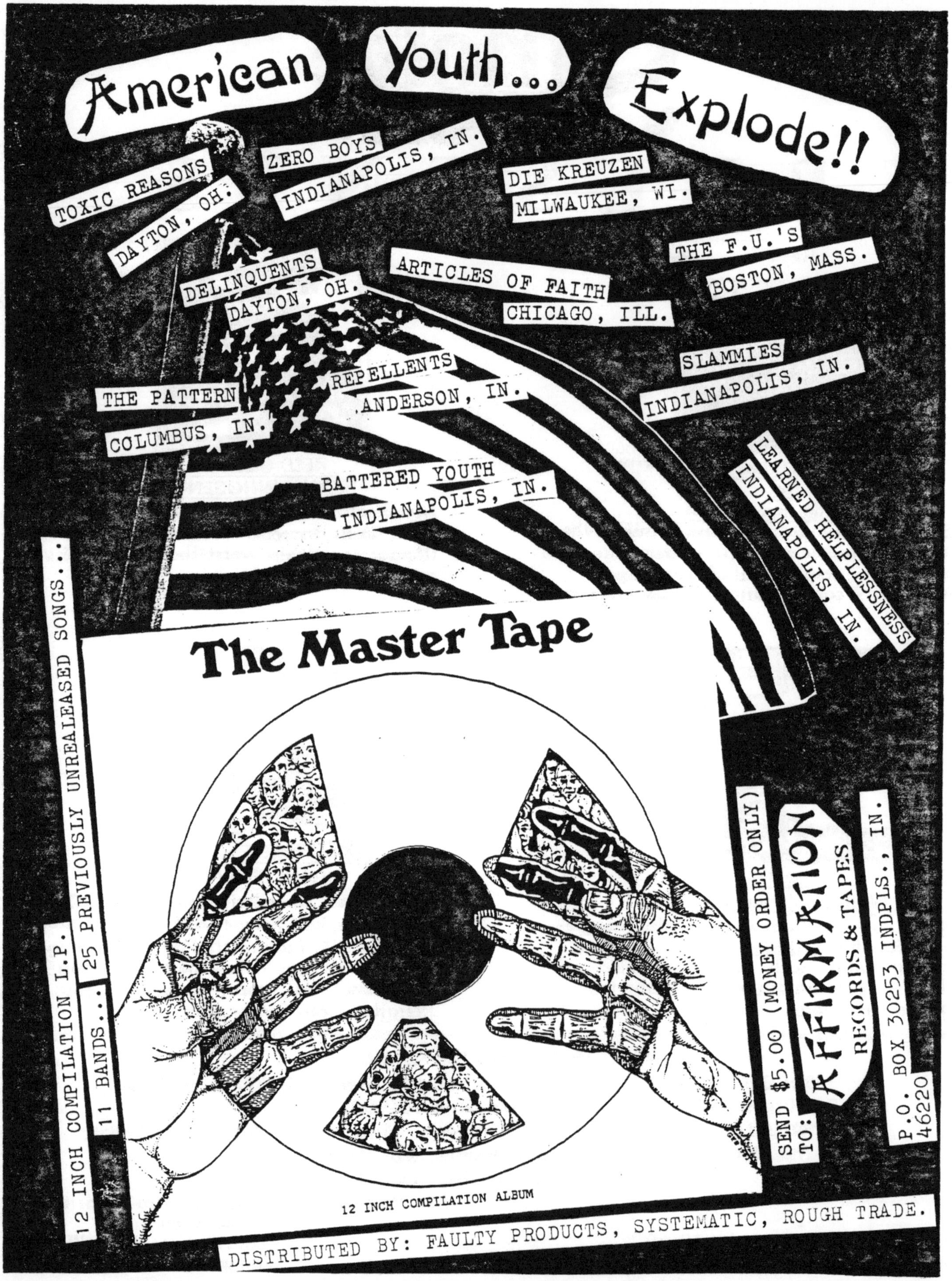

American Youth... Explode!!

TOXIC REASONS DAYTON, OH.

ZERO BOYS INDIANAPOLIS, IN.

DIE KREUZEN MILWAUKEE, WI.

THE F.U.'S BOSTON, MASS.

DELINQUENTS DAYTON, OH.

ARTICLES OF FAITH CHICAGO, ILL.

SLAMMIES INDIANAPOLIS, IN.

THE PATTERN COLUMBUS, IN.

REPELLENTS ANDERSON, IN.

LEARNED HELPLESSNESS INDIANAPOLIS, IN.

BATTERED YOUTH INDIANAPOLIS, IN.

The Master Tape

12 INCH COMPILATION L.P.... 11 BANDS... 25 PREVIOUSLY UNREALEASED SONGS...

SEND $5.00 (MONEY ORDER ONLY) TO: AFFIRMATION RECORDS & TAPES

P.O. BOX 30253 INDPLS., IN. 46220

12 INCH COMPILATION ALBUM

DISTRIBUTED BY: FAULTY PRODUCTS, SYSTEMATIC, ROUGH TRADE.

442

IRON CROSS

Sab-Vocals Dante-Drums John-Bass Mark-Guitar

AND IT TURNED OUT TO BE A TAMPON THAT SHE HAD FORGOTTEN TO TAKE OUT MONTHS AGO,SHE DIDNT EVEN KNOW IT WAS THERE,IT TOOK HER aWIlE TO GET IT OUT AND IT WAS EVIL LOOKING,MAYBE AN ILLO WILL HELP YOU GET THE IDEA-HA HA.... WRITE TO PUSHEAD....2713 KERR BOISE IDAHO

PIC by Tesco

TV:So you do wanna make any general statements or anything about your band.. Sab:I think it's a bit much for Mr.Yohannon who I've never met or even heard of to start slagging us off...I mean I don't see anything racist in the "Flex Your Head lyrics...TV:So what inspired you to name the band what you did... Sab;It's just a hard sounding name-that was the simple and only reason..its not a nazi symbol(as some would just l-ove to envision it,ED)John:Ya it goes back to the 1800's...John:It's just a hard sounding name you know..TV:Instead of calling yourself the Moral Urban Rea-gan Haters or some such shit...Dante: Youth Of Insane Children...TV:Your music has always been alot slower than most o-ther bands...Dante:We don't like thrash-Sab:We never wanted to play it-there's some bands that are really good at it but we never wanted to play it..TV:So John do you want to talk about being the new guy on bass?No one can accuse you of being new to this music(referen-ce to the fact he was the original bas-sist in the British band THE UNWANTED) TV:What were the early Roxy days like in 77?John:Great-alot different than it is now...it became fashionable like it is now very quickly...at the time it was like everyone was trying to outdo everyone else-see how shocking you c-ould be to people on the street and all of that--I mean people think it all st-arted in 77 but in 76 and even 75 there were punks there but there just weren't that many punks around-it was real und-erground at that timeTV:Was there a comm-unity at that time I mean did you chum around with Johnny Moped or..My band us-ed to hang around with guys in Generation X and Eater...TV:So what's your opinion of US bands?John:In general it's not what I like or am used to listening to --alot of the British bands and the"OI" bands...I like Fear because I think they're funny on stage and I like some of the Adolescents stuff...I support the bands here in DC...TV:So why did you n-eed a new bassist?Mark:Wendel had some problems..he wasnt being uh..Dante:He fucked up..Sab:He left us in the lurch 3 days before the Upstarts show...Mark: So we sat downstairs and practiced with John and it worked out fuckin great... Sab:Our second set was like the best we' ve ever playedMark:John fit in real well-

TV:What did you think of the Upstarts? All:BLAAAAAA BOOO HISS...JOHN We got kic-ked out of the dressing room...Sab:Me and Mensi had it out..Dante:Mensi got huffy-Dante:Their general attitude was like"Y-our not stars--We are"...John:They were basically taking the attitude that we're a big band--we're professionals-and what we say is right and anything you say aga-inst us is wrong and what Sab was saying was we've been listening to you for a long time and really like you and you come here and throw a load of shit on us...and tha'ts fucked up...Dante:He apologized on stage.. TV:So now you have your third bass player-- (laughter)Sab:4th...Dante:Fuck you guys try 19th...Mark:Ian even practised with us one time he was great..Dante:Eddie..Ian.. Toni..John..Wendell..Cynthia...we've had about 9... subject changes to....
Sab:I would like to know from reading issue #2 of max R+R how Mr Yohannon can possibly go to sleep at night with all of his worries + hangups... that magazine is so jam-med full of political, sociological rantings it reads like the communist workers party booklet.. Mark: Is he a real dick or what? Sab: It's like he's carrying the burden of the world on his shoulders... Dante: I feel sorry for him...SAB-I mean judging from his fanzine-maybe he's a red or maybe not-he's certainly left wing... his fanzine is shit-the only political System that works is democracy... and whether we live in a dem-ocracy or not right now is a debateable subject... I mean I'm not going to sit up on stage and quote Engals and Bakunin-the only politics I'm interested in are my politics(talk here about presidents/close proximity to governmental functions here in DC and how we all could care less)TV:At least Carter admited he lusted after women.Mark: Reagans son lusts after young men. Dante: Reagan doesn't know how to lust any more. Sab: What concerns me is who is shitting on me on a personal level. John: You've got to look at things realistically-the music can't really do anything on a grand-iose basis especially in a country this big-iose Alot of the songs this band has done have to do with life-and alot of it is kids and whats happening now... with you person-ally...
Write
2706 N. 4th St
Arlington VA
22201

OFFICIAL TOUCH AND GO PUSHEAD LAMORT INTERVIEW BRIAN SCHROEDER-A PERSON WHOSE ALTER EGO IS... PUSHEAD LAMORT--PUSHEAD=A BLEMISH ON SOCIETY LAMORT=DEATH(FRENCH TAROT CARD) TV:WHAT INSPIRES YOU TO DO A CERTAIN PIECE OF ART?PUS:INSPIRATION THRU IMAGINATION.SOME-TIMES YOU CAN'T OPENLY VOICE AN OPINION OR I-DEA WITHOUT SOME WIDE MOUTH TELLING YOU YOU DON'T KNOW WHAT YOU ARE TALKING ABOUT...WHAT IS THE PURPOSE OF A DEBATE WITH A BLOATED EGO? SO YOU GET IDEAS ABOUT THINGS YOU SEE HAPPEN-ING AROUND YOU IN EVERYDAY LIFE AND I JUST INT-ERPERATE THEM AS DEMENTED NIGHTMARES OR AS SU-CH.MOST PEOPLE PROCRASTINATE TOO MUCH TO MUCH TO EVER BELIEVE THAT SOMETHING IS WRONG.THEY ALWAYS WAIT TIL THE LAST MINUTE WHEN EVERYTHING IS CRUMBLING AROUND THEM.THEY ONLY LISTEN TO PAIN AND FEAR.IF SOMEONE CRINGES AT THE SIGHT OF A PUS-GORE PIECE THEN I'VE ACCOMPLISHED S-OMETHING.EVERYONE WHO TALKS ABOUT "BLOOD SAUS-AGE ILLO,THEY FELT THE PAIN AND THEY WON'T FOR-GET,MAYBE IT HIT AN INNER PHOBIA(OR CREATED ONE, ED)BUT NOBODY WILL EVER REALLY REALIZE THE REA-LITY OF SUCH AN ILLUSTRATION,IT'S JUST FICTION. LAUGHING AT THEM...BS:IT DOESNT HAVE TO BE BL-OODY OR SICK TO TO BE EFFECTIVE,BUT THE INSAN-ITY OF SOCIETY RUNS IN CIRCLES JUST TO BE IN FEAR.WHEN YOU CLOSE YOUR EYES THE SUBCONSIOUS STATE BRINGS OUT YOUR BRAIN WAVES IN DREAMS, IF THEY ARE NIGHTMARES YOU ARE LIVING A HOSTILE LIFE OR WISH TO..IF THEY ARE PLEASANT-IT IS SO-METHING YOU WISH FOR OR HAVE.EITHER WAY THE ANT-AGONIST IS ALWAYS FEAR AND THE PAIN IS PUSHEAD. TV:WHO BASICALLY DO YOU DRAW FOR? PUS:I AM NOT A ONE BAND PERSON OR AS SUCH.I ENJOY DRAWING WHO RATIFY AT EACH PIECE-THE PEOPLE OF APPRE-CIATION-THOSE WHO TAKE THE TIME TO LOOK AT WHAT IS THERE AND THEN POSITIVE/NEGATIVE IT.BASIC-ALLY I MUST LIKE THE BAND OR MAGAZINE FOR WHICH I DRAW..OR IT IS JUST A SELLOUT ON MY PART CUZ THEN THERE ISN'T MUCH FUN IN DOING ILLUSTRATIONS THINGS YOU REALLY DONT CARE FOR..DON'T WANT TO BE A COPORATE ROBOT.IT IS MY LEARNED ABILITY NOT THEIRS.PEOPLE I'VE DONE ART FOR..SHAWN/BYO,AB-BIE AND AL,DESTRUCTORS,NECROS,DISCHORD(RARE-JEFF HIDES THEM)MISFITS,ARTIFICIAL PEACE,MEATMEN, ROUGH TRADE,HEAD CLEANERS(SHESK) SKEEM@ GANG, FORCED EXPOSURE,'VOTE"(FINLAND)F.U.'S AND THE MIGHTY TOUCH AND GO PLUS MORE I'M FORGETTING. BS:ANNIE! IN EACH ILLUSTRATION I SUBLIMINALLY WRITE HER NAME IN WITH THE FOCAL POINT OR BA-CKGROUND.IT IS A LOVE APPRECIATION I SHARE WI-TH HER TV:WHEN DID YOU GET STARTED?PUS:STARTED WHEN I WAS 6-8 YEARS OLD-ENTERED ALL THESE JUNIOR ARTIST CONTESTS ALL THE TIME.WHEN I WENT TO SCHOOL TOOK LOTS OF ART COURSES,BUT THEY NEVER REALLY TAUGHT ME WHAT I KNOW NOW.
MY MAJOR INFLUENCES ARE FROM COMIC BOOK TYPE ILLUSTRATORS LIKE WRIGHTSON,NINO,EISNER,HO-GARTH,KIRBY AND NERBES.I JUST MARVELED AT THE PEN AND BRUUSH STROKES.IT WAS A SERIOUS FASCINATION THAT HELPED MY ART GROW.BS:NOW THAT I'M STARTED I DON'T WANT TO FINNISH..TV:WHAT ARE YOUR FAVORITE PIECES? PUS:HARD TO PICK FAVORITES-GOOD OR BAD THEY EACH CONTAIN CERTAIN LEARNING QUALITIES THAT HAVE HELP-ED MY STYLE PROGRESS."GARBAGE BABIES" AND "NO ESCAPE FROM THE DEAD" HAVE ITEMS I REALLY ENJOY.EVERYONE HAS A DIFFERENT OPINION OR CHOICE THOU.B.S.:LYNCH-ING SCEENE FROM "DAWN OF THE DEAD 2" AND "DRINK,D-RUG,DIE".IT'S A BUMMER WHEN GOOD ILLOS ARE USED FOR GIGS THAT GET CANCELLED BUT THEN THEY BECOME COLLECTORS ITEMS I GUESS.TV:HAS ANYONE THREATENED YOU OR BECAME ANGRY BECAUSE OF THE WAY THEY WERE DEPICTED IN ONE OF YOUR DRAWINGS?PUS:KINDA EARLY TO TELL EH TV?WATCH YOUR MAIL.BS:WHERE I LIVE I AM WELL KNOWN AND WELL HATED BUT MOST PEOPLE COULD NEVER TELL YOU WHAT I LOOK LIKE OR IF I AM PUSHEAD.I ONLY EXIST FOR THE EVIL OF MY ART TABLE AND THE PAINS OF CONTINOUS ILLUSTRATING, CRAMPS,BUTT SORES ETC. TV:WHAT ARE YOUR FAVE BAN-DS?PUS:ASK HIM HE KNOWS THE MUSIC:PUS:HARDCORE: DISCHARGE/GANG GREEN(RIP) SS DECONTROL/MINOR THREAT/ TERVEET KADET/NEOS/RUDIMENTARY PENI/7 SECONDS/ DISORDER/NECROS/MISFITS/FAITH/MEATMEN/DOUBLE O/ ADRENALIN OD/TARR BABIES/DESTRUCTORS/HUVUDUATT (HEADCLEANERS) AND (UK)SUBHUMANS TO NAME A FEW.. OTHER-PASSPORT ALLAN HOLDSWORTH HAPPY THE MAN ETC:TV:WHAT IS THE GROSSEST THING YOU'VE EVER HEARD?THE TIME THIS GUY I KNOW WAS FUCKING HIS GIRLFRIEND AND HE BUMPED INTO SOMETHING

FLEX YOUR HEAD

32-SONG D.C. SAMPLER $5.00 POSTPAID   DISCHORD 3819 BEECHER ST. N.W.   WASH. D.C.   20007

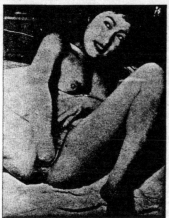

OUR READERS GROPING FOR THE ANSWERS

HEY YOU TESCO VEE
What the fuck is wrong with you?Why do you hate TSOL?So what if they're not like the Meatmen or Necros or other DC bands,They're an OC band!!And they're great!I'm good friends with Jack Grisham and believe me,they don't rip anyone off!As a metter of fact their new EP has already sold 20,000 copies and do you know how much Alternative tentacles gave them?200 dollars!!Bigfuck!! None of them are rich,Jack's the only one with a car(and a cheap one too!) Jack and Todd livewith their parents! Geez!Jack wants to kick your ass next time they go on tour!His address is: TSOL Global communications 3102 Ladoga Ave. long Beach Ca 90808 Write to him!I hope you dont hate me.I just wanted to set you straight.
               Steve Schulte
               Lakewood,Ca.
It would hurt alot more if he kicked my penis,my ass has padding on it..ED.

Dear Touch and Go:
In reference to your quote of the month in issue #19,Jack is exactly right.You see about 2or3 years ago Jack was in an intense band called Vicious Circle.These guys were fucking insane!!They had a following of fellow skinheads.These guys were radical.They would literally beat the shit out of another gang that came to a club came to a club called the Fleetwood in Redondo Beach.These guys had a rad reputation. The big thing a couple years ago in the South bay area home of Black Flag and in Huntington Beach was to have a skinhead.. I had a skin three years ago.The skins were people who liked to beat the shit out of each other and other people.Especially long hairs.Alot of these skins just evolved into other things.Jack is of those who evolved into something difference.TSOL has changed but when they first got together they were fucking great.
          South Bay punk and TSOL fan.

Hey Tesco-
In response to Raynerd Dean's letter: What a bunch o' Cal!This is obviously a bunch of sour grapes.Anything that starts out "Children of East Lansing (or any other small scene,anywhere has got to make you stop and think--- who the fuck does this card think he is?A priest?!"Oh Tesco I remember what it was like when punks were punks and women were glad of it.And now there's just me."Fuck all this Righteousness!(This Sage's 'words of wisdom" clutter the space you could have sold for 62¢ and we all would have been better off)I don't know or care about anybody else-but I don't need to read any So. Cal "mail" that tells me to enjoy myself and the scene!Besides he's gonna try and tell us that everyone E.L. is going to sport a skinhead within two years(or even my lifetime?)Horse shit or maybe Detroit?No way on earth sod! We all saw what happens to new wavers who go for a too punkish look-the Necros or somebody bloodies their scalp.Let me tell you-only in the media land of California or in the populated world of NY willl punk rock the fad ever happen.Those places shove people so closely together they are all dying for identity-and eventually the minority becomes the majority-at least as far as fads go.The only thing this chump says that makes sense(and it can only be deducted from his arguments) is that fashion sucks! You can't derive anything from the fact that a person has a mohawk or skinhead or black boots.Nothing!What we're talking about is the line that seperates posers from the real Mcoy.And you can't tell by looking at em most times.
You gotta see what's in their shrub before you pass judgment." Either way this guys "advice" sounds like they can't rise above the shit they're in and he shouldnt be trying to hold me/us down by screaming "the end is near!"Fuck that poop!It's typical:"We here in So. Cal started punk rock."Then it was"You people in the midwest still havent taken the "Black Flag" challenge.Now its "Punk Rock is dead,we saw it first"It's almost sounds like they're jealous because our "scene" still has unlimited energy and life!You can't suck it from me Baynard.Most Sincerely
                Doug from Attigaraphix
                E.L. MI

In reply to So.Cal GOTHIC SHOCK's editor letter and in response to Tesco's offer of space in T&G for such a reply!The question of whether it is a bad thing that punk is gaining in numbers can be answered in terms of what it is you like about it.To me it's the music.If 4 million copies of FEAR's album sold and only thousands of journeys,I wouldn't seek an identity insofar as becoming devoted to shit music.At the risk of sounding "out of vogue" even today there are a few long hair bands that play kick ass rock-n-roll...Keith of the CJ's digs Motley Crue,I like Motorhead's "Ace of Spades' and Tesco Implies Venom arent punk but are geat!I'm from Southern Cal and before i was locked back up in prison I had people from the original Masque scene tell me they'd sworn off going to gigs because of young skinheads.In the last Flipside one of LA's bands editorializes about the apathy to music and sheer juvenile arrogance of each new crop of 'punks' that are indeed proliferating-but the ones who don't love the music will be gone soon enough-and for those of us who do to gripe because alot of people are getting into it would be just as juvenile. For every young skinhead who gets tired of beating up punks and hippies and moves on to something else there will be two or three that grow up and concentrate on the music and living life instead of posing..when I was in high school it was massive drug abuse that became the in thing and those of us who thought we were different soon saw drugs become widespread-hopefully senseless violence and trendy acceptance wont spread as far as drugs have but regardless giving up on being a punk or being into punk isnt a positive thing-it's defeatist bullshit-I don't get bored or alienated by things I love...listen to the musicDIY and forget the scene.The midwest is no different than LA when it comes to more and more bands and more and more kids carrying the hardcore banner.Ray Dean should make his statements in his own zine and either decide he is or isnt a punk-none of the bands mentioned are hc straight ahead punk-they are great-but so are a hundred other LA bands=the more the merrier-the kids may not be united but they are all right!Signed Older but not wiser
          Defeated but not defeCAted on...the Ex R&R Bankrobber...

HEY Tesco
There's this kid we know who has burning rectal passion for the well known two faced nazi fag Rod Race. He desires the old beeef wagon parked up his anal garage.When his butt fags are not around he takes a warm hot dog and shoves it straight up his grungy ass and flogs his dog until he passes out.I think these kind of fags should have their balls sliced off so they lose their uncontrollable desires.
                    ANAL SERVANTS
to prank this fag call 332-1217

MY hair is blue black jus like ELVIS NOW!
DROP MEA

THE Woist!

Herein begins another Touch And Go exclusive....THE WORST ALBUMS IN HISTORY. This issue features 5 or so of some of the most scintillatingly bad records to ever be released...if you have any particular requests for LP's you would like to see featured here drop me a line.... HERE WE GO....

#1-VON LMO "FUTURE LANGUAGE"
This one incorporates the worst elements of Devo and bad Heavy Metal...only New York could have produced something so profoundly bad...hokey insipid lyrics about some future state of mind,,trashy instrumentation.and some of the dorfiest musical breaks....simply mind bogglingly poor...this record is so bad in fact it traverses the circular mental rating scale to actually become listenable in a laughable sense..me and the boys play it while watching porno movies..budget porno that is......................

MILK AND COOKIES
If you thought Sparks,or The Quick were the ultimate wimps foist your bad taste on this bunch...simpering faggots who cood and purred songs like "rabbits Make Love" and "Little Lost And Innocent" and made even the most sissified light-weight wanna gag...and now this sells for $15 and the only people that would buy it would be people who were either hopelessly gay,or very young or very bored...makes Manilow sound like Gengis Kahn...not good folks........

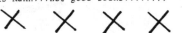

BUDGIE
Budgie were(are?)a three piece metal outfit from wales who have about 10 albums out...some of which I still maintain for the metal conoisor(sp?) are very good if you go for no holds barred,machine-like thud like their 1974 classic "In For The Kill"...but this was their first LP and PU this one popped outa someones butt..recorded like they liked the bass sound and forgot the other two guys...and waht could be dumber than this bands packaging...parakeets doing everything from riding horses to fighting battles in outer space...what the//???? A closet bad record for the folks like me and DS who bought this gem...

THOR-"KEEP THE DOGS AWAY"
From NY again..hmmmm we may have a trend here...this guy takes the cake...large and suntanned,sneering at us in a Presleyan pose that is supposed to instill in the pre pubescent consumer-a lust for something or other...so you aint sure..you buy the fuckin record and the company smiles...well not for too long cuz this one got cut out-but this boy has the very macho Ed Ames-call of Conan,me big wampum you slut vocals, and real thudlike backup(probably from some kinky haired jewish session men but you arent supposed to think about that)with whimsical titles like 'Military Matters" and "Thunder"...you guessed it this guy is big on muscle,image and libido and slim on talent,sellability and probably prick size....defiantely a bad record...

a Talk with a MINUTEMAN and a PLEB

The following was conducted with Mike Watt of the MINUTEMEN and Ken Starkey of the PLEBS....
TV:What is the true meaning of nirvana? MW:I think the Minutemen are too screwed up to know what nirvana is.Maybe it's knowing about everything or like everything's perfect.Shit I'm embarrassed. Ken:Not having to answer stupid questions like that.
TV:What gave you the inspiration to be rythmic,off beat,and full of conscienceness as exemplified by your records? MW:We like the idea of jazz,making music free with minimal bullshit.We're doing the best we can to play.I like the idea of a good worked out jam. Ken:Nature TV:What cuisines are in direct,mutual commaraderie with your particular lifestyles?
MW:George loves pickled eggs,pigs feet, sushi.I like marinated artichoke hearts, omelettes,avacodos,pinK's chili dogs, bobs,(made of beef hearts,gizzards,and chicken hearts.And anything my girlfriends parents have in their refrigerator.D.Boon likes food....
Ken:I'm into combination of breakfast cereals. TV:If homicide was suddenly legal,but just for you....
MW:We would quit the team.
Ken:Kill those who are responsible for the death and oppression of thousands of other innocent humanist people.
TV:What's the best record you've heard in recent times? MW:"Doc At The Radar Station" by Cpt. Beefheart."Pink Flag" by Wire.All the records by the Urinals and the Meat Puppets."A Can Of Bees"by the Soft Boys.Most everything by the Pop Group and Rip,Rig and Panic.Good jams from the 50's:Miles Davis,Max Roach,T.Monk,John Coltrane&Charlie Mingus. Some Parliment records("Mothership Connection")The first shit from a Certain Ratio.Roky Erickson.
TV:How does your environment affect your tuneage?MW:You answered your own question with the last one.We try to get as intense as the jams we hear.There's a feeling involved that's way more important than any kind of style or some sort of shit. Ken:Looking behind the orange curtain can make a person cloudy minded but if you can wade through all the bullshit it helps to strengthen my own personal thought.TV:What does the future hold? MW:We started our next album July 3. Some songs will seem longer.We'll get a little more flexible.D.Boon takes over as guitar warrior.
Ken:The death of capitalism...
TV:What type of audience jives with you,gives you boners etc.?
MW:People who go off and yell shit at us.Sometimes D.Boon jumps off of the stage on them,it's alot of fun. When we play we go off real emotional like(alot of sweat.)and feel better when everybody's spasing out with us. Ken:I don't think I've ever got a boner from an audience.
Q:How has your sound evolved since you began? MW:We've written over 70 songs. Every song is another notch on the big badge buff.We're more Minutemen now than we used to be.All of us are older now and are somehow the same but changed but not sure or what? Ken:Gino got a new clarinet,we're still working on our shit. We've got alot of new material but no time to work on it.
Q:Who makes the best red meat burrito in LA? MW:Carnitas Patzcuaro No.2.It's here in Pedro on Pacific and Santa Cruz. Ken:The same,most authentic.
TV:Ask yourselves some pointed questions. MW:Are we glad Tesco writes to us?Yes Do we think the world is complicated?Yes Ken:Do women jump in your head,scramble up your brain,and then jump back out? They sure do as well as trying to push their guilt onto you.....

THE WIPERS-"ROMEO"/"NO SOLUTION"
Trap Records Maintaining their
enigmatic "non" appeal with the
masses,all the while suiting my
tastes to a tee--converting few
here-mainly keeping the cult bas-
tions surrencified...the advent
of the power romance ballad?
write PO BOX 42465 Portland Oregon 97242

GG ALLIN-YOU HATE ME AND I HATE YOU":
Orange Records..does persistence p-
ay off...this guy probably fucked
his older sister and ate dog dew
or something and he wants whatever
image in decadence you want to foist on him...good thing there's no
lame Wayne Kramer riffing because
I think he's alot closer to stardom here...a singalong tune for
when the oven cleaner has your h-
ead spinning...but GG that sleeve
isn't gonna cut any mustard..how
about a picture of your massive
leather bag?Orange Records 639
Broadway #902 NY NY 10012.......

THE LURKERS-"THIS DIRTY TOWN"/
"WOLF AT THE DOOR" Clay Records
One of my ole faves minus Howard
Wall on the comeback trail...and
a winner it is...½ of it anyway-
b side is poopy but a side partys
in my pants and if you used ta like
em' you still will and if you never did you still won't...damn straight.....

SPECIAL DUTIES-"BULLSHIT CRASS"/YOU-
'RE DOING YOURSELF NO GOOD...Rondolet
Nothing as outstanding as their LP--
I lost touch with the Marxists that
put out all thoses similar singles-
but I hardly think with all the o-
ther more deserving penis's In this
big beautiful world we need to expose or repose on dogmatic doofs l-
ike the Crass...oh well..........
(but Steve Arrogant is still one of
the best singers going--besides with
his Steve Fix hair circa late 80' he
can't miss...)

ANTI ESTABLISHMENT-"FUTURE GIRL"
"No Trust" Glass Records
Every time I have to void my b-
owels I slap this one on to ex-
pedite matters -A side starts
out like John Denver and turns
into "WE SOUND LIKE THE DAMNED
SO BUY US CLODS"...blow me English half wits...

NUKKETEATTERI-"TERVETULOA HEL-
VETTIIN..."
Nothing that's going to change
the face of any scene...pretty
much standard rule of thumb-b-
arrage ala Varukers-but everything fits a little to nicely
into the sameness of what we've
all heard many times before...
I'll give em' another chance...

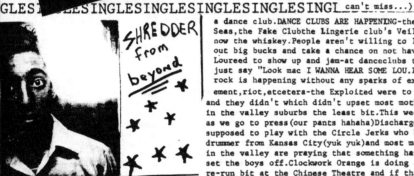

a dance club.DANCE CLUBS ARE HAPPENING-the Seven
Seas,the Fake Clubthe Lingerie club's Veil and
now the whiskey.People aren't willing to leaf
out big bucks and take a chance on not having
Loureed to show up and jam-at danceclubs they
just say "Look mac I WANNA HEAR SOME LOU.Punk
rock is happening without any sparks of excitement,riot,etcetera-the Exploited were to play
and they didn't which didn't upset most mothers
in the valley suburbs the least bit.This weekend
as we go to press(our pants hahaha)Discharge is
supposed to play with the Circle Jerks who have a new
drummer from Kansas City(yuk yuk)and most mothers
in the valley are praying that something happens to
set the boys off.Clockwork Orange is doing a huge
re-run bit at the Chinese Theatre and if that flick

I LIVE IN LOS ANGELES....I CARRY A SCHOOL ID.....
DUMDADUMDUM........This is the city,a blast of p-
alm trees and greasy taco joints.The story you a-
re about to hear is true.The names have not been
changed because no-one in L.A. wakes up before 4
in the afternoon anyways.Between Ray Milland and
Alan Ladd movies on TV at ungodly hours a so-called new "SCENE" or "SEEN" is hopping up from the
throes of uh er post-punk-pre-beatles-during Vel-
vet Underground kinda myoozic playing.Up and bum-
ming(cigarettes)are the voluptuous heavenly M-
arilyn Monroes of the 80's-the BANGS,all girls-
splashy guitars and totally void of the usual typical normal girl group nuances such as underwear
posing in top rock and cocaine magazines.Also aci-
dic and chemical are the Three O CLOCK,formerly
the Salvation Army,formerly youthful spunky song-
writers for the Dickies-this band of banditos is
the real mc coy in psychedelicatessan-man they
must even watch movies in revival theatres-the-
se guys are hip-dig um digum dig-um.Their album
is cacaphony minus the caca and the phoniness
so prevalent in british homosexual toy music.
At the greasy light headed head of all this cl-
amor is Dream Syndicate who say they sound nothing like the Velvet Underground and probably know
Lou Reed PERSONALLY!!Their EP is just like looking in kaleidascopes-we're talking colorful.The
Gun Club have an album in the wings(it be out
Shredmaniac get wid it.ED) produced by some of
the more social members of Blondie who coincide-
ntaly also probably know Lou Reed personally)
45 GRAVE have split up and reformed about 70
times in the past 6 hours with a bunch of new
members-Rob Ritter split for the most dirty low
down town this side of the Atlantic-Detroit(watch yor tongue whippersnapper,ED)(If I/m not mis-
taken Lou Reed has been there once or twice
IN PERSON)THE WHISKEY A GOGO IS CLOSED FOR SU-
RES AND FOR SHIRES AND FOR GOODSKI-last show
as a pale Plimsouls/Tom Petty thing smelling of

aint the happening movie then what's it going to
be then,eh,oh my brothers,a bit of old moloko etcet-
eraetcetera.The Necrosare coming to town and IT IS
GOING TO BE WUNNERFUL SEEING WHAT EVERYONE ELSE
HAS BEEN WAITING FOR FOR THE LAST THREE YEARS.
Minor Threat popped over charming and fresh giving everyone the shot in the arm they've been
begging for pardon the curved edge expression,,,
MINOR THREAT is as good as anything since the
Germs and no true blue punk could keep from r-
ocking their socks off.Anti Pasto and Chron Gen
came over and didn't do..so.fresh.ROCKBILLYBABA:
Every expunk and nonpunk from the subs has trimmed their hair for that ROCKABILLY LOOK or so the
L.A. Times tell me.Two days later the times reports
that MODS ARE THE SHINDIG OF THE DAY and display
mods in full gear bitching that PUNKS ARE SLOBS
AND THEIR VESPAS NEED FOREIGN PARTS.Life is complicated here.I bet we have as many punk rock emotional crisis as new york or lansing michigan.
Then again they're closer to Lou Reed.
          WATCHING CHANNEL FIVE AT FIVE,
               Shredder
          (What made L.A. famous
          made a problematic out of me)

cing either reorganization or dismember-
ment at the imminent departure of Eliot,
the Teen Beat idol and dreammate of hundreds of lonely Kalamazoo high school
girls...anyway VA was at the peak of their form this night,pffering tight well
balanced versions of all the legendary
VA hits.Kenny's voice was really strong
and he even stuck the mike in his mouth
and terrified everyone with his infamous demon roars..I hadn't seen the Necros since June 4,but after this show t-
hey're back at the top of my list...
"Satisfy" and "Take Em Up" were personal faves.They seemed upset that people
wer'ent dancing for em or something
but I wanted to get a good listen to
them and besides,just because my boots
arent bloody doesnt mean I did'nt love your show guys Misfits-now let's
not kid ourselves here-had the worst
sound quality of the night:it was so
loud and muddy that even some familiar songs were hard to recognize.Th-
ere was copious feedback throughout
the set and the Pa blew up in the
middle of M.C.I.G.O and Kill tonight"
a catastrophic set of technical cir-
cumststances which could have spelled disaster.But their astonishing
visual presence and power carried
the set and their onslaught,though
somewhat blunted was still capable
of whipping my fellow Misfit devotees into a frenzy and sending unin-
itiates off in slack jawed terr-
or.Pretty cool show over all...
review by CT..................

↓ ↓ MORE LIVE ↓ ↓ ↓

MISFITS/NECROS/VIOLENT APATHY/CRUCIFUCKS
at FOE LODGE #526 Kalamazoo Mi 9/26
The ghouls from beyond invade quiet Kalamazoo on a sleepy Sunday nite?Damn right
grandma and hide the kids.The Crucifucks
continued their reign as the Midwest's
most terrifying band,playing at will w-
ith everybody's brains.Doc was at his b-
est,cutting down from behind a nuwave ch-
ickie with a perfect knee-high tackle as
he began "Hinkley Had A Vision". The girl
came up to Doc after the set saying how
she was embarrassed to the point of tears,
the poor unfortunated child.....V.A.,Fa-

Twelve Inchez!

SS DECONTROL

THE KIDS WILL HAVE THEIR SAY

SS DECONTROL-"THE KIDS WILL HAVE THEIR SAY" X Claim/Dischord
Whenever I slap this mammy on the mat my bilge rat leaps outs me pants and flops around like a mackeral on the hot pavement...gee sorry folks I'll have to be serious concerning this piece because it is indeed a ranking candidate for LP of the season....as big and mean as one can find anywhere these days..living up to all my starry eyed and overly angst ridden expectations...real men listen to Decontrol-I didn't say that...heavy on the clean life and Al has his say...the singer sounds like he must be a raging bohemoth that stands at 6'9" and weighs in at a scanty 300...quit laughin I know what he looks like...how does such a diminuitive package sport your basic mega mouth...anyway as far as singers go they don't come much better than this...albums don't come better than this...

SONIC·YOUTH

SONIC YOUTH-NEUTRAL RECORDS
Interesting as shit and from NYC no less...this is one of those records that Greenworld would try to describe as all these amalgms of this and that...cool effects & an original approach...one of those you'll play when you are overamping on life...

MEAT PUPPETS LP SST Records by John Stabb...What can I say about this album-noisy funny often tuneful,indecipherable lyric al mind boggling noise.check it out and see if you don't talk backwards.It's more like an ep but these boys must smoke alot a cactus.Not for everyones ears.

M.D.C.

MDC-"MILLIONS OF DEAD COPS"
Radical Records
With a handle like this one must expect the reaction this band got when they hit Lansing...well a flyer with police obituaries and a splashing of red paint didn't help ease the local boys in blue's worst fear of getting blasted...so they called the hall that had been rented and the show was off...well moved to an outdoor location where Tolchock,Crucifucks,and MDC played--- until the cops shut it down...say so long to anything else happening at the Civic Players or in Lansing for that matter...a scene as fragile as this didnt need the adverse publicity this thing garnered regardless of who has the rights to do what...kid gloves were in order and...oh well I'll keep my yap shut...on to this record..well done lads...the band moves to Frisco the welcome mat of human rights punk rock...charging stuff,,right to the point...cept much as I hate cops,seems like killing them will only make humanity more oppressed particularly any type of underground movement that supports such a radical dogma but then it looks good on paper,and I love the way it sounds on plastic and I can sit and hide with my stereo and dream of armys of subversive baldies taking something or other by storm...but it's the men in black and white suits not cars that are really fucking us in the bleeding bunghole..."Millions Of Dead Politicians?"...."Millions Of Dead Plumbers"? "Millions of............

FAITH/VOID LP-Dischord Records
Our fellow indie label from the big town in the east do us again-Garsh if I give this one a bad review I won't be able to sleep on the floor at Dischord Haus ever again and watch those guys kill themselves,living off 7-11 sloppy joe turnovers and Big Gulp coke/dews...but I never lie and I don't have to cuz both sides have it...I'll spend my time on the less easily discerned because if you wanted my opinion you woulda asked for it and besides you all have this anyway...

THE MASTER TAPE-Compilation featuring TOXIC REASONS/SLAMMIES/BATTERED YOUTH/DELINQUENTS/ZERO BOYS/ARTICLES OF FAITH/REPELLENTS/LEARNED HELPLESSNESS/F.U.'S/THE PATTERN/DIE KREUZEN/Affirmation Records

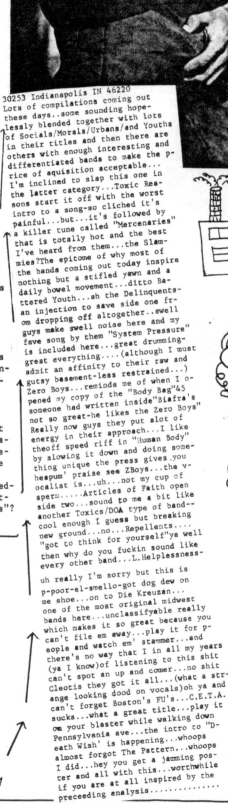

GUESS WHO????

30253 Indianapolis IN 46220
Lots of compilations coming out these days..some sounding hopelessly blended together with lots of Socials/Morals/Urbans/and Youths in their titles and then there are others with enough interesting and differentiated bands to make the price of aquisition acceptable... I'm inclined to slap this one in the latter category...Toxic Reasons start it off with the worst intro to a song-so cliched it's painful...but...it's followed by a killer tune called "Mercenaries" that is totally hot and the best I've heard from them...the Slammies?The epitome of why most of the bands coming out today inspire nothing but a stifled yawn and a daily bowel movement...ditto Battered Youth...ah the Delinquents-an injection to save side one from dropping off altogether..swell guys make swell noise here and my fave song by them "System Pressure" is included here....great drumming-great everything....(although I must admit an affinity to their raw and gutsy basement-less restrained...) Zero Boys...reminds me of when I opened my copy of the "Body Bag"45 someone had written inside"Biafra's not so great-he likes the Zero Boys" Really now guys they put alot of energy in their approach...I like the off speed riff in "Human Body" by slowing it down and doing something unique the press gives you heapum' praise see ZBoys...the vocalist is...uh...not my cup of sperm.....Articles of Faith open side two...sound to me a bit like another Toxics/DOA type of band-- cool enough I guess but breaking new ground...no...Repellents.... "got to think for yourself"ya well then why do you fuckin sound like every other band...L.Helplessness-

uh really I'm sorry but this is p-poor-el-smello-got dog dew on me shoe...on to Die Kreuzen... one of the most original midwest bands here...unclassifyable really which makes it so great because you can't file em away...play it for people and watch em' stammer...and there's no way that I in all my years (ya I know)of listening to this shit can't spot an up and comer...no shit Cleotis they got it all...(what a strange looking dood on vocals)oh ya and can't forget Boston's FU's...C.E.T.A. sucks...what a great title...play it ow your blaster while walking down Pennsylvania ave...the intro to "Death Wish' is happening...whoops almost forgot The Pattern...whoops I did...hey you get a jamming poster and all with this...worthwhile if you are at all inspired by the preceeding analysis...............

TOMMY LEE   VINCE NEIL   NIKKI SIXX   MICK MARS

 teen
Pin
up
no. ten

elektra

Great cover shot of Al Barile/SS Decontrol and friends fawning over a Seka poster. Seka was the fave porn star of punkers everywhere, and Al was/is one of P Rock's all-time good guys (as long as you don't use the word "Springa" around him!). Our last two issues were actually printed by Giant Printing in Arlington, Virginia, some Asians who didn't know any better (we were rejected by other printers, the story of my life). As I was driving home from the print shop, I was reading the issue while driving and crashed into a car stopped at a red light! Oops! Looking mighty slick now. Interview with Scream, one of DC's greatest and most unheralded units. Also features the greatest Minor Threat photo ever by Glen E. Friedman with Ian bearin' down so hard he may have bubbled in his seater, and judging from the look on Lyle's face, he did! The end was nigh for T & G and for the first wave of musclehead... It's hard to describe, but events were transpiring , and my mind-set and youthful exuberance for publishing were waning in a way that would soon make me step away from my beloved fanzine forever.

TOUCH AND GO

#21

THE SECRET DESIRES OF THE SEXIEST WOMAN IN THE WORLD!!

SS DECONTROL and FRIENDS...

Code of Honor

WHAT ARE WE GONNA DO?/WHAT PRICE WOULD YOU PAY?

Photo by Erich Mueller

Never desert your comrades in need,
In danger, or in trouble,
Never minimize your strength or power,
Never seek praise, approval, or sympathy,
Do not give or receive communication
Unless you yourself desire it,
Your self determination and honor
Are more important than your immediate life,
Never fear to hurt another
As long as it is in a just cause,
Be your own adviser,
Keep your own counsel,
Choose your own descisions,
Be true to your own goals,
Better to die than to live a lie.

new single $2.00

Fight or Die lp $5.00

from:

BETTER·TO·REIGN·IN

BIAH BIAH BLAH BLAND

...John Foster OP Mag

JUST A Thought...
A movie exists where a lady sticks her head up AN elephants Ass! Cool huh?

TOUCH and GO

COVER PHOTO...
GAIL RUSH
THE BOYS FROM BOSTON!!!

#21

T&G II

BOX 25305 WASH. DC 20007

YOUR EAST COAST—MIDWEST CONNECTION

TOUCH AND GO IS (supposed to be) PUBLISHED
EVERY COUPLE MONTHS.....................
EDITOR IN CHIEF--TESCO VEE
CONTRIBUTORS THIS ISSUE....JOHN SCHROEDER/
JOHN CRAWFORD/LEE ELLINGSON/JOE MC CREERY/
LYDIA AND ANNA/TODD SWALLA/WEE WEE+ COMIX/
PUSHEAD LAMORT/T. CALDWELL/SHANE WILLIAMS/
BYRON COLEY/1ESLIE CLAGUE/SHREDDER and all
else I forgot.....

Subsriptions
5.75 for 3 issues postpaid

LIVE REVIEW INSIDE!

GUN BLOWING UP LIGHTS

FLAMETHROWERS

KISS

BLUE FLASHPOTS

Touch+Go the mag that KEEPS you in tune with the tunes-on top of yer crotch—

Quote of the Month—
The same people who read OP are the same ones who thought the offense was great.
DS

Well welcome to the biggest bestest T&G yet..well ah hope anyways...took me too friggin long again but the old two job to pay the bills syndrome jus dont leave enough time for my beloved magazine... Since I have put out 20 issues at relatively low circulation I am debating a best of Touch and Go...by next issue I will have a better idea of what I want to do in that regard...needless to say I'll pick the most tasteless of stuff from the last 3½ years and put it all together with a smattering of new art and so on so folks like Jimmy J. who has all of em'll have ta snag one too...Please note the new PO BOX as the godamn guy at the other station gave me so much shit about all the packages...he's from India so on my last day I'm gonna scream...UNCLEAN!!! YOU FUCKIN' UNTOUCHABLE!!!!well..maybe I won't...anyway send all hate,love and stuff to my swell new big pull out drawer ...there's a couple new zines and a new record label here since last issue which is really cool...the scene here is smokin' hot these days with the spring thaw bringing on an onslaught of shows.. last weekend saw the GI's in probably their best performance in history...also Minor Threat with their gold lamea matching coats destroyed the Wilson Center.. One awesome show that also debuted Eric (00)'s new band as yet untitled...yet another band destined for stardom...anyway enjoy the issue.......Tesco..........

BIRTH DEFECT will be a cassette only project...any bands interested in participating contact Jeff H. 5417 Morgan So. Mpls Mn. 55419

I'm sure after reading T&G Forum there may be those of you who feel we are pulling a gang up on MaxR&R.. I don't necessarily agree or disagree with what is said by those who wrote in...I simply gave some anopportunity to speak their minds... I have nothing personal against any of the staff there...my conversations with them prove to me they are sincere i what they are doing and saying... I personally don't buy what they say-- and for them to lash back is too be expected...all i'm saying iseveryone should be free to express their views whether they be apolitical or otherwise...all I have to say is don't be a fuckin lizard on a log...if what someone has to say sounds like a workable philosophy then jump on it... There is no reason why anyone should have to hate because they disagree...

"Plastic Lip Service DISASTERS" -out NOW

HEAVEN
THAN TO SERVE IN

t+g forum (or against em' as it were)

Yesterday as I was plowing through the debut issue of Sierra Publications' excellent "Asshole" magazine I was overcome by the sickly sweet sensation of deja vu. A vast and stunning array of winkin'/blinkin' brown-eyes were staring me in the face, and 'though I was sure that I had never seen a display of bung-portals that was its equal, the sense of "having been there before" was unmistakable. Then it hit me; like a ton of fecal bricks. I had spied this many pouting sphincters before - sprayed up and down the contributors listing in "Maximum Rock & Roll". Assholes with red flags! Assholes with black flags! Assholes not afraid to let their freak flags fly! All their names were there for the world to see, and through their collective gaping flap has poured pile after pile of stinking bloody shit. Punk shit. Hippy shit. Shit. Shit. Shit.

Now, I may dig a little rea entry now and again, but that don't make me a shiteater; and in fact, now that I think of it, I guess ya could say that I'm not a dung fan at all. Nor am I a fan of dorks. Nor am I a fan of simps. And I especially hate anybody that trys to tell me what to do, say or think. It rankles me even more if it's some goddamn mealy-mouthed weako who's attempting to lay his plop-smeared rap on me in the name of "offering me some options", and this's just the sorta scam that the pipsqueaks at "MRR" are trying to pull. They fill their pages with the dogma of politically "enlightened" gimpsters like a Singapore peg boy fills his heinie with sailors' perfumed tube steaks. These elder statesmen wanna lay it all on the line for you. They wanna tell you just what this anarchy stuff's all about. They wanna get you in a dark room and show you slides of mushroom clouds while they rub their hands on your joint and murmur "War is bad" in your ear. They are crippled New Left gumbies who rode their little rubber horses to Berkeley when the Sixties collapsed of their own washed-out idiotic accord and they wanna PULL you down into the pot-suck Hell they call home.

In a letter to yours truly, Jeff "Gepeto" Bale and Tim "4-F" Yohannon hold the strings that wiggle the tongue of P-Rock's brown-nosed Pinnochio, Jello Biafra. Can you imagine 'fessing up to that? What's more, Bale goes on to state that Sacred Order and the Mentors suck. Not for any musical reason, mind ya, but because tunes like "Icky Bitch" are not possessed of suitably egalitarian sentiments. He passes the same verdict on Nig Heist's "Walking Down the Street" (a masterpiece in anybody's book), and compounds his stupidity further with the assertion that the Angry Samoans and the Meatmen have some dangerous right-wing tendencies. Who the fuck does this guy think he is? A commie version of my dad? This's exactly the same kinda crap old pop used to try to foist on me many moons ago. Look turd-boy, I spin disks for aggro and pleasure. If I wanted social commentary I'd watch the Superbowl. If I wanted some authority in my life I'd get my sweetie to tie me up. Ain't nobody gonna tell me that a song's no good 'cause its lyrics down espouse the party line; and if these fags are gonna try they better be ready for a fight. Fuck 'em, y'know?

Byron Coley
Santa Monica, CA

My case against Maximum Rock and Roll:

"What has two legs, hangs out on street corners, panhandles, sells dope, says 'That's cool man', is apolitical, anti-historical, anti-intellectual, and just wants to get fucked up and have a good time? A hippie? No, a punk!"

"Of course, punk now has a rapidly growing following, and it is perhaps inevitable that many of these newer people will be attracted by its superficial image, not its content. Thats where the media comes in. It's understandable that journalists from the corporate center or right would want to focus on the most negative aspects of the punk scene in order to undermine its potential for stimulating change, but it really hurts when the left reacts in defensive ignorance. The result of abandoning this vital cultural battlefield to the reactionaries could be disastrous. The example of NF -- the English skinhead phenomenon-- being manipulated by the National Front and British Movement should provide a dira indication of the dangers of such negligence."

Two great statements right? The second one, pompous as it is, claims that unless the burned out remnants of the sixties hippy left come and provide some sort of guidance and leadership for the punk scene it will fall into the hands of the Nazis. I mean punks are so dumb right? The first one, well besides being totally despicable strikes me as something you'd hear from some old time druggies trying to prove to themselves that young people are just as bad as they are. You'd figure the guys who wrote these statements have had absolutely no contact with punks, no knowledge of punks, or even the foggiest notion of what it is they are talking about right? But that can't be the case, because both of these gems come to us from the editors of Maximum Rock and Roll. "So what's the deal?" "Why are you bothering?" Nobody takes them seriously anyway, besides the magazine has a great record section.."

Good enough complaints against an article like this, but I'm chronically bored ok? Besides am I supposed to live in perpetual fear that somebody is going to say something mean about me if I dare to discuss unpleasant topics? Sounds like the kind of hell punk was supposed to get us out of.. Little town backstabbing and gossip are something I hate. I look down the rest of my life and all I see is constant bullshit., a guy has to pay them back once in awhile. Besides, Yohannon is a special case for me. When I was very young, growing up in NJ in the seventies, Tim Yohannon was the premier hippy of the entire state. He helped to found a magazine called ALL YOU CAN EAT..Copies are on file in th Rutgers Library in New Brunswick NJ if you don't believe me. I did volunteer work at state nuthouses that are filled to the brim with mad burnouts and cripples who believed that "LSd equals revolution" lie) If you ever get to see this mag, it is filled with sories about kids vs. pigs, pigs and drugs and how they won't let hippies take them, kill pigs fuck pigs, blah blah blah, and very little else, You see the editor is one of those folks who has made it his life's work manipulating kids for political purposes. He's the mummy from the time capsule. Back in the seventies the editors of all you can eat would never have dared fight the cops themselves

, but they sure as hell tried to get kids to do it for them. Today Dave MDC admits in the Xmas Flipside he isn't going to put any cops to the torch but also says he "wouldn't mind seeing others do it for him. Get the picture?

It's an old game, at the very least a new twist would have been nice...not this time. If you can ever find someone from the American radical movement and ask them about all this and they'll look at you like your nuts. Some of them are so paranoid they think punk was invented by the CIA,, to some of them this action is right up there withcradle snatching and man/boy sex clubs. The politics of Max R&R play right into the hands of the state, it's a fuckin' insult to a fellows intelligence. It's stupid.

OK, bigdeal, so who cares? Six Months and they'll be gone. I get letters from San Fransisco, even they say why bother, he's just a cranky old man. At least he puts good music on the radio, between the bullshit anyway. So I'll give you one. They don't need your love-just the appearance of your acceptance of them. Maximum R&R

has two purposes as i see it. One to give the appearance punk is under their control-that they have the power to make the scene do what they want. Two it makes them look like punk was their doing. our scene is alive-the sixties scene is dead or should be. I don't want to see punk turned into a media massacre, splashed all over TV, screamed about in the press as being made up of lunatics losers and those comitted to sensless vilence. Think about it. Think for yourself. Only fools fight for fools and die for nothing. Don't let yourself be used by people who manipulate and twist the facts. They speak in cliches and they think you are stupid. Fuck leaders. Fuck Manipulators.

John Tyson
NY, NY

Hey Tesco, Issue #20 is just as good as the others from your old place of residency. The new band interviews are great. But what really pisses me off is how you can say Husker Du suck shit. fuck. How many times have you seen them? They're fuckin' great. TSOL does suck somewhat, but not HuskerDu. In the hardcore scene you shouldn't be putting other bands down, there should be unity. Don't split the scene because that defeats the purpose of the scene. Another thing is why the FUCK did you make the teen pin-up #10 the Motely Crue? Their a fuckin bunch of longhaired goddamn freaks The type of music should be wiped off the face of theearth Jaff Hunting
Mpls, Minn
PS..Send some bands this direction. We need some out of state bands to get this area the boost in the arm it needs...
Jeff,,Being the opinionated ass that I am I don't usually lay back on the slams... Motley Crue suck yes, but the picture was worth a few belly laughs so I ran it... guess you didn't think so....ED

certain readers all wrote in and discussed the same topic so rather than respond individually I thought I'd run their letters and let vou decide...responsible replys welcome for next issue...

DOUBLE-O
5 SONG e.p.
OUT in MARCH
$2.50 P.P.
R&~~B~~DISCHORD

P.O.B.25054
WASH.,D.C. 2ooo7
make all checks payable to :
DOUBLE O

this tour also:Yes,*ce was not with them.
Instead,a new guy-Vinnie Vincent-played,who
was twice as good as *ce and looked just as
cool.The second song was"Detroit Rock City"
(The crowd went nuts)and then it was "Cold
Gin"-They went on hit after hit.If that
wasn't enough,they all got to do their own
solos.The coolest was when Gene did his,he
went onto the extension and started to puke
up blood.Then he would point to either side
of the stage and flame throwers would go
off-They went up a good 30 feet-I could
feel the heat from where I was sitting-not
to mention the stage was smoke-filled,and
the lights,and there were about 2 million
flashpots.Then the new drummer did his solo:
Again everyone left the stage,but this time
blue lights went on and so did the small
lights that were under each drum.So,then
the drum stand (gun turret) moved out onto
the stage and started turning side to side.
After about 5 minutes of severe drum poun-
din',the gun aimed up at the lights and,yes,
fired,blowing up one of the P.A. boxes and
a couple of lights.It then turned to the
other side of the stage and did the same.
Paul & Vinnie came out and did 5 minute solos each(Great,Fantastic,Cool,Jammin',Roc-
kin').

Throwers on the sides,100 Flashpots all
over,Big KISS sign,Smoke,Lights,Blue Flashpots along the front of stage and Gun-all
of these went off at the same time,ending
the KISS 10th Anniversary Show and the best
I've seen...................................GM

It's MUGGER!
proudly displaying
the tools of his
trade...(well 2 of
them any way)

photo-NAOMI
Peterson!

To start off,the Plasmatics opened(I hate
them).Their infamous Wendy O smashed a T.V.
(Boring),then was raised off the ground by
(Get this)a forklift truck(How cheap).They
were so boring-I had never heard any of the
songs before,but they all sounded familiar.
They even cut a fake "Strat" in half.Lucki-
ly,Brian brought an extra set of earplugs
with him,so I borrowed them-After that it
was alright.After that set by my fav. band
[Ho Ho],they started setting up the KISS
stage.To start with,the stage was made to
look like the front view of a tank.The ex-
tensions on either side of the stage were
the treads and the drum riser was the gun
turret-Yes,it moved back and forth & turned
left and right.They had a new guitarist

After they went offstage,they of course
were immediately called back on for an en-
core.Yes,they did "Love Gun" and went off
again,only to be called back on.They then
played(after throwing about 25 shirts into
the audience),get this,a 10 minute version
of "I WANT TO ROCK AND ROLL ALL NIGHT AND
PARTY EVERYDAY"(My fav. song apart from
"Detroit Rock City" and "Shock Me"),during
which Paul hurled a new Les Paul (Ha Ha)
at the stage,breaking the neck.He then of
course chucked it to the audience,who were
waiting like hungry dogs.The crowd sang a-
long(Fights,Rowdyism,Coolness)and at the
final cool moment at the end of the song,
they all got on top of the drum riser.It
then drove forward and started going side
to side blowing up things as before.How-
ever,on the final last note-the Flame

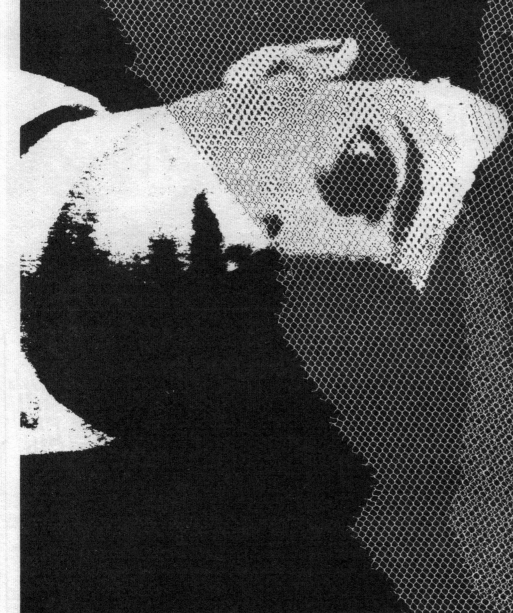

THE DANSE SOCIETY FANZINES

○ ○ ○ ○ ○ ○ ○ ○ ○

When and how was DANSE SOCIETY conceived?
DS:Before the Danse Society we were Danse Crazy..the bass player left and we got Tim. We have been TDS for about 2 years.
TV:From what I have gathered from write ups in the British press they would have you in the same category with a certain "new genre" of bands..what are your feelings in being listed with other bands such as 'Southern Death Cult' and 'Sex Gang Children'
DS:The reason the music press put us in this category is that they don't have the initiative to see us in our own right.All the new genre of bands have similar originality but not similarity in attitude and music..
TV:Would you consider your following a cult following?Are you searching for a 'mass' acceptance?DS:We don't mind who likes our music we are not searching for mass acceptance although we are not against it. TV:What is the inspiration for your songs lyrically and musically?DS:We all have different influences within our band,that is one of the reasons that our music cannot be compared with anything else,so we all write the music,we all put our own ideas into each song. TV:How is the club scene in England currently?Do you play out often? DS:We play quite often around England,about 12 dates every 2/3 months.Unfortun ately where the club scene was very good it is now deteriorating as people can no longer afford to go out as much as they used to. TV:Do you feel an affinity with any other European bands? DS:Not particularly.Not many European bands are well known in the country other than bands like DAF whom most of us like but I wouldn't go as far as to say we feel an affinity with them. TV:What are your musical backgrounds? DS:Steve and Gigsy(Paul Gilmartin)were in a futuristic band 'Y?' while Lyndon and myself(Paul Nash)were in a band (duo) called 'Lips-X' TV:Do you receive any indication of an American Audience? DS:Yes we have recently gotten quite a few letters from the USA which is surprising to us as we have no record distribution in the USA.
TV:Any desire to tour the US? DS:Yes when we have good record distribution and the demand has increased for us to play there-we will play. TV:What are your future plans?DS:To carry on in the form we have and perhaps to

do some soundtracks for films.
CONTACT THE DANSE SOCIETY ..
33 Finck St. London England SE1

Here be my list of fanzines with brief descriptions...if I forgot you sorry...thanx to all who have sent me zines'..if you did and I didnt reciprocate...write me and rag.....
In no particular order...
FORCED EXPOSURE-In my top 5 fave list,which I'll keep to myself so as not to swell any heads...this is seriously choice...$1.50 76 Bromfield St. Watertown,Mass 02172
REAGAN DEATH-I like this magazine because they are uncompromizing and arent afraid to take people to task..Great coverage of the Madison area...RD co Peter R.114 Gilman St #14 Madison,Wi 53703
THE TOILET-Coverage of the Milwaukee scene-no address listed
YOUR FLESH-Great coverage of the upper midwest scene-lot's of great photos..too bad about the cover..Peter &Ron co 1609 Lagoon #106 Mpls. Mi. 55405
CHAINSAW-Good overall coverage of the east and a good cross section of lots of different types of music Chainsaw Box 5356 Bethlehem Pa 18015
MAXIMUM ROCK AND ROLL- 4 iisues out in a very short time...also have a radio show that play all the underground hits..the political thing aint my bag..... alot of bands need this mag.. 6 issues $5 PO box 288 Berkeley,Ca 94701
END OF THE WORLD-Excellent in approach and execution...keep it up..634 W. Wisconsin Ave Suite #21 Milwaukee Wisc. 53203
RAW LEAKAGE-Of note is the great picture of the Effigies on this 2 pager..send a stamp 796 N. Lamont Dr. Cortland NY 13045
THRILLSEEKER-The first issue was thicker than a JC Whitney catalogue...brimming with goodness...besides the cover shot features Sky Stabb with his golden boy har'doo...get it.. new one?12515 Brewster Lane Bowie Md 20715
STRAIGHT EDGE-Issue 2 out by the time you read this...Abbie and Al are the best.... and their mag is great too...1850)Cean Ave 4D Brooklyn Ny 11230
SMAHED HITS-Pint size format packed with midwestern info and fun...I read it on the subway so the foreign people don't know why I'm laughing...2475 Normandy Dr. SE Grand Rapids Mich 49506
INSIDE VIEW-Hot photozine from Detroit.. Pics of all your faves...14887 Evergreen Detroit,Mich 48223
SUBURBAN RELAPSE-Has quietly worked its way into being one of the best anywhere...interviews from all over... Great exclusives that make me green.. This one has it...I ought to know..I've been reading these godamn things for 5 years now...PO BOX 610906 N.Miami Fl. 33161
Partyin' Press-All the fun thats fit to print from skating to (ugh)video games..send a stamp...box 457 Maumee Ohio 43537

CHURCH OF THE LATTER DAY PUNKS-Miss Carly..heart throb of many a rock hard stud has her say on a variety of topics...humorous,insightful..all you girls on the rah about participation support this...(and all you guys give her your $$ and maybe she will send you some ...uh..er..toys.. 611 Lawrence Ave Westfield NJ 07090
OP-Thick..literally and figuratively-no I'll be pleasant..such a noble effort deserves your support but I bang my dummy to a different drummer..mags

with personality..not clinical stodg-iness..they never review my thing here anyway...the editor thinks I'm sexist and racist..add him to the list...not only that they credit me with helping out on the south-western zine HEX who also fail to acknowledge my existence so likewise here...maybe if i do it for 3½ more years Foster will slap me on the buff puffs instead of labe-ling me and filing me away as so many left wingers seem to enjoy doing...box 2391 Olympia Wash 98507
VERSION TWO-THe first R Moore publication I've seen since Noise #7...Good job Bob..deserves a big hand for the Die Kreuzen Ep... a busy man and doing well in a thriving underground..Box 174 Xenia Ohio45385.....................
SICK TEEN-GO to a larger format Norb this thing is a pain in the bun to read...wouldnt bother me cept its worth reading!!708 St. Joseph St. Green Bay Wisc..54301

BLUR-Skinny zine from Kansas with well written reviews and a good perspective..PO BOX 3374 Lawrence Kansas 66044
ALTERNATIVE AMERICA-Save for Martin Rev this is dull..dull.. dull...how many people are going to wade through 5 pages of gaff from a walrus smack freak like Jeffrey Lee Pierce or the rest of this? I don't have time.... 814 ½ Massachusetts Lawrence Kansas 66044
TRULY NEEDY-Amillion pages thick and worth every cent,..covers wide range of music..new one out any time Box 2271 Rockville Md 20852
NEW BREED-One smokin hot new mag here...best new mag I've seen of late...lots of great pics..wild layout..get it palookas..c/o J.Clayton Ave. Charlotte NC 28205

SLAM-Another chaotic salty dog put out by a coupla roughnecks who dig muscle music...graphics from the Bowels of Satan...good for long stints on the stool for when my chronic colitus flares...882 Bank St.Akron Ohio 44305
TRIBAL NOIZE-I'll pass..529 E.13th St Apt 1C NYNY 10009
TENSION IN THE CATHEDRAL-Another thumbs up from the old man on this one-coverage of everything that is good in the punk rock kingdom...c/o Scott 156 Abbot Rd Concord NH 03301

CorrUGATED WHAT-Small no i mean tiny zine full of esoteric ramb-olo and assorted stuff...come on you closet peadophiles...order it c/o Lopsided 5 deforest lane Box 171 lagrangeville ny 12540
RIPPER-Smokin new issue has Batt-alion of Saints/Necros/and great exposure for new bands..also good interview with the Fuck Ups...get this for your frisco news... 1494 Teresita Dr. San Jose Ca 95129

VIOLENT APATHY

you once belonged

TOUCH and GO

↓↓↓↓↓↓
SEND All
discs, mags,
semi-nude photos-
(femmes only
por fAvor)
to BOX 25305
WASH, DC
20007

NOISE FROM NOWHERE

-PUSHEAD ©

$3 POSTPAID
TOXIC SHOCK   BOX 242 POMONA CA 91768

SEVEN INCH RELEASE
WITH

KENT STATE

MODERN INDUSTRY

MOSLEM BIRTH

MANSON YOUTH

OUT NOW! ON
☠ TOXIC SHOCK Records

DISTRIBUTED BY SYSTEMATIC & FAULTY

NOISE FROM NOWHERE t-shirt $7 postpaid. Pushead artwork in black & red on
white shirt. Available in small, medium and large only. HUGE MAIL-ORDER
catalog sent FREE with each order or send 50¢ for postage

LIVE POOP

BLACK MARKET BABY/UK SUBS at the 9:30
A snowy Sunday nite and Black Market
is back on track...great,but I liked
the old guitar player better,,,this
guy is wimpy and looked scared shit-
less...his guitar comes unplugged and
I thought he was gonna shit..but what
can you say about Boyd?He's the best
front man and belts out the tunes with
commentary to boot..like"Lets get going I've gotta be up for work at 6:30..
It's good to see one of the areas best
bands back on track...now I'm not one
to froth over Uk bands as a rule but
the SUBS kicked my ass from here to
bunfuck...showman who know how to incite the crowd...even the slow tunes
came off hot...by far and away the
best UK band I've ever seen...made
Discharge look like they didnt know
point #1 about a live performance..
Charlie Harper still brimmed with energy even though he has to be 39 and
Nicky Garrett is one smokin axe man...
Hot...hot...hot,...

        Been a partyin' scene out this
way dude.Friday the 3rd we were out to s-
ee the rumored V.A. new lineup debut.In
the new Lansing tradition since the CRU-
CIFUCKED have appointed themselves scene-
masters,things were spectularly uncertain.
Anyway the show was supposed to be at some
house by the Crest Drive In(Owned by a
"hippie anarchist no doubt,ED)WE passed
the Crest and blew a tire turning around.
Then(read carefully) we decided to pull
up under the canopy at the Crest so we
could change the tire out of the rain.
Turns out it was an exit and they have
the prongs designed to destroy the tires of anyone who tries to sneak in the
back..you guessed it.We ended up getting
the car towed and the tires patched and
then we drove home.Turns out the show
never happened 'cause one of the Crucifucks was working or something.So...
we drove all the way to Lansing just
so we could eat breakfast at Sambos
in GR. ya..its true the CRUCIFUCKS are
going off the emotional deep end..the
process has been germinating for some
time but somehow we're still taken aback by its force...Scott(bassist)turn-
ed the petulant little kid after John
defaced his MDC graffiti and wrote"IG
NORANT APPROACH" I'm sudienly sick of
it all the same way I'm sick of Articles
Of Faith-it's hard listening to a band
after you realize their a bunch of ass-
holes-approach before execution..later..-
                        Craig T.
                        Grand Rapids Mi

NECROS/BIG BOYS/NEGATIVE APPROACH/THE
FLESH COLUMNS atGraystone Hall Detroit
Jan 8th....Another cool hall show.this
wasn't as packed as the night before but
people really can't afford to dish out
8 dollars a weekend so that's understandable...but there was a good size crowd
of about 250 people.The Flesh Columns are
a new young band from Windsor,and they w-
ere really great.Very catchy songs here.
By the way they are a trio,2 guys on gui
tar n bass and a girl on drums who is really very good.It's cool to see girls doing something other than vocals.They were
fairly well received but it could have be-
en better,still...watch for them in the
future.NA were totally amazing.They opened with an untitled new song,and I myself think it is their best song to date.
They also played most of their EP and other new stuff like "I'll Survive" and "Friend or Foe?"Great set.Big Boys were next
and were as good if not better than the
night before.Except this night they did
their hit cover of "Hollywood Swingers"
which came across great live.We(Necros,ED)
Played also..we even did three new songs.
This was great show all in all,I had fun..
                        TODD SWALLA

T.Caldwell

461

THE ALLIED

Oh ya the line up goes...DOUG-VOCALS
PETE-GUITAR...BUD-DRUMS...MICK-BASS
WRITE THE ALLIED AT 818 CADIEUX
GROSSE POINTE MI 48230

HARASSMENT

Unsaid words are always heard
An excuse to start a fight
unknown reasons always exist
To violate our rights
Never knowin what we've done
To cause such a response
Never knowin what to do
or what it is they want
    Harassment from the police
    Harassment from our peers
    Unprovoked Harassment
    Harassment cause of fear
Always doing something wrong
But wrong in whose eyes?
Always gettin shit from people
And there's just one reason why
Knowing we're outnumbered
Knowing that we're few
Knowing that if we had to fight
That we could never lose
    Harassment from the police
    Harassment from our peers
    Unprovoked harassment
    Harassment cause of fear

LEAVE MY LIFE ALONE

They take my money and where does it go
It goes to somebody that I'll never know
They send me to school put me in a seat
and even if i don't learn I'm off the street
Leave my life alone
Leave my life a-lone-lone-lone
They got their policeman to keep me in line
And if I step out I'll be doing time
They'll put me in the army to fight their war
But I won't know what I'm fighting for
Leave my life alone
Leave my life alone-lone-lone

THE ALLIED were interviewed sometime in Dec. during their recent visit to the nation's capital....
TV:So fill me in how the scene is in Detroit now that I'm out of touch...
Doug:It's getting better now,there's like more new bands like the DISPLACED and FATE UNKNOWN,both great bands..there's a new band called the AFFILIATED are going to be really good..it's like the same faces at every show,there's like not that many new people coming..
Pete:At last nite's show there were alot of new really young kids...TV:But you don't see alot of the people from the Freezer days?Bud:The reason alot of the people don't go now is because the Clubhouse doesnt have a name like the Freezer did,so I guess the clubhouse isn't popular enough which is a stupid reason not to go to a show...TV:So none of the new bands never get to play the city club? Pete:The City Club aint booking hardcore shows lately,they were getting labeled as a hardcore club so alot of their new wave people wouldnt come..
Doug:They book a big show like Discharge on a Thursday night and they wonder why people dont come you know..so they say we're not making any money off those bands so we're not going to book them..
Mick:They don't even give any local bands like a Friday or Sat. night..
Bud:The only other bar giving bands a chance is Paychecks..TV:So is there alot of fights still?Doug:alot of that has died down like sure some drunk asshole comes and starts something then ya ther'll be a fight...then there's this stuff putting down the people into OI in the midwest now saying their trying to break up the scene and all that stuff..TV:Ya and I suppose I'm as guilty as anyone about spreading that(in reference to comments made in Forced Exposure I was talking shit to label and discredit the actions of a few on one particular

nite...yes i said things I shouldnt have and if i stepped on anybody's Doc Martins please accept my apologies,ED)Pete:Alot of those kids are really diehards and go to every show..Doug:They pay for every show,they put out magazines..TV:So what

happened as far as personnel changes? Pete:Rob Michaels was singing for us... Doug:At first we started out with me on vocals and this guy named spike on bass but he was more interested in going out with this girl than practising,so we sacked him,and I decided I wanted to go back to bass playing so we got Rob(ex of Bored Youth,ED)and the band was going again but then we found out Rob was going to college...so he goes off to college in Ann Arbor and leaves us with nothing so I decided to go back to singing and Bud: Mick came to the rescue...TV:So are you planning on recording and putting out a record?Pete:Ruthless Records wants to us out on their label..we're recording a demo with David Rice 2 weeks from now.. TV:So you would lay claim to an English influence overall as far as songwriting and such?Doug:It's just that me and Pete, that's mostly the kind of music we listen to,and when we write it comes through in our music.Pete:We've never tried to write a song and make it sound English..(talk here about the progressions of the scene in Detroit from the Bookies/nunzios stage through the Freezer and on to the Clubhouse)Pete:The Clubhouse is great for new bands like there was a show in Friday and there was like 6 new bands...(discussion here concerns Chicago and the difference between the over and under 18 crowds...) Doug:I said something like "Chicago doesn't deserve the EFFIGIES and this chick and this guy overheard me and bitched... TV:When a band gets to a certain point it seems the young kids always find cause to write them off..tsk..tsk...

T&G EDITORS' WANT LIST-if yall own any of these discs and want to score a healthy profit drop us a line...
1)SLEEPERS-(1st EP)
2)AVENGERS (1st EP on red or greenwax)
3)THROBBING GRISTLE-"HEATHEN EARTH"(on
4)SATAN'S RATS 45   blue)
5)PURE HELL 45
6)GENERATION X (mis-press)
7)MISFITS-"HORROR BIZ"(ON BLACK)
8)SNIVELLING SHITS EP
9)
10)LURKERS-FREE ADMISSION 45(on red)
11)BIRTHDAY PARTY"Nick The Stripper"(7")
12)999(78 rpm single)
13)THROBBING GRISTLE "UNITED"(clear)
14)SCREAMIN'MEE MEES 45s
15)SPK-early aus.45's)
16)MODERN ENGLISH-"DROWNING MAN45)
17)VIRGIN PRUNES-A NEW FORM OF BEAUTY"
(parts 2 and 3 ..10" &12")
18)VILETONES"LOOK BACK IN ANGER"45
19)LEATHER NUN CASSETTE(Industrial)
Top cash paid..all should be with picture sleeve...drop us a line...

SCREAM

TV:So are you guys pleased with how your LP turned out?
ALL:Yup..Pete:Only one mistake,on one song..I don't know if it was when they mastered it or what...Skeeter:It drops out for a split second and then comes back...one bad thing was the drum sound.. Pete:The sound coming out of Don's now is incredible..but the drum sound still needs to be louder...TV:So is this the first band for all of you guys?All:Ya.. So you've been together about..All:3 or 4 years..Skeeter:It took us a while to sort of get into the scene..the 1st time people heard us they weren't sure what we were trying to do Pete:We played the first Wilson Center show..Skeeter:And the crowd naturally rejected us because we were outsidersTV:Werent cool or something?Pete:At that time there was alot of that...and we werent as good then either..Skeeter:I think we were good but we were pretty lackadaisical(SP?!!) and Pete would be the only person really into it,but now were alot more veritile..I was pretty nervous if there was more than fifty people,because we were used to playing partys..Pete:We were still developing our sound and the Georgetown thing was a small crowd..the punk scene was small..Kent:And most of the punks come from Maryland and stuff.. TV:So you were grits huh?Pete:I saw this magazine at Ian's house called Capital Punishment that reviewed Black Market Baby and they called Scream "a bunch of jocks trying to be punk"...that basically was the attitude at the time...Skeeter: It was like Md and DC were united..there were a few people that really liked us.. we didnt spike our hair and we wore tennis shoes and not boots..we use this term boxed in and boxed out..you know the hippies,grits...Pete:Where we lived we started out playing parties and there were big crowds..but we still played our own music..we listened to the Sonics and that's how we learned how to play-listening to these old sixties songs... Skeeter:We had a great time..the hippies didnt like us because we were too fast and the punks didnt like us because we

wouldnt fit their image...we werent total thrash we were like melodic thrash.. Skeeter:We always had a 'throw it in your face style..like we might start off with a heavy metal song..Kent:we were all influenced by the Bad BrainsSkeeter: With me it was more like Hendrix...the stuff I hear in my head that I want to play is more like Hendrix..all of us write our own songs,even though Pete is like the master brain for writing..we try to throw him ideas so he doesnt have to do it all himself..it might sound stupid but I like to have three changes in each song..they dont even have to be chord changes or key changes but like climactic changes...TV:So how did they react to you out west...?Pete:It went real good,I was surprised..we all had a great time(all in the same truck? TV:No not the midwest I mean the west coast..Pete:Oh that we had a good time but it was a financial disaster..we just went out there..kind of a slipshod setup..Skeeter:We just wanted

to see what was happening out there... Pete:The best times we had was playing parties..we played one in Santa Cruz and one in Monterey..Skeeter:I like playing where the people are eye to eye and they're trashing all about you..you function better because its a person to person thing..TV:So what show was better in the mid west Detroit or Kalamazoo...All:Detroit...Skeeter:Kazoo was great..the scene is bigger in Detroit more established,,and Kalamazoo was more like just starting out...it was cool Violent Apathy played and what was that other band.. TV:The Virrelles? ALL..Ya..people didnt like em'..Skeeter:I like Violent Apathy-the lead singer makes it..TV:Kenny?He's the best!!(talk here about the early years as Skeeter gets nostalgic about getting a Strat and Franz instructing him inits use)Skeeter:When I was in school they used to call me a frock...cuz I was a jock and I used to smoke pot..ALL.YA WE'RE ALL FROCKS TRYING TO BE PUNK!!!!!Skeeter: Ya as soon as we got into this..like nobody at our school was into the music-we were actually playing at beer blasts-people would get so drunk they would almost start to get into it...even though the backs of their minds they were hating it..Franz:It was blind enthusiasm..

Everyone would get slushy drunk..when we would play there would be no place to sit down so everyone would have to stand up and Pete would just run and jump into people..Kent:Antagonize em'..Skeeter: Someone would be just about to drink a beer and there would be these girls that were made up and their lipstick and mascara is all running...Franz:We created something they'd never seen before..they started to understand it..TV:This was what about 2 years ago..Pete:Ya about the time TEEN IDLES were starting.. . TVSo what was your reaction when you saw them?Kent:I thought they sucked...the bass player sucked..All:yuks!!!Skeeter: Ian don't pay attention to that..... one string and one finger I thought it was great!!!To me Ian was like the fastest bass player cuz I hadnt seen the bad BrainsFranz:well when we saw the Teen Idles we were just as close minded as the punks were about us at the time...Skeeter:I thought they were just getting into the fuck this and that an d they made it a point to be so belligerant...the guitarist would like throw his guitar out into the crowd.. and hit people..I wanted to kill.. but after awhile you know I listened to their stuff on Flex Your Head and realized what they were trying to do.. Kent:I thought the Untouchables were good...Skeeter: Ya back then SOA were cool too..the Enzymes were the big band-they were the first HC band with two guitars.. (Conversation turns back to west coast and their aborted interview) Pete:How'd you hear about it?TV:I think it was John Stabb..Skeeter:Yohannon asked me what I though slamming was about..you know I could have made up some thing about how hard it is..the day to day struggle...but instead I said I don't try to hurt anybody...its more or less having fun..What it reminds me of is

this game called "Smear The Queer"when we were kids Pete:He asked Skeeter like what was slamming all about and Skeeter said its like this game called "Smear The Queer" and then Yohannon said.. "Well...thank you very much" Scream: (Laughter)Skeeter:No here were his

exact words "And with that closing statement"....Kent:He said "What does that mean?Pete:We shouldnt have done the interview like we did it with GI and us...we had a great time fuckin' around but...the next day he said to me "Look if I wanted interviews like that I could just go to any rock and roll bar..."He wants bands that come up there and make political statements which I'm willing to do anytime if he wants to sit down and talk politics, but it was an interview with 2 bands-we were having a good time,we were answering all his questions..and when Skeeter answered that question I guess he just got a bad attitude...I guess he's got alot of gay friends..Skeeter: Later I went back to him and said to him what kind of game it was..Pete:He tried to explainto Skeeter some psychological rap like his parents taught him was Queer was someone who wasnt right and he said "What if it was "Smear The Nigger?" Skeeter:I was about ready to rip his nose off...

_____

_____

Franz:Here we are at Tesco's bird sanctuary....(discussion on various topics) Pete:We used to have lots of trouble with the Faifax County police,I guess they had nothing else to do except bust up parties.. There are always cops who'll abuse their power but there's more that don't,you have to respect them for that...(conversation drifts to matinee violence)Pete:In New York it's like kill...I like playing up there cuz we get reactions like we used to get here...alot of em make fun of us....... DROP SCREAM A LINE....................

SREAM...
PO BOX 4965
FAllS CHURCH, VA 22044-0965

FAITH

photo L.CLAGUE

die kreuzen

TV' HOW DOES DIE KREUZEN VIEW THE WORLD?

KEITH: Someplace to live. If you want something, you have to work for it. Its not easy.
ERIK: Nothing will get done if you don't do it yourself.
DAN: Fucked up-people don't give a shit anymore. Newspaper haedlines read murders, wars, and sensless violence everyday

TV WHATS THE SCENE LIKE IN MILWAUKEE?
KEITH: There's more people than before.
E:People are a lot more supportive of what we do than, say, a year ago.
K:More people are getting bands together and doing things instead of just talking about it. Its to bad that we don't have anyplace to play now that Nikos is fucked...
D: Who cares about that place, kids can't get in anyways and half the scene is the kids.
K: There's a real lack of trendy people, which is great. People are doing what they want.
E: They're doing what they want instead of being afraid of what others will say or think.

TV WHAT WAS THE INSPIRATION FOR THE TITLE"COWS AND BEER"?
HERMAN: 'Cause everyone stereotyped Wisconsin or the midwest in general as being nothing but cows and beer.
D: That about sum that up!

HOW DO YOU SEE THE SCENE IN YOUR AREA AS OPPOSED TO OTHER AREAS?
E:Healthy
K:People come to all the shows.
H: Everyone around here knows what its about, they have something to do with it.
K:It requires commitment, and we have it.
E:there's a lot of input, people putting on shows, supporting us and others; Photographers, DJ's, everyone helps out.
H:Keeping the price down on shows and records helps a lot too.
K:More honest people, less leeches.
D:our scene is small, but it's very healthy.
E: People work together more.

TV HOW DID THE DEAL WITH VERSION SOUND COME ABOUT?
Husker Du had told us about "Charred Remains", and a few days later, we saw the add for it in NOISE. We answered it and Bob Moore said "Sure die kreuzen can be on Charred Remains" and he also asked us if we would like to do a record and split the costs with him, so we said ya! A year or so later;Ta da!! Cows and Beer!

TV WHAT IS THE BASIS FOR YOUR SONG WRITING?
K:It just comes out , we just sit there and do it. We think up parts and put them together.
E:Sometimes it takes a lot of work to fit the parts together.
H:Its gotta be fresh!
D:Its gotta please us.

TV WHAT ARE YOUR FEELINGS ON THE CURRENT STATE OF THE HARDCORE SCENE?
K:There are millions of bands playing now...
E:I think its really great.

D: Yeah, more people are into it.
K: People don't dismiss it anymore like they used to, they take it more seriously
D: There's more bands and more records every day
K: Everyone is really supportive. You can come from out of town and people are cool, lots of people helping each other out, like the Huskers.
E: We've gone as far as we have because a lot of people helped us out;now its our turn to help others. We're doing what we can.

WHAT SETS DIE KREUZEN APART?
K: We have good, well constructed songs.
E: We're not the typical skinhead or whatever type of band with our fists in the air screaming "revolt,revolt", people take you at face value and we don't want that face. We don't want to get labled.
D: When you labla something it becomes catagorized, and when you catagorize something you've gotten to the first step in ignoring it.
E: I think I read that somewhere...
H: We don't say we hate this so you should hate this...
K: Yeah, we just want people to think for themselves.
H: We want people to be aware of what's going on around them.

WHERE HAVE YOU PLAYED OUTSIDE OF YOUR HOMETOWN?
Chicago/ Minneapolis/ Columbus Ind./ New Berlin at Rock City!/ Madison/Indianapolis/ Rockford Ill.

IS THIS THE FIRST BAND FOR ALL OF YOU?
YES! We used to be cakked the Stellas, but die kreuzen has always had this lineup

FUTURE PLANS?
E: go to work tomorrow morning.
H: I hope I have a job tomorrow!
E: Get our record repressed, work on west and east coast tours, new recordings, help out local bands and bands that are just starting and live happily ever after.
ALL: Ha Ha Ha

Photo by Ron Schneider

9 SONG CASSETTE TAPE
PLUS LYRIC SHEET
SEND $.200 FOR THE TAPE
AND $.75 FOR POSTAGE

TO: DIE KREUZEN
634 W. WISCONSIN AVE #21
MILWAUKEE WI. 53203

da NIG HEIsT

start my own band called the Steve Corben Combo with me on guitar, Dez on bass and Spot on drums.
T:Whats' the future for the NH?
M:Well we got rid of our other guitar player.He was just a flake. we're gonna do our European tour. Thermidor kicked us off their label because we we'rent arty enough for them On "walking Down the Street" we were mor into an art thing.

SK"The band has to branch out into a more general audience to reach more people with their message. M:Our new release is gonna be out on SST/Cock-Sure records.
T:All stolen material.
M:Only one cover that Lou Reed song.
T:You do the writing?
M:It comes foom all over,but I write most of the songs,Dave has problems with premature ejaculation..T:How many times

can you come in a day??
D:Around here not too often.That's why we've got the band.
T:Any final words?
D:Nig Heist comes in your mouth,not in your hands..

Write these studs C/o SST Records PO BOX1 LAWNDALE,CA 90260

M:MUGGER (SINGER)
T:T&GO
D:DAVE (BASS)
SK:SYLVESTER "CHUCK"KING-(ROADIE)
S:SPOT
P:PICKLES (BAND MASSEUSE AND GURU)
M:Wow look at Dave's new Van Halen shirt.
P:Ya and dave's new Nig Heist pants.
T:I guess it pays to be image concious.
M:Yeah and it only costs 25¢
D:I paid it myself.Is that dedication or what?
M:Dez is the drummer,Dave's bass,Spot plays guitar when we play in LA.
D:And clarinet too.T:I thought Spot was booted.D:He was gonna sue us for kicking him out.
M:And he kinda gives good blow jobs Spot comere and tell us why you got kicked out of the Nig Heist.
T:What is the Nig Heist anyway?
D:It's the movement of the 80's..
P:It's the new religion
D:Going back to the primal urge so to speak,Mugger could you elaborate?
M:I could demonstrate.We're just into like.. you want me to point(digit to Pickle crotch) We just started a band cause Black Flag scored all the girls.Me and Dave thought if we started our own band and toured,with BF that we could release lotsa tension on tour.Be able to be good workers.D:Better workers.Up our product-ivity.
T:What was the original line up?
M:We recorded something for CHUNKS a long time ago and that was Spot on guitar..Merrill on bass.And the guitar player from the Mau Maus played/drums.We recorded it live in the studio.T:Did you guys play out like that?
M:Yeah,there was a place down the street from the Vex called Stage one and that was our debut/gig.I'm really insecure so it was hard for me to sing for the first time but these guys all talked me into it.Our first real gig-Dez played guitar(that's when he was still sjnger for BF)Spot played gtr and Billy from the D-escendents played drums.
P:It was a well thought out thing.
M:No Robo has too much class.
T:So you never had the Sex God in your ranks?
P:Muggers the new sex god for the 80's.
T:You mean Mugger's the Robo of the 80's?
M:Hey when Robo cross countrys he's got gro-upies piled in the air..
T:So do you guys always play with BF?
M:Mostly.
T:Obviously there are other select dates such as your good friends the Tolling Mi-dgets.DThat was our arty gig.
T:I was waiting for your slide show.
D:We were gonna show it on Boone's stomach but he started jumping up and down.

M:Our in connection for that show was that our old guitar players girlfriend's the lead singer in Twisted Roots.So we had the connect-ion with the New Wave scene.Now he's not our guitar player any more.He;s in the Circle Jerks.He sold out Nig Heist to be in the CJ's That's OK.
T:Another alumnus kicked downstairs huh?Don't any of them mo e up the ladder of success?
D:How could they top the Nig Heist?It's like Billy,then on top with the Nig Heist.The group es have the same pattern.First they go out with the Descendents,then BF,then they move up to the Nig Heist.
T:I was wondering about your influences.In write ups I've seen bands like Creedence Clearwater,Television and Pere Ubu get mentioned alot.
M:No we're really into this band called Husker Du.Those guys are just god in my book.
D:Basically they're an inspiration to me.
M:They all sing but I'm really into the dr-ummer.He really gives good blow jobs for a guy,his size.I'm really into Grant's hemmeroids, they aren't as big as Spot's bu they'll do.. before Spot popped his anyway..
T:What's the philosophy behind the Nig Heist?
D:You mean our message?We don't have a message. but we have a feeling we want to get across.A feeling we want to share with 50% of the audi-ence.M:No it's about 30% of the punk audience.
D:No actually about 5% of the audience.
T:You guys thought of doing any of those ladies only shows at Chippendales?
D:Yeah but it says fashionable attire recomen-ded and we can never get in.
M:Our message to the world is that we think people should splooey more.It's releasing your load.That's our message to the world. People should just calm down and get some poo-ntang even though I'm asexual.
T:Any plans for a big Nig Heist tour?
D:Well we may be going on a tour of Europe next week and we're taking BF and the Minutemen with us.
T:I was wondering when you recorded that last record?
M:See that Panasonic?That's the Nig Heist's port-able studio.It's one of Spot's ingenious schemes.
S:Yeah we recorded that at Total Access Studios.
T:Who plays guitar on that?
M:I do.Spot played drums and one of spots groupies played bass.
S:Hey lets get the story straight.
None of yoy guys can play.It's all tapes.
D:People think we actually play.We fool em/Actually we don't fool em.
S:Ya some guy in SF figured out its all done on tapes.It's like their smarter up there since Grace Slick gave birth to God.
M:It doesnt matter though cause those guys have oversplooeyetation.That comes from splooing too much over a long period of time.

S:You get dry.
M:Ya that's why the NH is so powerful. We got all this drive going from being asexual.T:Whose idea was the NH?
M:A long time ago when i was a punk rocker I hadda friend named Eugene. He's a half black,half white guy and he always used to steal cigarettes from me and despised me calling him a "nig" so I started calling him a "Nig Heist" And our first concept was to just steal all our songs,kinda like what the Circle Jerks did with their first LP.We were gonna steal "Police Story" from Black Flag. S:We stole all their equipment in-stead.T:I noticed that your version of "Here She Comes" makes a powerful anti drug statement..are the Nig Heist straight edge? D:Only 15 minutes at a time. M:We were into Straight Edge for awhile cause it seemed like the scam for broads.But we still went in the bathroom and smoked and drank.
S:I despise drugs of all kinds.
M:We're all straight cock.
D:I wanted to talk about Muggers' alcoholism problem.When we first started he useta get really plastered when we'd go on stage.His manager dr-ove him to it.
M:My manager was Raymond Pettibon.
D:He'd go to get him groupies and come back with little boys instead of little girls.
S:He couldn't tell the difference.
T:Has your success rate been better since NH began? D:Our success rate hasnt started yet.We'll see when we go on tour.
M:When we get back we're gonna book some gigs!D:We don't want people to have to pay to see us cause we never accept money for gigs. M:Yeah but we may have to cause we're supporting Merrell to go to art school.He's gonna be a big actor one of these days and he's gonna support us all so we're supporting him through Cal arts.
T:Who has the biggest cock in the band?
M:Ego wise or actual size?
T:Actual size.
M:She should know.
P:I havent seen them all..between M-ugger and merrill.M:What?
P:Are you talking about circumference or length?
T:Weight.
M:I would say Dez.Because this girl in Chicago gave us all blow jobs and she kept giving them to Dez.She told us he had the biggest cock.
T:I've heard you guys are veering off in a beatnick ot jazz direction?
D:Yeah well we have a progressive song called "Surf Board" where Spot plays clarinet. M:I was going to

PICS
UP
DA
BUNGER

CRUCIFIX

When it came out, or should I say by the time Universal put it out, our sound was totally different. Plus they did just about everything else totally backwards and never put out a second pressing. Our second record was independent 'cos we have found out that the only ones who can do things right is ourselves and consequently we were very happy with our single. TV:What is your opinion of US punks critical of so called "Limey Clones" ie punks who dress and act more like their UK counterparts? CF:For one punk is meant to be an individual thing and any punk should be able to look any fucking way he or she wants. The other thing is how is how

many US punks know what UK punks act like anyhow. It's a totally different thing. Chris our drummer once said "Crass and Discharge are our favorite bands-it's not because they're british, it's because they have the most to say"...TV:So do you think the world is doomed? CF:No, if everybody cares enough about our earth and themselves and they stand up and work for peace.. and make nuclear disarmament the most important cause.."War is so easy, peace is so hard"...TV:How have your out of town shows gone? Any plans to tour the country?? CF:We have played up and down the west coast and most of the time to favorable reaction. LA is really good and we still do fairly well in S.F. We should be touring the country in April and May.. from here to the east coast and back..TV:Any future plans? We hope to put out an album tour the world and release other bands on Freak Records
ANARCHY, PEACE, LOVE AND FREEDOM
                    CRUCIFIX 1983
(write PO BOX 331 San Fransisco, Ca 94101

TV;What is the state of the SF scene currently? CF:Not much is happening in SF proper-alot of bands are coming from the suburbs. Many are becoming more politically involved-which is good. Some of these bands are P.L.H., TRIAL, GRIM REALITY, and EXECUTIONER......... TV:Do you feel more of an affinity with the UK or US scenes? CF:As far as politics go we pay more attention to world politics than anything else. We are much more concerned with the threat of war which would involve all countries i.e. in a nuclear war the entire world as we know it would cease to exist. As far as US or UK politics go, of course we would

have to say we feel more of an affinity with US politics because this is where we live. And what the people in power are saying is what is affecting us every day of our lives. TV:Bands from the bay area generally seem to be of a more political bent-why do you think this is so? CF:We think this is so because the Bay Area in general is very politically active and this has always seemed to bleed over into the punk community. There are alot of liberals in our area, and because of this we almost always have conflicting politics with the rest of the country. Basically this is a big influence over the punks in general...TV:Were you happy with your 12"? Any particular reason your second record is independent? CF:No we were quite unhappy with our 12"

MEATMEN/FU'S/SS DECONTROL/NECROS/MINOR THREAT at the VFW hall in Boston......... Hows this for a bill? This has to rank up there with the best gig ever...since me and the boys went on first there wasnt a helluva lot of motion but there was no doubt that Boston is where the MM were most appreciated which proves what an intelligent scene they've got..tee hee...FU's were great..furious spasms of gut crunch and the crowd went nutso...when I just hear the name SS DECONTROL I sneer and my pecks swell in anticipation...the godamn lights for the video cameras made the power go off so there was only time for 6 or 7 songs but they still proved they are capable of total domination at the drop of a hat..(their new 12" is also awe inspiring) Fuck everyone..Springa's voice is unbeatable...his scorched bellowing is the best I've heard since Dez retired to guitar.. A band with a real message and if they fuck with your mind and body then I say great... NECROS now display a take charge steamshovel approach ...from the pounding sludge intro of "Andy's Shit For Brunch" to one of my personal new faves "Count Me Out" they played a great set...We all must admit it too.. Todd Swalla is the best drummer in the punk rock kingdom...sorry but as much as I love Minor Threat this wasn't the night..which still means they were better than most bands...it's just that I put them on such a pedestal that anything short of a million percent doesnt cut it...the sound just wasn't there...anyway we all had a great time seeing all the cool Boston Crew---we can't wait to go back...with our hot new band that is.....TV(thanx to Nancy and Al for the hospitality...)

471

SS DECONTROL
SSD

NEW SEVEN SONG
12" RECORD

"GET IT AWAY"

OUT MARCH 1

X CLAIM! records

NO. 3

472

Die KREUZEN-"COWS AND BEER" EP
Release #2 on the Version Sound label and a teeth sinker it is..I'm t-
aken aback again at the originality
and overall awesomeness of this com-
bo--with more and more generic crud
turning so called hardcore into nothing more than a pointless re-hash-
here's one bunch who are riding above
it all with solid ideas in tempo,ch-
anges and overall instrumentation...
The guitarist from one Midwestern
aggregation was overheard as saying
"That guitarist is so good it's depressing"...blows my ass to kingdom
cum....Po Box 174 Xenia,Ohio 45385

ARIZONA DISEASE-"Jr. Chemists"/"Les Seldoms"
Subterranean...A side is song about building
a fort ...ok strange and pubescent...no dull
and not worthy of anything...next "Spooky
Cooties" Drum voice and guitar..cutesy playful..simplistic...shitty...the B side is
worse...sorry....912 Bancroft Way Berkeley
Ca 94710

THE DANSE SOCIETY-"SOMEWHERE"/"HIDE"
Society Records
To say that this or any other DS record is their best would be misleading,
and a disservice to their previous efforts..let's just offer up "Hide" as
one of the most bone chilling drivers
of this or any season...a mixture of
the heady,the gutsy,the infectious...
all I can say is they have been one
of my fave bands for the last year
with no end in sight................

THE MARCH VIOLETS "GROOVING IN GREEN"/
STEAM"...,Merciful Release
OK so I'll get to the point..there
are two records out by this band
and two by the SISTERS OF MERCY
all on this label...all are very
excellant and very worthy of an
expenditure...its as simple as
that.........................

GG ALLIN "NO RULES"/A FUCK UP"
Orange Records......
Since I'm really not in the position of giving a fuck wat people think about me and my taste--
I like this moron's records..sure
he's the kind of guy who gets abused by the crowd wherever he goes-
probably screams back to New Hamp-
shire and butt fucks his sister--
no he did that last issue..he no
doubt is a sick puppy but this s-
ort of regressive era of Max's
sound on his records pleases this
old coneseur(SP?)...besides...he
gets more than his share of bad
press--which means he's doing
something right...right???
PO BOX 54 HOOKSET NH 03106
Hey he writes back)

MONTE CAZAZZA-Sordide Sentimental...
Not as sick as his earlier efforts but
still very worthwhile... une odd fellow
who dwells on topics that fans of Dean
Coral,or Ed Gein would enjoy...but here
he fails to capture my imagination in
any big way..as usual in this series y-
ou get the elaborate package with obscure art and various french passages
by noted authors...looks also like M-
onte is down on smut as the cliched
graphic of people fucking and meat
which will only cause him to fall from grace in my eyes because without
the exploitation and humiliation of
both sexes on a monthly basis via
large format glossies I would be one
unhappy boy...I'll give the package
a better grade than the tunes...you
can do better Monte baby..besides
you shoulda put it on Subterranean
not some frog label...french people
suck.... write BP 534 76005 Rouen
Cedex France.........

THE FUCKIN' FLYIN' A-HEADS "Swiss
Cheese Back"/"Watching Tv..Otaro
Records....From Hawaii comes this
indescribably catchy grunge classic-
the point being either someone is
pitted from years of being zitted
or somebodys just being silly..re-
gardless this 1980 bit of underground
noise is a personal favorite..PO Box
6335 Honololo Hi 96818

SOUTHERN DEATH CULT-"FATMAN/"MOYA"
"THE GIRL" Situation
Sorta funny-the person who wrote
one of the British weeklys saying
all this about US bands having t-
he 'dead thing' down first..a noble
effort but I hardly see the corre-
lation other than the name..the
sentiments here are hardly spook
city,but rather a well crafted b-
unch of songs,that I find interesting as hell..the off beat movement over there is back on track
with bands like SDC...solid debut..

WHITE CROSS-Zero Degree Records
Ok so what if ive got so many so
called hardcore records that make
me tense up as I forcefully wallow
in one plays...so what if originality
is giving way to a predilection for
a given style,heavily trodden with
an endless line of so called punks...
enter White Cross...took their time
and did it right...the music is baseball over da head...the lyrics??oh
well,I'll still say this is light
years better than most...Strongly
recommended...it gets my seal of
approval which basically amounts
to enjoying a listen while I'm
rifeling a load of screaming sp-
ermatazoa into the toilet......
PO BOX 14532 Richmond Va 23221

DER DURSTIGE MANN

ERiC HYSTERiC + CO. IN THE FLESH!!!

the message reach into what you are trying to say..ie are u a political band?Marcel:We are not a political band.Marcus:We are not anti American. The one we had for lunch yesterday was really alright! TV:WHat do each of you do when nobody is looking? Marcus:Being sober.Eric:Looking intelligent.Marcel:Sleeping.Oskar:Practicing.   TV:Who do you look up to,look down upon and try to overlook? Marcel:ET.   TV:What is the club scene

like in your area..what are the populations attitudes toward punks in your country?Oskar:There's only hippie clubs and students hang outs.Eric:Most people think punks are insane. TV:What do you think of pornography,public shows of drunkeness and the Vomit Visions first record?Eric:Three fine examples of the pleasures in life.. TV:What are your favorite hobbies,preoccupations,and foods besides each others bratwursts.. DDM:First two see last question..cant think of favorite food..TV:What is reality?ALL:Lots of bottles of whiskey, martini,beer,apfelwein...TV:Your opinion of the anarchy,unity all is well if it is punk rock school of thought

ERIC DOESN'T REAL- IT YET, BUT HE HAS COMMITTED A CRIME! THE POLICE KNOW IT. (his latest 45)!??

WE'RE GONNA. RAPE!KILL! PILLAGE! AND BURN! WE'RE GONNA RAPE KILL PILLAGE AND BURN!!

PUNK VIOLENCE!

COWAR..

as perpetrated by certain large US cities'   .Marcel: Punks are the old farts of today.. Eric:Most groups lack a thing called HUMOR...TV Are you pleased with your new EP? All of us like it.However the next record will be even better,with classics like :ZYKLON,ANTI DANGER LIGA, DEUTSCHLAND-TURKENSTAAT,PLASTIK,MADCHEN, VON DER THEKE...TV:Why do people pick their noses when they drive their cars? Eric:Don't know.Oskar:Sorry..havent seen you drive yet. TV:When was the last time you barfed your guts out? Marcel:Happens too often to be able to remember.have you played a show yet?DDM:No and we don't play to poseurs! TV:Favorite bands?Marcus: BLACK FLAG.Eric:RED CROSS Marcel:Cramps Oskar:"OI!" TV:Who writes the tunes/ Most songs M.Monoton-Words..Eric Hysteric Music; Final comment:PROST... contact DER DURSTIGE MANN BY WRITING... OBERTOR 6 6293 LOHNBERG/LAHN WEST GERMANY (oh by the way their name means THE DRUN- KEN MAN)...

DER DURSTIGE MANN
Marcus Monoton-Vocals
Eric Hysteric-Guitar
Marcel Roth-Bass
Oskar-Drums
Founded summer 82 at Frankfurt flea-market..Released EP "PROST" in Dec. 82 from session recorded 2 months e-arlier at 8 track studio in Heddern-heim(near Frankfurt)
TV:Where do you guys place yourselves ideologically amongst other German ba-nds like the ones on Rock O Rama... Zick Zack...or Idiot...
Eris:We're in a class of our own! Marcel:Most German bands are too tame and predictable.Mainly they are just sick copies of English Punk.The rest-don't want to waste time talking about Art-Musak..TV:What are your musical ba-ckgrounds..other bands etc...DDM:Import-ant influences:GERMS,RAMONES,KINKS(only 60's)HANS ALBERS...
TV:THE anti Americanism in Germany.. is it as widespread as it seems..does

INSURRECTION

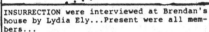

INSURRECTION were interviewed at Brendan's house by Lydia Ely...Present were all members...

Terry Scanlon(19)....vocals
Guy Picciotto(17)....guitars
Brendan Canty(17)....drums
Mike Fellows (17)....bass

Q:How did you all get together? Brendan: Deadline broke up because Ray and Christian went to college and then Insurrection had been kind of playing in my basement for a while and had done 3 shows before I even was in the band.It was just Mike and Guy doing this crazy shit ,doing some chaos and I had never seen them before and I just saw them on stage and said,"Fuck man,chaos kids" and then I got to know them.Guy:We were real impressed with Brendan's sound in Deadline...We thought he kept a pretty mean beat.Mike:He could play the skins.Guy:He was pretty much the King of the Big Beat.Back in the days when we were pretty much just the chaos guys,we were pretty much interested in just being cool and stuff and we figured he wanted to be in a band with us and we said it was alright.Brendan:It was kind of cool - they were more interested in being cool than in their music. Q:Why did Terry switch from bass(Deadline)to vocals(Insurrection)? Terry:......Brendan:He's a mute.He only sings. Guy: He has a mute stutter when he sings. Brendan:He's kind of embarassed.He can only sing;he can't speak. Terry: It just happened. Brendan: Evolution,it just happened.Q:Have you played a lot since you have been together? Guy: Four shows.The first was at the University of Maryland, but that doesn't really count because we weren't really together - It was half a show. 9:30 was our first real show. Brendan: It was great. Guy: We played with Faith and Double-O. After that,we played George Washington University with Iron Cross. Terry: And Social Suicide.Guy: We played a great party,like the total best, with Scam over in Virginia. Brendan: Scam are a good band. Look out for Scam. Guy: Scam are hot.We played New Year's Eve at another party at H.R.'s house and this all culminated in our trip to Detroit.Brendan: Our evolution to Detroit. Guy: We played with Negative Approach,Faith and the Allied - All great bands and a great scene. Mike: Jojo the dog-faced boy. All: Jojo the dog-faced boy and the cup...MTV... Corey's house...Taco Bell's...shit blood. Guy: I didn't take a shit the whole trip. That was three days that I didn't take a dump - That's not in the interview. Brendan: Three days before Guy took a dump - even after Taco Bell. Terry: Anytime he goes on a trip - He went on a trip with Deadline to New York and he didn't dump

there either. Brendan: The only place he'll shit is in his own bathroom...little-known facts...Mike: It's the truth! Guy shit at my house once and he blew up all over the bathroom. Brendan: There was shit all over the walls. Guy: It wasn't funny, man. I felt sick and then we bought laxatives instead of Pepto-Bismol. Hey,I don't want my mom to read this. Next question. Q: What bands do you like and what bands have influenced you? Brendan: Insurrection is the only band we like. Guy: Insurrection, Anti-Nowhere League. No bands influence us and no bands are any good. No, actually... All: We like all DC bands that are good: Scream, Faith, late Deadline - all the good bands. Q: Do you like Kiss? Guy: We like them, but they're not an influence. Brendan: Guy likes them - I only got turned on to them by their latest album. Mike: We're influenced by the Doors. Guy: They like the Doors. I like Kiss and the Beatles. Mike: The Doors are our biggest influence. Terry: Shut up, you little faggot. Mike: He likes hick music because he's a hick. Guy: He likes Leonard Skinhead. Brendan: He likes the Charlie Mountain Gang. Guy: Rosslyn Mountain Boys. No, we like the Damned, UK Subs, Beatles, early L.A. bands, Adverts. Brendan: MC5, Avengers. Q: What do you hate more than anything in the world? All: Girls! ....Enter Chris Bald of Faith....... Chris: What kind of hat is this? All: Peter Pan hat. Q: Why don't you like girls? Guy: Most of them are parasites. Terry: They don't have minds either. Chris: Yeah, no mimes. Terry: You've never seen a girl popping, have you? No! Brendan: They can't mime worth shit: they can't fake climbing a ladder; they can't do the wall bit. Terry: We case our rest. Guy: Girls like bands for the wrong reasons. I hate every girl except one - everyone's allowed one girl to like. Brendan: We like the gritty stuff, the magazines. We get into Fetish Times. Chris: Ughh ughh. Terry: Are you all going to

school, or what? Chris: This is Terry. He was lost out in the wilderness of Pennsylvania. Guy: He was out camping - Wilderness Survival. Brendan: We haven't practiced for the last three weeks because nobody could find Terry - Nobody was at his house - His whole family disappeared. We thought he'd moved, so we were going to get a new singer. We were walking down Wisconsin Avenue and there he was. It was really weird. Where were you again? Terry: Lorthian, Maryland. Chris: Lorthian.... That's a demonic name. Brendan: And he's still our singer. Q: Star singer? All: Yeah - our star singer. The best singer and the only singer we've ever had - our real rock star. Chris: Just like Chris Bald of Faith - he's insane. Guy: He's the only guy in Faith we really don't like. Faith'll be doing really good, then all of a sudden he'll start doing all these postures and moves. Terry: Remember this: "Only blue lights"? Guy: I remember that - the last person to do that was Flipper. Terry: That Flipper guy, he's a dick. Chris: How did they get the dolphin to fucking sing? Q: What do you usually do on a night out? All: Kill a few girls, drive, do the tunnels, spit blood. First we do baked beans and molasses at Terry's, pile into the Cougar(RIP), head for tunnels where we get sick, walk for hours and hours and we play 'Assemble the Pentangle', the game that isn't really a game. Then we hang the Awakening at (Hain's) Point. (Chris is being obnoxious and throwing stuff.) All: That's enough, Chris. Chris: I'm not Chris; I'm Peter Pan. Q: What does DOD stand for? Chris: Daisies Or Daffodils. All: DOD is a way of life - it stands for all that we are. Q: What are you? All: Us - Insurrection - Ourselves.

ALBUMS!

THE OUTCASTS-"BLOOD & THUNDER" Abstract Records

Although not normally predisposed to worship of those 'cross the Atlantic,I love the Outcasts...I'm sure certain of you bought this expecting another flash in the pan HC lp to give a load of lip service and a space in the back of the rack...lets see put it in your own verbose,opinionated asshole style verbiage,vee get to the point..hard assed pop?Power minus speed/?All the hot singles are here...plus some choice new stuff,..I guess in this boys case they have and always will strike that nerve...the best.....The Row,Ballydorn Rd. Killinchy,Co Down N. Ireland.........................

TANK-"FILTH HOUNDS OF HADES" Ok

so I love some heavy metal(the stuff that rocks/not jump on the cock stuff)This band is good despite the stupid lyrics(ex "blood and guts and beer) but this rocks my bones.. vocals remind ne of the Misfits and Ozzy..and for all the Damned fans(still a few?) Algy Ward("Ballroom Blitz" plays bass.."rock on good metal..Stabb

WARHEAD-Contagion Records

John and Dix Denney are at it again... eclectic noise from Weirdos from way back...I don't know exactly how limited this is but mine is stamped #83...A must for every record collection............. Contagion Records PO BOx 402 Hollywood Ca 90028

RANK AND FILE-Slash...The most nauseating

review of this had a headline "Safety Pins And String Ties"...to somehow even remotely equate the DILS with this is blasphemy.. Shows you what lengths people will go to be open minded...Country music is gutless refuse no matter how it's served up..the next big thing for a searching American audience...simply no way I can watch.....

ANGRY SAMOANS-"BACK FROM SAMOA".....
Never liked em'....still dont.......

VENOM "BLACK METAL" Neat Records
Installment #4 from a band who have most effectively combined the savage energy from two schools of music..this LP sees a cleaner sound with another dose of the sick,the perverse..they make no bones about their hometown.. It;s Hades and Sugar Daddy is Lucifer.. As a former early seventies metal fan I can safely say all competition look like pantywaisters...however they seem to be somwhere in between as far as audience goes...you know I could go on and on but all that really needs saying is Venom is the best yet in terms of power metal...nobody comes close...

SCREAM

SCREAM LP-Dischord Records
Guess it's no secret I'm biased in regards to products on this label..not a dud in the bunch with every release top notch...Scream has busted ass to get where they are today ...sloggin it out in the pits of the party circuit...but now you reign as one of the finest in the nations capital.. it was all worth it right bucks?Anyway this disc showcases their diverse mode of attack with a variety of styles and alternately serious and an occasional fun-ism thrown in for good measure...live the assault is deafening and with the aid of Don Zientara the fury is captured in the studio setting...technically speaking this is the best Dischord record-but then again every other one has its boner inducing aspects so for now this will do...get it....Dischord Records 3819 Beecher St NW Wash DC 20007

TSOL "BENEATH THE SHADOWS"
Altrenative Tentacles
Not much to say but here goes. This group has done better.The new addition of keyboards make The Damned imitation 2 obvious. Their idea of psychedelia would make any Seed,Prune,or Watchband cringe.Try again folks- review by Stabb...contact TSOL Box 655 Los Alamitos,Ca 90720

FANG-"LAND SHARK " Boner Records
You'll say "Tesco only likes it cuz it's on a label with a phallic name...no it's cuz some guy plays this tuned way low guitar that's just a little outa tune and it sounds mean and low and it rocks my angry red rocket into spashing forth a spring of the salty mucous cuz I dont' give the TV seal ta jus any old rekord I give em ta disks like this...and if you don like it the bassman Chris'll fuck yer bottom so wise up cum jobs... Boner Records 2146 Boner St. Berkeley Ca 94702

RF-7 "Fall In" Smoke 7 Records
This one will send even the most inpacted geriatric racing for the throne..absolutely the best record to come out of LA in ages...these guys have a handle on what makes severe social commentary--no cheap shots..just straight up the ass grinding dirge that makes my adrenalin level jump ten fold...and they've got the balls to make it stick...they do a song about the phenom of the 80's the "Coke Whore" Stupid cunts who fuck and suck even stupider pricks for cocaine...then they dedicate it to two femmes they probably know real well...it puzzles me that in all my devout wisdom,my worship of RF7 isn't duplicated all over...or is it? 7230 De Soto Ave Suite 104 Cahoga park Ca.91303 (Oh sorry Smoke Seven but take that piece of grunt"Sudden Death"and ram it where it be dark and odiferous..)

hail satanas

FRICTION

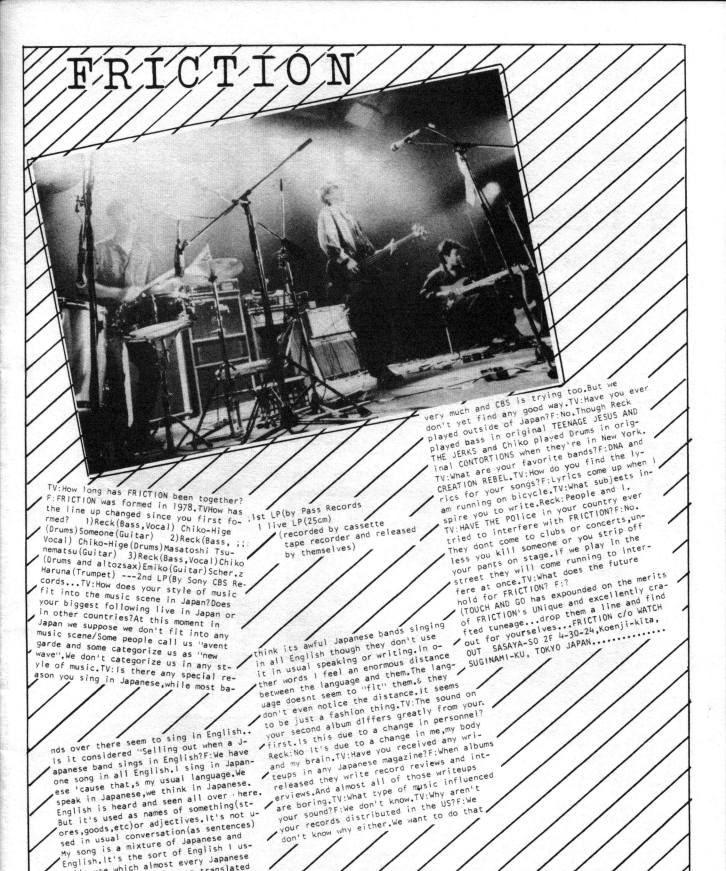

TV:How long has FRICTION been together? F:FRICTION was formed in 1978.TVHow has the line up changed since you first formed? 1)Reck(Bass,Vocal) Chiko-Hige (Drums)Someone(Guitar) 2)Reck(Bass, Vocal) Chiko-Hige(Drums)Masatoshi Tsunematsu(Guitar) 3)Reck(Bass,Vocal)Chiko (Drums and altozsax)Emiko(Guitar)Scher.z Haruna(Trumpet) ---2nd LP(By Sony CBS Records...TV:How does your style of music fit into the music scene in Japan?Does your biggest following live in Japan or in other countries?At this moment in Japan we suppose we don't fit into any music scene/Some people call us "avent garde and some categorize us as "new wave".We don't categorize us in any style of music.TV:Is there any special reason you sing in Japanese,while most ba-

;1st LP(by Pass Records 1 live LP(25cm) (recorded by cassette tape recorder and released by themselves)

nds over there seem to sing in English.. Is it considered "Selling out when a J-apanese band sings in English?F:We have one song in all English.I sing in Japanese 'cause that,s my usual language.We speak in Japanese,we think in Japanese. English is heard and seen all over · here. But it's used as names of something(stores,goods,etc)or adjectives.It's not used in usual conversation(as sentences) My song is a mixture of Japanese and English.It's the sort of English I usually use,which almost every Japanese understand.And not the one translated It might be because I've been in USA before and they're in my vocabulary.I

think its awful Japanese bands singing in all English though they don't use it in usual speaking or writing.In other words I feel an enormous distance between the language and them.The language doesnt seem to "fit" them.& they don't even notice the distance.It seems to be just a fashion thing.TV:The sound on your second album differs greatly from your. first.Is this due to a change in personnel? Reck:No It's due to a change in me,my body and my brain.TV:Have you received any writeups in any Japanese magazine?F:When albums released they write record reviews and interviews.And almost all of those writeups are boring.TV:What type of music influenced your sound?F:We don't know.TV:Why aren't your records distributed in the US?F:We don't know why either.We want to do that

very much and CBS is trying too.But we don't yet find any good way.TV:Have you ever played outside of Japan?F:No.Though Reck played bass in original TEENAGE JESUS AND THE JERKS and Chiko played Drums in original CONTORTIONS when they're in New York. TV:What are your favorite bands?F:DNA and CREATION REBEL.TV:How do you find the lyrics for your songs?F:Lyrics come up when I am running on bicycle.Reck:People and I. spire you to write.TV:What subjects inspire you to write.Reck:People and I. TV:HAVE THE POlice in your country ever tried to interfere with FRICTION?F:No. They dont come to clubs or concerts,unless you kill someone or you strip off your pants on stage.If we play in the street they will come running to interfere at once.TV:What does the future hold for FRICTION? F:? (TOUCH AND GO has expounded on the merits of FRICTION's UNique and excellently crafted tuneage...drop them a line and find out for yourselves...FRICTION c/o WATCH OUT SASAYA-SO 2F 4-30-24,Koenji-kita, SUGINAMI-KU, TOKYO JAPAN...............

o s o i o n g o l o e o s o

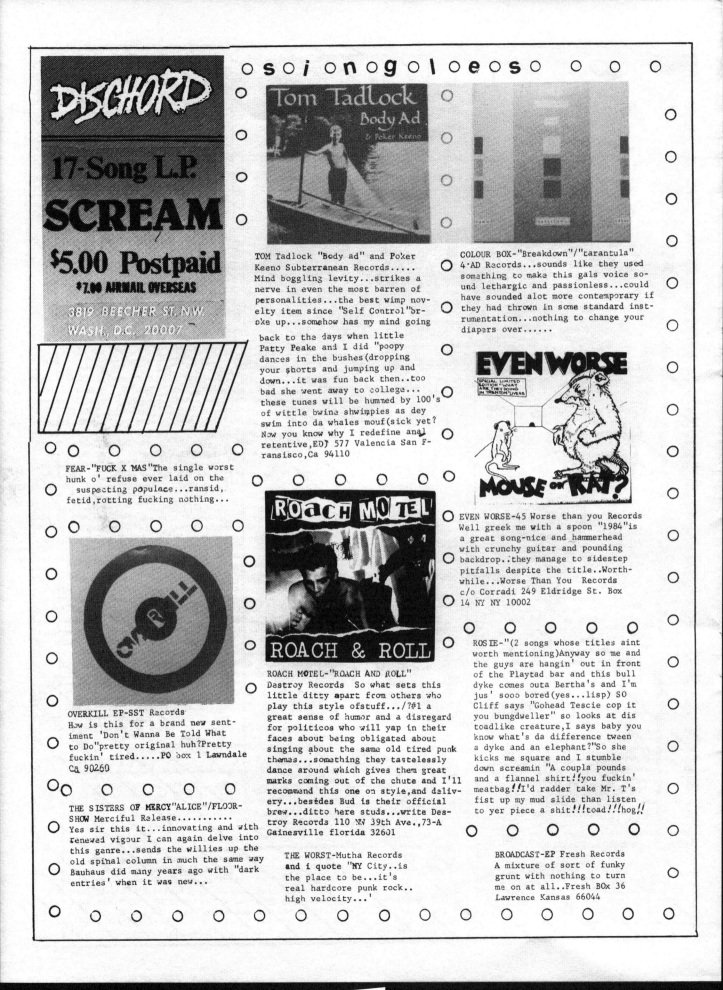

TOM Tadlock "Body ad" and Poker Keeno Subterranean Records..... Mind boggling levity...strikes a nerve in even the most barren of personalities...the best wimp novelty item since "Self Control" broke up...somehow has my mind going

back to the days when little Patty Peake and I did "poopy dances in the bushes(dropping your shorts and jumping up and down...it was fun back then..too bad she went away to college... these tunes will be hummed by 100's of wittle bwine shwimpies as dey swim into da whales mouf(sick yet? Now you know why I redefine anal retentive,ED) 577 Valencia San Fransisco,Ca 94110

COLOUR BOX-"Breakdown"/"tarantula" 4-AD Records...sounds like they used something to make this gals voice sound lethargic and passionless...could have sounded alot more contemporary if they had thrown in some standard instrumentation...nothing to change your diapers over......

FEAR-"FUCK X MAS"The single worst hunk o' refuse ever laid on the suspecting populace...ransid, fetid,rotting fucking nothing...

EVEN WORSE-45 Worse than you Records Well greek me with a spoon "1984"is a great song-nice and hammerhead with crunchy guitar and pounding backdrop..they manage to sidestep pitfalls despite the title..Worthwhile...Worse Than You Records c/o Corradi 249 Eldridge St. Box 14 NY NY 10002

OVERKILL EP-SST Records How is this for a brand new sentiment 'Don't Wanna Be Told What to Do"pretty original huh?Pretty fuckin' tired.....PO box 1 Lawndale Ca 90260

THE SISTERS OF MERCY"ALICE"/FLOORSHOW Merciful Release.......... Yes sir this it...innovating and with renewed vigour I can again delve into this genre...sends the willies up the old spinal column in much the same way Bauhaus did many years ago with "dark entries' when it was new...

ROACH MOTEL-"ROACH AND ROLL" Destroy Records So what sets this little ditty apart from others who play this style ofstuff.../?#1 a great sense of humor and a disregard for politicos who will yap in their faces about being obligated about singing about the same old tired punk themes...something they tastelessly dance around which gives them great marks coming out of the chute and I'll recommend this one on style,and delivery...besides Bud is their official brew...ditto here studs...write Destroy Records 110 NW 39th Ave.,73-A Gainesville florida 32601

THE WORST-Mutha Records and i quote "NY City..is the place to be...it's real hardcore punk rock.. high velocity...'

ROSIE-"(2 songs whose titles aint worth mentioning)Anyway so me and the guys are hangin' out in front of the Playtad bar and this bull dyke comes outa Bertha's and I'm jus' sooo bored(yes...lisp) SO Cliff says "Gohead Tescie cop it you bungdweller" so looks at dis toadlike creature,I says baby you know what's da difference tween a dyke and an elephant?"So she kicks me square and I stumble down screamin "A coupla pounds and a flannel shirt!!you fuckin' meatbag!!I'd radder take Mr. T's fist up my mud slide than listen to yer piece a shit!!!toad!!!hog!!

BROADCAST-EP Fresh Records A mixture of sort of funky grunt with nothing to turn me on at all..Fresh BOx 36 Lawrence Kansas 66044

dirk gunga beats the dummy

The most disgusting thing I can think of is observing my father,in his Lay-Z Boy fishing for his trouser trout while trying to tune in the Playboy channel he never paid for...people talk about a "scene" in Lansing..the only scene that existed in Lansing was some stupid leather jacketed clods hanging out in front of Bunches with a ghetto blaster playing punk rock'.. Every Thursday around dinner time I go to the North Gaurd station behind the White House and wait.Pretty soon a limo pulls up and an older lady gets out wearing a shawl a shawl and sunglasses and hikes up her dress.I whip out my dummy, shock her rectum,she leaves,and a few days later I get a check in the mail for $1000.Simple huh?To be in Times Square or some other heavy porn district with a pocketful of quarters and a tube of Go Jo is akin to being in the Glorious hereafter...you see collecting porn is quite different than say collecting stamps..what determines value in stamps is age and rarity..with porn its whatever sends the cardiac flow into your bag... if god was here right now I'd take some channel locks and strip him of his manhood.. Ever wonder why Whipping Boys upcoming LP is entitled "The Sound Of No Hands Clapping"? It documents the response they got on their last tour...my parents' sex life consists of my dad dressing up as a debutante and my mother as a marine sergeant,barking orders whild pop meekly submits to a thorough gouging of his coal chute via a strap on black rubber cod....my phallus has been referred to by many names...my little chili dog,my swinging passion fruit,my dirty creature my gravedigger...but the girls on P street affectionately call it "The Wedge" Henry Rollins diet is so vitamin packed he freeze dries his stools and sells them to third world countries as the Rollins P-Nut Clusters_{tm}...why does it take a mega buck movie about Ghandi to get americans inspired about this truly great person.. I've been indulging in a glass of my own golden frothy for many years...I was born with a two headed dick but the attending doctor lopped off the smallest of the two predicting correctly,problems later in life.

I always wondered what the red wig was doing in my dadas tool chest until one night I heard him screaming "Annie"!!! from the bowels of the master bedroom..why is there suddenly 9 out of ten hardcore bands all singing about the same tired subjects... who is Carol Schnek anyway?I'm surprised she didnt swear off punk rock altogether when Joe of the Crucifucks resisted her amorous advances...on Gary Coleman.. wouldn't you love to see that little tootsie roll skewered intra-rectally and hung over a flaming pit?Starting this month T&G will feature DIRK'S MAIL BAG--with answers to health and social problems... just drop me a line...this month... Dear Dirk...I'm laying in bed with a 16 year old girl,her deap cleaved mother, some crisco,and a green banana,but I can't get it up.What should I do?

Melwood Gorgo

Dear Melwood..Start the sluts lapping on each other,grease that banana and I'll be right over...the Meatmen have amarriage between their blood sacks and mild electric current..from the lame letters I've read in Ripper last issue I wouldnt be surprised if I saw a letter in there by my grandmother complaining of an itching colostomy bag..What could be worse than the blathering between songs by MDC?A 40 song set by Whipping Boy..everyone reading this right now has to drive to the Sunnyside retirement center in Downey,CA and blow Uncle Charley from My 3 Sons..alot of porn stars have dorfy faces so I generally sc issor their faces and slaughter my hog to their 4 limbed carcass..from years of polishing it,the skin on my crank has taken on the texture of fine hand crafted leather..after jousting with my girlfriend unsuccessfully for 20 minutes I usually give up..roll her over and dig my own grave..what could be worse than Tesco cutting a fart in a car on the way to a show in Detroit..?You got it...a warm up set by WB...catch ya next month..write me care of this magazine.......................

Guilty verdict in mutilation

By JOE SWICKARD
Free Press Staff Writer

Jeannine Clark was convicted Wednesday of mutilating her boyfriend's corpse in a 3½-day orgy of drugs and sex.

A Recorder's Court jury of six men and six women took an hour and five minutes to convict Clark, 22, after a three-day trial before Judge Michael Sapala.

Clark, who often had broken into tears during the trial, showed no reaction to the jury's decision.

CLARK CLAIMED she was forced under a death threat to pose for photographs with the mutilated body of her lover, Robert Beckowitz, who had been murdered as she held his hand.

Her claim was partially supported by the testimony Tuesday of James Glover, who pleaded guilty last year to Beckowitz's murder. "Right now, I'd say she didn't really stay of her own free will," Glover testified.

But both Clark and Glover said she could have fled several times.

CLARK CRIED uncontrollably as she recounted how Glover ordered her to begin the mutilation by emasculating

ONLY IN THE Motor City

MUTILATION, from Page 3A

Beckowitz's body "I went to do it but I couldn't do it," she said between heavy sobs. "I told him to go ahead and kill me, but I couldn't hurt Bob."

Clark, who faces up to 10 years in prison, will be sentenced Feb. 17.

Beckowitz was murdered July 14 in his home near Seven Mile and Telegraph by Glover, who said he thought Beckowitz was responsible for burning Glover's home.

The 6-foot-4, 250-pound Beckowitz was killed by a single gunshot to the head. However, an autopsy revealed that his body, which had been cut into 14 pieces, had been stabbed 84 times after death.

PHOTOGRAPHS found at the murder scene show a smiling, naked Clark apparently sawing off Beckowitz's head and striking sexual poses and committing sexual acts with severed parts of his body.

Prosecutor Thomas Bahen said the photographs, admitted as evidence, proved that Clark, 22, enthusiastically joined in dismembering her boyfriend. Bahen said Clark had many chances to flee, but chose to remain with Glover for 3½ days before going to the police.

"No one is going to know all of what happened, but those photographs are graphic evidence of some things that did happen," Bahen said. "Look at her face (in the photographs). Do you see fear, revulsion, disgust? I don't think you will find those things."

Bahen also said that the spinal-damaged Glover, who must use a cane to walk, needed Clark's cooperation to maneuver Beckowitz's hulking body.

DEFENSE attorney James Waske said Glover forced Clark to stay and to pose in the photographs, which could have been used to blackmail her into silence.

Clark said she had been holding hands with Beckowitz on a couch and watching the Benny Hill television program when Glover shot Beckowitz in the side of the head.

"Jimmy told me don't move and don't make any noise," she said. "He said I'd have to stay there a couple of days because he had to get rid of the body."

Clark said she did not protest because "I was afraid if I tried to say anything, he'd hurt me, too."

ALTHOUGH she said that Glover threatened to kill her if she disobeyed, Clark said she was allowed to leave the house by herself twice during the incident and that she returned both times. She bought film for Glover's camera during one of those outings, she said.

Glover, a snake tatoo on the top of his head barely visible through his cropped hair, testified he killed Beckowitz and "must have been" responsible for the mutilations and photographs. But he said he could not be sure because he was heavily drugged on synthetic opiates and amphetamines.

"It's a big puzzle . . . I cannot explain," he said.

With apoligies to all of you that sent me demo tapes...I simply didn't have my shit together to review them this time..Please don't hate me..you'll be so very unique if you don't..........TV..

super shredder spurtin

ANOTHER UPDATE FROM THE ONLY PLACE WEST OF INDIA THAT IS 85DEGREES IN JANUARY.
wail,simply wail,complicatedly wail,the world keeps spiinning,earth,wind,and
fire is still the best band around (flip to their "That's the Way of the World"
disc-marvy),and...
and tsol was rioted upon last night,as the cops ruthlessly chased children who
were CUTTING EACH OTHER UP WITH RAZ OR BLADES AND TAKING CHEAP DRUGS ON THE
STREET-it was such a pussy riot,looked like a buncha nine year olds having bad
acid trips,paralyzed,refrigerated,in fear,the cops probably felt guilty they
even bothered.the days of the blood drawing bad boys are over,let's be five foot
five (i am) and pretend to be in boots the size of our cars
band news,bland news,land news,panda bears:pears and flowers are over,salvation
army have shedded their paisley for what sounds a whole lot like what whoever
spoke of pop and art was thinking of,therearmormods in this town than there are
hairs in pete townsend's head-they hop to the untouchables (definitely a beboppin'
deal) and the northern soul records self respecting negroes would pay not to hear
and about da third of them own scooters and about an eighth of them own brains.
the t-bird roller rink is where people go to hear punk rock music,a scene which
i am,disrespectfully,unfamiliar with,but the band line ups are intense-circle jerks
and d.i.'s and wastd youth and and and...,i,uhmm,well,errr,no i'm not going to
complain in this update,let the babes run free in the forest.
did you see quincy's punk rock episode? i've seen bad but that's worse.howsabout
that cbs thing with film from the galaxy roller rink? gasp,yelp.
the english beat played the paladium,sold out and sneakers inners making the place
look like chicken of the sea tunacans.smelled like em too.i haaaaaate to be negative like this but it isn't a swingin' scene in la.a.,dig:no enticing new bands,
the gun club are gone,fear is as good as cherry flavored soda,the only place to
see the cramps is standing outside food king,all the socialites we love so much
have obtained diseases or moved to arkansas,all the homosexual painters poets and
boppers of the written words heardabout that gay cancer stuff and got scared away
into lofts downtown where they sit alone and watch television until they starve,
my dog ran away,and we just ran out of pepe passporte's tortilla dough shells.
life is pain,pain is no tortilla shells.
enuf melodie caca:last night i was on a bus on sunset and this lady with four suit
cases walks on the bus and she's obviously a regular and a nut and three fouths
and she sits next to me,fifty fuckin' empty seats and she has to sit next to lil
ole me,and she starts screaming YOOUUUUUU CANNNNN'T STOP ME,YOUUUU CAN NOT STOPPPPF
MEEEEEE,over and over and over and over like the manicest maniac fool i've ever
sat next to and man was she ugly,looked like a fuckin' sunkist prune,ughhh,and

finally someone in the bus yells "just call the cops" and the lady spins around
and says YOUUUUUCANNNNNNNNNOOOOOOMSTOPPPPPPMEEEEEEEEE!!!!! and the driver says
oki'llcallthecops and the lady said THEY WON'T STOP ME and just when the bus
driver picks up the phone the lady growls THEY WON'T STOP ME 'COS THEY WON'T FIND
ME and she throws the door open and grabs her bags and splits like lightning.see
what i mean? this place is suckin' hard cucumber man,pink cucumber.

that's the way of the world
plant your flower,grow a pearl,

SHreddED SHREDDerrrrrr.

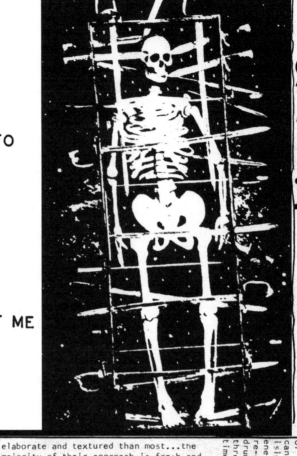
THE ALLIED/VOID/NEGATIVE APPROACH at the
9:30....Another matinee featuring a couple
of motor city units and a band from town...
twas good to see my pals from Murder town
once again...Allied were on first and played
a swell set...was the first time I had seen
them since the line-up change and the sound
was big and clean and full...they displayed
a great deal more confidence onstage and did
a rousing rendition of Blitz's "Youth"...
great set...then VOID who like an aquired taste get better every outing...when I first saw
them at the Wilson Center I wasnt quite sure
how to take them...the chaos they display live
makes their records seem tame...well this time
i was loading the cords as they chugged relentlessly through a ravagingly out of control set..
they even practised before the show i was told..
has to be seen to be believed...NEGATIVE APPROACH
is in no danger of losing their hold over balls
off the wall kings of speed-metal-attack as John
and Co. raged once again with new tunes to boot..
Their record doesnt quite capture the essence
of the bands live attack...all the adjectives
will be spared...see it...grab your crotch and
enjoy...the Detroit bands probably lost money
on the trip and hopefully this wont discourage
other out of towns from cruising in for a 1 off..

MARGINAL MAN/FAITH/MINOR THREAT at the
9:30 Club...jan. 83 So we pull up and
the line streatches down the block..
an obvious sellout,so quick confab between bands and mgt. results in the decision to have two shows..so we stood
around watching the skins beating on
the cards till Marginal Man came out..
the first in an afternoon of three guitar assault...their music is much more

elaborate and textured than most...the
majority of their approach is fresh and
the weak spots will be gone in time..
their arrangements obviously have taken
alot of working out...some very untypical
stuff from some gents who know what they
are doing minus the obvious hooks and
cliches and a definate blow to those who
say there is only one band in DC who can
play their instruments...tapir shit there
vas tree of dem today...next Faith featuring the legendary Eddie "Choppers"Mach-
etti late of the Untouchables on guitar
to compliment wonder boy Hampton on axe
duties,,and I was al last satisfied that
this great untapped resource of guitar
talent had found a home...this was by far
a superior set to the last time I saw
them..their timing was on and the sound
was dense and powerful...but as matinees
pass I cant help but loathe the goons
hired by the 9:30 to police the stage..
somewhere during Faiths set my mind wandered to a scene where someone drags these two buffoons into the crowd and turns
their heads into meatloafs..of course
tossing their slumped and non breathing
sacks of meat and broken bones back on stage.
for the vocalist in Social Suicide decide
what you wanna be dick-a bouncer or a half
assed singer...then came the pinultimate
in your basic punkrock dominion...Manuh
threat...does for my brain what a sloe
gin enema does for the rectum...now i
see why the line up change,well sort of
Lyle alone was great enough but the whole thing together is hot stuff...with

the new bassist Steve complimenting the
whole shebang with some pounding strokes
of the hand..so anyway now one and all
can expatiate on the merit of their decision...Ian was really going off...lotsa
energy all around..besides Jeff and Steve
re-define what a rythym section with bass
drum and guitar spitting identical...all
three bands were hot...no thumbs down this
time...TV

ARTIFICIAL PEACE/EXILED EP
Fountain of Youth Records
I tip my hat to Derrick and
Co. for getting a new label
rolling...this record could
be looked at as a start..cer-
tainly lacking in terms of production...not nearly what it
could have been but he knows
that and future projects will
undoubtedly be devoid of the
foibles encountered here...
a 7" and a 12" by the GI's
are planned..should be great...

baboon doooley meets Tim Why? DA PoPe of PunK

the good

MINOR THREAT 12"
SS DECONTROL-"GET IT AWAY"
DIE KREUZEN-"COWS AND BEER"
MISFITS-EARTH A.D. DEMO
ALL FUCKING VENOM
MARCH VIOLETS-"GROWING IN GREEN"
WHITE CROSS EP
THE MENTORS-"GET UP AND DIE"
THE DANSE SOCIETY-"HIDE"
RF-7-"FALL IN"
SCREAM LP
NEGATIVE TREND EP
CRIME-"ROCKIN' WEIRD"
OUTCASTS-"BLOOD AND THUNDER"
VIRGIN PRUNES BOX SET
NEGATIVE APPROACH
SUICIDE-"GIRL"
THE BIRTHDAY PARTY
SACRED ORDER-"ICKY BITCH"
FAITH/VOID
NECROS "COUNT ME OUT"

MINOR THREAT PHOTO BY GLEN E. FRIEDMAN

Welcome gang...let's just talk about why Socialism Sucks and why punk rock should <u>not have</u> "socially redeeming values".First off for anyone who really and truly is interested in political philosophers PLEASE READ BARBARISM WITH A HUMAN FACE by Bernard Henri-Levy--this book is written by a guy who used to work for Mitterand the socialist who is now leader of France,back when he was the opposition leader:and before that the author was part of the radical student uprising in France during the late 60's...In this book he refutes all forms of Socialist Doctrines.. he illustrates how Marxism has made capitalism what it is today if you can believe that...and his conclusions are in total agreement with my gut level feelings that the only appropriate response to oppression is individual action in the form of ART(read Punk Rock) and Individualism(read"thinking what you want)...he implies that to crave the power to change is really just another name for craving power when it is manifested by organized action...what it boils down to is that Tim Yohanon would be no better than Ronald Reagan if he had that much power--I'm a little off track now--Read that book for a broader view on the fallacy of socialism...Socialism is Barbarism(read Totalitarianism)With A Human Face...What I want to get over is Max R&R is helping create a gulf among punks by censoring works not politically correct...there is no place for censorship and sectarianism within the ranks of punk...and to compound the sin not only omitting the stuff but slagging it off and ridiculing it...Because of my status as a Federal prisoner my musical input is

limited-whatever tapes I can get in and whatever music I can pick up on KJHK the Lawrence Alternative Music Station as they dub themselves..so I do listen to Max R&R when I have the chance which is only rarely because I can't tune in until the other stations on nearby wavelengths go off the air and that's not until 1AM..most of my input has been from various zines I've read including the issue of RIPPER where they got a large spread to present their own ideas-that's the reason I'm urging people to read the book I mentioned since they gave a reading list of stuff to put stock in...sure they play alot of good stuff and give airplay to obscure young bands...but I'm almost sure that when they're seperating the wheat from the chaff they are doing so on the basis of politics rather than musical impact...I like the DK's well enough I suppose and I feel embarrassed for Biafra's welding himself to the prow of the MAX R&R flagship..but I also like the MISFITS..the point being that punk radio shows are far enough and few between that the ones that exist shouldnt be throwing out ½ of the greatest music because of various perceived ism's"...If I could hear the punk'greats anytime then I'd find it entirely appropriate to have a specialty show...featuring all the bands of one political persuasion..but as it is Max R&R is cheating its listeners..
SHANE WILLIAMS
Leavenworth,Kansas

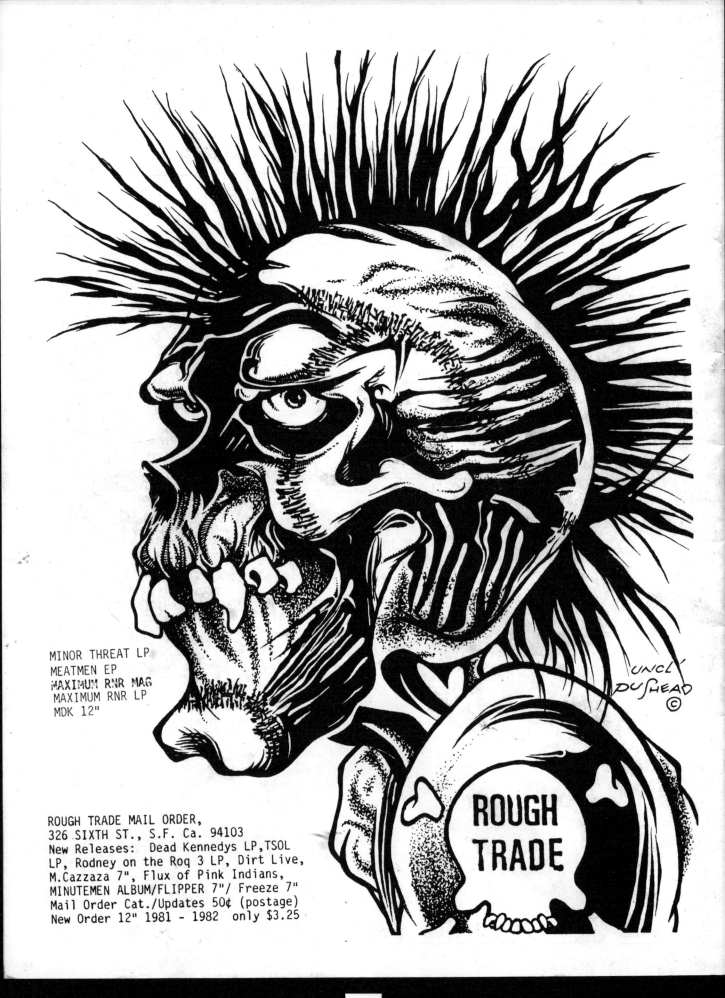

MINOR THREAT LP
MEATMEN EP
MAXIMUM RNR MAG
MAXIMUM RNR LP
MDK 12"

UNCL' DUSHEAD ©

ROUGH TRADE

ROUGH TRADE MAIL ORDER,
326 SIXTH ST., S.F. Ca. 94103
New Releases: Dead Kennedys LP,TSOL
LP, Rodney on the Roq 3 LP, Dirt Live,
M.Cazzaza 7", Flux of Pink Indians,
MINUTEMEN ALBUM/FLIPPER 7"/ Freeze 7"
Mail Order Cat./Updates 50¢ (postage)
New Order 12" 1981 - 1982 only $3.25

22

Here it is, last issue. Great cover shot of two guys who remain best friends to this day... Henry mesmerized by yes, a pool ball, Ian flippin' him off like a playful schoolboy. Don't remember the exact chain of events that would make this the last issue... But I've never lost my zeal for bands/music/and writing. Truth is, it was just too much money (and at this time, 1983, I was still not makin' much). Too much time, bands were breakin' up—the writin' was on the wall, indulge the pun. I'd like to think T & G left some sort of mark on the music world. I'll liken it to the mark left when my neighbor's garbage-truck-chasin' Chihuahua one day ran right under the truck and stuck to the tire for a few revolutions, leaving a bloody print every few feet... Okay, not very analogous but hey, it's messed-up/funny things like that that stick with you and force you to create a messed-up funny zine! I guess Ian said it best in our interview this year: The scene back then was a scattered, sometimes fractured, disparate, tribal union of souls nationwide/worldwide who shared one thing: a love for the music and a desire to spread the gospel of hardcore and independent music of great variety to anyone who gave a fuck. Say what you want about Touch and Go magazine, but there was no denyin' that thru all the potty-mouthed humor, vitriolic verbiage, and broad-brush pomposity, we truly gave a fuck!

TOUCH

AND

T GO

no. 22
$1.50

The fucking album is out !

SUICIDAL TENDENCIES

So go buy, beg for, steal, or at least listen to it... you'll be craving !

on FRONTIER

p.o. box 22
Sun Valley, CA 91352
$6.00 postpaid

490

TOUCH and GO
BOX 25305
WASH. DC 20007

your editor & sleazbag aristocrat... **TESCO VEE...** 10" (of course)

A **FIRST CLASS** Nobody!!!

CLASSY QUOTES...

"I'LL PLAY BASEBALL WITH YOR HEAD..."
THE MENTORS

BACK COVER BY Pushead..

COVER SHOT BY NAOMI PETERSEN.

Be sure and check out the new T&G classifieds which will appear from now on for those of you who wanna get ahold of something be it record/mag/tape/pen pal etc...example..WANTED-Female 12-40 who possesses eyes like two limpid pools of motor oil...whose lips are like two nitecrawlers having coitus in the musky depths of a peet bog...whose clam is like an ultra rare Arby's turned sideways (hold the horsey sause)And who wishes to monger the aging peckwood of one John Smith"...etc..you get the idea..seriously folks if collecting is your bag send those lists in...the results will stagger your mind...why am I doing this?Oh sheeit ahm jus filled with the spirit a good will...deadline for next issue is Aug. 30th OK???

WELCOME to yet another issue of T&G.. I'm getting closer and closer to Bi-monthly..who knows by next time I may be on track...There is a flurry of activity record wise with releases by BLACK MARKET BABY/a new record from FAITH/another 45 from IRON CROSS fe- aturing "Gray Morning", and two others.. MINOR THREAT has remixed their impos- sible to find 12" and the packaging t- his time up to snuff and all that...INSURRECTION will also be releas- ing a record...Eric formerly of DOUBLE

O is working overtime with his new band DOVE...Steve has left Minor Threat and is working with Richard and Bert of Double O along with Mike Brown formerly of UNITED MUTATION on drums...Paul Cl- eery is now the permanent bassist in IRON CROSS..he is formerly of Black Mar- ket...DC now has three viable record la- bels...DISCHORD/OUTSIDE/AND FOUNTAIN OF YOUTH...with R&B records also pl-

anning projects...Maryland's OBSESSED have a new 45 just out..(see review) In the Midwest the NECROS debut LP is due out any day and of course is a k- iller..a 7" by BLIGHT will finally see

the light of day soon...NEGATIVE APPR- OACH will be recording an album very soon(jump back) and the highly touted FLESH COLUMNS will also be recording for Touch And Go Records...THE ALLIED are slated for a release on Chicago's Ruthless label

SPECIAL THANKS TO..NAOMI Peterson, J Crawford, Bunde, Josh Friedman, Jim SAAH, Sean Duffy/Al Barile, Anna Preslar, John Schroeder, All of you who sent promos, rags etc...Anyone I forgot of course!

You tell me..what could be more stupid than this NO LABELS band slagging straight edge because one guy took a bruising at a show.. heresay, and rumor, and conjecture, and vindictivness don't add up to a valid argument..if they've got nothing better to do than bad mouth DC then they oughta hang it up..no there arent any philosophies minus holes...people expect to come to DC and see all these skins that are go- ing around blabbing about it and kicking the shit outa people who are drinking...folks this is a fucking media myth..the people who adhere to this philosophy are alot more silent and cool about it than th- ose who yap and are mis-informed.. Get the facts straight dicks......

Also thanks to Craig Taatjes!

TOUCH AND GO would like to apologise for failing to photo credit two pho- tos last issue..the VOID and DOUBLE O shots were taken by JIM SAAH who des- erves but didnt get..sorry for the fuck up..remember folks..never take anyone for granted..photographers are as much an integral part of the scene as anyone else..nuff said....

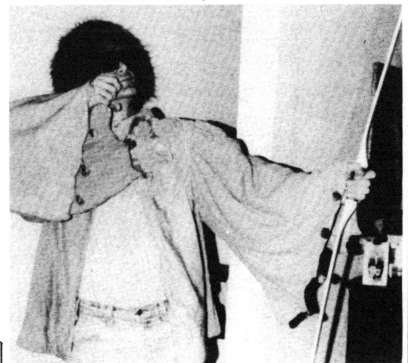

No it aint Handsome Dick..It's John"Sky" (don't call me Stabb)Schroeder in hisWi- lliam Tell phase...ya see he ate some eclairs that sat out too long n' he;s trippin' his brains out!!..nobody parties like this guy...!!!

FROM '77, HOLLAND HAD SEEN THEM COME AND GO; THE
PUNKBANDS. SOME WERE PRETTY DUMB, SOME HATEFULLY
STUPID, BUT SOME WERE ALLRIGHT I SUPPOSE.AS THE
ONLY EUROPEAN COUNTRY WHO HAD THEIR USA TELEVISION-
PROGRAMMES IN THE USA LANGUAGE, THEY FOUND IT OK
TO SING IN ENGLISH.
IN '77 EVERYBODY SAW THEIRSELVES A LITTLE AS PUNK
AND LISTENED TO BLONDIE AND THE JAM, WHILE OUR
OWN BANDS STAYED UNKNOWN. THESE BANDS WERE "IVY GREEN"
AND "SPEEDTWINS". THEY DIDN'T HAVE A LOT TO SAY,
BUT MADE AN LP ANYWAY. THE LP OF THE SPEEDTWINS IS
AS GOOD AS THE PISTOLS DEBUT.
IN '78 THINGS WERE CHANGING. THE MUSIC DIDN'T LOOK
SO ROCK ANYMORE, LIKE A YEAR BEFORE. THE LYRICS
BECAME IMPORTANT, WAY WAY MORE THAN THE MUSIC/..
WE HAD A FEW BANDS WHO WANTED TO BE LABBELED AS
RED; THE RONDOS WAS THE MOST WELLKNOW ONE. THEY
MADE AN ALBUM. ALSO VERY WELLKNOWN WAS THE EX.
THE EX MADE 2 ALBUMS AND EVERYBODY LOVED THOSE
BANDS. BUT THE MUSIC BECAME LOUDER AGAIN AND
IT WASN'T COOL ANYMORE TO LIKE THEM (WE DON'T
USE THE TERM COOL, BUT THIS STORY IS AMERICANIZED
FOR THE AMERICAN READERS¢
THE NITWITZ AND THE WORKMATES WERE LOUD AND AN EXAMPLE
FOR THE NEW BANDS, WHO WERE REACTING VERY LATE. THE
NITWITZ MADE AN LP. A NEW INDEPENDED RECORD LABEL
CAME OUT OF NOWHERE AND BROUGHT OUT RECORDS FROM
NOXIOUS, RAPERS, BIZON KIDS, LULLABIES, NIXE, RAKKETAX,
AND MORE. THEY ALL SOUND THE SAME AND THEY ALL AGREED
THAT LYRICS WERE IMPORTANT, BUT IF YOU READ THEM, YOU'LL
SEE THEY HAVEN'T GOT A LOT TO BE PROUD OF.
THE LAST FEW YEARS WERE IN THE NAME OF THE LOUDER
BANDS: JESUS & THE GOSPELFUCKERZ AND ZMIV. WE ALSO
DISCOVERED THE TAPE AS A CHEAP WAY TO BE HEARD AND
ON THE TAPE YOU CAN HEAR: PUKE, TOTAL CHAOZ, SURVIVAL
SQUAD, ASPERITYS, TRASHBAGZ, DDT AND MORE. I (PETER
ZIRSCHKY) PLAY IN FUNERAL ORATION, AND IS ON THE
TAPE "RAW WAR" BY X-CENTRIC NOISE IN ENGLAND AND
THE NEXT COM. TAPE BY "EIH".
IF YOU SEND ME A LIVE TAPE BY AN USA PUNKBAND, I'LL
SEND YOU A TAPE WITH 36 DUTCH PUNKBANDS.....

ADDRESSES:(ME)   PETER ZIRSCHKY, BURG ROELL STRAAT 203-2,
                 1064 BL AMSTERDAM, HOLLAND

(EIH-TAPES)   PAUL VD BERG, KOERIERSTERS WEG 21,
                 3815 NT AMERSPOORT, HOLLAND

(X-CENTRIC NOISE) X-CENTRIC NOISE TAPES
                   17 WEST END ROAD, COTTINGHAM,
                   NORTH HUMBERSIDE, HU16 5PL
                   ENGLAND

IN THE TONGUE IN CHEEK DEPT.

RACISM ALERT!!RACISM ALERT!!RACISM ALERT!!
AP)In a surprise move various and sundry
bands have moved into a new foray in the
world of punkdom..most notably an all
black band from NY has become the 'Bad
Crackers' who are reportedly beginning
each show with the challenge to the
audience'What's 10" and white?" With
the crowds of white fascist youth responding "NOTHING!!!" they also have
reportedly reworked some of their old
tunes into the now classic 'Fealess Honkey Killers'/
'I Luv I Women Fixing Me Dinner Wit Bare Feet On
A Dirt Floor'/and 'White Man Moonstompin'...in the
Motor City" we have Negative Watermelon with their
new hits "Ready To Grub"/"Rib Song"/"Sick Of Gooks"
with lead vocalist now ending "Fair Warning" with
that gentle refrain 'Don't Make me do what I dont
wanna do...cuz iiiiii'm a SEX MACHINE"!More details
on this new phenom as it develops...

Fockin great!
a manic masterpiece.!!!
Your single is a killer son.—
Heres our records

please send a Teen Idles
record to—
NECROS
c/o Barry Henssler
Box 421
Maumee, Ohio
         43537

Thanks
Tesco Vee

Tesco to Ian Snail Mail Missive #3

by FAT PAT

F A N Z I N E S

Here's the latest batch of publications,mags rags and periodicals I've recieved of late.. if I forgot yours write n' bitch OK?

TERMINAL-Large format with quality layout and incisive coverage...issue #12 features Husker Du/Black Flag/William Burroughs/ABC and more...great..$1 for sample copy PO Box 2165 Phila.Pa 19103

WARNING-As they so aptly put it this is Alaskas' only alternative..chaotic with multi colored pages..interesting bit on a guy who visited a high school to speak on"punk" also FEAR/Nina Hagen and record reviews.. good job folks...PO BOX 102993 Anchorage Alaska 99510

TENSION IN THE CATHEDRAL-Unfortun ately the last issue...Scott seems to have lost his taste for the music..tsk tsk..156 Abbot Rd Concord nh 03301

STRAIGHT EDGE-These folks take heat for saying what they think..which means I respect them a helluva lot..also happen to love their mag..this ish features Rattus/CJ's/Social Distortion/ and tons more..1850 Ocaen Ave 4D Brooklyn NY 11230 $1.50 by mail............

TRULY NEEDY-Another phone book from the folks at TN...How they manage to charge 80¢ is beyond me cuz mama printing is expensive..extensive interviews with Scream/Social suicide/Static Disruptors wide ranging record reviews..their scope is not limited..everyone has their say from fags like Howard Weulfing to studs like John Schroeder...Luv ya Barb-PO BOX 2271 Rockville MD 20852

THRILLSEEKER-What these guys have to say deserves saying more often ...63 pages..hey their chart has everthing from Bobby Darin to Ozzie..hey they even scored a Trouble Funk review.. extremely open minded...12515 Brewster lane Bowie MD20715....

SLUM WORDS-Ahh yes issue #2 gives me yet another pocket pistol w/ coverage of various scenes and NA/Iron Cross/Los Olvidados F-uckin great!!!185 South 16th St San Jose Ca 95112

LAST RITES-2 issues out of this great new Chicago zine..the new one features an ill informed T-sol/and reviews 1717 Sunnyside Beach Dr. Mc Henry Ill 60050

METAL MANIA-I know most metal blows moose meat but it's still cool to see an underground publication focusing on this type of music...features on big names and up and comers..Iau Kallen 1460 Webster St #5 San Fransisco Ca 94115 send $1

COMMUNIST ATROCITY-Political of a straṅe nature..never uh thought of it that way..ha ha..plays on cliches.. recently inspired to start up again.. send stamps...PO BOX 577 Elm Grove Wi 53122

TWISTED IMAGE-Large format newsprint from Frisco. latest is full of zines and such.record reviews and comix..2501 Haste St #414 Berkeley Ca 94704

BLATCH-Pint size from Oklahoma but hey dont hold that against em..this is a good zine..good layout and art..c/o Jymn Blanchard 501 Castle Rd. Bartlesville Ok 74003

MAX R&R-No. 6 is out w/Dicks,Skins=Nazis Effigies,Reports from all over,and records.. PO Box 288 Berkeley Ca 94701

PRIMITIVE NOISE-From the Windy City comes another half size..barely legible coverage of Chicagos scene and various other stuff.. Best part is a recount of the emotional scars of an attack by geese..great.. c/o Barry Stepe 11034 W.Doogan St Willow Springs Il 60480

O.G.SHITZ-OK so theres Mickey Mouse taking a dump on the cover..yuksville.. coverage of new bands The Convicted and Turmoil..write..13222 Siemon St. Garden Grove Ca 92643

GAGGING DOG-5 pages full of reviews and such..hilarious pic of a punked out Liberace..speaking of that virtuoso of the ivories can you picture that blond young buck boyfriend a his mounting his flabby bunger and wallowing in that quagmire??Geez I'd rather watch a South American snuff movie..then again I'll pass on both.. 1624Gaylon Dr Tempe Ari. 85282

TESTUBE NEWSLETTER-Distributor that deals in records and zines and such..some revi PO Box 89 Bascom Ohio 44809

BLUR-Zines dont haveta be chubby there bub to be choice..hey you know this place Lawrence makes the rest of middle America look pretty lame..and Ok I was a tad rough on Blakes Alternative AMERICA...what can I say except my prostate (affectionatly called by dingy doughnut)flared along with the colitus.... anyone would be an asshole with that little tandem now wouldnt they?write Blur atBox 3374 Lawrence Kansas 66044

MALICE-Vaults its way into my top whatever in short time..WHY???Because there is more to the world of music than fucking hardcore and opened minds these people are..everything from the obtuse to the chartreuse(whatever that means??)PO BOX 241022 Memphis Tenn 38124

Continued on page 25

FREE BEER PRESS-Hey from Osthemo Mich. I used to roller skate there..my grandaddy is buried there..single sheet. 4 sided..uncompromising to the point of becoming fuckfaces at times but I wont begrudge em that because too many zines kiss fuckin ass and at least these guys take a stand..good copy..good paper ..A+ guys...PO Box 412 Oshtemo Mich 49009

SMASHED HITS#6 of this little gem from southwestern Mich..lots of reviews and coverage..get it.. 2449 Normandy dr se Grand Rapids Mich 49506

of

venom

photo by KEVIN HODAPP

LIVE

INSURRECTION/HEART ATTACK/SCREAM at the 9;30
Sorry but we missed Insurrection cuz we were
late,got caught in traffic..excuses blah blah..
reports said they were great...Heart Attack
are I believed recently reformed and I was
pretty impressed with their songwriting and
delivery...the between song raps were a bit
forced but overall they rocked the place..
they now feature a two guitar line up when
they were previously a three piece..anyway
on to Scream...back after too long of a lay-
off...this scene aint so big that it can do
without any combo as mighty as dis...and of
course they played with your basic unbridled
intensity..they manage to look smoothly at
ease whilst the serious riffs be laying waste
to the meager hearing left in my drums...a
good matinee but a slim turnout...where were
you?

METALLICA/VENOM at the PARAMOUNT in NY 4/24/83
I'd be a bald face liar if I said I wasn't shitting when I heard Venom were coming over...it t-
urned out to be only two shows in NY(their Frisco
shows were cancelled)The opening act was from P=
ortland and had some good heavy riffs but the pan-
tywaister on vocals shot down anything they did..
too typical...something Venom is not...the drums
were a good ten feet up and this place they played was your basic light show rock palace which in
actuality is the only place they could have played considering the size of their stage show...so
this twisted voice comes on and as they hit the
opening chord the biggest blast knocked me back..
it had to have been ten bombs all going off at
once...it startled the fuck outa me and killed
every sperm cell I owned..the crowd up front s-
eemd unphased(we're talking the leather/patches
and studs brigade...we seemed to be the only
crossovers in the audience)The band raged through
all their faves "Countess Bathory"/"Black Metal"
a rousing "Teachers Pet"...their banter with the
audience kept the whole thing fuckin fun as shit..
The double bass featured the line "Fucking-Cunt"
as they affectionately call Abbadon..I mean this
place was Armageddon personified...smoke..flames..
bombs..and the most gut wrenching music I have
witnessed..Cronos' twisted features bellowing
contempuous lyrics accented by Mantas who would
screech the chorus in ear damaging intensity...
supposedly the first show had sucked and the
band kept saying "This blows the fucking shit
outa Friday night huh?"Their performance this
night was really tight and strong...I always
wondered what the faces would be to greet me
when it came judgment day...now I know..the
band promises to return as they so eliquently
put it..'We're going to come back and blow
your fucking asses to hell" or something to
that affect...Instead of "100 Days in Sodom"
it was "100 Days in NY"...so they lyricised
it...simply the most awesome thing I have
witnessed...I'm shitting....TV

     WHITEHOUSE/GI/KRAUT/NO TREND/SCREAM..somewhere
downtown DC)
Just caught the last few minutes of WHITEHOUSE from
England,venerable labelmates of the infamous COME
Organization...all the ear splitting feedback and
grate anyone could want..not tonight I guess..wrong
place,time and crowd...I have a few of their LP's
but a bit of this has to mentally absorbed in the
privacy of ones own abode...went out to get air and
drinks and missed some of GI but what I saw was good but shit no lights made it hard to enjoy Johns

GEE of **INSURRECTION**   photo by JIM SAAH

this guy wants to do shows...but a good
well planned 'event' beats the fuck out
of these hasty exercizes in futility...

antics..he did a scene from the upcoming movie release "GI Blood Massacre"..KRAUT were tight and to
the point..that is when their bigger than life ego
trips dont get in the way..."hea some postuhs eben
tho ya don desoive em"...OK so I wont let the fact
that their buttwipes cloud the fact that they're
competent at what they do...NO TREND need to lear-
n that to accomplish their goal of alienation and
a massive love to hate us syndrome they must at
least be competent musicians or competent manipulators or competent something...I wanted to
hate them really I did and got a mediocre mush
of nondescript half assed nothingness...for all
their antagonistic posturings its laughable they
have such a weak alternative...the aformentioned
combo droned on and on to the point where I couldnt hang out for Scream...a neither her nor
here evening........

WHITE CROSS/FANG/FAITH/NO TREND/THE JONSES
at the Lansburgh Cultural Center
First FANG cancelled then I guess FAITH
never intended to play or something,then
they substituted LEGAL WEAPON for FANG
then LEGAL WEAPON didnt show up..sound
fucked up?Sure was...most of the crowd
just hung out..this show was poorly organised and poorly advertised and was
in my estimation detrimental to the DC
scene...particularly when dealing with
out of towners who'll go off spouting
DC sucks when in actuality any show in
any city can bomb given enough strikes
against it...its all well and good that

baboon dooley in "FANZINE CONVENTION '83!"

SepPuKu-"Dekompostiones"Side Effekts Records...Pretty up front for this bunch...
they've set their trend I guess they can
wax whichever way they want.."Twilight Of
The Idols"is dank and ritual...like some
sort of pagan exchange..is it true all these guys are terminally ill?Some interesting observations on the back..how we are
entering another dark age of a passive electronic society as all cultures come to
simulate one another as western media spreads...this record has a sense of genuine
despair about it...now that I think about
it this is as disturbing as as any of their other releases...just proves their
diversity............................

THE EFFIGIES-"WE'RE DA MACHINE" Ruthless
Records...Ya you know they're one of my
faves...a 4 track 12" after all the waiting
is a bit of a let down especially with the
age of the material...with all the great
new tunes they've got going for them I
was hoping for an LP or whatever..this
will do for now..oh ya thanks alot for
the tape Babbin..support and be supported..

MARK STEWART AND THE MAFIA-"LEARNING TO
COPE WITH COWARDICE" Plexus Records
Hey I can take a hefty dose of politics
with the next guy and with this it goes
down alot easier than the customary set
to music adolescent "I wanna do it my
way"Cliche...here we have the plight of
humankind as Mr POP GROUP has always l-
et us in on what isnt any secret-that
injustice aint exactly hidden under any
rocks..."Blessed ARE THOSE WHO STRUGGLE"
can only be described as 'industrial
dub'...it stands as the psychotic masterpiece on this disc..black man lays d-
own the beat...screeching white man
documents in tones of anguish and torment..knocks this man back...I need it...

SHOCKABILLY-"EARTH VS SHOCKABILLY"Pretty
Wired stuff.Lotsa covers and done 'reel
psycho' w/a little 'shake of the hips"
thrown in.You've never heard "Purple
Haze" or "Day Tripper" put through the
ringer like this.Hendrix and Lennon are
twistin' in their boxes.Weak tummys are
to avoid this "mood rang"..sorta Reside-
ntish..Hmmm...reviewed by John Schroeder

VIRGIN PRUNES-"THE FACULTIES OF A BROKEN HEART"/
"WHAT SHOULD WE DO IF BABY TURNS BLUE" Rough Trade...OK so this is from last year I just copped
and I can't let an issue go by without expounding
on these guys' virtues...I'm still kicking meself
for not seeing them here but my folks were visiting
and they aint into the Prunes too much...these men
are very sick/bent/warped/theatrical..their music
varies with each release,with one thing a constant-
it's all fuckin great..this one was produced by
Wire's Colin Newman and is dedicated to Claude
Bessey(our loved one)Jeez ol Kickboy is still
out there somewhere..he always did have good
taste.........................

MIXED NUTS DON'T CRACK-Various Artists
Outside Records
Well recorded and executed for the most
part...a good documentation of DC's 'other
bands'..call them what you will..garage
experimental...they all have their licks
and hooks to vary this package enough for
repeat listenings..they are in a bit of
a position seeing that most people won't
be open minded enough to appreciate say
Chalk Circle along with United Mutation
who by the way are the fave on this..
they almost strike me of a parody of
speed only bands with a great raspy
animal on vocals...dont read their lyrics by the way or their impact is ruined...Nuclear Crayons hit with Catwalk
which is a jerked out ditty about something obtuse..the package comes with
elaborate foldout info and lyrics..but
somehow this works better in the dark
at 4 AM...also appearing here are Social
Suicide/Hate From Ignorance/Media Disease..all in all this is a necessity...
limited so hurry..Outside Records 3111
First St. North Arlington Va 22201

HATES-PANACEA"-Faceless Records
The Hates mode of attack seems to
have shifted slightly over the past
coupla years...their earlier singles
were cut outa rougher stock and wh-
en I first listened to this I was
instantly put off particularly by
"Houston" a Lee Hazlewood...but wh-
en Christian Arnheiter cuts loose
on the guitar this band is still
capable of some serious energy g-
eneration...still I liked the old
sound better...4200 W.34th St.Box
132 Houston Texas 77092

BIG BOYS-LULLABIES HELP THE BRAIN GROW"
Moment Records...There are a few things
in life I truly regret...not fucking that
big titted 16 year old when I was 13..not
fucking that big titted 21 year old when
I was 15..and not seeing the fucking BIG
BOYS when they were in town because everyone I talked to said it was cancelled..
I stuck my heel up my ass and walked around for days swearing at pedestrians,
and otherwise being miserable..you see
folks the whole idea is to set trends..
ya you know..as in not follow your heart and not everyone elses idea of cool...
this amalgm of funk/fun and cascading
gooood times splatters the competition
against da wall..both times this one
DC band comes back from their tour
(they'll remain nameless)I say "Hey
who was your fave band in the whole
country out of the 81 you seen'?"
da bald one say"BIG BOYS"/the peroxide funster sez"Big Boys" the pretty boy in da nasty green pinto sez
"BIG BOYS" so what am ah ta think??

WHITE FLAG-"S IS FOR SPACE" GASA TANKA Records
I'm a like...click it clicks..takes the whole
shebang into the furthest realms of the furthest nirvana of California asROCK AS A HARD
PLACE..parody of all time..a battleship steaming past the punks run aground...swerving
round all obstacles..humor.insight..self
taught and self mastered prophesy for the
80's... a how to for those a yearnin for the
truth and excellence in new music..goes be-
yon RED CROSS(blas-hemy,I'll burn in hell)
Epitomizes the chaos,the cliche,the bloated
and beasched whale of LA..burns past all of
us with a retching sense of purpose..but the-
n coming to the realization there is no pur-
pose(of course)I understand and folow meek-
ly..submissively in WHITE FLAGS WAKE...fuc-
king sperm screaming into my toilet...a healthy crap..a pizza with anchovies..all
that is good in the world..fuck.........

What ahm ta think is"Tesco ol man..
ya fucked up"..oh well until they
decide to come back ah jus console
meeself wit this slab of quintisse-
ntial goodtime cum serioso comment-
ata..write BIG BOYS 4808 AVE G
Austin Texas 78751

Smoked 7 FLESH
RECORDS

PRESENTS

"LUNG COOKIES"

A NATIONAL COLLECTION

FEATURING 16 BANDS
PLUS FANZINE!!

OUT LATE JUNE!

Smoke Seven
7230 De Soto Ave., Suite 104
Canoga Park, CA 91303

YOUR FLESH
FANZINE
1619 LAGOON #106
MPLS. MN. 55408

LAYOUT/Fleshpipe
PHOTO/BARBERO

POISON IDEA

T:Tom...C:Chris...J:Jerry....

I MIGHT BE MAD ABOUT THE WAY THINGS ARE TURNING OUT,
YOU MIGHT BE DEAD,THERE'S ONE WAY OUT
IT'S NOT UP, YOU BETTER THINK TWICE

I MIGHT BE MAD ABOUT THE WAY THINGS ARE TURNING OUT,
NO CHOICE FOR YOU,GOOD DEATH'S A BLESSING,
OPEN WIDE AND TAKE YOUR POISON,
COUNT YOUR BLESSINGS,BEFORE YOU LOSE THEM.

STAND ON BOTH FEET, HOLD MY OWN
NO GUN,NO WAY TO MAKE A MARK,
IMPRESSED, OBSESSED WITH PEOPLE I

TV:Would it bum you out if I said you reminded me a bit of the FIX? T:No I'm glad it didnt remind you of KISS,the FIX were great band and it's a compliment. J:People always say my voice sounds like Steve's I never thought so. TV:Whats Portland like to you guys? C:Terrible..J:Great,cold..T:Muscular.. TV:What inspired the cover concept on your EP? T:I'm a fan of Elvis's and his face and Christs' are the most universal faces in the world. Elvis is interesting to me because he's the American dream gone mad.Purest example of over indulgence. TV:How often are there shows?T:It varies..J:I go to everything,trendy,what have you about every week.C:? TV:Have any other bands influenced your style musically or lyrically? J:Lyrically-Furious Pig-Imperialist Pigs and the Pigs.T:Germs/Stooges/Syd Barret/ Discharge/SOA/and early Dischord shit we liked. C:Grinding teeth and knocking knees. TV:Opinion of porno/God/and drugs and their im-

pact on American Youth? T:The first and last allow you to ignore the second.C:Porno's great,God's ok but drugs are bad news..whatever you can stick in your ass is OK. J:I like porno in good humor,I don't believe in god and I take drugs and drink but hey I don't smoke.T:I don't smoke pot or cigarettes but I read tea leaves and sniff rose hips. Why does Reggae suck?J:Because they have rules,their rasta beliefs and shit.Religion; fuck it.TV:Amen..C:I used to like reggae until I saw the Bad Brains and $800 for 15 minutes and their hats looked corny.T:Being fashion and cleanliness conscious.I believe you should shave and wash your hair regularly. TV:Do you believe music is a tool for social change?T:Yes it has,starting with the Beatles The stones and Elvis..good or bad..C:It seems to be working out that way..T:Whether hardcore will is to be seen. TV:How has the re-

spons to your EP been?T:Good.J:All my pals like it,we have so much more new material though.TVSo the home town folks love ya or hate ya?C:Nobody loves me,but everyone seems to like the band..J:Nobody hates me but no-one will buy me a coke.T:It sure seems like we got treated like shit for a long time. TV:So what now?J:Tour..put out another record,tour..put out another re-T:And put out more bands on Fatal Erection, like Final Warning and Civil Defense..... they gang,,,write POISON IDEA at c/o Tom ROberts 939 NE 168th St Portland,Oregon 97230

THINK TWICE-

GIVE IT UP, GIVE IT UP, BURN IN HELL OR ROT INSANE.

12"

DIE DORAUS &DIE MARINAS LP-CBS Records
OK so they never had records this good when I was a toddling,runny diapered little shaver..they even played here recently and I dorked around and didnt make it again..what makes it is Die Marinas those 4 lovely lass' whose infectious alpine warbling is so satisfying even too a long in the tooth post pubescent like meself....great....

ACCEPT-"RESTLESS AND WILD" Heavy Metal World Wide Records
The opening cut is the most awesome driving pounding metallic onslaught I've had the pleasure to hear of late...there's something about double bass that just plain sends this boy inta orbit.. "Fast As A Shark" must be heard..a cut above the rest of this record but it still has many bright spots...the singer comes dangerous ly close to the melodic pretty boy at times but manages enough mean mouth grunge to keep this listenable Hey I've listened to alot of this stuff over the years...back in the early 70's I was your basic patches,hair and denim freak with Hard Stuff(remember them?) Budgie and the like regularly perusing the old tabel...so's yes I have somewhat of a basis for differentiation and I say this is <u>hot</u> stuff...............

COCTEAU TWINS-Peppermint pig"/"Laugh Lines" "Hazel" 4·AD Records...I know it isnt fair that will all the thousands of bands out there struggling for recognition..one such as this comes up with all the right ideas-with two 12" and an LP under their belts these folks are clicking with regularity-classic seperation between voice(femme) clang axe,and basso profundo..not for everyone but then neither is good taste...

DIE HAUT-"Der Karibische Western"
Sadly missed their 9:30 show..this is what I had always hoped Wall OF Voodoo would have sounded like instead of their lame Tulsa Bar band in a truck stop doing Devo covers sound..good drive and Chris Spedding guitar tremolo bar twang..nice..contact Zensor Belziger Strabe 23 1000 Berlin 62 W.Germany

ACID-GIANT records..Hey Cleotis willya check out that sleeve..skulls wit wurms, skulls wit jewels,skulls wit crosses stuck tru em'...but hey man we're talkin' sludge...p poor production...lousy lyrics featuring such ingenuous chorus lines as "Acid is the name-heavy metal is the game"Besides the woman croonin here is trying to vibratto here and it makes her sound like shit...from Belgium..steer clear...

GOVERNMENT ISSUE "Boycott Stabb" Fountain Of Youth" Records..soem swell guy or gal thought he would vibe Master Schroder and defame him on the construction site across from record and tape..so being the sport he is he immortalizes this..uh.."art" on this jammin' 12"..ahhh at last a recording of the classic song "G.I.."..a DC classic.. even the semi-muddy production cant mask the energy and creative songwriting herein...fore I be branded a biased son-of-a-ranter Ill close...buy..buy...consume.. enjoy...5710 Durbin Rd. Bethesda MD 20817

BLACK MARKET BABY '12 Song LP.'
OUT By AUGUST

GOVERNMENT ISSUE
THE Long Awaited 'MAKE AN EFFORT' 7" ep

OUT NOW
GOVERNMENT ISSUE
(Dischord/Fountain of Youth)
Boycott Stabb
12" ep

Fountain of Youth RECORDS

T$ JEE
BOX 25305
WASH dc 20007

LAST MINUTE RECORD REVIEWS.....
SONIC YOUTH "CONFUSION IS SEX" Neutral
Driving dischordant non melodys..like
a controlled experimentation..recorded
in a much more severe framework than t-
heir first effort...the guitar is as abrasive as they come...sounds like he's
butchering the thing..the ideas are r-
unning thick and red on this..varied-
not redundant..this one will make a
variety of tastes feel satisfaction..
CLOCK DVA-"ADVANTAGE" Polydor
When these guys tossed in the towel
I was a giving up..when the DVA things came out they were way too dance oriented to suit my tastes..but
then one Adi Newton realized his folly
and created a whole new Clock DVA..so
basically this is the follow up to
the classic "Thirst"...ahhhh..yes...

ng beforehand whether SOCIAL SUICIDE would play.Some-
one said they had broken up,which may or may not be t-
rue.I probably would have been happy not to see them
close the show,but when they took the stage they wer-
e only a three piece,with the bassist and guitarist t-
rading off on vocals.As such they were tight inspiring
and powerful.The absence of a lead vocalist(he is a b-
ouncer at 9;30 and unfortunately for the other band
members, a strong focal point, a smug focal point)did
them wonders.SOCIAL SUICIDE should breathe new life
as a three piece,if the decide to stay together....

Another Live Review !!

UNITED MUTATION/MEDIA DISEASE/NUCLEAR CRAYONS/HATE FR-
OM IGNORANCE/SOCIAL SUICIDE May 22 at the 9;30 Reviewed
by Josh.....It seems that Niteclub 930 is having second
thoughts about these Sunday hardcore matinees because a
couple of shows haven't been drawing well enough.In the
future,there will be matinees less often and with big n-
ame acts or special events,like this one,celebrating th-
e MIXED NUTS compilation LP.I guess around 100 to 125 p-
eople were there,a fair sized numder to come out and support these rather new inexperienced bands.(things in DC
are kind of happening on a smaller scale than one might
expect)Missing in action were CHALK CIRCLE,who are on t-
he album,but have since broken up....Arriving too late
to see United MUTATION(truly great vocals on the record

for sure),I caught the last three by MEDIA DISEASE and
think they need to get away from the stereotypical high
school/concentration camp subject matter,but if I was s-
till in high school I wouldnt hold it against them.It w-
as nice of NUCLEAR CRAYONS not to insist on headlining
the show.Probably the most important thing about them
is that the singer Lynch is the one who put out the record and organized the show.The band was happy to just
be themselves,loose and noisy.I believe they've played
out more than any of these other bands but arent on a-
ny superiority trip.They even broke out some toy instruments to sing Tammy Wynette's "Stand By Your Man".
HATE FROM IGNORANCE were playful and exciting showing
some real potential to be an interesting band for months and months to come...Alot of people were wonderi-

501

WHITE FLAG

Kiss alot.TV:Thats cuz anyone in any band that's worth their salt loves KISS...I mean is the pope white? Whos the biggest bufoon in CA these days..eg..the biggest dick?Pick:Well I can't say who is the biggest dick,but Al definately has the biggest dick..AL:No comment... so how long have you been a homosexual, Tesco?

TV:So describe your outlook on life/the scene/and the world in 25 words or less...(oh ya the band members are..Pat Fear/Al Bum/Jello B.Afro/Doug Graves/El Fee/ Pick Z.Stix,Tracy Element/Victor Kofdrop Richard S- ookey(not answering here) Pat:LA is huge and becoming impersonal,I used to go to shows and know everyone there.Most of the original punks have backed out be- cause the "media punks"made punk somewhat unpleasant. AL:The world is a mess,but the USA is still the best country in the world..there are no guns keeping you inside our borders..Jello:I've got a one way ticket to Moscow for any of those silly communist punks.. DOUG:Communist punks..what a contradiction,silly, silly,silly..TV:Bless you for saying that..when was WHITE FLAG conceived?PAT:DRUGS SUCK..EL:White Flag was conceived on December 25 about 1,983 years ago. TV:Hey there was no room at the inn was there?PICK: About a year ago,we decided that alot of punk had become it's own worst enemy,so we decided to re-in troduce some anarchy into it,nothing political,just fun,threatening punk values..TV:Still the original line up?Tracy:There is no line up.We have this cir- cle of people that all know the songs on different instruments,and whoever wants to play a particular show does,so thats our line up.PAT:And anyone who knows our stuff is welcome to sing and play on it at some point in the show,we like to get people in- volved..DOUG:The first record was me on bass,Pat on guitar and EL on guitar,Pick on drums and Al on vocals.He's the only person that always plays he's irreplacable.TV:OK so lay it out..your feel- ings on politico punkers..AL:Politics in punk are not our trip...but some people like it and thats

TV:You picked a bad time to ask me that cuz some 45 year old fag just kicked me outa his grocery store for wearing a Mi sfits"Bullet"-T/shirt...of course after I left after exchanging a few niceties) I thought to myself.."45 year old fags offend me..so I knelt down and prayed as hard as I could he would get AIDS and die very soon...thats how long I've b- een gay..AL:Was Mugger a good lay?TV:The best thing I ever saw Mugger do in the sex dept. was in Detroit he was going around asking for head from all these wenches he didnt even know..so he hauls off and slings one over his shoulder cave man style and as he's crossing the street she slips and cl-

umpo head first into the concrete..I dont think he got too much head that nite...so anyway ..how have people reacted to your name?PAT:Well the smart ones see what we are doing and are into us but there is a certain faction that say things like"YOU CAN'T call yourself that" and we get de- ath threats and stuff when we're on the radio.Some of them cum as soon as they hear the name..JeLLO:Some people are in- timidated by us,which seperates the inte- lligent ones from the uh less informed punks.AL:They've putt BLACK FLAG on a pedestal,made them into stars,which is what punk set out to eliminate,or at l- east create an alternative to.BF are our friends and they're all smart enough to see what we're doing.Henry is our biggest fan,really!!!TV:How is the LA

ok if they have an answer,I just hate people say- ing something sucks and not having an alternative. Communism and socialism suck,democracy is the on- ly system for me.If you dont like it here leave. Pat:Like you can be a communist here but try be- ing a democrat in Russia and see what happens rea- l fast..PICK:WE have a message,we're Pro USA but it isnt like we wont associate with someone who has different views...we like Articles Of Faith.. they are communists...so what..Jello.Politics in music is almost pointless anyway,even if you h- ave some profoundly innovative message nobody cares,like Bob Dylan wouldnt have sold any re- cords in the 60's if he had had the same mess- ages backed by Throbbing Gristle,art and politics makes boring art and useless politics in alot of cases.TRACY:Punk isnt going to change any- thing besides fashion and music.JELLO:I like

scene these daysBest bands?Jello:I don't go to shows unless we're playing because it's too far,RED KROSSS is the best band. PAT:I used to go to shows but I'm too cool now..no I'm just too poor,I used to go to the Starwood three times a week to see the GERMS/X/FEAR/and all the original bands.REDD KROSS/Social Dist- ortion/CH3/BANGLES/NIG HEIST/and POWER- TRIP are the best bands.except for W.A.S.P. and TEST PATTERN,heavy metal bands that are just radical beyond belief.I like Kiss alot too...TV:What type of women are hanging ar- ound after the shows waiting to get their butts pop...FAT:Big sleazy bitches in S.S. uniforms with leather whips and spike st- illeto heels that talk in authoritarian manners with German accents and give or- ders especially to ¡AL..PICKAnd he does whatever they say.Tracy:I like the male lesbians like the Naughty Women

your sister is eating em...besides why do Haitian people even exist.?Shit ask yourself some questions ok?WF:What are our favorite bands?PAT:KISS/X RAY SPEX/ GENERATION X/SEX PISTOLS/KISS/KRAUT/ BLACK FLAG/DEATH PATROL/CAHUENGA/REDD KROSS/TRAFFIC/SOCIAL DISTORTION/

and the NIG HEIST people,they crack me up.PAT: I wish more policeman would come to our shows.. TV:Whens the US tour?DOUG:Write to SST PO BOX 1 and ask for BLack Flag..We wont tour without them as a matter of principle unless we get 5 million a gig.PAT Or if we get to open for KISS but only on the condition that they dump the new guy and let me play lead for them.JELLO I'm too tired to tour,its hard enough to get from one room of the house to another at this point.TV:So are you the antithesis of BF?You both share the Black Sabbath influence huh? PAT:We're sort of the antithesis of what punk is now which is almost the opposite of what it was in the beginning.EL:Nobody in our band has any Black Sabbath records but we do "Paranoid" for our encore because AL looks like Ozzie.. our hardcore fans call themselves the OZZY YPUTH...weird huh?PAT:I have the first album OZZY YOUTH is like the KISS ARMY..EL:OH. DOUG:Black FLAG is fun,we're fun..this is music not social revolution,we're as much the same as they are different...TRACY:What did all that mean?DOUG:Nothing...

What;s the significance of that flying V axe?Yer wangs are shaped like that or wot? PAT:My flying V represents KISS and any.ot- her cool band I like.Dez played it once and looked awesome,he sang "Communication Break- down"with us in San Fransisco..we all got AIDS up there..AL:And Jeff from Red Kross s- ang "Watchin You" by KISS with us..PAT:And I sand "Strutter" and "Cmon And Love Me" with Red Kross..almost all the cool bands oute here are into KISS..TV:Who?I forgot... JELLO:I miss Ace alot..PAT:Ace is the best guitarist in the world.Pat Smear is the se- cond best and I like ADRENALIN OD/KRAUT and the MISFITS cuz they look like(you guessed it folks,ED)KISS.   TV:The world would be better place if what five people were dead? AL:You know that's a loaded question..PAT: Yeah there are five people in that other Flag band ha ha..JELLO:Black Flag are our friends..why do people think we're at war or something?DOUG:Because alot of people are silly,goobledeee goookky gump lump TRACY:What are you talking about?TV:We're talking about that store owner who makes sandwiches with AIDS on his fingers and

MEATMEN(send me a free record)AOF/DIE KREUZEN/ 5051/MINOR THREAT/RESIDENTS/KISS/MOTORHEAD/ DAMNED/BUZZCOCKS/ and LA's gods the GERMS... AL:DESCENDENTS/CODE OF HONOR/SSD/SOCIAL D./ MISFITS/SCREAM/GERMS/ADOLESCENTS/BAGS/REDD KROSS/VENOM/CIRCLE JERKS/MOTORHEAD/JELLO"KISS/ AND RED KROSS/ AND KISS AND THE GERMS AND SSD/ DOUG:THIN LIZZY and RED KROSS/PICK:TOy RAZOR/ AND TEST PATTERN/and UFO/and KISS and miNOR THREAT..EL:UFO and ADOLESCENTS and W.A.S.P. TRACY:NERVOUS GENDER and THE VANDALS..VICTOR: How come I didnt answer any questions in this interview?PAT I like TWISTED SISTER alot too especially the live stuff..JELLO:I hate music. It's much too much work,I want to go to sleep. Q:What do we think of Max r&r ?Pat:They ref- used to print an interview this girl did with us,said they didnt want to promote our viewpoint anyone that thinks that way deserves what we've got for them..JELLO:And thats a one way ticket to Moscow.DOUG:Have fun and be careful..AL:Jeff to the red courtesy ph- one..PATCheze out.TRACY:What is a MAXIMUM ROCK AND ROLL?......our album is called "S IS FOR SPACE and its seven bucks from GASATANKA REC- ORDS(checks payable to GASATANKA) 1241 N Harper Suite 6(Suite??what is this suite? pretty leggy secretaries dancing about in pink velveteen mini's lighting your cigars and grubbing on your dirty beef bayonets no doubt,ED)HOLLYWOOD CA 90046...GASATANKA is also putting out a compilation(who isnt? ED)album so send tapes and photos for consider- ation.WHITE FLAG has material ready for any compilations too. ALL:We don't care if it's a drag..surrender now and raise the White Flag..."

≡DAYGLO PEOPLE⚡

the following is an interview with DAYGO MEN
a band from Poland....TV:What inspired you to
start a band?DM:Probably the Martial law has
inspired us to get a band,we think so.The s-
econd reason of getting our band was a disso-
lution of "Solidarity". Then we saw they treat
society's will like a shit! We didn't want to
listen to their music,to their commercial li-
es-so we had to start our own music,OK.Anyw-
ay we always were very poor and couldn't allow ourselves to buy any music equipment.Fi-
nally we got a chance to borrow it-and we m-
ust be happy we ever have it! ....TV:What
is behind your name DAYGLO MEN? DM:Well when
"Solidarity" was born in 1980 then all over
the world you could hear news about Poland.
Everywhere every news paper was talking about our country which was like a reflex of
glow.Our country,Polish peeple are dayglo,
even they don't know it.The second meaning
is you know all Polish workers have a fucking grey life-we want them to be happy to be
dayglo in their life,although we know workers and all those poor people don't know t-
hey can live better,but........They're victims of this shitty system and believe in
their fucking God-who doesnt care about po-
ors.Yeah if you want to understand our name
you must live in Poland today....TV:Can you
get any US or UK records in Poland?Do they
tamper with your mail?DM:We really can't get
any.Have got alot of difficultys with getting them.OUr situation is hopeless,anyway
the people who go abroad and if they come
back to Poland then they bring some Western
records and sell themvery expensive:eg last
LP of "Flux Of Pink Indians" costs about
zloty 5000(polish money)And there is an average earing in Polnad about zloty 10000
isn't it funny?We are still in college so
we have no shitty money..yeah we believe
in the Westworld in Western punx-they'll
help us fuck 'nows anyway we can be wrong..
oh they doesnt tamper with our mail......
TV:Is it possible to record and cut a record of your own there?DM:What a funny question!..hm?Polish state run record industry
does not record punk music,commies don't
like us,we are like an ulcer on their arse.
We shit on their record labels.Although they say everything is society's property...
TV:how many punks would you say there was
in POland?DM:There is mre and more new pu-
nx these times,in Poland.A lot of them are

only average rowdies who like to do any riots
after alcohol.They are unable to think.The rea-
l punks or people like that want to about the
system and they know what they want being pu-
nx.We don't know a number of quantity of these people....TV:Are there ever shows in y-
our country where bands can play or is.it a-
ll underground?DM:Bands can play in Student's
clubs only very rarely.And two times for year
there is a bigger festival where punks can
present their music.We think that's shit 'coz
there is censorshit and punks have to change
texts etc.There is much problems to get places to play or practice,anyway have to survive
this situation.To be frank we prefer it all
to be underground!..TV:What are your songs
about?DM:Love peace and freedom and Ⓐ We sing
about everything what is bad for us and people
like us.We like free speech and when we're

playin and singing we make it as improvisat-
ion.You know we're not professionals..TV:What
are your favorite bands?DM:Each of us likes
different bands,tho we have some we all like.
e.g. THE PACKTHEATRE OF HATE/SUBHUMANS/DISCH-
ARGE/POISON GIRLS/KREUT/LOST CHERREES/CRASS
(a bit) etc etc...from the older bands we s-
till like T.REX +Bolan,DAMNED/DEAD KENNEDYS
We like SUBS too coz we're spent really nice
time with them when they were in Gdansk....

Detroit Piston

PICS OF THE stars...

TOM of DAYGLO MEN (POLISH BAND)

GLENN DANZIG PHOTO MARC BARRBILY

MONICA from HATE FROM IGNORANCE   photo Jim SAAH

STEVE RAWLINGS of DANCE SOCIETY

JOHN of VOID gets it where he NEEDS IT THE LEAST...

PHOTO BY Jim SAAH

pic by TV

PICS OF da STARS

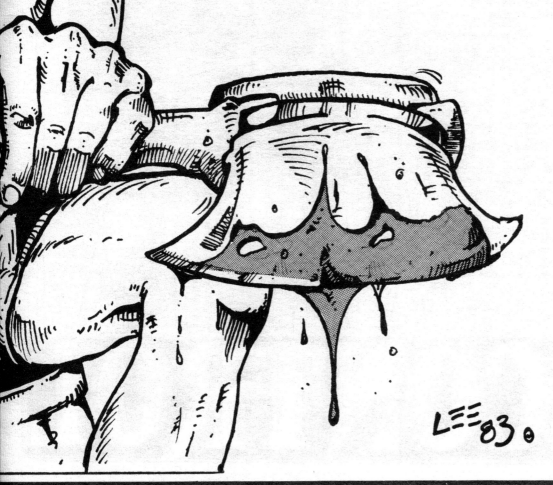

LEE 83.

SOCIETY SYSTEM

SS DECONTROL come on strong...physically,
mentally,emotionally..there is nothing
halfway about them...their live attack is
relentless and can be imposing to the unin-
itiated...their message is indellibly etch-
ed on every scrap of music...they have been
branded everything from neo-nazi's to mindless bullies..protagonists of a a "right
wing straight edge" philosophy...they seem
to feed on the myths,the stereotypes..all
the while strengthening the bond that exists
between crowd and band...yes as an outsider
to the Boston scene this will appear as somewhat conjecture..but I feel strongly that their
message is a powerful one...brimming with a
personal optimism that belies the menacing
nature of their attack...although still a
young scene the Boston thing has changed
over the last year as the band stated in
a recent interview with T&G.."The Boston
scene has expanded to large numbers in the
last year,with more and more kids coming
in from the suburbs"... Let's face it folks
the city of boston didnt have much to cheer
about until the likes of SSD/DYS/FU's and
the floundering GANG GREEN burst on the scene...the band remains conscious of what
is said about them but doesnt let it affect
their overall attack...(in a recent Boston
Rock poll"Hardcore"was biggest fad of the
year+"what hurt the Boston music scene the
most in 82")Sour Grapes from the art fags?
A little jealous that maybe all that media
that has so eluded them should suddenly be
laid waste on the likes of SSD?The band s-
aid it best.."We remain seperate and underground for the most part"...with the release of their new 12" entitled "Get It Away"
the secret is out folks..simply one of the
most powerful records ever made..."The Kids
Will Have Their Say" was representative
in it's time and place,but we werent pleased with its sound.GET IT AWAY is more characteristic of our sound,but 3rd phase SSD
should be the most reflective yet".indeed
where the first LP combined a mixture of
fast and slow,GET IT AWAY storms through
your living room with a two guitar onslaught..fuller and more direct..the reason
for the addition of a second axe man??

'We wanted to add to our sound and power,along,,
with adding fresh,new ideas.ANOTHER MARSHALL!!
Whereas alot of bands seem to shoot their representative wads upon first record/where SSD
is concerned there is a sense of resistance to
sameness...a need to change and mature as a
band with each outing...when any hint of stag-
nation begins to creep in they move on...
perusing this new turf with all the tact
and grace of a Sherman tank...needless to

Photo GAIL RUSH

say all do not share my enthusiasm with the
band..on a recent trip to Michigan they w-
ere greeted with mixed reactions "We had fun
on the road.Ann Arbor was good with alot of
young energetic kids..In Detroit the audience
had problems dealing with our enthusiasm".
Boston seems to share alot of similarities with the DC scene..indeed there is a
need for a steady all ages club(what city
doesnt need one?ED)Their first trip to the
nations capital was a bit tense with the
crew' from Boston mixing it up with the local-
s..certainly emotions run high among the
Boston regulars...things are in the works
for a return to town by SSD..their sched-
ules do not allow them the freedom to tour
like they would like..But dont fret all
you west coasters...they plan a west coast
tour between July 22 and Aug 8...Influences
range from the Bad Brains to AC/DC to Black
Flag to Minor Threat...but thankfully their
sound is their own...their message?"FREE
BODY FREE MIND FREE SOUL"..........
(indeed)...TV

DECONTROL

COUNTER ATTACK-Great new Philly zine.. interviews w/ White Cross/Ruin and others,,,states Philly is "less stagnant and cliquey than Boston or DC"..uhhh statements like that are pointless guys as is the trashing of Pushead..Whats the fucking point? 3201 Belgreen RD Phila Pa 19154

VD CAGE-Lots of bizzare art and some editorializing...lots of fun.. 2208 Parkside #117 Mesquite Texas 75150

IN TOUCH-A magazine for men who like to feel the hot bayonet in there amongst the polyps and dung but hey who gives a fuck there is a huge punk section here..granted they are a bit off trying to tantalize their audience with the hetero likes of one Hank Rollins but shit who does this hurt?I say any exposure is well and good when the collective HC scene is as small as it is...good pics Darby/Butthole Surfers and Henry...so what if there is also big greasy tools?..aint you ever seen a dick before? 7216 Varna Ave. North Hollywood Ca 91605

A² SQUARETOWN NEWS-Issue #7 huh?Shit I missed the other 6..It always pleases me to see Mich rags for such was my genesis..this Alice Royston has a good ear and a good"I'm ready to lay it on ya and fuck ya if you dont like what I have to say" attitude... well done... 1047 Olivia Ann Arbor Mich 48104..

WILLIG COMIC-good mix of the obscure and the obvious...stamps.. 4370 lowell Blvd #202 Denver Colo 80221

I WANNA-A biggie from Dayton with good incisive writing on all types of music..stamps Box 166 Wright Bro. Station Dayton Ohio 45409

BOYS AND GIRLS GROW UP-Jeez willya look at that cover...all slicked up and stuff..this is all art and musta been born on Mars..from the sublime to the stupid this is great toilet reading...very professional looking send $3 and you wont be sorry...po box 5718 Richmond Va 23220

7"

THE LATIN DOGS-"WARNING" EP Hadn't heard about these guys in quite some time so it was a welcome surprise when this slab happened into my po box..would've had a problem had it sucked because these guys are swell people.. fortunately this is not the case.. great songwriting that's light years above the competition.."World Powers" features a great scorching riff..Rank from the legendary southwestern Mich LIPS ARE BACK does vocal duties and does em up right again..LAB were producing musclehead back when garbage was the rule of thumb back in the days of Club Doo Bee..anyway the best tune here is a creeper called "Go To The Window".plodding severity..this bit of plastic comes highly recommended..probably limited so write today 172 College St. Springfield Mich 49017

GOVERNMENT ISSUE

12" E.P.

11 songs

FOUNTAIN OF YOUTH RECORDS

DISCHORD records

WITH: HOUR OF 1 G.I. SHEER TERROR AND MORE!

GOVERNMENT ISSUE

T&G classifieds (they're free!)

DEAD LINE FoR Classifieds iS August 30th for ISSUE #23

I.KRUMINS 22-121 St. Josephs Dr. Hamil-
ton Ont. Canada L8N 2GI..WANTED--B.flag
"Life Of Pain" promo/Crucifix 12"/Desc-
endents"Ride The Wild"/Fix-both 45's/
Fartz 7"/False Prophets "Overkill"/F-
unkadelic LP's "America Eats It's Young/
"Lets Take It To the Stage"/Impatient
Youth"Definition Empty"/John The Postman-
"Puerile LP"/Lesa-"Till The End Of The Day"/
Misfits-"Cough/She's Cool"/"Bullet"/ Neos
both 45's/Protex LP/Rude Kids-"Palisades
Park"/"Nar Sommere Hittat"/New Christs-
(anything)Necros(1st 45)trades wanted...
no cash.................................

WANTED-Back issues of Touch and
Go's...issues #1-7,9,11,15-18..
Will trade or pay..come on one
of you rubes must be done with
em by now...contact BYRON COLEY
847 19th ST Santa Monica Ca 90403

TOS PO BOX 14570 1001 LB AMsterdam Holland
Wanted-Necros 1st/Fartz 7"/Replacements "I'm
In Trouble"7"/Descendents"Ride The Wild"/De-
scendents"Unnational Anthem"/Controllers"Ne-
uron Bomb"/Killer Queers"/What Sampler 7"/
Braineaters Ep and Flexi/Any Urinals/also w-
ould like to trade for tapes of US bands...

TESCO VEE BOX 25305 WASHINGTON DC 20007
WANTED-Pee Wee Herman Pic disc/Throbbing
Gristle"Heathan Earth(blue wax)Avengers
1st(green wax)Virgin Prunes"A New Form
Of Beauty(cassette)Motorhead(1st LP)(on
white or other color) ANY MotorHEAD
foreign 45s"Louie Louie"(on colors)999
(78 rpm single)Leather Nun Cassette...
Nick The Stripper 7"(Birthday Party)
Autographed CRIME 45's(will pay $25 per)
Sham 69(foreign pic sleeves..especially
"Borstal Breakout" w/Pursey pointing at
button on lapel)Moors Murders   45($25)
Pink Military 45(pic same as LP)Eater
"Lock It Up"(7")The Infested(both 45's)
Bobby Sox "Scavenger of Death "/Connie
And The Cocksuckers 45/Slaugheer And
The Dogs "Boot Boys"(7")Unwanted "With-
duawel 78"/Motorhead 1st 45(Chiswick)
MC5 "Looking At You"(Skydog)Bad Actors
(45's other than "Strange Love"/Sisters
Of Mercy(1st)Adolescents"Amoeba"(gold
dj..will pay $75)Skrewdriver LP(w/xtra
track)Velvet Talks porn flexis.Abba
"Voulez Vouz Pic Disc(will pay $50)
Motorhead"No Class"(Fast Eddie sleeve)
Rude Kids LP or 45s(6) Will trade or pay
cash..have access to many records..send
want lists today for immediate reply...

DAVE STIMSON 708 N.Monroe ST. Apt #4 Arlington
Va. 22201 WANTED-(all are 7" and must have pic-
ture sleeves)THE GEARS-"Lets Go To The Beach"/
The Reactors-"Melt Down"EP/Fear"Living In The
City"/Flyboys-"Crayon World"/Dishrags-"The Past
Is Past"/Schoolgirl Bitch"Abusing The Rules"/
Stains-"Sick Of Being Sick"/Stanbys EP/Distor-
ted Levels 45/Hugh Beaumont Experience EP/(I've
got plenty of shit for trade,ie. singles by the
Fix(1st)Misfits/MDC Stains/Mentally Ill/October
Days etc.)Send Want lists....................
also have Deadbeats"Kill The Hippies"/ and Tooth
And Nail Compilation for trade...........;)

ERIC HYSTERIC-WANTED-Avengers 1st(colored wax)Descen-
dents"Ride The Wild"/"Hectic World"/Fear 1st 45/Mis-
fits"Cough/She's Cool/Misfits"Horror Biz(on black)Mi-
sfits"3 Hits From Hell"Ramones"I Wanna Be Your Boyfriend"/Vancouver compilation..will trade for your
wants..send list today...Obertor 6 6293 Lohnberg/Lahn
West Germany

FARK, SPASTIC RHYTHM TARTS, VIOLENT APATHY, CIRCLE JERKS
  at the East Hall Gym, April 15, 1983

SPA comes through this time. . . unfortunately, a high
profile band like the Circle Jerks tends to bring the jokers out
of the proverbial woodwork, like the pun croc guys here who cut
their hands, smeared blood on their faces and swore that the
state cops had messed them up while they looked oh-so-toughly
into each other's faces and screamed. . . pity the first two
bands had to get paid; the funniest thing about them was that
they were serious about it all as the dicks grooved to Farks
imitation of a single groove of "Sister Ray" on endless replay
and the Spastic Rhythm Tarts played their indecipherable tribal
noise while their Hare Krishna-ish following did scarf dances
and simulated sex shows...my God, what an ordeal. But at last
V.A. takes da stage with an amazing attack as Andy becomes a
little tornado behind his drums and the dicks grab Tommy's
guitar and pile on Kenny, who is desperately trying to escape.
The Circle Jerks inspire the meanest crowd action ever in Kazoo
and oh what a performance of non-stop musical blows (after they
figured out that they were tripping breakers because a circuit
was overloaded) and in my humble opinion Chuck rocks the world
with his drumbeats...better than their records... C.T.

HATE FROM IGNORANCE/FAITH/MARGINAL MAN /CRUCIFIX
Missed HFI due to our late arrival..oh ya this was
a Wilson Center Show...medium sized turnout..nice
night...shitty neighborhood..the DC bands really
shined this night...FAITH never sounded better..
the whole doubleguitarwhammy laid waste to us all..
lots a flyin guitars...real visual..great set...
MARGINAL MAN were simply awesome...they have a
great feel for dynamics...intro that build until
the whole arrangment is in flames (pretty analogous
huh?)10 times more powerful than their debut shows..
this is one instance when a good band(Artificial
Peace)breaks up to become a GREAT band...I like
CRUCIFIX...their records are both well done statements of purpose..but live they just couldnt
hold my attention..too Dischargy..their old s-
ound to me seemed more original................

TSOL/NO TREND at George Washington U.
No Trend were noisy and wore lots of
clothes and read articles about slam
dancing from People Magazine(if they're
not careful they'll sound melodic)TSOL
played and were great.Yeah they played.
Old stuff real fast.Some 1 said they're
bored w/old stuff(nahhh)the new material
reminded me of my fave band "Journey"
New keyboardist overpowered most every-
thing(but how cool,)I think they did
'Dust In The Wind' by Kansas.The singer
put his head and mikestand thru the c-
eiling(total A)It takes a real punk
rock band from Ca to show us how to be
cool.Many kids took over on vocals wh-
en I woke up.A nite of rock from true
rockers. reviewed by John Schroeder

THE DANSE SOCIETY at the 9:30 Club...
Ya I was your basic twitching diehard..show-
ed up hours early and had to wade through an
hourand a ½ play by someone named Richard B-
one...anyway finally DS...awesome is not even
close as an adjective here gang..from the north of England they come..away from the trend
a week London club scene..the music they play
is their own..on their own terms..devoid of
the lumping and labeling bestowed on them by
various parties..and lest you be deceived by
the name..this music is intense...relentless
pounding,guitar plus effect that gives it
a bigger than life sound..electronics yes..
but minus the fluff and painful predominan-
ce other various and sundry "new music"combos use that medium to cover up inherent
flaws and weaknesses....Its all there..
intros that utilize dynamics and build to
a fever pitch as the songs roar into full

tilt incredible drive...they played all
their greats "Hide","Come Inside" and a
great new one entitled "Love As Positive
Narcotic"..here we had a band that not
only lived up to my heady expectations
but far surpassed them..mind boggling
greatness....

forty fives
***

LET'S BARBEQUE

BIG COUNTRY-"Fields Of Fire"/"Angle Park"
Phonogram Records...Stripped of Dick Jobson's trappings of a pre-war Germany-Sk-
ids were the ultimate in shall we say m-
ajestic pop...here we have further proof
that the creative impetus therein was one
Stuart Adamson...and as Mr.Richard traverses pretentiously in his poet cum visionary malaise...his guitarist strikes
resonant chord in the positive,musically
progressing from whence he left off and
lyrically paint in the realm of I know
not what...it's all irrelavent...this
assemblage can doeth no wrong.........

BLITZ-"TELECOMMUNICATION" Future Records
You understand don't you???they were at
the top of the heap...adulation/a cult f-
ollowing stateside and a rabid bunch of l-
imeys worshipped their every move...so in
fighting destroys em and now its so passe'
to punk out--synthy drivel will prove our
versatility...ya well dix your base of fans aint into this grunt and even if they
were there are alot of bands doing it b-
etter...so sit smugly and watch the shit
fly..it's like slamming it into reverse
at 50 miles an hour...the bottom inevitably drops out..........boo.....hoo.....
PS..Notice now its Future Records...how
upbeat...how optomistic...I could gag...

BIG CITY 7" Compilation "Aint Too Pretty"
NY hasnt been without worthwhile releases
in the past year or so...the MOB,URBAN W-
ASTE and HEART ATTACK 45s all bristle with
ye old vitality..then there is such as MR.
Javi and Savage Circle...he slaps two of
his bands cuts on it probably saying to
himself self righteously "Hey by crackie
if I'm putting up the hogs I'm laying
down the tracks..."anyway this baby is
about as much fun as adobe squirt sessions following a 7-11 dung bag that
has expired..the high point is when the
needle is an inch off it on its way back...the ultimate in crud.............
Big City Records 2329 Vance St. Bronx NY
10469

PETER AND THE TEST TUBE BABIES--"ZOMBIE
CREEPING FLESH" Trapper Records...
After that abysmal LP this a welcome
surprise..a sense of humor(remember?)
and some creative tune writing..they
might have even took their time this
time..whatever..they scored........

ELECTRIC PEACE-BIG K Records
boing boing guitar and lux-ish voice..
harmony vocals..derivative from everything they've ever read or heard
of camp pop..good frisbee anyway....

ADRENALIN O.D. "LET'S BARBECUE" EP Buy
Our Records Records....
Hey what jammers...even has a snapshot
of the boys cooking out...great drivers
with big guitar..the drums are too buried in the mix but so what,this mamy rocks...hey Joisy be pumpin....write 2374
Steuben St. Union NJ 07083 if your record store don't stock this platter of
choiceness...

THE ROCKS-"I'LL NEVER BE THE SAME AGAIN" Love
Records Hey It's Butch Willis...Who?Ya I know even I hadnt heard of him till a couple
weeks ago..what we have here is a loon with
a guitar and his long low mournful ballad
bout love gone sour..hey I;ll give the gent
press..hes a local Maryland boy...besides
this is funnier than anything else I've
heard of late...mounds of guffaws,chortles
and titters gauranteed...

GODS GIFT "DISCIPLINE" New Hormones
Impassioned voice deadpans the nonsensical "na na na na na na Disipline"
..booooming drums..real garage sound..
this is their third record..must find
the other two..Neutral 415 Lafayette
NYNY 10003

TWISTED NERVE-"Five Minutes Of Fame"/"Strange Sensation" "Five Minutes Of Fame"/"St-
You sleeve it...range Sensation"
you have a diverse
or Rondolet..what you see is get unless
is 4,AD or type you see taste for unless
that cuts to Merciful sleeve is a Riot for the
to expand to the bone...Release what you get
where their listeners..maybe type of sound
these Blitz wanted to head..they're trying
guys are a rousing success..failed is

FATALITES"YEAH RIGHT"tape-Oh My God
Records "I Hate Insurance Companys"/
"Everything Sucks"/I Hate Girls"/"Gotta Piss"/"Fuck Everyone"The music here
is ghastly and the titles speak for the-
mselves.What more can I say? LE and A.P.

WARBOY"FUTILE LIVING"11 song tape-Confe-
ssional Records The songs here include
popular subjects:war,bored teenagers and
police but are by no means boring.Imagi-
native lyrics especially on "Law Enfor-
cer"catchy drum beats and snarly vocals
Push this band past the forgettables.
I dig the TV recording ala "Media Blitz"
at the beginning of "Cross Of Bigotry"
Besides the packaging is great..A.P.

YDI-15 Song demo...This is simply the best
fuckin demo I've ever had the pleasure to
receive...Vocalist is fucking awesome..sh-
reds his vocal chords so we can enjoy his
style..recorded loud and distorted..the k-
ind of stuff that makes the adrenalin go
ape..Last week I was struttin with my wa-
1kman and my machete and this was going
down and I went nuts at a produce stand/
hacking and bludgeoning my way to inner
peace..all you pansy ass copycats gotta
face it that these guys just scored heavily..in order to be heard you gotta be
louder-meaner-and more violent these days
and YDI got the market cornered...If you
do nothing else this whole fucking summer get this..Jackal 1304 N.26th St
Philadelphia Pa 19121..

TAR BABIES/MECHT MENSCH tape...Not much
to say except these to bands are two of
middle americas best..,disimilar approaches
but similar in great execution and relevant words...dont hesitate.. BONEAIR INC
311 S. Few St Madison Wisc. 53704

THE REJECTORS-21 SONG TAPE..Not really a demo-
more of an official release(?)Noble sentiment
backed up by some pedestrian songwriting..buy
their record..1207 SW 152nd Seattle Wa 98166

LAST WARNING-Er is Hoop Tapes Koerierstersweg 21 3815
NT Amersfort Holland ....All I know is ignore the mistakes,erratic drumming on what sounds like trash cans
atrocious quality and focus in on the vocals.Peter-
the singer,guitarist and song writer really makes use
of his throat,resulting in clinching,melodic,and pas-
sionate cues.The desperation really hits,particularly
on "Sinking Down" and the ballad like "Outside".Side
two is harder and faster and sounds live.Anyway this
band deserves a listen..A.P.

CONFLICT-"Americas Right"Unjust Tapes..A little old
but this band from Tucson has a great female vocalist/
lyricist Karen(the nurse)The music features fast drums
frenzied guitar,piercing vocals and tight stops.A truly
commendable piece of work.Try to get this..Mail $2.50
to KA 3033 E 6th Apt B2 Tucson AZ 85716 A.P.

PSYCHODRAMA-We're sorry Tape..Gotta feeling this
bunch of twistos must be seen live to be fully
appreciated...call it perfomance art or theatr-
ical shock value I think I must follow my calling and witness for myself..the music contained here is energetic electro with rythym machine..like mental hospital shit folks
if you are conjuring up images of anything
remotely healthy hey think again...someone
said they heave manure at the audience and
so on..hey I'm into it..degredation of man
as spectator is the ultimate art form.....
but hey theyn wrote on the tape "short hair=
short dick"..sounds like an obstreperous
jab in the air to me..4833 Walney Rd Cha-
ntilly Va 22021

OUTPATIENTS-basement tape...You know there's
something to be said for hearing these bands
in their infancy..when their youthful exuberance hasnt yet been watered...good grunge
here to eat your Captain Crunch with...the
bass player sounds like he's tootin crystal
methedrine..the mans fingers be liquid ligh-
tnin...yup..gotta get this one.too..whoops
lost the address..fuck...
Here it is!
24 Lord Rd
Westfield Mass 01085

WILLFUL NEGLECT-'82..Absolutely no information was s-
upplied so I dug into a dark dusty corner and leafed
through fanzines.Finally my search for truth was en-
ded.This two guitar band comes from St.Paul Minnesota
These guys get my approval.No titles were provided
but throughout the tape there was punchy vocals,fan-
tastic melodic guitar riffs and speedy work on the
skins.A must for all...

DEMOS Will Be
regularly-Sorry for
the wait gang!

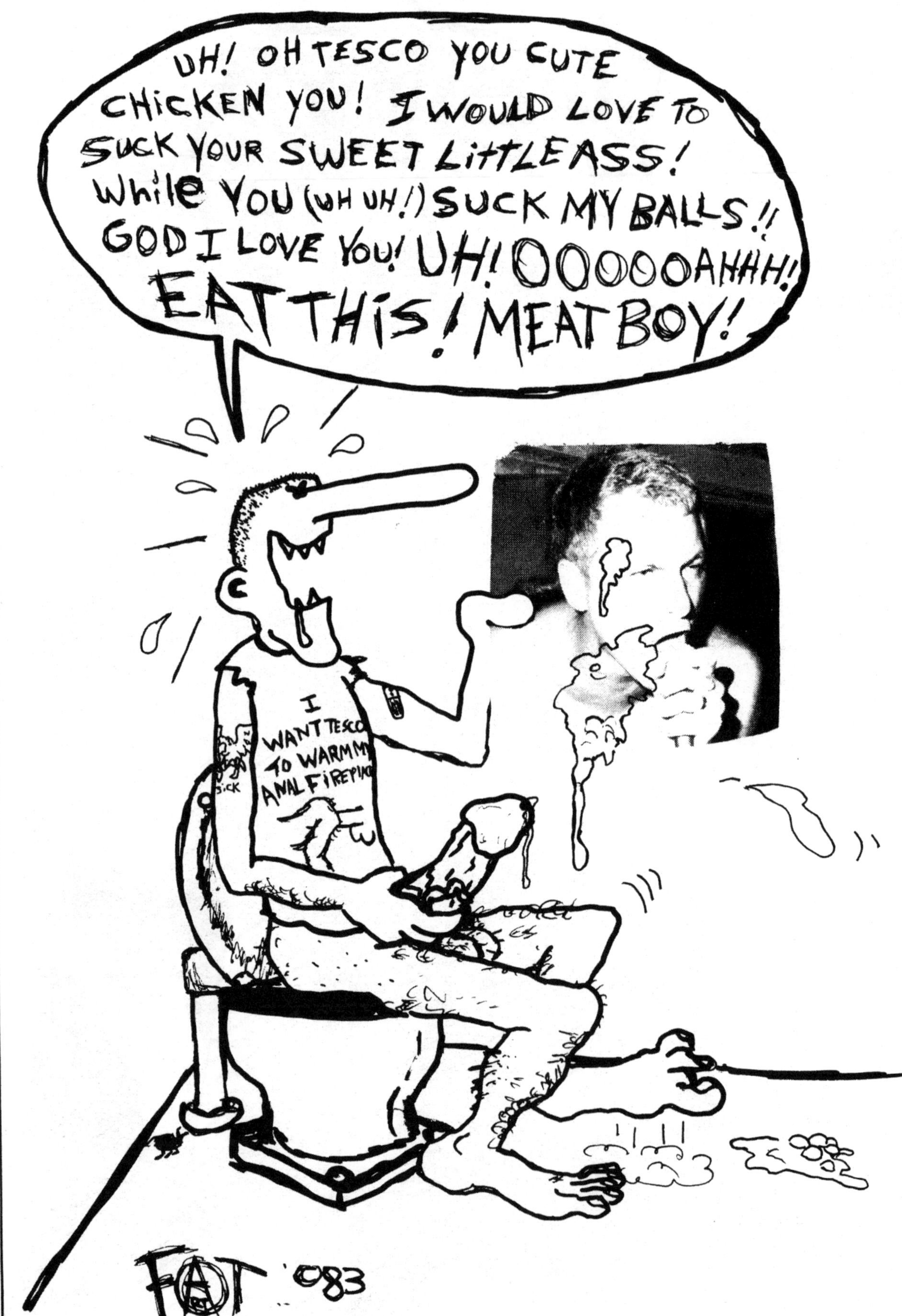

FROM THE "I CAN DISH IT OUT AND TAKE IT TOO" DEPARTMENT...YOUR EDITOR AS SEEN THRU AN(UNSOLICITED SO DON'T WORRY FOLKS)ABSOLUTELY WARPED DEPRAVED AND UNCLEAN MIND..(YOUR AVERAGE TOUCH AND GO R-EADER OF COURSE!!!)

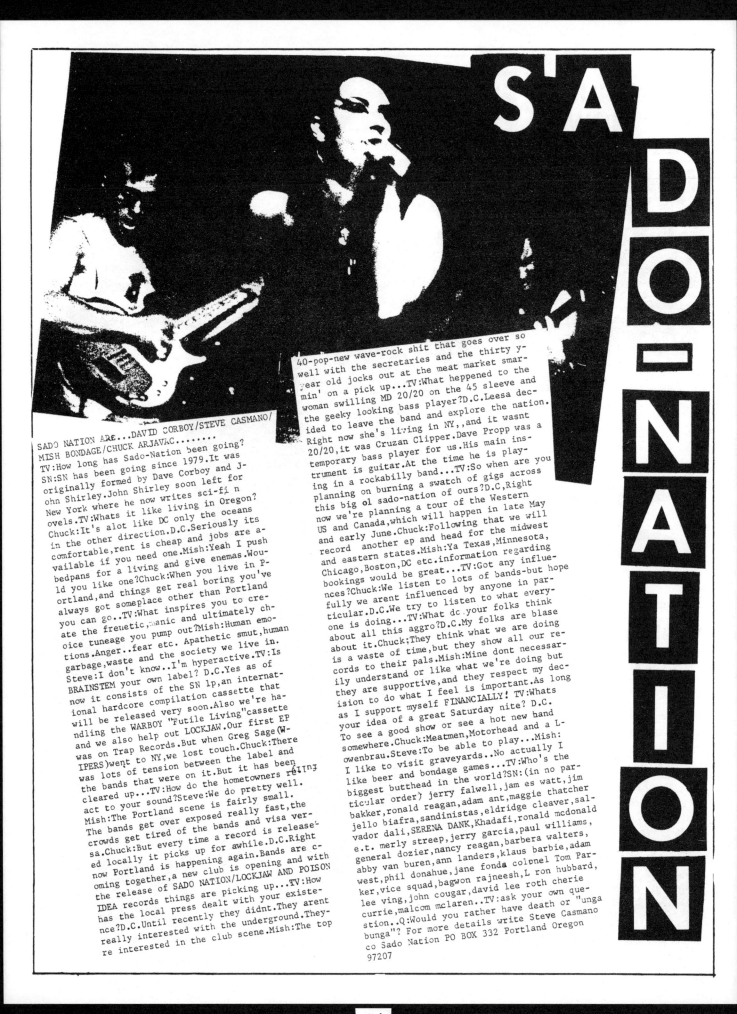

SADO-NATION

SADO NATION ARE...DAVID CORBOY/STEVE CASMANO/
MISH BONDAGE/CHUCK ARJAVAC.......
TV:How long has Sado-Nation been going?
SN:SN has been going since 1979.It was
originally formed by Dave Corboy and J-
ohn Shirley.John Shirley soon left for
New York where he now writes sci-fi n
ovels.TV:Whats it like living in Oregon?
Chuck:It's alot like DC only the oceans
in the other direction.D.C.Seriously its
comfortable,rent is cheap and jobs are a-
vailable if you need one.Mish:Yeah I push
bedpans for a living and give enemas.Wou-
ld you like one?Chuck:When you live in P-
ortland,and things get real boring you've
always got someplace other than Portland
you can go..TV:What inspires you to create the frenetic,manic and ultimately choice tuneage you pump out?Mish:Human emo-
tions.Anger..fear etc. Apathetic smut,human
garbage,waste and the society we live in.
Steve:I don't know..I'm hyperactive.TV:Is
BRAINSTEM your own label? D.C.Yes as of
now it consists of the SN lp,an international hardcore compilation cassette that
will be released very soon.Also we're handling the WARBOY "Futile Living"cassette
and we also help out LOCKJAW.Our first EP
was on Trap Records.But when Greg Sage(W-
IPERS)went to NY,we lost touch.Chuck:There
was lots of tension between the label and
the bands that were on it.But it has been
cleared up...TV:How do the hometowners relate
act to your sound?Steve:We do pretty well.
Mish:The Portland scene is fairly small.
The bands get over exposed really fast,the
crowds get tired of the bands and visa ver-
sa.Chuck:But every time a record is release-
ed locally it picks up for awhile.D.C.Right
now Portland is happening again.Bands are c-
oming together,a new club is opening and with
the release of SADO NATION/LOCKJAW AND POISON
IDEA records things are picking up...TV:How
has the local press dealt with your existence?D.C.Until recently they didnt.They arent
really interested with the underground.They-
re interested in the club scene.Mish:The top

40-pop-new wave-rock shit that goes over so
well with the secretaries and the thirty y-
year old jocks out at the meat market smar-
min' on a pick up...TV:What heppened to the
woman swilling MD 20/20 on the 45 sleeve and
the geeky looking bass player?D.C.Leesa decided to leave the band and explore the nation.
Right now she's living in NY,,and it wasnt
20/20,it was Cruzan Clipper.Dave Propp was a
temporary bass player for us.His main instrument is guitar.At the time he is playing in a rockabilly band...TV:So when are you
planning on burning a swatch of gigs across
this big ol sado-nation of ours?D.C,Right
now we're planning a tour of the Western
US and Canada,which will happen in late May
and early June.Chuck:Following that we will
record another ep and head for the midwest
and eastern states.Mish:Ya Texas,Minnesota,
Chicago,Boston,DC etc.information regarding
bookings would be great...TV:Got any influences?Chuck:We listen to lots of bands-but hope
fully we arent influenced by anyone in par-
ticular.D.C.We try to listen to what everyone is doing...TV:What do your folks think
about all this aggro?D.C.My folks are blase
about it.Chuck:They think what we are doing
is a waste of time,but they show all our records to their pals.Mish:Mine dont necessarily understand or like what we're doing but
they are supportive,and they respect my decision to do what I feel is important.As long
as I support myself FINANCIALLY! TV:Whats
your idea of a great Saturday nite? D.C.
To see a good show or see a hot new band
somewhere.Chuck:Meatmen,Motorhead and a L-
owenbrau.Steve:To be able to play...Mish:
I like to visit graveyards..No actually I
like beer and bondage games...TV:Who's the
biggest butthead in the world?SN:(in no particular order) jerry falwell,jam es watt,jim
bakker,ronald reagan,adam ant,maggie thatcher
jello biafra,sandinistas,eldridge cleaver,sal-
vador dali,SERENA DANK,Khadafi,ronald mcdonald
e.t. merly streep,jerry garcia,paul williams,
general dozier,nancy reagan,barbera walters,
abby van buren,ann landers,klaus barbie,adam
west,phil donahue,jane fonda colpnel Tom Par-
ker,vice squad,bagwon rajneesh,L ron hubbard,
lee ving,john cougar,david lee roth cherie
currie,malcom mclaren..TV:ask your own question..Q:Would you rather have death or "unga
bunga"? For more details write Steve Casmano
co Sado Nation PO BOX 332 Portland Oregon
97207

MOTORHEAD-"I GOT MINE" Bronze Records...Anytime one switches gears they leave themselves open to those who resist such change. Case in point is the opening melodia here which of course turns raunch as soon as Uncle Lemmy opens his mouth..I for one stand(alone?)on the merits of this 'new'Motorhead.. I happen to think that diversity is walkin arm in arm with greatness...FASTWAY can BLOWMAE...this is still the one...............

THE OBSESSED-"IRON AND STONE"/INDESTROY"/"SODDEN JACKAL" Invictus Records so I'm reviewing this cold...both times I went to see them things got fucked up so finnally a record...SOME plods and some moves..guitar is a fuzz monster and the volume has to be cranked but the paint starts peeling when it is...The axe delivery on "Indestroy" is choice city...B side is very much a "Sabs" soundalike(compliment)Great! PO Box 3744 Gaithersburg Md 20878

POISON IDEA "PICK YOUR KING" EP Fatal Erection Records
What can I say except this muthafucka roars thru your living room disembowling any animate object in it's past...singer ranks up there with the best..the same tormented snarling that made Steve Fix the enemy of every eardrum in Lansing back in its halcyon days...the whole band combines to make this one of this years best ep's..straight up......... ps·(the pressing plant mistakenly started pressing this on black.. (most are clear)uh oh-collectors be droolin now!!!)

THE BLOOD-"MEGALOMANIA" No Future Ok so the attitude should stop whence UK say US suck and verse vice uh..but the fact remains that most Britshit pales miserably to the likes of the US bands..sure they did it first(by the way the cat who did the scene thing in the latest Max R&R had some intelligent sentiment...unfortunately he's the exception)This un shows ya how Bushell's graspin at straws..pluggin this as hot is like too funny..bloated folk...

KAAOS-"TOTALINGEN KAAOS EP" Propaganda Records...Piddle paddle drum thrash with every minor chord Discharge ever ripped off Black Sabbath............. old Kaaos was better...............

7 SECONDS-"COMMITTED FOR LIFE" Squirtdown Records...Hey let's face facts..7 SECONDS are one of this countrys most committed/ hard working...simply stated one of the best..as far as vinyl output they have yet to actualize their potential..until this mammy which fully blazes and def-

PART 1 "FUNERAL PARADE" EP Paraworm Records..slow pulsating guitar with flange effect characterises this 6 songer..b orn of a vehemence against religion and some of what we have come to expect from the British.. don't eat animal flesh...the human race are all brainwashed idiots st-

BANG GANG'SHE RAN..BUT WE RAN FASTER' Matako Mazuri Records..HUh?What kind of a name is that?Anyway this jumpin ala the RANDOMS or sort of..stupid lyrics which hey doesnt mean they suck just that they are inane.."Stupid People"is hot..cliched opening refrain with serious yuksville words..hey you dont have to like this..its sloppy and garagy and sophomoric and ridiculous and you guessed it..I like it.. 3506 SPEEDWAY #204 AUSTIN TEXAS 78705
(I Picked mine,ED↓)

ewing in their own sweat and feces.. but a thread of optimism running throughout..the mood created here is very effective music wise and I'll leave it at that.. Mark F 4 Ludlow Close Bletchley Milton Keyes MK3 6BB England

inately will help open some ears..no longer a three piece..Steve's Rickenbacker sounds great..that plucking charge like EATER or BORED YOUTH..this platter must be had..72 S.Patterson Pl Sparks Nevada 89431

PICK YOUR KING E.P.

Poison Idea

45's

It's OK to wear a Revolutionary Fetus tee shirt this summer. Small medium or large $6.50 check or money order RUTE ON! to: R.F. TEE 7 Sopt TKR Kinnelon NJ 07405 (NOT AVAILABLE THROUGH ROUGH TRADE S.F.)

REVOLUTIONARY FETUS!!!
Out of the garbage cans into the streets!!
ACTUAL ILLUSTRATION

STRETCH MARKS

WHOS IN CHARGE

TV:Hey how close to the edge of the world is Winnipeg?SM:It's so close that last Saturday we were out drinking a few beers with some grain farmers(Moose Beer)and we got too close and fell.One of your nuclear space missiles picked us up and brought us back to Ottowa.TV:How big is the scene up there?SM:About this big for an average show we can get between 2-500 people at all ages show clubs and bars.It varies cause beer and admission is usually expensive.But we put on alot of our own shows and book out of town bands.TV:What inspires you guys to write the songs you do..get on the stage and go off ...fucking loony..etc..SM:Mostly the little brown bottles that contain 6.5% alcohol(More than we can say for that swill from south of the border)TV:You aint a shittin..SM:Ever try Old Stock?Four beers and you'll swivel. Actually the inspiration comes from knowing that if we jump alot(our average is 4.6 jumps a song)we may get laid alot by choice mamas,and all that war,nuwlear power corruption,acid rain,unemployment,apathy and all the things that an aware punk band is supposed to sing about and know.We dont know why we go fucking crazy etc.Basically it costs alot of money because our bass player breaks alot of equipment...TV:What inspired your name?Was it all those beached whales in Gent/Buf Swinger and Dude Magazines?SM:No we're all strtch marks of society and we're one more reason not to have kids...TV:What bands did you have in mind when you wrote "Professional Punks"? SM:At first it was written towards a Winnipeg band about a year ago but then as you look around there's alot of particularly English bands,40 year old biker rocks just jumping on the bandwagon $$$...TV:So what happens to you when the US and USSR start bombing the fuck outa each other? SM:In the last year the Stretc pad has renovated its house..we installed a bomb shelter 80 feet underground..our superior survivalist leader Trevor Winthrop Baines informs us every week on how to mutilate a mutant..TV:Huh/???..Got any fave bands? SM:The Pack/Man Sized Action/Riot 303/ Minor Threat/Youth Brigade/Kiss/Aerosmith Code Of Honor/Gene Krupa/Articles Of Faith and the Meatmen until they stopped being neat and sold out to the corp-

structure and started worshipping the structure and they begged Max R&R for forgivness.TV:Hey you guys TV:Whos the Lennon..TV:belch...TV:If you've sense of humor...Calgary?SM:I'd know it biggest dick in Calgary then you'd know it ever been to Calgary Ron Hadley photos has to be Rockin Ron this.Actual street ra- 303.We have proof of the manor street ra- of Ron Whizzin off the Calgary n- mp.Ron won third prize at the Calgary n- stampede.TV:If you had Beki Bondage first ude and passed out?(hows your loads on her face for a classy what would you do?(hows that perverted que- question?ED)SM:Funny you were here she stion.seems last time they position minds pleaded to be put in that good.SM:Well respected and blew four loads on her?SM:Well together other bands are up there?SM:Well TV:What we have the Apache Mohican(are we up here we have a pretty far out you can un- band,they're American lingo so you can some- talking good American there are personal- derstand us eh?)Actually lingo are leav- good Crisis/Unwanted/Societys Grudge/and ity more..TV:Future plans?SM:We're straight lots more..TV:June 13th..drive straight ing Winnipeg to LA doing on the 18th.. through we're supposed a join up with of then we're supposed and play alot of certain American band home in Aug to form US cities piece..write STRETCH MARKS AT a five Piece..write Manitoba B3C 3YA Box 11A3 Winnipeg Manitoba B3C 3YA Canada

CHICAGO SCENE REPORT -

The scene is fluctuating in almost every aspect; bands play regularly, then go into hiding for months, some clubs book many HC shows in a few weeks period, then ignore HC for several months and audience support is the biggest question mark. The Minor Threat show drew lots of people while a Necros or a Husker Du show draws a small audience. On with the band report; Negative Element have just released their ep Yes, We Have No Bananas, it has 8 songs and well worth getting and it's on Version Sound. They have been playing out sporatically and are planning another record on their own label already. Rights of the Accused are releasing an ep also on Version Sound/Feedback records called Mean People Suck. Rights have been playing out pretty often, especially after Anthony (drummer) finally got his cast off his ankle in early May. Opened for Minor Threat and Necros shows. Steve (bassist) has just released a Chicago area compilation tape. Effigies have also releaseda 12", 4 song ep called We're Da Machine and play out here every 3 months or so. Besides the new ep being on their label Ruthless, it is releasing a 6 song ep by Naked Raygun in a month or so. N.R. went on a 2 week tour of the east coast in late March and gig here every month or so. Santiago (ex-Naked Raygun guitarist), Pierre and Bob (both ex- Trial by Fire/Strike Under) have formed a power trio. Playing out May 29th for first time with ex-Chicago band Bag People. Should produce some wild, high energy stuff. Evil Eye are most of the members from Juvenile Delinquants and are great. Have girl singer, Carol, who has a great stage presence, look for lots of great things from this group. End Result, a trio that plays everything except drums and keyboards are playing out once in a while and will be on the Lung Cookies and Master Tape II compilations out this summer. They are also working towards releasing a single this fall. Articles of Faith are releasing a 2nd single and going on their 2nd tour in the middle of June. Rumors have it that the drummer is leaving the group in the near future Anti-Bodies have finally found a permanent drummer and are playing out often. They also recorded some cuts for the Mastertape II comp. Six Feet Under have added a new singer (Pat) and are looking for a new bass player and old singer (Ray) is forming a band with ex-DV8's guitarist. Two young bands; Verboten and Bloody Nails are on the Chi-Comp tape and play out seldomly. Seismic Waves are from Evanston (a suburb just north of Chicago) and played out a lot this winter, but then stopped. Shows lately include Minor Threat, MDC, Necros, Husker Du, Cirle Jerks, Tar Babies, Mecht Mensch, Misfits. Coming: Void. No Trend, J.F.A., No Label, Dead Kennedys, Big Boys and maybe Sin 34. Hall shows and Cubby

Bear are best places to play. Bands please call Steve at Cubby Bear (312) 327-1662 or me (312) 866-6727 for shows, Crucifix and Meat Puppets both didn't get shows here and we're the ones who loose out. Starving Dogs Tape is $4 for tape and booklet, send to:STARVING DOGS, 11034 W. Doogan, Willow Springs, Ill. 60480.

SEAN DUFFY/LAST RITES

Party Line Dept...
WHIPPING BOY-Thanks for the free publicity! YOU!! Send your want lists in for next issues Record Swap-T+6 assures you results! Your editor is taking a short break after this issue -The new issue (#23) will be out probably in early Sept. For All of you newcomers who can't stand us Since Last issue Welcome Aboard!

PS...IF YOU'VE
   ALREADY
     ORDERED
ONE AND
  YOU'VE BEEN
WAITING FOR
  MONTHS...WE'RE
REALLY SORRY
AND WE'LL FIRE
YOUR'S OFF AS SOON
    AS WE
       CAN

MINOR THREAT

BACK IN STOCK

OUT OF STEP

It's Been...

REMIXED, **$3.50** REMASTERED
AND THE COVER'S
FIXED!

3819 BEECHER ST. N.W.
WASHINGTON D.C. 20007

Future Projects: FAITH / DEADLINE / INSURRECTION /
            MARGINAL MAN / SCREAM ?
               Who Knows When...

We've started keeping books And paying taxes, so
  We're broke, BUT WE'RE LEGAL!!!!!

TARBABIES

JJ:Vocals/Robin Bass/Bucky-Guitar
Dan- Drums

TV:How are things in Madison these days?
JJ:Getting bigger and better all the time.
Robin:Things have been growing alot.The
WilMar's been getting known as a cool p-
lace to go.Plus all the younger people
have been showing up.There's still 40,000
college jerks-still out there.Dan:there's
been alot of shows the last coupla months.
There's more bands playing here and more
local bands compared to before.Bucky:Mad-
isons not like any other twon I've ever
lived in.Everyone trys so hard with all
their rallys and demonstrations to be p-
olitically hip but we're pretty flimsy
 compared to some other areas as far as
activism goes....TV:So wheres the hangout..
what's the Friday nite happening?JJ:Well
theres either bands or parties or both
or we hang out at the punkerhouse and
watch TV,groove to some tunes and get loose..Dan:You can always skate something.
TV:What other bands,,,Robin:There's alot
but one worth mentioning especially is
the Appliances,they've been together
for 5 years-not a hardcore band but d-
efinately hardcore music..JJ:Millions
of em..Bucky:We have a band up here
called Killdozer that are real good.
Their "La Grange"(ZZ TOP)cover is the
big hit around here.Dan:Too much commercial TRASH besides TB's and MM)Ki-11
dozer,NFOD The Appliances/SFB/IManent
Attack/Choir Boys/Knucklhead/Los Monos
Mudmen/ ...TV:Where all have you guys
played?Dan:Chicago at Cubbybear/Milwau-
kee at surf n turf skateboard park/Nikos
and Lost Dutchmans,Minneapolis at Goo-
fys and 1st Ave.Madison Merlyns and the
Wil Mar community center where Robin and
JJ have got alot of cool shows together.
and the best fucking basements in Mad-
ison.TV:OK so opinions on James Watt/
7-11 Big Gulps/college students/skateboa-
rds/abortion/wall walkers and the world
at large?Robin:Like wow man...JJ:College
students-some are,most arent-abortion-yes
skateboards suck-Wall walkers?The world
at large?Bucky:The world is sick.The human
race is a disease.It's almost funny;Dan:
James Watt is a crazy baldhead;Mountain Dew
quarts blaze on big gulps..Skating is alot
of fun..TV:Got any fave bands?Dan:Die Kreu-
zen/Black Flag w/ Dez singing..Bucky:Black
Flag 1983..JJ:Minutemen/Black Flag/Crucifuc-
ks/Husker Du/Jeff Beck/ Led Zep/Minor Threat
and on and on..TV:You have a record coming
out right?JJ:Ya theres always some new expense or hassle that comes up holding it back.
TV:Had any local trouble with cops/reds/jocks?
JJ:Cops hassle us for skateboarding on the
street,biking on the sidewalk and whatever
else they find to pin on us to cure their
boredom.We had alot of that 1 Or 2 years
ago and they know who we are and
where we are.Bucky:I hate straights.people
who just creep through life doing everything
the safe way.I dont think they're alive because they've never gone out and found life for themselves....write TAR BABIES c/o
Robin Daview 311 S.Few ST Madison Wisc
53704

Unmitigated Bullshit....
↓↓↓↓↓↓↓↓↓↓↓↓↓↓↓↓↓↓↓

NO TREND/SCREAM/VOID/DEAD KENNEDYS at the Lansburg
Cultural Center (Review by John Schroeder)First off
the price was 2 high(8 dollars?)If I didnt slide
my way in I wouldn't have paid the price.Got there
early..by 3:00..many folks crawling the woodwork
waiting in line.I've never seen such a pack of try-2
Hardcores(WHATTA CIRCUS!)By 8:00 they opened up
and allwere in.Finally a real stage built and what
stacks of power(DK's Gear)It looked like a rockin
show to be sure.No Trend played and much has been
said about them(too much,ED)and that's that.For
all interested they have a new girl bassist(nuf
said)After that all da sudden the promoter said
"Fire marshalls just shut down the show(huh??)
Well not 1 patron left.Many made noise and much
too everybodys surprise DK lead singer Jello Biafra jumped onstage and formed an impromptu J.B.O
(The Jello B.Orchestra)with 200 people worshipping
the almighty 1.Accapella versions of hits like
"Nazi Punks Fuck Off" and "Let's Lynch the Landlord"
were chanted(oh boy)(oh gawd,ED)Is there a double
live LP in the works?Soon the crowd was getting
real edgy.Ends up the fire boys let them play for
1 more hour(turned out to be ½ hour)Void left...
Scream were pissed Dead K's played like 10 songs
and I'm sorry but I dont see it anymore,but the
majority of the crowd saw something in them.
It was non-stop crash bang boom and dive mania.
I usta love them but lost interest after awhile.
Sad too say most think they got their moneys
worth...(poor fools)JS(Ya no shit...the phenom-
enon continues...only support a band with the
big name...only go to a show to see a media
creation that reeks of overblown egos/wallets
and of total disregard for anything but themselves...it doesnt matter the 9:30 is cutting
back the matinees for poor turnout..it isnt
important that SCREAM or VOID could totally
blow the DK's asses away...it doesnt even matter if you wanna shell out$8 of your hard
earned cash for these phonies...Hats off to
DYS in Boston for refusing to play with these mental midgets...and for the boycott
staged there I salute you...this is the fuckin big time folks and it stinks...the beginning of the end but then we're way past
that stage now arent we?ED)

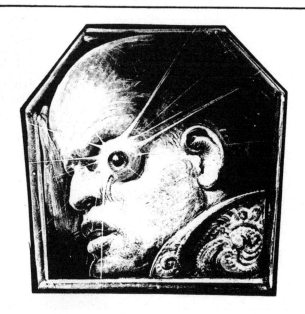

Top Pix

12"

7"

SS DECONTROL-"GET IT AWAY"
SADO NATION-"WE'RE NOT EQUAL"
VENOM-"COUNTESS BATHORY"(Live)
MARK STEWART AND THE MAFIA LP
BLACK FLAG "NOTHING LEFT INSIDE"(Live)
SONIC YOUTH-"CONFUSION IS SEX"
GOVERNMENT ISSUE "BOYCOTT STAB"
NECROS-"CONQUEST FOR DEATH" LP
SISTERS OF MERCY 12"
ALL COCTEAU TWINS
DANSE SOCIETY LIVE
COSEY FANNI TUTTI TAPE
BIG BOYS-"LULLABIES HELP THE BRAIN GROW"
YDI DEMO
CLOCK DVA-"ADVANTAGE"
WHITE FLAG LP
CH3-"AFTER THE LIGHTS GO OUT"
PAGANS-"LIVE LP"

POISON IDEA EP
CHRIS AND COSEY "OCTOBER"
MISFITS-"EVILIVE"
ACCEPT-"FAST AS A SHARK"
THE WEASELS-"BEAT HER WITH A RAKE"
MENTORS-"GET UP AND DIE"
MARCH VIOLETS-"CROW BABY"
DIE KREUZEN "COWS AND BEER" EP
BOBBY SOX-"SCAVENGER OF DEATH"
OBSESSED EP
NEGATIVE TREND EP
7 SECONDS-"COMMITTED FOR LIFE"
SPEAR OF DESTINY "THE WHEEL"
AGENT ORANGE (Dutch)"YOUR MOTHER SUCKS COCKS IN HELL"EP
THE LATIN DOGS "WARNING" EP
SUICIDE-"GIRL"

523

AMERICA'S SLEAZOID, TRAPEZOID, TABLOID...

FEATURING SSD/SADO NATION/WHITE FLAG/& TONs MORE!!!

<u>999 Times</u>, May 1979—the genesis of my literary ascent. The entrance stage left of one Tesco Vee, clad in nothing but a transparent cloak of 999 adulation. Be it real or misplaced, I was gonna write about my fave band, goddammit! Nick Cash had this fab pair of pink, pegged slacks on one of the platters, and I lusted after those jodhpurs so desperately, I called up Trash & Vaudeville in NYC and told 'em I wanted some... They said wha?? Probably handcuffed the receiver and guffawed at the pencil-necked hayseed from Michigan asking for such pantaloons. So they said, "Ya, send us money and we'll send you some"... Three weeks and $50 later a pair of Kelly green straight-legged dress pants arrived in the mail. Nice... Maybe it was for the better... Me in pink pegged slacks woulda looked mighty fruitcake. Hell, I just wanted to be like Nick! So here I am lashing out at 999 haters, pouring Yankee adulation over those cats like there was no tomorrow. Laugh away at the feebleness of my attempt, tease me ad nauseam about it, at least I had the stones to reprint it here , and at least there is a picture of tit torture in it, and what could be as unrelated to 999 as that?

May: #1

Save your money

AS8502

999 NINE NINE NINE

Times

The only rag for the 9.9.9. devotee.

- This issue contains...

Interviews (sort of)

Album reviews

Plagarism

1 Live review

Photos

Nothing about other bands!!

45s and other junk

High fashion

Crossword puzzles

A cure for Herpes-3

March '79'

Published in Michigan... Home of absolutely Nothin

999

999 Live at Bookies 870 Club
March 29, 1979

New Musical Express said the band was invited
to this country. Whoever was responsible danke.
Bookies is a pansexual paradise according to
New York Rocker. Well I didnt note any patrons
having coitus with cooking utensils but it is
a great little spot to see Nick Cash and the
boys. Warmup was a hometown favorite called
Coldcock that reaffirms my view of Detroit As
the capital of nothing. 999 launched into
Out Of Reach which instantly stirred the
sold out throng into amidwest pogo circa 77
(everything gets here 5 light years late)
The set included all your favorites, My Street Stinks,
My Desire, Homicide ,Lets Face IT,Feelin Alright
with The Crew(for us? oh really Nick you shouldntve)
and of course Emergency(yours truly and another bloke
got to belt out a couple choruses on this tune (sigh)
who sez people-punk ala Sham, Skids is dead? Go's
without saying twas best gig this sod's ever saw . If
this quartet ever graces your burg with their presence
dont miss it!

*Boycott
Trouser Press.
They had the
balls to slag
off the 2nd album.*

*Runner up
in 999 record review
contest!*

"SEPARATES"
999
United Artists Records import

999 write a bible of consumptive love and
violent death then shred their own myths,
hopes and fears to ribbons before your
very eyes. Guy Days spins out guitar
cliches from the Beatles to Creedence
Clearwater, stands them on their heads
into filthy maelstroms of sound that
always climax in someone getting their
feelings hurt. Nick Cash's voice goes from
documentary-like detachment to irra-
tional obsession, sneering sarcasm to an
iron-hided romance in the space of a
breath. The cynic locked in a perpetual
death duel with the idealist, the idealist
coming out on top (I think). Martin
Rushent gives the band a fuller, richer
sound than the last album comparable
to Chris Thomas' Pistols work. While
pretending to conform to rock 'n roll
limits, 999 throws an acid poison in the
face of accepted standards and goes them
one better.

Chris D.

*Reprinted
without
Slash's
permission*

from Bomp →

all their records

7-77 — I'm alive
11-77 Nasty Nasty
1-78 Emergency
4-78 Me + My Desire
8-78 Feelin alright
      with the crew

2-78 First album 999
10-78 Homicide
7 or 8 78- Waiting
11-78 -Action EP
12-78 second album
      Seperates!!!

America calls 999

999 leave for an American tour
at the end of March, and have
already been snapped up for
club engagements in Philadelphia, Boston, New York, Toron-
tok San Francisco, Los Angeles,
Detroit, Washington and
Chicago — including three
nights at the Whiskey in L.A. —
despite the fact that they have
no record deal at all in the
States. It seems the tour has
been set up solely on the
strength of their reputation here
at home.

They'll be away until the end
of June and, on their return, will
play a few selected dates
around Britain. As reported last
week, they headline the first of
the new Sunday-night rock
shows at London Lyceum on
February 18 and — as they have
not played in London since
November — this will be their
only concert in the capital for
nine months.

Ed Case, temporarily replac-
ing Pablo Labritain on drums,
will accompany 999 to America.
Labritain's arm, broken in a car
accident, is healing well but
won't be strong enough for him
to play. He is currently undergo-
ing physiotherapy treatment.

INTERVIEW WITH NICK CASH(twas more like a short conversation)

Cash;How ya doing,where did you get the badge?
me;Made it
me,How many gigs have you had over here?
Cash About 15 or 16.
me; Hows the response been?
Cash; Real good considering our label hasnt released
      anything over here.
me;Of course UA are too worried about their friggin movies.
Cash; Ill stop by later and give you some promos(exits)

Did I say something wrong?

MISC.

NATHAN,

PLEASE SEND ME A COPY
OF THE TEEN IDLES EP
BEFORE I FORGET WHAT A
PUNK RECORD'S SUPPOSE TO
SOUND LIKE. THANX.

SEND TO: DS
            c/o TOUCH & GO
            P.O. BOX 26203
            LANSING, MI
                48909

SLASH

BOX 48888 L.A. CA., 90048
(213) 654-2876

15¢
U.S. POSTAGE
OLIVER
WENDELL
HOLMES

Touch & Go
614 S. Putnam #2
Williamston, Mich
48895

Thanx for your issue
#1. keep sending it, well
send you Slash.
Okay?

Kickboy

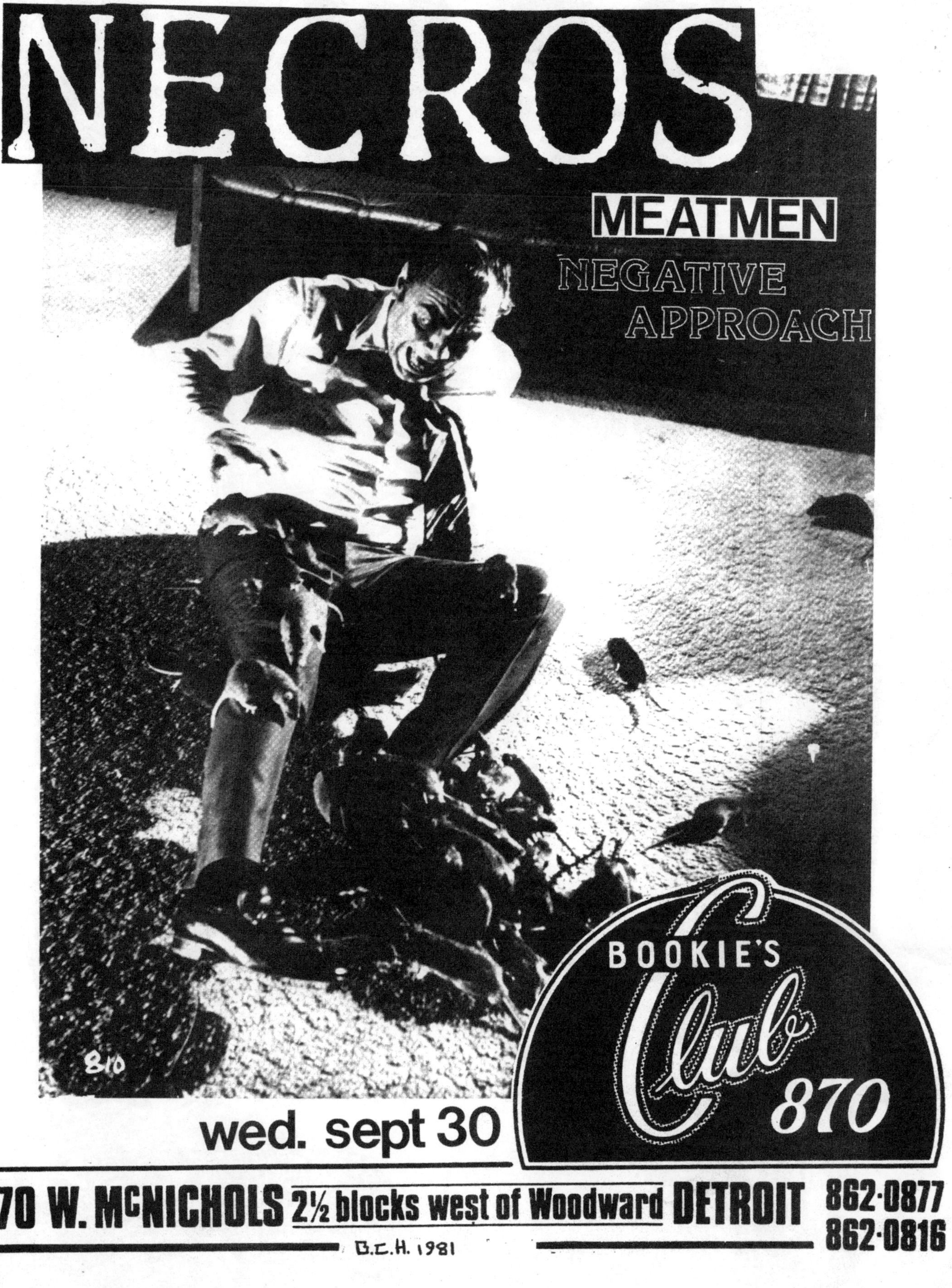
NECROS
MEATMEN
NEGATIVE APPROACH
810
BOOKIE'S
Club
870
wed. sept 30
870 W. McNICHOLS 2½ blocks west of Woodward DETROIT
862-0877
862-0816
B.C.H. 1981

FLESH EATERS
UNDERTAKERS

TUES. APRIL 21 WHISKY

the
FLESH EATERS

A MINUTE A SECOND
TO PRAY TO DIE

RUBY RECORDS

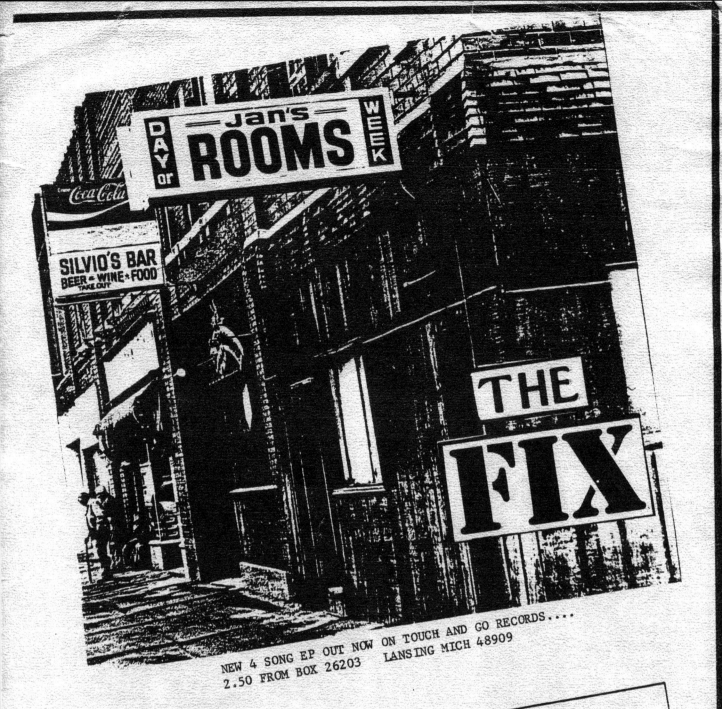

NEW 4 SONG EP OUT NOW ON TOUCH AND GO RECORDS.....
2.50 FROM BOX 26203   LANSING MICH 48909

SIDE ONE

COS THE ELITE
TRUTH RIGHT NOW

SIDE TWO

S I G N A L
OFF TO WAR

UPCOMING TOUR.......
DEC. 12 OBANIONS...CHICAGO
DEC.13 BEAT EXCHANGE NEW ORLEANS
DEC.16 AUSTIN TEXAS
DEC. 17 TACK CLUB SANTE FE
DEC. 18 BACKSTAGE CLUB TUCSON
DEC. 19 MADISON SQUARE GARDEN PHOENIX
DEC. 22=23 MUTE CLUB SAN FRANSISCO
DEC. 24 DUNCANS PUB RENO
DEC. 25 MABUHAY GARDENS SAN FRANSISCO
DEC. 29 DUNCANS PUB RENO
JAN. 2 CRAZY ALS INDIANAPOLLIS

NECROS

TOUGH AND GO REKORDS POB 26203 Lansing MI 48909

barry henssler-vocals
andy wendler-guitar,bass
todd swalla-drums
jeff lake-bass on "police brutality"

WILSON CENTER

15TH AND IRVING STS. N.W. APRIL 30TH

MINOR THREAT
IRON CROSS
FAITH
ARTIFICIAL PEACE
DOUBLE O
VOID

JAN 22ND

AT 8:00

H.B. WOODLAWN HIGH SCHOOL
4100 N. VATICAN LANE
ARLINGTON

IRON CROSS

Artificial PEACE

Capitol punishment

VOID

BLACK MARKET BABY

S.S. DECONTROL

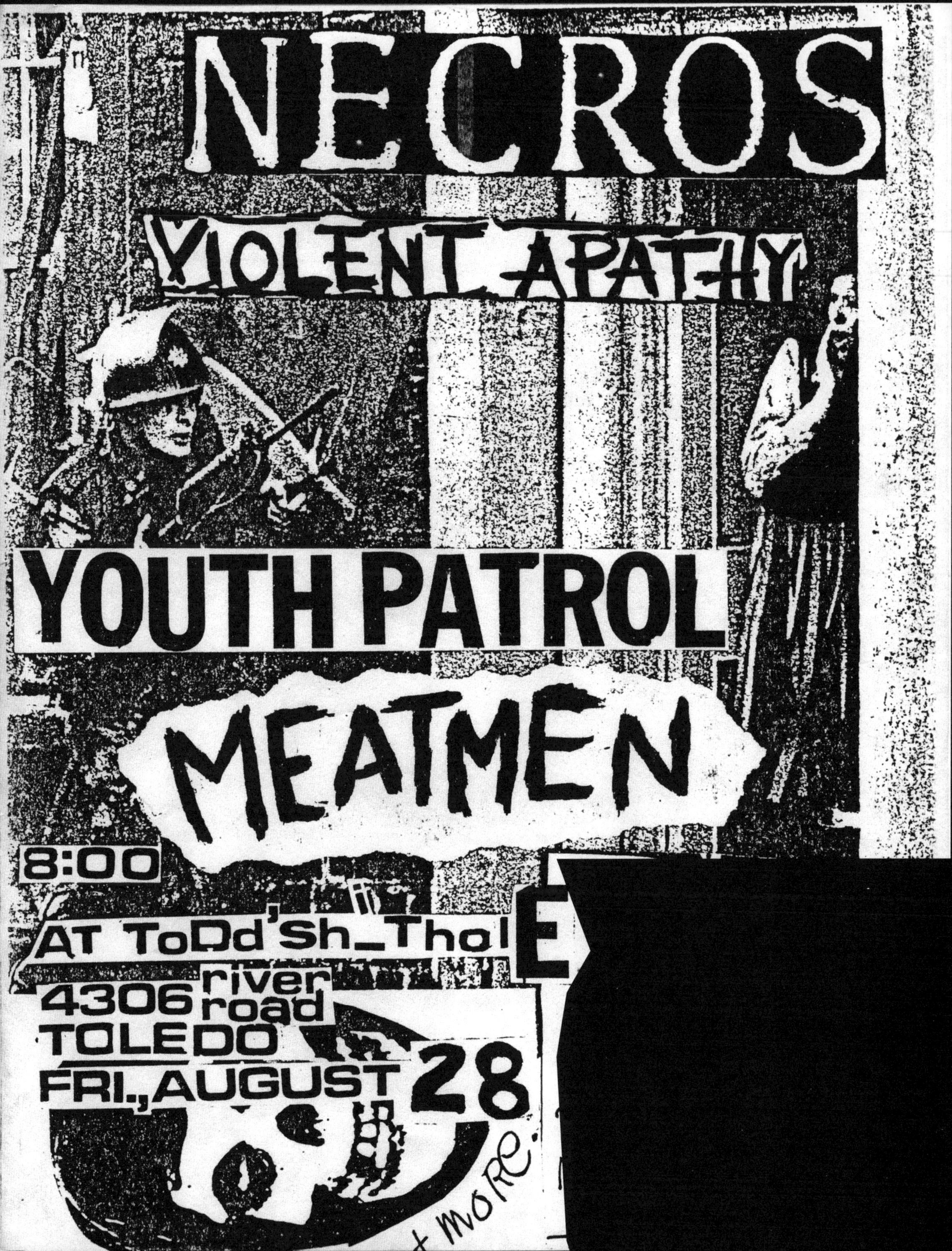

NECROS
VIOLENT APATHY
YOUTH PATROL
MEATMEN

8:00
AT ToDd'Sh_Thol E
river
4306 road
TOLEDO
FRI., AUGUST 28
+ more

NECRO

VIOLENT APATHY

NEGA
A

SAT. DEC 12
THE CROOKED BEAT
39

BORED YOUTH

IVE
ROACH

MEATMEN

Youth Patrol

mcdonald's   **SUBURBAN ANGER**

TOUCH and GO

PROCESS OF ELIMINATION ep

RECORD RELEASE GIG

cass
troit

SUPPORT MIDWEST HARDCORE

GReeTings...
we be pleazed to meaf you....

ORIGINAL LINE UP 81-82

NECROS

MEAT MEN
mmA
BLUD SAUSAGE

NEGATIVE APPROACH

YOUTH PATROL   Violent Apathy

SAT., OCT. 3

Bands start at 7:30

AT: Endless Summer SKATE PARK
ON LITTLE MACK near masonic

more info call 419-382-1731

When is a plywood extension a springboard?

The f.i x

CORONATION TAVERN...
WINDSOR
SEPT. 5 (Saturday)
w/ special guests

MEAT MEN
BLOOD SAUSAGE

Wow! Black Flag at Club DooBee.

BLACK FLAG
THE FIX
and THE NECROS

Sunday Mar. 22ND at
Club DooBee

corner of Marsh + Lake Lansing

one hot piece of talent!

only $3.00

at the NEW BEAT CLUB
643 9th St nw (St. Hyacinth hall)

L-7
&
N.A.

NEGATIVE APPROACH

$3   JUNE 5, 1982

can't tell no one what to do